The Harry Potter Companion

by

Acascias Riphouse

© Copyright 2003, Acascias Riphouse
All rights reserved.
No part of this book may be reproduced, stored in a retrieval system, or transmitted by any means, electronic, mechanical, photocopying, recording, or otherwise, without written permission from the author.

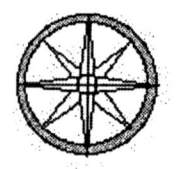

To My Guiding Star, Tig

Text Copyright © 2003 Acascias Riphouse
Illustrations by Henry Starbright © 2003 Henry Starbright

All rights reserved. Published by Virtualbookworm, the Virtualbookworm DESIGN, and associated logos are trademarks and/or registered trademarks of Best Books.

HARRY POTTER and all related characters and elements are trademarks of Warner Bros.

If you purchased this book without a cover, you should be aware that this book is stolen property.
It was reported as "unsold and destroyed" to the publisher, and neither the author nor the publisher has received any payment for this "stripped book."

Nor part of this publication may be reproduced in whole or in part, or stored in a retrieval system, or transmitted in any form or by any means, electronic (including posted on websites), mechanical, photocopying, recording, or otherwise
without written permission from the publisher.
For information regarding permission write to Virtualbookworm.
Attention Permissions Department, PO Box 9949, College Station, TX 77842

ISBN 1-58939-582-4

Printed in the U.S.A.

First printing, May 2004

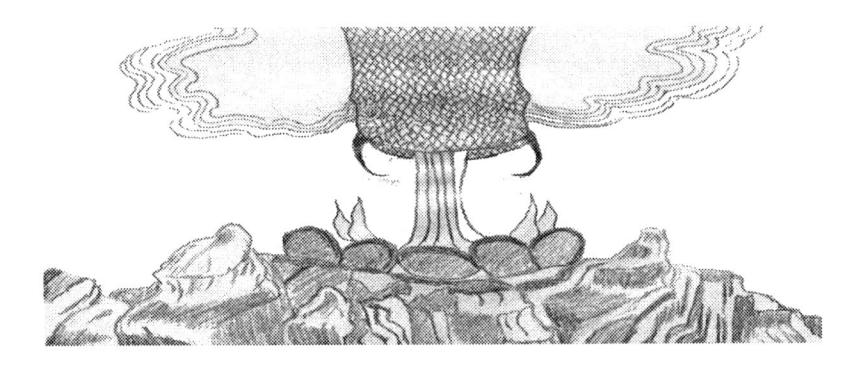

Contents

Introduction	9
Part I. Wizard Lifestyle	11
Acronyms and Abbreviations	11
Wizarding Government and Non-Governmental Organizations	13
The International Confederation of Wizards	13
The British Ministry of Magic	16
Getting to the MoM	17
MoM Levels	19
By Level: The Departments	20
Assorted MoM Offices	36
Assorted MoM Facts	38
MoM Personnel	39
Non-Governmental Organizations	40
Schematics A to G*	
The Lively Arts	42
Music	42
Song	42
Dance	43
Books and Literature	43
Poetry	44
Theater	44
Language	45
Tapestry	45
Embroidery	46
Painting	47
Photography	47
Sculpture	48
Metal Crafts	48
Heraldry	49
Seal Carving	49
Other Pastimes and Interests	50
Games and Cards	50
Sports	51

3

The Harry Potter Companion

Collecting 52
Inventing 52
Knitting 53
Learning 53
Fanciers 53
Cooking 53
Charity Work 54
Reading Matter.. 54
Newspapers 54
Magazines... 55
Books 55
    By Author.. 55
    By Title 57
    By Topic 60
    By Publisher 62
    Well-Known Authors.. 62
Brooms and Quidditch 63
Types of Brooms 63
Who Owns What Broomstick.. 64
Racing Broom Companies 65
Broom-Servicing Products... 65
Quidditch, The Game 65
    Rules 65
    Fouls 66
    Special Moves 66
    Positions and Players 67
    The Pitch and Equipment.. 67
British and Irish League Teams by Nation........................ 68
Cups.. 69
Quidditch World Cup 1994 69
    Teams Playing in QWC 1994 70
Schematic H
Expressions 71
Wizarding Expressions... 71
Strictly British 72
Rag and Bone.. 74
Clothing and Accessories 74
Health 78
Money.. 79
Terminology 80
Weights and Measures 81
Wizards and Modernity... 81
Technology 81
The Environment 82
Health 83
The Status of Women and Children................................ 84
Race 86
Political Structure 87
Social Structure 88
Social Terminology 90

4

Religion in the Wizarding World 94
Part II. Hogwarts.. 98
  Hogwarts, An Overview.. 98
    The Founding 98
    School and House Banners 99
    Students.. 99
    Teachers... 99
    Transfer Students..100
    Signing Up...100
    Getting Accepted...100
    Getting to Hogwarts 101
    Electricity and Magic 101
    The Floors...102
    The School Hierarchy..102
    The Terms 103
    Classes..103
    School Rules and Procedures 104
    During The Voldemort Years 104
    Schematic I
  Hogwarts, The Facilities 105
    The Castle and Interior 105
    By Floor...106
    Towers...110
    Other Parts..110
    Schematics J-N
  Harry and The Underworld 114
  Hogwarts, Grounds and Outbuildings 117
    Schematic O
  Hogwarts, Offices 120
  Hogwarts, Staff..123
    Former Staff 123
    Former DADA Teachers..123
    Partial Listing of Current Staff 123
    Schematic P
  Annual Sorts 124
  Houses..124
    House Government 128
    Schematic Q
  Points..129
  Detentions 132
  The House Cup 134
  Clubs 134
  Career Advice 136
  Classes 136
    Breakdown of Founders' Classes..142
    Harry's Classes 143
  Exams...148
    Basic Exams..148
      Harry's Basic Exams...148
    OWLs..149

THE HARRY POTTER COMPANION

- Harry's OWLs 149
- NEWTs 150
- Feasts 150
  - Start of Term Feasts 150
  - Halloween Feasts 151
  - Christmas Feasts 151
  - End of Term Feasts 152
  - Other One Time Feasts 152
- Hogsmeade Weekends 153
- Harry's Presents 154
- Foods 156
  - Food Lists 156
  - Recipes 162
- The Quidditch Cup 169
  - Quidditch Matches 170
  - House Teams 171
- Triwizard Tournament 174
- Magical and Nonmagical School Supplies 177
  - School Lists 177
  - Equipment 178
  - Types of Wands and Who Owns Them 180

Part III. General Wizardry 183
- Magical Talents 183
  - Inherent Magical Talents 183
  - Learned Magical Talents 185
- Charms, Hexes, Jinxes, Spells and Curses 186
  - Incantations 188
  - Charms 191
  - Hexes 195
  - Jinxes 195
  - Spells 196
  - Curses 197
- Potions 198
  - Magical Products 201
  - A Few of Filch's Banned Products 202
  - Weasleys' Wizarding Wheezes' Products 202
  - Wizarding Food and Candy Products 204
- Magical Beasts 205
  - Diseases 224
- Animals: Non-Magical 224
  - Birds 225
  - Fish 229
  - Insects 230
  - Mammals 230
  - Reptiles 235
- Plants: Magical or Used in Magic 238
- Stones: Magical or Used in Magic 243
- Magical Gadgets, Gizmos and Devices 246
  - Wizarding Transport 258
  - Harry's Scar 263

ACASCIAS RIPHOUSE

Portraits Etc. 269
   Portraits 270
   Photos 273
   Statues 274
   Tapestry 275
Part IV. Biography: Wizards Abbot-Ravenclaw 276
   Alphabetical Listing of Wizards A-Ra 276
      Schematics R-T
   What Year? 347
   First Name Please! 348
Part V. Biography: Wizards Riddle-Zonko and All Other Beings 354
   Alphabetical Listing of Wizards Ri-Z 354
   Other Magical Beings 386
   Werewolves 399
      The Moon and Lycanthropy 402
   Spirits 405
      Ghosts 406
         Ghost-Related Stuff 410
      Poltergeists 411
      Assorted Spirits 411
   Muggles 412
      Muggle Stuff 422
         Assorted 422
         Days 422
         Games 422
         Trains 423
      Schematic U
Part VI. Where and When 424
   Places 424
      Diagon Alley and Environs 425
      Hogsmeade 430
      Other Wizarding Places 432
      Little Hangleton 440
      Little Whinging 440
      London Area 442
      Other Muggle Places 442
   Schematics V-Zc
The Timeline of Events 445
   1000 BC - July 1, 1996 445
Part VII: Schematics. 497
   A: A History of Wizarding Government 498
   Ab: Wizarding Government Structure
      from International Level to MoM Level 499
   B: British MoM Departmental Flow Chart 500
   C: DRCMC Flow Chart 501
   D: MoM Levels Guide 502
   E: MoM Level 2 503
   F: MoM Level 9, Dept of Mysteries 504
   G: MoM Level 10, Courtroom 10 and Environs 505
   H: Standard Quidditch Pitch and Balls 506

THE HARRY POTTER COMPANION

I: Hogwarts' Grounds 507
J: Hogwarts' Floor Guide...508
K: Ground Floor, Hogwarts 509
L: Great Hall, Hogwarts...510
M: The Chamber of Secrets 511
N: Sorcerer's Stone Protections 512
O1: Hagrid's Cabin and Environs 514
O2: Hagrid's Cabin, Detail 515
P: Filch's Form...516
Q: Harry's Tower Room 517
R: Family Trees: Harry and Voldemort......................................518
S: More Family Trees 519
T: The Black Family Tapestry: An Excerpt................................520
U: Muggle Games..522
V: 4 Privet Drive: Lower Floor and Grounds.............................524
Vb: 4 Privet Drive: Upper Floor and Harry's Room 526
W: Privet Drive and Environs: Little Whinging 527
X: Riddle House and Property 528
Y: Headquarters, OoP: Sirius Black's House.............................529
Z: Hogsmeade Village...530
Za: The Burrow 532
Zb: The Burrow 533
Zc: Dumbledore's Scar: Map of the Underground.................534
Za: The Burrow 532
Za: The Burrow 532

All schematics are placed at the end of this volume. Most have more than one chapter they might be associated with. Notations on the Table of Contents merely indicated the most appropriate chapter.

Acknowledgements 535
About the Author..537

INTRODUCTION

GREAT TALES MAKE PEOPLE THINK as much for their flaws as their perfection. Because each individual brings a rare selection of knowledge to their reading of a text, each may see different things in the same story. As an American, I thought little of Harry's trip from Paddington to Little Whinging on July 31, 1991. It was not until I read the now slightly outdated but still enlightening *A Charmed Life: The Spirituality of Potterworld* by Francis Bridger, an Englishman, that I discovered one could not catch a train from Paddington Station to Surrey as no trains departing Paddington crossed the River Thames. Francis' knowledge of trains presented a problem, a gap in an otherwise logical line of events. I tried to think of how Harry's experience could be lined up with Francis' revelation. My presumption was that perhaps the trains did run from Paddington to Surrey in 1991 when Harry traveled on it. Or perhaps the train he meant was the Underground, which can be used to reach Surrey.

Having resolved that detail, I began to think of other gaps in Harry's story. Why did Animagi bother to use their talent? Transfiguration had all of the same virtues, without any of the drawbacks. What made them do it? How did Voldemort get his wand back in 1994? He had after all dropped it 13 years previous in Godric's Hollow and fled a vapor to Albania without it. How could Molly be Sirius' first cousin? The more I thought, the more questions began to form. Eventually I had to know the answers. I began piecing bits of information together and creating answers that held their own against tests of logic. For some questions, many answers were possible, for others, only one. The complied results became the heart of this book. To this was added all relevant details available on various subjects mentioned within the 5 books of the series since these were often overlooked and relevant to how answers were worked out. It does no good to discuss Animagi for example if no one understands what they are.

Details of *Quidditch Through the Ages* and *Fantastic Beasts and Where to Find Them* were generally not included. These works, while interesting, for the most part had no direct bearing on the books of the series. They are stand-alone works, covering in detail their respective specific subjects, Quidditch and magical beasts. Most readers will have these books. Those who don't may easily purchase them and benefit a worthy charity in doing so. For those not aware, these 2 works were written by JK Rowling to benefit Harry's Books Fund, a part of Comic Relief UK. For my part, it would be unthinkable to cull every detail from these works as it could potentially undercut their sale, which in turn would remove needed funds from the hands of those for whom they were intended. Though some well-meaning individuals have gutted these books and set their contents up on websites for fans to peruse, this is in reality a despicable act of theft from a charity working to help young people all over the world learn to read. I

The Harry Potter Companion

encourage you to buy the books if they are not in your possession and remove the pertinent information if it is on a site you control.

Returning to this book, it is really more of a Pensive just easier to carry around. Here one can consult on various overlooked points of fact, reflect on obscure information and ponder widely interconnections that may not be immediately apparent. Many things revealed here might be very surprising to some and, since over 2,100 pages of text were assiduously dissected, broken down and analyzed for detail, there is sure to be something of interest here for everyone, even the most ardent know-it-all. In places, some sacred cows have been slain. Where I have flagrantly flown in the face of standard interpretation, I have tried to note it and explain my case. I have not relied on material beyond the books if it contradicts published record, and, while I have respected canon, it cannot be let to fly in the face of logic and common sense. Please feel free to disagree, for your thoughts may be right - in the end.

As future volumes of the Harry Potter series are produced I will be adding all relevant material to updated editions of this work until a final volume is available sometime after Harry's last adventure is published. To this end, suggestions for additions to future volumes are welcome. Due to zoning restrictions and health codes, I am not permitted to accept owls, Howlers or hate mail, but the odd criticism, correction or kvetch will be given every consideration if kindly put. For obvious reasons (see Part I, Wizards and Modernity if the reasons are not obvious), email is impossible, but I can be reached by Muggles and wizards alike through:

Best Books
Box 3002
Thousand Oaks, CA 91359-3002
Attn: A. Riphouse.

Acascias Riphouse
The Old Bench
Spit Corner
Peel, IoM
June 28, 2003

Part I. Wizard Lifestyle

Acronyms and Abbreviations

IN AN EFFORT TO CONSERVE SPACE acronyms and abbreviations will be used. Some are already in use, such as SPEW or Jr, others are not. Both are grouped in the classes they would most likely be used in. Punctuation with acronyms and abbreviation will not be used.

DA: Dumbledore's Army.
DADA: Defense Against the Dark Arts.
NEWT: Nearly (or Nastily) Exhausting Wizarding Test.
OWL: Ordinary Wizarding Level.
Pr: Professor.
SPEW: Society for the Protection of Elf Welfare.

ICW: International Confederation of Wizards.
IWC: International Warlocks' Convention
MoM: Ministry of Magic.
Dept: Department.
DIMC: Dept of International Magical Cooperation.
DMAC: Dept of Magical Accidents and Catastrophes.
DMGS: Dept of Magical Games and Sports.
DMLE: Dept of Magical Law Enforcement.
DMT: Dept of Magical Transport.
DoM: Dept of Mysteries.
DRCMC: Dept for the Regulation and Control of Magical Creatures.

THE HARRY POTTER COMPANION

NGO: Non-governmental organization. An organization not attached to or governed by a nation, such as the United Nations High Commission for Refugees, a charity that aids refugees fleeing war, famine and other misfortunes.
PM: Prime Minister of Britain.
UN: United Nations.

QWC 1994: Quidditch World Cup 1994.
TT: Triwizard Tournament.

G: Galleon(s).
S: Sickle(s).
K: Knut(s).

FB: Newt Scamander's book *Fantastic Beasts and Where to Find Them*.
QTA: Kennilworthy Whisp's book *Quidditch Through the Ages*.

HQ: Headquarters.
MIA: Missing in action.
OoP: Order of the Phoenix.

aka: Also known as.
eg: For example.
et al: And the rest.
etc: And so forth.
ie: That is.
v: versus
yr: year

am: In the morning.
pm: In the evening.

AD: Meaning "the year of our Lord," in those years after the death and resurrection of Jesus Christ.
BC: Before Christ.
91/92: The years during a school year are abbreviated as follows: 91/92, 92/93, 93/94, 94/95, 95/96 and so forth.
Jan: The months of the year are abbreviated as follows: Jan, Feb, Mar, Apr, May, Jun, Jul, Aug, Sep, Oct, Nov, Dec.
b: born.
c: circa, meaning on or about the time noted.
d: died.

pint: A liquid measure equal to .473 liters. There are 2 pints to a quart and 4 quarts to a gallon.
oz: Ounces.
mph: Mile per hour.
": Inches.
': Feet.

Jr: Meaning junior, the son of.
Sr: Meaning senior, the father of.

WIZARDING GOVERNMENT AND NON-GOVERNMENTAL ORGANIZATIONS

This section covers the ICW, its legislation and subcommittees, the British MoM, its legislation and departments, and various non-governmental organizations operating in the wizarding world. This is by no means an exhaustive list. It is simply all that it is currently known.

THE INTERNATIONAL CONFEDERATION OF WIZARDS

The history of the formation of the ICW is shown on schematic A but it warrants some discussion. As the schematic shows, in 1280 European warlocks were meeting as a group and, less than 9 years later, an international body of warlocks was established. However, while many nations, including Britain, enfranchised women in the 14th century not all nations did the same. This issue finally split the International Warlocks' Convention (IWC) irreparably and in 1692 the ICW was formed to give women complete political equality at the international level. The British MoM went with the new ICW while other MoMs opted to continue to be headed by the IWC.

Despite their fundamental differences on women in government, there was always a spirit of cooperation between the ICW and the IWC and it would be incorrect to assume that relations between them were anything but cordial. In point of fact many IWC rulings were simultaneously adopted by the ICW. For example, the ban on dragon breeding by the IWC in 1709 was adopted by the ICW in the same year. Although it was several centuries before the MoMs could reconcile and full political power was finally transferred from the IWC to the ICW, when it did occur there was little disruption caused to the average wizard's life, great rejoicing among witches and no significant changes in points of law.

Since the British MoM opted to go with the ICW in 1692, we will focus our discussion on that body. The ICW first met in France in 1692. At that time Pierre Bonaccord, noted troll lover and all around extremely forward thinking warlock, became the body's first elected Supreme Mugwump. After overcoming many obstacles and almost a year of discussions, a large degree of international unity was reached. Today the ICW, with representatives from every wizarding nation or geographic designation, meets each summer, usually in Jul, in France under the chairmanship of the Supreme Mugwump to discuss, resolve and legislate on important matters of mutual or international concern. See schematic Ab for an overview of the ICW in relation to the MoMs.

The ICW is currently similar to the Muggle UN. While each wizarding area has an individual MoM, the ICW oversees all MoMs in all countries or geographic designations without exception. Any violation of an ICW decree can lead to severe penalties for the nation or MoM where the violation took place. However, all MoMs are required to obey the ICW only in matters where a signed treaty or other formal agreement exists between a MoM and the ICW. In a case where no treaty or agreement between the ICW and a MoM exists, sanctions cannot be levied and penalties cannot be imposed. For example if 2 wizards elect to duel in Transylvania, their respective MoMs may be dismayed, but there is no ICW or MoM breach of existing treaties as Transylvania has not signed the International Ban on Dueling.

In cases of treaty breaking, the ICW can employ sanctions and penalties. A sanction the ICW might impose on a nation or MoM is a fine for breaking the International Code of Wizarding Secrecy. With regards to Beasts, frequent fines are levied for kelpie sightings against Scotland, a single member nation within the British MoM, and for yeti sightings against the Tibetan MoM. If continued breaches occurred and the offending MoM or nation was unwilling or unable to deal with a situation, the ICW might elect to send a task force out to deal directly with the problem. In both of the above cases, the ICW opted to send a task force to assist existing but insufficient containment efforts.

International Confederation of Wizards' Conference: Representatives of the MoM to the ICW meet face-to-face annually at the ICW Conference which takes place in France during the summer, usually in Jul. The French play a significant role in the ICW's administrative and judicial process, and the ICW headquarters has long been located in France. Given Dumbledore is the chairwizard of the ICW, it indicates the British play a more central role in the ICW's legislative processes and thus the actual doings of the annual conference. This is not to imply one MoM is any more important than another but simply to remark that what began as an essentially Eurocentric system, has stayed that way.

A large but equal number of delegates from each MoM attends the conference, which can last a number of weeks depending on what items are on the agenda and how passionate the delegates feel about them. It is a very important event, affecting millions of wizards, and is always covered by the various national wizarding newspapers. Rita Skeeter attended for *The Daily Prophet* in 1995, giving a somewhat slanted view of the conference and its Supreme Mugwump, however, her articles were widely read proving a high level of interest to the wizard on the street. Far more than say the average Muggle shows in the doings of the UN or even the doings of her or his own national government.

During the year, while delegates are apart, MoMs provide meeting space for ICW delegates. The British Seats for the ICW are in the MoM building in London on Level 5 where all the international offices and departments reside. These delegates, appointed by the various MoMs, engage in discussion of needed international legislation, decide which issues or areas of dispute are to be brought up at the next annual conference, oversee the implementation of agreed to ICW legislation, treaties or other ICW obligations such as providing team members to a specific task force and liaise with their own MoM's officials about entering into currently existing treaties and other ongoing matters.

By necessity, a standing body composed of international wizards appointed by the various MoMs is attached to the ICW. This body is located in France and works full time on overseeing the application and implementation of current ICW agreements, treaties and legislation. It also has the responsibility of coordinating the annual ICW conference and seeing to the various needs of the delegates, such as providing translators, making sure sufficient catering is available and finding secure lodgings for this large group of wizards. It is unknown how many wizards make up the ICW as delegates or as full-time employees. One would suspect around 2,000 delegates and 5,000 employees would be sufficent.

International Confederation of Wizards, 1692 Conference: At the first meeting of the ICW, significant amounts of legislation were passed that continue to effect wizards today. Among the laws this conference established was a wizard's right to carry a wand at all times. This legislation is significant because, although it was created at a time when Muggle persecutions were extremely fierce and the wizarding community was planning its retreat into hiding so confrontations with Muggles would be minimized, it now gives anyone of any age a right to carry around in her or his pocket a weapon capable of killing a dozen or more people at a time. Wizards clearly have always felt that the responsibility of wand ownership is one most individuals can bear responsibly, no doubt in part because of the fact they grew up bearing it.

International Statute of Wizarding Secrecy of 1692: aka the Statute of Secrecy. Passed by the ICW in 1692, it makes every MoM directly responsible for the consequences of magical sports played within their territories and requires wizards to refrain from using magic anywhere near the Muggle public (section 13) except in cases of using magic to save the wizard's own life. There are, in addition, many other sections and applications of the Statute which are too numerous to discuss here.

International Code of Wizarding Secrecy: The Code contains the Statute of Wizarding Secrecy of 1692 as well as all other ICW legislation. All laws (statutes) are contained within a country's Penal Code. If a wizard breaks the Code of Wizarding Secrecy, she or he might not be breaking the Statute of 1692. But if she or he breaks the Statute of 1692, she or he would certainly be breaking the Code.

In 1750, Clause 73 was inserted into the Code to make the MoMs responsible for the various magical Beasts, Beings and Spirits dwelling within their territories. Which is interesting as the Beast, Being and Spirit divisions currently used by the MoMs wasn't developed until 1811, or 61 years later. Anyway, it is this clause that makes a MoM responsible when a Muggle spots a yeti, is harassed by a ghost or moves into a house where the former owner's ghoul failed to get relocated.

International Confederation of Wizards' Quidditch Committee: This committee researches Quidditch as it is played today and is responsible for standardizing Quidditch pitches, balls and rules around the globe. It has a hand in various regional, national and world cups, from the aspect of insuring all international rules are observed and supplying referees who meet exacting standards.

This is but one of many committees the ICW has to deal with various issues important to wizards. Committees operate only as a last resort where an issue is perhaps widely disputed, such as the rules of Quidditch. Listing all committees at the ICW would fill a volume in itself and such committees are not relevant to this discussion.

International Task Force: Currently there are only 2 international task forces operating, one in the mountains of Tibet and one in the area of Loch Ness, Scotland. An international task force is a last resort used only when a MoM is unable or unwilling to deal with certain breaches of magical law. It is sent out by the ICW to deal with the situation directly. The ICW will set up a committee if the situation doesn't yet warrant sending out a task force but requires closer scrutiny.

Decree for the Reasonable Restriction of Underage Sorcery: This legislation, passed in 1875 by the ICW, in short forbids wizards under 17 doing magic outside of school but there are many other parts to this decree. For instance, Paragraph C of the decree says a wizard can't do underage magic in front of Muggles while Section 19 says a wizard can do underage magic to save her or his own life and Clause 7 says underage magic may be used in front of Muggles in exceptional circumstances that include threats against the life of the wizard or any Muggles present at the time. Clearly it's a very complex piece of legislation with a loophole for practically anyone.

International Ban on Dueling: As of 1994, this piece of ICW legislation was signed by all MoMs except the MoM in Transylvania. The ICW vowed to continue to work with Transylvania to try and resolve this matter, ie, get them to sign.

THE BRITISH MINISTRY OF MAGIC (MOM)

When known, various offices and committees will be grouped under their department. See schematic B, the MoM flowchart, for specific relationships. The MoM currently has 7 departments:

- Dept of Magical Law Enforcement
- Dept of International Magical Cooperation
- Dept for the Regulation and Control of Magical Creatures
- Dept of Magical Games and Sports
- Dept of Magical Transport
- Dept of Magical Accidents and Catastrophes
- Dept of Mysteries

MoM History: The Wizards' Council established prior to 1269 was the first form of wizard government in Britain and directly preceded the current British MoM. At the time it was established, it did not include many areas of responsibility that are now considered a standard part of the British MoM's jurisdiction. Over time, as Britain developed, various individual MoMs (Scotland, Ireland, Wales, Cornwall) joined together to become the British MoM. For wizards, the term British refers to an area specified by wizards, not a Muggle government. This is why today's British MoM includes areas thought of traditionally as British, such as the nation of Ireland, as well as large parts of what Muggles call the nation of Britain.

As any wizarding territory can opt out of a Muggle designated nation, just as Transylvania opted to form a separate MoM from Romania despite being considered one nation by Muggles, certain territories traditionally associated with Muggle-designated Britain are actually considered separate areas to wizards and thus have individual MoMs. The Falkland Islands, Gibraltar, the Isle of Man and the Channel Islands, to name but a few, all have their own individual MoMs. They each remain on friendly terms with the British MoM but feel they can best address their own unique needs and difficulties by having a local governing body.

The current British MoM, representing the nations of England, Wales, Scotland, North Ireland and Ireland proper, seems to have been established sometime prior to 1674 when the British and Irish Quidditch League was pared down to today's 13 MoM-approved teams. It is likely too that the British MoM was established prior even to 1650, since the first Quidditch European Cup was held in 1652. Most likely the British MoM was established around the date 1600 and represented more of a name change than any actual shift in the body itself or how it went about its daily business. The Wizards' Council simply became the MoM and the Chief or Chieftainess became the Minister of Magic. The process of electing this official stayed the same, as did the job description of the office.

Today, as in 1269, the individual at the head of the governing body is all-powerful. And today, as in 1269, the governing body considers its main function to be keeping Muggles ignorant of the wizarding community so that wizards don't get Muggles asking for magical solutions to all their problems. Wizards, like any normal being (excepting house-elves), fear exploitation of their powers by Muggles and, flying in the face of any compelling evidence that any Muggle has ever wanted to exploit them (kill them yes, exploit them no), wizards' tax Galleons continue to go toward paying the MoM to cover up any trace of wizardry.

However, an exception this rule is the Prime Minister of Britain who has always been informed of the presence of wizards within Britain and, given the opportunity, usually willingly works with the MoM on matters of mutual concern, such as the escape of dangerous criminals like Sirius Black. It must be said that while the MoM is always willing to obtain additional help from a PM, it is unwilling to give additional help to a PM in return. During the Voldemort years (1970-1981), the MoM spent a good part of its time and money attempting to hide what was going on from Muggles, including 4 successive PMs. This was difficult as Muggle-killing occurred with alarming regularity and the MoM itself was in complete disarray having many of its employees acting under the Imperius Curse of notorious Death Eaters.

Despite the fact terror, confusion, distrust and panic reigned at the MoM, the MoM continued to avoid asking for help on all but the most glaring cases of magical destruction. The PM-MoM cover-ups continued till 1981 when the murder of 12 Muggles was committed by Peter Pettigrew on a street crowded with Christmas shoppers. The Muggle public was informed by the PM, then Margaret Thatcher, that a gas line had broken and exploded, Sirius Black went to jail and the MoM went back to operating in secrecy. The MoM did not ask a PM for help again until 1993, when Sirius Black escaped. It is unclear if Muggle PMs have their memories modified upon retiring from office but, given the MoM's passion for wizard protection, it seems likely.

After Voldemort's defeat, the Minister of Magic during this period, Millicent Bagnold, continued in her position another 10 years. She eventually retired in Dec 1990 having completed a successful reconstruction of the MoM and having restored a measure of safety, peace and normalcy to the wizarding community. Many wizards wanted Dumbledore for the new Minister of Magic, however, though he won the popular vote, Dumbledore's commitment to Hogwarts was more compelling and he refused the post. So in 1991, Cornelius Fudge, by default, became Minister of Magic and the MoM has taken a decided turn for the worse ever since. Even 5 years down the road, in 1996, Fudge continues to show no sign of running the MoM in any way but that which aggrandizes him personally.

Overlooking Fudge and his recent term in office, the MoM has always been considered an interesting, even fun, place to work. Arthur loves his MoM work so much he passes up promotions and needed pay raises to stay where he is. The MoM performs important services for the wizarding community and MoM employees are generally well respected, though not generally well paid. Often MoM employees, even Heads of departments, must seek outside sources of income to supplement their meager earnings. Newt wrote books, Arthur enters drawings offering a cash prize, Ludo gambled excessively and Moody, on a MoM pension, came out of retirement to teach at Hogwarts. However, Molly, who knows well the vicissitudes of MoM employment, wants her children to work there because a small steady paycheck is better than none at all.

GETTING TO THE MOM

The MoM is located in central London. To reach it from 12 Grimmauld Place, exit the Underground after 4 stops, go down a side road to a section with smaller less imposing buildings until reaching a side street that contains shabby-looking offices, a pub, an overflowing skip and an old red phonebooth.

THE HARRY POTTER COMPANION

Visitors' Entrance: The Visitors' Entrance is the old red phonebooth located just before a heavily graffitied wall. It is missing several panes of glass and its telephone hangs crooked on one wall. Using the phone dial 62442, and wait for a woman's voice to speak into the phonebooth. After stating one's name and purpose, a small square silver badge with both inscribed on it will come out of the change return. The phonebooth will then sink down into the ground making a grinding noise. One remains completely in the dark until the phonebooth reaches Level 8, the Main Entrance and Atrium. For security purposes, the phonebooth lift permits travel only between the street and Level 8. To reach any level within the MoM one must use the MoM's internal lifts.

Atrium: Located on Level 8, the Atrium serves as the Main Entrance and is the first hall visitors to the MoM see. Many gilded fireplaces reside on either side of the splendid hall for employees or visiting wizards to arrive or depart the MoM via the Floo Network. Ongoing floo traffic causes a continuous soft whooshing noise to be heard throughout the long hall. Most wizards prefer to arrive or depart the MoM by the Floo Network and queues often form at the fireplaces during various peak travel times. Magical fires are kept burning only during business hours (approximately 8am-6pm). When the MoM closes each night, the fires are turned off.

The Atrium has a polished, dark wood floor, a peacock blue ceiling inlaid with gleaming gold symbols that continually move and change position and walls paneled with shiny dark wood. Looking from the phonebooth into the Atrium, one sees on the left wall in-bound fireplaces and on the right wall out-bound fireplaces. Wizards are permitted to Apparate into the Atrium area during office hours, but may not Apparate into any other part of the building. Halfway down the hall, beyond the fireplaces but directly in line with the phonebooth, is (or was, till Jun 1996) the magnificent Fountain of Magical Brethren.

Fountain of Magical Brethren: This fountain contains a "larger than life" grouping of golden statues standing in the midst of a circular pool of water. The tallest and central figure is a wizard with wand erect. Surrounding him are a beautiful witch, a male centaur, a male goblin in a pointy hat and a male house-elf. The 3 creatures gaze adoringly up at the witch and wizard as if they were gods. Jets of water issue from the wands of the witch and wizard, the point of centaur's crossbow laid arrow, the tip of the goblin's hat and the ears of the house-elf. All coins thrown into the fountain go to St Mungo's.

Dumbledore, during his battle with Voldemort in Jun 1996, brought all the figures of the fountain to life to protect Harry. They were very much the worse for wear afterwards and doubtless they will be repaired though probably not by Dumbledore who wholeheartedly disapproved of the message the fountain presented, ie, that wizards are gods to be looked up to, adored, even worshiped. He feels this wizard-centric view is what allowed Voldemort to gain a toehold among the MoM oppressed, disenfranchised and humiliated in the 1970s and 1980s and, since it hasn't changed, what will allow him to gain a toehold again in the 1990s.

Security Desk: At the far end of the Main Entrance hall, beyond the Fountain of Magical Brethren, to the left of a pair of golden gates, is the security officer's desk located just under a sign that says "security." Security personnel are easily recognizable as they wear peacock blue robes and silver badges. At the desk a guard will search each visiting wizard with a Secrecy Sensor, which obviously doesn't work all that well or Lucius Malfoy wouldn't have continued to get in, then takes her or his wand for registration.

Wand registration is a short simple process. The wand is placed on a brass instrument similar to a baby's scale or a set of scales with only 1 plate. Once a wand is placed on it, it will vibrate. A slit at the bottom of the instrument will eventually spit out a narrow strip of parchment with the wand's relevant details: length, core substance and years in use. In Harry's case the slip read: 11" with a phoenix feather core and used for 4 years. The guard will keep the parchment on a small brass spike and the wand will be returned to its owner as legally no one can deprive a wizard of carrying a wand at any time, even in the MoM, even in Courtroom 10.

Lifts: Beyond the golden gates is a smaller hall with 20 or so lifts in it. The lifts are covered by golden wrought-iron grills and are of an old Victorian-style. They move on pull chains which tend to clatter and jangle rather loudly. These rattling lifts can take a wizard, or Interoffice Memo, to Levels 1-9 but cannot go to the street above or Level 10 below. As wizards cannot use electricity to operate the lifts, they are most probably moved by trolls, located somewhere on or under Level 10, manually pulling on the chains.

Once an elevator grill shuts, with a bang, the chains start to move. Inside each lift are buttons numbered 1 to 9 that correspond to the levels reachable by lift. Simply select the level number and wait. A woman's cool voice, the same voice that was in the phonebooth, will announce each level as the lift stops. As with Muggle lifts, once a lift is going up, it goes all the way up before going all the way down. Unlike Muggle lifts, they have swaying candle lamps at the top that are usually surrounded by flapping Interoffice Memos in the form of paper airplane which one hopes are inflammable.

Although one can catch a lift that is already headed up or down and one can certainly punch a button, the lifts will stop at every floor and open their grills irregardless of what buttons are pushed. This makes sense on a broader scale as Interoffice Memos have no fingers with which to push buttons. They only depart the lifts when their particular floor is announced. If the doors of the lifts didn't open on every floor, every trip up or down, how could Interoffice Memos travel from place to place efficiently?

MoM Levels

The following list of what is on each level should not be considered exhaustive. For a visual aid, see schematic D of the MoM levels. Remember that Level 1 is the level nearest to the Muggle street while Level 10 is farthest under the street. Level 8 is where all visitors enter the building either via the phonebooth lift or the Floo Network. Apparition can be done into and out of any part of the MoM, as Voldemort and his Death Eaters proved, but Security and MoM regulations insist Apparition only be conducted in the Atrium.

Level 1: It is unknown what is on this level but it is presumed to have the Office of the Minister of Magic and offices of attendant personnel who assist in running that office.

Level 2: Dept of Magical Law Enforcement, Improper Use of Magic Office, Auror Headquarters, Wizengamot Administration Services.

Level 3: Dept of Magical Accidents and Catastrophes, Accidental Magic Reversal Squad, Obliviator Headquarters, Muggle-Worthy Excuse Committee.

Level 4: Dept for the Regulation and Control of Magical Creatures, Beast, Being and Spirit Divisions, Goblin Liaison Office, Pest Advisory Bureau.

Level 5: Dept of International Magical Cooperation, International Magical Trading Standards Body, International Magical Office of Law, International Confederation of Wizards, British Seats.

Level 6: Dept of Magical Transport, Floo Network Authority, Broom Regulatory Control, Portkey Office, Apparition Test Center.
Level 7: Dept of Magical Games and Sports, British and Irish Quidditch League Headquarters, Official Gobstones Club, Ludicrous Patents Office.
Level 8: The Atrium, floos, Security, internal lifts. The phonebooth brings visitor here.
Level 9: The Department of Mysteries. The hallway walls are bare and without windows. A plain black door at the end of the hall goes into the department itself while an opening to the left of the door leads down some steps to Level 10. No lift goes further underground than Level 9.
Level 10: This high-security area has rarely been used since 1982. This level has cells for prisoners awaiting trial and Courtroom 10. The bare stone walls in the corridor are graced only with torches in brackets. The doors here are heavy and wooden with iron bolts as well as keyholes. Courtroom 10 has a grimy, dark door with an immense iron lock and heavy iron doorhandle.

BY LEVEL: THE DEPARTMENTS
Departments and offices are listed by level. Associated terminology will be defined within the sections they apply to, ie, Aurors will be explained in Level 2, where Aurors work.

Level 1
Unknown. It is presumed to have offices associated with the Minister of Magic.

Level 2
Dept of Magical Law Enforcement: It is the largest department of the 7 departments in the MoM and the one to which the 6 other departments all, with the possible exception of the Dept of Mysteries, must ultimately answer or be responsive to. Barty Crouch Sr was Head of this department from sometime prior to 1970 until 1982. The DMLE is currently run by Amelia Bones, who took over from Barty Sr in 1983.

Aurors Headquarters: Aurors are powerfully magical Dark wizard hunters. All Aurors are loyal to the MoM and its objective of ridding the world of Dark wizards, though a few aren't too sure the MoM knows what it's doing and are working with Dumbledore's OoP on the side just in case. Rather like the American FBI or the British MI5, MoM Aurors deal with internal threats, in other words, those extremely magically powerful individuals whose actions are illegally Dark and taking place within the British MoM's jurisdiction. While a certain level of Dark activity is personal choice, illegal Dark activity is that which so heinous as to be criminal (treason, torture, murder) or so glaringly obvious as to pose a security risk to the wizarding world (Muggle-baiting, Muggle-killing, attempting to take over the world, etc).

Being an Auror is a particularly dangerous job and not one the average highly talented wizard would wish to apply for. Alastor "Mad-Eye" Moody, a now retired Auror, has many missing body parts from his days working as an Auror during Voldemort's first attempt to rise to power. Frank and Alice Longbottom are both permanently insane directly because of their work as Aurors. Still others have ended up dead. Both Harry and Ron claim they would like be Aurors but it remains to be seen if they can make the outstanding grades needed, 5 NEWTs at the E level, or survive Auror Training, a 3-year-long and very difficult process.

The last new Auror added to the force was Tonks in 1992. No new Aurors were added between 1992 and 1996. Given the importance of this job to the MoM, one would think that any qualified person applying for and surviving Auror Training would be added to the force. It would seem either wizards don't apply or applicants wash out in large percentages. It's doubtless a little of both. Still, with Voldemort and his Death Eaters on the loose, what Aurors the MoM has they are likely to lose rather quickly and an educated guess says the MoM will be actively recruiting new Auror candidates very soon.

Current Aurors besides Nymphadora "Tonks" Tonks, include Kingsley Shacklebolt, Mr Williamson, Mr Dawlish and a witch with a patch over her eye. Auror Headquarters is quite large and there are many Aurors, but exactly how many Auror there are and who they are is unknown. Aurors probably prefer it this way for safety reasons. As Moody's life proves, one can make a lot of bad enemies as an Auror. It is better that no one but MoM employees ever know who all the Aurors are than have them listed in *The Daily Prophet* and picked off one at a time. To this end, Aurors also have no uniforms, badges or other identifying marks. All work is plain clothes or undercover.

Auror Headquarters: The office is located just down the hall from the lift and through a pair of heavy oak doors. There are many cubicles in the Auror Headquarters and in general the Aurors are a pretty messy bunch. There is a second set of oak doors at the back of the room, so Aurors do exhibit a certain amount of paranoia and like to have at least 1 back-up means of escape even in their own office.

Auror Training: This 3-year program requires candidates have 5 or more E level NEWTs before even applying. NEWTs in DADA, Potions, Transfiguration and Charms are required, in addition to whatever else the candidate may have NEWTs in. After being accepted the candidate is given to a battery of psychological tests and numerous training courses. Once the program is successfully completed a trainee can, if she or he still chooses to do so, become an Auror. Courses one might take during training include Concealment and Disguise or Stealth and Tracking which rely heavily on the candidate knowing how to Transfigure and Untransfigure. Being able to work with potions and antidotes is also very important as Aurors risk almost constant very skilled and often subtle assassination attempts. And of course nothing matters more than the personal practice of CONSTANT VIGILANCE!

Magical Law Enforcement Squad: These squads deal with infractions of magical law, excluding Dark wizards. They have regular foot patrols, Hit Wizards and other things that one shudders to think about under their control.

Hit Wizards: These wizards are similar to a SWAT team, but have as their objective killing the target. They are best described as assassins or, more kindly put, snipers. Once a Hit Wizard is called in, it's all over.

Magical Law Enforcement Patrols: These patrols go around on foot looking for shady activity. They deal with anti-Muggle pranksters, wizards that engage in Muggle-baiting and the like. They also deal with wizards engaged in non-Muggle-related offenses such as indiscreetly sending up shooting stars, releasing large numbers of owls in daylight as part of a mass mailing campaign, attempting to smuggle flying carpets into the country or enchanting and flying Muggle cars.

Anti-Muggle Pranksters: These wizards do things just to annoy Muggles such as create regurgitating toilets. Wizards of this persuasion see Muggles as less than human and therefore fair game.

Muggle-Baiting: The use of witchcraft to harm Muggles in some way such as selling them shrinking keys. It's a punishable offense, but cases are hard to prosecute as most Muggles don't realize they're being baited. For instance, Muggles will never admit a key magically shrank by itself but will cling to a non-magical answer despite all contrary evidence and insist they lost it.

The Council of Magical Law: aka Wizard Court. This court is lower than the Wizengamot. The trials held here are jury trials headed by the Head of the DMLE. A small jury composed of a defendant's peers votes by a show of hands on the defendant's guilt or innocence. Unlike Muggle courts, there are no lawyers for either side for cases tried this court. Cases are prosecuted by the court and defendants must present their own defense. Like Muggle courts, this is an open court where average wizards and the press are welcome to come and watch the proceedings.

In cases where the defendant is a highly dangerous criminal, such as a Death Eater, the council uses Courtroom 10. The Council of Magical Law, not the Wizengamot, is the body which tried most of the Death Eaters and assorted associated followers of Voldemort in Courtroom 10 during the 1970-1982 period. Although these individuals had committed crimes of a serious nature, they were tried here because their guilt was a foregone conclusion and it was thought best to make a public example of them.

Wizengamot: aka Wizard High Court, Full Wizard Court. Headed by the Chief Warlock, currently Albus Dumbledore, and comprised of a body of 50 members called Elders, who are all quite elderly, the wizards who form the Wizengamot wear distinctive plum-colored robes with an elaborately embroidered silver W on the left breast. This court presides over only the most serious of cases and all attending Elders act as jury deciding the verdict by a show of hands. During a trial, any member of this court may act as an Interrogator and put questions to the defendant or any witnesses appearing. A Court Scribe will take down all the proceedings. As in the lower court, the court and the defendant each act without the benefit of lawyers. Persons directly involved in the cases may attend, such as the arresting Aurors, witnesses or the family of a victim, but this is a closed court permitting no outsiders or members of the press. This is not to say this is a secret court as court records may be accessed by the public, but it is certainly very quite about its doings.

Wizengamot Charter of Rights: Among other things, this charter allows the accused to present witnesses in support of her or his defense case. On the surface this sounds fair especially as, reflective of British Muggle law, British magical law considers everyone innocent until proven guilty. However, close inspection shows the legal system to be extremely biased in favor of the courts. By denying independent lawyers for both parties, prosecution and defense, it is extremely unlikely anyone brought up on charges will be found innocent. While advantageous for the MoM, it does leave wizards at large short changed when it comes to justice.

For instance, of legal age is 17 in Britain's wizarding world, whether or not one is still in school. This is why Fred and George in 1996 could leave Hogwarts if they chose and not be in any legal trouble for doing so. However, it also means that at 17 one can be tried and disciplined as an adult even if one is in school. By law, Harry should never have been tried as an adult by the Wizengamot at age 15 for doing underage out-of-school magic and there was no legal precedent for such an action. But it is this sort of jackassery that Cornelius Fudge has pushed the courts into and Amelia Bones has failed to circumvent or counteract.

The legal system is a reflection of the Head of the DMLE and the Minister of Magic. If the Minister of Magic is corrupt, it is the duty of the Head of the DMLE to observe legal procedure, protect the court system and make sure justice is not subverted. Sadly, Madam Bones appears disinterested in doing any of this. This is no surprise however as a competent Head has been missing from the DMLE for over 25 years. Under Barty Sr the courts were a stage from which he promoted himself to a gullible wizarding public. Under Amelia the courts are Star-Chambers Fudge uses to crush any political opposition. Whatever the MoM's original intent for the courts and the charter, they are long gone now and wizards stand a better chance of justice in Muggle courts.

Disciplinary Hearing: This type of hearing is for underage magic and similar, very minor, breaches of magical law. It is supposed to be a very low-key affair with the Head of the DMLE, and perhaps a couple of other wizards in the department, meeting with the accused in an office setting. A parent or guardian should also be present if the accused is underage. The hearing should feature reviewing the circumstances of the alleged illegal action, allowing the accused to present her or his case and any witnesses, then deciding on an appropriate disciplinary action, if any is required, or clearing the individual completely and expunging any record of the crime.

Misuse of Muggle Artifacts Office: Arthur Weasley is the Head of this office. It has only 1 other employee, a warlock named Perkins who is Arthur's assistant. This office deals with bewitched things that are Muggle-made and liable to fall back into Muggle hands. Occasionally Muggle-baiting suspects are brought in for questioning or even prosecuted by this office. A wizard intentionally selling a bewitched tea set to an unsuspecting Muggle is a good example of Muggle-baiting. Once a Muggle is attacked by the sugar tongs or scalded by the kettle, Arthur's office steps in. Usually in such situations Memory Charms are applied to the Muggle to cover up the event, the offending items are retrieved (and added to Arthur's collection) and the incident is fully investigated to see how it happened and if any wizard is responsible.

This office has the authority to act on tips and conduct raids on the homes, workplaces or storerooms of individuals suspected of enchanting Muggle objects for resale to Muggles. In the summer of 1992 Arthur was a party to 9 raids in 1 night and proved he was not above raiding even fellow Order members such as Mundungus "Dung" Fletcher, who in turn proved he was not above hexing Arthur to escape with his goods. While Arthur's Muggle protection work sometimes puts him at odds with some OoP members, occasionally he can do an OoP member a good turn. His office was able to get Moody off on a lesser charge with a fine and warning for his exploding dustbins when the Improper Use of Magic Office was ready to step in and send him to prison.

The MoM doesn't have much respect for the work of this office as demonstrated by its location. See schematic E for an overview. This office is located on the far side of Level 2, as far from the elevators as possible. There is no direct route to it and to reach it one must exit the elevator, go down the hall, around the corner and Auror Headquarters. Exiting Auror Headquarters through a second set of oak doors, one must turn left into another corridor then right into a dimly lit, shabby, dead-end corridor. At the end of the corridor are 2 doors. On the left is a broomcloset and on the right is a door with a tarnished plaque which reads: Misuse of Muggle Artifacts Office.

Arthur's office is smaller than the broomcloset and lacks even one enchanted window, which most hallways of the MoM have. It is littered with enchanted Muggle objects such as hiccuping toasters and gloves that twiddle their thumbs. With 2 desks crammed into the miniscule office there is barely room to move let alone work. In addition, all the walls are lined with file cabinets on top of which are tottering piles of files. What wallspace there is has been covered with posters of cars, dismantled engines, diagrams of how to wire a plug, post boxes, and other of Arthur's Muggle-technology obsessions. Perkins seems a bit overwhelmed by it all, but Arthur likes it and it probably reminds him of his shed at home.

Registry of Proscribed Charmable Objects: Part of the Misuse of Muggle Artifacts Office's work is deciding what objects shouldn't be charmed because they might fall into Muggle hands. Teapots, gloves, toilets, doorknobs and keys are just a few of the items on the registry's list. Carpets are also defined as a Muggle Artifact by the registry, so flying carpets, while prevalent and acceptable across the Middle East, can't be imported into Britain and those attempting to smuggle them in would be in serious violation of British law. However if one had a flying carpet in the family already, under grandfather laws it could probably be kept, though not flown.

The Muggle Protection Act: A bill that Arthur had been working on for some years and was shepherding through the legislative process in the summer of 1992. Its aim was to further increase the protection of Muggles from abuse by wizards. The bill was objected to by some wizards, namely Lucius Malfoy who tried to discredit Arthur to stop it passing, but in the end it was passed. No doubt the numerous attacks on Muggle-born wizards at Hogwarts in 92/93 prompted a more serious effort by the MoM to protect Muggles at large, much to Lucius' chagrin.

Improper Use of Magic Office: Mafalda Hopkirk appears to be the Head of this office as her signature is on all the correspondence. It handles cases of underage magic or the misuse of magic, such as illegal Animagi turning into beetles and eavesdropping on private conversations in restricted areas. The office apparently can detect misused magic if it's blatantly misused, but beyond that its detection methods aren't all that accurate. For instance, these methods didn't detect that the Hover Charm done at 4 Privet Drive in Jul 1992 was done by Dobby. The office believed because Harry was the only wizard living in the house, he must have done the magic which is logical but incorrect. This flaw in the office's data collection and interpretation methods means many wizards are wrongfully cited or prosecuted each year.

The office also tends to be highly reactionary and overzealous. Citing the Decree for the Reasonable Restriction of Underage Sorcery, 1875, Paragraph C, Harry was threatened with expulsion from Hogwarts after Dobby's Hover Charm usage. This despite the fact this office doesn't have the right to expel anyone from Hogwarts because Hogwarts, in 1992, was an independent organization not controlled by, or required to answer to, the MoM in any way. While the MoM might have found some alternative means of punishing him, at no time was Harry allowed to come into the MoM to explain what had happened and have his record cleared. He was not even asked to. He was presumed guilty in the eyes of this befuddled office and stayed that way.

In the summer of 1995 Harry was forced to use underage out-of-school magic for the first time ever in order to save his own life as well as that of his cousin, Dudley Dursley. The Improper Use of Magic Office, using the bogus 1992 Hover Charm charge that Harry was never allowed to clear, prosecuted Harry for a second offense, by the Wizengamot, at age 15. To say this office is inept as well as unjust is an understatement. Yet, it's continually allowed to interfere with young wizards' lives unchecked. It can, and does, even provide criminal records (that are in fact false) to the MoM when young wizards apply for work and have their background routinely investigated as part of the process.

The Improper Use of Magic Office not only sticks its nose in children's business, it manages to get itself involved in messing up older wizards' lives as well. Using its authority to get involved in cases of magic that risk being noticed by Muggles, which is an offense under Section 13 of the ICW Statute of Secrecy, this office attempted to charge Moody for his projectile-shooting, noise-maker, intruder-alert dustbins. This crime was such a terrible breach of Section 13 that Moody risked going to Azkaban. Fortunately Arthur got to the scene of the crime first and Moody got away with a caution, if one can call 10 months in a trunk under the Imperius Curse of a notorious Death Eater fortunate or a caution.

In point of fact, Moody had every legal right to protect himself against perceived threats, especially if the MoM was unwilling to provide him adequate protection or a fresh start with a new identity somewhere else when he retired. As the MoM long considered Moody's behavior outrageous, they were entirely unwilling to protect him or even take his safety concerns seriously. As later events in 93/94 proved, his precautions were entirely justified and didn't go far enough. This office and the MoM will be extremely lucky not to get hit with a lawsuit for A) failing to protect him and B) attempting to prevent him from protecting himself, a basic human right.

Animagi Registry: By law an Animagus must register with the MoM. The registry was primarily designed to help an Animagus should a transformation go wrong or find an Animagus when, after transforming, she or he forgot she or he was human and took up life as the animal she or he became. The registry shows what animal an Animagi becomes and lists her or his distinguishing markings. Should an Animagus choose to engage in activities that are unlawful, eg, becoming a beetle to trespass and spy, the registry can help officials spot them and move to protect others by trapping and arresting them. Penalties are very severe for not registering and include prison, however the registry is kept at the Improper Use of Magic Office which, given its level of incompetence and willingness to pin crimes on innocent wizards, makes it easy to see why so few Animagi choose to register.

The registry is very small as there have only been 7 Animagi in the century c 1890-1990 who chose to register. Of the known registered Animagi, Pr McGonagall (tabby cat) is the only one Harry has knowingly been acquainted with. Who the other 6 are, or if they are even alive, is unknown. It would seem that all 7 could still be alive during Harry's early life and school years. The registry is a bit of a conundrum itself. It claims to register wizards as soon as they discover they are an Animagus and states that all the registered Animagi seem to have had this talent from birth. This would imply a month-old infant could, and would, change into an animal and back again. However since being an Animagus is considered very rare, it may be Animagus abilities develop later than birth or even infancy and most wizards hide the fact they are Animagi. Rita Skeeter (beetle), the only known unregistered "natural" rather than created Animagus, obviously didn't develop her talent in infancy or childhood where her parents might have spotted it and knew enough to hide her gifting when she did develop it. This would all imply she became an Animagus in her teens while at boarding school and that Animagus abilities may be connected to puberty for some individuals.

Looking beyond Rita to other known and unregistered Animagi, we see that all of these are Animagi by talent, making the Animagus abilities on the whole seem a little less rare. Peter Pettigrew (rat), Sirius Black (dog) and James Potter (stag) all became Animagi through diligent study and practice. Since even a wizard as "talentless" as Peter can become an Animagus, it must be considered a natural talent available to all wizards and acquirable if one is willing to put one's mind to figuring it out. This being the case, there may be many 1,000 of unregistered "taught" Animagi. However, since most wizards are responsible in their use of magic, they aren't much of a worry. Dark wizard Animagi on the other hand pose a major threat, but they are unlikely to register. Thus the registry idea is really a bit useless.

Although it has never been said what exactly Tom Riddle got his medal for Magical Merit for during his school years, it would not be surprising to discover he found the secret to becoming an Animagus by talent rather than birth. Certainly Tom, as Voldemort, seems a little more than likely to have the ability to turn into a snake. He may even be on the registry as one of the 7 known Animagi. But beyond that, Tom was a great scholar, perhaps the greatest ever in the wizarding world. He could find out things and make connections others couldn't, such as where the Chamber of Secrets was, how to get into it and what it contained, which even Dumbledore couldn't do. If anyone discovered how to become an Animagus through sheer intelligence and talent, it must be Tom Riddle.

Which leads us back to James, Sirius and Peter. They must have had some basis for thinking they could figure out how to become Animagi before actually trying to do so as all wizards know Animagi transformations are danger-fraught even for natural Animagi. This indicates someone previous to James et al's student days had already achieved Animagi transformation by talent and left a record of doing so. Tom Riddle probably wrote a paper on it, which was subsequently put in the Restricted Section. James, with his Invisibility Cloak, was then able to acquire it. Using Tom's essay as a guide the trio was then eventually able to figure out the process since James and Sirius were the most talented students, Remus was the most intelligent student and Peter the hardest working student in entire school.

It seems likely too that Dumbledore, being as magically powerful and talented as he is, is probably also on the registry as an Animagus from birth since he was teaching Transfiguration at Hogwarts in the 1940s and being an Animagus seems to be plus in landing that position. What exactly he could turn into is a mystery. Why he would even want to given it would be far easier for him, or anyone, to Transfigure into an animal and keep his humanity is an even bigger mystery. Perhaps individuals with this talent feel a primal need to become fully animal. This is really all that could explain Animagi transformations when Transfiguration is easier, safer, legal and has all the benefits of Animagi without any of the drawbacks, if indeed the drawbacks exist. See Animagi in Magical Talents, Part III, for a further discussion.

Level 3
Dept of Magical Accidents and Catastrophes: This very important department handles all the really big snafus in the wizarding world that memory modification just can't cover up either because too many people are involved or the event happened too publicly and the whole world already knows about it. Fudge was Junior Minister (ie, second-in-command of the department) here in 1981 when the Peter Pettigrew-Sirius Black mass Muggle murder incident took place. Arguably the biggest snafu in British wizarding or MoM history, the successful handling of this event probably got Fudge tapped for the Minister of Magic job a decade later.

Accidental Magic Reversal Department: This "department," really an office, reverses unintentional magic that has consequences beyond what the average wizard can deal with. This office stepped in and deflated Marge Dursley then modified her memory after Harry accidentally blew her up. Harry didn't know how to deflate her and was out of school and underage to do the magic needed to deflate her. In addition, as a Muggle, memory modification was essential for preserving Harry's status as a wizard as well as the existence of wizards in general. No penalties attach to cases of accidental magic, though all wizards are urged to exercise self-control to prevent such events.

Accidental Magic Reversal Squad: Squads consist of trained Obliviators and others who go out in teams, usually of 2 wizards, to help reverse incidents of accidental magic and modify the memory of any Muggles that might have witnessed the accident. They are also the group that assists Splinched wizards, so the individuals on these squads clearly have a high level of magical skill and enjoy doing reams of paperwork.

Obliviator Headquarters: An Obliviator is a specialist who performs Memory Charms on people when they see something they shouldn't like dragons. Arnold "Arnie" Peasegood is an Obliviator with the Accidental Magic Reversal Squad. An Obliviator warlock in plus-fours was at QWC 1994 modifying Mr Robert's memory 10 times a day. Gilderoy Lockhart might have been a great Obliviator if only he'd used his skills for good instead of evil.

Office of Misinformation: This office becomes involved only in the very worst wizard-Muggle catastrophes or accidents. Often this office will work with the Muggle PM to cover up an event of magic too glaring to be ignored. When Peter Pettigrew killed 12 people (13 only if one counts the 12 Muggles plus Peter himself who was thought to have died but did not) with a curse, this office disseminated the lie that it was a gas explosion and the PM obligingly did the same.

Muggle-Worthy Excuse Committee: These folks cook up the stories wizards circulate when something goes terribly wrong and a magical catastrophe occurs. They probably have several banks of filing cabinets full of ready-to-use excuses to offer Muggles.

Level 4
Dept for the Regulation and Control of Magical Creatures: This is the second largest department in the MoM, only the DMLE is larger. It divides itself into 3 main branches: Beast, Being and Spirit Divisions with many more subdivisions. For an overview, see schematic C.

Beast Division: This division is responsible for all MoM classified Beasts. It uses a 5X system to rate a beast's level of dangerousness, with 5X being the most dangerous possible and 1X being dead boring. For a discussion on how beasts are rated and why, as well as a look at which beasts have garnered what rating, see FB. For a look at the beasts themselves, see Magical Beasts in Part III of this book.

Ban on Experimental Breeding: While the MoM has no desire to limit the creativity of wizards, over time the breeding of new species has almost always led to disappointment and disgust, if not actual death and destruction. This ban, the work of Newt Scamander, was wisely passed in 1965. The ban makes the creation of new species illegal in territories under the jurisdiction of the British MoM, which means Hagrid broke this ban by creating the blast-ended skrewts in 93/94. Of course, wizards are free to travel to other MoM jurisdictions with less stringent rules on breeding if they feel they must experiment.

Centaur Liaison Office: This office was established for the use of centaurs but as of June 1996 not one has ever used it. There is a certain stigma attached to wizards working in this office. Whether centaurs know or care about the office's existence is debatable. Perhaps Firenze will be able to use it to have the MoM liaise with his herd for his successful, death-free, repatriation.

Committee for the Disposal of Dangerous Creatures: This committee executes creatures that pose an immanent risk to Muggles or wizards. The committee sends out a MoM official and an executioner armed with a weapon for the actual disposal. The law requires that all parties hear the official execution notice read aloud, then sign it, before the execution can take place. It's considered an impressive office to work for despite the actual nastiness of work. The dishwasher at the Leaky Cauldron told a veela at QWC 1994 he worked for this office after falling under her spell.

Dragon Research and Restraint Bureau: Dragons are a natural resource in the wizarding world. Without dragons, many magical potions, not to mention wands, would never work. Their existence must therefore be insured so that future generations of wizards can actually do magic. Many risk-loving individuals, like Charlie Weasley, work as both researcher and restrainer. Researchers study dragon behavior, find environments suitable to dragon needs and rescue dragons hatched or otherwise acquired by well-meaning but rather stupid individuals. Restrainers capture wild dragons that are in unsafe areas, recapture dragons that have gone rogue and restrain dragons to keep them out of reach of both Muggles and wizards.

While it's true that Muggles need to be protected from dragons, dragon-Muggle interaction has always been extremely rare. In cases of dragon attack on Muggles, the bureau sends out wizards to subdue the dragon and relocate it to a safe area as well as administer Memory Charms to the unfortunate Muggles who witnessed the attack. As for wizard poachers that are attacked, if the dragons don't eat them alive, the MoM certainly will when they turn up in hospitals with suspicious burns or bites. The excellent work of the bureau has resulted in no dragon attacks on Muggles since 1932 and no wizards or Muggles killed by dragon attack in several centuries. Bravo!

Ghoul Task Force: This office is primarily for the removal of ghouls from formerly wizard-owned homes that have now passed into Muggle hands. The task force will try to relocate a ghoul to a new wizarding home, as ghouls are very desirable pets, but only if it is of a harmless variety. Murderous ghouls must be removed to derelict dwellings or completely uninhabited areas and chameleon ghouls unfortunately are often too difficult to find to relocate.

Pest Sub-Division: This sub-division deals with infestations of magical beasts such as bundimuns, nogtails, chizpurfles and the like. They keep albino bloodhounds and other interesting things used in magical beast infestation removal around the office, which makes it quite an entertaining, if slightly smelly, place to work. See FB for more detail on the various beasts they are involved with.

Pet License Office: The actual name of this office eludes discovery, but wizards who wish to own certain obviously magical beasts, such as crups, require a special license from the DRCMC. Prospective owners are usually required to pass a test to insure they fully understand how to care for the creature they wish to own, know how to disguise it in Muggle areas and are aware of all safety procedures to observe if the adopted creature is considered dangerous.

Werewolf Capture Unit: Being in the Beast Division, this unit only works with those werewolves currently in wolf form. The capture unit's job is to capture werewolves who are injured, ill, running free in populated areas or otherwise in situations where they pose an immanent threat to others or are in danger themselves. Captured wolves are detained until they can transform back into wizards and afterwards given needed aid and assistance or just a good talking to.

Werewolf Registry: Another Newt Scamander idea, the registry was established in 1947 and all wizards must register once they become werewolves. Unlike the Animagi Registry, this registry really does have the safety of the werewolf in mind. The capture unit when called out to deal with a problem wolf can check the Werewolf Registry and find out if there are any werewolves living in the area. If the wolf is a known werewolf, the unit can take proper precautions to insure the wolf is not destroyed or harmed while simultaneously taking proper precautions to insure the safety of locals and unit members. The registry is only for British werewolves so the capture unit is occasionally stuck dealing with real wolves or even wizards who turn out to be foreign werewolves on holiday in Britain.

Spirit Division: This division handles ghosts, poltergeists and assorted spirits. Some office in this division would have been responsible for ordering Moaning Myrtle confined to Hogwarts after haunting Olive Hornsby for years. Currently, no actual offices within this division are known, though there does seem to be a ghost postal service.

Being Division: Muggles, goblins, wizards, werewolves (in human form), hags, vampires and house-elves would all deal, and be dealt with, by this division. Having to juggle the needs and desires of many different magicals, it is one of the more extensive divisions and the offices listed below represent only a small fraction of those in the division.

Goblin Liaison Office: Cuthbert Mockridge is Head of this office. Given the number of riots and rebellions goblins have raised in Britain over the last 400 years alone, the fact that goblins control all the wizarding world's money and the fact that goblins are anti-wizard, it must be a pretty interesting, sometimes dangerous, office to work for and one that requires diplomacy, guts and strong defensive magic skills.

Office for House-Elf Relocation: This office relocates the unfortunate elf who finds herself or himself living in a home where there is no longer a blood descendant (or spouse of a blood descendant) of a particular lineage to work for and thus needs to find a new family to enslave herself or himself to. In theory, this office should have been able to help Dobby and Winky but trying to help house-elves that wish to be paid or are disgraced was doubtless beyond even their capability.

Werewolf Support Services: This office helps newly bitten people adjust to their condition by giving them information on the disorder and ways of containing it, organizing local support packs where werewolves can let their hair down with others of their kind and helping them find work or a place to live where their condition will not be aggravated by the ignorance of others. At least that's what it's supposed to do. Despite the very compassionate wizards running this office, they've had a difficult time making a difference in werewolves' lives due to the MoM.

Werewolves are considered part-humans by the MoM and the MoM has never been interested in helping part-humans in any meaningful way. It has in fact been the chief promoter of negative legislation as well as negative attitudes regarding part-humans, most particularly werewolves. Anti-werewolf legislation, designed by Dolores Umbridge then Senior Secretary to the Minister of Magic, passed into law in 1993 and made the average werewolf's plight even more desperate by cutting off any possibility of getting a job and thus income to survive on. Hopefully these attitudes will start to change, laws will be reversed and decent amounts of funding for the support office and cure research will be allocated now that Dolores has left the ministry and the MoM needs all the allies it can get.

Level 5
Dept of International Magical Cooperation: This department works on anything that has to do with other MoMs and their jurisdictions. The DIMC helped organize QWC 1994 and the 1994 attempt to revive the TT. Barty Crouch Sr was the DIMC's much respected Head from 1983 until 1994 when he disappeared and was later found to have been murdered by his son.

International Magical Trading Standards Body: This body works on important things like standardizing the minimum thickness for an imported cauldron. Percy worked here for part of his first year at the MoM and later became assistant to Barty Crouch Sr, jumping numerous more qualified individuals for the post. Ultimately he began handling the day-to-day office affairs for Barty Sr and did so for a number of months in 93/94. It would seem the International Magical Trading Standards Body is a good entry-level place to work if one wants to fast track to the top.

International Magical Office of Law: This office works out cross-national complaints and assists other MoMs in concluding legal matters that cross borders such as smuggling chimera eggs or extraditing criminals that have sought refuge on foreign shores, though it appears to have failed in the case of Voldemort. His whereabouts were well known to be Albania, 1981-1993, and several witless wizards stumbled onto him, but he was never apprehended, perhaps in part because he was a noncorporeal vapor.

International Confederation of Wizards, British Seats: This is where the British delegation for the ICW gets together to talk about what needs to be addressed in future conferences as well as the implementation of current ICW rules and regulations in their jurisdiction. These individuals are not a part of the legislative body of the British MoM, for which there is no space designated anywhere at the MoM. The MoM's elected legislators, who are a much larger group than the ICW representatives, meet in another building located in London, much as the British Muggle Parliament has a building of its own and all other various British ministries are housed in other buildings.

Level 6
Dept of Magical Transport: This department is in control of all forms of wizarding transport including the Knight Bus. They have the authority to administer the Apparition Test, can fine people for creating an illegal Portkey or pull an unsafe broom off the market. Any form of transport is controlled or regulated by this office and any transport-related issue or crime is addressed by this office.

Floo Network Authority: This office oversees the Floo Network and Floo Network Regulators.

Floo Network: All wizards have at least one hearth, usually in the kitchen of a home or in the public area of a business, that is hooked up to the Floo Network. All wizards' hearths hooked together form the Floo Network which may be used for place-to-place travel or magical fire conversations (ie, floo calls, floo phone) within a contiguous landmass of a MoM. Wizards of all ages may use the network for either purpose. A hearth does not have to have a magical fire going for a wizard to arrive at another hearth or receive a call from another hearth, but a wizard must depart from or place a call from an existing magical fire. It is presumed that one cannot floo travel (or floo call) internationally because there is no way to magically tie floos across an ocean. The fact no one built a fireplace at QWC 1994 to bring wizards from overseas and no one ever makes an international floo call seems to confirm this.

Floo Network Regulator: Regulators are wizards that are in charge of the day-to-day operations and functioning ability of the Floo Network. Floos can be watched by a Regulator to see if and when someone's using a floo as a point of arrival, but a Regulator cannot tell who is using the fire or where the incoming wizard or call originated. Marietta Edgecombe's mother is a Regulator.

Floo Regulation Panel: The panel oversees which floos get hooked up, when and for how long. They are also the authority that sees to it that floos are disconnected when wizards move out of a house. Arthur has (possibly now had) a friend on the panel that he persuaded to hook up the Dursley's fire for a day in Aug 1994 so he could pick Harry up and transport him to the Burrow. Normally Muggle fireplaces are never supposed to be hooked up to the network and after what happened at the Dursley's they probably never will be again.

Broom Regulatory Control: This office is in charge of broom safety and regulation. It tests brooms to see that they're up to certain safety and design standards, pulls brooms off the market if they are found to be unsafe, studies broom-related or flight charms and sends inspectors to various broom companies to make sure all manufacture is done in an approved way. There is no age limit for broom ownership nor flight test to qualify as a broom rider but all manufacturers must number their brooms and register the buyer of a broom with the Broom Regulatory Control office. This is so the office knows who to contact if a stolen broom is found, a broom is found at the scene of a crime, a Muggle gets a hold of flying boom or a flyer is injured by some malfunction inherent in the broom.

Portkey Office: This office arranged the time-activated Portkeys for QWC 1994 ticket holders to insure orderly arrivals and departures. It's the only authority that can legally create a Portkey, however, anyone can create a Portkey using very basic magical skills and there is no way for the office to detect the creation or usage of an illegal Portkey unless it's done right in front of a MoM official. While it's understandable and commendable that the MoM wishes to control Portkeys to prevent serious accidents, they are fighting an uphill battle.

Apparition Test Center: The center tests people age 17 and up on their Apparating and Disapparating abilities. The test can be passed with distinction or failed rather miserably. Some people have to take it 2 times (Charlie Weasley) to pass and though there is no limit as to how many times a wizard may repeat the test, at a certain point an embarrassment factor kicks in and riding a broomstick, taking the Knight Bus or using the Floo Network for a period of time doesn't seem so bad.

Level 7
Looking out from the lift one sees a slightly messy corridor lined with posters of Quidditch teams hanging crooked on both the walls.

Dept of Magical Games and Sports: This department has been in charge of all magical games and sports played in the MoM's territory for several centuries. Ludo Bagman was the most recent Head, from sometime after 1982 until Jun 1995. Under his administration the DMGS, in conjunction with the DIMC, helped organize QWC 1994 and the 94/95 attempt to restart the TT, which is not too shabby as a legacy.

British and Irish Quidditch League: Although teams are individually owned and operated by various wizards or wizard consortiums, this office establishes the League teams and rules of the game, organizes pitches where League games may be played without the observance of Muggles and sells tickets to all matches. How exactly private ownership can benefit a specific owner, or owners, with the MoM controlling everything including ticket sales is a bit nebulous. There is probably no monetary benefit to team ownership which is why Ron claimed with *infinite* money already in his possession he would own a Quidditch team.

It's been said that this office was set up and promulgated the first official Quidditch rules in 1750. This is 58 years after the ICW made the MoMs responsible for magical games and sports played in their territories and 76 years after the DMGS supposedly already existed and limited the number of teams playing to 13. All one can do is admire the League's fortitude and all those who played World Cup games for 227 years and European Cup games for 98 years without agreed upon official rules or even DMGSs and disagree violently with world-renowned Quidditch historians like Kennilworthy Whisp.

Official Gobstones Club: There are many Gobstones players throughout Britain and this office oversees local clubs, organizes tournaments in secure areas, standardizes the rules and equipment of the game and encourages wizards to get involved in the sport. Played at the keen amature level rather than professional level, it nonetheless has many ardent fans and followers.

Ludicrous Patents Office: Over the years wizards have created many unique things, as well as tinkered around with other wizard's creations to make something new and improved. To this end, this office establishes patents for all manner of magic including charms, potions and devices to name but a few. Most of what passes through their doors is pretty ludicrous, but every now and again a real winner like Mrs Skower's All-Purpose Magical Mess Remover or Bertie Bott's Every Flavor Beans comes along and makes wading through all those genuinely inane patent requests worthwhile.

Level 8
See Getting to the MoM for complete information on this area.

Level 9
Dept of Mysteries: This department is fairly hidden as its work is top secret. People who work here are called Unspeakables because they are unable speak about what they

do. Located on Level 9, one must exit the lift, go down the long stone corridor, through the plain black door at the end and into a circular room with black walls, 12 black doors, a black marble floor and blue-flamed candles. The 12 doors are handleless, unmarked, and rotate, usually after a door has been opened then closed again, to confuse intruders. Individuals who work here know that by simply stating aloud the door or area needed, the right door will open automatically. Four of these doors have an X burned into them since Jun 1996.

Of the 11 chambers (the 12th door goes back to Level 9's corridor and the lift), only the contents of 5 are known to Harry. See schematic F for an overview of the entire level including the various chambers. The exact placement of all but the chamber devoted to Time are unknown. The chambers are said to contain the great forces of the universe and Unspeakables spend their lives studying these deep mysteries. Broderick Bode, who worked in the DoM till he was murdered, seems to have been studying time which for obvious reasons is closely connected to prophecy and he might have been studying that as well.

Brain Room: This long rectangular room has lamps on golden chains hanging low above a few empty desks. In the very middle of the room is an enormous glass tank big enough for 6 teenagers to swim in. The tank is filled with deep green liquid that is probably a magical solution of some kind and contains a number of pearly white brains drifting lazily about in it. The brains are rather unattractive, looking something like slimy cauliflowers. Each one has long ribbon of tentacles hanging off it which display many moving images on them as if they were frames on an unwound roll of magical film. Whose brains these were, why they are being studied and what their actual function at the MoM is, is a mystery. One would speculate that extreme human intelligence is what is being studied but this presupposes the brains are in fact human and intelligent which cannot be ascertained of a certainty.

Attempting to touch any of the brains is not advised as they tend to wrap themselves tightly around anyone touching them like an octopus on a rock and are incredibly difficult to disengage even by magical means. A brain's intent, once it touches a living being, is to implant its entire thought contents into the new mind. This process does however take some time to complete during which the connection must be fully maintained for the transfer to take. Ron was accidentally attached to a brain for 20 to 30 minutes and had to be treated with Obliviating Cream to make him forget what the brain passed on to his mind. However, the result of Ron's contact with the brain remains to be seen.

Obviously some of the brain's contents were passed on to Ron or the use of Obliviating Cream would not have been necessary. Madam Pomfrey felt the cream was working but whether Obliviating Cream can actually eliminate the brain's thoughts completely is questionable. It may only be able to cover them up, much like a Memory Charm. Certainly if the brain made Ron so intelligent he never had to study to ace his exams or so magically talented he could put Harry and Hermione to shame, he'd probably be ok with what happened. But if the brain's leavings somehow changed his personality, or gave him 2 personalities – like Harry, he'd likely be quite upset.

Death Chamber: A slightly creepy place, this rectangular room is larger than the Brain Room with a sunken stone pit in the middle. The surrounding space is comprised of levels of stone, set in amphitheater style, all around the room. It has all the hallmarks of an ancient Greek theater, complete with stark odd bits of scenery on a raised stone dais in the center of the pit. In this specific case, the scenery is a tall, ancient, cracked and crumbling stone archway with a tattered black curtain (or veil) fluttering in the middle. If one tries to look through the veil from the front, one sees only dark empty space, not the opposite side of the room, but when looked at from the back, one sees though the veil to the front of the room.

From beyond the curtain one can hear the whisper of many voices. Both Luna and Harry heard these voices and Luna believes they are the voices of the dead. Luna's theory seems confirmed by later events, ie, when Sirius passes through the arch while still alive yet Dumbledore insists he is suddenly dead. In addition, Dumbledore says the room is called the Death Chamber. Given Dumbledore's high status as Supreme Mugwump, we must assume he is well aware of what is in the MoM despite the fact that the room is supposedly top secret. This doesn't necessarily mean Dumbledore is telling Harry the whole truth of the room, but he must be given the benefit of the doubt.

Returning to the archway, although it is not a Dark object it is very dangerous and kept in an highly restricted area. Harry's experience proved if looked at too long or at too close a proximity, the archway will enchant or lure a wizard into wanting to step up on the dais and walk through the black veil. Given going through the veil means ending up where the dead are and, even if one wasn't dead before passing though, one is by some means made dead at the time of passing through the veil, one must consider this an highly enchanted object much like Tom Riddle's Diary. So why does the MoM have it, who are the dead in it, how did they get there and what does the MoM do with the arch today? It's a mystery.

Hall of Space: This room holds a model of the universe, or at least the solar system of which Earth is a part. All 9 planets, and one must assume the sun as well since the planets can only be seen due to the sun, seem to be there. Like actual space, there is no perceivable gravity and most individuals, unless they are quite hefty, upon entering the room must proceed to float across it to reach the opposite door and natural gravity again. During Jun 1996, Luna, Ron and Ginny passed through this room. Luna, in defending herself and the others against several Death Eaters, was forced to use a Reductor Curse on the planet Pluto and totally destroyed it as part of her escape plan. Unfortuante as this was, it can most likely be repared with a Reparo spell, unlike the damage done to the Hall of Prophecy.

Sealed Chamber: This room was unopenable by Harry even with Sirius' enchanted open-all knife. This room is always kept locked because, according to Dumbledore, it contains a force that is more wonderful and more terrible than death, human intelligence and all the forces of nature. It is the thought by many to be the most mysterious of all the subjects available for study in the DoM. Harry apparently possesses this force in quantities while Voldemort hasn't any at all. One must assume from the given hints that this room contains pure, unadulterated love. What this room is officially called is unknown.

Time Room: This room is directly across from the entrance door and the hallway (even if the circular room spins, it doesn't change where the rooms actual are, only where they appear to be). At the far end of the Time Room is the only means of entrance into the Hall of Prophecy proper, a doorway without a door. The Time Room is itself is a long rectangular room full of the odd mechanical clicking of many clocks and many flecks of dancing white light coming from the bell jar. There are clocks of all kinds and sizes, sitting on desks and shelves, hanging on walls and free standing on the floor. The room also holds the MoM's Time-Turner collection, which is quite extensive.

A door to the right (as one heads to the Hall of Prophecy) opens to a small dark cluttered office with bookcases full of large heavy books. At the end of the Time Room, before going into the Hall of Prophecy, stands a towering crystal bell jar as tall as Harry at 15 which contains Time itself. The jar stands on a desk, has porous sides one can put one's hand, or other body part, through and is full of billowing, glittering wind. In the heart of the jar is a tiny jeweled egg that gives birth to a hummingbird which grows, dies and falls back into the egg to be reborn again and again.

In Jun 1996 a Death Eater's head fell into the jar and his head regressed to a baby's and back again, over and over. Hopefully his head can be stuffed back into the jar, left to grow and then be taken out at the appropriate time. It would be very difficult to prosecute a warlock in a regressed state of mind. On the other hand, if the state is irreversible, it seems a stiff enough punishment on its own. Logic would dictate that Mr Crabbe or Rastaban Lestrange encountered the bell jar. Given the thickly muscled necks of both men once upon a time, but Rastaban's time in prison wasting away, it seems Mr Crabbe was the one whose head fell into the bell jar.

Hall of Prophecy: This room, located just beyond the Time Room, is as high and wide as a great cathedral (think Chartres or St Paul's). It is full of row upon row of high towering shelves filled with small dusty spun-glass spheres. Some spheres have a weird liquid glow in them, others are dark and dull like blown lightbulbs, but all have tiny yellowing labels with the initials of the person who gave the prophecy, to whom it was given, and what or who it is about affixed to the shelf just below each orb.

Torches in brackets give light between the tall aisles of shelves but no warmth to the room overall. However, though the Hall of Prophecy is cold, when Harry touched the orb containing Sybill's prophecy about him and took it down from the shelf it was warm. It may be that the orbs are always warm, which seems unlikely given the room is filled with orbs yet is cold or, more likely, the orbs are always cold till the proper person touches them, at which point they become warm and release themselves from the shelf to which they were magically secured. Removal of an orb by any person not the intended recipient, is impossible and those who try are rendered mad. This condition is not easily remedied and weeks of intensive potions therapy by Healers at St Mungo's may be required.

The numbers on the rows of shelves starts low by the Time Room and runs higher the further from the Time Room one goes. There were above 97 rows of prophecy orbs when Harry and 5 members of the DA first went into the Hall of Prophecy in Jun 1996. Unfortunately, 12 Death Eaters joined them there and insisted upon dueling in the hall. Needless to say a lot of damage was done. How many rows of orbs were lost is unknown but many 1,000s must still remain in the hall to be studied. Hopefully neither the Death Eaters nor the DA will be back for a visit anytime soon.

Level 10

Reachable only by stairs from Level 9, it is the high-security area of the MoM. It contains only cells and a courtroom. There is one corridor, ending in the courtroom, which is made of stone and dimly light by torches in brackets along the walls. One presumes there is no access for officals of the court or case-involved wizards other than the corridor.

Courtroom 10: This high-security courtroom is where Harry ended up when he first took a tumble into Dumbledore's Pensive in 1994. The courtroom was used by the

THE HARRY POTTER COMPANION

Council of Magical Law to try Voldemort's supporters and collaborators from 1970-1982. It was not used again until Aug 1995 when Harry was tried in it for using underage magic in front of his Muggle cousin to save both their lives, well, their souls, from dementors who were running rampant in Little Whinging's alleyways. Given the resugence of Death Eaters, it will probably see use again in the near future. See schematic G for an overview of Level 10.

Courtroom 10 is deep underground and located just off a long windowless corridor that is rough stone on all sides including the ceiling. The corridor is lined on either side with the battered old doors of numerous prisoner holding cells and is very bleak and depressing. At all times when known criminals were held here pending their trial, such as in the days of the many Death Eater trials, it was not unusual for dementors to be watching over the corridor and escorting the prisoners between their cells and the courtroom.

The grimy dark door to the courtroom has an immense iron lock and heavy iron handle, which may be because iron is supposed to have the power to defeat most witchcraft. The courtroom walls, ceiling and floor are all made of dark unadorned stone. It is a square room is dimly lit by torches and has amphitheater seating on all 4 walls. The galleries seat about 200 wizards with all seats having a clear view of the center of the room where the defendant's chair sits. The gallery directly opposite the entry door is high above the others and used by the Interrogators, MoM officials or representatives and the Court Scribe. Those seats on the left side of the defendant, as she or he faces the court, are for the jury. The Head of the Council of Magical Law acts as Judge.

Although dementors might escort prisoners to and from the courtroom, they never stay in the courtroom, so an alternate means of restraining the defendant was devised. The defendant's chair, or chairs if there are multiple defendants as in the case of the Longbottom's torture case, has restless chains lying around the bottom of it. The chains are invested with a sensory mechanism and rattle around clinking threateningly if a suspicious person is near them. If a convicted criminal sits in the chair, the chains glow gold and snake around the individual's arms. They don't react at all when faced with an innocent person, as in Harry's case.

ASSORTED MOM OFFICES

These offices are known to exist but where they are located or which of the 7 departments they might be affiliated with is unknown.

Committee on Experimental Charms: While charm inventors like the late Mrs Lovegood are encouraged to push the bounds of knowledge, safety standards need to be observed and no experimental charm should be disseminated to the public before being tested and approved for use. This office does ground-breaking research on new charms to make sure they are safe for use, looks for cures to charms that are seemingly irreversible and gets involved in cases where wizards have died or been irreparably injured by a charm.

It is probably under the DMAC, given the dicey nature of an experimental charm. There are some tangible personal risks to working in this office. Gilbert Wimple, who wokrs with the committee, has had job-related horns for some time. But it is important work that needs to be done. Given the damage Hermione's Sneak Jinx has done to Marietta Edgecombe, 3 months uncurable and counting, one can see how vital the work of this committee is. Hermione herself will be lucky not to end up charged with creating and using an illegal charm.

Magical Maintenance: This office handles the MoM's building maintenance. Maintenance decides what fake weather the enchanted windows will show on all levels. The last time they wanted a pay raise, the enchanted windows had 2 months of hurricanes before the dispute was settled. Clearly the MoM doesn't have house-elves to do the cleaning and maintenance. It would seem that maintenance would have to clean Level 9, but it may be so top secret the Unspeakables must to do it themselves. It would after all be rather dangerous for maintenance wizards to be poking around many of the rooms in the DoM.

Wizarding Examinations Authority: This body sends wizards out to do wizarding students' OWL and NEWT exams. The team is usually composed of ancient wizards with loads of skill and talent themselves. Madam Marchbanks and Pr Tofty are with this group and did the 1996 OWLs, and one assumes NEWTs, at Hogwarts. If there are other wizarding schools in Britain, and one must assume there are since Hogwarts takes only the *best* of the British wizarding world, the Wizarding Examinations Authority would also do those schools' exams also since those schools would be under the British MoM and have to meet the MoM's standard of magical excellence.

Wizarding Standards of Education Office: What this office is named is open for speculation; that it exists is undeniable. Since there were 21 Educational Decrees before Dolores Umbridge started churning them out at Hogwarts in 95/96, there must have been a MoM office setting standards of education for a number of years beforehand. This body would be responsible for writing all the Educational Decrees, setting standards of education, sending out the wizards of the Wizarding Examination Authority and anything else related to education.

Presumably the following legal measures were all removed after Dumbledore was restored as Head of Hogwarts. Legally the MoM had no right to pass Educational Decrees 22-29, as Hogwarts is not part of the MoM government structure. How the MoM could go on to give approval for the whipping of students, which is not even a legal punishment for adults, is beyond comprehension. If this office is under the Improper Use of Magic office in the DMLE, which seems most logical, it can hardly be helped to note the utter irony.

Educational Decree 22: Aug 30, 1995. In the event the Headmaster of Hogwarts cannot provide an appropriate or adequate candidate for a teaching post, the MoM will select one at its own discretion.
Educational Decree 23: Sep 8, 1995. Creates the position of Hogwarts High Inquisitor and appoints Dolores Umbridge to fill that position.
Educational Decree 24: Oct 9, 1995. Bans all student organizations, societies, groups and clubs that have 3 or more students and are meeting regularly without the High Inquisitor's knowledge or approval.
Educational Decree 25: Nov 5, 1995. Makes the High Inquisitor the supreme authority at Hogwarts and gives her the ability to override all other teachers' punishments, sanctions or removals of privilege.
Educational Decree 26: Jan 16, 1996. Bans all teachers from giving students information that is not strictly related to the subjects they are paid to teach.
Educational Decree 27: Feb 23, 1996. Expels anyone possessing a copy of the Mar 1996 *The Quibbler*.
Educational Decree 28: Apr 16, 1996. Appoints Dolores Umbridge to replace Dumbledore as Head of Hogwarts.

THE HARRY POTTER COMPANION

Educational Decree 29: May 13, 1996. Permits Filch to use the corporal punishments he's always longed to against students.
Approval for Whipping: May 1996. Permits Filch to whip students. Dolores Umbridge got this from the MoM more so Filch would be on her side more than any sadistic desire to see students whipped, though she does seem to prefer severe or painful physical punishments for most infractions.
Order of Dismissal: A parchment form Dolores Umbridge uses for legally sacking teachers. It must be signed by the Head and then countersigned by the Minister of Magic to be valid.

ASSORTED MOM FACTS

Class A Non-Tradeable Goods: Severe penalties are attached to the importation or sale of these goods. At no time and for no purpose is it acceptable to have these goods. Acromantula, dragon and chimera eggs would fall into this category according to the DRCMC.
Class B Tradeable Material: A dangerous material which may be traded, but the trade of which is subject to strict control and use guidelines by the MoM. Romanian Longhorn horns, erumpent horns with Exploding Fluid and bulk billywigs would likely fall into this category.
Class C Non-Tradeable Substance: Substances that are not to be traded but can be owned if the owner agrees to MoM regulation and inspection, does not sell, trade or otherwise disseminate the item and owns the item only for study or research purposes. Venomous tentacula and its seeds are in this category. Hogwarts has venomous tentaculas legally. Fred and George have venomous tentacula seeds without the MoM's knowledge to sell in Skiving Snackbox candies to an unsuspecting public.
Code of Wand Use: This code stipulates the regulations regarding wand use as set out by the MoM. Clause 3 states that a non-human creature cannot carry or use a wand at any time, for any reason, ever. Winky was sacked by Barty Crouch Sr for breaking this clause. Technically, because the wand was in her hand, she was carrying it. That Barty Crouch Jr put it there was an extenuating circumstance and one which she could not reveal due to being an house-elf.
Guidelines for the Treatment of Non-Wizard Part-Humans: These guidelines set out the treatment of vampires, hags and other species which are part-human, but not wizards. These beings may or may not have magical powers. The guidelines state, among other things, that these beings can't stamped out or otherwise harmed just because they are part-humans or non-wizards. Such beings are however 2nd-class citizens in the MoM's eyes, have lesser rights that are subject to wizards' whims and are often illegally mistreated even by those whose job is to protect them.
Interdepartmental Memos: Memos are written on pale violet paper with Ministry of Magic stamped along the edges. The paper is then folded into an airplane and launched toward the nearest door. The airplane then flies up the corridors into the first open lift and circles around the lamp at the top till its floor is announced. It then zooms out to whomever it's addressed. Memos do flap their wings to keep airborne and like the lamplight in the lift making the charm used on them probably moth rather then airplane related.
Law 15 B: This law is focused on attacks on wizards by non-human but intelligent creatures, like centaurs or merpeople.
MoM Bill: A bill is a proposed piece of legislation. Given the MoM has bills, there must wizards to vote on them. This body is not the British Seats of the ICW but an elected body that has as its main functions representing the wizards of their respective

constituencies and voting on new British MoM legislation. As of yet this body has not been named and seems to do whatever Fudge wants.

MoM Cars: Although no one is supposed to enchant Muggle artifacts, such as cars, the MoM has a number of enchanted, old-fashioned 1950s cars it occasionally uses for transporting special people, presumably mainly Fudge and visiting dignitaries. These cars magically expand to hold many people and trunks, can slide through narrow gaps in traffic and are able jump ahead of traffic that is standing still at a light without being noticed.

MoM cars come with MoM drivers, who look like Muggle chauffeurs. They will touch their hat in salute, open and close the doors for passengers and even help with unloading luggage. In certain rare cases wizards working at the MoM may borrow cars, with drivers, for certain uses. Arthur was allowed to borrow some MoM cars, with drivers, to take Harry and the Weasley clan to King's Cross Station in Sep 1993 when Sirius Black was believed to be after Harry.

MoM Owls: The MoM tried owls for internal mail delivery at some point in the distant past but had to give them up because they were too messy. However the MoM does use owls, usually barn owls, for all external deliveries. There must be, therefore, an owlery somewhere within the MoM, and a passage from the owlery to an above ground outlet for the owls to fly out from to hunt or make deliveries. Presumably the outlet is high up and out of sight as it would look very odd to have owls popping out of the curbside drains, manholes or trashbins.

Order of Merlin: This honor is given by the MoM and comes in 1st, 2nd and 3rd class. It is a somewhat dubious distinction as Order of Merlins are often awarded for giving money to the MoM or a MoM charity such as St Mungo's. Dumbledore holds a 1st class, Newt Scamander a 2nd class for his work in Magizoology and Gilderoy Lockhart a 3rd class. Fudge said he would try to get Pr Snape a 2nd class for capturing Sirius Black, and maybe even a 1st class. It isn't said what Dumbledore or Lockhart did to receive their honors. Dumbledore likely did something sterling, such as save the world, while Lockhart likely gave a wad of cash.

MoM Personnel

The following is a very short, very partial list of MoM employees. They must number in the hundreds but we've only heard of a few.

Ludo Bagman: Former Head, DMGS. He left office in Jun 1995.
Basil (Unknown): DMT, Portkey Office.
Bob (Unknown): DRCMC, Beast Division, Ban on Experimental Breeding section.
Amelia Bones: Head, DMLE.
Broderick Bode: An Unspeakable in the DoM until he died in Jan 1996.
Croaker: An Unspeakable in the DoM.
Barty Crouch Sr: Head, DIMC till he died in May 1995.
Cornelius Fudge: Minister of Magic since 1991.
Amos Diggory: DRCMC.
Madam Edgecombe: DMT. A Floo Regulator with the Floo Network.
Mafalda Hopkirk: DMLE. Improper Use of Magic Office. Probably the Head.
Bertha Jorkins: DMGS till she died in the summer of 1994.
Walden Macnair: DRCMC, Beast Division. Executioner for the Committee for the Disposal of Dangerous Creatures till he was put in prison as a Death Eater in Jun 1996, he is a friend of Lucius Malfoy.

Eric Munch: DMLE. Security at MoM.
Cuthbert Mockridge: DRCMC, Being Division. He is Head, Goblin Liaison Office.
Arnold Peasegood: DMAC. Obliviator on an Accidental Magic Reversal Squad.
Perkins: DMLE. Misuse of Muggle Artifacts under Arthur.
Augustus Rookwood: Former Unspeakable with the DoM in the 1970s and early 1980s. Imprisoned as a spying Death Eater in the early 1980s, escaped in Jan 1996, reimprisoned in Jun 1996.
Newt Scamander: Retired from the DRCMC.
Kingsley Shacklebolt: DMLE. Auror.
Nymphadora "Tonks" Tonks: DMLE. Auror.
(Unknown) Dawlish: DMLE. Auror.
Dolores Umbridge: Former Senior Undersecretary to the Minister of Magic. She has been on the lam since Jun 1996, probably to avoid prosecution for criminal activity during 95/96.
Arthur Weasley: DMLE. Head, Misuse of Muggle Artifacts Office.
Percy Weasley: Currently Junior Assistant to the Minister of Magic since the summer 1995.
Gilbert Wimple: He's with the Committee on Experimental Charms.

Non-Governmental Organizations (NGOs)

This section includes societies, groups and organizations that influence the MoM or the society of which they are a part. This does not include recreational, social or student clubs.

Dark Force Defense League: A group of anti-Dark wizards which one assumes actually is active against the Dark side. However, they have Lockhart as a member so what they actually do, if anything, is open to debate. It is probably more like a club or society for wizards who dabble in dealing with Dark creatures.
International Association of Quidditch: Hassan Mostafa of Egypt is the current Chairwizard. This association lobbies on behalf of Quidditch as a sport, as well as supports the development of the game and encourages wizards to play it, support it or get involved in other ways.
International Federation of Warlocks: This body criticized Fudge for warning the Muggle PM about Sirius Black's escape in 1993. It is a group of internationally prominent and powerful warlocks, some of whom are representatives to the ICW. Their censure is more personally embarrassing than politically damaging.
Order of the Phoenix: A secret society founded in 1970 by Dumbledore, its purpose was and is to fight Voldemort. Only overage wizards who have left school can join it because the risk of death is quite high. Having fought Voldemort and his supporters 1970-1982 and lost over 50% of its members, the Order went semi-dormant in the post-1982 years. A few members were asked to casually keep an eye on Harry, without is knowledge, but the bulk of the OoP were fully released from duty. Arabella Figg and her cats did the bulk of watching in Little Whinging, but Dedalus Diggle seems to have taken over for her every now and again especially when Petunia took Harry out of the Little Whinging to London or elsewhere.

The Order was fully revived in Jun 1995, again to fight Voldemort and his supporters, and over 20 members were enlisted or renlisted. Dumbledore set up Sirius Black's house at 12 Grimmauld Place, London as the Order's headquarters in 1994 in preparation for Voldemort's reappearance. Currently the Order is busy tracking known

Death Eaters, recruiting wizards overseas and in Britain and standing a 24/7 guard over Harry who is ultimately the only wizard with the power to destroy Voldemort forever. It remains to be seen what their role will be now the MoM is aware of Voldemort's return and telling the public. As the MoM was completely inept at dealing with Voldemort's last rise to power, it would be foolish of members of the Order to reveal themselves. Most probably the Order will remain secret and continue its work, as it did previously, until Voldemort is actually finally destroyed.

Original Members of the OoP: The Order had a 50%+ death or destruction rate from 1970-1982. At that time the ratio was said to be 1 of the Order to 20 Death Eaters which means there were as many as 400-500 Death Eaters, possibly more. Of this number, very few were ever caught or killed. Order members included:

>Sirius Black
>Edgar Bones: killed with his entire family
>Caradoc Dearborn: MIA - presumed dead
>Dedalus Diggle
>Elphias Doge
>Aberforth Dumbledore
>Albus Dumbledore
>Benjy Fenwick: dead
>Rubeus Hagrid
>Frank and Alice Longbottom: tortured to total insanity
>Remus Lupin
>Marlene McKinnon: killed with her entire family
>Dorcas Meadowes: killed
>Alastor "Mad-Eye" Moody
>Peter Pettigrew: became a Death Eater in 1979 or 1980
>Sturgis Podmore
>James and Lily Potter: killed
>Gideon and Fabian Prewett: killed in action
>Severus Snape: a Death Eater secretly working for the Order since 1980.
>Emmeline Vance

Molly wasn't in the original Order but Arthur might have been from things he's said.

New Members of the OoP: The following is a list of people who joined or rejoined the Order when Dumbledore reactivated it in Jun 1995.

>Sirius Black: killed Jun 1996
>Dedalus Diggle
>Elphias Doge
>Albus Dumbledore
>Aberforth Dumbledore
>Arabella Figg
>Mundungus Fletcher
>Rubeus Hagrid
>Hestia Jones
>Remus Lupin
>Minerva McGonagall
>Alastor "Mad-Eye" Moody
>Sturgis Podmore
>Kingsley Shacklebolt
>Severus Snape

Nymphadora "Tonks" Tonks
Emmeline Vance
Molly Weasley
Arthur Weasley
Bill Weasley
Charlie Weasley

It is unknown if Fred and George Weasley have become members since leaving school in 1996.

The Salem Witches' Institute: Located in Salem, Massachusetts. A group of American witches from this organization went to QWC 1994. Possibly it's a girls' school that focuses on training in music or are, but more likely it's a think tank that studies witchcraft and witches, an organization that helps shape US MoM policy on or advances the cause of witches throughout America, or a teaching hospital specializing in witch-only illnesses or training witches to be Healers.

THE LIVELY ARTS

In this section many of the arts wizards enjoy will be discussed. These are by no means the only arts wizards practice, just some of the more prevalent ones.

MUSIC

Music is much loved by wizards and most individuals seem to possess some form of musical ability. Harry can play the flute, albeit not well, but enough to put Fluffy to sleep. Hagrid can carve a flute that actually works which means he too must play one now and then. Seamus, who is a known Kestrels fan, dwarves and Pr Quirrell would all seem to be harpers. Even wizards who don't play music at least like and in some cases love it. Nearly Headless Nick likes the sound of a good musical saw orchestra. Dumbledore enjoys chamber music and calls music in general magic beyond anything they do at Hogwarts. Even the wizard on the street prefers music to most other distractions as the many listeners to WWN programing attest.

WWN: Wizarding Wireless Network. A radio station for the wizarding community that plays mostly music and even has programs devoted to popular singers.

SONG

Song is an extremely popular art form among wizards. Nicholas Flamel was an opera lover. WWN has at least one program featuring popular singers. Each year the Sorting Hat makes up a new song to great acclaim. Hogwarts has a school song that can move Dumbledore to the occasional tear. The dwarves sing songs they, or others, have composed while accompanying themselves on the harp. Puddlemere United, has a song so popular it was recorded by a famous singer. But not only wizards or beings enjoy song, the merpeople (Beasts) are very accomplished singers, though rather unappreciated, and Peeves (a poltergeist) is extremely musical, though most wish he weren't.

Celestina Warbeck: A popular singer.
Beat Back Those Bludgers, Boys, and Chuck That Quaffle Here: Puddlemere United's team song, which Celestina recorded and sold to benefit St Mungo's. Whether this proves the popularity of Celestina, the song or Puddlemere United is unclear, but they make a great triple threat.

The Hobgoblins: A popular singing group formerly headed by lead singer Stubby Boardman.
Weasley Is Our King: A popular Slytherin Quidditch song with lyrics by Draco Malfoy. There is also a crown-shaped badge which uses the title as a logo. It later became a popular Gryffindor song, with somewhat altered lyrics.
The Weird Sisters: A very popular contemporary singing group. Kirley McCormack is their well-known guitarist and other band members play drums, several guitars, a lute, a cello and bagpipes. The band is composed of at least 8 extremely hairy wizards who dress in artfully ripped and torn black robes. They are however not against color or contemporary fashion and sell colorful Muggle tshirts with their logo on them. Tonks has a purple one with THE WEIRD SISTERS on it.

This was the musical group Dumbledore booked for the Yule Ball in Dec 1994, and everyone approved of his choice, including the Beauxbatons, so they must have a worldwide wizarding following. They played a slow mournful tune for the champions and their dates to open the Yule Ball then went on to play for the next 4 hours. Young and old seem to appreciate them and they are certainly the most popular music group in the British wizarding community though they seem to be a mostly Scottish band with roots in the Portree area.
The Witching Hour: A WWN radio program that features popular singers.

DANCE

Dance has always been popular among wizards. So much so that most of Hogwarts' teachers and students know how to and dance quite well. The TT in 1994 included as an essential part of its activities a formal ball, the Yule Ball, and we can presume it always did so from the 13th to the 18th century during those years it was held. At the 1994 Yule Ball, both Heads and all the students from Beauxbatons and Durmstrang knew how to dance. But not just wizards dance, many magical creatures and even ghosts like to trip the light fantastic.

Dobby will do a little dance when happy, a troupe of dancing skeletons performed for Hogwarts' Halloween Feast in 1992 and who can forget the veela repeatedly dancing before and during QWC 1994? The school ghosts did formation gliding one year, a type of dance to them considering dance in the period in which they lived and what dance was like then, but at a formal ghost function, Nearly Headless Nick's Deathday Party, all the stops were pulled. At least 250 ghosts were seen waltzing in Dungeon 5 by Harry, of which approximately 230 were visiting ghosts of all eras, who had obviously kept abreast of dance despite the fact they were dead.

Although dancing may not be everyone's cup of tea, it appears that most wizarding children get dance lessons. Parvati could not only dance at age 14, she could lead. Hermione was a fine dancer who doubtless had been given lessons as the only child of 2 parents making good incomes. The fact that Ron didn't like to dance didn't mean he couldn't and in Harry's case desire wasn't the problem but the fact he couldn't because he'd never been given dance lessons. The Dursleys, who had given Dudley lessons of every kind, had simply never given Harry the same opportunity.

BOOKS AND LITERATURE

Wizarding culture has quite a brisk market for books. As no one can use computers or TV as a means of communicating knowledge, the written word is vital to obtaining information. Home libraries are popular and where people can afford it, holdings seem abundant. Molly Weasley has a mantle full of cookbooks and books on housekeeping.

School libraries are substantial and doubtless there are circulating libraries in the wizarding world as well.

Books are popular gift items to give as well as receive. Dumbledore is always getting books as presents for Christmas and, though he insists he'd rather have warm woolly socks, this doesn't curb the folks that give him the books, who seem to think them excellent presents. Harry has received books as gifts from Ron, Hermione, Hagrid, Sirius and Remus, and been very pleased with all of them. Hermione loves books to point of being an incurable book collector. Even Hagrid, while not exactly bookish, occasionally steals one or two from the Library for reference.

There are several publishers of books, comics, magazines and newspapers in the wizarding world. Pubs like the Leaky Cauldron seem to keep a selection of all of these for their patrons. See the section on Reading Matter for full detail. And while journalists (Rita Skeeter) can be fairly off-center and publishers distinctly corruptible *(The Daily Prophet)* or ridiculously radical *(The Quibbler)*, suffice it to say that most authors are decent people who turn out worthwhile material and writing on the whole is a very well respected career path in wizarding society.

POETRY

Poetry is another widely embraced passion among the magical and one with a very long history. Magical spells have often involved lengthy, poetically structured verse, and this is unsurprising as rhymed poetry is easier to remember than prose. Spell poetry goes back 1,000s of years. Subject-specific poetry, poetry for poetry's sake, was already popular when 11th-century Scots Gaelic wizard poets began writing about Quidditch and ancient by the time 15th-century Norwegian wizard poets joined them. Today such poetry is considered a long-standing part of wizarding culture but one would do well to reflect on the intimate connection of wizards' poetic development in Europe and the spread of Quidditch. Passion moves people to poetry and Quidditch moves people to passion.

Moving on, magical beings besides wizards and many magical beasts love writing a good length of poetry, particularly when set in that ancient form, the couplet. Pr Snape is quite a good poet, having come up with a logic puzzle set in couplets to protect the Sorcerer's Stone. Gringotts' doors surpass his achievement and prove goblins have long been extremely poetic. The couplets advise thieves to think twice before attempting to pluck treasure from goblin vaults, and strike a good blend of ominous threat and artistic merit. Sphinxes, as the base of their riddles, always use poetic couplets, as Harry discovered in TT Task 3. Even Peeves and Draco have a way with poetry and, regrettably, song.

THEATER

Playwriting and of course performances of plays have been around in the wizarding world for many centuries. Although the majority of plays fail to stand the test of time as high art, they nevertheless represent an area of endeavor for wizards. For instance, a 15th-century French wizarding playwright might have her or his masterwork remembered chiefly for its passing Quidditch reference, but it doesn't negate the fact that the author was actually, with the 2-4 hours of dialogue, attempting to address contemporary issues in wizardry, such as dangerous Transfigurations, through a cautionary play.

This art form is less widely embraced than say portrait painting but not from any inherent dislike of theater or the lack of quality plays. It is merely because it is difficult to get 100-500 wizards together nightly, or for weekend matinees, without Muggles noticing. Barring theater produced in Hogsmeade, theater ownership by wizards is not lucrative and certainly the desire for secrecy among wizards has led many a young playwright into poverty and destitution. As a quick scan of the various departments of the MoM proves, the government will support any clearly Muggle-visible magical sport or game, but the arts are left to private citizens. And this is probably a good thing since so many wizards love the arts and enjoy pursuing them on their own, without MoM interference.

LANGUAGE

There is vast interest in foreign languages among wizards and many speak at least 2 languages. Dumbledore speaks several languages. Barty Crouch Sr spoke 200. Fleur Delacour went to Britain to better her English and most of the Beauxbatons seemed to speak English quite well. All the Durmstrangs spoke English as a second language, probably because it was Karkoff's first and he wouldn't learn any others, but that just shows how talented the Drumstrangs were, and are.

Bill Weasley is surely fluent in Ancient Egyptian, Hieroglyphics, Gobbledegook and probably modern Arabic. Charlie doubtless speaks Romanian by now if he didn't before going to Romania to work. Percy must be fluent in a few languages or he wouldn't have ended up in the DIMC. The ICW, wizards most important government institution, seems to have as its main language French, and possibly English as a secondary language, despite it being an international body. This means that wizarding translators must be abundant and available or most of the ICW members speak the 2 main languages.

What is unique about this love of language is that no schools teach languages. Hogwarts, a very advanced and respected secondary school, has no language department and doesn't offer any languages as electives. This means of course that all wizards who speak another language, or several, choose to learn a specific language knowing they must teach themselves and are amazingly apt pupils. While this makes Barty Sr and other polyglots quite remarkable in some ways, it's not wholly unexpected to find self-taught polyglots in the wizarding world.

By and large wizards are more naturally adept at acquiring languages, attach more value to being fluent in several languages and have more need to communicate, cross-species as well as cross-nationally. In addition, wizards are, and have always been, a small segment of otherwise larger societies and as such feel a greater need to be in contact with wizards as a whole rather than Muggles of their own nationality. The creation of the TT in the 11th century was a recognition of that cross-cultural need, as was the creation of the World and European Quidditch Cups. Surprising as it seems, but according to Dumbledore true, Quidditch always been the great leveler and the great uniter of the wizarding world.

TAPESTRY

Tapestry has long been a popular textile art among wizards, particularly witches of the upper classes. In an age when painting was crude and photography unheard of, the record of history both social and political was formed on the looms. Tapestry, in a sense, is a living thing for just like photos, the beings woven onto them move about displaying a specific moment in time. They can interact with people passing by and be helpful or not. Like photos, tapestries are unable to speak however their subjects cannot leave their particular tapestry.

Tapestry graces the hallways of Hogwarts and one particularly fine example on the 7th floor is that of Barnabas the Barmy attempting to teach trolls to do ballet. The Hogwarts' school banner and House banners are also tapestries. It would make sense, though it has never been stated, that as tapestry the figures on these banners are alive and can move. The individual House banners would be exciting and safe enough, however, given the 4 species on the main school banner, lion, badger, snake and eagle, movement on it would likely lead to them eating each other.

EMBROIDERY

Embroidery is an important part of wizard culture though a great deal overlooked. It shows up on everything in the wizarding world. Robes and hats might be embroidered with moons and stars in silver tambouring, Quidditch robes are embroidered with a player's last name across the shoulders, the Elders of the Wizengamot have a silver W embroidered on their purple robes to show their office. Yet in the absence of modern equipment to create inexpensive machine-embroidered works, a significant investment of time and money goes into creating handmade embroidery. Embroidery therefore visually displays to onlookers the importance or wealth of the wearer.

Dumbledore is a classic example of persons of importance wearing embroidery. There is hardly an item of clothing in his wardrobe that isn't embroidered on in some fashion. He has embroidered hats and robes for fancy occasions. In his private hours he wears a purple dressing gown embroidered in gold. As head of the Wizengamot he has embroidered robes showing his status as an Elder. Other wizards time and again refer to his sense of style, not just in his wizardry or the way he operates, but how he presents himself and his clothing. Given house-elves fondness for needlework, they surely must do a bit of embroidery as part of their labors and this may be how Dumbledore's clothes became so embroidered. On the other hand, Dumbledore has never appeared underfunded, especially if he's going around telling Harry the Sorcerer's Stone's wealth-producing ability is not such a great thing, so there is no reason he couldn't or wouldn't simply purchase embroidered goods on his own.

Pr Lockhart had wealth enough to buy embroidered goods and did so to bolster his status among other wizards as well as swell his already enormous ego. He was a photo opportunity waiting to happen and always had to look his best. It says just how important embroidery is to wizards when a wizard of his fame and reputation, not to mention vanity, has to be decked in it 24/7. Ludo, Head of the DMGS, and needing to look his best for the Yule Ball probably got his purple robes with yellow stars on credit, but it points up the fact that for supremely special occasions, the well heeled are expected to break out the embroidered robes and hats. But what about the less well heeled?

As usual they must make their embroidered goods or go without. Molly doesn't have a single embroidered article in her wardrobe. A quilted gown is as close to fancy needlework as she gets. She is relatively poor and this is exactly what one would expect to find in a poor wizard's wardrobe, an absence of embroidery. Sybill Trelawney on the other hand is another story altogether. She embroiders her own handkerchiefs as a pastime but carries them in a very obvious manner. Why? Because carrying embroidered things enhances her status in the eyes of others. She's a textbook case of a person who feels abused and degraded who does anything she can to get respect, even if that means hours of tedious or difficult embroidery.

PAINTING

Painting is a very popular pastime among wizards as the walls of almost any wizard's home, office or shop can attest. The very fact that a copy of a painting still has to be painted means there are numerous wizards employed in this fashion. However, wizards aren't the only ones who like to break out a brush and canvas. Dobby enjoys painting as a hobby, and in keeping with the wizarding world's main painting obsession, he is a portrait painter, though many may not appreciate his work. Why are wizards and others so fascinated by painted portraits? Primarily one supposes because portraits are alive and can interact with their surroundings and even speak. How exactly portraits come to reflect the sitter's personality is down to the magical solvents used in the pigments when the canvas is being painted. Like wizard photography, anyone can do it.

Often the same exact same portrait of a notable wizard is hung in several places, meaning it's been repeatedly painted by professionals or amateurs. Particularly popular portraits might hang in Hogwarts, at the MoM, in St Mungo's, on the wall of someone's home, anywhere. Since portraits can be very helpful (Sir Cadogan) or not (Phineas Nigellus) wise wizards like keep plenty of them around. Dumbledore has 12 in his office, 1 of which saved Arthur Weasley's life. But painting is not now and never has been done for functional reasons. Muggles paint because they love it and preserve something of beauty that they enjoy and wizards paint for the same reasons.

A large, angry looking wolfhound gambols about in the frame next to Sir Cadogan's. While not my pleasure, it was some wizard's favorite dog once and she or he clearly wanted to keep it around as a source of inspiration and comfort when it was long gone. The forest the Fat Lady hid in after surviving a slashing by Sirius Black in 1993 was some wizard's favorite spot. Why shouldn't or wouldn't she or he go out one autumn day and paint the sliver beeches and golden alders so they can still stand rustling in the wind after they've all been torn down for progress and parking lots?

This brings us to maps, a subsection of painting. It must be said, since the Fat Lady hid in a map of Argyll, that maps are painted as well. Upon entering a map, the entering figure can hide in it because they shrink to an appropriate relative size, and are thus able to slip into a town, a wood or a cave and hide. Depending on the size of a map, the casual observer might detect general movement such as a herdsman driving his cows out to pasture each day and back, a stream bursting its banks in spring or a large flock of birds migrating south for the winter, but finding an individual in hiding would require careful study, making maps a very good place to take a powder.

PHOTOGRAPHY

Photography is a wizarding profession as a well as a hobby. Bozo is a photographer for *The Daily Prophet*. Possibly there are art photographers as well. Certainly some of the Chocolate Frog trading cards use photos (Dumbledore) as well as photos of portraits of those long deceased. Photographs are not as popular as portraits, possibly because of their ephemeral nature, being just paper and chemicals, or their dependence on Muggle technology, most of which wizards don't know how to operate and don't care to learn about. But photography continues to be an area of interest all the same, usually among the young.

As wizarding photography was completely dependent on the existence of Muggle cameras, it followed the development of Muggle photography over the course of some 100 years. The first Muggle cameras were invented and in general use by circa 1850-1870. A period of time then elapsed before wizards became interested in Muggle cameras and started thinking up ways to improve them. Since Hagrid has pictures of himself with his wizarding father from 1940 or so that don't move, the special developing solution that makes photos move must have been discovered after that.

We know that by the time Harry's parents were in school, the discovery had been made. But pictures are of his parents at school or later. So, logically, somewhere around 1950 the discovery must have been made, then, over the next few years, it went from rich man's toy to middle-class child's hobby. The interesting thing about wizarding photos is that they never led to the development of wizarding movies in the cinematic sense. This is possibly because most equipment used to make movies these days is electrically driven and would be too difficult to magically reproduce.

Frankly, it is a much more interesting to think up a story, pull it from the mind of the author and throw it in a Pensive where it can be experienced. Of course Pensives are very rare, so until they can be massed produced most wizards will stick to reading. The fact that Dumbledore has to loan Pr Snape his Pensive implies there is only 1 in the entire world. The fact that it's carved with runes implies it's very old magic, which has perhaps passed out of living memory. But, someone with initiative will someday find a way to do it and once they do, this author will be buying one and having a wander through *The Phantom Tollbooth*, among other treasured classics.

SCULPTURE

Sculpture from stone would seem to have had many followers over the years given Hogwarts is stuffed with it. Some stonework is magical, some not. Statuary that is purely decorative (doesn't talk or move) was in the MoM's Atrium as the Fountain of Magical Brethren. From Dumbledore's actions, it would appear that any powerful wizard can make statuary alive after a fashion. This would make a stonework subject's abilities limited only by what powerful magic its wizarding creator or subsequent owner could do. And this seems entirely reasonable.

A Medieval bust of a wizard sits muttering to itself in Latin in one of Hogwarts' halls. The wizard subject obviously imbued it with his magical personality once it was carved. The 2 gargoyles flanking the ground floor staffroom move about and are simply stuffed with snide personality. Who's personality are the 2 snide gargoyles expressing? They could be expressing their carver's but it would not have been beyond one of the founders to magick them up. The gargoyle in front of Dumbledore's door says nothing, but moves when the password is given. Godric probably gave this gargoyle, who stands in front of his old tower's door, life but not speech as no one seems to have liked silent and willing obedience to his every word more than he.

METAL CRAFTS

Related to statuary is metal craft. Metal charming has a long history as nothing makes a more lasting impression than the gold of an ornament or the steel of a blade. The Fountain of Magical Brethren's statues were all crafted of gold, or a metal resembling gold, and doubtless created by some skilled wizard metal charmer. It is possible, though highly doubtful as the goblin figure was rather insulting to goblins, that the statues were cast by goblins. Goblins are particularly gifted in all manner of metal crafts from casting money and engraving goblets to fashioning armor and charming carts to do their bidding.

Dumbledore bought or acquired in some fashion a goblin-wrought indestructible helmet for Hagrid and Olympia to take to the giants Abroad which implies he at least is on good terms with some goblin factions. Sirius Black's family had goblin-wrought silver goblets several centuries old. The MoM uses goblin-cast coins. The Sword of

Gryffindor is very likely goblin wrought and engraved though it was (possibly) magicked up later by Godric. Wizard metal charmers may do good work, and the Golden Snitch is certainly proof of that, but when looking for superior quality metalwork wizards that can afford to go to a goblin craftsman do.

HERALDRY

Heraldry is of great interest to wizards. Every family of standing has a crest and a motto (the Blacks), schools have crests and mottos as well (Hogwarts), there are special letter seals carved with crests (Hogwarts), crested rings for gentlemen (Mr Black), crested House banners (Hogwarts) and even crested coaches (Beauxbatons). Given all the interest in heraldry, there is probably a body within the MoM that helps individuals and organizations develop then register a crest much as the College of Heralds does in Britain though the name of this office within the MoM, if it exists, is unknown. Some families and organizations would of course already have a crest and motto, the Black's dates back to the 1290s, but how it would be determined today who gets a crest and motto is speculative in the absence of any actual aristocracy. One supposes the holder of an Order of Merlin might be entitled to a crest and motto if she or he didn't have them already.

SEAL CARVING

Related to heraldry, seal carving is an ancient art that goes back thousands of years before the time of Christ. In olden days everyone used a seal. In Asia seal carving is a high art and seals are collected by many for their beauty as well as their sentiment. They come in many styles and are made of many natural carveable materials from jade to soapstone. In Europe however metal seals were long favored over stone seals as they could be easily formed into a piece of commonly worn jewelry like a ring or a pendant. Europeans used seals with coats of arms or initials to seal their letter or legal documents. Britain even uses the Great Seal for the making a bill the law of the land. Once stamped with the Great Seal, a bill is law.

One hastens to add, for any treasure hunters reading this book, that Britain has and uses a Great Seal but it is not *the* Great Seal. The current seal is a copy of the Great Seal which was chucked in the Thames River by James II. At the time it was tossed, c 1688, the Thames was not the sort of place one could or would dive in but a foul gutter of water filled with raw sewage, dead bodies and other distressing things. James II tossed the seal in the river to show his utter disgust at being dethroned by his misguided subjects, ungrateful daughter and mercenary son-in-law. That no one looked for the Great Seal and just decided a copy was good enough is unsurprising.

Hogwarts has at least 2 seals, one for letters and house-elf tea towels and one for Library books, but it probably has others. These are magical seals and the resulting seals they produce are usually multicolored or unusual in other ways such as stamping goldleaf lettering onto red wax. Although having and using a seal may seem like ridiculous affectation or Romanticism to Muggles, seals do serve a purpose in the wizarding world. There are no self-sticking envelopes or lickable glue parchment rolls. The only way to close such things is with wax. A seal pressed into the wax forces it to hold tight. So a seal is actually a handy and necessary object for wizards who always need to be sending owls.

THE HARRY POTTER COMPANION

OTHER PASTIMES AND INTERESTS

Wizards have a wide variety of interests outside the arts and crafts mentioned above. This section touches on a few of those. Quidditch however is in a separate section devoted entirely to that game.

GAMES AND CARDS

One of the most popular wizarding games is Gobstones. It is so widely played that there are clubs in many villages and towns and even a full-time Official Gobstones Club office at the MoM. It would seem younger people play Gobstones like marbles while older folks use larger balls and play it like lawn bowling. Obviously, given the nature of the stones themselves, it makes sense to have the MoM oversee players of this game to make sure proper precautions are observed around Muggles.

All ages enjoy wizard's chess, with its living pieces, but there is no overseeing body for players and there appears to be no clubs. Clearly as chess, it is more of a private game and the MoM encourages this as it's difficult to have large chess clubs or tournaments go unnoticed by Muggles when game pieces talk and move of their own accord. Gobstones in that respect is a bit easier to hide. However, wizard's chess is more interesting to those who prefer games of mental strategy to games of physical skill. Wizard's chess is a game Pr McGonagall plays, Ron is excellent at and Harry likes learning.

All the above is not to say that wizards play only magical games. Wizards are human beings, just like Muggles, and as such they share many interests. Games that are culturally prevalent and enjoyed by Muggles are always enjoyed by wizards of the same culture as well. Kennilworthy Whisp is a big fan of backgammon. Dumbledore likes tenpins. Harry and Ron are always playing tic-tac-toe and hangman. See schematic U and the Muggle Stuff section in Part V for more information on these games. And then of course there are the ever popular card games.

Card games in general are popular with adult wizards and Hagrid plays cards regularly at the Hog's Head, usually more for fellowship then illegal goods though the latter are oftentimes more easily acquirable. Young wizards also have their fun with cards, but cards of a more magical variety. Ron has a pack of Self-Shuffling cards he keeps in his room at the Burrow, while Fred and George and many other Hogwarts' students are fond of Exploding Snap. Ron even gets creative with Exploding Snap cards and thinks it's good fun to build card houses with them. The exploding may be unique, but any Muggle could identify with Ron's love of executing a house of cards.

Gobstones: A game similar to marbles but which uses stones that squirt a nasty smelling liquid (possibly stinksap) into the a player's face when she or he loses a point thus adding insult to injury. Stones can be made of various materials, including gold, and come in various sizes from marbles to lawn bowls. They become useless during a game once they expel their contents but they can be refilled, if done with care, and used for a lifetime. The exact number of stones that make up a set or a game is unknown.

Wizard's Chess: The chess pieces are alive and actually do combat with an opponent's figures. It's very similar to directing troops in battle, barring the back talk from one's soldiers. One purchases one set of 16 men (for one side only) and one board. Ron's set is white but to be practical the men are probably able to turn their garments inside out to be black (or some other color) as well. On the other hand, it may dragged off the board by its fellow pieces where it will huddle limply with other defeated pieces or simply slump against the wall or table seeming to be dead. They can be a little melodramatic at times but it adds interest to an otherwise slow game.

Pr McGonagall created a gigantic, faceless, stone wizard's chess set as a protection for the Sorcerer's Stone in 1992, which Ron was able to defeat. Ron, Harry and Seamus are all chess players. Seamus has a black set and Harry received a set of unknown color from a Christmas cracker at the feast in 1991. Harry plays well, but not as well as Ron. Hermione is dreadful at wizard's chess but Ron likes playing her because it's the only thing she's bad at and he feels her character will be improved by losing at something. Hermione's playing proves the logical move and the strategic move are not always the same thing.

Exploding Snap: A favorite card game of Fred and George. It is played with an exploding deck of cards. The explosion is usually very loud and involves smoke and flames. The cards are apparently self-repairing so one can get a quantity of games out of a single pack. Percy disapproves of Exploding Snap but Fred and George, while they were at school, used to play it with Ron and Harry all the time during vacations and even on the Hogwarts Express. They are of course on Filch's list of banned items and like Gobstones can only be played in the common room or out of doors.

SPORTS

Broom sports are popular all over the wizarding world and many countries have a unique broomsport to engage in. See QTA for additional information on these sports. However, Quidditch is geographically the most widely played broom sport, the one with the largest number of wizards playing it and certainly the one most bet on in those MoM jurisdictions where betting has been legalized. For Quidditch lovers in Britain there is even a Museum of Quidditch, located in London, which contains Quidditch artifacts dating back many centuries. See the section on Brooms and Quidditch for more on this fascinating sport.

Some wizards like to engage in Muggle sports, as Sir Patrick proves. Sir Patrick is very fond of polo, though he plays it with his head. The Headless Hunt, which he heads, is obviously engaged in fox hunting of a spectral kind, given it's spectral horses. And while some Muggle sports can be fairly innocuous in the hands of wizards, ie, head juggling – which may or may not involved the use of multiple ghosts' heads – others can be highly dangerous, ie, dueling. Though recent efforts have been made to ban dueling, it will likely always be a part of wizarding culture in sporting clubs if not in practice. Dueling for many cultures satisfies social as well as political affronts thus preventing mass bloodshed among feuding families and even national wars.

Wizard's Duel: This type of duel is done with wands only. There is no physical wand-to-wand or wizard-to-wizard contact but real duels use real magic that can do serious, even mortal, harm and seconds are always required to care for the injured or cart off the dead. A duel can become very rapid fire and wands may be whipped about so fast and furious that they look like swords. However with most wands being 7-16" and the majority being around 10", a wizard's duel might look distinctly odd to many Muggle observers, in fact rather like dueling with pencil sticks. In the end though it's the skill and power of the individual wizard not the size of her or his wand that counts.

COLLECTING

Collecting is another fascination wizards share with Muggles. Wizard children, Hannah Abbot and Ernie Macmillan among them, love Chocolate Frog Trading Cards. They are popular to collect, so one meets many people collecting and trading and, with so many different cards available, the fun can last for years. Many older wizards enjoy collecting vintage broomsticks (Whisp) and a number of Quidditch fans enjoy collecting figurines (Ron) and memorabilia of their favorite players (Dean), teams (Seamus) or games (Harry).

Dumbledore is a collector of magical instruments and gizmos and other wizards must share his interest given Dervish and Banges stays in business. Molly collects her favorite author's books (Lockhart). Hermione collects books in general, as does Dumbledore. Dobby is a sock collector who seems to collect badges as well. Dementors are soul collectors, which appears work related but is really just them doing something they love. Arthur collects Muggle technology. Harry has a thing for broom-related products.

Pr Snape collects rare potion ingredients and uses them as decorations in his classroom and study. Filch collects chains and instruments of torture. Dolores Umbridge collected kitten plates. Moody collects Dark Detectors. Pr Sprout, Uncle Algie and Neville share a love of collecting rare plants. Lucius Malfoy and Mr Black (Sirius' dad) collected Dark Arts items. Hagrid collects rare and often illegal creatures when he can. Mrs Black (Sirius' mom) collected house-elf heads. Many wizards seem to have a thing for goats. In short, everyone that's anyone in the wizarding world seems to collect something.

INVENTING

Many wizards enjoy inventing and almost every area of endeavor has its share of inventors. Broommakers are always striving to improve their products, as the release of the numerous brooms like the recent Cleansweep 9 and 11, the Nimbus 2000 and 2001, and the Firebolt can attest. Many wizards are working in experimental medicine, hoping to invent much needed cures, or at least aids, like the recent Wolfsbane Potion which has done so much to improve so many werewolves' lives. Mrs Lovegood had an interest in experimental spells which sadly killed her but the fact there is an entire committee devoted to experimental charms at the MoM implies it's a very popular area for wizard inventors to work in.

Of course not all inventing is as serious as brooms, medicine and experimental charms. Arthur Weasley likes to magically tinker around with Muggle artifacts to try and come up with something interesting and useful, despite the fact it's against the law. Hagrid is always breaking the Ban on Experimental Breeding to create something new and dreadful, which he invariably loves. The Weasley twins, work exclusively on inventing joke items and though Hermione says they only know showy magic, tinkering with magic itself ultimately expands the bounds of magical knowledge, if it doesn't get one jailed or killed.

KNITTING

There seems to be a number of wizards and beings of both genders that are interested in knitting. Hagrid was knitting the first day Harry met him and later the fruit of his labor was found to be a tea cozy in his cabin. One assumes all house-elves learn to knit as part of their education but Dobby raised his knitting to a high art. Dobby created socks with Snitches and broomsticks on them that were at least very clever, if not matching. Hermione taught herself to knit for the SPEW cause, and is improving, but will occasionally magick her needles to knit by themselves. Why exactly everyone likes knitting is difficult to say, perhaps it is a soothing as well as productive creative outlet. And too, in the absence of knitting machines, someone's got to do it.

LEARNING

For those wizards whose interests lie in self-improvement, there are courses available to allow them to enhance their magical skills in the privacy of their own homes.

Kwikspell: A correspondence course in very basic witchcraft and wizardry that is generally used by the less talented. The course, of unknown cost, is said to be all new, fail safe, quick result and easy. It presupposes the learner knows nothing,eg, Lesson One offers some useful tips on holding one's wand. After applying, a person will be sent a purple envelope containing a sheaf of parchment with curly silver writing on it. Filch was taking the course, at least he had the first lesson on his desk in 1992, but so far noticeable improvement seem lacking. The course has many adherents who claim to have been helped and it's unclear how long the course is or how soon one can expect a result, but in Filch's case it's been almost 4 years with no result.

FANCIERS

Fanciers are those wizards who are particularly interested in a specific breed of animal. For example there are many kneazle fanciers, but even more fancy hippogriff fanciers. Newt Scamander's mom was a breeder of fancy hippogriffs for pleasure as well as profit. These magnificent creatures are so popular that every year calendars featuring them, which are considered quite nice gifts at Christmas for even the general wizarding public, are produced by the cartload.

COOKING

Wizards and Muggles share a love of cooking, though wizards are by necessity forced to cook as magic interferes with electricity and thus common appliances such as refrigerators, microwaves, blenders and toasters are useless to them. The average wizard, lacking a house-elf to do the cooking, must learn to fend for herself or himself with a nothing but a wood burning range similar to Mrs Weasley's or a simple hearth and cauldron similar to Hagrid's. Few and far between are the advanced magically powered gas-lit ovens such as Mrs Black had in her home.

Chefs vary but many wizard chefs today engage in the same healthful cooking Muggles do because both are human and new research on diet and exercise does not go unheeded just because Muggles made the discovery first. Kennilworthy Whisp enjoys vegetarian cooking, the Weasleys have a fruit orchard that features apples, Hogwarts has gone organic with its vegetable patches and Hagrid grows or catches his own food. Most wizards eat at least a balanced diet, though there is a decided passion for high-cholesterol foods. One can always spot a wizard by the amount of fatty foods on her or his plate. See the section devoted to Foods in Part II.

Although health is certainly in, this doesn't means sweets are out. Molly is very adept at candy and desert making and the Weasleys make strawberry ice cream in the summer. Mrs Malfoy sends Draco sweets from home, every single day, which she must make, buy or have about her mansion. Hagrid is always making tea goodies like treacle fudge, though mainly its only edible to those with giant-strength teeth, jaws and stomachs. Dumbledore can often be found coming downstairs in the night for his favorite drink, hot chocolate. Hogwarts' house-elves are always willing to hand out a tray of doughnuts and eclairs as well as provide extreme deserts at feasts and even Hermione eats them when out of sight of her dentist parents. No wizard ever turns down a sweet.

Charity Work

Some wizards enjoy doing charity work and Dumbledore is no exception. He will go to any length for a good cause, up to and including prying a book from Madam Pince's abnormally strong fingers so that it might be printed for charity, namely Comic Relief UK, Harry's Books Fund. In addition Dumbledore even writes forewords for this Muggle charity. St Mungo's is a popular wizard charity and singing sensation Celestina Warbeck and Puddlemere United combined efforts to support it though song. Hermione set up SPEW as a charity to help house-elves, whether they want help or not, yet one can't help but think that Kreacher might have been turned from the Dark side if only someone had started such a charity a century back. All good wizards find a way to get involved in a charity.

Reading Matter

This section contains all published reading materials including newspapers, magazines and Hogwarts' textbooks. Books are listed in alphabetical order by author (if the author is known) and by alphabetical order by title (for books where the author is unknown). Books listed by topic, by publisher and by well-known authors are also included for easy reference.

Newspapers

The Daily Prophet: A wizarding community newspaper that's been in publication since at least 1883. *The Daily Prophet* exists solely to sell itself and at 5K a day for owl delivery, it does a very brisk business. Fudge, as head of the MoM, occasionally uses his influence to make the paper toe the party line and suffice it to say this paper has no issue spreading lies and half-truths, engaging in slander and smear campaigns or hiring Rita Skeeter as a special correspondent.

The Sunday edition is called The *Sunday Prophet,* the late edition, when it is published, is called *The Evening Prophet* and for short the paper in all its forms can be called *The Prophet*. The Wednesday edition is known for its zoological column. Each year the paper sponsors "*The Daily Prophet* Grand Prize Galleon Drawing" and in Jul 1993, Arthur Weasley won it and a 700G cash prize.

The Daily Mail: The Muggle paper Vernon reads every morning at breakfast. A British paper known for its conservative views.

Magazines

The Quibbler: A well-intentioned but not well-informed monthly magazine produced by Mr Lovegood of Ottery St Catchpole. Articles are likely to be of an unintentionally spurious or inflammatory nature and the cartoons are usually badly drawn. The wizards who write for the magazine, according to Luna, do so because it's an honor or just to see their names in print. Since there are no paid reporters, the magazine operates cheaply and thus is inexpensive for readers. It's politically anti-Fudge and anti-MoM,

will print anything *The Daily Prophet* won't or can't (eg, Harry's account of Voldemort's rebirth in Little Hangleton) and is widely read.
Transfiguration Today: A magazine which venerable old warlocks seem to take great delight in arguing about.
Which Broomstick: A monthly magazine for broomstick riders. It does articles on the various models and the latest gear and gadgetry for broomsticks. It's very similar to Muggle car magazines but lacks lurid pictures of half-naked witches sprawled across broomhandles, which is doubtless why Molly allows Ron to read it.
Witch Weekly: A weekly magazine for the housewitch community. Molly claims she reads it for the recipes, but it is very gossipy and she does seem to peruse those pages as well. Rita Skeeter was published in *Witch Weekly*, in Mar 1995. It carried her article on Harry's love life which also accused Hermione of toying with young gentlemen's hearts. This magazine gives out the Most Charming Smile Award annually.
The Adventures of Martin Miggs, the Mad Muggle: Ron's favorite comic book character. He has a stack of comic books related to this character in a corner of his room at the Burrow. This publication on the whole does little to bolster a young wizard's respect for Muggles or teach them about Muggles' lives, but it is entertaining.

BOOKS

In addition to regular books, which might or might not have wizard pictures in them, there are also magical books. Usually magical books are imbued with some form of Dark magic such as the ability to burn one's eyes out when reading it or one like the old witch of Bath had that one could never stop reading.

BY AUTHOR

A History of Magic: By Bathilda Bagshot. Hogwarts' textbook for History of Magic.
Break with a Banshee: By Gilderoy Lockhart. Hogwarts' DADA textbook in 92/93.
Gilderoy Lockhart's Guide to Household Pests: By Gilderoy Lockhart. Molly keeps this book on the kitchen mantle at the Burrow.
Gadding with Ghouls: By Gilderoy Lockhart. Hogwarts' DADA textbook in 92/93.
Holiday with Hags: By Gilderoy Lockhart. Hogwarts' DADA textbook in 92/93.
Magical Me: By Gilderoy Lockhart. The autobiography he was signing at Flourish and Botts in Aug 1992.
Travels with Trolls: By Gilderoy Lockhart. Hogwarts' DADA textbook in 92/93.
Voyages with Vampires: By Gilderoy Lockhart. Hogwarts' DADA textbook in 92/93.
Wanderings with Werewolves: By Gilderoy Lockhart. Hogwarts' DADA textbook in 92/93.
Year with the Yeti: By Gilderoy Lockhart. Hogwarts' DADA textbook in 92/93.
The Standard Book of Spells (Grade One): By Miranda Goshawk. Hogwarts' textbook for Charms for 1st year students.
The Standard Book of Spells (Grade Two): By Miranda Goshawk. Hogwarts' textbook for Charms for 2nd year students.
The Standard Book of Spells (Grade Three): By Miranda Goshawk. Hogwarts' textbook for Charms for 3rd year students.
The Standard Book of Spells (Grade Four): By Miranda Goshawk. Hogwarts' textbook for Charms for 4th year students.
The Standard Book of Spells (Grade Five): By Miranda Goshawk. Hogwarts' textbook for Charms for 5th year students.

THE HARRY POTTER COMPANION

The Dream Oracle: By Inigo Imago. Hogwarts' Divination textbook for 5th year students. They are battered leather books kept in the Divination classroom and pulled down only during class. They are used for dream interpretation.

Magical Drafts and Potions: By Arsenius Jigger. Hogwarts' textbook for Potions.

The Diary of Tom Riddle: By Tom Riddle. A small, thin book with a shabby black cover, it started life as a Muggle diary printed in Vauxhall Road, London. It has T. M. Riddle written on the first page and appears to be a blank diary for the year 1943, however, it is actually a Dark item that became Dark after Tom Riddle magicked it up as a means of causing yet more trouble for future generations long after he was dead. Once written in, the diary absorbs the ink into its pages till it vanishes altogether then Tom writes back (his writing also vanishes after a short time). The diary is a vehicle for reincarnation only if Tom can get a diarist to confide a lot of personal information to him and in turn confide a lot of his personal information back to the diarist.

The book also contains Tom's memories and serves as a time portal. It can suck a reader into the diary and show her or him Tom's memory of various events from 1943. Tom kept the Diary even after he became Voldemort and seems to have given it to Lucius Malfoy, his chief Death Eater, sometime between 1970 and 1981. The diary was in Lucius' possession for many years until, in 1992, he surreptitiously gave it to Ginny Weasley in hopes of discrediting Arthur and his Muggle Protection Act. It's doubtful Voldemort told Lucius the diary could reincarnate him as Lucius is at best a slippery friend. More likely Voldemort told Lucius the diary could cause a person to open the Chamber of Secrets and let a monster out that would kill Muggle borns.

What is particularly interesting about the diary being in Lucius' hands is that Lucius must have wondered who T. M. Riddle was in looking at the diary and done research to find out more about him. This means of course that Lucius probably knows that Voldemort is Tom Riddle, and a half-blood and ipso facto a Mudblood. This would seem to be confirmed when Lucius has no reaction to Harry's statement that Voldemort is a half-blood, while Bellatrix goes ballistic over it. What does all this mean? In essence Lucius is only interested in power, whose got it and how he can get it away from them. The pureblood philosophy is one he believes in only in so far as it will gain him the power he seeks.

Fantastic Beasts and Where to Find Them: By Newt Scamander. Hogwarts' textbook for Magizoology and a supplemental text for Care of Magical Creatures. It's the quintessential work on magical beasts and has been through 52 editions since it was first published in 1927. It describes 75 magical beasts in vivid, often graphic or blood-curdling, detail.

Defensive Magical Theory: By Wilbert Slinkhard. A completely useless Hogwarts' textbook for DADA used in 95/96. Chapters include such things as basics for beginners (Chapter 1); common defensive theories and their derivations (Chapter 2); makes a case for using non-offensive responses when magically attacked (Chapter 3); and seems to be the leading proponent of nonretaliation and negotiation (Chapter 34). The author apparently doesn't believe in violence or is a coward of gigantic proportions.

One Thousand Magical Herbs and Fungi: By Phyllida Spore. Hogwarts' textbook for use in Potions and Herbology.

A Beginners' Guide to Transfiguration: By Emeric Switch. Hogwarts' textbook for Transfiguration years 1-3.

The Dark Forces: A Guide to Self-Protection: By Quentin Trimble. Hogwarts' DADA textbook for 91/92.

Unfogging the Future: By Cassandra Vablatsky. Hogwarts' thick black Divination textbook for 3rd years. It is a very good guide to basic fortune-telling methods including palmistry, crystal balls and reading bird entrails according to folks at Flourish and Blotts but it doesn't seem to have benefited Harry, who failed his OWL in Divination by misreading a crystal ball.

Curses and Counter-curses: Bewitch Your Friends and Befuddle Your Enemies with the Latest Revenges: Hair Loss, Jelly-Legs, Tongue-Tying and Much, Much More by Prof. Vindictus Viridian: A book that interested Harry when he saw it in Flourish and Blotts in Jul 1991. He wanted to buy it to be able to curse Dudley but Hagrid steered him away from it.

Magical Theory: By Adalbert Waffling. Hogwarts' textbook for Magical Theory, years 1 and 2 only. After that it's probably a supplemental text for Transfiguration and Charms.

Quidditch Through the Ages: By renowned Quidditch expert and author Kennilworthy Whisp. First published in 1952, it has remained a best-seller to date. Hogwarts' Library has only a single copy that's usually always checked out. Hermione read it for flying tips during her first year. Harry tried to read it but Pr Snape confiscated it.

Home Life and Social Habits of British Muggles: By Wilhelm Wigworthy. Published in 1987, it explains all about the Muggle life. It's Hogwarts' textbook for Muggle Studies.

BY TITLE

Achievements in Charming: A book Hermione read to bone up for the OWLs.

Ancient Runes Made Easy: A book that Hermione uses for her Ancient Runes homework.

An Anthology of Eighteenth-Century Charms: A book Harry looked through for a charm to breathe underwater.

An Appraisal of Magical Education in Europe: A book Hermione read that mentions Beauxbatons.

Asiatic Anti-Venoms: A book Harry looked at for a 5th year Potions essay.

Basic Hexes for the Busy and Vexed: A book Harry looked at for help with TT Task 1. It includes such hexes as will produce Pepper Breath, Horn Tongue or Instant Scalping in the intended victim.

Broken Balls: When Fortunes Turn Foul: A book Harry saw in Flourish and Blotts' fortune-telling section.

Charm Your Own Cheese: A book Molly keeps on the kitchen mantle at the Burrow.

Common Magical Ailments and Afflictions: A book Hermione might look in to find out about a scar burning.

A Compendium of Common Curses and Their Counter-Actions: A book found on the shelves of the Room of Requirement.

The Dark Arts Outsmarted: A book found on the shelves of the Room of Requirement.

The Dark Forces: A Guide to Self Protection: Hogwarts' DADA textbook for 94/95.

Death Omens: What to Do When You Know the Worst Is Coming: A book Harry saw in Flourish and Blotts' fortune-telling section. The manager of the store advised Harry against reading it. Its cover shows a huge black dog with gleaming eyes - The Grim.

Dragon Breeding for Pleasure and Profit: Hagrid took this book from Hogwarts' Library to study up on how to raise Norbert.

Dragon Species of Great Britain and Ireland: Hagrid looked at this Hogwarts' book in the Library before Norbert was born.

Dreadful Denizens of the Deep: A book Harry looked through for a charm to breathe underwater.

THE HARRY POTTER COMPANION

Enchantment in Baking: A book Molly keeps on the kitchen mantle at the Burrow.
The Encyclopedia of Toadstools: A book that hit Lucius Malfoy in the eye during his fight with Arthur.
Flying with the Cannons: A book on the Chudley Cannons that Harry read in 1994.
Fowl or Foul? A Study of Hippogriff Brutality: A book Ron researched for Buckbeak's appeal.
From Egg to Inferno, A Dragon Keeper's Guide: Hagrid looked at this Hogwarts' book in the Library before Norbert was born.
Great Wizarding Events of the Twentieth Century: A book Hermione bought for background reading in Jul 1991. Harry is in it for defeating Voldemort in 1981.
Great Wizards of the 20th Century: An Hogwarts' Library book that was searched by Harry, Hermione and Ron for Nicolas Flamel.
A Guide to Advanced Transfiguration: Hogwarts' Transfiguration textbook for 6th and 7th year students.
A Guide to Medieval Sorcery: A book Harry looked through for a charm to breathe underwater.
The Handbook of Do-It-Yourself Broomcare: This book came with Harry's Broom-Servicing Kit. It includes information such as *A Charm to Cure Reluctant Reversers.*
The Handbook of Hippogriff Psychology: A book Ron researched for Buckbeak's appeal.
Hogwarts, A History: A book Hermione reads religiously. It seems to answer almost all questions about Hogwarts. However, Hermione finds it a highly biased and selective look at Hogwarts, which glosses over all the nasty aspects of the school. This of course implies the author knew all the nasty aspects, which she or he did not, and purposely kept them back. Hermione was particularly disaffected by the lack of any information on the Chamber of Secrets or house-elves – both of which were of course secrect. The book is over 1,000 pages long.
Important Modern Magical Discoveries: An Hogwarts' Library book that was searched by Harry, Hermione and Ron for Nicolas Flamel.
Intermediate Transfiguration: The Hogwarts' Transfiguration textbook for 3rd, 4th and 5th years. It shows such semi-useful things as how to turn owls into opera glasses.
The Invisible Book of Invisibility: A very expensive book which Flourish and Blotts lost 200 copies of. It was, after all, invisible.
Jinxes for the Jinxed: A book found on the shelves of the Room of Requirement.
Madcap Magic for Wacky Warlocks: A book Harry looked through for a charm to breathe underwater.
Magical Hieroglyphs and Logograms: Hermione's additional reading book for 5th year Ancient Runes.
Magical Water Plants of the Mediterranean: A book Pr Moody (Barty Jr) gave to Neville hoping Harry would ask for help from his friends. It has information on gillyweed in it which would have been useful to Harry in accomplishing TT Task 2.
Men Who Love Dragons Too Much: A book Harry looked at for help with TT Task 1. But it only talks about talon-clipping charms, how treat scale rot, and other dragon healthcare magic.
Modern Magical History: Hermione bought this book for background reading in Jul 1991. Harry is listed in it.
The Monster Book of Monsters: Hogwarts' textbook for Hagrid's Care of Magical Creatures class, an elective class Harry, Ron and Hermione take. It is a green leather-covered book with gold writing Harry received from Hagrid for his birthday one year. It's seemingly alive and snaps at people and other books using its covers, which it flaps

with great effectiveness. It moves sideways like a crab by standing on its edges and prefers to hide in dark places such as under a bed or in a cupboard. Though it lacks actual teeth, it does have a fearsome bite capable of causing great pain and destruction. It is soothed only by stroking its spine with a finger, but Harry opted to close it with a belt.

Moste Potente Potions: A Hogwarts' Library book in the Restricted Section. Hermione checked it out for the Polyjuice Potion recipe it contained.

Nature's Nobility: A Wizarding Genealogy: A large heavy book Sirius found, and threw out, during the house cleaning at Grimmauld Place in Aug 1995.

A New Theory of Numerology: A book Harry gave Hermione for Christmas 1995.

Notable Magical Names of Our Time: An Hogwarts' Library book that was searched by Harry, Hermione and Ron for Nicolas Flamel.

Numerology and Gramatica: An Hogwarts' textbook Hermione has for Arithmancy.

Olde and Forgotten Bewitchments and Charmes: A book Hermione looked through for a charm to breathe underwater.

One Minute Feasts - It's Magic: A book Molly keeps on on the kitchen mantle at the Burrow.

Powers You Never Knew You Had and What to Do with Them Now You've Wised Up: A book Harry looked through for a charm to breathe underwater.

Practical Defensive Magic and Its Use Against the Dark Arts: A set of books given to Harry by Sirius and Remus for Christmas 1995. They each have superb moving color illustrations (one assumes photographs rather than true illustrations or drawings) that demonstrate all the counterjinxes and hexes they describe.

Predicting the Unpredictable: Insulate Yourself Against Shocks: A book Harry saw in Flourish and Blotts' fortune-telling section.

Prefects Who Gained Power: A study of Hogwarts Prefects and their later careers: A book Percy was found reading in a Diagon Alley junk shop in Aug 1992. One assumes that Tom Riddle becoming Voldemort is not mentioned.

The Rise and Fall of the Dark Arts: Hermione bought this book for background reading in Jul 1991. Harry is in it as is the sky-projected Dark Mark.

The Rune Dictionary: A book Hermione has for Ancient Runes class.

Saucy Tricks for Tricky Sorts: A book Harry looked through for a charm to breathe underwater.

Self-Defensive Spellwork: A book found on the shelves of the Room of Requirement.

Sites of Historical Sorcery: It mentions Hogsmeade. Hermione read it one year on vacation.

Spellman's Syllabary: Hermione's additional book for 5th year Ancient Runes.

Sonnets of a Sorcerer: A Dark magic poetry whose readers were forced to speak in limericks the rest of their lives.

A Study of Recent Developments in Wizardry: An Hogwarts' Library book that was searched by Harry, Hermione and Ron for Nicolas Flamel.

Theories of Transubstantial Transfiguration: An Hogwarts' Library book that beat up Dumbledore when he thoughtlessly doodled in it.

Weird Wizarding Dilemmas and Their Solutions: A book Hermione looked through for a charm to breathe underwater. It includes such things as making nose hairs grow in ringlets.

Where There's a Wand, There's a Way: A book Harry looked through for a charm to breathe underwater.

The Harry Potter Companion

By Topic

Animal & Beast Related
Break with a Banshee
Dragon Breeding for Pleasure and Profit
Dragon Species of Great Britain and Ireland
Dreadful Denizens of the Deep
Fantastic Beasts and Where to Find Them
From Egg to Inferno, A Dragon Keeper's Guide
Fowl or Foul? A Study of Hippogriff Brutality
Gadding with Ghouls
Gilderoy Lockhart's Guide to Household Pests
The Handbook of Hippogriff Psychology
Men Who Love Dragons Too Much
The Monster Book of Monsters
Travel with Trolls
Year with the Yeti

Arithmancy
A New Theory of Numerology
Numerology and Gramatica

Being Related
Holidays with Hags
Nature's Nobility: A Wizarding Genealogy
Voyages with Vampires
Wanderings with Werewolves

Biography
Great Wizards of the Twentieth Century
Notable Magical Names of Our Time
Magical Me (autobiography)
Prefects Who Gained Power

Charms
Achievements in Charming
An Anthology of Eighteenth-Century Charms
Olde and Forgotten Bewitchments and Charmes

Cookbooks
Charm Your Own Cheese
Enchantment in Baking
One Minute Feasts - It's Magic

Curses
A Compendium of Common Curses and Their Counter-Actions
Curses and Counter-curses

Dark Arts
The Dark Arts Outsmarted
The Dark Forces: A Guide to Self-Protection
Defensive Magical Theory
Practical Defensive Magic and Its Use Against the Dark Arts (series)
The Rise and Fall of the Dark Arts

Divination
Broken Balls: When Fortunes Turn Foul
Death Omens: What to Do When You Know the Worst Is Coming
Predicting the Unpredictable: Insulate Yourself Against Shocks

ACASCIAS RIPHOUSE

Unfogging the Future
Education Related
An Appraisal of Magical Education in Europe
Herbology
Encyclopedia of Toadstools
Magical Water Plants of the Mediterranean
One Thousand Magical Herbs and Fungi
Hexes
Basic Hexes for the Busy and Vexed
History
Great Wizarding Events of the Twentieth Century
A Guide to Medieval Sorcery
A History of Magic
Hogwarts, A History
Important Modern Magical Discoveries
Modern Magical History
Sites of Historical Sorcery
A Study of Recent Developments in Wizardry
Jinxes
Jinxes for the Jinxed
Medical
Common Magical Ailments and Afflictions
Muggle Related
Home Life and Social Habits of British Muggles
Poetry
Sonnets of a Sorcerer
Potions
Asiatic Anti-Venoms
Moste Potente Potions
Magical Drafts and Potions
Quidditch
Flying with the Cannons
Handbook of Do-It-Yourself Broom Care
Quidditch Teams of Britain and Ireland
Quidditch Through the Ages
Runes
Ancient Runes Made Easy
Magical Hieroglyphs and Logograms
The Rune Dictionary
Spellman's Syllabary
Spells
Madcap Magic for Wacky Warlocks
Powers You Never Knew You Had and What to Do with Them Now You've Wised Up
Saucy Tricks for Tricky Sorts
Self-Defensive Spellwork
The Standard Book of Spells (series)
Weird Wizarding Dilemmas and Their Solutions
Where There's a Wand, There's a Way
Theory
Invisible Book of Invisibility

Magical Theory
Transfiguration
A Beginner's Guide to Transfiguration
A Guide to Advanced Transfiguration
Intermediate Transfiguration
Theories of Transubstantial Transfiguration

BY PUBLISHER
Little Red Books
A History of Magic by Bathilda Bagshot. Published in 1947.
Home Life and Social Habits of British Muggles by Wilhelm Wigworthy. Published in 1987.
Obscurus Books
Fantastic Beasts and Where to Find Them by Newt Scamander. Published in 1927.
WhizzHard Books
Quidditch Through the Ages by Kennilworthy Whisp. Published in 1952.

WELL-KNOWN AUTHORS
Bathilda Bagshot
A History of Magic
Miranda Goshawk
The Standard Book of Spells (series)
Arsenius Jigger
Magical Drafts and Potions
Gilderoy Lockhart
Break with a Banshee
Gadding with Ghouls
Holidays with Hags
Magical Me
Travels with Trolls
Voyages with Vampires
Wanderings with Werewolves
Year with the Yeti
Newt Scamander
Fantastic Beasts and Where to Find Them
Wilbert Slinkhard
Defensive Magical Theory
Phyllida Spore
One Thousand Magical Herbs and Fungi
Emeric Switch
A Beginner's Guide to Transfiguration
Quentin Trimble
The Dark Forces: A Guide to Self-Protection
Cassandra Vablatsky
Unfogging the Future
Pr Vindictus Viridian
Curses and Counter-curses
Adalbert Waffling
Magical Theory
Kennilworthy Whisp

Quidditch Through the Ages
Wilhelm Wigworthy
Home Life and Social Habits of British Muggles

BROOMS AND QUIDDITCH
Working with the expectation that everyone has a copy of *Quidditch Through the Ages* by Kennilworthy Whisp, this is a short overview on the subject of brooms and Quidditch.

TYPES OF BROOMS
No matter how jazzed up or decorative a broom is these days, it still began its life as a common broom available at any cleaning supply shop. Any wizard can make a flying broom with a few basic spells, but specialist-made brooms fly better, longer and are a consistently safer product. The power and complexity of spells put on brooms today make them very difficult to tamper with, but a powerful wizard could (though only a Dark wizard would) attemp to tamper with one.

The Bluebottle: A family broom that was advertised at QWC 1994. It has a built-in Anti-Burglar Buzzer among other exciting features.
Cleansweep 5: A professional League Quidditch broom in the 1950s.
Cleansweep 11: It does 0-70 mph in 10 seconds, with 70mph being its top speed. The handle is Spanish oak with anti-jinx varnish and it has built-in vibration control among many other features. It was released sometime in summer 1995.
Comet 260: Given Draco's comments, it was probably released in 1991.
Comet 290: Released in summer 1995, it can accelerate 0-60 mph in 60 seconds only with a decent tailwind. Meaning the Comet 260 is slower.
Firebolt: Released in Jul 1993, this broom became an international standard broom used by the Irish national side at QWC 1994. It has an ash handle with hand-painted, individual registration numbers, can accelerate to its top speed of 150mph in 10 seconds and has an unbreakable Breaking Charm. It has a slimmer handle than a Cleansweep, birch twigs for its broomtail, perfect balance and pinpoint turning. Needless to say, it costs 100s of Galleons. Its maker is unknown.
Nimbus 2000: The Nimbus 2000 was the fastest, most aerodynamic broom ever made when it was released in Jul 1991. Its sleek shiny mahogany handle has Nimbus Two Thousand written up at the top in gold and its tail is comprised of neat, straight, aerodynamically arranged and trimmed twigs of unknown species. It does have slight flaws such as listing to the tail end and a tendency to develop a drag after a few years but it's still a very desirable broomstick. The top speed is 65mph.

Harry received a Nimbus 2000 in Sep 1991 from Pr McGonagall so he could play on the Gryffindor House team. The best broom on the field in 91/92, its usefulness was unfortunately short lived. In Nov 1993 Harry fell 50' from this broom during a game and the broom, lacking a rider, drifted over to the Whomping Willow in the prevailing winds. The willow beat it to bits, which Ron retrieved and Harry lovingly put away.
Nimbus 2001: Released in Aug 1992, it was a highly improved model that made the Nimbus 2001 look very shabby indeed. The maximum speed probably topped out at round 85-90mph. The entire Slytherin team was mounted on this broom in 92/93 thanks to Lucius Malfoy. Due to the Chamber of Secrets being opened the season was cut short leaving the broomsticks' usefulness to the team in question. However, in

93/94 a full season was played and Gryffindor proved that quality broomsticks are no match for quality players.
Other Older Brooms: Silver Arrow and Shooting Star.

Who Owns What Broomstick

Cho Chang: Comet 260. A really nice broom, but it can only top out at under 60mph. It is no match for Harry's Firebolt broom which tops out at above 150mph. Luckily he's polite enough to give her a sporting chance when their teams play each other.
Madam Hooch: She first learned to fly on a Silver Arrow.
Draco Malfoy: He had a Comet 260 at home during 91/92. In 92/93 he was upgraded to a Nimbus 2001 when his father bought a set of them for the entire Slytherin House team in a deal that allowed Draco to become the team's Seeker.
Harry Potter: His broomstick was a Nimbus 2000 from Sep 91- Nov 93. After it was destroyed, he received a Firebolt from Sirius, Dec 25, 1993, which he continues to ride.
Ravenclaw Team: All team members rode the Cleansweep 7 in 93/94. A good quality broom, but Cho continued to ride her Comet 260 anyway whenever she played Seeker.
Slytherin Team: All team members rode the Nimbus 2001 in 93/94. Presumably they continue to ride on the Nimbus 2000s since they are team brooms.
Nymphadora Tonks: Comet 260. As an Auror, owning a good broom is imperative. Which says a great deal about the Comet 260, but if she wants to have a long and healthy career she should at least invest in a Nimbus 2001. No doubt Moody already has one for quick escapes.
Fred and George Weasley: They each have a Cleansweep 5, which are about 40 years old. The Cleansweep 5 was a professionally used Quidditch broom in the early 1950s. However Oliver Wood suggested in Sep 1991 that a Cleansweep 7 (the most recently released Cleansweep at the time) would be second choice only to a Nimbus 2000. So a Cleansweep 5 is not really that outdated.

The Cleansweep company only uses odd numbers for its brooms, so broom model 7 is really only the next model after model 5. In 1991, to stay competitive with newly released Nimbus and then later the Firebolt, Cleansweep began biannually releasing updated broomsticks. By Aug 1995, the most recent release was the Cleansweep 11, which Ron received as a present.
Ginny Weasley: What broomstick she rides is a good question. She must have a very good one if she can play Chaser or Seeker on it. On the other hand, her brothers all have relatively old brooms and her family is quite poor. One must assume she begged her parents to give her a combined multi-year birthday and Christmas present in 1994.
Ron Weasley: He has a Shooting Star till 1995. The company making this broom went out of business in 1978, so the broom is at least 23 years old. The charms on it are so worn down that butterflies can now pass it without straining themselves. However, it does stay in the air. Given the broom, it's no wonder Ron was always playing Keeper at the Burrow for his brothers. Ron's parents got him a Cleansweep 11 in Aug 1995 for becoming a Prefect. The new broom was competitive enough to get him on the House Quidditch team as a Keeper and a player rather than a reserve.

Racing Broom Companies

Cleansweep Broom Company: Maker of the Cleansweep.
Comet Trading Company: Maker of the Comet.
Nimbus Racing Broom Co: Maker of the Nimbus.

Universal Brooms Ltd.: Maker of the Shooting Star, this company closed in 1978. Their brooms loose altitude and speed as they age which makes them safe for beginners and consequently perfect as Hogwarts' school brooms in the 1990s.

BROOM-SERVICING PRODUCTS

Broom-Servicing Kit: Made by Fleetwood, it comes in a sleek, black leather case with Broom-Servicing Kit stamped across it in silver. The case unzips to reveal a large jar of Fleetwood's High-Finish Handle Polish, a pair of silver Tail-Twig Clippers, a tiny brass compass one can clip to one's broom for long journeys and a copy of *The Handbook of Do-It-Yourself Broomcare*. Hermione gave a kit like this to Harry for his birthday one year.

Tail-Twig Clippers: Silver, sharp and fairly sturdy since they are for cutting wood. Think upscale pruning sheers.

Fleetwood's High-Finish Handle Polish: Brooms, like wands, are wooden products and require periodic cleaning, oiling so they don't crack and polishing to preserve the object from water damage. Fleetwood's gives a broom that little bit of extra beauty as well as protection.

QUIDDITCH, THE GAME

Quidditch is originally an English game which dates back to the 11th century. It takes its name from Queerditch Marsh where an early, very crude, version of this game was played. Popular world wide among wizards, almost every child grows up playing Quidditch or some form of it.

RULES

There are many rules, the following are the 10 most pertinent ones. Consult QTA for a detailed assessment of all known Quidditch rules.

1 There is no altitude limit for players but they cannot cross over the bounds of the pitch.
2 Captains, and only Captains, may call a time out by signaling the referee. This is the only time before the end of the game that a player's feet may touch the ground without the team receiving a penalty for it.
3 The referee may awards penalties but those individuals who are assisting the referee as bounders may not.
4 A team's Chaser always takes the penalty by flying from the central circle to the scoring area. All other players must keep well back.
5 While a Chaser may seize the Quaffle from an opposing player, they may not seize any portion of another player's anatomy.
6 Trickery, as long as it involves no actual physical contact, is encouraged.
7 During a game there are no substitutions allowed in case of injury. The team must play without that player, even if that player is the Seeker or Keeper.
8 Reserve players may only play if the game has not yet begun.
9 The game ends only when the Snitch has been caught by one of the Seekers, or by mutual agreement or consent of both captains.
10 Wands may be taken on to the pitch but not used on opposing players or their brooms, the referee or any officals, the balls or members of crowd (unless they choose to imitate dementors).

The Harry Potter Companion

Fouls

Although the Transylvanians managed to pull off a whopping 700 fouls in the first QWC in 1473, there are only about 10 common fouls in modern Quidditch, of which 5 have turned up on Hogwarts' pitch:

Blagging: Seizing an opponent's broom, usually by the tail, to slow, stop, or hinder, Draco. Any player might be caught fouling another player this way.
Blatching: Flying in such a way as to intentionally collide with another player, Marcus. Any player might be caught fouling another player this way.
Blurting: Locking broomhandles with another player with the intention of steering her or him off course, Draco. Any player might be caught fouling another player this way.
Cobbing: While some use of elbows is expected and acceptable, the excessive use of elbows to keep opponents at bay is a foul, Montague. Any player might be caught fouling another player this way. Only a referee can determine how much elbowing it too much elbowing.
Quaffle-Pocking: Tampering with the Quaffle so that its rate of fall is increased or it falls in an odd manner such as zigzaging or loop-de-looping, Dobby. Technically Dobby was guilty of Bludger-Pocking since he tampered with the Bludger. Any player might be caught fouling another player this way.

Special Moves

There are 13 known special moves in Quidditch, of those, 3 have been used and 2 practiced by Hogwarts' players, and 3 were seen in QWC 1994.

Bludger Backbeat: A Beater hits a Bludger backhanded and over her or his shoulder. Fred tried this but not during a game.
Dopplebeater Defense: Both Beaters hit the same Bludger at the same time to increase the iron ball's power and velocity on impact with an opposing player. Fred and George have done this during a game.
Double 8 Loop: A Keeper blocks the goal hoops by making a looping figure 8 around all 3 hoops. Ron has used this technique during games.
Hawkshead Attacking Formation: Chasers form an arrow pattern and fly toward the goals as a group to intimidate the Keeper and any opposing team player who might seek to deflect their attack. Used in QWC 1994 by the Irish team.
Porskoff Ploy: A feinting move used by Chasers. The Chaser with the ball flies to a high altitude but then throws the ball to a team member flying yards below. Used in QWC 1994 by the Bulgarian team.
Reverse Pass: A Chaser throws the Quaffle over her or his shoulder to another player, hopefully one of their own team. Angelina has done this during a game.
Sloth Grip Roll: A player hangs upside down from the broomstick by both her or his hands and feet, like a sloth, usually to avoid an oncoming Bludger but actually to avoid anything in-coming. Angelina made the team practice this move when she was Captain.
Wronski Feint: aka the Wronski Defensive Feint, or if one is Hermione, the Wonky Feint thing. A rather painful feinting move used by Seekers. A Seeker, pretending to see the Snitch, hurtles downward hoping that the opposing Seeker will panic at missing the Snitch and do the same. The feinting Seeker pulls up hoping the other Seeker will but not be able to. Used by Bulgaria in QWC 1994 to great effect.

ACASCIAS RIPHOUSE

POSITIONS AND PLAYERS
Each team is made up of 7 players but may have as many reserve players as they like. Each game has 1 referee, who is usually helped by as many assistants as they require stationed around the pitch to make sure no boundaries are broken. Specifics for each position follows.

Referee: There is only 1 referee per game. This highly skilled office requires an expert flier with uncommonly good eyesight and neck muscles as well as a thorough knowledge of the game and a strong belief in pacifism. Referees rarely die during a match these days but in the past they have been known to vanish from them unexpectedly and turn up in the Sahara Desert months later.

Beaters: There are 2 Beaters per team. Their duty is to protect their team members from Bludgers. Equipped with bats for deflecting Bludgers, these positions are usually occupied by male players with plenty of upper body strength and an excellent sense of balance. Beaters may not score with or handle the Quaffle or Snitch.

Chasers: There are 3 Chasers per team. These positions usually go to women who are light, fast and have excellent hand-eye coordination. Only the Chaser with the Quaffle may enter the scoring area. Chasers may not touch the Snitch.

Keeper: There is only 1 Keeper per team. A Keeper guards the goal posts and scoring area. Keepers generally are to remain within the scoring area, though they can fly out of that area to intimidate or head off opposing Chasers. A Keeper may not touch the Snitch.

Seeker: There is only 1 Seeker per team. Seekers are usually the smallest, lightest and fastest players. This position requires excellent flying skills, sharp eyes and the ability to fly one or no handed. Harry has all these skills and the ability to focus so intensely as to be able to see an object moving in slow motion. Seekers get fouled more frequently than other players and the most serious accidents seem to happen to them, however, it's considered the glamour job and the position that gets the most attention and adulation. The Seeker may touch the Snitch but not the Quaffle.

THE PITCH AND EQUIPMENT
See schematic H for a quick overview of the pitch and balls. The following gives detailed information on both topics.

The Pitch: An oval shape, 500' long and 180' wide, the pitch has a small 2' center circle where all players initially gather at the start of a game. After the balls are released by the referee from the center circle, players may go into air. There are 3 golden scoring hoops (of unknown diameter) at either end of the pitch, each standing 50' in the air. The pitch is usually surrounded by a raised stadium and built on bog or marsh land, which makes for softer landings when a player falls from her or his broom and is generally far away from human (Muggle) habitation.

Quaffle: A seamless scarlet leather ball 12" in diameter, the Quaffle is enchanted to stick to a Chaser's hand and fall slowly through the air when dropped. Each Quaffle that makes it completely through a goal hoop is worth 10 points; it doesn't matter which hoop it goes through, it's still only 10 points.

Bludgers: These are 2 iron balls 10" in diameter and bewitched to chase or attack the player closest to them.

The Golden Snitch: aka the Snitch. A walnut-size gold ball with silver wings that look similar Dumbledore's half-moon glasses. It is bewitched to elude players and aviud capture as long as possible and the charms on a Snitch can last for 100s of years so once one escapes a pitch it's almost impossible to recover. Capture of the Snitch, which can occur only once in a game, is worth 150 points and ends the game.
Robes: Quidditch robes are generally much longer than regular robes. Team members always have their name embroidered on the back of the robes, just like a jersey. They come in a wide variety of colors and usually also sport team emblems on the front or back.

BRITISH AND IRISH LEAGUE TEAMS BY NATION

Please note that England has a disproportional number of teams due to having had more teams when the number was pared down in 1674 by the DMGS (though some teams continued despite being downgraded). Teams that are in Muggle-designated Britain but to wizards are separate areas with regional MoMs, such as the Channel Islands or Isle of Man, are not included.

Appleby: England, has the Arrows.
Chudley: England, has the Cannons. Ron's favorite team. They were ninth in the league (of 13) in the 1990s, which is about as close to the top as they've been in 100 years or more. Robes: bright orange with giant double black Cs and a speeding black cannonball. The cannonball appears to be speeding, it is not magically enhanced to fly on robes, banners, Ron's bedspread, etc.
Falmouth: England, has the Falcons.
Puddlemere: England, has Puddlemere United. Oliver Wood started on their reserve team in 1994 after graduating Hogwarts. Dumbledore's favorite team.
Tutshill: England, has the Tornados. They have been Cho Chang's favorite team since she was 6. They went on a winning streak in the 95/96 season. Supporters tend to wear a sky blue badge with 2 gold Ts on it that is not magically enhanced.
Wimbourne: England, has the Wasps. They wear black and yellow horizontally striped robes with a wasp emblem on the chest and apparently many former players keep and wear their robes after retirement. Ludo Bagman formerly played Beater for the Wasps in the 1970s and 1980s before becoming Head of the DMGS.

Ballycastle: North Ireland, has the Bats. And a really beautiful city with a great annual faire!
Kenmare: Ireland, has the Kestrels. Seamus' favorite team.

Montrose: Scotland, has the Magpies.
Portree: Scotland, has the Pride of Portree. Kirley McCormack is from Portree and usually has family playing on the team.
Wigtown: Scotland, has the Wanderers. Kennilworthy Whisp's favorite team.

Caerphilly: Wales, has the Catapults. "Dangerous" Dia played on this team, during what years is unknown.
Holyhead: Wales, has the Harpies.

CUPS
League Cup: Any member team of the League can potentially win this every year. Competition for this cup involves only those teams playing in 1 League. In the British and Irish League there are 13 teams striving for the cup.

European Cup: Played every 3 years, all the League teams of Europe usually compete in this event. Played consecutively since 1652, but not in years the World Cup is played (represented by an x) or when various events (eg, WWI and WWII) required it to be canceled. Recent European Cups include: 1991 x 1997 2000 2003 x 2009.

World Cup: Played every 4 years consecutively since 1473, it cancels the European Cup in the years they overlap. It is also subject to cancellation due to various catastrophes. The competition is open to any nation that can form a team no matter whether they have a League or not. Recent World Cups: 1990 1994 1998 2002 2006 2010. QWC 1994 was announced as the 422nd World Cup. Given there were only 521 years between 1473 and 1994, that would mean only 130 World Cups could have been played at a maximum. Ludo was probably overexcited by the event itself and meant to say the 122nd cup, meaning 8 cups had not been played due to large-scale wars or other problems such as the Black Plague.

National Teams: aka the national side, or the international team. These are teams formed of the best players in any one country regardless of what team or league the player might normally compete on or be resident in. These teams compete for the QWC. For a long time only European countries put together national teams but in the last few QWCs, as international travel has become easier, teams from the Americas, Australasia and Africa have put together excellent teams and made very good showings.

QUIDDITCH WORLD CUP 1994

QWC 1994 was a huge event, the final game of which took over 500 people more than a year to set up. The DMGS tried to make the cup as accessible to everyone as possible and sold a variety of tickets. The cheaper the ticket the earlier one had to arrive at the site of the game. The Lovegoods and Fawcetts had the cheapest tickets and had to arrive 2 weeks before the match. Arthur got his very pricey large parchment tickets free from Ludo and didn't have to arrive till the day of the match. The Diggorys also had expensive tickets that allowed them to arrive the day of the match.

The MoM set up a designated Apparition point (in some woods near the stadium) for wizards choosing this method of arrival. Wizards good at Apparition or not traveling with minors were able to use this method if they lived within or could travel to a distance of about a 300-mile radius from the site. Wizards coming from great distances like Africa or America and traveling with minors could use broomsticks or Muggle airplanes. Those within the British MoM's jurisdiction could use time-activated, date-specific Portkeys to reach the site.

Security, always a big issue when 100,000 wizards congregate in a single place, was especially tight in the case of QWC 1994. Full anti-Muggle security was maintained, wizards were asked to refrain from using magic or dressing or acting like wizards, and a compliment of Obliviators were on hand 24/7 in case of security breaches. The national teams traveled to a special pitch on a deserted moor set up by the DMGS, by unknown means. Surrounding the pitch was a very tall, golden stadium, every inch of which had been covered in powerful Muggle-Repelling Spells prior to the event.

Throughout the site of the QWC many saleswizards were selling various merchandise related to the event. Velvet-tasseled programs, action figurines, scarves,

The Harry Potter Companion

flags, rosettes, hats and the like were all widely available, though quite pricey. Bookies were on hand to take bets, as was Ludo Bagman who was virtually the gaming center of the event despite his clear conflict of interest and use of borrowed goblin money to fund his racket. A gong signaled those throughout the campsites when the game was ready to start and a lighted pathway directed wizards to the stadium's staircases.

The stadium was designed to hold a minmum of 100,000 wizards and it appears every seat was filled. The golden walls of the staium is said to have surrounded a field large enough to hold 10 cathedrals comfortably, which is a bit odd as the Quidditch pitch is a standardized 500' by 180' and professional pitches are not larger than say Hogwarts' pitch just because a game is more important or professional. It was probably the stadium seating that was the size of 10 cathedrals. Built onto the stadium cross from a large blackboard, where writing appeared pitching the various products of those companies sponsoring the event, was the Top Box.

Cornelius Fudge had the Top Box made for himself, Ludo and Barty Sr, and other dignitaries he'd invited to attend the game. Purple carpet on laid the stairs that led up to the Top Box, which was positioned at the halfway point of the field and set as high up as possible in an effort to make the seats eye level with the competition. Inside the box were 20 purple and gilt chairs set in two rows of 10 seats. The second row was furthest from the railing, the first was closest to the action.

Second Row: (left to right) Winky, Barty Jr, Ludo, Minister Oblonsk, Cornelius, Lucius, Draco, Narcissa.

First Row: (left to right) Harry, Ron, Hermione, Ginny, Fred, George, Bill, Charlie, Percy, Arthur.

Teams Playing in QWC 1994

The two teams playing in QWC 1994 were Bulgaria and Ireland. A display from the team mascots, in this case, leprechauns and veela, preceded the QWC match. Referee Hassan Mostafa then released the balls and spirited play between the two teams ensued, punctuated by vigorous attempts to subvert the game by veela.

Bulgarian National Team:
Robes: Scarlet.
Chaser: Dimitrov
Chaser: Ivanova (probably female)
Chaser: Levski
Keeper: Zograf
Beater: Vulchanov
Beater: Volkov, male
Seeker: Viktor Krum, male

Technically, Ivanova is a woman's name because of the ending -va. Ludo says however that the player is male. He may have been mistaken in his excitement, or she may look a bit mannish. Where gender is not listed as a certainty it is unknown, though -ov is a male ending.

Irish National Team:
Robes: Green.
Chaser: Troy
Chaser: Mullet, female
Chaser: Moran, female
Keeper: Ryan

Beater: Connolly, male
Beater: Quigley
Seeker: Aidan Lynch, male
   Where gender is not listed as a certainty, it is unknown. One presumes since the Chasers are a famous trio that all of them are female, especially as most of the best professional Chasers are female.

Final Score: Bulgaria v. Ireland 160-170. Ireland won the cup, though Bulgaria caught the Snitch that ended the game. The cup is large and made of gold, which is probably gilded silver rather than solid gold. It takes a couple of husky wizards to carry it. Usually the cup is presented by the Minister of Magic of the country hosting the event to the winning team. In this case Fudge presented it to the Irish team.

EXPRESSIONS

This section contains common wizarding expressions translated for Muggle readers followed by British language helps for those who wonders what bins or prats are and don't have friends in Britain to consult.

WIZARDING EXPRESSIONS

Bring and fly sale: A swap meet.
The cat's among the pixies now: Meaning the worst has happened. The Muggle version would be the fox is among the chickens or the wolf's among the sheep.
Do a Crouch: Meaning turn in one's own kin. Named after Barty Crouch Sr.
Do a Weasley: Meaning to leave school early and in a spectacular manner. Named after Fred and George Weasley.
Fell off the back of a broom: Meaning stolen goods. Similar to fell off the back of the truck.
Galloping gorgons: A wizarding expression of surprise or amazement. Gorgons are snake-haired women thought to turn those who look at them to stone.
Galloping gargoyles: A wizarding expression of surprise or amazement.
Gormless gargoyle: Meaning the stupid idiot.
Got ploughed: To fall for the Wronski Feint such that the Seeker ends up on the ground, or in it.
Gulping gargoyles: A wizarding expression of surprise or amazement.
Hold your hippogriffs: Meaning wait or slow down. Similar to hold your horses.
Like some common goblin: Meaning to act like a common criminal. Goblins have a genuine knack for ending up on the windy side of the law.
Losing a Knut and finding a Galleon: Meaning not what one was looking for, but finding something even better. Similar to lose a penny, find a pound or dollar.
Merlin's Beard: An expression of shock. Rather like Good Heavens.
Might as well be hanged for a dragon as an egg: Meaning, if one is going to do something illegal, it might as well be a spectacularly illegal rather than minorly illegal as the punishment is the same. Similar to might as well be hanged for a sheep as a lamb.
No good crying over spilled potion: Meaning one can't change what's already happened. No good crying over spilt milk would be the Muggle equivalent.
Pull a Pettigrew: Betray a cause one claims to believe in or person one claims to have friendship for.

A tale worthy of Harry Potter: Meaning a ridiculous lie.
Umbridge-itis: An illness students would claim to be suffering from as soon as Pr Umbridge appeared in class Umbridge-itis is in reality Skiving Snackboxes.
Wasn't room to swing a kneazle: Meaning a tight place. The Muggle equivalent would be there wasn't room to swing a cat.
What in the name of Merlin: A wizarding expression, of shock. Similar to the Muggle expression "what in the name of God (or Jesus)," but completely unrelated to a belief system that centers around Merlin or credits Merlin's name with inherent divinity or power.
Working like house-elves: Meaning to work very hard or all the time. Similar to working like demons or dogs, back in the days when demons and dogs actually worked for a living.

STRICTLY BRITISH

In this section are common British words and their American equivalent or sufficient explanation to understand what the inherent meaning is.

Abroad: Meaning not on British soil, usually implying somewhere on the Continent of Europe. Although the British are but 13 nautical miles from the Continent, there is a feeling that the Continent is as foreign a place as the moon and its peoples equally beyond reach or understanding. Abroad is usually said with a mixture of disgust, horror and foreboding, and in writing generally capitalized, "he went Abroad," as if it were a place in its own right.
Alice band: A hair band.
Balaclava: A ski mask minus the face covering bit. It covers the head and shoulders.
Berk: An evil idiot.
Bin: A trashcan.
Blimey: Similar to "wow" or other expressions of shock or surprise.
Bonfire Night: aka Guy Fawkes Night, Nov 5.
Budge up: Move over.
Budgie: aka budgerigar. A parakeet.
Bung: To stop something up, to give someone something to shut them up.
Cheek: also, cheeked, cheeky. Meaning to be impertinent, sassy or otherwise affronting.
Christmas Cake: A fruitcake, covered in marzipan and white icing.
Christmas Pudding: Usually a plum cake that's been steamed, doused with brandy and set on fire.
Codswallop: Lies or untruths.
Collywobbles: The willies or hebe-jebies.
Conk: Slang for nose.
Cracker: An empty cardboard cylinder, similar to an empty toilet roll, stuffed with candy, wrapped in bright paper and tied at either end. Inside the tube is a strip of paper coated in gunpowder which cracks when two people pull the cracker apart by tugging on opposite ends.
Crumpet: A small, flat circle of baked bread. Americans would call it a Thomas' English Muffin.
Crikey: A common expression of surprise or amazement or even admiration. Australians are justly fond of this word.
Dead: Meaning really, as in really useful.

ACASCIAS RIPHOUSE

Dodgy: Not quite on the level, possibly illegal.
Dresser: A cupboard with shelves for dishes and drawers for kitchen utensils.
Effing: A slang substitute for the very crude 4-letter word starting with f.
Fairy lights: Meaning strings of Christmas lights, not actual fairies holding lights.
Fancy: Meaning to really like.
Flutter: A wager.
Fringe: Bangs of hair.
Galumph: To gallop in a lumbering way.
Git: An idiot.
Half past: also Half. In terms of time it means 30. Half three is 3:30. Half past 3 is also 3:30, not 3:15 as Americans mean when they use it.
Haversack: A backpack that's worn over one shoulder.
Holidays: A vacation.
Holidaymakers: Vacationers.
Hosepipe: A garden hose.
Jumper: A sweater.
Kip: Meaning to camp or lodge.
Knickerbocker Glory: A parfait made with ice cream.
Lift: An elevator.
Lounge: Living room. Usually the word of choice for the rich or those who are not wealthy but social climbing.
Net Curtains: Usually meaning lace curtains.
Newsreader: A newsanchor.
Nick: Meaning to steal.
Pastille: A type of aromatic (peppermint, cinnamon, etc) or medicated candy.
Pasty: Meaning a meat pie with a folded crust. Similar to a popover just with meat and veggies in it.
Peaky: Meaning ill looking.
Pillock: A fish, but used to mean brainless idiot.
Plus-Fours: Bermuda shorts.
Porridge: Oatmeal.
Post: The mail.
Prat: Someone non-upperclass and stupid. Whereas a ponce is someone upperclass but stupid.
Ruddy: A form of the British swear word bloody.
Shirty: Meaning to be rude.
Skip: A large dumpster.
Skive: also skiving. Meaning skipping something, (class, dinner, etc) by making an excuse of some sort.
Snogging: Meaning to hug and kiss.
Spare: also going spare. Meaning to go crazy or be crazy.
Take the mickey out of: Meaning to tease.
Term: This can mean a term, 1 of 3 in every school year, or 1 entire school year.
Ticked: Meaning to check or cross off.
Tin: Canned, as in canned goods.
Titchy: Tiny.
Tosh: Nonsense.
Trainers: Sneakers.
Treacle: A type of sugar product.

The Harry Potter Companion

Trifle: A layered sponge cake soaked in sherry and topped with fruit, custard or whipped cream.
Tripe: A food but also used to mean ridiculous.
Underground: The subway, subway system or subway trains.
Whelk: A type of mollusk.
Wotcher: A greeting that's popular in London.

Rag and Bone

In this section is anything that couldn't be found a home elsewhere. It includes a wide variety of information about a wide variety of subjects. Logically, all these topics share the fact that they relate to the average wizard's lifestyle.

Clothing and Accessories

Cloaks: Cloaks are usually floorlength, at least short, 15th-century Elizabethan cloaks don't seem to be in demand. Cloaks come in all styles and all colors, but most are floorlength and designed to match a set of robes rather like the coat of a suit. Cloaks can however be made in a different color and used to accent a set of robes. Fudge has a pinstriped cloak that usually contrasts with his bottle green suit. Rita Skeeter has a fur-trimmed cloak matching her winter robes. Durmstrang students, whose school is in a cold climate, have fur-trimmed cloaks but the shaggy matted fur surely contrasts with their blood-red robes.

Cloaks have all manner of fastenings from fancy jeweled gold ones to plain grey steel ones. Hogwarts' uniform cloaks are black with silver fastenings. Real silver? probably not. But many styles of silver to be sure or who could tell their cloak from the 1,000 others lying about? Cloaks can also come with or without hoods. Hogwarts' cloaks have hoods, which given the climate in Scotland is more necessity than a fashion statement. However, Pr Snape always wears a hooded cloak, even in his dungeon classroom which is certainly a fashion statement as he can't possibly need a hood underground, indoors.

Invisibility Cloaks come in only one color but they allow a wizard to become invisible as long as it is covering the wizard entirely. These cloaks always have hoods and are floorlength, which makes invisibility easier. They are usually also quite voluminous. Harry is able to fit 3 people under his cloak, not comfortably since Ron has grown 6" but, all the same, 3 people. And while Invisibility Cloaks are extremely rare, Traveling Cloaks are extremely common and everyone seems to have at least one, sometimes more.

Traveling Cloaks can be sleek and tailored (Karkoff) or wide and voluminous (Moody) depending on the wearer's taste or needs. Certainly there are no hard and fast rules about the color of a Traveling Cloak, but black seems tradition and most common. Moody wears a black, extra voluminous one to hide his wooden leg. Lucius Malfoy wears a tailored black one wherever he goes and thinks of it as a fashion statement, basic black, basically elegant. Fudge also has a black one in his collection. But Dumbledore's is purple, because it's his favorite color. It's all just a matter of taste.

Earmuffs: This item of clothing is one that Dumbledore as well as Pr Sprout wear in winter. Pr Sprout prefers hers to be fluffy and pink. Dumbledore's are probably purple. Most students and staff seem to use their scarves as earmuffs, wrapping them around their heads to cover their ears. Earmuffs are particularly helpful in all seasons when dealing with mandrakes and Pr Sprout seems to have a large and varied collection of them for student use, which may also mean she's an earmuff collector.

Glasses: In spite of advanced medical practice that can mend bones instantly, no one in the magical world seems to have cured nearsightedness or farsightedness. All vision-impaired wizards use glasses rather than contact lenses. Possibly because use of contact lenses disrupts magical ability. Certainly we know that eye contact is important from the basic jinxer to the advance Legilimens. It may be that while a glass lens is not disruptive of eye contact a plastic lens that can be shifty and easily bent or warped could be.

Handkerchiefs: These come in all manner of color and style. Pr McGonagall's is lace trimmed. Pr Trelawney's is embroidered by her own hand. Hagrid's is large and checked. What's particularly interesting about them is there doesn't seem to be anyone in the wizarding community that doesn't always carry a handkerchief at all times (this includes wizard ghosts). Even other magical beings like house-elves carry them. For those Muggles looking for magicals in their community, cloth hankies (carried by those wearing glasses) are the most visible sign.

Hats: Most wizards buy hats to match a set of robes they wear, but some always wear a black hat no matter what color robes they wear. Hats generally stand about 3' tall and most wizards, and goblins, stick with the classic tall, pointed, 17th-century wizard's hat so famously associated with Puritan and Pilgrim Muggles. However, Gran seems to wear a stuffed vulture on a Muggle-style hat which was common when she was a girl in the 1910s. Certainly the "bird on a hat" theme was most prevalent then, though Muggles preferred other types of bird. Fudge wears a lime green bowler. Winky has a blue hat with ear holes. Dobby likes knitted hats. It would appear that hats are purely a matter of taste or lack thereof.

Wizards always, always wear their hat. Always. Even shopping, even at dinner, even on trains or in coaches, even dancing, even when playing Quidditch, even on holiday, even riding on broomsticks and even in classes. Indoors, outdoors, day or night, wizards always always wear their hats. Always. The only exceptions to this rule are sleeping, bathing and swimming. Why exactly wizards have this hat fetish is open to speculation. It seems to be a simple case of doing what's culturally appropriate or trendy but they may be protecting their heads since the mind is the source of much magic.

Jackets: Jackets can come in any material. Most younger wizards have modern Muggle-style clothing for wearing about town but as is usual with wizards, the style might be Muggle but the material is decidedly wizard. Fred and George bought themselves dragon skin jackets (of lurid green scaly material, probably Common Welsh Green) which were very expensive but Muggle in style. Given the toughness of dragon skin and the number of dangerous things Fred and George do, they've probably made a wise investment.

Purses: Most witches carry a common Muggle-looking purse which may or may not be enhanced with an expanding charm or other wizarding features. Molly's purse seems to have everything she wants in it, which is quiet a lot. At first glance one might say it's been magically expanded however logic suggests if that were true and it did have all Molly wants in it, it would be too heavy to carry. Her purse must instead have a charm on it that gives it that ability to produce whatever the person reaching into it is looking for, similar to the charm on the Room of Requirement.

Watches: Most everyone in the wizarding world carries a watch. Younger folks seem to wear wristwatches that are mostly gold, which is very distracting when one is looking for a Golden Snitch. Older folks, like Dumbledore, carry pocketwatches which are more stylish but some can require more skill on the part of an owner to discern the time since not all watches have hands and numbers. Some watches are astronomic, replete with planets and must be read like a star chart. Others have hands but in place of numbers are things that the owner ought to be doing. Some people prefer their clock to be an hourglass pendant, similar to a Time-Turner, while still other's like a wrist-worn sundial. There are probably skilled watchmaking wizards constantly developing new ways to tell time every year and it's up to the buyer to figure out what she or he can most easily read.

Jewelry: It would seem that jewelry is common in the wizarding world. Warlocks of importance might have a crested ring in addition to a wedding ring, fancy cloak fastenings of expensive metals, fobs that double as seals, cuff links for closing the sleeves of robes or, like Dumbledore, fancy silver-buckled shoes. They might wear an ornament or badge on their hat to affix a feather or hold a fancy strap around the crown. Many gentlemen carry fancy walking sticks with embossed metal heads, enjoy a nicely jeweled set of buttons on dress robes or carry little silver or enameled boxes in which to carry their favorite smoking tobacco in style. Truly sentimental gents might even have a hand-painted ivory cameo of their wife or sweetheart with an expensive setting that they wear around their neck or on a pocket chain.

Witches are women first and always women and therefore most like to wear their finery every day. Pr Trelawney may go overboard, with bangles, necklaces and rings but Madame Maxime on fancy occasions wears an opal necklace and opal rings for daily wear. Pr Umbridge is fond of old ugly rings, worn on every finger. Parvati likes bangles on both wrists and butterfly hair ornaments. Madam Rosmerta likes her fancy spangled shoes. Even Rita Skeeter has jewel-encrusted glasses. Add to this many of the same accouterments the warlocks have such as buckled boots, fancy cloak fastenings, pedant or ring seals and cameos and one quickly realizes that goblin jewelers and wizard metal charmers must be kept very busy indeed.

Socks: Wizards, and other creatures, do like their socks. Dobby loves mismatched pairs of socks and even knits them. Vernon has given old socks to Harry as a present. Harry gave Lucius Malfoy a sock, which ended up setting Dobby free. Dumbledore complains he can never get anyone to give him socks, particularly warm woolly ones. And Harry was able to buy socks for every day of the year at a wizarding shop in Hogsmeade proving they had at least 183 pairs in stock.

While no one can say why socks are an obsession with so many beings, suffice it to say they are. And one can't help but notice that it's a healthier obsession than most Muggles have. Socks are useful, healthful and attractive. A good pair of socks can last for years, and are passed around so there's no waste. Talented knitters can make their own while professional sock knitters must make a very good living indeed. Dobby, with his excellent knitting skills and superb design talents, could do worse than open his own sock shop in Hogsmeade.

Robes: Robes should always be floorlength, covering one's shoes, but not so long that they drag. Most robes slip on over the head or button up the front, have numerous pockets inside them, some of which are up to 16" long for wands, and feature sleeves that go all the way down to the wrists (which is why no one ever sees the Dark Mark on anyone's arm). Some wizards just wear underwear under their robes (Pr Snape) while others wear Muggle clothing like tshirts and jeans (Harry). Robes come in many colors, styles and materials but usually they match the wearer's hat.

Most adults seem to have one color outfit they like and always wear it. Pr McGonagall prefers to wear green robes. Pr Snape always wears black robes. Pr Lockhart wore a wide assortment of colors that complimented his forget-me-not blue eyes. Dumbledore likes dark cool colors like midnight blue, forest green or purple. All students have to wear a uniform robe, hat and cloak, which varies depending on the school. Durmstrangs wear blood red, Beauxbatons sky blue and Hogwarts basic black. Most wizards (barring Rita Skeeter) and wizarding students choose to express their fashion personality only on those occasions when dress robes are called for.

Dress robes come in a variety of colors, styles and expensive materials. All adult wizards have at least one set of dress robes. All 4th-7th year students at Hogwarts are required to have dress robes for various formal functions that crop up. Fleur Delacour has silver-grey satin robes. Parvati has turquoise robes. Hermione likes floaty robes. Pansy has frilly pink robes. Draco's robes are black velvet with a high collars like a priest's or vicar's. Harry's are just like his school robes but bottle green.

Ladies might have robes that are floaty, ruffled or decoratively trimmed. They may come in any color, print or pattern and are usually made of expensive materials, such as silk, organza or satin. Pr McGonagall has red tartan robes, which might be related to her sept. Gentlemen can be equally posh wearing robes in stylish cuts that are trimmed in gold, embroidered or made of rich fabrics. Ludo's are purple with yellow stars and moons. Dumbledore's are usually embroidered. Minister Oblonsk's were black but trimmed in gold ribbon or braiding.

Quidditch robes differ from regular and dress robes in that they are made of cotton, wool, linen or other semi-durable fabrics and cut much longer. Additional length may seem to make little sense given more material means more drag while in flight but it stems from an early tradition in which people wore robes and nothing else play Quidditch. A great deal of embarrassment for Quidditch players who wore regular-length robes while rocketing over the heads of spectators ensued. When players finally realized what was happening, lengthy robes were quickly adopted.

Scarves: Most wizards have and wear scarves during the winter season. A large number of adults at Hogwarts have tartan scarves which is unsurprising given most have lived in the Highlands of Scotland for a decade or more. Many adults and students seem to prefer to wear their scarves around their heads in place of earmuffs which is odd, but doable if one tucks the ends up under one's hat to secure them. In addition to a regular scarf for daily wear, most students and teachers have a scarf especially for wearing to Quidditch matches.

The wearing of a purely decorative scarf sporting one's team's colors is traditional at all British sporting events. That being the case, Hufflepuffs wear yellow and black striped, or yellow scarves with a black badger; Gryffindors red and gold striped, or red with a gold lion; Slytherins green and sliver striped, or green with a silver snake; Ravenclaws blue and copper striped, or blue with a copper eagle. And while Dumbledore is supposed to remain unbiased in such matters and doesn't wear any kind of scarf, he does only turn up at Gryffindor games which leads one to believe he is in reality just a bit biased toward his old house.

Where exactly students acquire a Quidditch scarf is a bit of a mystery. One supposes one can be bought in Hogsmeade, but that's not until a student's 3rd year. It is more likely that students knit them themselves, magically or by hand, or have a house-elf do it. Certainly there is a lot of creative effort put into Quidditch scarves, banners, hats, etc and it would behoove older students to aid younger ones in decking themselves in their House colors before a game. There may even be a standard House scarf issued to each student, after they have been sorted into their Houses, when they first arrive at their dorm rooms, perhaps placed on their bed

Shoes: Most students seem to wear Muggle sneakers or the like for daily wear, even at Hogwarts. For warlocks boots seem to be the fashion. Bill, Dumbledore, and a male

Auror at MoM all wear boots. Dumbledore goes for traditional black, silver-buckled, 17th-century style boots. Fudge, the Minister of Magic, has some pointed purple boots. More modern warlocks seem to go for dragon skin boots if they can afford them. Dragon skin is particularly showy as most dragons come only in spectacularly garish or lurid colors. What ladies wear is hard to discover as they usually have long robes covering their shoes. One might guess they would opt for any attractive Muggle footwear.

Suits: For gentlemen not exactly wizards, like Hagrid or Filch, suits seem to be the order of the day with special suits for special occasions. Hagrid has a black moleskin suit for daily wear and a brown one for events like the Yule Ball. Filch normally wears a brown suit but has a set of moldy tails he wears at Christmas. Most wizards wear robes at all times but an exception to this rule would be Fudge. He seems to always wear a pinstripe suit perhaps because like Vernon he's trying to be impressive and superior.

Umbrellas: Despite the Impervius Charm, all wizards seem to prefer to own and use an umbrella. On days there are Quidditch matches and it rains, students are out in their hats, carrying umbrellas. To accommodate a 3' hat the umbrella shafts must be about 6' tall. Certainly only Hagrid's umbrella appears normal in size but he's a half-giant. It might simply look normal in his large hand. It would still stand out though as it is pink and flowery and most students have black umbrellas.

Health

Complimentary Medicine: In the wizarding world, complimentary medicine is old Muggle cures such as stitches. These cures don't work on wizards most of the time and many wizards are unwilling to even try them.

Dragon Pox: A magical illness of a contagious nature. Probably similar to chicken pox.

Lycanthropy: The werewolf syndrome.

Mediwizards: Parahealers. Some were at QWC 1994, to tend the injured players and administer medicinal kicks to the referee.

Pipes and Smoking: The wizarding community seems to smoke pipes exclusively, probably because they are well aware of the benefits pipe smoking has over cigars or cigarettes. However, benefits aside, only a small percentage (less than 1 in 100) of the adult wizarding population smokes. Witches and warlocks smoke in about equal numbers but no positive or negative value is ascribed to those who smoke or to smoking. Wizards do it, do it publicly and no one mentions smoking bans or second-hand smoke.

Pipes come in a wide variety of styles, from modern 19th-century, short-stemmed pipes that are easily portable to the long-stemmed pipes of the early 18th century which are not. They can be intricately carved or simply turned, made of rare exotic woods or local white clay. The rich might have pipes with inlaid bowls or silvered stems and even velvet-lined cases for their pipes. The Leaky Cauldron seems to keep the old pub tradition of loaning out pipes to visitors, which sounds unhygienic, but the smoldering tannins and searing smoke is somewhat antiseptic.

Wizard pipe tobacco is unique as it gives off various color smokes and smells when burned. Smoke may be of any color one chooses and may or may not dissipate. Dung's tobacco results in very thick green smoke which gathers around him and provides a ready smokescreen for his illegal doings or getaways. Some magical tobacco smells are good, others fairly bad. Dung's is like acrid old socks which surely discourages anyone from pursuing him. One would think, since ladies smoke, more delicately scented, possibly floral, spicy or perfumed smells are available.

Scrofungulus: A magical illness of a contagious nature. One dreads to speculate, but it would seem to be a fungal type scrofula.

Spattergroit: A disease that leaves one's skin pock-marked and gruesome looking. The remedy is liver of toad bound to one's throat while standing naked before the full moon in a barrel of eels' eyes. It was suggested by a Medieval Healer's portrait at St Mungo's that Ron had this. Actually Ron had freckles.

Vanishing Sickness: A magical illness of a contagious nature that makes its victims disappear, one assumes totally but perhaps partially.

MONEY

Wizard Money: There are 3 types of coins in the wizarding community: Knuts which are bronze, Sickles which are silver and Galleons which are gold. Their values in relation to each other is as follows:

29 Knuts = 1 Sickles
17 Sickles = 1 Galleon

The approximate relation of US and UK money to wizarding money is, as of 2003, as follows:

493 Knuts = 1 Galleon
67.04 Knuts = 1 US dollar
96.33 Knuts = 1 UK pound

The conversion of wizarding money to US or UK currency is as follows:

1 Galleon =   7.35 US dollars   or 5.12 UK pounds
1 Sickle =   43 US cents   or 30 UK pence
1 Knut =   1.5 US cents   or 1 UK pence.

Harry thinks wizarding money is strange looking. Ron calls Muggle money weird looking. So we must assume that the 2 don't look much alike. Harry calls wizard money coins so they must bear some similarity to coins. However, only Sickles are stackable. Given all this, perhaps wizarding money looks more like its name. Sickles are likely flat and curved like a farmer's sickle and therefore stackable. Knuts, which owls collect for *The Daily Prophet* may resemble small nuts and be round and squat like sunflower seeds. Galleons may be shaped like ships they are named after. Of course this is only a discussion of British wizarding money and other MoMs have their own unique wizarding money that bears no resemblance to what the British MoM uses.

Galleons: Although we don't know much about wizarding money, we do know that Galleons have serial numbers on their sides which refer to the goblin who cast the particular coin. These numbers would be 8 digits long presuming the system Harry and the DA were using was similar to 01122045 which is British for Dec 1 at 8:45pm. It is possible that sickles are stamped out given their flatness and Knuts are cast like Galleons, but goblins rarely let anyone tour their minting facility and don't like answering too many questions about their moneymaking, so it's difficult to say for certain.

Money Bags: Most wizards use pouches or bags to carry their money. These can sometimes be made of mokeskin, which is considered the best type of pouch to have, but a pouch can be made of any type of leather. They usually resemble the drawstring leather bags of the Middle Ages. No one carries a wallet, checkbook, credit cards or other Muggle money-related ephemera for several very good reasons. Wallets only work with flat, paper money which wizards don't have, the credit card system is electricity dependent which wizards can't use and checks, it would seem from Sirius' purchase of Harry's Firebolt, are unnecessary since one can simply give a company a vault number.

TERMINOLOGY

Anti-Muggle Security: This security measure was in effect at the QWC 1994. It means a wizard must, as much as possible, dress and act like a Muggle so as not to attract Muggle attention.

Blood Debts: When a wizard saves another wizard's life, it creates a bond between them. Dumbledore says it is magic at its deepest and most impenetrable, but gives no furth explanation leaving Harry somewhat at a loss as usual. Peter Pettigrew owes a blood debt to Harry and this will prove a difficulty for Voldemort, sometime in the future. Peter has already gone a bit soft on hurting Harry and tried, only a few months after being saved by him, to persuade Voldemort not to use Harry's blood for rebirthing.

Chief Warlock: The wizard in charge of the Wizengamot. It's Chief Witch when the position is held by a woman. Dumbledore is the current Chief Warlock.

Grand Sorcerer: It has not been stated what this wizard is in charge of. One presumes that it's Grand Sorceress when the position is held by a woman. Dumbledore is the current one. Possibly this is the head of the as yet unseen legislative branch of the British MoM.

Heptomology: Given the prefix, either a type of divination involving the number seven, hepto = seven, or a type of divination involving the reading of livers, hepatic = liver. The latter a Roman technique of questionable virtue. The former possibly based on the very ancient belief that the number 7 is a divine number.

Orthinomancy: A type of divination that involves reading bird entrails. The Romans were very fond of it, but apparently it did not reveal to them the very important information that if they continued invading other countries, in the future their empire would collapse.

Supreme Mugwump: This individual is the Chairman or Chairwoman (also called Chairwarlock, Chairwitch, Chairwizard) of the ICW. Dumbledore is the current one. The individual is elected by other ICW members and one assumes can only be removed by the ICW members or if the MoM which appointed the individual removes them as a representative. Thus it was Fudge who removed Dumbledore as a British representative to the ICW and therefore Dumbledore couldn't continue to be the Supreme Mugwump even if the ICW wanted him to.

Seer: A prophetic person who is able to tell the future, or a portion thereof. They are very rare. Muggles and wizards can be born with this talent. It is thought to be primarily inherent but some individuals feel it can also be acquired over time, through study and practice. Biblical record would seem to indicate both trains of thought are vaild.

WEIGHTS AND MEASURES

Wizards are very proud of their national heritage. They are more interested in preserving their unique individual cultures as they are, than creating a universal wizarding culture. All British wizards use traditional British weights and measures even though Britain itself has gone metric. Wizards never use the metric system. This makes them a bit easier to spot about town since they are always looking at their conversion charts.

For those that don't know the old British system, a chart follows with the most useful weights and measures.

Weights
  Ton = 2,000 pounds = .907 metric tons
  Pound = .454 kilograms
  Ounce = 28.350 grams

Capacity
  Gallon = 4.546 liters
  Quart = 1.136 liters
  Pint = 56826 cubic centimeters

Length
  Mile = 1.609 kilometers
  Yard = .9144 meters
  Foot = 30.45 centimeters
  Inch = 2.45 centimeters

Area
  Acre = 4047 meters.

Hands: This is used for measuring horses. One hand is equal to 4", considered the width of a man's palm. Mr Ollivander remarks he took a tailhair from a 17-hand unicorn stallion, 17 x 4" = 5'6" at the top of the withers. A very large horse, at least to those of us that are 5'4" and couldn't even see over its back.

WIZARDS AND MODERNITY

The following is a discussion of contemporary wizarding culture touching on many different points. Headings are given in case readers wish to skip directly to a particular section of interest.

TECHNOLOGY

Wizards grow up in a world lacking technology animated by electricity, thus as adults they generally prefer to stick to what they already know. This is not to say wizards are against advancement through technology, they are not. They simply, as most Muggles do, pick and chose from what's available based on what will work for them. For instance a cast-iron wood-burning stove with oven and pots and pans is preferred by many witches to cooking over an open hearth with a cauldron and spit. Wood-burning stoves were new technology in the 19th century and readily adopted by wealthy housewitches at that time. When later still, in the 1890s, gas was discovered for lighting, heating and cooking, some creative and very wealthy wizards (like the Blacks) found a magical way to adapt it to heating magicals' stoves and boilers as well.

The split between wizard and Muggle society got larger slowly, over the 19th and 20th centuries, with each new piece of technology that Muggles could use and wizards could not, because it depended on electricity. Wizards, confronted with being marginalized by the inability to use advanced Muggle technology, adapted to run magically what technology they could and, failing a successful conversion, relied on older technology and methods. The Knight Bus is transport for the elderly, underage or stranded and is used because of its ability to carry many people without being conspicuous to Muggles. But runs magically, not on fossil fuels or electric batteries. The same is true of the MoM's cars and even Arthur's Ford Anglia. The Hogwarts Express on the other hand is even older technology. It is a pre-electric vehicle and runs on coal and water. It is now only used by wizards on a limited basis to Muggle avoid suspicion.

Wizards do have some technology of their own invention, it just doesn't run on electricity. Dumbledore's office is stuffed with instruments, all working, all run by magic. These devices are small and serve limited magical purposes. Wizards are certainly trying to bridge the Muggle-magical technology gap and shops like Dervish and Banges, that specialize in making and repairing magical instruments, run a steady business. Wizard inventors are always coming up with new devices but what can be done by magical technology is always limited to what magic itself can do.

In many instances where magic fails completely, manual or animal labor picks up the slack. Molly does her family's cooking and washing. Hogwarts runs on house-elves' labor. The postal workers sort the mail by hand and by hand tie it to various owls that do the actual delivery work. Hippogriffs and winged horses are used for basic and long-distance transport. Nifflers are used for mining. Fairies are used for Christmas lighting. Sphinxes replace the best Muggle anti-theft systems, as does the occasional troll. And while all this may seem a great burden at first, the use of human or animal labor and magic does have advantages. The most important one is that wizards' lives create little or no waste.

What isn't self-repairing, like Dumbledore's instruments and office, can be repaired with a simple spell. Books go through many hands till they are worn out completely, justifying the loss of a tree to produce it. Robes have many owners before they end up rags. Furniture and goods stay in families virtually forever, unless a case like Sirius and his house crop up. In general though, once purchased an item last virtually forever, cutting down on consumerism. When at last a wand or a broom brakes it can go for firewood. In essence, a wizard's life and lifestyle from start to finish are environmentally responsible and infinitely sustainable.

THE ENVIRONMENT

Wizards show tremendous respect for their environment. Unlike Muggles, wizards still recognize their utter dependence on the Earth. Without the wood for wands or brooms, there would be no magic and no magical transport. Without raw minerals, plants and animals, no potions. Without magical beasts, no wand cores and fewer needed clothing articles or transport. So wizards at every turn try to preserve that from which they derive the tools with which to release the magic within themselves. They use natural renewable resources which don't produce toxic waste when disposed of and work patiently and diligently with the earth in order to sustain their way of life.

If certain plants can only be picked during certain phases of the moon. no one forces a magical plant to grow by stuffing it in a closet with 24 hour full-spectrum lights beating down on it. No one pours tons of chemicals over it to make it bigger so there's more usable elements. No one tries to trick it into producing the desired root, seed, leaf, whatever. If a potion is dependent on the cycle of the moon, no wizard is foolish enough to attempt to try and force the moon to do her or his bidding. Everything is done with the rhythm of the Earth. If that means no Veritaserum can be ready for a month, then there's no Veritaserum for a month.

Everything is kept recyclable and nothing is created or used that is environmentally damaging. Pr Sprout composts in her greenhouses and teaches her Herbology students to do the same. Magical products like Doxycide only stun doxies so they can be removed to another area. Doxies are not killed simply because their annoying or wizards have the power to kill them. There is an ethical environmental consciousness pervading the wizarding world that is actively at work. The centaurs are justly mortified at a large stupid giant ripping out trees in their forest. Pr Snape is upset the Whomping Willow was run into by a car. Hagrid cares enough to do what was best for Norbert even though in his heart he wanted to keep him and loved him like a child. Dumbledore doesn't demand the Forbidden Forest be cleaned out and made safe, even though a colony of arcomantulas lives there.

Which brings us to creatures magical and not. Creatures are treated with great respect by wizards because they need them and they know future generations of wizards will need them. There are no extinct magical or nonmagical species due to wizards acting irresponsibly. Muggles may have killed off a species wizards' used in their magic, but wizards never have done so. From minor species with no magical purpose like the golden snidget to dragons whose every fiber are magically useful, all species involved with wizards are protected by international law. Reserves are set up to insure species will have what they need to continue to exist. The MoMs pay wizards study all the species that they are involved with. The harvesting of these resources is done with care and always a view to insuring the survival of those creatures wizards will always need for magical purposes.

Magicals' one destructive act is the use of animal furs, which may be distasteful to Muggles, but the fur is from a renewable resource, biodegradable and used for needed warmth by those without central heating, like Durmstrangs, or those whose work is primarily out of doors, like Hagrid. And while where on the subject of clothes, one of the biggest burdens on the planet, it must be noted that they are of minimal importance to wizards. An individual might own 3 or 4 sets of robes and a set of dress robes but true a clothes horse, like Pr Lockhart, is very rare. Wizards may go overboard on socks but this is a minor vice. This limited purchase of clothing means that the manufacture of clothes is kept on a human scale and usually within the community in which they are sold. Cottage industry abounds. Small shop owners are many rather than few. Quality of life is good for a majority of people who live in a stable economy where not much changes over the centuries.

Finally, wizards don't create weapons of destruction, mass or otherwise. Wizards may still die in wars but not ones that kill millions or destroy the cities, villages and open spaces of entire countries for decades to come. By carrying around a wand every day from the time they are very small, wizards have learned to use this potentially lethal weapon responsibly. Barring occasional freaks of nature like Tom Riddle and Salazar Slytherin (only 2 freaks in 1,000 years one might add), wizards won't create things that might linger around for decades and kill or maim completely innocent people. They could. They have the knowledge. But they don't. They choose to reject any weapon beyond a wand and never to use a wand to kill another being.

HEALTH

It would seem from the wizard Healers at St Mungo's that wizards don't use any medicine that involves penetrating the skin of a living person. Surgery is out of the question in a society that rejects stitches and removing body parts, or parts of body parts as wholly unacceptable. But accidents do happen. Harry was deboned, Eloise cursed off her nose. These magically caused incidents were reversible. But others are not. Moody is living testimony that once a limb, nose, buttock or other part of one's anatomy is destroyed, there is no getting it back magically. Perhaps a magical eye can fill a socket, but a female Auror working with Kingsley Shacklebolt wears a patch over her eye indicating that not everyone can or chooses to go that route.

Which brings up the subject of vanity as it regards health. The wizarding world is not obsessed with 3% body fat or everyone having the look of a fashion model. Oh granted, there is vanity. But Mrs Figg is outside shopping in carpet slippers. Harry's hair sticks out and up in all directions. Moody doesn't get a prosthetic leg or have plastic surgery to get a nose. Pr Sprout leaves her hair grey. No one tells Dumbledore, Madam Marchbanks or Pr Tofty they are too old looking. And while Gilderoy Lockhart may have been drooled over by middle-aged witches, no one in the wizarding world is joining a gym, jogging 5 miles a day or having liposuction to emulate him. Wizards are who they are and that's acceptable, even if it's unusual.

But back to medical treatment. If traditional Muggle practices are out, what's in? Obviously magical potions play a large role in healing. But what else? The Healers must work with the body to help it repair itself so all noninvasive techniques would be acceptable. These would include the following: vitamins, chiropractic, herbal medicine, naturopathy, homeopathy, acupuncture, aroma therapy, massage, physiotherapy, color therapy, crystal therapy, steam baths, magnetic therapy, colonics, casts, traction, amulets, talismans, fasting, prayer and even shock therapy. Many of these techniques have worked for thousands of years for Muggles as well as wizards.

The fact that most modern Muggle doctors may frown on most, if not all, of the above treatments doesn't mean they are ineffective. Aspirin was an herbal remedy once. Bone setting was once thought ridiculous by Muggle doctors, who much preferred to chop a broken limb off. And I need hardly remind wizarding readers that much of modern Muggle medicine is based on the availability of machinery operated by electricity and thus are simply not a usable option for wizards. It would be impossible to do open heart surgery without a blood-circulating machine and who would be foolish enough to try it when even common Muggle cures like stitches don't work on wizards? So, given the limitations, wizards do the best they can with what they've got and it's worked well for them for many 1,000s of years.

Of course, it must be admitted that wizards don't have a cure for everything and not everyone who checks into St Mungo's leaves shortly after. Some patients are very damaged and must go to a ward for long-term care. It may take many months or even years before a breakthrough occurs, if it ever does. However, St Mungo's long-term care wards has few patients and even most of those must get well over time. It might also be remarked that the Longbottoms are in a long-term ward at St Mungo's indicating cases of mental illness are treated at the hospital. Given the low number of insane wizard in the hospital, and the Longbottoms are only insane because of torture, mental illness must be nonexistent or generally curable in the wizarding world, making wizard medicine quite excellent.

THE STATUS OF WOMEN AND CHILDREN

In reviewing the data, it appears there has been complete political equality for women since the 1300s and possibly earlier if one assumes that women participated in British politics well before one became a Chieftainess of the Wizard's Council. Of course internationally, the struggle for women's rights was a long and hard-fought battle with victory arriving only in the 1600s for some and the 1900s for others. Today women however have benefited greatly from their foremothers struggle and are serving in every job capacity the MoM has to offer, including Minister of Magic.

The Minister of Magic before Fudge was a woman, Millicent Bagnold, and she had the unenviable task of guiding the MoM through the turbulent Voldemort years during the 1971-1982 period as well as the aftermath and reconstruction. The Head of the DMLE the largest and most influential department in MoM is currently Madam Amelia

Bones and has been so since c 1983. Madam Umbridge was Senior Undersecretary to the Minister of Magic for many years up until her sudden and much welcome departure in 1996. Nymphadora Tonks is the only Auror to be added to the force since 1992, in other words, only a woman has made the cut.

Women work outside the home if they choose to and not just at the MoM. Madam Malkin owns one of the top clothing stores in Diagon Alley. Another witch in Diagon Alley owns the Magical Menagerie, a respected shop as much for its knowledgeable owner as its unique collection of animals. Madam Rosmerta owns the Three Broomsticks pub and inn and had done so for about 20 years. Dilys Derwent was Head Healer at St Mungo's in the 1700s and went on to serve as a very respected Head of Hogwarts. Hogwarts staff is half female with the current Deputy Head a woman, Minerva McGonagall. And women at Hogwarts don't just teach "feminine" subjects either. Madam Hooch teaches flying and Quidditch and is as much of a jock as any warlock could be. Minerva teaches Transfiguration, arguably the most complex and difficult magic taught at Hogwarts.

But does this mean the only acceptable role for women is working outside the home nowadays? Certainly not. Many women chose to stay home and be housewitches and mothers. Molly Weasley does this and no one criticizes her for being "just" a housewitch and a mother. It would seem Narcissa Malfoy, though probably currently in prison for conspiracy to commit murder among many other things, was a housewitch before getting involved with Kreacher. Mrs Black was surely a wealthy housewitch if she had time to sit for a life-size portrait to be painted. Mrs Lovegood was a housewitch with a passion for experimental spells.

Women who chose to be housewitches, wives and mothers are not criticized or looked down upon by others and these roles are considered honorable and worthwhile in the wizarding community even if a witch chooses to marry a Muggle. Women are, in short, free to pursue whatever course of life appeals to them. Women can be authors or inventors, Quidditch Captains or conservationists, record setters or recording artists. In the wizarding world, there is nothing a woman can't do, and do well, and no one ever tells her otherwise. Another wonderful part of equality for women is that it has spilled over to create greater equality for children as well via the trickle-down effect.

Children are by and large greatly cherished and respected in wizarding society. Few children come from a broken (Riddle) or abusive (Snape) home and few children are unwanted (Barty Jr) or disowned (Sirius) by their parents. These stable loving homes turn out generally stable loving people. Where the home is unstable and unloving, there are of course a large number of children likely to end up Slytherins and Death Eaters. Judging from various sources, children are encouraged to exhibit their magical talents as early as possibly. Kevin was doing magic at 2, Newt was dissecting horklumps at 7 and Neville was bouncing out windows at 8. But it is just because magical talent turns up early in a child's life that parents cannot risk sending them to Muggle schools.

Wizarding children are therefore home schooled until they are ready for a proper magical education at age 11. Some may balk at this suggestion but it seems unlikely that wizard children would be sent to Muggle schools and thus risk exposing the entire the wizarding world through their use of accidental magic. Also Ron states he has never seen Muggle money and clearly knows nothing of how to use a telephone. He would have been familiar with both if he'd gone to a Muggle school. Wizard primary school also seems unlikely since there are not enough wizards living in any one place to form a school, except of course Hogsmeade, where there is an ongoing hag problem.

So, given the home schooling aspect, it must be presumed that parents, mostly mothers, educate their children till the age of 11, or in those cases where parents are wealthy a tutor can be hired. Children therefore represent a major commitment and a major investment of time for parents. At age 11 a wizarding child is sent to a wizarding boarding school far away from Muggles where advanced magic may be safely taught. This represents a major financial outlay for parents, but for most children secondary school represents the only formal education they receive as there appear to be no wizarding universities. Thus at 11 a wizarding child is out their own, making decisions about what to eat, when to go to bed, and whether to do their studies. Responsibilities far in advance of many Muggle children of that age.

At 13 they are going to places like Hogsmeade and perhaps drinking mildly alcoholic beverages. As Ron says in the Three Broomsticks, he can order firewhisky, which is to say hard liquor, if he wants. That this is an accepted practice among wizards shows parents recognize that youth at 13 are of an age where they can be trusted to make their own decisions about some adult matters. Ginny at 13 began dating and at 14 was on her 2nd boyfriend. At 15 we find Roger Davies publicly kissing a female student in Madam Puddifoot's, and Harry experiencing his first date, his first kiss and his first break up, while Hermione at the same age is juggling the attentions of 2 very ardent suitors, Ron and Viktor. It is clear that most students have gone through several romantic attachments by the time they reach 17.

But is that a good thing? Perhaps. At the age of 17 in the UK (18 in the US) a person achieves legal majority, meaning adulthood. We know that at 16 Sirius left home for good and no one made an effort to force him back either legally or by emotional appeal. At 17 Sirius had his own home, Percy started work at the MoM and Fred and George opened a business in Diagon Alley. Clearly if adulthood is 17, at 17 one needs to be ready to be an adult. How could this happen if children were not allowed major responsibilities or kept from making their own decisions about their own lives prior to age 17? To suddenly be confronted with adult responsibilities at 17 after never being allowed to grow into an adult in any way but physically would be criminally negligent parenting.

Thankfully, most wizard children are spared from over-protective or controlling parents by the boarding school system. While it is true that most Muggle boarding schools bear *no* resemblance whatsoever to Hogwarts, wizards in general have had to raise the standard of boarding school education and boarding school care since every child is subject to it. This is true throughout wizarding Europe as well. Beauxbatons were hardly over awed by Hogwarts and Durmstrang, while they may have been a bit impressed, had a perfectly adequate and appropriate school for the sort of studies they were learning. Wizarding schools are all about equal in schooling, facilities and accommodation and wizarding parents clearly feel these schools provide an appropriate level of independence and protection as well as a stable place to gain a solid education.

RACE

Wizards would seem to consider race a non-issue. Anthony Goldstein is likely Jewish, but this was no hindrance to becoming a Ravenclaw Prefect and he is not harassed for it. The Patil twins, of East Asian possibly Indian origins, are considered the prettiest girls in their class by Seamus' account. They could hardly be that by a White boy in a racist environment. Seamus is not looked down on because he's Irish. Harry dated Cho Chang, from her name a Korean-Chinese girl.

Angelina is Black but became Quidditch Captain and went to the Yule Ball with Fred who is White and no one objected to either. Kingsley Shacklebolt, also Black, has gained the job of Auror, a highly difficult job to get. Ginny is dating Dean at the end of 1996 and while this may shock Ron, it is not because Dean is Black and Ginny White.

It's because Dean is Ron roommate and Dean dating Ginny poses a potentially awkward situation for Ron, who certainly doesn't want to hear Dean discussing his sister's virtues with fellow roommate and close friend Seamus.

Make no mistake though, racism does exist in the wizarding world. It simply has nothing to do with the color of a wizard's skin. Nonpurebloods are discriminated against by purebloods, non-wizards by wizards, part-humans by full humans and werewolves by everyone. There is also wizard racism against Muggles as a whole, which accounts for a large part of Voldemort's popularity and the better part of those who commit Muggle-baiting crimes. For whatever reason, some human beings will always feel it necessary to discriminate against others in order to feel better about themselves. In this respect, wizards are no different than any other human beings.

POLITICAL STRUCTURE

As has been touched on in other sections, wizarding society embraces complete democracy and equality as a goal if not a practical standard. All wizards regardless of color, race or gender are equal. Though there might be rich and poor, Muggle borns and purebloods, all are equal in the eyes of the law. British wizards' lives being similar to British Muggles' lives, all wizards have an equal vote when it comes to electing government representatives or leaders. However one can't blame the people for Fudge. The people wanted Dumbledore as Minister of Magic, but he declined. Fudge won the post by default and ought to be recalled if wizards had any sense at all. But it's yet to happen.

It is apparent there is a judiciary branch (DMLE), an executive branch (Minister of Magic) and a legislative branch at work at the MoM. It seems likely the Head of the legislature is the Grand Sorcerer, and perhaps is currently Dumbledore, but there is no way to confirm this. Though we see little of the legislative branch and have no idea where it's located, it can be presumed to exist simply because Lucius Malfoy attempted to discredit Arthur's Muggle Protection Act. Lucius had influence with the MoM, if he could have buried the bill quietly he would have. But, Lucius was forced to publicly discredit Arthur. Why? Because public officials respond to public pressure. Lucius was creating public pressure so that representatives in the legislature would be at the mercy of their constituents, who after hearing Ginny had killed Muggles herself, would press their representatives to veto the Muggle Protection Act bill.

It is interesting to note, despite all the democracy and equality rhetoric, wizards look down on the poor more than the nonpurebloods. British wizards are a capitalist society and what really counts is having gold and lots of it. Gold influences the Minister of Magic, the MoM and even the awarding of Order of Merlins. While the MoM gets money via taxation, a gift to the MoM never hurt any giver as Lucius Malfoy can attest. It is however a bit odd that a culture that isn't based on industrial capitalism is so greedy. Given wizards live in a preindustrial culture, land and those who hold land should be more valuable as partners to the MoM as they would have the most wealth and influence over society.

Which brings up another oddity. In a society where land-based wealth is preeminent, aristocracy generally develops and continues until industry becomes preeminent. Yet wizards appear never to have had an aristocracy. Muggle kings have certainly given titles to wizards, Nearly Headless Nick was either born a knight or earned the title, likewise Sir Patrick and the Bloody Baron, but the Wizards' Council, later British MoM, never created one. Voldemort may continue to insist he's a Lord, but one cannot simply make oneself a lord. While it's difficult to understand how

British wizards managed to avoid developing an aristocracy. Perhaps because wizards in Britain already had a Muggle monarch to deal with they didn't feel they needed a wizard one as well.

Social Structure

Except for Hogsmeade village, every wizard lives out her or his life in Muggle communities. Wizards are encouraged to be a hidden culture by the MoM who tells wizards to wear Muggle clothing when in public places, stay indoors during the day if possible and avoid attracting Muggle attention to themselves by say creating exploding dustbins, flying a Ford Anglia and the like. Although there is always some limited interaction between the Muggles and wizards, most wizards don't know anything about Muggles or the Muggle world and don't want to. As Percy says the student who chooses Muggles Studies in school is considered to be going for the soft option and he says this despite the fact it's what his father likely did. So there is a certain stigma attached to wizards who like Muggles or think there is actually something worth learning about or from them.

Even with a person of Arthur's enthusiasm for all things Muggle, there is little concrete knowledge among wizards of how Muggle things work (computers, ticket turnstiles, microwaves, etc.), or what Muggles lives are like (plumbers, electricity, basketball, money, etc) and this is not really all that unusual. Wizards, like most people, are simply more interested in and involved with their own society on a day-to-day basis. But what is this society like? Well, as in all societies there are good and bad wizards. The Dark wizards are generally the most talked about since they are the ones that pose the greatest risk to wizard society by taking actions that tend to be noticeable to Muggles.

As most Dark wizards think Muggles are either less than human or something the world could do without entirely, they feel free to engage in Muggle-baiting or worse Muggle-killing. Muggle-baiting is enchanting a Muggle object to be either dangerous or frustrating to Muggles (shrinking keys, biting doorknobs, regurgitating toilets, etc) and rather common while Muggle-killing is thankfully rare, though it was done a plenty by Voldemort and his followers from 1970-1982. All MoMs have made these acts illegal and attach serious punishments to them, but Dark wizards continue to engage at them at a steady rate. Though this is not altogether good news. The lack of an increase in crimes against Muggles in proportion to an ever-shrinking number of wizards suggests the percentage of wizards going Dark is on the rise.

Dark wizards have many nasty beliefs, but one can understand that they dislike living a hidden life because of Muggles and resent the fact they have superior talents but are forced to limit the usage of their powers because they might expose the wizarding world to Muggles. The MoM's policy of protecting Muggles from the truth, wholly at the expense of wizards, virtually created the setting for Voldemort's rise to power in the 1970s and continues to do so in the 1990s. The MoM bolsters the belief that wizards are superior to Muggles, and even to their fellow magicals, yet continually turns around and slaps wizards down when they try to use those powers. The MoM is classically passive-aggressive and is singlehandedly creating the sort of resentment toward itself and Muggles that Voldemort thrives on.

But I digress. As in most traditional societies, and wizards do have a traditional society, there is respect for the elderly, who often work to a very advance age (over 100). There is no inherent desire to be young or prolong youth by unnatural means, quite the reverse. The young are respected as the next generation, but the elderly, who have wisdom few can attain without turning grey, are more respected, even by the young. It is the elderly that are in charge of important positions within the MoM. The Wizengamot is filled with Elders age 80 and up. The Wizarding Examination Authority seems to be staffed exclusively by wizards age 90 to 100+. The average age of a Minister of Magic is 60 with Department Heads mostly attaining that status in their 50s.

It would seem although men and women are equal, this has not led to a breakdown of traditional British moral norms or gender relationships. Marriage, between a man and a woman, is a traditional and very respected social institution and, while divorce appears unavailable to wizards, second marriages are permitted to those who are widowed. No one engages in co-habitation, premarital sex, adultery or multiple wives or husbands. Homosexuality, bisexuality and transgender Transfigurations also seem unheard of. Marriage seems to be the social norm for those who form romantic attachments, but these marriages appear to go bad rather quickly.

Most of the married adult wizards appear to be extremely unpleasant and most single adult wizards, who have never married or are widowers, appear to be extremely pleasant. Single adults also represent a majority of all wizards, indicating a slightly unusual anomaly, a traditional society that values and accepts singles. Singles adults represent the majority of wizards Harry knows. A few singles are bad to be sure, but the bad to good ration for single wizards is 1:100 compared marrieds who run 2:1. Wizards may feel marriage doesn't bring out the best in them, as statistics seem to indicate, and may therefore avoid marriage since there's no social stigma attached to being single.

Statistics relating to marriage, however, may be skewed for other reasons than personal choice not to marry. There are some wizards who appear to be single but may be in relationships of a unique sort. Remus Lupin might have a mate, she just might be a wolf. As wolves are monogamous, he wouldn't seek out a human relationship after forming one with a shewolf. But can the relationship be defined as a marriage? Difficult to say. This same question would apply to wizards marrying veela (who are beasts) and vampires (who are dead). These same issues come up when dealing with other magical beings. Giants marry, but what about house-elves, goblins and the like? Are Dobby and Winky a couple? Are they married?

Given Kreacher's family on the wall at Headquarters, house-elves do get together and have children. Their social structures seem similar to wizards' but Kreacher speaks only of his mother and grandmother, indicating a matrilineal society. Goblin society on the other hand seems patrilineal, but we have yet to see a female goblin. They must exist as family of them was killed in Nottinghamshire in the 1970s but what does family mean to a goblin? Does goblin culture allow the females to be seen or are females dominant and simply prefer to tend their children while sending their male out to do the wage-earner work? We just don't know.

Other interesting features of wizarding society include a desire to be extremely individual. Except for a few names such as Tom, Millicent or Augustus, each person's Christian name is entirely unique. See First Names Please! in Part IV. Parents obviously want their children to be raging individuals and go out of the way to make sure they are, even if its only by a slight variant in spelling: Rodolphus, Radolphus and Rudolphus being a good example. However, despite generally raging individuality, bad wizards are easy to spot as they are almost always blonde. If one considers the number of Dark (all 3 Malfoys, Barty Jr, Karkoff), corrupt (Ludo, Rita), odd (Luna, Firenze), weak (Sturgis), untrustworthy (Lockhart), or stuck up (Fleur) wizards, they are all blonde.

This "blondes are bad"(or at least have negative personality traits) rule applies to Muggles as well (all 4 Dursleys). Why this should be so is unknown. As a blonde, I'm offended by my own analysis, but as a scientific researcher, the facts are undeniable. So, what about other hair colors? Redheads are always good (Weasleys - Percy is misguided not bad, Dumbledore, Lily). Brunettes are more likely to be nice (Hermione, the Creeveys) than not (Dolores). Greys seem to be all good (Moody, Lupin, Pr Spout), but those born with white hair don't seem to exist in the wizarding world. People might go white or are white blonde, but they are not born white haired so it remains to be seen how they turn out.

Black-haired wizards are really a mixed lot. They either very extremely swing good *and* bad (Harry, James Minerva, Sirius, Severus, Peter, Cho) or they are bad to the bone (Tom, Mrs Black, Bellatrix). Harry can be violent and temperamental, James was an arrogant bully, Minerva degrades and ridicules a fellow teacher in public, Sirius tried to kill Severus, Severus was a Death Eater and Peter became a turncoat. Cho is stupid (despite being a Ravenclaw) and manipulative. Tom Riddle of course went bad very early in life and has stayed that way, Mrs Black was insanely bad and Bellatrix Lestrange is about as bad as anyone can go and still be human. The black-haired folks are a dicey bunch and best treated with care or avoided if possible.

Other wizarding world oddities include the unusually high number of only children (Neville, Harry, Hermione, Draco, Severus, James, Peter, Barty Jr, Tonks, Hagrid, Tom Riddle, Lockhart), twins (Weasleys, Patils, and most likely the Dumbledores, Prewetts and Lupins) and families that have only 2 sons (The Black brothers; the Lestrange brothers; the Dumbledore brothers, the Prewett brothers, the Creevey brothers, and the Weasley brothers, Arthur and Billius). Statistically speaking the figures for such groupings of children are way above the Muggle average. Very few in the wizarding world seem to have the statically more typical Muggle family of 1 boy and 1 girl or all girls (except the Delacours, Blacks and maybe the Patils).

The complete absence of anyone in any way physically handicapped is also atypical. Given a person may be handicapped and magically powerful, a few handicapped persons should be at Hogwarts, though Harry has yet to meet one. It may be that there are no handicapped people in wizarding society, either because they are all cured at birth or they are never born. But this doesn't set explain individuals who become physically handicapped later in life. If an Auror can lose an eye and not have it be repairable or replaceable, they can lose both eyes and go blind. Davey Gudgeon is a case in point. Suppose he had lost an eye to the Whomping Willow? He would have been partially sighted the rest of his life. Perhaps handicapped students are sent to a special wizarding school that is designed for and has cirrculum suited to their needs. One hopes this is the case.

SOCIAL TERMINOLOGY

To help those not familiar with the wizarding community, a list of the relevant terminology applicable to wizards follows.

Death Eater: A person who has sworn her or his life and loyalty to Voldemort. Generally they have an indelible brand on their inner left forearms. When Voldemort touches any one of their brands, it turns black (normally it's russet or red) and all Death Eaters must immediately Apparate and join him. Apparently Voldemort himself doesn't have a brand (called the Dark Mark) of his own. It is not clear how Death Eaters know where to Apparate to once the brand is activated, but maybe the mark acts like a homing device and takes its bearer to within a few yard of wherever the bearer of the initially activated brand is currently standing.

Only a Death Eater knows how to conjure the Dark Mark (yes, this is also called the Dark Mark and yes it is very confusing). Only they call Voldemort the "Dark Lord" which the poor sod wasn't even bright enough to think up himself but had to steal from the Dark Lord, Sauron (of JRR Tolkien's *Lord of the Rings*). No Death Eater can say Voldemort's name because they are apparently all "unworthy" to speak it. This is a tradition Voldemort stole from the Jewish tradition, relating to God, whom Voldemort also thinks he is. At certain times Death Eaters are obliged to kiss the hem of Voldemort's robes, a tradition from Ancient times. However, Dumbledore always calls him Tom and treats him like a naughty puppy, which must be hugely irritating for an ego the size of Voldemort's.

Voldemort's Death Eaters are themselves a rather name-shy bunch. They always have their hoods up and usually wear masks with slits for eyeholes. They are never supposed to know the names of all the other Death Eaters, but since most of them were in school together they do. Anyone the Death Eaters were unacquainted with before Little Hangleton is known now, since Voldemort, who knows every Death Eater, went listing off their names when they are in a group in Little Hangleton. As if that weren't enough, a year later Lucius Malfoy, the top man among the Death Eaters, went barking out everyone's name in the DoM. Names can hardly be that much of a secret now. It is likely this sort of ongoing stupidity that caused Pr Snape, considered Lucius' lapdog by many, to become a double agent for Dumbledore's OoP.

Death Eater philosophy, such as it is, seems to hinge on cleansing the magical world of nonpurebloods and possibly Muggles as well. Many wizards embrace Voldemort's views for reasons stated earlier in this essay. Many, such as Mr and Mrs Black, didn't like his cruel and violent methods and so did not join Voldemort's ranks, but they did subsequently cool their heels and let him do the dirty work since they agreed in principal with what he was doing. Apparently no one knew then or knows now that Voldemort is actually half Muggle and therefore a Mudblood. Harry blurted it out in front of the Death Eaters, but it was quickly dismissed as a lie. It remains to be seen what effect, if any, this information might have on his followers when they have some leisure to think and do some rudimentary research. Certainly it would behoove the MoM to run this information, complete with a genealogy, in *The Prophet*.

When Voldemort disappeared in 1981, many of his 400-500 Death Eaters claimed to have been acting under the Imperius Curse, pretended to return to the good side and went on with their lives. Some kept up Voldemort's work in secret ways, like Lucius Malfoy trying to torpedo the Muggle Protection Act in 92/93. Some stayed loyal to Voldemort, tired to find him and went to prison, though these were the rare exception. Some were killed by Aurors rather than letting themselves be taken alive and face Azkaban. Most seem to have just crawled back into the woodwork and, since the MoM never had a handle on the scope of the Death Eater problem or a list of names to work with, there is a good chance Voldemort may get many of his 400-500 back.

The following is a list of dead Death Eaters as of 1983.

> Regulus Black: dead because he tried to quit
> Voldemort's service, killed by Death Eaters
> Evan Rosier: dead, killed by Aurors
> (Unknown) Wilkes: dead, killed by Aurors.

A list of Death Eaters according to Voldemort, meaning these were the only people he knew had the Dark Mark brand and the only people he called Death Eaters in Little Hangleton in Jun 1995:

> (Unknown) Avery
> (Unknown) Crabbe
> Barty Crouch Jr: Dementor's Kiss
> Antonin Dolohov: in prison
> (Unknown) Goyle
> Igor Karkaroff (former)
> Bellatrix Black Lestrange: in prison
> Rodolphus Lestrange: in prison
> Lucius Malfoy
> Walden Macnair
> (Unknown) Nott
> Peter Pettigrew
> Severus Snape (former).

As one can see from Voldemort's list, although he commented on several missing Death Eaters, including some in jail, he did not mention the following as people Death Eaters:

> (Unknown) Jugson: in prison
> Rastaban Lestrange: in prison
> (Unknown) Mulciber: in prison
> Augustus Rookwood: in prison
> (Unknown) Travers: in prison.

It is impossible to know, when he commented on 2 of the Lestranges being in prison, which 2 he meant since there were actually 3 Lestranges in prison. When the 10 Death Eaters broke out of prison, the 5 men not mentioned by Voldemort in Little Hangleton were broken out as part of the 10. Of the 5 on the list above, 4 turned up in the MoM. Those in the MoM were:

> (Unknown) Avery
> (Unknown) Crabbe
> Antonin Dolohov: escapee
> (Unknown) Jugson: escapee
> Bellatrix Black Lestrange: escapee
> Rastaban Lestrange: escapee
> Rodolphus Lestrange: escapee
> Walden Macnair
> Lucius Malfoy
> (Unknown) Mulciber: escapee
> (Unknown) Nott
> Augustus Rookwood: escapee

Of those raiding the MoM, only one escaped, Bellatrix. This left 4 of the Death Eater escapees at large. So the following list is of the only known Death Eaters to be at large as of Jul 1996:

> Bellatrix Lestrange: escapee
> (Unknown) Goyle
> Peter Pettigrew
> (Unknown) Travers: escapee
> Male Death Eater 1: escapee
> Male Death Eater 2: escapee

Of this list, the last three were never mentioned by Voldemort as Death Eaters in Little Hangleton. One assumes, since they were part of the break out, their loyalties are with Voldemort but whether they have a brand and are true Death Eaters is speculative.

Half-and-Half: Half-and-half wizards are those magical children born to a nonpureblood wizard and something else (giant/veela/Muggle/etc). People in this category include: Hagrid, Seamus.

Half-Blood: A person that's the product of any individual or being not a pureblood + a pureblood is a half-blood. Most wizards these days are half-bloods if one looks back far enough into their history as wizards would have died out long ago if they hadn't taken to marrying Muggles. People in this category include: Harry, Tonks, Voldemort.

Madam: A witch over the age of 17, whether married or unmarried. Madame is the French version. Usage of either of these in front of Muggles would lead them to believe the woman is married as this is the traditional usage of madam(e). An interesting side note, with married couples the wife's name precedes the husbands: Lily and James Potter, Molly and Arthur Weasley, etc.

Master: This is the proper title for an underage male warlock. Mister is used if they are of age.

Miss: This is the proper title for an underage female witch. Madam is used if they are of age, whether married or unmarried.

Mudblood: A derogatory term used for any nonpureblood. Even products of a Muggle-born wizard + a pureblood wizard would be considered Mudbloods. Mudblood, meaning dirty or common blood, is the very worst and most insulting name used for nonpurebloods. Purebloods like Malfoys think they are better than others because of their heritage, however, Draco as a pureblood is not as good a wizard as Hermione a Muggle born. Bloodlines are no indication of ability.

Muggle Born: Wizards born to completely nonmagical parents and families. Persons in this category include: Hermione, Lily, Justin Finch-Fletchley, Dean Thomas. Perhaps Dumbledore is in this category as well. It might help explain his great love for Muggle borns if he was one himself.

Pureblood: A wizard born to a witch and a wizard of pureblood status. Persons in this category include: Draco, Sirius, Ron, Neville, Ernie Macmillan. Practically all the pureblood wizards are related because they intermarry. There are very few choices if one only wants to marry another pureblood because there are hardly any left. Some purebloods think magic shouldn't be taught to anyone but purebloods, Salazar Slytherin for one.

Squib: A completely non-magical person born to wizarding parents. People in this category include: Mrs. Figg, Argus Filch. There is some stigma attached with being a Squib so some choose to move into the Muggle world where they're considered normal. The birth of a Squib is very rare. Squibs do seem to have some very limited magical ability. Both Argus Filch and Mrs Figg can talk to and command a cat. No Muggle could do that.

Warlock: A male wizard. They also go by the title Mr if of age or Master if they are younger.

Witch: A female wizard. They also go by the title Madam if of age, or Miss if they are younger. Mrs may be used if they are married, but wizards generally use Madam for married and single witches.

Wizard: A male or female magical human or part-human.

RELIGION IN THE WIZARDING WORLD

Let me be clear, before anyone sends any letters: this is *not* a discussion of my personal beliefs, this is an analysis of what wizards are doing in their own world and what they themselves believe. This is neither a condemnation of nor an apologetic for wizardry, Christianity or Christian wizards. It is an exploration of facts as set down by others.

It would be difficult to deny that Britain has long been a traditionally Christian culture. Likewise it would be difficult to deny that people tend to practice the faiths predominately associated with the culture they have been raised in. British wizards are no exception to all this and Christianity, therefore, plays a significant role in the wizarding world in general and Harry's life in particular. Wizards can embrace Christ because they do not see any inherent conflict between wizarding and what Christ preached. This is because wizarding skills are something a person is born with, like a certain shape nose or color eyes. It is unalterable part of the person and not one which they have a choice about. Muggles may see this difference as inherently evil, but is it?

Many years ago in the 1980s, a woman in England developed an unusually high electrical charge in her body which caused every electrical appliance she touched to break. She was featured in *Popular Science* waving happily amidst her broken hoovers, irons and blenders. Perhaps 100 years ago, when bioelectricity was not known let alone understood by the masses, she might have been drowned as a witch. But today Muggles understand that the body is electric and that some people are more electric than others. It's science, like the electric eye that opens the door for them at the grocery store or the lamp that turns itself on when they clap their hands.

When Muggles understand the why of things, or know that there are others that do, they call it science. When they don't, they usually end up with tagging someone a witch or something as witchcraft and destroying that person or thing. This is tragic because wizards are just human beings exactly like Muggles, except they have a few unusual capabilities. They have chosen to call themselves "wizards" but are they biblically speaking wizards? Not as long as the talents wizards are born with are used within the proscribed limitations of the faith they practice. Given the very narrow definition of witchcraft in the Bible, it is easily identified, so that all one needs do is compare it to what individual wizards are doing to draw the correct conclusion about where anyone stands.

Magic involving necromancy, talking to or calling up the spirits of the dead, is expressly banned by the Bible and the Christian faith. But no one at Hogwarts or in the rest of the wizarding world is doing necromancy. As close to dead as anyone has got is Voldemort. Priori Incantatem wasn't Harry trying to talk to the dead. It was freak accident that caused shadows of old spells to regurgitate themselves, which in turn spoke to Harry of their own volition. The shadows were not the actual dead speaking to him. Moving on, one can hardly accuse those speaking with ghosts of practicing necromancy. Ghosts at Hogwarts are simply there, according to Nearly Headless Nick by choice and, most of the time, appear completely unbidden. It is doubtful that speaking to the ghosts is engaging in necromancy as ghosts are simply there to speak as they will, which no one can stop.

Divination, the practice of trying to find out the future from sources other than God, is a banned practice by the Christian faith, and one which Dumbledore didn't even want it taught at his school. So why is it there? Because Dumbledore felt it was best to have Sybill on his team, after she gave a prophecy regarding Voldemort's destruction. Surely if Voldemort could have, he would have kidnapped Sybill to find out more about the prophecy she'd given then killed her to prevent her giving others to those who might wish to harm him. But Dumbledore prevented all this by taking her on staff at Hogwarts. It would hardly have been wise or even kind of Dumbledore to send her away from Hogwarts, but he couldn't hire her as anything but a Divination teacher without explanations she likely wouldn't have believed.

When Harry confronted Sybill about a prophecy she gave him, she didn't remember it, didn't believe him and completely scoffed at the idea. But this brings up an interesting fact, she doesn't know she's prophetic, but nevertheless she is, and prophecy has never been banned by the Bible, in fact its practice is highly encouraged. So is keeping a prophet around a bad idea? No, the Bible tells believers to be kind to the prophets or suffer a terrible fate. So Dumbledore took in a prophet who happens to teach Divination. But is Divination a respected subject at Hogwarts? Indeed no. It is an extremely belittled subject, even by Dumbledore, and no one believes in it but the truly gullible. Sybill herself keeps to her Tower mostly so as not to be confronted about her Gift which she herself believes is bogus.

Firenze was taken on as a Divination teacher after Sybill was sacked. But was this to continue Divination as a subject? No, again it was to rescue a friend in need. Firenze needed a place that was safe to hide out from his murderous herd. Dumbledore took him in. It's true Firenze taught Divination, but in a most unusual way. He began by telling his students he didn't put too much faith in divination, even centaur divination, as centaurs had been wrong before. He was hardly making a case for the study of divination in any way. And, in point of fact, Harry failed his OWL in Divination and both he and Ron are not going to take it at NEWT level. They wish they had never gotten involved in Divination in the first place, but it was too late to switch electives when they realized this, and having to take 2 electives, they were forced to continue.

Though it is covered in Divination, astrology in particular speaks to the heart of the divination question, so a discussion of it follows. Consulting the stars with the express purpose of using them, rather than God, to determine the course of one's life is a sin. This fact is unquestionable. But what about using astrology for the express purpose of getting closer to God? Motive, not action, is usually the problem with arts of divination. Anything can be a good thing if used for godly purposes. This is proved by the assorted Magi who determined Christ's birth and showed up in the right place at the right time because of reading the stars.

The Magi discerned the truth from the stars because they were looking for God in them. One might add, as the biblical record indicates, everyone else had to be told the news by God sending a messenger. Only the Magi found God with out anyone telling them the details. The centaurs are reading the stars as the Magi might have, to discern the truth about world events, not to find the winning lotto numbers. And it must be said, if one is going to point a finger, Muggles would do well to point it at their weathermen, who predict every day and forecast into the future via their various scientific methods purely for personal gain. This is divination of the expressly banned variety and likely why they are always wrong and people who put their faith in their projections usually come off the worse for it.

Branching out to a discussion of Christianity in the wizarding world, Gringotts' doors are inscribed to say that thievery is a sin. Not a moral failing, not a crime, not an outrage against society, a sin. If the wizarding world had no concept of sin, coming from Judeo-Christian worldview, why on earth would the goblins use the word sin? Goblins certainly don't beat around the bush as a species and they are generally *very* up front about their balance sheets. Would goblins allow themselves to be misconstrued on such an important topic as money, their money, by using a word that no one in their community actually understood? It's extremely doubtful. So British goblins apparently embrace a Judeo-Christian worldview and believe that wizards do as well.

And of course how would the wizarding community understand swearing if there were no God? Does damn mean anything, if one lacks a concept of damnation? What can Good Lord, good Lord, my God or Gwad, really mean except that they recognize an actual Lord or God if the person is choosing to cap the initial letter? What can "God Rest You Merry Hippogriffs" mean if there is no God? Sirius might have changed the lyrics to reflect his feelings about hippogriffs having little reason to like men after unjustly spending 13 years in prison but he didn't change the God part. Which brings us to the subject of Christmas and religious holidays traditionally associated with Christians.

Focusing in on Hogwarts if Dumbledore, or wizards in general, had fundamental conflicts with the Christian faith, such events as Christmas and Easter would be written off as winter or spring celebrations at their schools. In such countries where Christianity is not a part of people's general social milieu, and ever where it is such as America, this happens with great frequency. But it doesn't happen in the British wizarding world. Hogsmeade, a 100% wizarding village, like Hogwarts, decks the halls 100% for Christmas. Dumbledore even leads students and teachers in religious carols - to which no one objects. The armor is bewitched to sing a specifically Christian carol "O Come All Ye Faithful."

And Christmas is not just a Hogwarts' holiday or a Hogsmeade holiday or a Dumbledore holiday, the Weasleys celebrate Christmas, Dobby celebrates Christmas, Hermione celebrates Christmas, Sirius celebrates Christmas, Flitwick and McGonagall celebrate Christmas. Even the Fat Lady and the other Hogwarts' paintings celebrate Christmas. Considering the supposedly natural antithesis of wizardry and Christianity, this is quite irregular behavior on the part of wizards, unless they really are Christians. A lone voice might cry, but the Yule Ball is pagan. Alas, it is not. Up until very recently Christians in Scotland (1900), who were Christians to the point of dying for their faith, referred to Christmas as Yule. When the TT was begun in the 13th century, Yule was what Christmas was called by Christians. So it is incorrect to assume the Yule Ball is in any way pagan.

Taking a look at Easter, though as of yet there has been no the annual celebration of Easter, it is a 3-week holiday called Easter holiday. Though many students choose to stay at the castle, the holiday is not overlooked by the Weasley family. Molly sends her children, Harry and Hermione traditional Easter Eggs. No one seems to think it strange. Hermione in fact one year is upset because her egg is so much smaller than Harry's and Ron's. Why? Because she knows the Weasley family celebrates Easter and has probably gotten eggs before as a friend of Ron's. Hermione and Harry are not offended by the eggs. No one at school comments on the weirdness of the eggs. So, other students besides Weasleys must celebrate Easter and think it a perfectly normal thing to get an Easter Egg from home during the season.

Halloween, which is All Hallow Even, is another Christian holiday, one which has to do with the dead. It is particularly celebrated at Hogwarts on the same scale as Christmas. Given the number of ghosts at Hogwarts (20 at least), it seems appropriate that this religious holiday which features the welfare of the dead should be celebrated. Yes the bats come out as decor, the skeletons appear as entertainment and Nearly Headless Nick may reenact his death, but this is traditionally how Halloween has been celebrated by Christians for hundreds of years. There is nothing inherently pagan in all this. Why shouldn't All Hallow Even be celebrated as it always has?

In thinking of ghosts at Hogwarts, one is forced to ask how the Fat Friar, a Catholic Christian monk, could continue to be a part of Hogwarts if he felt being a wizard was incompatible with his faith? He is clearly a person of great personal faith in choosing to become a Friar after graduating Hogwarts and was probably not the only wizarding monk but despite his belief in his own salvation, the Friar chose not to cross over into Heaven. According to Nearly Headless Nick, the Friar chose to remain at Hogwarts. Why? To continue his Christian mission of love among the students and staff of the school. The Friar is exemplifying in the highest possible way true Christianity, love that is sacrificial.

Yet none of the Hufflepuffs want the Friar removed as "too religious" or "forcing the Christian faith" on them. Quite the contrary, they love him. Likewise no students of the wizarding world objects to the use of BC and AD which recognizes the birth and dominion of Christ. No one is using BCE and CE. No one is asking refusing to use BC and AD. No one is complaining about their use and telling Mr Ollivander to change to his sign because he's offending other wizards. One has to ask why, particularly in an era when people thrive on demanding political correctness at the expense of other's right to free speech? It can only be because the wizards are by and large Christians and feel comfortable in going on using ancient Christian vernacular.

Moving to Harry's life, from the point of view of the Christian religion, Harry could not have a godfather, which is a religious office defined by the church, if Harry had never been baptized in the Christian faith. Sirius could not be a godfather to Harry if he was not also baptized in the same denomination of the Christian faith. Presumably they are both either Catholics or Episcopalians, denominations that have godparents. Given the bent of most of the ghosts at wizarding Hogwarts, Catholic seems the likely choice. Dumbledore also appears Catholic as he peruses in his spare time *Theories of Transubstantial Transfiguration*. The word transubstantial, which means to change one thing into another, and makes no sense in relation to word transfiguration, which means exactly the same thing, unless the author is using transubstantial as an adjective for Transubstantiation, the Catholic doctrine of Christ actually becoming the Eucharist, in which case the title then makes perfect sense.

Finally, because there is no clear expression of other faiths besides Christianity around Hogwarts or in the wizarding world doesn't mean they don't exist. Given the wide assortment of surnames at Hogwarts, one would expect any number of people to be believers of other traditions. Some may be Jewish (Goldstein), Hindu (Patil), Buddhist (Cho), Catholic (Finnigan) or any other faith. Perhaps the referee of QWC 1994 was Muslim given his name, Hassan Mostafa, though Egypt does have a large Coptic Christian population as well. In either case, there is no inherent reason why any wizards of any culture around the globe should not be fully participating in a religion of their choice, including that great and ancient wizard-loathing one, Christianity.

PART II. HOGWARTS

HOGWARTS, AN OVERVIEW
HOGWARTS SCHOOL OF WITCHCRAFT and Wizardry is a 7-year, boarding secondary school (equivalent of 5th - 11th grades, US) located in the far North or Northwest of Scotland. It accepts only the most promising talent in Britain, though it will also take foreign students occasionally. Hogwarts was founded by the 4 greatest wizards of the 10th century who wished to create a school - far away from Muggles – dedicated to instructing wizarding children in magic. See schematic I for an overview of the property.

THE FOUNDING
Hogwarts was founded in the 900s by 4 of the most accomplished wizards of their age: Godric Gryffindor a bold, brave warlock from a wild moor - possibly a Welshman; Rowena Ravenclaw a fair and extremely intelligent witch from a glen - possibly an Irish woman; Helga Hufflepuff a sweet hardworking witch from valley broad - possibly a Scottish woman of German extraction; and, Salazar Slytherin as shrewd ambitious pureblood warlock from fen (the Fen Country?) - possibly a Englishman of Spanish or Portuguese extraction.

After the school was built and up and running, 2 of the founders had a falling out, Godric and Salazar. Apparently the two men had issues, then words and finally things got so bad Godric picked a fight with Salazar (more than likely challenged him to a duel) and Salazar decided he'd had enough of Godric and left in disgust. There is no indication either of the witches had any problems with Salazar or wanted him to leave. So, Salazar might have been difficult to work with, choosing only to teach purebloods magic, but it was Godric that pushed until Salazar left.

Given the Head's office is now Godric's old office, one is forced to think that Godric wanted to be Head, instead of perhaps rotating Headship between the 4 founders, and Salazar was the only one standing in his way. Godric thus wanted to get rid of Salazar in order to seize power. On the other hand, it seems that Salazar always sensed a break was going to come, even before the castle was finished, and during the building of Hogwarts put in the Chamber of Secrets on the sly, sticking a basilisk in it and creating an opening for the basilisk on the 2nd floor of the castle, the same floor where the door to Godric's tower office is. Either way, it paints a pretty ugly picture of both warlocks and one feels sorry for Helga and Rowena having to work with them.

School and House Banners

The school banner is very large and has a giant golden H surrounded by the individual House symbols: snake, lion, eagle and badger. The school banner's background color is unknown, but probably purple. It's also unknown as to whether the banner's animals are alive and moving about. One supposes they do, given all other tapestries in the school are living things and move. The school banner is only displayed on very special occasions, during the TT Welcome Feast for instance and perhaps at the Start of Term Feast. It probably dates to the 10th century and the founding of the school. Perhaps it was woven by Rowena or Helga.

The 4 Houses each have a banner in their house colors with the appropriate, probably moving, animal. Slytherin has a green banner with a silver snake, Gryffindor a red banner with a gold lion, Hufflepuff a yellow banner with a black badger and Ravenclaw a blue banner with a copper eagle. Each banner is gigantic and designed to cover the entire wall behind the High Table in the Great Hall. They are only displayed on special occasions, such as when the House Cup is awarded to a particular House at the end of the year or during a TT Welcome Feast. These too probably date back to the 10th century and were woven, personally or magically, by the individual founder of each house.

Students

Hogwarts has 7 grades and about 1,000 students. There is a diversified co-ed student body with many different races represented. The school is fully co-ed, as are all activities, clubs and sports there, but the dorms are completely separated by gender and the girls' dormitory has added defensive measures to protect it against male visitors or intruders. One presumes all shower and lavatory facilities are gender divided as well.

Given there are 1,000 students divided into 4 Houses, that's 250 students per house. If students are further divided further into 7 grades, that's 36 student per grade, per House. This means about 144 students would be inducted into Hogwarts each year and each House table in the Great Hall would have to seat at least 125 students per side to accommodate them all. Allotting a meager 2' per place setting, a table would need to be at least 250' long. If one includes room to put the High Table and walk, the Great Hall must be the size of an American football field.

Teachers

As for the number of teachers at Hogwarts, one must first look at class size. Often it is said a teacher teaches a double class, meaning in this case there would be 72 student to a double class. Even allowing that a wizard could teach a class of this size class effectively, they are also said to teach regular classes. Looking at Transfiguration as an example, there is no possible way that Pr McGonagall could teach all the Transfiguration classes to each House at each grade level in a week. Using classes for 7 grades, times 4 Houses, times 2 classes a week as an average, she would have to teach 56 classes a week.

This can't possibly be done by a single person for the simple reason there are but 25 periods of 1.5 hours available for teaching per week. Since every single class is not a double class, Hogwarts would need at least 3 teachers to cover Transfiguration. Figuring then 3 teachers per subject to cover any core class, Magizoology, Flying, Potions, History, Transfiguration, Charms, Herbology, DADA and Astronomy alone would take 27 teachers. Factoring in electives like Arithmancy, Muggle Studies, Ancient Runes, Care of Magical Creatures, Divination and perhaps others as well, and there would be a need for a good 15-20 more teachers, teaching full time. This would create something like 40-50 teachers at the High Table and living at the school.

TRANSFER STUDENTS

Normally a student starts a school at age 11 and stays until she or he graduates at age 17 (or 18). It is unknown if Hogwarts accepts transfer students, but it was implied by Viktor Krum that people do ask to transfer schools at least occasionally and Dumbledore said he would welcome any Beauxbaton or Durmstrang student that wished to come to Hogwarts. This would imply the ability to transfer schools. On the other hand, Dumbledore, at the time he made his statement, was speaking to 7th year students age 17 and up with no need to study at Hogwarts as their studies were completed.

SIGNING UP

Parents can put their child's name down with Hogwarts from the time they are born and Lily and James Potter did this for Harry, but the number of students actually accepted into Hogwarts each year is widely variable and based on many factors such as talent, aptitude, maturity, personality and parentage. A student usually must be 11 to start the school, but if a person is extra smart, extra mature and happens to be born in Sep, like Hermione, she or he can get in at age 10. Due to the variances of birth dates, some students start the first year at age 11, and turn 12 the first day of term. Some may have only turned 11 a day before the start of term. This explains why some students are so much more physically or emotionally mature than others.

GETTING ACCEPTED

Acceptance letters are always of thick heavy yellowish or yellow parchment and addressed in emerald green ink (this seems to be the school ink, as most Hogwarts documents have green ink writing). On the back of the envelope is a purple wax seal stamped with Hogwarts' coat of arms: the letter H surrounded by the 4 House mascots: Lion (Gryffindor); Eagle (Ravenclaw); Badger (Hufflepuff); Snake (Slytherin).

Acceptance letters are sent by Pr McGonagall, the Deputy Headmistress to worthy 11-year-olds (not their parents as Muggles might expect). They usually arrive the 3rd week of Jul but may sometimes be as late as Jul 31 in arriving depending on where the potential students are and whether the letters can reach them easily or not. Replies of acceptance or decline are to be sent back to Pr McGonagall by owl and need to arrive not later than Jul 31, for reasons unknown since school starts Sep 1. The acceptance letters are sent out the first year and each year the student is eligible to return to school.

Letters will always contain a list of books, clothing or supplies needed for the upcoming school year.

GETTING TO HOGWARTS

Hogwarts is a hidden place and difficult to find. If a Muggle looks at it, all they see is an old ruin with a sign over the entrance saying danger, do not enter, unsafe. The only way students are supposed to travel to Hogwarts is via the Hogwarts Express. Under exceptional circumstances students may take the Knight Bus, but at no time should they use magical means, like flying Ford Anglias, broomsticks or winged horses, such travel is not illegal to use, just considered showing off and irregular.

Upon arriving at the Hogsmeade station, first years will take boats across the lake to the Castle. The boats take students across the Lake and under the cliff the castle stands on. There is no secret entrance and students must then walk up to the castle's frontdoors. Upon leaving to return home they will again use boats to travel from the castle to the station. The reason for students doing so is unknown, but the trip probably activates some ancient protective magic and was likely the only way to get to the castle when it was originally built.

Second years and above, upon arriving, are picked up in thestral-drawn carriages. Students taken up the track from the train station to a road that leads to the entrance of Hogwarts, recognizable by the wrought-iron front gates flanked by pillars on either side, with statues of winged boars on top of them. They then travel up a long steep drive to the frontsteps of the castle. Second years and above return to the station the same way at the end of the year (or to go to the train for Christmas vacation, at which point it seems 1st years must go back and forth on the boats).

Boats and Stagecoaches: At 144 students (1st years) and Hagrid, a total of 37 boats would be needed if students sit 4 to a boat and 1 boat for Hagrid alone. About 100 stagecoaches are said to come for 2nd years and above at the Hogsmeade station but at 4 persons to a coach, they'd need at least 216 coaches and as many thestrals if they are single-horse drawn. Few coaches seat 8 people unless students are opting to ride 2 in the driver's seat and 2 in the rumble seat, which one doubts they would be willing to do on cold and rainy nights.

ELECTRICITY AND MAGIC

The more magic around, the more it disrupts the flow of and counteracts the effects of electricity. Since Hogwarts has over 1,000 magicals at any given time, the concentrated levels of magic there would make it pointless to bring any electrically operated equipment to school as it would just go haywire and become useless. Even the area around Hogwarts, which includes the wizard-populated Hogsmeade village, is effected for many miles because there is just so much magic in the air. This is not say that magic does everything by Hogwarts. It does not.

Over 100 house-elves do the washing, cleaning and cooking and while elves may use the formidable magic they possess to do some things, most of their duties require manual labor and plenty of it. Students have to write out their papers by hand as no magical word processors exist. Recording devices can't tape a lecture if a student misses it, to Hermione's chagrin. Elevators don't exist, so everyone has to deal with the staircases themselves. Apparition is impossible within Hogwarts or it's grounds, so if one is late to class, running is the only alternative. All this must be particularly hard on handicapped students who must exist, though Hogwarts doesn't appear to have any.

The many protective spells on Hogwarts, designed mainly to interfere with magic done by someone outside the school trying to harm those within, also prevents students attempting advanced, illegal, or dangerous magic (except becoming Animagi apparently). As Dumbledore stated, these spells would normally have prevented a Legilimens creeping around in a student's mind. That the protective magic on Hogwarts couldn't prevent Harry's mind being affected was only because Harry's mind *is* Voldemort's mind. That they exist point up the strongly defensive nature of the spells used at and on Hogwarts and its grounds.

THE FLOORS

Being in Britain, Hogwarts naturally uses European floor reckoning, this means that the floor the Great Hall is on is called the ground floor and the floor above the Great Hall is called the first floor. It's difficult to navigate the various floors, even if one does know which floor one is on, as there are many shortcuts, odd double (meaning they go up 2 floors rather than 1) or movable staircases and secret passageways. Students often lose their way because they are not paying attention to where they are going, but even when they are it can be difficult. It took Harry about a week to learn how to find his way from Gryffindor Tower to the Great Hall by himself. Fred and George liked the challenge of navigating Hogwarts, but other students would surely be glad of a map. This may perhaps in part be why the gang of 4 (James, Sirius, Remus and Peter) concocted the Marauder's Map.

THE SCHOOL HIERARCHY

The ranking at the school normally is the School Board of Governors, the Headmaster, the Deputy Headmistress, Heads of Houses, the teachers, other staff members, the Head Boy and Head Girl, the 24 Prefects and finally the general student body. This is approximately 1 Prefect for every 40 students, which is an entirely reasonable number of persons to manage.

During 95/96 there was a coup attempt on Hogwarts by the MoM and the MoM got rid of the Board of Governors and added a Hogwarts High Inquisitor, who ranked above the Headmaster. The High Inquisitor later added the Inquisitorial Squad, a group of students who ranked above the Head Boy and Girl and assisted the High Inquisitor in her mission. The MoM returned autonomy to Hogwarts in Jun 1996 and both the High Inquisitor and Inquisitorial Squad became defunct positions. The school is now safely back in the hands of the Head and, one assumes, the reinstated Board of Governors.

School Board of Governors: Hogwarts has a board of 12 governors which oversees the running of the school. The appointment or suspension of a Headmaster is entirely up to the governors. Governors also hear about incidents such as Buckbeak attacking Draco and are obliged to take action if parents seek redress on any such issues. Lucius Malfoy was a school governor for a number of years, but was eventually fired in 1993 for pressuring the other 11 governors (by threatening to curse their families) into suspending Dumbledore from the Headmaster position.

The board was temporarily replaced in 95/96 when the MoM voted itself control of Hogwarts and, oddly, not one governor even complained. Eventually the board was restored in Jun 1996. The current 12 wizards serving on the Board are unknown, as is how they are appointed or removed, or what power they have besides hiring and firing

Heads. Clearly people can be thrown off the board since Lucius was, but it's unclear if it's the other board members who throw a member off the board.

Order of Suspension: In order to remove a Headmaster an order of suspension must be signed by all 12 wizards on the school board of governors for Hogwarts. This rule was vacated in 95/96 when the MoM tried to take over Hogwarts. As of Jun 1996 it is back in force.

Hogwarts High Inquisitor: This post existed only during 95/96. Pr Umbridge held the position and used it to control every aspect of school life. The position was done away with in Jun 1996.

The Inquisitorial Squad: This group existed only during the 95/96 year. A small group of Slytherin students who were supportive of Pr Umbridge formed the main nucleus of this squad. Draco, Pansy, Millicent, C. Warrington and Montague were all a part of it though there were other students as well. Their emblem was a little silver captial I that they wore as a badge. The squad members were basically enforcers and used their position to dock points from students of other Houses. They read all the inbound or outbound owls, among other silly things, and were so hated that they were continual victimized by students with better wizarding skills as a punishment. The squad became defunct as of Jun 1996.

THE TERMS

The school's first term begins Sep 1. There are 3 terms: Winter (Sep 1 - Christmas vacation), Spring (Post-Christmas vacation to Easter vacation), Summer (Post-Easter vacation to the start of summer vacation), with a late summer vacation running from approximately Jul 1 till Aug 31. There are also two 3-week breaks, one at Christmas, during which most students go home, and the other at Easter, during which most students stay at school and study. In total there are about 38 weeks of school, with homework generally assigned over the Easter and summer breaks.

CLASSES

Classes run Monday to Friday from 9am to about 6pm at the very latest. All 1st and 2nd years have assigned classes. All 3rd to 5th years have a minimum of 2 elective classes they pursue until OWLs are taken. A maximum of 12 subjects total can be taken for OWLs and NEWTs. After the OWL exams, continued education to the NEWT level in a specific class is subject to the discretion of the professor who teachers the class and usually based on the student's OWL result in that subject.

Students have weekends free to do whatever they wish. For 3rd-7th year students there are certain Saturdays (usually about 4 each year) on which they are permitted to leave the school grounds and visit Hogsmeade village. Quidditch is played once a month on Saturdays, beginning in Nov and ending in May or Jun, with most of the school attending all the matches unless of course they are Petrified, dragged off into the Forbidden Forest to meet a giant by Hagrid or choose to go to the Library to study. Sundays have no activities of any kind and are probably so because of the observance of the Christian Sabbath.

School feasts occur Sep 1, Oct 31, Dec 25, and in late Jun the night before students leave. On Halloween classes are run all during the day of the feast. There does not appear to be an Easter feast, or a graduation ceremony of any kind, but there may be both. At a minimum one would expect a graduation ceremony since parents are paying good money to see their child educated. Since Easter is an observed holiday and one which many students stay over at school during, one would expect an Easter Feast and or Passover Feast for those of Christian or Jewish affiliations respectively. One would also expect there to be a church or chapel in Hogsmeade, as well as at the school, where students can attend services since they are not allowed to leave the school most weekends.

Bells: Bells, of the traditional church bell type that must be change-pulled, probably by Filch, sound from castle to announce the start of morning classes, the 10-minute change between of classes, the start of afternoon classes and at the start of lunch and dinner. Their peals ring out for several miles so it is no use telling a teacher one didn't hear them.

SCHOOL RULES AND PROCEDURES

General Rules: These are just a few of the common ones.
 All 1st – 4th year students must be in their Houses by 8pm.
 All 5th – 7th year students must be in their Houses by 9 pm.
 Students should not be outside the castle proper after dark.
 No magic of any kind is allowed in the hallways, between classes or any other time.

 Certain magical items are forbidden in the school hallways.
 No fighting is allowed, either physical or magical, at any time.
 No yelling is allowed in the castle, particularly the Great Hall.
 Library books must not be taken outside.

Emergency Rules: When in an emergency situation certain special rules apply that supersede the general rules.
 Quidditch matches and training sessions are canceled.
 Teachers must escort students in a group to their next class.
 Students are to be in their dorms by 6pm.
 Students must not leave their dorms after 6pm unless escorted by a responsible party: a Prefect, professor or school ghost.
 Prefects, professors and ghosts will patrol in pairs after dark looking for unusual activity in the castle.

DURING THE VOLDEMORT YEARS

Hogwarts was one of the last safe places in the wizarding world during Voldemort's initial rise to power in the 1970s and 1980s. Dumbledore was Headmaster then and Voldemort feared to confront him knowing from his school days how much more magically powerful Dumbledore was. But the fact remains that Voldemort did want to take the school, probably to purge it of Mudbloods, but this is a guess. It's never been fully articulated what he planned to do with Hogwarts once he got it or why he wanted it in the first place.

It seems odd that Voldemort would even want Hogwarts given Hogwarts' Headmaster Dippet was extremely nice to him, made him a Prefect, allowed to stay during his 5th and 6th year summer vacations, then made him Head Boy, not to mention giving him awards for magical merit and services to the school. Why does he want to destroy the only place that was ever really nice to him? Theoretically, he might desire to exact revenge on the school because of what happened to his ancestor, Salazar Slytherin, but why Voldemort would seek satisfaction for a clan that would have rejected him as Mudblood is a bit unfathomable.

HOGWARTS, THE FACILITIES

This section covers the castle and its interior locales. It is arranged by floor then alphabetically with the floor. For an overview of the various floors, see the Hogwarts' floor guide schematic J. For locations not within the castle, see the Hogwarts, Grounds and Outbuildings section. For a specific teacher's offices, see the Offices section. Information about classrooms are in the Classes sections.

The Castle and Interior

The castle has 7 floors, but there are also towers that rise at least 7 floors above the 7th floor, such as Gryffindor Tower which is known to be shorter than the Astronomy Tower. The castle has numerous towers and turrets only a few of which are shown on the schematic for clarity sake. In addition to towers above the castle, there are at least 5 different underground levels beneath the castle including dungeons and living space. The large Great Courtyard, a popular place for students huddle in between classes when the weather is bad, connects several parts of the castle while a smaller courtyard, off the Great Hall, is a popular place for students to hang out after lunch when the weather is good.

The castle's interior is unusual in that it has 142 very individual staircases. Some staircase wide and sweeping, some are narrow and rickety, some have a vanishing step in the middle that one has to remember to jump, some lead somewhere different but only on Fridays and some are even double staircases, directly connecting 2 floors by skipping over 1 floor. The doors are equally mysterious. Some have to be asked politely to open, others require tickling in exactly right place and still others are actually solid walls just pretending to be doors. There are hundreds of coats of armor, which are generally no help at all in finding one's way about as they wander at will, as do people in pictures, but the statues and tapestries all make reliable interior landmarks.

There are numerous internal secret passageways leading to places within the castle, somewhat erroneously thought of as shortcuts by the daring, and 7 external secret passageways leading to Hogsmeade and other places beyond the bounds of Hogwarts. Of the internal passageways, Filch and Mrs Norris know them all. Of the external passageways, Filch knows of only 4. Of the remaining 3: one is behind a mirror on the 4th floor, but caved in during the winter of 1992 and is now completely blocked; one is at the foot of the Whomping Willow and leads to the Shrieking Shack; and, one is through the hump of the hump-backed witch statue on the 3rd floor and leads to Honeydukes' basement.

Hogwarts' corridors have high windows that let the light through in bars. The halls are lit by torches at night, and sometimes during the day in winter when they are extremely cold, drafty and dark. The castle is so drafty in winter that loose windowpanes let in wind that can be strong enough to blow out the indoor corridor torches. The windows are all mullioned windows, meaning they are made up of little squares of glass, and once a little square is broken it doesn't seem to get repaired, possibly because it's a low priority on Filch's list. Classroom windows all tend to rattle in winter, and classrooms themselves tend to be cold, except the Potions classroom where there are no windows and one has a cauldron fire to huddle around.

Most classrooms are lit by a chandelier rather than torches or candles on desks. They have the usual classroom features, a chalkboard, a wastebasket, numerous individual chairs and desks for the students and with a large desk and chair at the head of the room for the teacher. There are no fireplaces in classrooms. Only the Great Hall and House common rooms ever have fires. All of the staff offices have fireplaces, but

The Harry Potter Companion

teachers may or may not light them. Pr Snape for instance never lights his hearth except momentarily to make an angry floo call. Pr McGonagall, always has her fire going, no matter what the weather or season. There are no fires or fireplaces in students' dorm rooms or bathrooms.

The Kitchens always have a fire going for cooking purposes and they may possibly be the source of the 24/7 hot water that's piped up to the Prefects' Bathroom and one hopes other bathrooms as well. On the other hand, Hogwarts might have a gas-heated boiler of enormous proportions hidden in a basement somewhere. After all hot water for over 1,000 people every day is a tall order. Like the Quidditch pitch, hot water for bathing is not something the founders would have originally built into the castle as hygiene in c 900 meant never, ever bathing if one could avoid it. The gargoyle sink that spits only cold water in Pr Snape's dungeon is probably an original fixture and only intended for hand washing. But one assumes c 1800 that the students and teachers became a little more interested in bathing and at that point flush toilets, hot and cold running water, bathtubs, and other amenities were installed.

Finally, given that Pr Flitwick was assigned the task of teaching (not charming) the doors of the castle to recognize Sirius Black, some walls amuse themselves by pretending to be doors, some doors are picky about how they are opened and some staircases move on Fridays, it seems reasonable to assume that the castle is a sentient life form. Just as the founders put their brains into a hat, (now the Sorting Hat) that is very much sentient, so too they might have put themselves into the castle as well. What limitations the castle might have as a sentient being is hard to say. Obviously it can't talk, or hasn't yet. It moves, but only its interior. It must see, or it couldn't recognize Sirius and there'd be no point in attempting to teach it to do so. Can it hear, smell, taste or feel? Perhaps it can. It may even be able to do more besides.

BY FLOOR

The Ground Floor
See the schematic K for an overview of this area.

Classroom 11: Located on the Ground Floor in the corridor leading off the Entrance Hall on the side opposite the Great Hall, it is usually never used. It was magically turned into a forest for Firenze in 95/96 after he was forced to leave his herd and become a teacher of Divination at Hogwarts.

The Courtyard: It is a large courtyard very near the Great Hall where students usually hang out after lunch if the weather is good. From the courtyard one can go in a sidedoor, down a corridor and up a double staircase to reach the DADA classroom on the 2nd floor.

The Entrance Hall: Standing at the front of the castle one sees the large oak frontdoors at the top of the stone steps. These huge doors have no door knocker on the outside. Inside, the doors have a sliding lock, probably an iron or wooden bar of some kind. Armor flanks the doors on either side and is always there and doesn't wander away (though the suits may change the guard now and then). The hall itself is huge and paved with giant flagstones. The stone walls are lit with flaming torches at night and the ceiling is so enormously high up, probably 7 stories = 70 ft, it can't be seen. There is a magnificent marble staircase leading to the upper floors opposite the frontdoors but what color the marble is is unknown. At the top of the staircase are 4 large carved stone niches were the House hourglasses stand. On the right side of the hall are the doors into the Great Hall and a janitor's closet. On the left side is the door of the Pre-Sorting chamber where 1st years wait before going into the Great Hall and a hallway with empty classrooms off of it.

Girls' Bathroom: Located on the ground floor, it's where Hermione was attacked by the mountain troll. Leaving the Great Hall, turn with Hufflepuffs toward their dorm, slip down a side corridor, turn into the next corridor which has a large stone griffin in it. At the dead end of the griffin's corridor is a corridor that runs horizontally, turn left. The girls' bathroom will have a key in its door.

Great Courtyard: There is a courtyard in the center of the castle, around which people walk to classes, located just off the Great Hall somewhere. Balconies hang out over part of it creating protection from rain and sun. Ron, Hermione and Harry have a favorite corner to stand in during windy days in the winter.

The Great Hall: See schematic L for an overview. Located off the Entrance Hall, double doors lead into the Great Hall. The Great Hall is strange and splendid place and the location for all meals, feasts and social occasions such as dances. Its ceiling is bewitched, probably with a Protean Charm, to look like the sky outside so that at any given moment one can tell what the weather is doing. The hall is lit at night with 1,000s of dripless candles that float in midair over the tables and often decorated for feasts. At the back, behind the High Table at the head of the hall, there are tall windows high up at the top of the wall through which the owls fly every morning. One can look into the hall from outside the castle, even when one is short (like Harry at age 12), through the long windows that face the drive.

House tables run vertically to the High Table at the top of the hall with Hufflepuff usually the closest to the doors, then Slytherin, then Ravenclaw and finally Gryffindor against the far wall, though this is subject to change. Each table seat about 250 people and has an equal number of chairs, not benches, around them. Whenever the students gather, even for meals, the place is a forest of pointed black hats because wizards ALWAYS wear their hats. The tablewares are simple during the year and there are no tablecloths but during feasts special gold, self-replenishing, self-cleaning wares are used. The table linens are always white for feasts, on all tables, rather than House colors.

High Table: The High Table is where all the staff eat, except Pr Trelawney, who prefers to dine in her tower. Dumbledore always sits in the center on a special chair which is large, high-backed and gold. Pr McGonagall usually sits next to him. Hagrid always sits at the extreme left of Dumbledore, nearest the Gryffindor table. The table seats approximately 40-60 teachers.

Staffrooms: There are at least 2 staffrooms, one on the ground floor and one on the 2nd floor, but there might be one on every floor. The ground floor staffroom has 2 snide-talking stone gargoyles guarding its door and is located very close to the Great Courtyard.

Violet's Chamber: Located through a door behind the High Table, it is a small chamber with a candle-filled chandelier and a fireplace opposite the door. It's walls are lined with paintings of witches, including Violet, and warlocks who seem to be former Heads, but one finds it difficult to picture Vi as a Head. On the other hand, there are side-by-side portaits of a warlock with a walrus mustache and a wizened witch there and the 2 of them fit the descriptions of 2 former Heads.

First Floor
Little is known what this floor holds other than Pr McGonagall's office.

Second Floor

The Harry Potter Companion

Broomcloset: There is one around the corner from the DADA classroom.
Corridor: Located near Myrtle's bathroom, the windows have a small crack at the topmost pane and there is usually water all over the floor due to Myrtle having a tantrum. This is where the basilisk first struck in 1992.
Moaning Myrtle's Bathroom: A girls' bathroom. The bathroom has a brass doorknob and can be seen from the head of a main staircase. Myrtle was a student who died in the bathroom in 1943. She was killed by the basilisk that used one of the bathroom's sinks as a point of entry into the castle. There are 4 stalls in the bathroom and Myrtle lives in the toilet of the end stall. The stalls have wooden doors that are flaking and scratched and have keyholes with the keys left in them. One of the doors is hanging off its hinges. Myrtle can usually be found floating above her toilet tank (an old style, raised-tank Crapper), or sulking in the toilet's U-bend.

On one of the bathroom sink's copper taps, there is carved a tiny snake. This tap has never worked according to Myrtle. When the snake is spoken to in Parseltongue, the tap glows with a brilliant white light and spins, the sink then sinks out of sight through the floor, leaving exposed a large pipe wide enough for a man to slide through. This is the entrance to the Chamber of Secrets and the place from which the basilisk emerged when called by Tom Riddle. This brings up 2 interesting points, 1) it must have seemed quite odd for the original Tom Riddle to be in the girls' bathroom all the time (but the 2nd time around Tom possessed Ginny, who could use it without question) and 2) where did Salazar get copper piping in the 900s?

The bathroom is a gloomy and depressing place with a large dirty mirror that is cracked and spotted hung above a row of chipped sinks and a damp floor that reflects the dull candlelight. Only a few low-burning stubs set in holders light the room. There is usually an out of order sign on the bathroom door because of flooding caused by Myrtle having a tantrum. No one uses this bathroom if they can help it because of Myrtle's rather irritating presence. However, Hermione found it was the perfect place for doing illicit potionmaking and it was in this bathroom, using an old cauldron perched on the toilet with a water-proof fire under it, that Hermione whipped up the Polyjuice Potion.
Pictures: In a corridor near a portrait of a mawkish witch in a meadow and a painting of several card-playing wizards, Fred and George set off their Wildfire Whiz-Bangs to cause a distraction to Pr Umbridge.
Staffroom: It is a long, paneled room with no windows that is full of old mismatched chairs, mostly squashy armchairs and dark wooden chairs. It has few features barring a fireplace and ugly wardrobe cupboard full of teachers' cloaks and robes (and occasionally boggarts).

Third Floor
Trophy Room: The crystal trophy cases contain silver and gold cups, shields, plates and statues. The cases are probably carved rock crystal. There are about 100 cups, as well as lists of old Head Boys and Head Girls, and any awards the school has ever given such as for Magical Merit or Special Services to the School. The room is always unlocked, has doors at either end and windows to let the moonlight and sunlight in. If one goes out one door and turns the corner, down a long gallery full of suits of armor, around a doorpost, down 2 more corridors, through an opening covered by a tapestry and down the hidden passageway, one comes out near the Charms classroom, which is some distance from the Trophy Room, but still on the same floor.

Fourth Floor

ACASCIAS RIPHOUSE

Not much is known about it except one of its corridors has a large vase. It also has a boys' bathroom that Montague ended up in 2 days after he got put in the Vanishing Cabinet. He unfortunately materialized in one of the toilets and was profoundly disoriented by the time he was discovered and extracted.

Fifth Floor
The Prefects' Bathroom: Located in the same corridor as the statue of Boris the Bewildered, the entry is the 4th door to the left beyond the statue. Entry is by password only and in 94/95 the password was pine fresh. It's a beautiful room lit by a chandelier and everything in it is white marble including the rectangular swimming-pool tub sunk in the middle of the floor. Jewel-topped golden taps, about 100, surround the edges of the tub. Each tap's jewel is a different color. The taps each produce something different: giant bi-colored bubbles or steam, hovering perfumed clouds, thick white foam like a raft or water jets that made bounced on across the surface of the water to name a few.

Every comfort is supplied and in one corner, near a gold-framed painting of a mermaid with long blonde hair on a rock, house-elves have left a pile of fluffy white towels. The mermaid is the only painting in the room, probably the only painting that likes water or being wet with steam. There is a diving board at one end of the bath, so it must be quite deep at least a one end. Long curtains of white linen hang at the windows, though it's doubtful anyone can look in on the 5th floor. However, Moaning Myrtle tends to spy on male Prefects out of the taps. This can be a good thing if one needs help in solving a golden egg type problem, but slightly disconcerting otherwise. She does not always make her presence known and it would be impossible to tell whether she is there or not at any given moment. Use of a towel at all times is advised.

Sixth Floor
All that's known to be on this floor are Sir Cadogan's picture and a few others.

Seventh Floor
Room of Requirement: aka the Come and Go Room. It is nearer the Owlery and Library than the dorms and opposite the tapestry of Barnabas the Barmy being clubbed by trolls. One can only find it when one has real need of it and once found it is always equipped with what the seeker needs. A seeker walks past the blank stretch of wall 3 times, thinking about what she or he needs, and evemtaully a highly polished door will appear between a window and a man-sized vase. A brass doorhandle allows the door to be pulled open.

Dobby found a bed and antidotes to Butterbeer for Winky in it, Dumbledore found chamber pots, Filch found cleaning materials and Fred and George found a broomcloset in which to hide from Filch. For Harry, there was a large room with flickering torches, wooden bookcases filled with books on DADA, a wealth of large silk cushions on the floor and rows of shelves at the far end filled with all sorts of Dark Detectors. The door even had a key sticking out of the interior lock for extra safety.

It would be remiss not to comment on the fact that Dumbledore found room full of chamber pots. He was obviously looking for a bathroom. Whether the room is old fashioned and presented him with chamber pots or whether that's what Dumbledore was thinking of is something we may never know. Certainly, given Dumbledore's age, he may well have been thinking of a chamber pot since they were commonly used in many homes up until the 1930s and which many people preferred rather than having something as "disgusting" as an indoor toilet.

No one appears to use the room for personal gain, such as thinking about the tests one might have to take and getting a copy with the answers, finding a cure a debilitating disease such as Lycanthropy, or thinking about Galleons to pay off some bet or bill. It may be that the room cannot make money. It may also be limited to produce only what exists, thus if a cure for some disease did not exist, it couldn't be produced. Likewise, while it may help students prepare for tests, it may have been forbidden to help students cheat on tests. Every magical thing has its limitation, these are probably not the only ones.

TOWERS

The Astronomy Tower: aka the Tallest Tower, tallest astronomy tower. This tower is out of bounds to all students except at Astronomy class time. Norbert was dispatched to Romanian from this tower. The tower is up the marble staircase, then 2 more flights of stairs, to its entrance, then up a spiral staircase that is at least another 9 floors up. Seemingly it would only be 11 floors up making it shorter than Gryffindor Tower which is 15, but the 2 flights of stairs might be double staircases, putting the entrance on the 5th floor or higher. It is probably about 20 stories up.
Dumbledore's Tower: See Dumbledore's Office.
Gryffindor Tower: See Houses.
The North Tower: The tower is at least 1 story tall and has windows. Accessibly by circular trapdoor in the ceiling of the 7th floor, a ladder is let down for students to climb up. It is where Divination classes are taught and Sybill Trelawney lives. See Classes for a description of the classroom.
The Owlery Tower: aka the Owlery or West Tower. The Owlery is at the very top of the West Tower. There is a spiral staircase in the tower that must be climbed to reach the Owlery's entrance. It is a tall tower with a circular stone room at the top. It is cold and drafty, as there is no glass in its many windows, and school and student owls roost in the rafters here. At any given time one can find 100s of owls sleeping or eating here. Most owls go out hunting at night and come back in the morning. The floor is covered in straw, droppings and skeletons of regurgitated mice, voles and other unlucky creatures. This tower is where Buckbeak landed and let Harry and Hermione off before flying away with Sirius. From the bottom of the tower staircase, one can go down 2 more staircases and down 2 corridors, and one arrives at the hospital wing.
Ravenclaw Tower: See Houses.
West Tower: aka the Owlery Tower.

OTHER PARTS

This section includes major areas or wings of the castle that are devoted to a single purpose, such as the Hospital Wing.

Chamber of Secrets: See schematic M. Created by Salazar Slytherin in c 900, this chamber contained a basilisk until 1994. For many centuries no one actually believed it existed except descendants of Slytherin. Slytherin created the chamber so only someone with his talent, being a Parselmouth, could open it. The Chamber was first opened by Tom Riddle in 42/43. Tom Riddle was the true Heir of Slytherin and as a blood descendent of Slytherin was a Parselmouth. Tom discovered the chamber by doing library research. One girl, Myrtle who was a Muggle born, died from looking at the basilisk but this may have been bad luck and stupidity rather than an intentional killing. After all, most students know enough magizoology not to look into a basilisk's eyes!

Lucius Malfoy knew about the Chamber, although it was opened 10 years before he was born. Undoubtedly Voldemort told him about it when he gave Lucius the diary for there was really no other way Lucius could have learned about it. It would seem no one thought much about the Chamber for nearly 50 years (1942-1992) till Lucius got Ginny Weasley to open it. Unfortunately Voldemort had already sewed the seeds of the Chamber's desctruction in 1981 when he accidentally passed the Parselmouth ability to Harry. So, when Lucius got Tom Riddle to open the Chamber again in 92/93 by possessing Ginny Weasley, Harry was able to enter the Chamber, save Ginny and destroy the basilisk, Tom and the enchanted diary that allowed Tom to possess Ginny in the first place.

The Chamber can be reached only by speaking Parselmouth to the snake scratched on the copper sink fixture in Myrtle's bathroom, then sliding down the large, slimy, dark pipe under the sink. The Chamber is so deep underground that it is thought to be under the Lake, which would put it a good couple miles down. There is a tunnel at the bottom of the pipe which has dark slimy walls and a wet floor littered with small animal bones. It leads to the Chamber's door, a solid wall with two entwined snakes carved in it. Their eyes are set with emeralds and they look strangely alive but are not. Speaking Parseltongue, one must command the wall to open. It cracks in half and the halves slide into recesses in the wall, like pocket doors. One can then enter the long, dimly lit chamber where there are towering stone pillars supporting the roof, which is so high up it can't be seen but obviously it is still underground.

Carved twisting serpents with hollow eye sockets form the pillars and a greenish gloom hangs in the chamber. For some reason Salazar never magicked up the stonework serpents, which is somewhat inexplicable, and prefered to rely on the basilisk. Beyond the last pair of pillars is a huge statue of a warlock standing against the back wall between two pillars. The giant statue has an ancient face with a long thin beard that falls almost to floor. It is dressed in sweeping wizard robes but they don't cover the 2 grey stone feet on the floor. This is a likeness of Salazar Slytherin and we must assume its flattering despite the monkey-like face since he made it, which is scary. The basilisk comes out of Slytherin's mouth when called in Parseltongue. The mouth opens very wide and out the basilisk pops.

There is no longer a live basilisk though the Chamber continues to exist. It doubtful anyone would open the Chamber due to the stench of rotting basilisk. However, the Chamber is impressive magic and should be put to some good use. Perhaps it can be cleaned out by Slytherins and used as a playroom, racquetball court or indoor practice Quidditch pitch for their House. Certainly the existence of the Chamber does raise the question of what other sorts of magical traps Slytherin may have left at Hogwarts. It also gives Pr Binns a great deal more reason to treat myth and legend as historical fact.

Dungeons: There are currently at least 5 usable Dungeons under the castle. Other underground dungeons have been converted to serve as classrooms, student housing and even safety measures for the Sorcerer's Stone. For a look at the various rooms and devices used to protect the Sorcerer's Stone see the schematic N. These rooms are located at the lowest level of the known dungeons in the castle. Only the Chamber of Secrets is further underground.

The Hospital Wing: The hospital is in a wing of its own. The entrance seems to be on the 3rd floor. The entrance to the Hospital wing has 2 doors, which can be locked and a lot of windows to let in light. The hospital wing has numerous beds that never seem occupied despite the 1,000 students. They are usually made up with white linens, none of which seem to bear the school crest. Each bed has a bedstand and there are curtain partitions which can be pulled for privacy. One can see Hagrid's from the Hospital wing's windows.

Hospitalized 91/92
Neville: potions class accident
Neville: broken wrist from a flying accident
Neville: fight with Crabbe and Goyle
Ron: dragon bite on his writing hand
Harry: Voldemort attack, 3-day coma

Hospitalized 92/93
Harry: arm was deboned
Colin Creevey: Petrified
Sir Nick: Petrified
Justin Finch-Fletchley: Petrified
Hermione: Polyjuice Potion accident
Penelope Clearwater: Petrified
Hermione: Petrified

Hospitalized 93/94
Harry: dementor attack
Ron: broken leg
Hermione: dementor attack
Moody: kidnapping

Hospitalized 94/95
Elois Midgen: to have her nose reattached
Ms Fawcett: beard removal
Mr Summers: beard removal
Fred Weasley: beard removal
George Weasley: beard removal
Goyle: boils on his nose
Hermione: growing front teeth
Hermione: bubotuber pus on her hands

Hospitalized 95/96
Katie Bell: nosebleed
Alicia Spinnet: eyebrows growing out of control
Marietta Edgecombe: Hermione's SNEAK jinx - she was not cured
Jack Sloper: knocked out with his own bat
Montague: confusion
C. Warrington: cornflake-like skin condition
Pansy: sprouted antlers
Pr Umbridge: shock
Ginny: broken ankle
Neville: broken nose
Ron: brain injuries
Hermione: dueling injuries.

Kitchens: Located beneath the Great Hall, only house-elves work here. Harry knew where the kitchens were in his 1st year but apparently never told Hermione or Ron. To reach the kitchens, turn left after coming down the marble stairs and go to the door behind which are some steps into a broad corridor with pictures of food. One picture will have a suit of armor near it and be of a bowl of fruit. Tickle the huge green pear it squirms, chuckles and turns into a large green doorhandle. Pull it open and go down some steps into the kitchens. The hallway where the paintings are also contains the doorway to Hufflepuff House, which must make sneaking off for a midnight snack very handy.

The kitchens are one room as large as the Great Hall above them, but, despite the fact it is probably only 10' underground, it also has with an high ceiling. There are 4 long wooden tables in the kitchen, one below each of the House tables. The dishes are sent up through the ceiling to their counterpart tables by elf magic and retrieved the same way. Since there is no 5th table, one wonders how the elves get food to the High Table. Anyway, there are mounds of pots and pans, brass not iron or steel, heaped very hygenically round the room against the stone walls. The floor is made up of flagstone. There is a great brick fireplace at the far end of the room, which usually has a stool before it with Winky on it, drunk. At least 100 elves hang out in the kitchens, so apparently Hogwarts has more than 100, and all the true Hogwarts' house-elves (the enslaved ones) all wear a uniform tea towel stamped with the Hogwarts' crest and tied like a toga.

The Library: It is said to have 100s of narrow rows and 1,000s of shelves with 10s of 1,000s of books, which makes it gigantic with holdings of something near 1, 000,000 books. Given the size of the Library, it has its own wing with an entrance on the 2nd floor. The Restricted Section is at the back, cordoned off by a rope, but it has very low swags and is easy to step over. Madam Irma Pince is the only librarian and very particular about her books. However instead of nondamaging bookplates, she gives all the books a red wax seal on the cover which says property of Hogwarts library with the impressed Hogwarts in gold letters.

The Library has portable lamps available at the front desk, one would assume for students to go looking in the stacks which are quite dark because of all the tall narrow rows and shelves. The Library has a number of tables and desks each with night candles on them which are lit when it's dark or gloomy. In other words, fire + books! The Library closes at 9pm normally, but is open later during exam times. At night it is pitch-black and can be very eerie which is probably why Madam Pince doesn't have her quarters anywhere near it. The Restricted Section books generally whisper among themselves, occasionally making louder noises if upset, and can be hostile to intruders.

The Restricted Section: This section is at the back of the Library and roped off, so students know it's out of bounds. Students need a signed note from one of the teachers to even look into any of the Restricted Section books and they are rarely checked out. These books contain powerful Dark magic that is never taught at Hogwarts but older students studying DADA occasionally need to use them because they do have to know what they are or could be up against. Only the librarian can go into the Restricted Section and bring out the book the student needs.

These books are Dark and need special handling because they can act in strange and unusual ways. Titles found here might have peeling faded gold letters in foreign languages or no title at all. A book might perhaps have a bloodstain on it or give a piercing bloodcurdling shriek when opened. One might hear a faint whispering coming from the books when they know someone is in their section other than Madam Pince. It's best to find a really stupid teacher like Pr Lockhart to bang out a permission slip or note and leave this section to the professionals rather than to try and take a Dark book surreptitiously.

Harry and The Underworld

While on the topics of Dark things and things underground, it seems appropriate to slip in a discussion of Harry's most reoccurring issue, the underworld, and those in it, the dead. Why Harry ends up in the underworld, or is so sought out by its denizens, is open to speculation. It may be because the Slytherin nature, which loves all things Dark and subterranean, was imparted to him by Voldemort when he was attacked as an infant. He may feel the draw of it and know he must continually do battle with and hopefully eventually overcome it. It may be that he has a need to confront death and achieve "resurrection" as a single persona rather than Voldemort's twin or counterpart. His continual battle against Voldemort is after all as much to save himself as the wizarding world. Or it could have nothing to do with Slytherin or Voldemort at all.

Focusing on the theme of the underworld, one sees that Harry physically ends up in the underworld with regularity. He lives at the Dursley's for 10 years in the cupboard *under* the stairs until 1991. He confronts Voldemort underground to save the Sorcerer's Stone in 1992. He then confronts Tom Riddle even deeper underground to save Ginny from the Chamber of Secrets in 1993. One might say that the latter 2 events were simply a case of Harry's willingness to do what must be done and Voldemort was choosing the underground venues. But in 93/94 Harry voluntarily spends a good deal of time in underground tunnels making trips to Hogsmeade. At the end of the year, to save Ron, he ends up in an underground tunnel again, this time to reach the Shrieking Shack and his ultimate confrontation with Sirius Black.

In 1995, Harry ends up in a graveyard, the underworld of the dead. Later in that same year Harry ends up in the underworld of the MoM, when he is force to go to Courtroom 10 for his misuse of magic hearing. For the following school year, 95/96, the underground of Harry's mind, his subconscious, is attacked until ultimately Harry ends up at the MoM, almost as far underground as possible, in the most mysterious place of place of all, the DoM, to rescue Sirius and confront Voldemort. Even if Harry is not of his own volition chosing the venues for all these events, he still ends up in the underworld. Harry doesn't resist the call of the underworld. Even when Hermione gives valid reasons why he should not go into the DoM, he rejects them and choses the underworld against all logic. Why?

To answer this we must look at Harry and his relationship with the dead. The dead seem to have a more than average interest in Harry for reasons not entirely clear. These reasons may become clear later on, but for now it's impossible to discover their motives. Harry's motives for being interested in the dead, on the other hand, are quite obvious. Since practically everyone Harry cares for is dead, he has more cause than most to be interested in the dead. This interest is not entirely unremarked upon even by his closest friends or impartial magical objects. As the Mirror of Erised revealed, Harry's deepest and most profound desire is to be with his family, who are all dead. However, Harry is by no means suicidal. He simply recognizes that all the people really cares for are dead, and more than that were murdered, were unjustly made dead before their time. This bond between Harry and the murdered dead seems to have formed with the death of his parents

It is as a result of being unable to help his parents, who were murdered while he was in the same house, that Harry develops a belief that people will die without his intervention. Since he did not intervene to save his parents, he attributes their death to the lack of his intervention. This is ridiculous, but this is $2 + 2 = 4$ thinking is typical of the very young. Hermione calls Harry's condition a hero complex but in reality it is nothing of kind. Harry's desire to save people doesn't stem from the fact that he needs or wants to be a hero or be thought of and admired as such. It stems from a need to atone for not helping his parents, for not doing anything at his parents' death, by not letting history repeat itself. No risk to himself personally is too great to be borne, if by such hazzards he can prevent his history from repeating itself.

Harry does have a psychological complex, it's just not a hero complex. Harry has a saviour complex. He needs to save people. In order to do this he feels he needs to act when people are in danger of death. His motivation is himself and his need. That someone is saved is secondary, though he never consciously recognizes this. This is why when Cedric dies before him, as he stands helplessly by, he dreams about it for months afterward. Harry didn't know Ced well enough to be distraught over his death. However Harry did have a memory of the curse that killed Ced being used on his parents. Cedric's death forced Harry to relive his worst case scenario – standing helplessly by when someone is murdered. Harry was unable to break the cycle. At the root of cycle is need, Harry's need to be a saviour. But what fans the need is Harry's belief system. Harry's worldview lacks the concept of resurrection. There is only life or death in a mortal realm.

The life and death v. death and resurrection worldview issues grow as Harry ages. It begins with Sirius Black. Sirius comes out of Harry's dead and finshed past. Harry is an orphan, till Sirius becomes his gaurdian. Some semblance of a family, of a parent, is ressurected from the dead. In seeing Scabbers transformed into Peter Pettigrew, Harry bears witness to a ressurection. He is confronting someone long thought to be dead. The idea that dead isn't really dead is further bolstered a year later when Harry is forced to confront Barty Crouch Jr, another person long though to be dead. These 2 men are, due to magical transformations, resurrected from the dead before Harry's very eyes. They are living proof that death is not always final.

During the course of the TT Harry is confronted with ressurection on a personal level during Task 2. Harry is forced go underwater (underworld) to bring Ron, who is in a state of living death, to the surface where he can breathe. In other words, Harry must resurrect him - shades of Opheus and Eurydice. In Harry's mind, he has only an hour to resurrect the one most dear to him. Harry believes Ron will die after the hour. This flies in the face of all Harry knows about the TT: the precautions are being taken to prevent anyone's death, but most of all the innocent non-champions. The need to save outweighs rational thought. Harry waits to make sure Hermione and Cho are rescued and when he is confronted with Gabrielle, who has no rescuer, he rescues her himself. Harry saves people even if they don't need to be saved, because his need overrules everyone else's.

At the end of Task 3, Harry ends up quite literally in the valley of death, the valley setting of the graveyard of Little Hangleton. Here Cedric dies, while Harry is helpless to prevent it. Here also, Harry shares a part in resurrecting his mortal enemy Voldemort to a human form. When Priori Incantatem occurs, Harry is forced to communicate with shadows of the dead, including the newly dead Cedric who requests a form of resurrection out of the valley of death when he asks Harry, at great personal risk, to drag his lifeless corpse back to his parents. The murdered dead, including Harry's own parents, are resurrected and actively take part in defeating Voldemort and aiding Harry (and Ced) in escaping the Death Eaters. Death and resurrection. Death and resurrection. Death and resurrection. It would be difficult for anyone, even Harry as blinkered as he is by his own problems, not to consider the fate of person after death at this point.

The following year, 1996, Harry ends up underground (underworld) again, on Level 9 of the MoM, in the Chamber of Death, hearing the voices of the dead. Harry is confronted by the existence of immortality. But it doesn't really sink in except on a subconsious level. It is not until Harry is forced to stand helplessly by and witness the death of Sirius – a death he caused by forcing Sirius to come and rescue him after Voldemort had lured him to the MoM – that the shoe beings to drop. This is the 5th time Harry has been unable to prevent death. Lily and James, Frank Bryce, Cedric Diggory and Sirius Black all died with Harry as helpless witness. Harry is forced to see that he not only can't save anyone, even his trying to save people has backfired.

Consciously he still doesn't acknowledge his saviour complex. Instead he snaps, has a psychological meltdown, and goes after Sirius' murderer to do something very out of character – use an Unforgivable curse on her. His bid to exact revenge via torture fails because of lack of will but it attracts the attentions of Voldemort, who, in the form of a snake, attempts to crush Harry to death. It is in this moment that Harry's subconscious mind at last breaks through. Harry admits dying wouldn't be so bad, as it would mean he could be with Sirius, the only parent he has ever known and loved. Harry has made a leap of faith. He presumes that Sirius has already experienced a heavenly resurrection, that he is in a better place, and that he himself will experience the same if he dies.

Harry is finally able to look past the dead, the underworld and the mortal life, to resurrection, eternal life and eternal love. Harry has broken the cycle, perhaps not physically yet, but psychologically. The need to save people, to not let them die, was *his* need. He presumed that this life was all that people had and all that could be had and with that worldview, one must do anything to insure the survival of oneself and others. But with the idea that there is something better beyond this life, that death really is the last great adventure in an unknown country, Harry can live with the fact that death happens and he doesn't need to obsessionally "save" everyone.

Yes, Harry should want to help people, to strive to prevent others from being murdered or otherwise harmed, but not from a sense of his own need, not to bolster a skewed worldview where every death becomes his fault. Harry's need made him reckless even dangerous to himself and those he sought to help. But without that irrational need, Harry really can get on with his true task, saving the world, in a rational and effective manner. But credit where credit is due. Harry never has and likely never will become the "hero" on his own. He is rash and never once fully understood the circumstances he was in before acting. He reacts rather than acts. It is Dumbledore that comes to the rescue and saves the day, and usually Harry from the situations he's needlessly put himself into.

Dumbledore saved Harry from the Mirror of Erised, and from Pr Quirrell (Voldemort). Dumbledore saved the Sorcerer's Stone. Fawkes and Sorting Hat, both Dumbledore's, saved Harry from Tom Riddle. Dumbledore saved Harry when he falls from his broom and Sirius and Buckbeak by telling Harry and Hermione to use the Time-Turner and helping them get away with it all. It's Dumbledore that's kept the Order watching over Harry all his life. Dumbledore told Harry about the Room of Requirement. Dumbledore saved Harry from prosecution by the MoM. Dumbledore protected Harry from Voldemort with living statues. And the list goes on and on, but the meaning is clear.

It is only with Dumbledore's help that Harry goes from being a near disaster to truly heroic. It is only with Dumbledore's help that Harry lives long enough to make his physiological transition from child obsessed with needing to save people to adult that has put aside his own need and is actually able to save people. And without Hermione and Ron, Harry would be an utter failure all together. Does this make Harry less a hero? No. An essential truth of life is that as individual human beings, we are not very heroic figures, but with friends at our side, we can be. Just because the Beatles said it first, doesn't make it any less true, we get by with a little help from our friends.

Hogwarts, Grounds and Outbuildings

Given what individuals have said throughout the years a good deal of information is available on where things are in relation to other things. This makes them fairly easy to plot. A few locations are of course up to individual interpretation but for a general overview of Hogwarts' grounds see schematic I.

The Beech Tree: This tree has been by the Lake since James' time and probably many years before. It is a popular place to spend warm sunny afternoons doing homework or just watching the Giant Squid bask in the shallows.

The Castle: Set high on a cliff overlooking a usually calm lake and surrounded by mountains that become icy grey in winter, the castle is also surrounded by the Forbidden Forest. Passing through the magnificent wrought-iron gates flanked by stone columns topped with winged boars, the long sloping drive leads up to the castle steps and the oak doors of the Entrance Hall. Coming out of Hogwarts between the gates, if one turns left and continues down the road eventually one ends up going into Hogsmeade village. This road connects to the main street and goes through the town and out to the mountains. A turn off along the road before the town's main street will lead to the Hogsmeade Station.

The Forbidden Forest: The forest is on the edge of the school's property and appears to surround the castle. It contains acromantula spiders, thestrals, stoats, rats, unicorns, boar, trolls, werewolves, pheasant, the flying Ford Anglia and Neville's lost school broom, among many other things. The trees there are towering, gigantic and densely packed together. Beech, oak, fir, yew and sycamore all grow there. The forest is cool, damp and dark even in the summer. Its floor is covered with an almost impenetrable undergrowth including dead leaves, treeroots, stumps and brambles. There is a path through the forest but about a half-hour in, the trees get so thick that the path becomes almost impossible to find let alone follow. There is a stream running through the forest that helps to keep it moist and moss grows on trees in the vicinity of the stream.

Hagrid's cabin stands just beside the forest. A narrow winding track of earth made by Hagrid runs from near his house into the forest where it splits a short way in. Hagrid often goes hunting in the forest with his crossbow and Fang and most of his fresh meats seem to come from here. He says that nothing in the forest will hurt him or Fang, and it seems to be true, but then again, little could harm Hagrid with his giant blood and Fang runs at the first sign of danger. About an hour's walk into the forest, where the ground starts to slope downward into a cleared hollow, is Aragog's residence. Many centaur herds also live in the forest. The centaurs aren't very friendly most of the time but they don't like humans or wizards much and think of the forest as their *personal* property. Since Oct 1995, a semi-civilized giant named Grawp has also been living illegally in the Forest.

It is said that Hagrid can walk from his cabin so far around the perimeter of the Forbidden Forest that the Lake and the castle fall out of sight. This would imply that the forest runs completely around the castle and that the grounds extend very far away from the castle, especially as Hogwarts sits on a cliff and would be easy to spot for some distance. It may be that the forest goes over the mountains surrounding the castle and when Hagrid follows it over the mountains, then the castle disappears from view. Either way, the magic protecting the castle extends to the limits of the grounds, wherever they may be.

The Greenhouses: There are at least 3 greenhouses at Hogwarts. To get to them one must leave the castle by the front steps, the only way to leave the castle, and cross through the school's vegetable patches, which must be quite extensive figuring 4 persons can be fed by 1 acre. With 1,200 people at Hogwarts, there must be 300 acres of vegetable patches. The Whomping Willow is across the lawns from the greenhouses and one can see it and Hagrid's cabin from the door of Greenhouse 3. Simple rather harmless magical plants are kept in Greenhouses 1 and 2. These plants are not lethal or otherwise dangerous to students. Greenhouse 3 is always kept locked and only Pr Sprout has the keys, because it contains all the dangerous plants such as mandrakes, Abyssinian shrivelfigs and bubotubers. This greenhouse smells of earth, dragon dung fertilizer and the heavy perfume of various flowering plants such as the giant umbrella-sized blooms of the Venemous Tentacula which dangle from the ceiling. Pr Sprout also composts inside the greenhouses, which leads one to think NEWT level Herbology is only for those with a decided lack of olfactory senses.

Hagrid's Cabin: For an overview of Hagrid's cabin and its setting, see the schematics O1 and O2. Hagrid teaches Care of Magical Creatures just beside his house, near the Forbidden Forest. Draco, Crabbe, Goyle, Harry, Ron, Hermione, Lavender, Parvati, and Dean all take the class but it remains to be seen who can hack NEWT level studies with Hagrid as a teacher if skrewts are OWL level. There is a large makeshift paddock about a 5-minute walk from the cabin and this is where Hagrid pens interesting, often dangerous, creatures for class or puts up Olympia's 12 visiting abraxans.

Hagrid's cabin is small, wooden and abuts the Forbidden Forest. He doesn't mind living near the forest because he knows nothing in the forest would, or even could, hurt him. Or at least that was the case up until Mar 1996 when Hagrid broke centaur law by saving Firenze from being kicked to death. The centaurs have since been extremely hostile toward humans of any kind and one is not sure they wouldn't torch Hagrid's place with flaming arrows if given a further provocation beyond Grawp. Hagrid has a long history of doing things detrimental to the forest, starting in 1943 with the release of Aragog into it and continuing to 1995 when he brought a destructive giant into the forest.

Outside the frontdoor of Hagrid's cabin, one might see a large crossbow and a quiver of arrows, a pair of galoshes and a water barrel. On the side of the house is his only water source, a well, probably with a kelpie in it. In the back is a fenced vegetable garden growing runner beans, peas and other vegetables. There is also a chicken coop in the back and a pumpkin patch a few yards away near the trees. His battered, flowery, pink umbrella with the spearlike end is usually resting against the back wall of the cabin. Because he doesn't have running water, he presumably has an outhouse and a shower facility near his cabin somewhere.

Hagrid's cabin has windows with curtains. He has a huge high bed with a patchwork quilt over it in one corner and a fire glowing in another opposite it. The hearth generally has a huge black iron cauldron in it, Fang's basket and Hagrid's chair beside it and a hearth rug in front of it. The fireplace has a mantle which always has a tin of homemade treacle fudge in it, but only giant jaws find it edible. Hagrid likes to bake but, living alone, he can cook as well. He prefers dishes heavy on the meat, usually of creatures he's caught in the forest, and he always has a ceiling full of smoked hams and pheasants hanging over his kitchen table. The occasional stoat also makes it onto the menu.

Since his place is a one-room cabin, there is no formal kitchen. Hagrid has a scrubbed table with chairs, a crockery cupboard with doors and a large copper basin with water that acts as a sink. Near his bed is a large double-door wardrobe with a mirror inside it. A chest of drawers beside the bed rounds out Hagrid's collection of furniture. Now and then some interesting creature may be found in the cabin, such as a dragon in the hearth or hippogriff on the bed. On those occasions Hagrid, who isn't allowed to borrow library books, usually takes a book from the Library for reference purposes and hides it under his pillow. He always returns it later.

Probably the curses Madam Pince puts on her books don't effect Hagrid because of his giant blood. It is also probably why he can drink mulled mead out of a pewter tankard the size of a bucket and not get the least bit drunk. Although, small amounts of firewhisky seem to make a big impact on him. Normally Hagrid sticks to tea and he enjoys inviting his friends round for tea. He makes tea with teabags and has a copper kettle he puts in the fire (on a trivet probably) to heat up the water. He is quite good at knitting and has made a little cozy for his teapot. If one went to his place for tea, one would probably have some fruitcake or other baked goods. Going for dinner isn't recommended as one will likely be offered "beef" casserole, but find bird parts in it.

The Lake: Located just south of the castle, this large lake is the first thing most students see of Hogwarts. From the platform in Hogsmeade, there is a steep narrow downward sloping path to the lake. It is thick with pine trees on either side, but no dangerous creatures. After going around a bend at the bottom of the path, 1st years arrive at the Lake and their first view of Hogwarts castle on its cliff. The Lake has mostly grass and a few trees around it and most students hang out there in good weather. No one ever seems to fish in the Lake, but this may be out of respect for the merepeople who really need the fish there for survival.

The Lake is very dark and deep, and quite cold, underwater there is only about 10' of visibility, but at one there are shallows (probably 12' deep) where the Giant Squid likes to bask. During heavy rains the Lake can burst its banks and turn the school flowerbeds into little streams but this is very rare. In winter the Lake freezes over and turns the color of chilled steel but no one seems to ice skate on it. There are many creatures in the Lake: an entire village of merpeople, grindylows and even sharks. It has small silver fish as well but no one fishes there. Given the giant squid and merepeople who have seen sharks live in the Lake, it must be a saltwater body. Being located in Scotland that would make it a sea loch. It was the scene of TT Task 2 and champions had to swim in it, but no one seems to swim in it normally.

The Quidditch Field: The pitch is on the west side of the Castle surrounded by a stadium that seats about 800 and was probably build in the 12th century when the game was becoming widely popular in other contries. Since the game was not around when the founders built the school, they couldn't have built the pitch or the stadium. The stadium is raised high in the air so students can see the action, but everyone brings binoculars anyway. The pitch is used for classes in Quidditch as well as games and practices. On either side of the pitch are locker rooms for the playing or practicing teams to change in but there are no House-exclusive locker rooms. Practice balls are kept in the Madam Hooch's office or sometimes the locker rooms and can be borrowed any time for practices. A single broomshed is located a little way from one of the locker rooms and is where all 4 teams keep their brooms – which surprisingly hasn't caused any problems despite the Slytherins going in and out all the time. Beyond the pitch is part of the Forbidden Forest, which it tall and acts as a screen, but the whole of Hogwarts is invisible to Muggle eyes, so the forest may be irrelevant to hiding the pitch and stadium.

The Whomping Willow: See Magical Plants.

Hogwarts, Offices

Offices reflect individual taste and from that aspect are very interesting. But in a boarding school setting many offices are connected to living quarters in some way, so in a sense, these rooms aren't offices so much as private studies and part of the teachers' homes.

DADA Office: Obviously this room has gone through so many transformations it's difficult to say what it will look like next. But, such as it has been decorated in the past, can be noted. It is located on the 3rd floor, near the Charms classroom, and the windows face the Quidditch Pitch. There is an ugly stone bust of a medieval wizard sitting on a column muttering to himself in Latin in a corridor near the office and a suit of armor in the corridor where the office is located. There is also a swiveling staircase near the office though it is normally not used as the one in the corridor itself is the one normally used.

There is no information for when it was Pr Quirrell's office, doubtless he didn't have any people up to visit with Voldemort living in his head. It would seem from Hagrid's comments that Pr Quirrell held the DADA position for a number of years before turning loyalties and subsequently dropping dead. When the office was Pr Lockhart's it contained countless framed photos of himself, all winking and flashing dazzlingly white teeth, unless it was late, in which case they were usually in hairnets or curlers. He had a large shiny desk with candles but no paperwork on it. The walls were also lit with candles that shone brightly, otherwise how would one be able to see his pictures? In the evenings he would answer his fan mail rather than bone up on his DADA skills here. Possibly the office is connected to living quarters as he kept socks in the desk drawer and had his trunk in his office with his robes packed the minute he wanted to flee.

Under Lupin the office took a decidedly scholarly turn. The office had a tea kettle and teabags at the ready for visitors. Assorted Dark creatures lurked in tanks, boxes or desk drawers. And of course there were chipped mugs and a variety of old battered books. Though Lupin's things were all worn and beat-up looking because he was poor, most scholars' offices and homes would look about the same, even if they were very well off. Scholars are simply pack rats who don't care much about cleaning. Others would think him eccentric not poor. With Barty Jr, pretending to be Moody, the office was filled with Dark Detectors and Moody's trunk was kept under the windows where Barty could keep an eye on it. It seems rather odd that no one who visited Moody in his office, like Pr McGonagall or Dumbledore, noticed that their face was in the Foe Glass. Didn't they wonder why "Moody" thought of them as foes? Perhaps not, given he was so paranoid.

When Pr Umbridge took over the office, all the surfaces in the office were draped with lace: doilies, covers or cloths, but she refrained from putting up lace curtains. She set up several vases full of dried flowers around the office, each vase on a doily. A collection of ornamental Technicolor kitten plates was affixed to one wall. Each plate had a large kitten that was able to move about the plate – probably due to photo transfers. Some kittens had electric blue eyes and each wore a different bow on their neck. A luridly flowered tablecloth covered her desk which also usually also had pink parchment and a small box of Floo Powder on it. A small lace-covered table with a straight-backed chair stood beside her desk and served for students doing detentions. A chintz-covered armchair served as her personal chair.

ACASCIAS RIPHOUSE

As she progressed in power a wooden block with gold letters saying "headmistress" all in caps appeared on the desk – because she couldn't get into the Head's office, Gryffindor Tower. At one point she even had Harry, Fred and George's brooms chained and padlocked to a stout iron peg in the wall behind her desk. A new door was put on the office after Fred and George's brooms left. She always seemed to keep the fire going, perhaps so she could spy on people using the Floo Network rather than because she was cold. She left the school rather abruptly after recovering from a centaur attack and is probably in jail or on the run for illicitly sending dementors after Harry. Hopefully the house-elves will pack up for her.

Dumbledore's Office: The entrance to Dumbledore's tower office (Godric's old office) is around a corner on the 2nd floor, behind a large, mute and extremely ugly stone gargoyle. Usually the password is candy related; the passwords: 92/93 Lemon drop; 94/95 Cockroach Cluster; 95/96: Fizzing Whizbee. The password causes the gargoyle to come to life and step aside revealing a blank wall. The wall then splits in two to reveal a moving spiral staircase that appears to be going continuously upward.

The spiral staircase takes one up a dizzying amount of turns, implying it's up a number of floors, and stops at the top of the tower near a gleaming oak door with a brass door knocker in the shape of a griffin. Behind the oak door is a circular room that is large, beautiful and full of odd little noises. There are many interesting sliver instruments here, including a Lunascope. Most stand on spindle-legged tables whirring, clicking, ticking or emitting small puffs of smoke of various colors. Whenever these instruments get broken, they repair themselves, as do the furnishings of the office.

There are curtained windows, one facing West from which the sunset can be seen, and one facing South from which the Quidditch stadium can be seen. A black cabinet is somewhat opposite the desk to the right of the door as one enters. It contains the Pensive, tea making things, an old cauldron and other items. Behind the door is Fawkes' perch. The walls are covered with 12 portraits of old headmasters and headmistresses, all usually sleeping in their frames, or pretending to be sleeping. Phineas Nigellus, Dilys Derwent, Everard (Unknown), the gilmet-eyed witch, and (Unknown) Fortescue all are here and Dumbledore can often be heard conversing with the portraits when alone.

The claw-footed desk is huge and highly polished with a high chair behind it. On the desk stands a silver ink pot and a handsome scarlet quill that is possibly one of Fawkes' shed out ones. Behind the desk on a shelf is Godric's sliver sword in a glass case and next to that is the Sorting Hat. Dumbledore appears to live in the tower as well, as he often seen coming down the marble staircase in his bedclothes, indicating he lives on an upper floor. Though probably he lives in the portion of the tower just below his office.

As a side note it is interesting to reflect on the fact that Moaning Myrtle's bathroom, the entry point for the basilisk, and the entry to Godric Gryffindor's tower are on the same floor. One doubts this all coincidence and one suspects that Salazar Slytherin was at one point the Potions Master and had thoughts of nipping upstairs, releasing the grown basilisk and pointing it toward Godric's office, or the DADA classroom where Godric likely taught, then nipping back downstairs and pleading ignorance to all that went on above him. Though one hastens to add this is all conjecture.

Filch's Office: It appears to be in a windowless room on the ground floor, directly below a classroom. The office is a dingy room lit by a single oil lamp suspended from the low ceiling. It smells faintly of fried fish. Filch keeps large rolls of parchment in his desk drawers so he can fill out reports on each student he catches. He then gives the reports to Dumbledore. See schematic P for a look at the form. A moth-eaten chair sits next to his desk and on the desk are long black quills in a pot and an ink pot. If a student arrives at the right moment, she or he might see a large glossy purple envelope with silver lettering on the front sitting on his desk. This is the Kwikspell course that Filch has been taking since 1992. On the wall behind Filch's desk hang a highly polished and well-oiled collection of chains and manacles and he keeps a horsewhip somewhere.

In the office somewhere are posted the 437 items that are banned from use in hallways or any other place inside Hogwarts castle. No one has actually every gone to his office to look at the list but he adds to it every year. There are wooden filing cabinets lining the walls and each drawer is labeled with the names of pupils. One cabinet is marked Confiscated and Highly Dangerous. This is where the Marauder's Map was found by Fred and George. These cabinets contain details on every student that Filch ever caught and punished. Fred and George, unsurprisingly, managed to get an entire drawer to themselves in under 3 years. He wages constant war against the students however the students seem to be winning rather handily as he is outnumbered 1,000 to 1 (or 1,000 to 2 if one takes Mrs Norris into account).

Flitwick's Office: His office is on the 7th floor, 13th window from the right of the West (Owlery) Tower.

McGonagall's Office: Her office is located on the 1st floor. It is a small room with a large fireplace and usally a fire. The room holds her desk and chair and a couple of chairs in front of the desk. She keeps a tartan-colored tin filled with cookies (Ginger Newts) on her desk and shares them with students who come to her office. Her office door closes automatically and may lock itself as well. The Quidditch Cup is kept on the fireplace mantle where it will be immediately highly visible to any visitor, particularly Pr Snape.

Snape's Office: Going down the narrow stone staircase from the Entrance Hall that leads to dungeons, one finds a door on one side, halfway down the cold passageway. This is the door to Snape's office. There is also a door that opens from the office into the Potions dungeon. His private store cupboard is in one of the corners of the office. In it are the more dangerous or rare magical items he might use for making seriously advanced potions. Bicorn horn and boomslang skin are of few of the items one would find there. Hermione and Barty Jr (Moody) broke into it and stole items for Polyjuice Potion.

His office is quite shadowy due to it being torch-lit, underground and without windows. He keeps the fireplace dark and empty except when making a floo call. The office is noted for its cheerlessness and coldness. Harry and Ron had dinner here once, after the Whomping Willow incident, and were forced to look at walls lined with shelves on which 100s of glass jars, with float slimy revolting bits of animals and plants suspended in various color potions, reside. Behind his desk are a particularly nasty large slimy something suspended in green liquid and a frog in purple liquid. His collection of pickled things in glass jars is ever expanding.

Pr Snape seals his office with a spell no one but a powerful wizard, either Dark or Aurorlike, could break but it doesn't seem to help. It is probable that Pr Snape lives in the dungeon area, but his office is certainly not connected to his quarters or he'd have known Barty Jr (Moody) had broken in. The odd thing about Pr Snape's office is that though it's repeatedly broken into, and he knows ingredients are missing, he never realizes what potion the stolen ingredients are being used to make, despite the fact he's an expert at potions and very few potions could require *both* boomslang skin and bicorn horn.

HOGWARTS, STAFF

The following listings of staff, past and present, are all listed in the biography section for those wishing more information. Obviously, not all current staff members are known as there must be about 50 teachers on staff at any given time.

FORMER STAFF

Dilys Derwent	Former Headmistress
Armando Dippet	Former Headmaster
Everard (Unknown)	Former Headmaster
(Unknown) Fortescue	Former Headmaster
Phineas Nigellus	Former Headmaster
Mr. Ogg	Former Groundskeeper
Apollyon Pringle	Former Caretaker
Pr Kettleburn	Care of Magical Creatures thru 92/93

FORMER DADA TEACHERS

Pr Quirrell	Until Jun 92
Gilderoy Lockhart	92/93
Remus J. Lupin	93/94
Barty Crouch Jr (Moody)	94/95
Dolores Jane Umbridge	95/96
Unknown	96/97
Unknown	97/98

PARTIAL LISTING OF CURRENT STAFF

Pr Binns	History of Magic
Albus Dumbledore	Headmaster
Argus Filch	Caretaker
Professor Flitwick	Charms
Rubeus Hagrid	Keeper of the Keys/ Gamekeeper/ Care of Magical Creatures
Madam Hooch	Flying/Quidditch
Minerva McGonagall	Transfiguration
Irma Pince	Librarian
Poppy Pomfrey	Nurse
Pr Sinistra	Astronomy
Severus Snape	Potions
Pr Sprout	Herbology
Sybill Trelawney	Divination
Firenze	Divination
Unknown teacher	Muggle Studies
Unknown teacher	Ancient Runes
Professor Vector	Arithmancy

What exactly the Keeper of Keys does or has the keys to is unknown. One assumes the front gates but keys is plural.

ANNUAL SORTS

To be Sorted, is to be placed in a House by the Sorting Hat. The Sorting Ceremony is what the procedure is called. The following is information on how the Sorting Hat sorted new students since Sep 1991. Only information that is known is recorded. Given 144 students are inducted each year this can only be considered a very partial list at best.

The 91/92 sort:
Gryffindor: Lavender Brown, Seamus Finnigan, Hermione Granger, Neville Longbottom, Parvati Patil, Harry Potter, Dean Thomas, Ron Weasley
Hufflepuff: Hannah Abbot, Susan Bones, Justin Finch-Fletchley, Ernie Macmillan
Ravenclaw: Terry Boot, Mandy Brocklehurst, Michael Corner, Anthony Goldstein, Padma Patil, Lisa Turpin
Slytherin: Millicent Bulstrode, Vincent Crabbe, Gregory Goyle, Draco Malfoy, Theodore Nott, Pansy Parkinson, Blaise Zabini,
Unknown: Morag MacDougal, (Unknown) Moon, Sally-Anne Perks.

This event was not recorded for 92/93
Gryffindor: Colin Creevey, Ginny Weasley
Ravenclaw: Luna Lovegood

This event was not recorded for 93/94

The 94/95 sort:
Gryffindor: Dennis Creevey, Natalie McDonald
Hufflepuff: Eleanor Branstone, Owen Cauldwell, Laura Madley, Kevin Whitby
Ravenclaw: Stewart Ackerley, Orla Quirke
Slytherin: Malcolm Baddock, Graham Pritchard
Unknown: Emma Dobbs

The 95/96 Sort:
Gryffindor: Euan Abercrombie
Hufflepuff: Rose Zeller

HOUSES

Houses are like a surrogate family for the students. Having a House gives a student instant friends and companions. Students of the same year and House take classes together, sleep in the House dormitory together, eat at the same House table, and spends free time in the same House common room. Each House at Hogwarts has a long and noble history and produced a number of outstanding wizards over the years. The 4 Houses are named after the 4 founders and each House takes only the kind of students its founder would have. Each has a House Ghost, House dormitory, House colors and a House Head.

Gryffindor: Founder: Godric Gryffindor. This House takes only those who are brave and daring, have nerve or practice chivalry. Ghost: Sir Nicholas de Mimsy-Porpington. Location: Gryffindor Tower. Colors: Red with gold lion. Head: Pr McGonagall.
Gryffindor Tower: The tower's entrance is at the end of a corridor on the 7th floor. The Fat Lady guards the entrance which is a circular hole raised a couple of feet off the

ground. The Fat Lady will not swing open unless the proper password is given. Once through the hole, a student arrives in a bright, cheerful, cozy, round common room which is full of countless dilapidated, squashy armchairs. It also has a large fireplace with a threadbare, hole-ridden hearth rug, a noticeboard, an old chest of drawers, some long desks and some rickety old tables and chairs. It is here that students read, do homework, talk or socialize. The room is candlelit rather than torchlit and personal pets wander freely throughout the tower.

Two doors, opposite the fireplace, lead off the common room, each to a stone spiral staircase. One door is to the girls' dorm, the other to the boys' dorm. Up at the very top of the boys' spiral stone staircase is the 7th floor of the tower (15 floors up from the grass in total) and the door to circular room Harry, Ron, Neville, Dean, and Seamus share every year. See schematic Q for details of the room. The door originally had a plaque that read First Years on it in 91/92, but it changed to Second Years in 92/92 and presumably has changed every year after.

Harry's room has 5 four-poster beds hung with deep red velvet curtains and canopies. There is space under the bed rather than drawers, which would be more helpful. Their trunks are placed at the end of their beds where they remain all year and serve as a sort of spare storage area. Beside each bed is a bedcabinet where school supplies, robes, etc are kept. They also have bedstands, where Harry puts his glasses each night, and which have jugs of water and goblets on them. There is an additional stand with a silver jug of water and silver goblets by another window in the room as well.

Harry's bed is near a high narrow window and light is always falling on it. He can see Ron's face from his bed as well as Neville's. His Hungarian Horntail figurine camps out on his nightstand (imagine grabbing that rather then one's glasses in the morning!). There is a window by Neville's bed and from Harry's window in the room one can see the Forbidden Forest and the Whomping Willow so it must face North-Northeast. One assumes Neville keeps his frog somewhere in the room. Seamus and Dean don't seem to have pets they bring, but they may have owls. All the boys wear pajamas, dressing gowns and slippers, while the girls wear nightgowns or nightdresses, dressing gowns and slippers.

One presumes Hermione Granger, Lavender Brown, and Parvati Patil, are roommates, as they are all 1st year girls, and perhaps others from the unknown list for their year as well. One also presumes their rooms are set up similar to the boys, but they may not be. The girls' dorm has a special feature, the boys' doesn't. If an univited boy get to the 6th step of the girls' dorm staircase, it sets off an alarm, a long loud Klaxon-type wail. The steps shift into a giant slide and the offending party is sent back to the common room, chastened but unharmed. There is no protective device for the boys' dorm and girls may enter it if they will, as Hermione did one Christmas morning. It would seem that while the founders were willing to protect the girls, they were only willing to protect the girls that wanted protection. This says something about Godric Gryffindor, who created the tower, and it isn't very chivalrous.

Given that 35 students join each House each year, this would mean, at 5 students a room, 7 dorm rooms are needed for each year within a house. For the entire 250 students of the House approximately 50 rooms would be needed. Presumably 25 of the rooms are for girls and 25 are for the boys, but there's no guarantee that each year will be exactly split in half by gender even if the school strives for this. Probably an expanding charm is used on the tower to create the needed space. Bathrooms, separated for boys and girls, are likely in the lower part of the tower, or dungeons of the tower, and accessible by unknown means.

THE HARRY POTTER COMPANION

Passwords: In 91/92: Caput Draconis, pig snout. In 92/93 wattlebird. In 93/94 Fortuna Major, and later many different ones, including scurvy cur, oddsbodikins, flibbertigibbet. In 94/95 balderdash, fairy lights, banana fritters. In 95/96 Mimbulus mimbletonia.

Noticeboards: These are in every House common room for students of that House, as well as by the door of most Houses for other students of other houses to put notes on. The outer noticeboard of Gryffindor Tower is on a wall next to the Fat Lady. Slytherin House has no outer noticeboard as they prefer not to associate with Mudbloods. On Gryffindor's common room board there are notices about trading cards, various educational decrees, used books for sale, club meeting dates, dates of Hogsmeade weekends, lost and found items and so forth.

Students Who Have Been or Are In Gryffindor:
See Note 1 at the end of this section.
Euan Abercrombie
Katie Bell
Lavender Brown
Colin Creevey
Dennis Creevey
Seamus Finnigan
Hermione Granger
Angelina Johnson
Lee Jordan
Neville Longbottom
Natalie MacDonald
Parvati Patil
Harry Potter
James Potter
Alicia Spinnet
Dean Thomas
Arthur Weasley
Bill Weasley
Charlie Weasley
Fred Weasley
George Weasley
Ginny Weasley
Molly Weasley
Percy Weasley
Ron Weasley
Oliver Wood

Slytherin: Founder: Salazar Slytherin. This House takes the cunning, the ambitious and purebloods (though Voldemort was a notable exception). Ghost: The Bloody Baron. Location: Under the dungeons. Colors: Green with silver snake. Head: Pr Snape.

It has been said that there was not a single witch or wizard that went bad that wasn't in Slytherin, including Voldemort. Although Slytherin has wizards that went bad, so surely do other Houses. After all, people also believe all Parselmouths are bad and Harry isn't. This statement about Slytherins, if it were true, would mean that Barty Crouch Jr, Sirius Black (who was suspected of being bad for 15 years) would both have been Slytherins. While it is true they were both purebloods, and probably Slytherins as well, Peter Pettigrew who also went bad, but was never suspected of it, seems to have been a Hufflepuff (working 5 years to become an Animagus) if ever there was one, despite his loyalty issues.

Slytherin Dungeon: Using the entrance to the dungeons, go down the stone steps, through the labyrinth of passages, deep under the school, past a side room and down into a passageway where there is just stretch of bare, damp, stone wall. The wall is the entrance. The common room is a long low room much like a snake's lair. It has walls of rough stone walls and round greenish lamps that hang from the ceiling on chains. An elaborately carved hearth fireplace surrounded by rather severe high-backed chairs round out the room. There is usually a fire going in the hearth, which makes sense as reptiles like to bask in heat.

Password: In 92/93 Pure blood. This is the only one known.

Students Who Have Been or Are In Slytherin:
See Note 1 at the end of this section.
(Unknown) Avery
Malcolm Baddock
Miles Bletchley
(Unknown) Bole
Millicent Bulstrode
Vincent Crabbe
(Unknown) Derrick
Marcus Flint
Gregory Goyle
Daphne Greengrass
Terence Higgs
Rodolphus Lestrange
Draco Malfoy
Lucius Malfoy
(Unknown) Montague
Theodore Nott
Pansy Parkinson
Graham Pritchard
Adrian Pucey
Evan Rosier
Tom Riddle/Lord Voldemort
Severus Snape
C. Warrington
(Unknown) Wilkes
Blaise Zabini

Ravenclaw: Founder Rowena Ravenclaw. This House takes the wise, those with a ready mind or love of learning. Ghost: tall lady? Location: Ravenclaw Tower. Colors: Blue with copper eagle. Head: Pr Flitwick.

Ravenclaw Tower: All that is known is that they have a tower on the West side of the castle for their House.

Students Who Have Been or Are In Ravenclaw:
See Note 1 at the end of this section.
Stewart Ackerley
Terry Boot
(Unknown) Bradley
Mandy Brocklehurst
(Unknown) Chambers

THE HARRY POTTER COMPANION

Cho Chang
Penelope Clearwater
Michael Corner
Roger Davies
Marietta Edgecombe
S. Fawcett
Anthony Goldstein
Luna Lovegood
Lisa Turpin
Padma Patil
Orla Quirke

Hufflepuff: Founder: Helga Hufflepuff. This House takes the just and loyal, the patient and true or those unafraid of toil. Ghost: The Fat Friar. Location: underground, opposite the kitchens. Colors: Yellow with black badger. Head: Pr Sprout.

Hufflepuff House: Coming down the marble stairs, turn left. They use the same broad, well-lit basement corridor that goes to the kitchens. The door to Hufflepuff House is opposite a picture of the fruitbowl that is somewhere near the entry to the kitchens. Nothing more is known. It would seem to be underground, and, given badgers (the House symbol) live in burrows underground, it would make sense. The House is probably not as deep underground as Slytherin.

Students Who Have Been or Are In Hufflepuff:
See Note 1 at the end of this section.
Hannah Abbott
Susan Bones
Eleanor Branstone
Owen Cauldwell
Cedric Diggory
Justin Finch-Fletchley
Ernie Macmillan
Laura Madley
Zacharias Smith
(Unknown) Stebbins
(Unknown) Summers
(Unknown) Summerby
Kevin Whitby
Rose Zeller

HOUSE GOVERNMENT

The school Houses have a hierarchy through which the students are governed. The Head of House is the top, followed by Head Boy and Head Girl. The 2 student Heads are over the 24 Prefects.

Head of House: The Head of a House has the right to expel any student in his or her House, but not any student of another House. Heads, like other teachers, can deduct points from and give detentions to a student of another House. The Head of House (like the MoM itself) does not have the right to expel students or confiscate the wands of students not proven guilty of a crime (Hagrid being a notable exception to both rules).

Head Girl and Head Boy: A student is chosen to be a Head Girl or Head Boy in their 7th year only. These 2 students are in charge of the Prefects and oversee them as well as the other students. It is possible to be made a Head without ever being a Prefect though that is unusual. James Potter became Head Boy without being a Prefect. Former Head Boys include Percy Weasley and Tom Riddle. Former Head Girls include Lily Evans.

Prefects: Each House has 6 Prefects (2 in 5th year, 2 in 6th year, and 2 in 7th year) for a school total of 24. Prefects (12 girls and 12 boys). Students can only be made a Prefect in their 5th year. If it doesn't happen then, it won't happen later unless some extraordinary circumstance like the death (Cedric), incapacitation, expulsion, or elevation (to Head Girl or Head Boy) of a Prefect takes place. Once students becomes a Prefect, they stay Prefects till graduating. Prefects may become Head Girl or Head Boy, but this is not always the case.

Prefects are to assist the Head Girl and Head Boy and any teachers who request their help. They get instructions from the Head Girl and Head Boy on the Hogwarts Express then patrol the train during the journey. Around the school they enforce the rules and can take points if they feel it's necessary, but only from their own House's students. Prefects are supposed to help younger students get their bearings, assist teachers with things like patrolling halls with Filch, decorating for Christmas and watching over 2nd years when they are kept in on breaks. Prefect can get sometimes get clubby and tend to sit only with other Prefects at meals.

From at least 1942 to 1995 all Prefect badges were silver. In the 95/96 school year badges became a version of the banner of the House the Prefect represented. Ron's badge was gold with a lion on it. One assumes Slytherin's were green with a silver snake, Ravenclaws blue with a copper eagle and Hufflepuffs yellow with a black badger, but this is never said. New Prefects in 95/96: Hermione and Ron, Draco and Pansy, Ernie and Hannah, Anthony and Padma. Former Prefects include Bill and Percy Weasley, Tom Riddle, Remus Lupin and probably Lily Evans.

POINTS

In the realm of punishments any teacher may give points to or take points from any student of any House. A Prefect may not award points to any student but they may dock points from students of their own House. Points are given for shows of excellence, heroism, intelligence or other similar virtues by students. Points are taken for infractions or large breaches of school rules. At most a teacher will take or give 50 points. Most awards are 5-10 points. It is interesting to note that Pr Snape is the only person ever to take just 1 point, which is exceedingly kind and from him most unexpectedly so. Dumbledore is the only one ever to award more than 50 points (usually 60-200) at a clip.

The points are stored in 4 House hourglasses located in niches in the wall at the top of the marble staircase so that students can see them as they go down to their meals in the Great Hall. Immediately as points are deducted, stones magically fly up. As soon as they are added, they magically they fly down. Apparently the castle hears everyone speaking and adjusts totals according to what it hears. Each House has an hourglass filled with gems in that reflect a House color. Ruby: Gryffindor; Emerald: Slytherin; Sapphire: Ravenclaw; Yellow Diamond (possibly): Hufflepuff.

The following is a list of what students lost or gained points for their house, why, how many points and who awarded or deducted the points.

The Harry Potter Companion

Points 91/92:
+??, Hermione, for knowing about Switching Spells, McGonagall
-1, Harry,
for cheek, Snape
-1, Harry,
for not helping Neville, Snape
-5, Ron,
 for fighting with Draco, Snape
-5, Hermione,
for taking on a full-grown mountain troll, McGonagall
+5, Harry,
for knocking out a troll as a 1st year, McGonagall
+5, Ron,
for knocking out a troll as a 1st year, McGonagall
- 5, Harry,
for taking *Quidditch Through the Ages* outside, Snape
- 5, Ron,
for grabbing Draco, Snape
-20, Draco,
 for wandering around castle at night, McGonagall
-50, Neville,
for wandering around castle at night, McGonagall
-50, Harry,
for wandering around castle at night, McGonagall
-50, Hermione,
for wandering around castle at night, McGonagall
+50, Ron,
for great chess playing, Dumbledore
+50, Hermione,
for cool logic in the face of fire, Dumbledore
+60, Harry,
for pure nerve and outstanding courage, Dumbledore
+10, Neville,
for courage, Dumbledore

Points 92/93:
+10, Hermione,
 for knowing the uses of mandrake, Sprout
+10, Hermione,
for knowing the dangers or mandrakes, Sprout
+10, Hermione,
for knowing Lockhart's secret ambition, Lockhart
-5, Ron,
for mouthing off, Percy
+50, Harry,
 ? for flying?, ?? Percy mentions
+200, Ron,
for the defeat of basilisk, Dumbledore, he also was given a Special Award for Service to the school
+200, Harry,

130

for the defeat of basilisk, Dumbledore, he also was given a Special Award for Service to the school

Points 93/94:
- 5, Hermione,
for helping Neville, Snape
+10, Neville,
for defeating the boggart twice, Lupin
+5, Parvati,
for defeating the boggart, Lupin
+5, Seamus,
for defeating the boggart, Lupin
+5, Lavender,
for defeating the boggart, Lupin
+5, Dean,
for defeating the boggart, Lupin
+5 Ron,
for defeating the boggart, Lupin
+5, Harry,
for answering a boggart question, Lupin
+5, Hermione,
for answering a boggart question, Lupin
-10, Harry,
for being late to DADA, Snape
-5, Harry,
for not sitting down in DADA, Snape
-5, Hermione,
for being an insufferable know it all, Snape
-50, Ron,
for throwing crocodile heart at Draco, Snape
-50, Slytherin (Marcus, Draco, Crabbe, Goyle)
for pretending to be dementors, McGonagall

Points 94/95:
-50, Gryffindor (Harry and Ron),
for fighting with Draco, Snape
-10, S. Fawcett,
for being in the bushes at the Yule Ball, Snape
-10, Mr Stebbins,
for being in the bushes at the Yule Ball, Snape
-10, Hermione,
for discussing her social life in class, Snape
-10, Harry,
for reading magazines in class, Snape

Points 95/96:
-10, Harry,
for talking about Voldemort, Umbridge
+10, Hermione,
for vanishing her snail, McGonagall.
+5, Hermione,
for knowing what a bowtruckle is, Grubbly-Plank
+5, Hermione,

for knowing what wood lice are, Grubbly-Plank
-5, Hermione,
for disrupting class with questions, Umbridge
-5, Angelina,
for shouting in the Great Hall, McGonagall
-5, Harry,
for not keeping his temper around Umbridge, McGonagall
-10, Harry,
for fighting, Snape
+10, Hermione,
for knowing about thestrals, Hagrid
-50, Harry,
for *The Quibbler* interview, Umbridge
+20, Harry,
for passing a watering can, Sprout
- 5, Hermione,
for rude comments, Draco
- 5, Ernie,
for contradicting, Draco
- 5, Harry,
 for being alive, Draco
- 5, Ron,
for not having his shirt tucked in, Draco
-10, Hermione,
for being a Mudblood, Draco
-10, Harry,
for trying to curse Draco, Snape
+50, Harry,
for alerting the world to Voldemort, McGonagall
+50, Ginny,
for alerting the world to Voldemort, McGonagall
+50, Ron,
for alerting the world to Voldemort, McGonagall
+50, Hermione,
for alerting the world to Voldemort, McGonagall
+50, Luna,
for alerting the world to Voldemort, McGonagall
+50, Neville,
for alerting the world to Voldemort, McGonagall

DETENTIONS

Any teacher or other staff member may give detentions to any student of any House. Prefects may not give detentions to anyone but in very extreme cases a Prefect (or a teacher) may speak to an offending student's Head of House. Detentions are reserved for the very worst offenses when either point taking has been ineffective or the rule breaking was so egregious only a detention will serve. Magical punishments, as well as physical punishments, are never used and strictly forbidden.

    The following is a list of detentions, which includes the name of the student, why the detention was given, who awarded it and, if known, what the detention involved.

Detentions 91/92:
Harry, Hermione, Neville and Draco,
for wandering around castle at night, McGonagall
Finding the wounded unicorn in the Forbidden Forest with Hagrid and Fang was the detention.

Detentions 92/93:
Harry,
for the slug incident, McGonagall
Assisting Lockhart, with fan mail was the detention.
Ron,
slug incident, McGonagall
Polishing silver in the Trophy Room with Filch was the detention.

Detentions 93/94:
Ron,
for criticizing the way he teaches DADA, Snape
Cleaning hospital bedpans without magic was the detention.
Marcus, Draco, Goyle, Crabbe,
for pretending to be a dementor, McGonagall
Neville,
for letting Sirius get his passwords, McGonagall
Not being allowed to know the passwords and having to stand outside and wait for someone to come or go from the common room to get in or out was the detention.

Detentions 94/95:
Neville,
for melting his 6th cauldron in Potions, Snape
He had to disembowel a barrel full of horned toads for the detention.
Harry,
for fighting with Draco, Snape
He had to pickle rat brains for 2 hours for the detention.
Ron,
for yelling, Snape
He had to pickle rat brains for 2 hours for the detention.

Detentions 95/96:
Harry,
for insisting Voldemort's alive, Umbridge
He had to do lines with the Dark magic quill for 1 week for the detention.
Harry,
for saying Quirrell had Voldemort in his head, Umbridge
He had to do lines with the Dark magic quill for 1 week for the detention.
Harry,
for saying Draco was stupid, Umbridge
He had to do lines with the Dark magic quill for 1 night for the detention.
Harry,
for punching Draco, 1 week, McGonagall
It was changed to a lifetime Quidditch ban by Umbridge.
Fred and George,
for punching Draco, 1 week, McGonagall
It was changed to a lifetime Quidditch ban by Umbridge.
Crabbe,
for hitting a Bludger after the game, Umbridge

He had to do lines, possibly with the Dark magic quill, for 1 week for the detention.
Lee Jordan,
for pointing up a flaw in Educational Decree 26, Umbridge
He had to do lines with the Dark magic quill for the detention.
Harry,
for doing *The Quibbler* interview, Umbridge
He had to do lines with the Dark magic quill for detention.
4 Entire DADA classes,
for Umbridge-itis, Umbridge
Pr Umbridge gave up trying on this matter.

THE HOUSE CUP

The Inter-House Championship winner receives the House Cup. Over the years students have just come to call it the House Cup or the House Championship. Points won in Quidditch matches are also applied toward existing House Cup totals which may have been earned in other ways. This is why the winner of the Quidditch Cup also usually wins the House Championship. In some years there is no record of a House Cup being awarded, that is not to say it wasn't, simply that there is no record or reference to it so it can't be said with certainty who won, though one always presume Gryffindor.

1992:
Gryffindor: 482. They won the House Cup.
Hufflepuff: 352
Ravenclaw: 426
Slytherin: 472
1993: Gryffindor wins the House Cup.
1994: Gryffindor wins the House Cup.
1995: The House Cup was not awarded due to Cedric's death in the TT.
1996: There was no record of a House Cup awarded this year.

CLUBS

There are numerous clubs, also called societies, for students who want to get together with others who share like interests. These are some known ones, but with 1,000 students there are doubtless many more.

Charms Club: Students get together and practice or learn about Charms here. Vicky Frobisher is a member of this club and very passionate about it.
Dueling Club: Headed by Pr Lockhart with Pr Snape assisting, this club met between Dec 1992 and May 1993 in the Great Hall at 8pm on Thursdays. The High Table and House tables were removed and a golden stage lit by 1,000s of candles floating in midair was set up along one wall to serve as Pr Lockhart's teaching venue. Given a sharp increase in fear for personal safety due to basilisk attacks, most of the school attended this club for the duration it was run.

In a proper duel, wands are raised like swords, swung overhead then down, with each person casting a deadly spell at their opponent, but the club aimed for teaching students to disarm each other using only their wands. It was in a meeting of this club that Harry, along with the rest of the school, discovered that he was a Parselmouth.

Some of the known attendees were Harry, Ron, Hermione, Seamus, Dean, Lavender, Neville, Justin, S. Fawcett, Ernie, Terry, Draco, and Millicent.

Dumbledore's Army: aka the DA. Formed in Oct 1995 it's unknown if the club will continue now that there is no reason to hide it. In this club, Harry secretly taught a group of students DADA techniques and allowed them to get practical experience by using them on each other. The club was kept secret initially because of Pr Umbridge's unwillingness to let students practice real magic. Everyone who joined the had to sign, unwittingly, a jinxed parchment that Hermione created so that if any signatory ratted out the club, a jinx activated which, with purple pustules, spelled sneak in capital letters across the offender's face.

Signatory members of the DA include:

Gryffindors
2nd year Dennis,
4th years Colin and Ginny,
5th years Ron, Hermione, Neville, Dean, Lavender and Parvati, and
7th years Katie, Alicia, Angelina, Fred, George and Lee.

Ravenclaws
4th year Luna,
5th years Padma, Anthony, Michael and Terry Boot, and
6th years Cho and Marietta

Hufflepuffs
5th years Ernie, Justin, Hannah and Susan, and
6th year Zacharias.

In alphabetical order: Hannah Abbott, Lavender Brown, Katie Bell, Susan Bones, Terry Boot, Cho Chang, Michael Corner, Colin Creevey, Dennis Creevey, Marietta Edgecombe, Justin Finch-Fletchley, Seamus Finnegan, Anthony Goldstein, Hermione Granger, Angelina Johnson, Lee Jordan, Neville Longbottom, Luna Lovegood, Ernie Macmillan, Padma Patil, Parvati Patil, Harry Potter, Zacharias Smith, Alicia Spinnet, Dean Thomas, Fred Weasley, George Weasley, Ginny Weasley, and Ron Weasley.

No Slytherins were invited to attend the club and were not made aware of its existence primarily due to the fact that the Slytherins were 100% behind Pr Umbridge and her ridiculous ideas but also because no member of the other 3 attending Houses had any friends who were Slytherins. Slytherins don't usually befriend non-Slytherins and rarely make trustworthy friends even when they do.

Gobstones Club: People in this club meet to play Gobstones. This is a popular sport and many wizards form local community leagues. The MoM has an office entirely devoted to looking after Gobstones Club members. Gobstones seem to come in 2 forms, 1 small like marbles and the other large like lawn bowling. Either can be played at Hogwarts. Most often students seem to play the smaller version in their common rooms, which results in much offensive odor and mess.

SPEW: aka The Society for the Promotion of Elf Welfare. Ron is SPEW's reluctant Treasurer, Harry is SPEW's reluctant Secretary and Hermione is SPEW's very vocal and proactive President and fundraiser. SPEW supporter badges come in a variety of colors and are 2S each. Harry and Ron bought badges but never wear them. Hagrid absolutely refused to join. Dumbledore hasn't joined but seems to believe in the rightness of Hermione's ideals, if not the practical execution of them.

Hermione is always trying to persuade others to join the cause and collects money in the House common room by rather aggressively shaking a tin at fellow students. Neville contributed to get rid of Hermione, but isn't really a supporter of the movement. It remains to be seen if anyone else will join. SPEW's manifesto is to stop the abuse of magical creatures, mainly house-elves, by wizards and to encourage wizards to lobby for a change in house-elves' legal status. SPEW would like to see house-elves recieve fair wages and better working conditions in the short-term and laws about wand use changed in the long-term. SPEW would also like to see an elf working in the DRCMC, as something other than a slave, because they are underrepresented there.

Hermione would like to take SPEW to the next level as a career goal. This may be in direct conflict with the house-elves' aims of remaining employed and unnoticed. Most of the house-elves at Hogwarts are offended by Hermione and her aims and have banned her, politely, from the Kitchens, while refusing to clean Gryffindor Tower in protest. Hermione remains in the dark about her behavior offending the elves, but one doubts that she would or could be deterred from attempting to help them anyway. Only Dumbledore really seems to see the point of SPEW, which in itself lends substantial weight to the cause.

CAREER ADVICE

Advice is given to 5th years during their 3rd term, to discuss various career options and what NEWT studies will need to be pursued in order to attain that career. Students (usually) meet privately with the Head of their House to discuss their intentions. Harry and Ron want to be Aurors. Hermione wants to do something worthwhile, like advance SPEW to the next level. A few examples of wizarding career paths follow.

Healer: One needs E level NEWTs in Potions, Herbology, Transfiguration, Charms and DADA.
Muggle Relations: An OWL in Muggle Studies will do. Which either says something about Arthur's abilities as a student or his passion for Muggles, probably the latter.
Banking: Requires Arithmancy, DADA and Charms NEWTs, among other things. Gringotts is looking mainly for Curse Breakers, who need love of adventure and travel among other more magical skills.
Security Troll Trainer: Unknown requirements, but a NEWT in Care of Magical Creatures couldn't hurt.
Auror: This post requires top grades and E level NEWTs in a minimum of 5 subjects. DADA, Transfiguration, Charms and Potions are required NEWTs. The other NEWT is up to the student.
DMAC: They are looking for help but the requirements are unknown. Probably a NEWT in charms, with especially good marks in Memory Charms, and the ability to lie under pressure make a positive impression.
Cultivated Fungus Trade: Unknown requirements, but they are looking for help. One assumes a NEWT in Herbology and a love of dark places would be a plus.

CLASSES

The following section provides information on classes taught at Hogwarts, including where they are located, who teaches them and what is taught in them. The listing is alphabetical with elective classes interspersed with required core classes.

Ancient Runes: A 3rd year elective. The teacher and location for this class are unknown. Hermione chose this elective. Reading Runes was a practice of Germanic peoples from the 3rd to the 13th centuries AD. It involves making interpretations based on throwing small stones carved with Rune letters that can mean a variety of things depending on the situation one is enquiring about. This coursework was probably started at Hogwarts by Helga Hufflepuff.

Based on the interpretation words, the language being used for this class is Gothic. The 24 Runes being used would therefore be Algiz, Ansuz, Berkano, Dagaz, Eihwaz, Ehwaz, Fehu, Gebo, Hagalaz, Ingwaz, Isa, Jera, Kenaz, Laguz, Mannaz, Nauthiz, Othala, Perthro, Raidho, Sowilo, Thurisaz, Tiwaz, Uruz and Wunjo.

Ehwaz: Means interpretively partnership according to Hermione. Most people feel it interpretively means growth, change, movement, that sort of thing. The word translated literally is horse. This Rune looks like the capital M. It was on Hermione's OWL in Ancient Runes. She got it mixed up with eihwaz. Probably the only thing she got wrong on all the OWLs, so not much to worry about.

Eihwaz: Means interpretively defense, among many other things. The word translated literally means tree, or yew. This Rune looks like a backwards Z. Let's hope Hermione didn't throw this stone herself, otherwise it would appear Voldemort (and his yew wand) may feature heavily in her future.

Arithmancy: A 3rd year elective. The teacher is Pr Vector. The location is unknown. Hermione chose this elective and thinks it's very sensible. It involves using numbers and numerical calculations to understand or predict things. This coursework was probably started at Hogwarts by Rowena Ravenclaw.

Astronomy: A core course for years 1-5. The teacher is Pr Sinistra. The location is the Astronomy Tower. This class involves learning about the planets and stars and their movements. This coursework was probably started at Hogwarts by Salazar Slytherin as astronomy is important to many magical practices, particularly potions, which involve certain planets being in certain positions when ingredients are gathered. For instance the phase of the moon effects Fluxweed. Pick Fluxweed at the wrong time and it can't be used for Polyjuice Potion. Muggles are just beginning to rediscover the use of astronomy in caring for plants, it's called Biodynamics.

Jupiter seems to be a major focal point in wizarding astronomy. Harry is almost always learning about it or its moons, every single year. Astronomy's written OWL involved naming all of Jupiter's moons. The OWL practical was filling out a starchart, no doubt including the moons of Jupiter. So perhaps the focus on Jupiter was entirely justified after all. But as of yet no actual mention of why Jupiter is so important has cropped up. Mars, bringer of war, has cropped up, but not Jupiter.

Care of Magical Creatures: A 3rd year elective. This coursework was probably started at Hogwarts by Salazar Slytherin, who was so good with basilisks. It has been taught by Hagrid since 93/94, and occasionally Pr Grubbly-Plank fills in. The location is near to Hagrid's cabin or in the Forbidden Forest. Newt Scamander's *Fantastic Beasts and Where to Find Them* is a supplemental text for this class but *The Monster Book of Monster* is the main text, which says a lot about the direction the class is headed. Harry, Ron and Hermione all take it, as do Crabbe, Goyle and Draco. Someone opting to pursue this class to the NEWT level might end up a dragon researcher like Charlie Weasley or working in the Pest Advisory Bureau at the MoM.

The class features many magical creatures, from the completely harmless to the positively deadly. Creatures that might be covered in this course in the 3rd year are hippogriffs, flobberworms and salamanders. By the OWL year, bowtruckles, porlocks, kneazles, crups, knarls, nifflers and unicorns would be covered. Although centaurs and merpeople have chosen to be classed as Beasts, they are never studied in Care of Magical Creatures as it would be highly offensive to them and highly dangerous to the students.

Charms: A core class for years 1-5. This coursework was probably started at Hogwarts by Helga Hufflepuff. It is taught by Pr Flitwick in a classroom on the 3rd floor in the Charms corridor. At the end of the Charms corridor there is a door which lets one into the usually always empty for some reason right-hand side of the corridor. It was guarded by Fluffy in 91/92 when it was the entrance to the passageway to the Sorcerer's Stone.

Charms class usually begins with Pr Flitwick taking of the role. Summoning Charms, Cheering Charms, and Silencing Charms are all things a student would learn in this class. Although it is said that charms don't last as long as spells, charms are serious magic and can be every bit as dangerous as spells. Experimental charms can get a wizard jailed if not killed.

Defense Against the Dark Arts: A very important core class for years 1-5, especially now Voldemort is active again. This coursework was probably started at Hogwarts by Godric Gryffindor. It was taught by Pr Quirrell through 91/92; Pr Gilderoy Lockhart in 92/93, Pr Remus J. Lupin in 93/94, Pr Barty Crouch Jr (posing as Alastor "Mad-Eye" Moody) in 94/95, and Pr Dolores Jane Umbridge 95/96. It has for some time been considered a jinxed job and Dumbledore has to take whoever is willing to take it just to fill it. The DADA classroom is located on the 2nd floor. It has glass windows running along the back wall, a chandelier for winter lighting and the usual wastebasket and chalkboard.

Under Pr Quirrell, the classroom smelled of garlic, but students did learn DADA. Under Pr Lockhart, it was severely vandalized by Cornish pixies and no one actually learned anything. Under Pr Lupin the class became practical and students were finally given their first practical lessons. He covered boggarts, red caps, kappas, grindylows, hinkypunks, werewolves and vampires. Under Barty Jr (Moody), a very talented Dark wizard in his own right, 4th years got an introduction to and training in defending themselves against Unforgivable Curses when normally 6th years would only be allowed to see what an illegal Dark curse look like.

Under Umbridge, the DADA class once again took a giant step backward. She assigned her students to reading about theories of DADA, with emphasis on non-magical non-violent defense, and never allowed them to do any practical magic or even have their wands out in class. This was in line with MoM policy on DADA instruction at the time but ridiculous all the same. It was at this point Hermione and Ron suggested to Harry that he start a club for DADA, which he did. The group subsequently became Dumbledore's Army. Dumbledore strangely enough has never stepped in to teach DADA himself, which he could, not even to save the school from MoM control.

Divination: A 3rd year elective. This coursework has only been taught at Hogwarts since Jan 1980 when Sybill was hired. It is usually taught by Sybill Trelawney in the North Tower. The entrance is found by going up a 6th floor spiral staircase, with a picture of a group of women in crinoline dresses at the bottom and a group of sinister looking monks at the top, to the 7th floor and the circular trapdoor in the ceiling with a brass plaque that reads: Sybill Trelawney, Divination teacher. The classroom is reached by climbing up a silver ladder, let down at class times, through the circular trapdoor.

Pr Trelawney sits in a tall wingback chair, usually with a miniature model of the solar system in a glass dome under it. The model has 9 planets and a fiery sun all hanging in thin air inside it and they move to show where every plante is currently; it's for astrological purposes. She always sits near the fireplace, which gives off a heavy perfume smell and her classroom is generally hot and stuffy. She keeps all the windows closed with the curtains drawn and has red scarves thrown over the lamps which gives the classroom an odd pink glow.

In addition to the poor lighting, suffocating warmth and the heavy, sickly, sort of perfume smell, the small circular room is filled with fat overstuffed little poufs, 20 or so small circular, very spindly, tables and chintz armchairs. The mantel is crowded with loads of divination-related junk and there are shelves running around the walls of the room which have dusty looking feathers, stubs of candles, packs of tattered playing cards, dream analysis books, countless silvery crystal balls and a vast array of blue and pink teacups on them.

Hermione took Divination for a while in her 3rd year but dropped it two-thirds of the way through the 1st year because she thought it was just ridiculous twaddle. Harry and Ron stayed with it till OWLs but have decided not to continue Divination studies at the NEWT level. Dean, Neville and Seamus, who were also in it, don't think much of it either. Only Lavender and Parvati seem to actually like the class and Sybill, though Parvati's interest in Firenze is probably all that will keep her taking NEWT level Divination studies.

Divination is only possible to those who have a Gift already according to Pr Trelawney, which makes the class itself of little or no use. First year divination might include tea leaves and crystal ball reading, 2nd year divination astrology and 3rd year divination dream interpretation. Harry and Ron make up most of their homework, but Sybill doesn't seem to notice. No one, including Dumbledore, believes in divination or has any real respect for it. Pr McGonagall goes out of her way to ridicule it to every 3rd year class at the start of term. Only the centaurs seem remotely good at divination.

During 95/96 Pr Firenze, a centaur, took over the Divination class in midyear. He claims the wisdom of centaurs is impartial and impersonal and that they watch the skies only for massive changes in world events, not personal fortune. It can take almost a decade for centaurs to be sure of what they are seeing and even then Firenze advises one shouldn't put too much faith in the final interpretation as centaurs are sometimes mistaken. Centaurs divine by the burning herbs (sage and mallow) and observing the shapes of the fumes and flames. It takes many, many years to learn to read the signs and one doubts anyone will be in school long enough to pick up on centaur divination techniques.

Centaurs do seem to know what they're doing when it comes to divination. The centaurs knew that the calm years after 1981 didn't mean the war with Voldemort was finished for good, as many wizards thought. However, centaurs believe that Harry is doomed to die and Voldemort destined to win out in the end. This is made worse by the fact centaurs feel obliged to do nothing to change the outcome they see in the stars because they take a vow not to interfere with events they perceive. Firenze is a more forward-looking centaur and will do anything he has to keep Voldemort from winning the coming battle, including letting Harry ride on his back and teaching centaur divination to humans.

Flying and Quidditch: This seems to be a 1st and 2nd year course taught by Madam Hooch. Since Quidditch was only invented in the 1100's and flying a broomstick in the late 900s, one doubts the coursework Madam Hooch teaches was originally part of the founders' curriculum. If flying was taught, it was likely done by Godric Gryffindor. Flying nowadays is taught on a smooth flat lawn on the grounds, rather than the Quidditch pitch. The school has brooms students learn to fly on. First years are forbidden to bring brooms to school, so without the school brooms, they can't learn to fly. School brooms do have a few problems though. They vibrate if a student flies too high, which may be partially why Neville fell off, or they always fly slightly to the left, as if they are out of alignment.

Year 1 seems to be basic flying techniques. Year 2 is probably devoted to refining students flying skills and improving their Quidditch skills. Most students from wizarding families seem to grow up riding a broom from the time they are infants. So by year 2 there's very little left to learn. Since second year students can be on the House Quidditch teams, indicating most 2nd year students are flying at an advanced level, there's not much point in pursing further lessons. By year 3 flying falls off Harry's schedule and it doesn't seem he's excused from class because he plays on a House team.

Herbology: A core class for years 1-5. Pr Sprout teaches this class in the greenhouses behind the castle. The coursework was probably originally taught at Hogwarts by Salazar Slytherin. In this class students learn how to care for and use all manner of magical plants and fungi. This all-practical class is generally physical work such are repotting, fertilizing or pruning. Students in the 3rd year and up usually work in Greenhouse 3 where the more exotic and dangerous plants are, such as Abyssinian shrivelfigs, mandrakes, and venomous tentaculas. Pr Sprout has good control over her plants, but she keeps the greenhouses locked all the same.

Pr Sprout is an environmentalist and uses natural dragon dung fertilizer, keeps a compost bin in each of her greenhouses and teachers her all her classes to compost. She doesn't even mind taking a beating to care for a rare plant, such as the Whomping Willow. Herbology is the one class that Neville really excels at and Pr Sprout even compliments Neville's work in her class to other teachers. Neville's love of herbology extends to owning rare plants that even the greenhouses at Hogwarts don't have, like Mimbulus mimbletonia.

History of Magic: A core class for years 1-5. The coursework was probably started at Hogwarts by Godric Gryffindor since all knights if they were worth their salt knew many ancient histories and lore as well as how to fight. Taught today by Pr Binns, the only ghost teaching at Hogwarts, History of Magic takes place on the 1st floor in the very largest classroom of the school. It is the most boring class of all and only Hermione is able to stay awake during it to take notes. The most exciting thing that ever happens is Pr Binns drifting through the chalkboard at the beginning and end of class.

Here students learn about such things as the 1637 Werewolf Code of Conduct, the uprising of Elfric the Eager, the Medieval Assembly of European Wizards, the International Warlocks Convention of 1289, the goblin rebellions and riots of the 18th century, the Giant Wars, Medieval witch burnings, the formation of the ICW and the 1749 breach of the Statute of Security. If this class is optional beyond the OWL level, one doubts Harry will take it, but he really ought to if he wants to understand as an Auror who all the Dark wizards are, how they got the way they are, what their up to now and why.

Magical Theory: There is a textbook for this class, but no mention of the class, classroom or teacher. The coursework was probably originally taught at Hogwarts by Rowena Ravenclaw. The class teaches students the basic theories and principals of magic, how it works, why it works, things one should never do and so forth. It would seem one doesn't have to take this after the 2nd year. Presumably after 2 years, Magical Theory simply gets incorporated into the everyday studies of Charms, Transfiguration and Potions since, at advanced levels, theory has very specific applications in very specific contexts.

Magizoology: There is a textbook for this class but no mention of the class, classroom or teacher. This coursework was probably taught at Hogwarts originally by Helga Hufflepuff. This branch of magical science is concerned with the study of magical creatures. One presumes it is a 1st and 2nd year class only. Since Care of Magical Creatures is a 3rd year course, one assumes that a student must know about a creature before possibly caring for it. A foundation course of Magizoology would give students a good grounding for Care of Magical Creatures, or if they opted not to take that option, they would still have sufficient knowledge of magical creatures in case they needed a part of one for a potion (unicorn), had a problems with one (grindylow) or wanted to acquire one (crup).

Muggle Studies: A 3rd year elective. This coursework, if it was a part of the founders' original curriculum, was probably taught by Godric Gryffindor (to the further irritation of Salazar). The teacher and location of the class are unknown though the class is probably on the 1st floor. The textbook is *Home Life and Social Habits of British Muggles*. It is all about Muggles. Essays for this class include topics such as electricity and explaining way Muggles need it. Ernie Macmillan started this class with Hermione, who took it even though she is Muggle born to get a wizard's perspective, but she dropped it after a year. An OWL in this subject allows one to work in Muggle Relations. Percy says other wizards think of this line of study as a soft option.

Potions: A core class for years 1-5. This coursework was probably originally taught by Salazar Slytherin. It is taught by Pr Snape in the dungeon. The classroom is a cold, creepy place with pickled animals floating in various color potions stashed in glass jars on shelves all around the walls. This class always starts by taking role after which students work in pairs around a shared cauldron. About 20 cauldrons (40 students) are set between wooden desks on which students put their brass scales and jars of ingredients. Potions a student might learn are the Draught of Living Death, Hair-Raising Potion, or Shrinking Solution. The classroom has only 1 sink in the corner for cleaning up. The spigot is in the shape of gargoyle and its mouth spits out cold water, and only cold water. Occasionally Pr Snape makes Neville or Harry stay after class and clean foul things off the tables.

Students must line up outside the closed, sealed door of the Potions dungeon and wait to be let in. Apparently it's always locked otherwise either because Pr Snape is paranoid or because he's tired of people breaking into his personal store cupboard via the classroom door entrance. Each day a potion is prepared. Daily marks are given and a student gets a zero if a potion isn't turned in and or Pr Snape hates her or him. Advance potions might be made over the course of several classes. Class is a weekly torture for everyone who is not a Slytherin, but especially Harry with whom Pr Snape has personal issues. The only good thing about Potions is that in winter students can warm themselves around fire under their cauldron. Harry, Ron and Hermione always take the very back table.

One must get an O on the OWL in Potions to get into NEWT Potions. It remains to be seen if Harry can get an O in Potions, or if Pr Snape would take him even if that happy circumstance arose. One expects that if Harry did pass with an O there would be nothing Pr Snape could do prevent Harry taking the class except quit and rejoin Voldemort for good, which he just might do. Perhaps Dumbledore will take pity on Severus and get one of the other Potions teachers to pick up a few of his classes, like any class that Harry's in. On the other hand, Harry may be in Pr Snape's class because as a member of the Order he can keep an eye on Harry.

Transfiguration: A core class for years 1-5. This coursework was probably originally taught by Rowena Ravenclaw. It is taught by Pr McGonagall, usually in a classroom on the 2nd floor. Pr McGonagall changes her desk into a pig and back again as a first class 1st years' demo and herself into a tabby cat and back again, with a faint pop, as a first class 3rd years' demo. Turning things into other things is a very difficult skill to master and some of the most complex and dangerous magic that students learn at Hogwarts. This class is always hard work, though it's Hermione's favorite and the one she has been most interested in since the day she arrived.

First years start by turning matches into needles and progress from there. Second years turn beetles into buttons or a pair of white rabbits into slippers and progress from there. A 3rd year might learn about Animagi. A 4th year might turn hedgehogs into pincushions. A 5th year might try changing Guinea fowl into Guinea pigs. Human Transfiguration is said to be a 6th year topic, but in previous years, 92/93 to be exact, Pr McGonagall did teach a 4th year classes this, having students turn each other into badgers (so probably a Hufflepuff class).

A student must get an E on the Transfiguration OWL to get into NEWT level Transfiguration. Only Hermione is really good at this subject. Everyone else needs to put in more effort. Transfiguration is a powerful magical tool but it has it limits. For example, dragons are too big to Transfigure into something more manageable even for someone very skilled in the art and, rather tragically, Transfiguration is never used as a punishment. Though it has been used as a weapon in the past with unexpectedly horrible results. See FB, Quintaped.

Breakdown of Founders' Classes
The following list shows which of the founders might have originally taught a specific class at Hogwarts.

Helga Hufflepuff
Charms
Ancient Runes
Magizoology (can't be studied at NEWT level)
Unknown elective

Rowena Ravenclaw
Transfiguration
Magical Theory (can't be studied at NEWT level)
Arithmancy
Unknown elective

Godric Gryffindor
DADA
History of Magic
Flying (can't be studied at NEWT level)
Muggle Studies

Salazar Slytherin
Herbology
Potions
Astronomy
Care of Magical Creatures

One presumes, since several students have taking 12 OWLs that 12 classes are available in which to take NEWT level studies. Since only a few of the electives offered at Hogwarts are known, it is safe to assume that there are, and probably always were, other electives that make up the number 12 at least.

HARRY'S CLASSES

There is a lot of confusion with Harry's classes. So the following schedules reflect Harry's schedule as near as is possible. Underlined classes reflect that they are confirmed to be correct. Other classes have been inserted based on information such as Charms is a morning class. Still others are inserted at random because without any exact reference it's impossible to say exactly where they might belong.

Third years are said to add 2 electives, but still keep their core curriculum subjects but this would seem incorrect. Magical Theory, Magizoology and Flying/Quidditch lessons all end after year 2, as reflected in final exams, and it seems reasonable they would end. If 1st years learn to fly, 2nd years learn to play Quidditch and wizard children grow up flying brooms and play Quidditch from before the time they can walk, as observational (QWC 1994) and verbal (Seamus, Draco, Ron) evidence would indicate, students certainly don't more classes in either.

With Magical Theory it would seem a necessary basic class for 2 years, but eventually it becomes subsumed into intermediate studies of Transfiguration, DADA, Charms, and Potions. Theory becomes irrelevant without eventual practical application but in advance application, a theory is very specific to how it is used and best left to experts in the specific field using it. Likewise after 2 years of Magizoology, all students are at least aware of these creatures at a fundamental level and have the basic information and knowledge they need to do magic. If an individual then wants to do Care of Magical Creatures afterwards to build on that knowledge, they are well prepared.

Hermione's electives are shown on the schedules in (parentheses) to differentiate them from Ron and Harry who share a large part of their schedules with her. For much of 93/94 she has 5 electives, during the 2nd term of that year she drops to 4, and finally at the end of that year she drops to 3, which she keeps through to her OWLs. Sometimes her electives take place when Harry and Ron's electives do, sometimes they do not. As with the rest of the schedule, these electives are underlined if they are confirmed in some way.

Typically at Hogwarts breakfast is 8-9am on weekdays and, 8:30-10:30am on weekends. Classes run 9am-12:30pm with 10 minute breaks between classes. Lunch runs approximately 12-1pm. Afternoon classes run 1-5:30pm. Classes generally end before 6 pm. Dinner is usually served 5-7pm. Quidditch practices take place about 2 times a week, but can be as much as 5 times a week before an important game. Detentions can be anytime but are usually at 7pm, after dinner, until about midnight. Umbridge went for 5pm detentions so students would miss dinner. Pr Snape opts for 6pm Occlumency lessons, so Harry can at least eat before being mentally attacked.

Possible Schedule First Year Gryffindors 91/92:
Mon:
   9:00 Herbology
   10:10 DADA
   1:00 History of Magic
   2:40 Magical Theory

THE HARRY POTTER COMPANION

    7:00 Quidditch Practice
Tue:
    9:00 Herbology
    10:10 Charms
    1:00 Magizoology
    2:40 Transfiguration
    7:00 Quidditch Practice
Wed:
    12 -2 am Astronomy
    9:00 DADA
    10:40 History of Magic
    1:00 Magizoology
    2:40 Magical Theory
Thu:
    9:00 Herbology
    10:10 Charms
    1:00 Transfiguration
    3:30-5:30 Flying
Fri:
    9:00-12:00 Potions
    Afternoon free
    7:00 Quidditch Practice

Sat/Sun: No classes

Classes (2 @ week/1.5hr): Charms (morning class), History of Magic, Magizoology, Defense Against the Dark Arts (morning class), Transfiguration, Magical Theory, Herbology.
Classes (1 @ week/2hr): Astronomy, Flying.
Classes (1@ week/3hr): Potions.
Flying: Double with Slytherins.
Potions: Double with Slytherins.

Possible Schedule Second Year Gryffindors 92/93:
Mon:
    9:00 Herbology
    10:10 Transfiguration
    1:00 DADA
    7:00 Quidditch Practice
Tue:
    9:00 DADA
    10:40 History of Magic
    1:00 Magizoology
    2:40 Charms
    7:00 Quidditch Practice
Wed:
    12-2am Astronomy
    9:00 Magical Theory
    10:40 Potions
    1:00 History of Magic

    2:40 Quidditch/Flying
Thu:
    9:00 Magizoology
    10:40 Herbology
    1:00 DADA
    2:40 Potions
    8:00 Dueling Club
Fri:
    9:00 Herbology
    10:10 Transfiguration
    1:00 Charms
    2:40 Magical Theory
    7:00 Quidditch Practice

Sat/Sun: No classes

All classes are 2 @ week/1.5 hr except Astronomy which is 1 @ week/2hr and DADA which is 3 @ week/1.5hr.
Herbology: Double with Hufflepuffs Mondays and Fridays.
Potions: Double with Slytherins on Thursdays afternoons only.
DADA: It may be that Dumbledore feels DADA is vital now that Voldemort is back and therefore increased the DADA classes, especially for Harry who must ultimately deal with Voldemort on his own.

Possible Schedule Third Year Gryffindors 93/94:
Mon:
    9:00 Potions
    10:40 DADA
        (Ancient Runes)
    1:00 Herbology
    2:40 History of Magic
    7:00 Quidditch Practice
Tue:
    9:00 Care of Magical Creatures
        (Arithmancy)
    10:40 Charms
    1:00 Divination
    2:40 DADA
    7:00 Quidditch Practice
Wed:
    12 -2 am Astronomy
    9:00 Divination
        (Arithmancy)
        (Muggle Studies)
    10:40 Transfiguration
    1:00 Care of Magical Creatures
    7:00 Quidditch Practice
Thu:
    9:00 Potions
        (Muggle Studies)

(Ancient Runes)
  10:40 History of Magic
  1:00 DADA
  8:00 Anti-Dementor Lessons
Fri:
  9:00 Herbology
  10:40 Transfiguration
  1:00 DADA
  2:40 Charms

Sat/Sun: No classes
  7:00 Quidditch Practice

All classes are 2 @ week/1.5hr but DADA which is 4 @ week/1.5 hr.
Potions: Double with Slytherin Monday and Thursday.
Herbology: Double with Hufflepuff Fridays only.
Care of Magical Creatures: Double with Slytherins on Wednesday.
DADA: It is taught 4 times a week. Perhaps because Dumbledore felt the last DADA teacher was so bad, students were a year behind and 8hrs a week of hands-on DADA seems appropriate.

Possible Schedule Fourth Year Gryffindors 94/95:
Mon:
  9:00 Herbology
  10:40 Care of Magical Creatures
  1:00 Divination
      (Arithmancy)
Tue:
  9:00 History of Magic
  10:40 DADA
  1:00 Transfiguration
  2:40 Divination
      (Arithmancy)
Wed:
  12 -2 am Astronomy
  9:00 Herbology
  10:40 Charms
  1:00 Care of Magical Creatures
  2:40 (Ancient Runes)
Thu:
  9:00 Transfiguration
  10:40 Potions
  1:00 DADA
Fri:
  9:00 History of Magic
  10:40 Charms
  1:00 Potions
  2:40 (Ancient Runes)

Sat/Sun: No classes

All classes are now 2 @ week/1.5hr.
DADA: Seems to be 3 times a week 1.5hr, more catch up work one supposes.
Herbology: Double with Hufflepuffs on Monday.
Care of Magical Creatures: Double with Slytherins
Potions: Double with Slytherin.
Divination: It's said to be a double class but it's never said who they double with.

Possible Schedule Fifth Year Gryffindors 95/96:
Mon:
   9:00 History of Magic
   10:40 Potions
   1:00 Divination
       (Arithmancy)
   2:40 DADA
   6:00 Remedial Potions aka (Occlumency
Tue:
   9:00 Charms
   10:40 Transfiguration
   1:00 Care of Magical Creatures
   2:40 Herbology
Wed:
   12-2am Astronomy
   9:00 Divination
       (Arithmancy)
   10:40 Transfiguration
   1:00 Care of Magical Creatures
   6:00 Remedial Potions aka Occlumency
Thu:
   9:00 Herbology
   10:40 Potions
   1:00 (Ancient Runes)
   7:00 Quidditch Practice
Fri:
   9:00 History of Magic
   10:40 Charms
   1:00 DADA
   2:40 (Ancient Runes)

Sat/Sun: No classes
   1:00 Quidditch Practice

All classes are now 2 @ week/1.5hr.
Detentions: Those with Pr Umbridge start at 5pm, so students miss dinner.
Potions: Double with Slytherin, on Monday.
DADA: Double, but it's never said who with, on Monday, and back to just 2 @ week.
Charms: Double, but it's never said who with, on Monday.
Transfiguration: Double, but it's never said who with, on Monday.
Care of Magical Creatures: Double with Slytherins always.
Herbology: Double with Hufflepuffs always.

Divination: Double, but it's never said who with, Monday.

EXAMS

Exam grades affect the type of work a student is qualified to do. The more subjects a student does well in, the more things that student is qualified to do. This is why the British often used "qualifications" to mean grades a student received while in school or subjects a student took in school. Percy's response to "What are your qualifications?" would be 12 NEWTs with E grades. Going back to employments, Percy with 12 NEWTs is qualified to take almost any job, besides being qualified to work at the MoM. Fred and George, with 3 OWLs apiece, and no NEWTs at all . . . . Well, it's a good thing they opened their own joke shop because no one would hire them to do anything except perhaps to be a ticket conductor on the Knight Bus. In addition to an exam qualification, a student would also need a recommendation from a teacher, to vouch for her or his work as well as her or his character. This can come from any teacher, but a recommendation from the head of the student's House is best. This is why when Pr Snape threatens students of his House with the possibility of a less than glowing recommendation, they take his threat very seriously.

BASIC EXAMS

Final written exams for students years 1-4 and 6 are usually given the 2nd week of Jun in large classrooms that can accommodate about 145 students, or all students in the same year of study from all 4 houses. These exams are limited by time, length of the parchment and the size of a student's handwriting. New quills, bewitched with Anti-Cheating Spells, are given to exam takers at the start of each exam and all the standard methods of cheating are highly discouraged.

All classes, except perhaps Magical Theory, History of Magic or other strictly academic classes, require the student to take a practical exam to demonstrate a certain level of ability as well as knowledge has been attained. Some teachers give the practical exam in a group, others give it individually. After exams there is a free week. Students receive their basic exam marks the 3rd week of Jun. Students must pass these exams to remain in school and go on to the next year, usually (Marcus Flint's parents probably pulled strings).

HARRY'S BASIC EXAMS

So far Harry has had basic exams for years 1-4 and sometimes not even then. What basic exams he has taken are discussed in this section.

91/92: Harry must have passed, since he was accepted back the next year. He mentions only a few exams.
Charms: The practical was done individually. Students had to make a pineapple dance across Pr Flitwick's desk.
Transfiguration: The practical was done in a group. Students had to turn a mouse into a snuff box with points given for how pretty it was, but taken if it had whiskers.
Potions: The practical was done in a group. Students had to make Forgetfulness Potion.
History of Magic: The written exam was done in a group and consisted of 1 hour of answering questions about wizards who'd invented various magical items such as self-stirring cauldrons.

92/93: Exams were due to start Jun 1, 1993, but were canceled by Dumbledore. Everyone was given a pass for that year.

93/94: The exams were held the 2nd week of Jun. Harry must have passed since he was accepted back the following year. He mentions only the following exams.

Transfiguration: The practical involved turning a teapot into a tortoise.

Charms: The practical was to demonstrate the use of Cheering Charms.

Care of Magical Creatures: The practical was to keep the flobberworm alive for 1 hour.

Potions: The practical was to make Confusing Concoction.

History: The written was about Medieval witch hunts.

DADA: The practical involved getting through an obstacle course of various Dark creatures such as grindylows, red caps, hinkypunks and boggarts.

Divination: The practical was to read a crystal ball.

94/95: Harry was a champion in the TT and all champions were excused from taking exams. He got an automatic pass, but one assumes he would rather have taken his regular exams instead.

OWLs

Aka Ordinary Wizarding Levels. These are given to 5th year students only, in place of normal exams. Special examiners from the Ministry's Wizarding Examination Authority are brought in to administer the exams. One subject is tested each day. The written exams take place in the Great Hall in the morning. The practical exams are given in the same place in the afternoon. Only the Astronomy practical is given at a different time and place, at night on the Astronomy Tower. OWL results are sent to students by owl sometime during Jul. OWLs are extremely grueling and OWL results determine which students can go on to NEWT level studies. Students will not be accepted into NEWT level studies with certain teachers if they don't meet the individual instructor's standards.

OWLS Grading System:
- O, outstanding
- E, exceeds expectations (excellent)
- A, acceptable
- P, poor
- D, dreadful
- T, troll (this may have been a joke, probably actually terrible).

Harry's OWLs

Harry took his OWLs in Jun 1996. Only one subject per day was tested. The OWLs took 2 weeks to complete and covered 9 subjects for Harry and Ron, 10 for Hermione. Theory or written exams were taken in the morning at 9:30am in the Great Hall. Students sat at small individual tables facing the High Table at the top of the hall where the examiners sat. In the afternoon, following the written exam and lunch, practical exams in the same subject as the written exam were taken at 1:00pm in the Great Hall. The Astronomy practical was given at 11:00pm on the Astronomy Tower because that's when the stars were out and where they were most observable.

Week 1:
Mon: Charms, featured Cheering Charms
Tue: Transfiguration, featured Switching Spells
Wed: Herbology, featured fanged geraniums

Thu: DADA, featured making a Patronus for Harry
Fri: Ancient Runes (Hermione)
Week 2:
Mon: Potions, featured a question on Polyjuice Potion
Tue: Care of Magical Creatures, featured unicorn diets
Wed: Astronomy, featured Jupiter, again
    Divination (Harry and Ron), featured tea leaf reading
    Arithmancy (Hermione)
    Astronomy, practical, featured mapping Orion
Thu: History of Magic, featured the formation of the ICW.

NEWTs

Aka Nearly Exhausting Wizarding Tests or Nastily Exhausting Wizarding Tests. NEWTs are taken by 7th year students only. Beyond the 5th year, advanced studies are taken only at the individual teacher's discretion and usually based on the student's grades in that subject on the OWLs. NEWTs can be taken in all core classes and any elective a student has been studying since the 3rd year. Because Harry wants to be an Auror, and to be an Auror one needs at least 5 NEWTs with E grades, he will be taking NEWTs in Transfiguration, Potions, Charms, DADA, and possibly Care of Magical Creatures, Herbology and Astronomy.

FEASTS

Every year Hogwarts has a certain number of feasts. They are arranged here in a generally chronological order as they happen through the year. Additional feasts are noted at the end. These include all one time events, like the Basilisk Feast. Some feasts have decorations associated with them, others don't. Foods typically are served in 2 courses, the main and dessert courses. All feasts use special gold tablewares. The plates and goblets will refill themselves repeatedly until the feast ends, at which point they will vanish the remains, then vanish themselves.

START OF TERM FEASTS

Always held on Sep 1, just after the Sorting Ceremony, it's to welcomes new and returning students. Dumbledore opens the feast by welcoming new students and saying a few words on the occasion. After this, the feast begins. There are no decorations associated with the feast but food is abundant. Main courses might include roast meats, chops, sausages, bacon, steak, potatoe of every description, vegetables and Peppermint Humbugs. Dessert courses might include blocks of ice cream in every flavor, pies, tarts, eclairs, doughnuts, trifle, fruits, Jell-O and pudding.

    At the end of the feast Dumbledore gives same start of term notices (announcements): students are not to go into the forest, no magic can be done in hallways between classes, Quidditch trials begin the 2nd week of term and anyone who want to play for a House team should speak to Madam Hooch. After the announcements Dumbledore shoots out of his wand a gold ribbon with the school song printed on it which hangs in the air. Each then person picks a favorite tune (any favorite tune) and everyone sings producing a rather pleasantly discordant song. Dumbledore will sometimes conduct the song and even cry a small tear over it. After the song is over, students are then dismissed and Prefects guide the 1st years to their new Houses.

Start of Term Feast 1991:
Dumbledore added an unusual notice. He instructed them to stay away from the right-hand side of the 3rd floor corridor unless they wished to die a painful death.
Start of Term Feast 1992: Harry and Ron missed it due to the Whomping Willow disciplinary meeting they had with Dumbledore, Pr McGonagall and Pr Snape in Pr Snape's office. They had dinner in Pr Snape's office afterwards, courtesy of Pr McGonagall.
Start of Term Feast 1993: Harry missed it due to the dementor attack that occurred on the Hogwarts Express.
Start of term Feast 1994: The only things new were the white linen tablecloths on House tables. Hermione spilled pumpkin juice on Gryffindor's after learning Hogwarts had house-elves.
Start of Term Feast 1995: Pr Umbridge interrupted Dumbledore's announcements and made a speech, to the horror of all.

HALLOWEEN FEASTS

Always on held Oct 31, the decorations usually include things like a 1,000 live bats fluttering on the walls and 1,000 more swooping over the tables in flocks and causing the candles to flicker.

Halloween Feast 1991: This year was remembered for its disruption by the mountain troll that attacked Hermione. Food was later sent to the various common rooms.
Halloween Feast 1992: This year the usual live bats appeared but Hagrid's vast pumpkins carved into huge lanterns big enough for 3 men to sit in were an interesting addition. Dumbledore booked a dancing skeleton troupe for entertainment. It ran 7pm - 12 midnight but Harry, Ron and Hermione went to Nearly Headless Nick's Deathday Party instead, missed the feast completely and unfortunately found the basilisk's 1st victim afterwards.
Halloween Feast 1993: Decorations included 100s of candle-filled pumpkins, clouds of live bats fluttering about and flaming orange streamers snaking across the stormy ceiling. At the end of the feast, the ghosts did formation gliding then Nearly Headless Nick reenacted his botched beheading to great acclaim.
Halloween Feast 1994: It began at 6:00pm. This feast was noted for the Goblet of Fire being placed in front of Dumbledore on the High Table and coughing up a 4th Champion for the TT.

CHRISTMAS FEASTS

Always held on Dec 25 at noontime, the Great Hall is usually decorated well beforehand. Hagrid brings in 12 fir trees from the Forbidden Forest and sets them in the Great Hall. Festoons of holly and mistletoe are run all around the Great Hall's walls and the trees are trimmed by Pr McGonagall and Pr Flitwick. The rest of the school is festooned for Christmas by Prefects, with individual teachers dressing up their classrooms according to taste and ability.

At the feast itself, the tables are always trimmed with piles of Christmas crackers. Among foods served turkey and chipolatas seem to be enduring Christmas Feast favorites. The feast is held at 12 noon, so there is a Christmas tea later in the afternoon sent up to the House common rooms and usually consisting of leftovers. Turkey sandwiches, crumpets, trifle and Christmas cake, as well as the ubiquitous pumpkin juice are served.

Christmas Feast 1991: Decorations included 12 towering fir trees trimmed with tiny sparkling enchanted non-melting icicles, 100s of glittering candles and golden glasslike bubbles. Stacks of Wizard Crackers with interesting gifts inside them were placed every few feet along all the tables and foods included roast turkeys, potatoes, chipolatas, peas, gravy, cranberry sauce and Flaming Christmas Puddings for dessert.

Christmas Feast 1992: The Great Hall was decorated with 12 frost-covered Christmas trees and thick ropes of holly and mistletoe crisscrossed the enchanted ceiling from which warm and dry enchanted snow fell. Alcoholic eggnog that got Hagrid a bit high was served. Dumbledore led students in a few of his favorite carols and, after 3rd helpings of Christmas Pudding, most students left. It was just after this feast that Hermione drugged Crabbe and Goyle with Christmas cupcakes and Harry and Ron, using Polyjuice Potion, questioned Draco in Slytherin's common room. Hermione ended up in the hospital later in the day because of a Polyjuice Potion accident.

Christmas Feast 1993: Holly and mistletoe streamers were put in the corridors and lights shone from inside every suit of armor. The usual 12 trees were crowned with golden stars. Dinner included turkey, potatoes and chipolatas and lasts about 2 hours. Everyone wore party hats, except Pr Snape. The usual House tables were removed this year because so few students stayed over. There was only one table for all 12 people, later 13. Seated face-to-face in 2 rows:

Row 1: Dumbledore, Snape, (Trelawney), McGonagall, Sprout, Flitwick, Filch;
Row 2: 1st years (Derek & ?), a 5th year Slytherin, Harry, Ron, Hermione.

Pr Trelawney joined the feast late, making 13 for dinner. Pr Lupin was ill with Lycanthropy. One assumes other teachers went to visit family or friends.

Christmas 1994: This feast was replaced by the Yule Ball.

Christmas 1995: Harry did not attend this feast. He and the Weasleys spent Christmas at Headquarters with Sirius. Headquarters was decorated with holly garlands and gold and silver streamers, glittering heaps of magical snow scattered about to hide the threadbare carpets and a large stolen Christmas tree trimmed with live fairies. The stuffed house-elves were dressed with Santa hats and beards, doubtless by Sirius to offend Kreacher.

END OF TERM FEASTS

This feast normally occurs in late Jun on the night before the Hogwarts Express takes students back to London. Decorations include the Great Hall decked in colors of House winning the House Cup. The banner of the winning House, replete with animal symbol, hangs behind the High Table covering the entire wall.

End of Term Feast 1992: Jun 1992. The Great Hall was decorated in Gryffindor colors.
End of Term Feast 1993: This feast was replaced by the Basilisk Feast.
End of Term Feast 1994: There was no mention of a feast, but they surely had one. Harry was hospitalized at the time due to dementor attack.
End of Term Feast 1995: This feast was replaced by the TT's Leaving Feast.
End of Term Feast 1996: Nothing was recorded of this event.

OTHER ONE TIME FEASTS

Feasts are listed in chronological rather than alphabetical order.

Valentine's Day: Feb 14, 1993. Held during breakfast, bacon was served and the Great Hall was covered in large, lurid pink flowers while heart-shaped confetti fell from a pale blue ceiling (into the food). Musical valentines were delivered all day by dwarfs dressed in Cupid wings. Pr Lockhart arranged the event as a morale booster and was dressed in lurid pink robes to match the decor. All the other teachers were extremely angry about the affair. A whopping 46 people sent Pr Lockhart cards and Harry got musical one with words composed by Ginny Weasley.

Basilisk Feast 1993: May 29, 1993. This feast replaced the End of Term Feast. Dumbledore declared it to celebrate the end of the basilisk and the closing of the Chamber of Secrets. It was called so suddenly everyone attended in pajamas. It ran from very late in the night to the following morning. Everyone that had been Petrified was cured by then and even Hagrid turned up, at 3:30am. Trifle was served. Gryffindor was announced as the winner of the House Cup. Exams were canceled, as were DADA classes through the end of term, due to Pr Lockhart's illness.

Welcome Feast: Oct 30, 1994. It occurred to welcome the Beauxbatons and Drumstrangs to Hogwarts for the TT. Each school showed up in a rather bizarre and grandiose manner to display their magical prowess. Durmstrangs showed up in ship from a whirpool in the Lake, while Beauxbatons showed up in a flying coach pulled by abraxan horses. At this feast all the House banners were displayed in addition to the school banner.

The Yule Ball 1994: Dec 25, 1994. This feast is a part of every TT and called the Yule Ball. Everyone 4th year and above stayed over Christmas to attend. The lunch that day, that proceeded the ball, consisted of turkey, Christmas pudding and piles of crackers. The castle was done up with everlasting icicles hanging on the banisters of the marble staircase and in the Great Hall 12 trees decked with luminous holly berries and real hooting golden owls. The armor was bewitched to sing religious carols like "O Come All Ye Faithful" but only knew a part of the words.

Leaving Feast 1995: This feast replaced the usual End of Term Feast and was called Leaving Feast because the students from Durmstrang and Beauxbatons were leaving. Decorations included black drapes on the wall behind the High Table, for Cedric. A toast was made to Cedric Diggory's memory and another toast to honor Harry. Dumbledore told everyone that Voldemort had returned. Dumbledore also told the visiting students that he would welcome back anyone that wanted to come back, (the Durmstrangs had been abandoned) in an attempt to reach out to the foreign students. But most students were 17 and graduates, so he may have meant back as in, to join the Order and help fight Voldemort rather than back to Hogwarts as a student.

HOGSMEADE WEEKENDS

For 3rd year students and above, there are a certain number of Saturdays each year during which, if students have signed permission slips from a parent or guardian, they are permitted to go to Hogsmeade village. It is open to older students only, normally, because of the hags that reside in the village. Dennis Creevey was permitted to go as a younger student, probably because his father permitted it and his brother agreed to be responsible for him. As smaller children, they are perfect hag fodder and really unsafe unless in a pair. It was probably as much for Colin's protection as Dennis' enjoyment that this rule was bent. It is difficult to say how many Hogsmeade weekends there are each year. It seems to vary depending on what else is happening at the school. About 4 seems normal. The 3 in 94/95 may have been due to TT events. The 2 in 95/96 were probably because Umbridge was such a controlling cow.

THE HARRY POTTER COMPANION

93/94: Oct 31, Dec 11, Apr 21, Jun 8.
94/95: Nov 21, Jan 18, Mar 6.
95/96: Oct 7, Feb 14.

HARRY'S PRESENTS

In this section is a list of all Harry's known Christmas and birthday presents in chronological order. Although it would seem like the Dursleys didn't send Harry anything in 1993 or 1995 for Christmas, one presumes that they did and there simply wasn't a full listing of all his presents. Since the Dursleys would never send Harry anything if they didn't have to or use an owl (which they must to get something to Hogwarts), yet appear to do both for Christmas 1991, 1992 and 1994, it would seem logical that the Christmas presents, and possibly birthday presents, are related to keeping Lily's charm active and the only reason the Dursleys continue to give them.

Birthday 1990:
Dursleys:
A coat hanger
An old pair of Vernon's socks
Birthday 1991:
Hagrid:
A snowy owl, Hedwig
Christmas 1991:
Hagrid:
A handmade wooden flute that sounds a bit like an hooting owl
Dursleys:
A 50 pence piece, which Harry gave to Ron
Molly:
A Weasley sweater, emerald green, but with no initial on chest
A large box of fudge
Hermione:
A box of Chocolate Frogs
Anonymous (Albus):
An Invisibility Cloak that was James Potter's.
Other Gifts (from Wizard Crackers):
A pack of non-explodable, luminous balloons
A Grow-Your-Own-Warts Kit
A wizard's chess set
Birthday 1992:
The MoM:
A warning from the Improper Use of Magic Office
Dobby:
He held up all Harry's birthday cards and mail so Harry never received any of it.
Christmas 1992:
Hagrid:
A tin of treacle fudge that needs to be softened in fire before eating
Dursleys:
A toothbrush
Molly:

A handknit Weasley sweater
A large plum cake
A Christmas card
Hermione:
A luxury eagle-feather quill
Ron:
A book: *Flying with the Cannons*
Birthday 1993:
Hagrid:
A birthday card
A book: *The Monster Book of Monsters*
Hermione:
A birthday card
A Broom-Servicing Kit, which includes a broom compass
Ron:
A birthday card
An Egyptian Pocket Sneakoscope
Christmas 1993:
Molly:
A Weasley sweater, scarlet with a gold Gryffindor lion on it
12 mince pies
A Christmas cake
A box of Nut Brittle
Anonymous (Sirius):
A Firebolt
Birthday 1994:
Hagrid:
A birthday card
A cake
Hermione:
A birthday card
A cake
Ron:
A birthday card
A cake
Sirius:
A birthday card
A cake
A letter
Christmas 1994:
Hagrid:
A box of sweets including Harry's favorites: Every Flavor Beans, Chocolate Frogs, Drooble's Best Blowing Gum and Fizzing Whizbees.
Dursleys:
A single tissue
Molly:
A new Weasley sweater, green with a dragon on it
Numerous homemade mince pies
Hermione:
A book: *Quidditch Teams of Britain and Ireland*

Ron:
A bag of Dungbombs
Sirius:
A penknife with attachments to unlock any lock and undo any knot
Dobby:
A pair of socks, one red with broomsticks and one green with Snitches, handknit by Dobby.
Birthday 1995:
Hermione:
Honeydukes Chocolate
Ron:
Honeydukes Chocolate
Christmas 1995:
Hagrid:
A furry brown wallet with fangs, probably moke.
Molly and Arthur:
A Weasley sweater
A number of mince pies
Hermione:
A homework planner that is slightly abusive and harassing
Ron:
A huge box of Every Flavor Beans
A broom compass
Sirius and Remus:
A set of books: *Practical Defensive Magic and Its Use Against the Dark Arts*
Tonks:
A small model of a Firebolt which actually flies
Dobby:
A portrait of Harry that Dobby painted himself.

FOODS

The following is a list of all consumable foods and drinks, along with how often they are mentioned and who loves or hates them. Do note the wizarding diet is a little high in fats, sugars and cholesterol-causing items and Muggles are advised not to try it.

FOOD LISTS

Breakfast Foods
Fruit 'N Bran Cereal 1
Cereal 2
Cornflakes 3
Sugar 4
Porridge (Oatmeal) 7
Porridge with Treacle 1   Harry Fav
Crumpets 3
Bread 4
Bun 1
Muffins 1
English Muffins 1
Toast 17   Harry & Hedwig Fav

Marmalade 6
Doughnuts
   Plain 2
   Jam 2
Bacon
   Fried 14
   Rinds 1
   Sandwiches 2
Eggs
   Unspecified 10
   Fried 2
   Scrambled 3
   Easter 2
Sausages
   Fried 9
   Sausage Rolls 1
Kippers 3

Snack Foods
Chips 1
Crisps 1
Peanuts 1
Assorted Nuts 1
Low-Calorie Snacks 2
Sugar Free Snacks 1

Fruits
Strawberries 1
Bananas 1
Cherry 1
Grapes 1
Grapefruit 1
Unspecified 1
Prune 1
Lemon 1
Pineapple 1

Vegetables
Potatoes
   Unspecified 7
   Roasted 4
   Boiled 3
   Mashed 3
   Fries 1
   Baked 2
Tomatoes
   Cold canned 1
   Fried 1
Pumpkins 2
Peas 3

Harry Fav

Carrots 3
Onion 1
Wilted Salad 1
Salad 1
Cabbages 2
Runner Beans 2
Leeks 1
Grated Celery 1
Cauliflower 1
Sprouts 1
Turnips 1

Soups
Goulash 1   Harry Fav
Bouillabaisse 1
Canned Vegetable Soup 1
Stew 1
Soup 1

Lunch
Hamburgers 1
Shepherd's Pie 2
Loaf of Bread 1
Large Ham 1
Cornish Pasty 1
Cottage Cheese 1
Sandwiches
   Unspecified 1
   Turkey 1
   Corned Beef   Ron Hates
   Bread and Cheese 1
   Stoat 1   Hagrid only
   Chicken and Ham 1

Condiments
Gravy 2
Ketchup 3
Marshmallows 1
Cranberry Sauce 1
Butter 4
Salt 1
Unspecified Sauces 1
Garlic 1
Cream Sauce 1

Dinner Meats
Roast Beef 2
Roast Chicken 2
Pork Chops 2   Dumbledore Fav
Lamb Chops 3

ACASCIAS RIPHOUSE

Unspecified Chops 2
Steak and Kidney Pie 3   Harry Fav
Mince Pies 2
Meat Pies 4
Chipolatas 2   Dumbledore Fav
Roast Turkey 4   Christmas Fav
Loin of Pork Roast 1
Chicken and Ham Pie
Chicken Legs 2
Chicken Casserole 1
Beef Casserole 2
Meatballs 1
Dragon Steak 1   Hagrid only
Steak 1
Salmon 2
Raw Liver 1
Tripe 1
Rabbit 1
Salami 1

Puddings
Main Course Puddings
   Unspecified 2
   Yorkshire 3   Ron Fav
   Christmas 4
   Steak and Kidney 1
   Black 1
   Savoury Multiple

Dessert Puddings
   Rice 1
   Petunia's covered in whipped cream and sugared violets 1
   Treacle 1   Harry Fav
   Chocolate 1

Desserts
Bath Buns 1   Hagrid
Doughy Cookies 1
Treacle Fudge 3   Hagrid
Treacle Pudding 1   Harry Fav
Chocolate Eclairs 2
Eclairs 1
Jell-O 1
Trifle 4
Custard Creams 2
Biscuits (cookies) 1
Nut Brittle 1
Spotted Dick 1   Ron Fav
Chocolate Gateau 1

The Harry Potter Companion

Pale Blancmange 1
Ginger Newts 2   McGonagall Fav
Pies
   Assorted 2
   Apple 3
   Lemon Meringue 1

Crumbles
   Rhubarb Crumble w/ Custard 2   Harry Fav
Tarts
   Pumpkin 1
   Jam 1
   Treacle 2   Harry Fav
   Custard 2   Dumbledore Fav

Ice Creams
   Chocolate 2
   Knickerbocker Glory 2
   Chocolate and Raspberry with Nuts   Hagrid Fav
   Blocks of every flavor imaginable
   Strawberry and Peanut Butter   Harry Fav
   Homemade Strawberry   Weasley Fav
   Lemon Ice Pop 1
   Fortescue's Choco-Nut Sundaes
   Multiple   Harry Fav

Cakes
   Chocolate Multiple
   Rock w/ raisins 2   Hagrid
   Christmas Multiple
   Assorted 6
   Plum 1
   Fruit 4
   Cream 1

Candies
Mars Bars 1   Harry Fav
Bertie Bott's Every Flavor Beans 4   Harry Fav
Drooble's Best Blowing Gum 3   Harry Fav
Chocolate Frogs 10   Harry Fav
Pumpkin Pasties 4   Harry Fav
Cauldron Cakes 4   Harry Fav
Licorice Wands 2
Lemon Drops 2   Dumbledore Fav
Pear Drop 1
Peppermint Humbugs 3
Toffee 4
Fizzing Whizbees 2
Honeydukes Chocolate 4
Sugar Quills 3

Acascias Riphouse

Cockroach Clusters 2
Pepper Imps 2
Chocoballs 1
Levitating Sherbet Balls 1
Nougat 1
Coconut Ice 1
Assorted Chocolates 1
Toothflossing Stringmints 2
Ice Mice 2
Peppermint Cream Toads 2
Exploding Bonbons 1
Blood-Flavored Lollipops 1
Acid Pops 1
Jelly Slugs 1
Fudge Flies 1
Wine Gums 1
Fred and George Weasley's joke candies are listed on the Magical Devices page.

Drinks
Water 1
Milk 8
Tea 30
Coffee 5
Orange Juice 3
Dandelion Juice 1
Pumpkin Juice 12
Hot Chocolate 4
Cocoa 1
Sodas
   Pumpkin Fizz 1
   Gillywater 2
   Sodawater and Cherry Syrup with Ice 1
Alcoholic Drinks
   Butterbeer 13
   Beer 1
   Mead 2
   Mulled Mead 2
   Wine
      Regular 5
      Elderflower 1
      Nettle 1
      Turnip 1
Hard Liquors
   Sherry 2
   Brandy 5
   Red Currant Rum 1
   Odgen's Old Firewhisky 2

THE HARRY POTTER COMPANION

RECIPES

In case someone wants to know what tea or dinner might be like at Harry's, Hagrid's, Hermione's, Ron's, or Dumbledore's house, the following recipes are broken down and arranged into meals. Bon appetite!

Tea
Bath Buns	Hagrid
Treacle Fudge	Hagrid
Rock Cakes with Raisins	Hagrid

Dinner
Bouillabaisse	Hermione
Roasted Potatoes	Hogwarts
Rhubarb Crumble with Custard	Harry
Goulash	Harry
Mashed Potatoes	Hogwarts
Treacle Tart	Harry
Cornish Pasty	Ron
Boiled Potatoes	Hogwarts
Spotted Dick	Ron
Chipolatas	Dumbledore
Baked Potatoes	Hogwarts
Custard Tart	Dumbledore

Bath Buns

2 c	Flour
1/4 c	Sugar
3 T	Shortening
1	Egg, well beaten
3 t	Baking powder
1/2 c	Seedless raisins
1/2 t	Salt
1 T	Sugar
	Milk
1/2	Lemon rind, grated

1. Sift flour with baking powder and salt then add shortening
2. Add grated lemon rind, sugar, egg (save a little of the egg), raisins and enough milk to make a soft dough that can be molded
3. Mold small amounts into round buns
4. Brush the saved egg to brush over the tops
5. Place on well-oiled baking sheet.
6. Bake in a preheated 450°F for 12-15 minutes
7. Brush tops with 1T sugar moistened with a little cream
8. Serve hot

Serves 12

Acascias Riphouse

Treacle Fudge
- 1/2 c   Light cream
- 3/4 c   Packed brown sugar
- 1/4 t   Salt
- 4 oz   Unsweetened chocolate
- 2 T   Unsalted butter
- 1/3 c   Molasses (not blackstrap)

1. In a bowl mix cream, sugar, and salt
2. In a heavy saucepan, melt the chocolate with butter
3. Remove from the heat and stir in molasses
4. Add the chocolate mixture to the cream mixture
5. Pour into a buttered pan
6. Chill for 2 hours
7. Cut into squares and serve

Rock Cakes with Raisins
- 1 c   Flour
- 1 t   Baking powder
-          Pinch of salt
- 1 t   Nutmeg
- 4 oz   Butter
- 3 oz   Brown sugar
- 3 oz   Raisins
- 1   Egg
-          A little milk

1. Sift flour and salt into bowl and add butter
2. Add sugar, raisins, nutmeg, beaten egg and only enough milk to make stiff dough
3. Place in rounded portions on greased baking sheets
4. Bake in a preheated oven at 425°F for 15-20 minutes

    A staple at English boarding schools, these individual cakes are served with afternoon tea. They don't keep well and after a day they take on the characteristics of rocks. Serve fresh
Makes 4-6 cakes

Shellfish Bouillabaisse
- 3 oz   Lobster meat (uncooked)
- 3 oz   Scallops (uncooked)
- 4 oz   Shrimp (uncooked)
- 2 oz   Crab legs (shelled)
- 4 oz   Clams (raw)
- 3 t   Olive oil
- 1   Onion (chopped)
- 1/2 c   Celery (chopped)
- 1   Clove garlic (minced)
-          Pinch of rosemary
- 2 T   Sherry
- 1 c   Tomato pulp
- 1/2   Lemon (sliced thinly)

THE HARRY POTTER COMPANION

    2 c   Fish stock
    1 T   Sugar
    2 T   Salt
    1¾ T   Cayenne pepper
    3¾ T   Saffron

1. Make fish stock
2. Place the olive oil in a heavy sauce pan and add the onion, celery, garlic, parsley and rosemary and saute for 5 minutes
3. Add the shellfish, all uncooked items (cleaned and shelled), and the sherry
4. Simmer for 5 minutes
5. Add tomato pulp, lemon slices, fish stock, sugar, salt and pepper
6. Cook on a low flame for 10 minutes
7. Add the saffron at the last minute, stir well and serve
Serves 8

Roasted Potatoes
    8-9   Potatoes cut in 1" pieces or 5" thick wedges
    1 c   Olive oil
    1 T   Salt
    1 T   Pepper

1. Toss cut-up potatoes with enough olive oil to coat lightly
2. Season with salt and pepper (or garlic salt), rosemary, etc
3. Arrange in an even layer on lightly oiled shallow baking pan
4. Roast in a preheat oven at 425°F for 20 to 30 minutes or until tender, stirring occasionally
Serves 8

Rhubarb Crumble with Custard
    1.5 lb Rhubarb, trimmed and scrubbed
           Juice of 1 lemon
           Pinch of nutmeg
    6 oz   Brown sugar
    2 oz   White sugar
    6 oz   Plain flour
    3 oz   Butter
For Custard:
    2 T   Custard powder
    2 T   White sugar
    20 oz Milk

1. Cut rhubarb into 1" chunks and layer it with the brown sugar in a 2-pint capacity ovenproof dish
2. Sprinkle with nutmeg and lemon juice
3. Add the butter into the flour with fingertips until the mixture resembles fine bread crumbs
4. Stir in the white sugar
5. Sprinkle the crumble mixture on top of rhubarb and press down firmly

ACASCIAS RIPHOUSE

6. Bake in a preheated oven at 400°F for 30-40 minutes
7. Rhubarb makes its own juice and top will brown slightly when ready

Custard:
1. Add custard powder and sugar together in bowl and mix to a smooth paste with 2 T milk taken from rest
2. Bring remainder of milk to a boil and pour on the paste in bowl, stirring well
3. Return to pan and boil for 1 minute, stirring all the time
4. Serve hot custard over hot crumble
Serves 8

Goulash

2 lb	Beef chuck
1 t	Salt
2	Onions, white or yellow
2 T	Lard or shortening
2 T	Imported sweet paprika
2	Bay leaves
1 Qt	Water
4	Potatoes, peeled and diced
1/4 t	Black pepper

1. Cut beef into 1" squares, add 1/2 t salt
2. Chop onions and brown in shortening, then add beef and paprika
3. Let the beef simmer in its own juices along with salt and paprika for 1 hour on low heat
4. Add water, diced potatoes and remaining salt
5. Cover and simmer until potatoes are done and meat is tender

Prepare egg dumpling batter:

1	Egg
6 T	Flour
1/8 t	Salt

1. Add flour to unbeaten egg and salt and mix well
2. Let stand for 30 minutes
3. Drop by teaspoonfuls into Goulash
4. Cover and simmer 5 minutes after dumplings rise to surface
5. Serve hot with dollops of sour cream
Serves 6

Mashed Potatoes

7	Potatoes, cut in 1" slices
1/2 c	Milk
1 t	Salt
1/4 c	Butter

1. In large saucepan, add potatoes to 2" boiling water to cover
2. Return to a boil

3. Reduce heat and cook, covered, about 12 minutes or until tender; drain
4. Heat potatoes over medium-low heat for 1 minute to evaporate excess moisture, stirring occasionally
5. Using electric hand mixer or potato masher, mash potatoes
6. Mix in milk, butter and salt

Serves 6

Treacle Tart

1	9" pie shell, with additional pastry for lattice top
2 c	Treacle (molasses may be substituted)
1.5 c	Fresh white breadcrumbs
1 t	Lemon juice
1	Egg, beaten with 1t of water

1. Mix the syrup, breadcrumbs and lemon juice and spread them into the pie shell
2. Roll out the remaining pastry, cut it into 1/4" strips and form a lattice top over the filling
3. Brush the pastry with the egg and water mixture
4. Bake in a preheated oven at 350°F for 10 minutes
5. Reduce the heat to 300°F and bake for another 20 to 25 minutes, or until the filling is lightly set
6. Serve hot with whipped cream or vanilla ice cream Serves 6

Cornish Pasty

Pastry:

3 c	Flour
1.5	Butter sticks, cold and cut into pieces
1.5 t	Salt
6 T	Water

1. Blend flour, butter, and salt until well combined
2. Add water, one tablespoon at a time to form a dough
3. Toss mixture until it forms a ball
4. Knead dough lightly against a smooth surface with the heel of the hand to distribute the butter evenly.
5. Form into a ball, dust with flour, wrap in wax paper, and chill for 30 minutes

Filling:

1 lb	Round steak, coarsely ground
1 lb	Boneless pork loin, coarsely ground
5	Carrots, chopped
2	Large onions, chopped
2	Potatoes, peeled and chopped
1/2 c	Rutabaga, chopped (or turnip)
2 t	Salt
1/2 t	Pepper

1. Combine all ingredients in a large bowl

ACASCIAS RIPHOUSE

2. Divide the pastry dough into 6 pieces, and roll one of the pieces into a 10-inch round on a lightly floured surface
3. Put 1 1/2 cups of filling on half of the round
4. Moisten the edges and fold the unfilled half over the filling to enclose it. Pinch the edges together to seal them, and crimp them decoratively with a fork
6. Transfer the pasty to a lightly buttered baking sheet and cut several slits in the top.
7. Repeat steps 1-6 till all dough is used
8. Bake in a preheated oven at 350°F for 30 minutes
9. Put one teaspoon of butter through a slit in each pasty, and continue baking for 30 minutes more
10. Remove from oven, cover with a damp tea towel, and cool for 15 minutes
Serves 6

Boiled Potatoes
    7 Potatoes

1. Wash and cook the potatoes with their skin in salted water for about 25 minutes
2. Add rosemary to the water for a nice effect
Serves 6

Spotted Dick

2 oz	White breadcrumbs
2 oz	Self-raising flour
4 oz	Shredded suet
8 oz	Prepared stoned raisins
1/8 t	Salt
1/2 t	Grated nutmeg
1/2 t	Ground ginger
1/8 t	Mace
1 oz	Whole candied peel, finely chopped
	grated zest of one orange
3	Eggs
3 t	Brandy

1. Mix breadcrumbs with suet and flour in a large bowl
2. Add raisins making sure that none are stuck together
3. When these ingredients are well mixed, add the salt, nutmeg, ginger, mace, candied peel and orange zest, mixing thoroughly
4. In a small bowl beat the eggs well and add them with the brandy to the mixture, stirring for at least 5 minutes 5. Pack the pudding basin with the mixture, cover with grease-proof paper and foil and tie down with a string
6. Steam for 4 hours, making sure that the saucepan doesn't boil dry
7. Serve with hot custard
Serves 4

Chipolatas

6 c	Lean pork
2 c	Fat pork
2 c	Rusk
1 c	Scalded ground rice

The Harry Potter Companion

1 T	Coriander
1 T	Pimento
1 T	Nutmeg
1 T	Thyme
1 T	Cayenne
1 T	White Pepper
2 T	Salt

1. Combine pork, rusk and part scalded ground rice
2. Add coriander, pimento, nutmeg, thyme, cayenne, white pepper and salt and mix thoroughly
3. Fill the sheep casings, 16 per pound
3. Fry the finished chipolatas

Serves 12

Chipolatas are often mistaken for cocktail sausages, but the latter are just a miniature version of the ordinary pork sausage. In Britain chipolatas are usually served at Christmas with turkey.

Baked Potatoes
    15 Potatoes

1. Preheat oven to 425°F
2. Thoroughly scrub the potatoes
3. Pierce jackets in several places to allow steam to escape
4. Wrap individually in aluminum foil
5. Place potatoes on oven rack or baking sheet
6. Bake 40 to 55 minutes or until tender when pierced with a fork
7. Serve with butter, sour cream, garlic butter or seasonings

Serves 12

Custard Tarts

3/8 c	Sugar
2 T	Cornstarch
1.5 c	Milk
2	Egg yolks
1 t	Vanilla extract
12 oz	Package ready-made puff pastry
1 c	Flour for rolling

1. Place the sugar in a pan with 5T of water and gently bring to a boil, stirring until the sugar dissolves
2. Dissolve the cornstarch in a little of the milk
3. Whisk the remaining milk, egg yolks, vanilla extract and cornstarch mixture into the sugar syrup
4. Gently bring to a boil, stirring until smooth and thickened.
5. Cover the custard and allow to cool
6. Open out the sheet of pastry and roll out a little more to a thickness of 1/8"
7. Cut the pastry into 4" circles and use them to line a small bun pan
8. Refrigerate until the custard is cool
9. Spoon the cooled custard into the tart cases then bake in a preheated oven at 400°F for 20 minutes until the tarts are golden brown

10. Serve warm or at room temperature
    Serves 16

Cooking Measurements
For those working in metric measurements, metric equivalents are given for each old British measure.

t: teaspoon, 1 teaspoon =5 ml, 3 teaspoons = 1 tablespoon.
T: tablespoon, 1 Tablespoon = 15 ml.
c: Cup, 1 cup = 16 ounces = 500 ml.
oz: ounce, 1 ounce =31.25 ml.
Qt: quart, 1 quart =.946 liters.
lb: pound, 1 pound = 450 grams.

THE QUIDDITCH CUP

Teachers, and even the school ghosts, follow all the House Quidditch matches closely because the cup is won by the points accumulated over a season, not by the number of won games. If total accumulated points are high, but wins are low, a House can still win the cup. Points won in Quidditch are added to House hourglasses, making them important to the winning of the House Cup as well. Each House team plays the 3 other House teams only once during the year making a total of 6 games played each year. Matches are usually played at 11am (or 1pm) on Saturdays starting in Nov. Games are usually not played in months with major holiday vacations, such as Easter or Christmas when the teams have not had time to practice.

Each House team has 7 regular players and may have as many reserves as they wish. Gryffindor always has no reserve players, though they have often needed them, and only replaces players after an injury, ban or expulsion has occurred which is less than wise captaining. New members are added teams during the 2nd week of term, when tryouts are held. Teams all have use of the 2 locker rooms during matches or practices. Quidditch robes, embroidered with a player's last name across the back, are kept by the individual players in their respective trunks. All brooms belonging to team members are kept in a broomshed with an unlocked wooden door that is near the pitch. All the Quidditch balls are kept locked in a wooden crate or a trunk in Madam Hooch's office. Dobby was able to tamper with the balls using his extremely strong house-elf magic, but wizards wouldn't be able to get to the balls let alone tamper with them unless they were very powerful.

There are 700 ways to commit a foul, but only 10 fouls are commonly seen nowadays during a game. Only players with no sense of sportsmanship or fair play would sink so low as to foul another player and needless to say frequent fouls occur during Hogwarts' matches when Slytherin House is playing. A captain may ask the referee for an inquiry if something questionable happens but this is rare as Madam Hooch is an excellent referee and does almost all of Hogwarts' matches. On the one occasion Pr Snape did referee a game, it was only because he felt that Harry was in danger of being attacked by Pr Quirrell and he felt himself the only one able to combat such Dark magic. Like Pr Snape's DADA knowledge, his Quidditch knowledge is not all that good and the game was rife with fouls, however, he did protect Harry and that was his main purpose.

The Quidditch stadium runs around the entire field, holds about 3/4 of the student body (there are always those few that would rather study) and benches are raised high in the air for a better view. Students bring binoculars, carry signs made of sheets and wear decorated hats, flags, rosettes, scarves or other items displaying the colors or mascot of their House team. Most students will support their own team first and any team playing against Slytherin second. Heads of Houses usually attend their House's games and sometimes even all games. Hagrid goes to Gryffindor games because Harry, and later Ron, both play on this team. Dumbledore rarely attends games but can see them from his office widow. When Dumbledore does attend games, it's usually because Gryffindor is playing or because it's the final game of the season and he needs to be there to present the Quidditch Cup to the winning Head of House, or team captain.

The Quidditch Cup itself is a huge silver cup with all the details of previous winners on it. It is usually inscribed similar to this Gryffindor, 1971, James Potter. It's said to be kept in the Trophy Room except when it's being awarded by Dumbledore to a team captain or Head of House after the last match of the year but it always seems to be sitting on Pr McGonagall's office mantle so, go figure. Each year the winning House is inscribed on it with the year and the captain's name. The year Harry joined Gryffindor's House team, Gryffindor's last cup win was in 84/85 during Charlie Weasley's stint at Hogwarts. Slytherin went on a 7-year streak of wins from 85/86 thru 91/92. The cup was canceled in 92/93 due to basilisk problems but Gryffindor was finally able to pull out a win in 93/94. There was no cup awarded in the 94/95 season due to the TT, but Gryffindor reclaimed the cup in 95/96.

Quidditch Matches

The following is a list of games that were known to have been played or were probably played. The Referee is Madam Hooch unless otherwise noted.

91/92 Games, Slytherin Cup
Slytherin v. Hufflepuff
Slytherin must have won to have ranking S1, H2 at start of the Gryffindor game.
Gryffindor v. Slytherin
Gryffindor wins 170-60, moves into 2nd place - above Hufflepuff. S1, G2, H3. Known Game.
Gryffindor v. Hufflepuff
Ref: Snape. Gryffindor wins in 5 minutes, 150-20, and moves into 1st place for the cup, knocking off Slytherin. Dumbledore attends. G1, S2, H3. Known Game.
Hufflepuff v. Ravenclaw
Ravenclaw wins. G1, S2, R3, H4.
Slytherin v. Ravenclaw
Slytherin wins. G ties S, R2, H3.
Gryffindor v. Ravenclaw
Ravenclaw wins. Gryffindor losses the Quidditch Cup to Slytherin. Final ranking: S1, G2, R3, H4. Known Game.

Although Slytherin, Gryffindor and Ravenclaw each won 2 games a piece and Hufflepuff no games during this season, Slytherin must have won its 2 games by more points than Gryffindor, and Gryffindor in turn won its games by more points than Ravenclaw. Presuming a minimum of 300 points (for 2 Golden Snitches) for Slytherin and Gryffindor the additional points must be made up of Quaffle points, which prove to be the deciding factor. This shows the importance of Chasers on a team as equal to that of a Seeker, though Chasers get little of the Seeker's adulation or praise.

92/93 Games, No Cup Awarded
Slytherin v. Gryffindor
Gryffindor wins, 150-60. Known Game.
Gryffindor v. Hufflepuff
Canceled by McGonagall. Known Game.
  These are the only known games played. Due to basilisk attacks the games were called off. The Quidditch Cup was not awarded in 1993.

93/94 Games, Gryffindor Cup
Gryffindor v. Hufflepuff
Hufflepuff wins, 150-50. Dumbledore attends. Known Game.
Hufflepuff v. Ravenclaw
Ravenclaw wins, 50-250. Known game.
Ravenclaw v. Slytherin
Slytherin wins. Known game.
Hufflepuff v. Slytherin
Slytherin wins.
Gryffindor v. Ravenclaw
Gryffindor wins. Known game.
Gryffindor v. Slytherin
If Gryffindor wins, they move into 1st on points. Gryffindor wins, 230-20. Known game.
  Dumbledore awards the cup on the spot. Pr McGonagall puts it in her study.

94/95 The TT, No Cup.

95/96 Games, Gryffindor Cup
Slytherin v. Gryffindor
Gryffindor wins, 40-160. Known Game.
Hufflepuff v. Gryffindor
Hufflepuff wins, 240-230. Known Game.
Ravenclaw v. Slytherin
Slytherin win?
Ravenclaw v. Hufflepuff
Ravenclaw win?
Slytherin v. Hufflepuff
Hufflepuff wins. Known Game.
Gryffindor v. Ravenclaw
Gryffindor wins. Known Game. Gryffindor takes the cup.

HOUSE TEAMS
The following is a list of teams and their players as far as they are known or indicated. The year of a player as well as their position is noted. Adrian Pucey must be an exceptional player as he seems to have played in almost every position. Things in (parentheses) indicate uncertainty.

91/92 Teams
Gryffindor: Robes: Scarlet Red.

Captain: Oliver Wood, Keeper, 5th yr.
    He was Captain 90/91,
Chasers:
  Angelina Johnson, 3rd yr.
  Alicia Spinnet, 3rd yr
      Reserve, 90/91,
  Katie Bell 3rd yr.
Seeker: Harry Potter, 1st yr.
Beaters:
  Fred Weasley, 3rd yr.
      Played 90/91
  George Weasley, 3rd yr.
      Played 90/91

Slytherin: Robes: Forest Green.
Captain: Marcus Flint, Chaser, 6th yr.
Chasers: Adrian Pucey, 2nd yr.
      (Montague? 2nd yr?)
Seeker: Terence Higgs, 7th yr.
Keeper: Bletchley, 2nd yr.
Beaters: ? Derrick, 4th yr.
      ? Bole, 4th yr.
Other positions and players unknown.
Slytherin is an all male team that leers at girls.

Hufflepuff: Robes: Canary Yellow.
  Unknown team members.

Ravenclaw: Robes: Sapphire Blue.
  Unknown team members.

92/93 Teams:
Gryffindor: Same as 91/92.

Slytherin: Seeker is new.
Captain: Marcus Flint, Chaser 7th yr.
Chasers: Adrian Pucey, 3rd yr.
      (Montague? 3rd yr?)
Seeker: Draco Malfoy, 2nd yr.
Beaters: ? Derrick, 5th yr.
      ? Bole, 5th yr.
Keeper: Miles Bletchley, 3rd yr.

93/94 Teams:
Gryffindor: Same as 91/92.

Hufflepuff:
Captain: Cedric Diggory, Seeker, 5th yr.
Other positions and players unknown.

Ravenclaw: All on Cleansweep Sevens; but Cho is on a Comet 260.
Captain: Roger Davies, 5th yr.
Seeker: Cho Chang Seeker, 4th yr.
Other positions and players unknown.

Slytherin:
Captain: Marcus Flint, Chaser, 8th yr.
Chasers: C. Warrington, (2nd yr?)
 ? Montague, (4th yr?)
Keeper: Adrian Pucey, 5th yr.
Seeker: Draco Malfoy, 4th yr.
Beaters: ? Derrick, 6th yr.
 ? Bole, 6th yr.

94/95 Teams:
In this year there was no Quidditch played due to the TT.

95/96 Teams:
Gryffindor:
Captain: Angelina Johnson, Chaser, 7th yr.
Chasers: Katie Bell, 7th yr.
 Alicia Spinnet, 7th yr.
Beaters: Fred and George, 7th yr.
 Replaced midseason.
 Andrew Kirke, (year?)
 Jack Sloper, (year?)
Seeker: Harry Potter, 5th yr.
 Replaced midseason.
 Ginny Weasley, 4th yr.
Keeper: Ron Weasley, 5th yr.

Slytherin:
Captain: ? Montague, Chaser, (6th yr?)
Chasers: C. Warrington, (4th yr?)
 Adrian Pucey, 6th yr
Keeper: Miles Bletchley, 6th yr.
Seeker: Draco Malfoy, 5th yr.
Beaters: Vincent Crabbe, 5th yr.
 Gregory Goyle, 5th yr.

Ravenclaw:
Captain: Roger Davies, Chaser, 7th yr.
Chasers: ? Bradley, (year?)
 ? Chambers, (year?)
Seeker: Cho Chang, 6th yr.
Other positions and players unknown.

Hufflepuff:
Chaser: Zacharias Smith, 6th yr.
Seeker: Summerby, (year?)

Other positions and players unknown.

TRIWIZARD TOURNAMENT

The TT was established some time prior to 1291, as a friendly competition between the 3 largest European schools of wizardry Hogwarts, Beauxbatons and Durmstrang meaning each school was well established by that time. As the name implies 3 student wizard champions, 1 from each school, compete against each other, in 3 magical tasks. Each competing school took a turn hosting the event, which took place only once every 5 years meaning they would have to host only once every 15 years.

The TT was considered a way to establish ties across the borders, but eventually, in 1792, the death toll got so high they stopped having it. It's unknown what school was hosting when things went wrong but it seemed to have been Beauxbatons. For over 200 years the event languished till in 1994 an attempt was made to restart the TT. The British MoM's DIMC and the DMGS worked together to organize the event, under very controlled conditions, and Hogwarts agreed to host. Given the outcome, the TT was probably again called off in perpetuity.

Triwizard Tournament of 1792: A cockatrice went on a rampage and injured all 3 school judges sitting on the panel. It was at this point they decided to stop doing the TT. Obviously it didn't matter how many students died, but injure a judge and, well, that's just too much.

The Welcome Feast: Oct 30, 1994. A traditional part of the TT in which the hosting school welcomes the other 2 participating schools. The arriving schools usually do so in a spectacular fashion to impress the other schools with their magical abilities. The Welcome Feast in 1994 was to honor of the 12 Beauxbatons students, 12 Durmstrang students and their respective Heads, Olympia Maxime and Igor Karkoff. During the feast the Goblet of Fire was displayed and students were told how it worked and how they could enter if they met the age requirement.

The Weighing of the Wands: This ceremony occurs before a TT starts. Each champion's wand is inspected by a qualified wandmaker then spell-tested to make sure that it is functioning optimally. Mr Ollivander was brought in to weigh the wands for the 1994 TT.

Triwizard Tournament of 1994 (94/95): The DIMC and the DMGS were the main bodies responsible for this attempt to restart the TT. They felt they had come up with a way to insure no one would die and maximum safety for competitors, judges and spectators could be maintained. The main change to the competition was to require all the competitors be 17, of legal age. It was the 1st and only time ever the TT imposed the age limit. An Age Line was even set up to prevent students under 17 from entering their names into the Goblet of Fire. The reason for the age limit was that legally the MoM wasn't responsible if someone chose to enter at age 17 and got killed. In addition to the age limit the MoM insured that all TT tasks were controllable, meaning adult wizards could intervene if champions got into trouble or requested help.

Incentives to enter included 1,000G in personal prize money, being exempt from end of the year exams and being able to ask for help, ie, cheat. Champions were not allowed to ask for or accept help from teachers or judges (though Ludo offered his help to Harry), however, the rules say nothing about champions asking for or accepting help from anyone else, including other champions. Disincentives included not being able to easily decline to be a champion once chosen, begin hit with some serious consequences for breaking a magical contract is one declined being a champion and of course dying in some unusually painful or otherwise horrible way while competing.

For each of the 3 tasks students were only told the day and time it would start, often a few months in advance of the actual task. Only when one task was completed were students told about the next task. Champions were to be given no hint of what was going to happen for some tasks and for others they were given a cryptic clue to help them prepare without actually knowing fully what the event entailed. The 3 tasks are to supposed to test different aspects of a champions character as well as their magical skills, which as 17 should be very advanced. A panel of 5 judges, 3 of whom are the Heads of the competing schools, awards points at their own discretion for each champion after each task is completed. Each judge can award a maximum of 10 points for each task.

The Panel of Judges in 94/95 was composed of Ludo Bagman, Albus Dumbledore, Olympia Maxime, Igor Karkoff and Barty Crouch Sr. Percy filled in for Barty Sr at Task 1 and Task 2. Cornelius Fudge filled in for Barty Sr, at Task 3 when Percy was put under investigation by the MoM. The champions for the TT were Harry for an unknown school, Cedric Diggory for Hogwarts, Fleur Delacour for Beauxbatons and Viktor Krum for Durmstrang. An official winner was never declared by the judges although Cedric and Harry both reached the TT Cup at the same time and ought to have been declared joint winners. Ultimately Cedric and Harry were considered to have won. Cedric was killed and got the honor for winning, Harry received the cash prize by default after Mrs Diggory told him to keep it. But Harry felt guilty for keeping it, so, he gave it to Fred and George to open their joke shop.

Task 1: This task was to test a champions daring and courage in the face of the unknown, in this case a dragon. The object was to steal from a nest of real dragon eggs a fake golden egg without getting hurt by the mother dragon or destroying any of the eggs or the dragon. This task occurred Nov 24, 1994. In theory no champion was supposed to know she or he was to be facing a dragon. In fact, all of them knew they were facing a dragon, because someone else told them. This was not abnormal for a TT task because cheating is a traditional part of the TT.

Cedric was 1st. He drew a Swedish Short Snout. It took him 15 minutes. He Transfigured a rock into a live Labrador Retriever as a diversionary tactic. He received a facial burn. His score was 38.

Fleur was 2nd. She drew a Common Welsh Green. It took her 10 minutes. She put the dragon to sleep with a charm. She had her skirt burned. Her score is unknown.

Viktor was 3rd. He drew a Chinese Fireball. It took him about 8 minutes. He used a Conjuctivitus Curse that blinded the dragon but she squashed half her eggs by accident so points were deducted. His score was 40.

Harry was 4th. He drew an Hungarian Horntail. It took him about 5 minutes. He used his Firebolt to get the egg and was not injured. His score was 40.

One does wonder why the students didn't simply Accio the egg itself and spare themselves and the mother dragons some difficult moments. As William of Occam pointed out out long ago, the simplest solution is often the best. But, given magical schools are more vocational schools, they don't teach courses in Logic. One expects the fault lay with inadequate curriculum for intelligent students rather than stupid students.

The Golden Egg: The egg which the champions rescued contained within it a clue to surviving the second task. If a champion could solve the clue, she or he would be able to prepare for the next task. By opening the egg a loud screechy wail was released, the sound of merpeople singing. When held underwater one could hear them singing in English, surprisingly enough, though one is sure they were still singing Mermish. The song gave the clue that the second task was set underwater and involved something a champion held dear. This allowed champions time to find a way to breathe underwater though if they'd been a bit smarter they might have just hid the thing they held dear and spared themselves a soaking.

The Yule Ball: This traditional part of the TT took place on Dec 25, from 8 pm to midnight. It's considered an opportunity for students to socialize with, or date, students from the other schools. The ball was open to 4th years and above, though one could invite a younger student as one's date if one wished. Dress robes were required for the event though Olympia wore a gown. There was no Christmas tea that year as the ball included a feast which precede the ball. Champions entered in procession after everyone else was seated at dinner and sat together at a large round table at the top of the hall where the 5 judges also were seated. Unlike regular feasts at Hogwarts, people ordered from menus by stating what they wanted and it simply appeared.

After dinner the champions and their dates opened the ball by dancing the first dance by themselves: Fleur and Roger, Cedric and Cho, Viktor and Hermione, Harry and Parvati. After this all the other students were permitted to join the dancing. The ball was attended by some 1,200 people, of which probably 800-900 were Hogwarts teachers and students. Hogwarts was festively decorated indoors and out, 800 barrels of mulled mead were served and the Weird Sisters were brought in special for the event. Everyone had a good time but Harry and Ron, and their dates Parvati and Padma. The evening ended with a last dance after which students were dismissed to their respective Houses.

Mead is an alcoholic beverage, which calculating 800 barrels which are fixed at 31 gallons per barrel equals 24,800 gallons of mead. Dividing this by 1200 drinkers would mean each person would need to drink 20 gallons (approximately 320 cups) to consume it all. While Hagrid and Olympia could do this without passing out, one doubts anyone else could. One presumes there is still a large stock of barrels in the basement of Hogwarts. Perhaps it will be brought out for Christmas, for the next 20 years. Certainly it *may* improve will aging. On the other hand, having tasted mulled mead before, this author can honestly say, 1 or 2 glasses over the course of a lifetime would be plenty for most people.

Task 2: The task involved rescuing a hostage who was tied up in the merpeople's village at the bottom of the Lake. Champions had to come up with a way to breathe underwater for a long period of time, about an hour, to reach the hostage. This task occurred Feb 24, 1995, when the Lake was freezing cold but not froze over. Champions had had approximately 3 months to work out the clue from their eggs and should have been well prepared. As it was, only Cedric was ready for the task, having solved the clue early and found the proper magical solution, which he was able to execute correctly.

Fleur had to abandon completing the task because of a grindylow attack. Her score was 25.

Harry freed Ron, and Gabrielle, but lost time waiting for other champions to rescue their hostages. His score was 45.

Cedric used the Bubblehead Charm to rescue Cho. His score was 47.

Viktor Transfigured himself into a shark, badly, and saved Hermione with Harry's help. His score was 40.

Task 3: The object of this task was to get through a giant booby-trapped maze and grab the TT Cup. The first champion to touch the cup would receive full marks and win the competition irrespective of her or his total score. This task occurred on the evening of Jun 24, 1995. The maze was comprised of 20' hedges grown on the Quidditch pitch and filled with odd dangerous creatures and areas that were rigged with unusual spells. Those leading in points got a slight (maybe 30-60 seconds) head start into the maze. Harry and Cedric entered the maze together first followed later by Viktor and later still by Fleur. Officials surrounding the pitch, identifiable by red stars on the top of their hats (McGonagall, Barty Jr [Moody], Flitwick) or back of their vest (Hagrid), were to patrol the outside of the maze looking for red sparks.

Champions were to shoot red sparks up in the air to signal that they or another champion was in trouble and needed help. Despite the available help Fleur was Stunned by Barty Jr, Viktor (under Barty Jr's Imperius Curse) tortured Cedric with the Cruciatus Curse then was Stunned himself by Harry, Cedric was killed by Peter Pettigrew with the Avada Kedavra Curse after ending up in the Little Hangleton graveyard and Harry had his blood used for Voldemort's rebirthing potion, ended up dueling for his life with Voldemort and finally had to out run a pack of Death Eaters dragging Cedric's corpse. Clearly this was not the safety-oriented TT the MoM had hoped for. However, the important thing to remember is that no judges were hurt.

MAGICAL AND NONMAGICAL SCHOOL SUPPLIES

If it's something students are told to bring to Hogwarts because it was in a list sent to them by Pr McGonagall, or something they usually bring it's listed in this section. This section starts with the various lists students are sent each year and ends with a look at student equipment.

SCHOOL LISTS

Year 1
Equipment

1 pewter cauldron, standard size 2	(Potions - Snape)
1 set of phials, glass or crystal	(Potions - Snape)
1 set of scales, brass	(Potions - Snape)
1 telescope	(Astronomy-Sinistra)
1 wand	(Charms – Flitwick & Transfiguration – McGonagall)

All students need to bring parchment rolls, ink, a tapemeasure and quills.

Students are allowed to bring an owl, cat or toad, but no other animals, though Ron brought a rat and Lee Jordan a tarantula.

First years are not allowed to bring or have a personal broomstick at school, but Harry had a waiver from Dumbledore.

Uniforms
3 sets of plain black work robes
1 plain black pointed hat
1 pair of gloves made of dragon hide or similar protective material
1 black winter cloak with silver fastenings
All clothes are to carry name tags as all uniforms look alike and the house-elves, not to mention the students, could never tell their laundry apart if they didn't have tags.

Booklist

The Standard Book of Spells (Grade 1)	(Charms - Flitwick)
A History of Magic	(History of Magic - Binns)

The Harry Potter Companion

Magical Theory (Theory - Unknown)
A Beginners' Guide to Transfiguration (Transfiguration - McGonagall)
One Thousand Magical Herbs and Fungi (Herbology - Sprout & Potions - Snape)
Magical Drafts and Potions (Potions - Snape)
Fantastic Beasts and Where to Find Them (Magizoology - Unknown)
The Dark Forces: A Guide to Self-Protection (DADA - Quirrell)

Year 2
Booklist
The Standard Book of Spells (Grade 2) (Charms - Flitwick)
Break with a Banshee (DADA - Lockhart)
Gadding with Ghouls
Holiday with Hags
Travels with Trolls
Voyages with Vampires
Wanderings with Werewolves
Year with the Yeti

Year 3
Booklist
The Standard Book of Spells (Grade 3) (Charms - Flitwick)
Unfogging the Future (Divination - Trelawney)
The Monster Book of Monsters (Care of Magical Creatures - Hagrid)

Year 4
Booklist
The Standard Book of Spells (Grade 4) (Charms - Flitwick)
Intermediate Transfiguration (Transfiguration - McGonagall)

Dress Robes: They are required for 4th years and above, who would likely be coming to the Yule Ball. Ron had second-hand, long, lace-trimmed, maroon velvet robes during this year but was thankfully bought new ones by Fred and George for his 5th year. Harry has some just like his school robes but in bottle green to bring out his eyes. Hermione has some floaty pale blue robes.

Year 5
Booklist
The Standard Book of Spells (Grade 5) (Charms - Flitwick)
Defensive Magical Theory (DADA - Umbridge)

Books are always chosen by the professor teaching the course and this is why the DADA books change every year, though one presumes with a steady teacher, the book would remain the same for all 7 years. Except for Charms and Transfiguration, classes use the same textbook for the entire 7 years. Elective courses also seem to use the same book from the first year to the NEWT year, which is unfortunate for those taking care of magical creatures. Divination, which has only one purchased textbook, has supplemental texts that Sybill keeps in her classroom and loans out to students, which is very cost effective.

EQUIPMENT

Brass Scales: These are needed for the weighing of materials used in Potions, though they seem to be popular with all magicals as the house-elves use them in the Kitchens.

ACASCIAS RIPHOUSE

It's unclear why they need to be brass, other than Pr Snape may take pleasure in the fact that it's a lot of work for students to keep them polished. However, goblins also prefer to use brass scales and goblins are as exacting in the measurements as anyone can be.

Cauldrons: These come in all sizes and metals: copper, brass, pewter, silver, gold and can be self-stirring and even collapsible. Collapsible cauldrons come in a handy if one needs to carry them around a lot, self-stirring is good for those who are busy and can't watch their cauldrons and smaller ones are nice if one is whipping up potions in a confined space, like a toilet stall. Pewter, standard size 2, cauldrons are required for Hogwarts. Neville has been through 6 cauldrons in 5 years due to various accidents. Poorly made imported cauldrons were something of an obsession with Percy for a while. Harry wanted a gold cauldron but Hagrid wisely stopped him as gold melts at a very low temperature.

Phials, Glass or Crystal: aka vials. Phials are needed for Potions. Glass would probably be better than lead crystal ones since they would be less breakable, but rock crystal phials would add a very interesting twist to potionmaking since such phials would have the capability of acting like a conductor of heat as well as electric charges.

Scrolls: Parchment scrolls are generally self-rolling. When one is finished with them, they just roll up. A scroll can probably come in many sizes starting at about 5' long by 8" wide, and going up by 5' length increments and 2" width increments to about 60' long and 20" wide (for architectural plans, diagrams, or even art).

Tapemeasures: All students have these to measure their homework assignments which are always given in feet and inches rather than pages or number of words. Mr Ollivander has one he keeps in his coatpocket that has silver markings, is voice activated as well as manually operated and will work even on its own.

Telescope: Students are required to have one for Astronomy classes. Harry's is brass and collapsible. It must be a fairly good one to see *all* the stars of the constellation Orion.

Wands: There are wandmakers in every country. Usually wandmakers go to collect the wood from a wand-tree (usually findable by the presence of bowtruckles) and the magical core materials themselves at great personal risk. Probably a sense of adventure, great skill with wood, an artistic bent and good instincts about people and magical beasts are necessary to be a good wandmaker. Wands are fairly inexpensive considering they last a lifetime with proper care; Harry's wand cost only 7 Galleons ($ 51.45 US or 35.83 pounds UK).

Prices vary only with the difficulty in crafting a particular wand, the rarity of the wood or the difficulty of obtaining the magical core item. All wands have as their core a powerful magical substance such as a unicorn tailhair (difficult to obtain) or a dragon heartstring (deadly to obtain). No two wands are the same, due to the many core and wood combinations and the fact that no two magical beasts are the same, but two wands that share a core substance from the same creature, such as a tailfeather from the same phoenix, are called twin wands. It is difficult to use twin wands against each other as Priori Incantatem (see below) is likely to result.

A wizard can't do her or his best magic with a borrowed wand and will never get as good a result using another wizard's wand, but she or he could still do some pretty impressive magic. This 1-wand-1-owner relationship may explain Neville's otherwise inexplicable lack of talent. One admits his magical abilities were slow to make themselves known compared to other pureblood children but since arriving at Hogwarts he's been forced to use his father's wand (probably because Gran is sentimental rather than cheap). He's been working at a disadvantage magically speaking and may be profoundly magically gifted but unable to prove it. Thankfully his father's wand broke in Jun 1996 and Gran will now be forced to get him a wand of his own for the coming school year.

Buying a new wand can be a much more exhausting process then scrounging up the Galleons to pay for it so the help of a professional wandmaker in determining the right wand quickly is vital. If after whipping a wand overhead and swishing it down, nothing happens, that wand is not for the right one for the wizard swishing it. The wand should not do uncontrollable or lackluster magic when used, but it should give some indication of performing quality, controllable magic in the wizard's hand. In Harry's case, when he held the wand right for him, it emitted some colored sparks of dancing light.

Once purchased a wand should be treated with care, unlike how Charlie Weasley apparently treats his! Mr Ollivander specifically asks after his wands to make sure they are well treated because he knows the importance of wandcare to doing magic. Wands, like any piece of wood, require oiling and polishing and even periodic cleaning. If a wand dries out it might crack or catch fire when doing particularly powerful spells. If the wand does break, the broken pieces of the wand still have power and can be bound up with Spellotape but this is not advised.

A wand broken cleanly in half, as Hagrid's was, is safer to use than a damaged wand like Ron's which was almost snapped near the end. Either way they will work, though not nearly so well as they did originally. Ways to know if a wand is damaged or on its last legs: it sparks at odd moments; it emits a thin grey smoke that smells of rotten eggs; it makes a popping noise; it misdirects a charm; or it backfires charms. If a wizard experiences any of these occurrences with her or his wand, she or he should stop using it immediately and get a new one.

Types of Wands and Who Owns Them

James: Mahogany, 11". It was pliable, had a bit more power than most and was excellent for Transfiguration work. An Ollivander wand. This wand was apparently lost or destroyed in 1981.

Lily: Willow, 10.25". It was long and swishy and nice for charm work. An Ollivander wand. This wand was apparently lost or destroyed in 1981.

Hagrid: Oak, 16". Despite being oak, it was rather bendy. It was broken in half in 1943. At 16" it was one of the longest wands around. An Ollivander wand.

Harry: Holly, 11". The core is a tailfeather from Fawkes, Dumbledore's phoenix. The wand is probably silvery-white since that's how unstained holly looks. It is nice and supple. An Ollivander wand.

Voldemort: Yew. 13.5". The cores is a tailfeather from Fawkes, Dumbledore's phoenix. The wand was purchased in 1939, blown up and lost in 1981, recovered in 1994. It's a very powerful wand, made even more powerful by being in Voldemort's hands. An Ollivander wand.

Ron: He had Charlie's old battered and chipped wand, with its unicorn tailhair core sticking out from 1991-1993. Its useful life ended May 29, 1993 after Obliviating Pr Lockhart's memory. He bought a new Ollivander wand Aug 31, 1993. Willow, 14". It has a unicorn tailhair for a core, as Charlie's did, so it may be that unicorn tailhairs work for Weasley boys in general.

Fleur: Inflexible rosewood, 9.5". The core is one veela hair apparently given to the wandmaker by her grandmother – a magical beast. Mr Ollivander thought it was a temperamental wand but it does emit attractive pink and gold sparks. Maker unknown.

ACASCIAS RIPHOUSE

Cedric: Ash, 12.25". The core was one tailhair plucked from a particularly fine, 17 hand, unicorn stallion. The wand was pleasantly springy and Ced kept it in good condition by polishing it regularly. It was lost in Little Hangleton's graveyard when Cedric was killed there in 1995. An Ollivander wand.

Viktor: Hornbeam, 10.25". It has a dragon heartstring core. The wand is rather thick, quite rigid and very powerful in a raw uncontrolable sort of way. A Gregorovitch wand.

Priori Incantatem: aka the Reverse Spell Effect. A very rare and strange effect that occurs when two wands with the same core material (twins) are used against each other. The wands will not work properly and when the wand beams intersect they become connected and remain so unless effort is made by both parties to disconnect them. If the wand remain connected any length of time they will start to vibrate heavily, both wizards will be lifted slightly into the air and set down in the nearest large clearing. If the connection continues to be unbroken a gold thread will start to spin a crisscrossing dome over the 2 wizards involved. An unearthly and beautiful sound like the phoenix song will be heard coming from the vibrating golden threads. Eventually a large bead of light will form in the middle of the connecting beam and, depending on whose will is stronger, the bead will be forced toward one of the wandtips. Whichever wandtip the bead of light touches, that wand will begin to regurgitate the spells it's done in reverse order.

Given that it is a rare effect, not too much is known about it. This might explain why many wizards wrongly believe the ghost of *every* spell cast by the wand pops out in reverse order when Priori Incantatem occurs. Appearing from Voldemort's wand when it got Priori Incantatem were: Cedric Diggory, Frank Bryce, Bertha Jorkins, Lily Potter and then James Potter. No shadow of any Cruciatus Curses appeared, yet Harry saw Voldemort do it to Avery and had it done to himself. No shadow of the spell the produced Peter's new hand appeared either. Clearly Voldemort did other magic with his wand beside kill people with the Avada Kedavra Curse yet none of those spell regurgitated. So every spell is not regurgitated, only the ghosts of those spells that killed people.

So what does this say about Priori Incantatem? Well, it would seem that only the most powerful of spells still have ghosts that can be regurgitated after the passing of many years. Harry's parents died 13 years before their shadows appeared. But even Priori Incantatem has its limits. No shadows before Harry's parents appeared, and Voldemort had killed plenty of people before them. So it would appear there is a time limit of about 13 years on what a wand can regurgitate. One might also observe that only ghosts of murderous spells appeared. Voldemort had surely done other powerful spells and other spells involving people but they didn't regurgitate. Only the Avada Kedavra, and whatever killed James Potter, seem to produce a ghost. Something to think about.

James Potter is an odd case. Obviously Voldemort used some spell on James that killed him, over time, or it would not have regurgitated, but what that spell was, is unknown. It couldn't have been an Avada Kedavra as James did not die before Lily. The events must have been something like James and Voldemort dueled, James was mortally wounded by a spell that he was only partially able to fight off; Voldemort went into the nursery and killed Lily who threw herself in his way; he immediately attempted Harry's murder, but instead vaporized himself. This vaporizing of Voldemort had the effect of leveling the house to rubble. James, who was dying anyway at that point, was the crushed to death when the house collapsed died, though he would have died anyway from the spell, eventually. Given the number of unique

THE HARRY POTTER COMPANION

magical spells Voldemort had come up with, and the great threat that James was alive, Voldemort may have concocted a special death spell for use on James. More than this, cannot be speculated.

Note 1: This list of students, and those that follow for other Houses, should not be considered exhaustive. These lists are of student definitely confirmed to be in a certain House.

Part III. General Wizardry

Magical Talents

Inherent Magical Talents

THESE ARE TALENTS USUALLY ASSOCIATED with wizards from their birth and considered to be unacquireable by education or exist as a talent unique to only certain individuals.

Animagus: Being able to turn into one (and only one) form of fauna. All wizards with this talent must be registered with the MoM's Improper Use of Magic Office's Animagi Registry. Being unregistered can get one into a lot of trouble, but it also gives one wider latitude to do interesting things. The drawbacks of not registering is Azkaban and why the MoM keeps an eye on them through the registry is, supposedly, that transformations can go horribly wrong and a wizard might not ever recover if no one knew to give her or him aid. However one cannot assume that it's true that transformations can go even slightly wrong, just because the MoM says so, given the MoM's motivation to keep tabs on Animagi.

Maybe one Animagus, once, badly transformed due to some reason entirely unrelated to being an Animagus. But, given the very small number of Animagi registered, where would the MoM find a large enough sample population to prove that transformations can go wrong? Seven Animagus are not enough to be able to tell what Animagi can and can't do let alone what might have caused a bad transformation. None of the 7 seems to have ever had a problem transforming. An additional unregistered Animagus was born, Rita Skeeter, but she's never had any problems transforming.

The 3 that were self-created: Sirius Black, James Potter and Peter Pettigrew, did it through study and hard work. Sirius and James became Animagi in 3 years, Peter in 5. If it can be an done by oneself if one is intelligent enough to figure out how to do it, and these self-taught Animagi never had a single transformation go wrong, over an entire lifetime of repeatedly becoming Animagi, it severely undercuts the MoM's position that Animagi are somehow a danger to themselves and should register to get MoM protection. It's unclear why the MoM so fears Animagi. One expects the usual paranoia about anyone different. But whatever its excuse, the MoM's position on Animagi looks very queer indeed.

There are a few interesting misconceptions about Animagi due to their rarity. Some wizards believe that becoming an animal is to be limited in the same ways as the animal. For instance, if one turned into a cat, one would have a cat's mind and might easily forget where one was going incognito and start chasing mice instead. This is not only insulting to cats (Pr McGonagall), and other animals, it's untrue. If Peter Pettigrew, a talentless wizard, can stay a rat for 12 years rat without ever losing his human mind, so much so that he cannot only read a newspaper, he can fully understand the implications of what he's read, how can he be said to have a rat brain?

Another misconception is that if one stayed in an animal form too long, one might lose oneself and might not be able to return to a human state. While Peter might have been forced to return to his human state after some years, and restored to human form by Sirius and Remus, it doesn't mean he couldn't have returned to his human state himself. In fact, Sirius, who himself was an Animagus, knew that Peter could, otherwise what would have been the point of him *asking* Peter to turn himself back? Sirius knew, from being a dog for a very extended period of time that a wizard doesn't lose her or his mind or her or his ability to transform.

So, is an Animagus fully human when an animal? Good question. Sirius states his emotions were less complex as a dog. But we know that Peter's emotions remained entirely intact to the point that his hair fell out and he got sick with fear. An educated guess would say Sirius simply preferred to think his emotions were less complex when in fact the truth is more along the lines of when Sirius was in his dog form dementors were unable to sense his canine emotions and therefore were unable to suck his emotions out. The fact the dementors were more bearable to be around when Sirius was a dog and dementors though Sirius was going mad while he was in dog form, confirms dementors can't sense, read, interpret or suck animal emotions. Additional discussion of Animagi can be found under the entry for the Animagi Registry in Part I.

Bluebell Flames: Being able to produce portable, waterproof flames of a bright blue color that can be carried around either in the hand or in a glass jar seems to be a special talent. Lupin and Hermione have it, others don't.

Levitation: There are no magic spells, charms, etc, will allow wizards to fly when in their human form, however levitation is a common gifting among wizards. Unfortunately levitation only allows a wizard to hover 5 feet above the ground, enough to get a wizard in trouble with Muggles, but not enough to do a wizard any real good.

Metamorphmagus: Metamorphmagi are very rare. The ability to completely magically change one's appearance at will seems to be something one is born, but people said that about Animagi too and it wasn't true. Tonks was born a Metamorphmagus and is able to change her appearance to make herself appear different and even older. But can she change her gender? Or become much younger? It wouldn't seem so. Could she become an animal? Probably since she turned her nose into a pig snout for the amusement of Ginny and Hermione. Possibly it is minorly painful to metamorphise as Tonks is always screwing up her eyes and making strained expressions while transforming. However she seems to be able to do it multiple times in a very short space of time, just for fun, so it must not be too painful or straining on the physical body.

Parselmouth: The ability to speak to and understand Parseltongue and command snakes is an extremely rare gift. Generally one must be face-to-face with a live snake to evoke this talent, or at minimum will oneself to believe that a drawing, stuffed animal, etc, of the snake is alive. If speaking Parseltongue, the speaker believes she or he is speaking in a human language but observers hear it as hissing. It's considered a mark of a Dark Wizard and there would seem to be some truth to that as Salazar Slytherin, Voldemort and Harry, because Voldemort cursed him, are known to be able to speak Parseltongue, the language of snakes. This is not to imply that Harry is a Dark wizard, merely to point out that the only reason he has this gift is because a Dark wizard gave Harry a part of himself, which happened to include the ability to speak to snakes, when he cursed him.

Seers: The ability look into the future and interpret what one sees correctly is a very rare gift. It is said to run in families. It apparently skips 5 generations according to Sybill. She seems to be right.

LEARNED MAGICAL TALENTS

These are talents generally considered to be acquireable by education. They can be commonplace or obscure.

Apparition: The ability to Apparate and Disapparate, to vanish from one place and appear in a different place almost instantly, is a commonly learned talent that almost all wizards over 17 have at their command. Apparators are those who have the ability to legally Apparate. The Apparition Test is the test given by the DMT and it must be passed before a wizard can begin to use Apparition as a means of personal (and only personal) travel. No one under 17 can use Apparition (or even Apparate with an adult) or take the Apparition Test. The test can be passed with distinction (meaning an above average grade) or failed repeatedly. When done incorrectly it can lead to nasty complications like Splinch. One can, technically, Apparate over 300 miles, the maximum distance depends on the individual skill or the wizard, but it is not recommended that anyone Apparate between continents. Apparition becomes increasingly unreliable over very long distances and should only be used by highly skilled wizards for attempting to cross large bodies of water to reach other continents. One cannot Apparate or Disapparate within Hogwarts or even into or out of Hogwarts' grounds due to special enchantments that prevent it.

Splinch: also Splinched. The sorry state of leaving half of oneself behind when one Apparates so that half of one's body or body parts, such as just an ear, toe or kidney, is in one place and half or parts are in another place often miles away. It is not painful, but when it happens the unfortunate wizard can't move either way. Such events are not common, thankfully, but when they do occur they require the DMT to send out a team to get the wizard back together and use Memory Charms on Muggle bystanders. The DMT hates these cases because they generate lots of paperwork, but there is no fine or punishment for a wizard who ends up Splinched.

Divination: Tea leaf reading, crystal ball gazing, astrology, runes, arithmancy, tarot cards, etc, are all forms of divination. Some feel that divination can be learned, others claim one must be born with a Gift. The centaurs claim divination can be learned, but they say one can only see the big universal picture, not the little everyday happenings.

Legilimens: A Legilimens is a wizard who has the ability to look into others' minds by magical means. This magic is called legilimency and its opposite is occlumency. The incantation used is Legilimens. Dumbledore, Pr Snape and Voldemort all have this ability. Legilimency lets a wizard extract thoughts, feelings and memories from another being's mind. It requires the ability to interpret the findings correctly. Eye contact is usually crucial in legilimency. Time and space usually matter as well.

At a place like Hogwarts, guarded by many ancient spells and charms to protect those who live within its walls from physical or mental harm (another reason Pr Snape is at Hogwarts probably), it should be impossible to accomplish. But, in Harry's case the usual rules don't apply. His mind is Voldemort's, and vice versa. On the other hand, the curse that gave Harry the Parselmouth ability might also have given him the ability to use very high level legilimency and occlumency skills against anyone including Voldemort. The fact Harry got so far into Pr Snape's very closed mind suggests this to be so.

Occlumens: A wizard who practices the obscure branch of magic known as occlumency has the ability to seal her or his mind against magical intrusion and influence by another wizard by allowing the Occlumens to shut down all feelings and memories. It gives the wizard the ability to lie to others and get away with it even if she or he is Legilimens by another. Legilimency is the opposite of occlumency. Presumably the incantation is also Occlumens. Voldemort and Pr Snape are both excellent Occlumens. Dumbledore is only fairly good at by comparison.

In order for occlumency to work, one needs to be able to let go of all emotions or thoughts and make one's mind blank and calm. Feelings and memories must also be banished. If there is nothing in the mind, there is nothing an enemy can get out of it through legilimency such as thoughts that contradict any lies one might have been telling. The ability to repel another's mind with the one's own means not having to resort to repelling them with a wand. Pr Snape seems to have habitually practiced occlumency since 1980 if not earlier. This is no doubt why he is such an expert in the field and why there is always an odd cast to his eyes.

Harry was given some very unsuccessful occlumency lesson by Pr Snape in 95/96 in hopes Voldemort wouldn't continue to get into his mind. It had the reverse effect and weakened Harry's mental defenses to the point that it turned him into an aerial that picked up Voldemort's every mood swing. This is not to say that Harry couldn't be a good Occlumens eventually, with practice, against Voldemort. Harry might well have inherited the ability to be a superb Occlumens through Voldemort's failed curse. Also the fact that Voldemort was able to hide some information from Harry (the fact that Sirius wasn't at the MoM being tortured) indicates that Harry should be able hide things in his mind from Voldemort.

CHARMS, HEXES, JINXES, SPELLS AND CURSES

As a general rule, one thing all magic seems to have in common is the harder one wants the projected magic to hit the target, the more likely it is one must raise one's wand overhead, in a circular motion (as if building up centrifugal force with which to launch the magic), before releasing the magic at the intended target. This lassoing action must have the effect of strengthening or accelerating the spell considerably or no one would take the risk of raising their wand over their head thus presenting a perfectly clear target for a well placed Stupefy to the torso.

Another thing most magic seems to have in common is if there is an incantations it is likely to be in Latin or in the native speaker's language. Why does magic have an affinity for Latin? Possibly because using an ancient tongue eliminates the worry of Muggles picking up on the fact magic is being done. All things being equal, most people ignore others if they speak in a foreign language. Also, using Latin prevents magical mishaps. Orchid if used for magic, might crop up in sentence, creating a chance that it will set off some unfortunate accidental magic. Orchideous on the other hand has a 1 in a billion chance of turning up in daily conversation.

Of course whatever the word, all magic requires a hefty intention behind it. Pack will not cause any packing for someone non-magical. Pack may fail to produce a spectacular result if one doesn't like packing - Tonks. And Muggles could never use a magical word and gain a magical result. Some magic is of course language specific. A French incantation running to a stanza, when rendered into English would never work. A foreign word for which there is no English equivalent would also fail; the German Treppenwitz comes to mind. It means that witty remark one thought of as one was leave, ie, long after it could be used effectively. These are perhaps also reasons so many wizards are polyglots. The more languages, the more magical abilities.

The following definitions have not been approved by the MoM. They are just observations.

Charm: Charms don't have a very long life expectancy according to Hermione. But Ron's 40-year-old broom still flies, albeit slowly and not well. Thus a conflict arises. It would appear that all charms degrade over time. But how long the charm takes to degrade is equal to the talent of the person charming the object, the power of the charm itself and the ability of the person or thing being charmed to be charmed. The word charm is often interchanged with spell, but a charm is different than a spell. A charm can be very advanced but still not be a spell. A charm may or may not use an incantation. Charms are generally dependent on wand movements rather than incantations or a combination of both. Usually a charm involves a localized object (Ludo's voicebox, Fluffy's doorlock) or a temporary timeframe. They are not intended to be permanent or even long-lasting magic. Even a memory charm is only supposed to hide one memory (localized object) for the lifetime of the person involved (temporary timeframe).

Hex: Hexes usually have a component that makes the party on the receiving end experience some physical form of pain. Sometimes minor permanent damage can occur with a hex. Arthur Weasley still has scars from where Mr Ogg hexed him during his days at Hogwarts. Hexes are painful but survivable. They are usually used defensively and generally no magic is required to remove their effects. A counterhex is to stop a hex from hitting its target, not stop the effects of a hex.

Jinx: Usually used to harass, vex or annoy another. Generally, though all levels of outcome are possible, no jinx is ever fatal. In using a jinx one must maintain eye contact without blinking. Unlike hexes, a jinx must be magically stopped to stop its affects. A counterjinx is a jinx used in defense against another jinx to hopefully stop the jinx or make it ineffective before it hits its target. It doesn't remove the effects of a jinx that's already hit. A jinx usually requires removal by magical means.

Spell: The word spell is generally applied to any charm, hex, jinx or curse as well as to an actual spell. A true spell is an advanced form of magic that always involves an incantation. Its effects, unlike charms, do not wear away. Spell damage, unlike a jinx or hex, can be permanent or even mortal. The sort of wand movement done with a spell is less relevant to the spell than for aiming the spell at a target. Dumbledore seems to use wand "twiddling" as an enhancement to his magic, but this may be a purely aesthetic enhancement, to do with his sense of style rather than have any practical purpose. A spell is usually the type of magic needed to apply magic to a wide area, be permanently effective or life threatening. For instance a Four Point Spell which seems to involve only the wand, really involves direction based on the position of an entire planet. Vanishing Spells can be permanent, what's vanished is gone forever. Shock Spells are so dangerous they can only be used by medical professionals.

Curse: A curse is always magic with the intent to do grievous bodily harm. The harm may be minor, major or mortal. It always takes a countercurse to end the effects of a curse. Take Moody's advice practice CONSTANT VIGILANCE and never get hit with one. The 3 Unforgivable Curses are criminal magic, punishable by an automatic life sentence in Azkaban.

INCANTATIONS

All incantations are listed alphabetically, regardless of classification, ie, charm, hex, etc. Not all incantations have proper classifications in the sections following.

Accio: A Summoning Charm. Use of this incantation brings whatever one wants. Harry used it to get his Firebolt for TT Task 1. Molly used it to find hidden Ton-Tongue Toffees. Distance is not an object as long as one's summoning skills are good. One can even Accio an animal against its will, which may mean one could Summon a person as well if one's talents were advanced enough.

Alohomora: A spell used to open locked things. It can be used on locked doors or windows, padlocks, safes and another type of lock. Hermione used it to open the door to Fluffy's room and the window of Flitwick's office.

Aparecium: An incantation used to make invisible ink visible. Hermione tried it on Tom Riddle's Diary.

Avada Kedavra: One of the Unforgivable Curses. It causes instant death. Usually the curse is accompanied by a bright flash of green light and a rushing sound like something flying through the air - perhaps the sound of rushing death. There is no countercurse or no magical way of blocking it, however one can always duck or try to get a phoenix to swallow the curse whole. This curse requires very powerful feelings behind it, as well as powerful magic, to make it work. All the 4th years together in Harry's DADA class couldn't hurt Barty Jr (Moody) if they tried. They didn't have the skills and they didn't have the desire to see him dead. One must truly want the target being dead in order for it to be effective. A half-hearted "I wish you were dead" will not finish off the target, though it may cause momentary intense pain. Use of this curse on any magical being (as defined by the MoM) results in an automatic life sentence at Azkaban.

Avis: Mr Ollivander used this incantation to test Viktor's wand. It creates a blast like a gun and a number of birds shoot out. The blast might simply have been Viktor's wand though.

Colloportus: An incantation used to magically seal a door shut. Hermione used it in the DoM.

Crucio: The incantation for the Cruciatus Curse. An Unforgivable Curse. It produces a torture of terrible pain on the victim's body. Harry says it feels like hot knives stabbing him all over him body. But the type of pain experienced may be individual. The curse can be general, involving the whole body, or particular, involving just a body part. If used long enough it can drive the victim to permanent insanity. The Longbottoms were victims of this curse. Use of this curse on any being (Being as defined by the MoM) results in an automatic life sentence at Azkaban. Again, one needs to really want to torture the victim and enjoy torturing for it to work.

Deletrius: An incantation used to cause something to vanish.

Densaugeo: An incantation that causes the 2 front teeth of a person hit by it to grow at an alarmingly fast rate. Draco hit Hermione with this incantation accidentally.

Diffindo: An incantation used to split something apart. Harry used it on Cedric's brand new book bag to make it split open, and also on the brain that attacked Ron. It did work on the bag, but it didn't work on the brain.

Dissendium: The incantation used to open the hump of the hump-backed witch statue on the 3rd floor at Hogwarts.

Engorgio: The incantation for the Engorgement Charm. Hagrid used it on his Halloween pumpkins one year, to spectacular result.

Ennervate: An incantation to bring beings back to their senses after being knocked out. It was used on Winky by Amos Diggory.

Evanesco: An incantation that causes things to vanish. Bill used it to make the 12 scrolls vanish, presumably he was able to call them back. Pr Snape uses it to get rid of cauldrons full of badly made potions mixture, presumably he would never want to call this stuff back. It is a type of Vanishing Spell.

Expecto Patronum: The incantation to work the Patronus Charm. It produces a Patronus which will protect one from dementors.

Expelliarmus: An incantation for the Disarming Charm. It's used to disarm another wizard of a wand or other hand-held object. It generally produces scarlet light. Pr Snape almost knocked Pr Lockhart out with it at Dueling Club.

Ferula: An incantation that produces bandages around wounded limbs. Pr Lupin used it on Harry.

Finite: An incantation that ends something.

Finite Incantatem: An incantation used to stop the effects of almost all other magical incantations. It was used by Pr Snape to stop the effects of all the incantations being used during Dueling Club.

Flagrate: An incantation that puts a fiery cross (X mark) on whatever it's directed at. Hermione used it on the doors of the circular room of the DoM.

Incarcerous: An incantation that causes ropes to shoot out of a wand and tie up whomever the wand is pointed at. Pr Umbridge used it to bind a centaur, with regrettable results.

Incendio: An incantation used to create fire. Arthur used it on the Dursley's hearth so the Floo Powder could be used.

Impervius: An incantation used to make whatever it's used on impervious. Hermione used it on Harry's glasses to make them repel water.

Inanimatus Conjurus: It would seem to involve conjuring up inanimate objects from thin air. Harry had to write an essay about it in his 5th year.

Imperio: An incantation used for the Imperius Curse, one of the Unforgivable Curses. It puts the cursed under the command of the curser. It can be fought, but it's rare anyone wins immediately. Most people do manage to shake it off eventually. Use of this curse on anyone results in an automatic life sentence at Azkaban.

Locomotor Mortis: An incantation for the Leg Locker Curse. It causes ones legs to stick together so all one can do is bunny hop. It was used by Draco on Neville once, and Hermione reversed it. Too bad Harry didn't use it on the spiders in the Forbidden Forest.

The Harry Potter Companion

Locomotor Trunk: Locomotor is the incantation used move inanimate objects. It causes the object to levitate a few inches off the ground and one can then guide it with a wand. In this case the object being moved was a trunk. Tonks used it on Harry's trunk.

Lumos: An incantation that creates light at tip of a wand.

Mobiliarbus: Molbili is an incantation that allows one to levitate an object a few inches off the ground and then move them apparently without a wand. Arbus is tree. Hermione used it to move an entire Christmas tree at the Three Broomsticks.

Mobilicorpus: Mobili is an incantation that allows one to levitate an object a few inches off the ground. Corpus is body. Sirius moved Pr Snape's body using this spell and directing it with a wand as it levitated.

Morsmordre: This incantation is known only by Death Eaters. It produces the sign of Voldemort - The Dark Mark which is made of green smoke and rises from the wandtip high up into the sky. It fades away after a period of time, a few hours or so. Barty Crouch Jr used it at QWC 1994.

Nox: An incantation to stop light coming out the tip of a wand. The opposite of Lumos.

Obliviate: An incantation used to do an Obliteration Charm. It has a variety of applications. It can obliterate someone's memory, partially or completely, erase footprints in the snow, wipe a chalkboard clean or a host of other fun things.

Orchideous: An incantation that Mr Ollivander used to test Fleur Delacour's wand. It causes a bunch of orchid flowers to sprout from the end of a wand.

Pack: An incantation that is supposed to pack a trunk. Tonks uses this charm to pack all Harry's things. Andromeda Black Tonks is so good at this charm that the socks will even fold themselves.

Peskipiksi Pesternomi: An incantation that is supposed to stop pixies. It was used by Pr Lockhart. It either doesn't work, or he didn't have enough magic in him to make work. One tends to think the latter.

Petrificus Totalus: An incantation used for the Full Body Bind. It causes the body to go completely rigid, with arms at the sides, legs together and mouth shut. It leaves one flat on one's face and stiff as a board with only one's eyes movable. It was regretfully applied to Neville by Hermione.

Portus: An incantation used to turn an object into a Portkey. Any object can be made a Portkey but only the DMT has the right to issue a Portkey. It's illegal to just make a Portkey oneself. However the DMT has no way to know if or when a wizard makes or uses a Portkey. Dumbledore used a blackened kettle from his cupboard to turn into a Portkey. When the incantation is said, the object will vibrate and glow with an odd blue light. When it comes to a rest and turns back to normal color it is ready for use.

Prior Incantato: An incantation used to make a wand regurgitate a ghost of the most recent spell the wand performed. Amos Diggory used it on Harry's wand at QWC 1994. Completely unrelated to Priori Incantatem, for which see the entry for wands in the Equipment section of Part II.

Protego: An incantation used to produce a shield which will deflect most spells (in the general sense of the word) and cause them to bounce back onto the person who sent them. It is a type of Shield Charm. An actual shield may be produced or simply an unseen resistant force. Harry used this to defeat Pr Snape's Legilimens attack, but it also had the effect of letting Harry force his way into Pr Snape's mind because of the bounce-back effect. Voldemort used it to produce a real shield, to hide from Dumbledore's magic. Harry used it keep his prophecy orb from fly out of his hand in response to Bellatrix's Accio.

Quietus: An incantation that returns a magically magnified voice to normal. Sonorus would be the opposite incantation.
Reducio: An incantation that reduces or shrinks things. The opposite of an Engorgement Charm or Enlargement Charm.
Relashio: An incantation that is supposed to send sparks out the tip of a wand. If one happens to be underwater at the time it will send out a jet of hot water instead. Harry used it on the grindylows in the Lake during TT Task 2.
Reparo: An incantation that is used to fix anything that is broken. Hermione used it to fix a train compartment window Ron broke. Though it will fix the broken object, it will not restore any contents that was spilled or lost when the breakage occurred.
Rictusempra: An incantation used to produce nonstop laughter. A type of Tickling Charm. A silver light is usually emitted from the wand as well. Harry hit Draco with this during a duel.
Riddikulus: An incantation to deal with boggarts. They don't like being laughed at, so the key is to repeatedly force the boggart into the shape shift into something that one finds laughable. After enough shapeshifting , the boggart vanishes.
Scourgify: An incantation used to clean something. Harry used it Hedwig's cage.
Serpensortia: An incantation that causes a long black snake to come out of a wand. Pr Snape had Draco use it on Harry during a duel.
Silencio: An incantation used to silence something. A Silencing Charm 5th years learned to use on bullfrogs and ravens. It requires a sharp jab of the wand.
Sonorus: An incantation that magnifies one's voice about 100 times its normal volume. One directs the charm with a wand to one's throat or other noise-making object. Ludo used it on himself so he could commentate QWC 1994.
Stupefy: An incantation used to stun something or someone. A type of Stunning Spell. Usually the wand emits a red beam. It could be used on dragons if one had enough 6 or more people using it together.
Tarantallegra: An incantation used to cause nonstop dancing. Draco hit Harry with it during a duel.
Unknown: Possibly vino (wine) was the incantation. Mr Ollivander used it to test Harry's wand and made a fountain of wine shoot out of the tip.
Unknown: Possibly fumus (smoke) was the incantation. Mr Ollivander used it to test Cedric's wand. He shot a stream of silver smoke rings out of it.
Waddiwasi: This incantation causes whatever object the person is holding it on to fly up their nose with great force and speed. Pr Lupin used it on Peeves. The object was chewing gum. The incantation seems to get more use at certain times of the year, such as during Christmas dinners.
Wingardium Leviosa: An incantation used to make an object fly. A swish and flick wand movement is required. Ron used it to knock out a mountain troll in the girls' bathroom during Halloween 1991.

CHARMS

Incantations may or may not be given. For some charms the incantation is simply unknown.

Anti-Cheating Charms: These are used on all exam pens to keep students from cheating.
Banishing Charms: These are used to make thing go away from one, but not disappear entirely.

Breaking Charms: These are used on brooms to make them stop.
Bubblehead Charm: This charm puts a bubble of air over one's head so one looks like one is wearing a fishbowl. Cedric and Fleur used it in TT Task 2. It got to be fashionable under Pr Umbridge's reign.
Cat Fur Charm: Fred and George used it to cover themselves with cat fur. Possibly a variation of the charm that put Agnes in the Janus Thickey Ward.
Cheering Charms: Theses make one cheerful, or if done wrong giddy, giggly or downright hysterical with glee.
Color Change Charm: This charm makes things change color. Harry mixed it up with the Growth Charm on the OWL practical exam for Charms.
Confundus Charm: A charm used to confuse persons or things. A really strong one was used by Barty Jr (Moody) to confuse the Goblet of Fire and allow him to submit Harry's name under a 4th school for the TT.
Cushioning Charm: It creates a magical invisible cushion. Used primarily on broomsticks.
Disarming Charm: A charm used to disarm another wizard of a wand or other hand held object. Produces scarlet light. Pr Snape almost knocked out Pr Lockhart with it. Expelliarmus is the incantation.
Disillusionment Charm: It makes whatever it's applied to shift colors like a chameleon so it can blend in with the surrounding environment. It is commonly used mainly on magical animals to conceal them from Muggles but one supposes Aurors get a bit of use out of it as well. Like all charms, it isn't permanent and must be periodically renewed. To Disillusion is to perform this charm on someone or something. Moody did it to Harry to transport him to Headquarters. Harry thought it felt like someone has smashed an egg on his head, the cold contents of which he could feel run trickling down his body.
Drought Charm: It is used to dry up puddles, ponds and the like. It is not powerful enough to dry up the Lake, which is a part of the sea.
Engorgement Charm: This charm makes things swell up, sometimes very unpleasantly. It was used by Hagrid (illegally) on the Halloween pumpkins. Ton-Tongue Toffees also uses this charm. Engorgio is the incantation.
Enlargement Charm: It will make anything bigger. Barty Jr (Moody) used it make a spider large enough for a class to see. Fred and George put one on Harry's interview in *The Quibble*r to make it into a wall hanging. It can even make a person as big as Hagrid, permanently if done incorrectly. Reducio is the opposite incantation.
Entrancing Charms: They are a type of enchantment that causes a person to fall in love with, or become entranced by, another person. Pr Lockhart mentioned them Valentine's Day 1992.
Fidelius Charm: An immensely complex charm only a very skilled wizard could preform involving the magical concealment of a single secret, apparently multiple secrets don't fit, inside a living human being's soul. The information is thereafter impossible to find because it's hidden inside the selected person or Secret-Keeper. As long as the Secret-Keeper doesn't tell the secret, no one can find the secret they are looking for. In the Potter's case, they couldn't be found by Voldemort after they went into hiding even if he were staring in their living room window. A moment's thought proves this quite interesting, because it means that the charm was hiding the Potters themselves, not the location of their safe house. Thus the Potters were the secret kept in Peter Pettigrew. And that is a disturbing thought.

Flame Freezing Charm: This charm allows a wizard being burned at the stake to fake their death. The charm renders the flames mild in temprature, gentle and tickling. It was very popular during the Middle Ages and the 17th-century witch hunts.
Flashing Paint Charm: A fairly tricky charm that makes paint flash different colors.
Flying Charm: This charm is used on broomsticks to make them fly.
Freezing Charm: This charm was used by Hermione on pixies to immobilize them. It causes all motion to stop on the thing or being it's used on.
The Full Body Bind Charm: This charm causes the body to go rigid, arms at the sides, legs together and mouth shut. It leaves one flat on one's face, stiff as a board with only one's eyes able to move. It was used by Hermione on Neville. Petrificus Totalus is the incantation.
Gripping Charm: A charm invented so the Quaffle could be held with one hand without the use of a strap.
Growth Charm: A charm to make things grow larger. It was on Harry's OWL practical exam in Charms.
Hair-Thickening Charm: A charm that causes hair to thicken but if misused might cause one's eyebrows to grow down to one's mouth. Pr Snape accused Alicia Spinnet of using it rather on herself than admit Miles Bletchley did it to her. He also referred to it as a hex which is probably a mistake as Alicia had to go to Madam Pomfrey for help, indicating she needed reversal which would not be needed if it were an actual hex.
Homorphous Charm: A charm that supposedly can cure werewolves by turning them back into completely normal people. Pr Lockhart probably made it up.
Hot Air Charm: A charm that involves a complicated wand wave, but produces hot air from a wand tip. Hermione uses it to dry her robes when they get wet from rain or trailing in snow.
Hover Charm: A charm used to cause things to hover in the air. It was used by Dobby on Petunia's dinner party dessert to great effect.
Imperturbable Charm: A charm that causes objects to be Imperturbed. If used on a door, nothing cannot harm the door in anyway. Even if things are thrown at it, they will just bounce off. There is no way for anything to pass by, under, or around the door. Molly used it on the kitchen door to prevent Extendable Ears getting in.
Impervius Charm: It is used to make whatever it's used on impervious. Hermione used it on Harry's glasses to make them repel water. The incantation is Impervius.
Levitation Charm: A charm that causes something or someone to levitate in the air at which point it can be guided with a wand to the appropriate height and place. It was on the OWL practical exam in Charms. Lee Jordan used this to place nifflers in Pr Umbridge's office. Mobili is probably part of the incantation.
Memory Charms: These are charms used for memory modification, mostly to cover up a memory a Muggle might have of seeing magic used. They create a sort of short-term memory loss. The memory is still there, but it is not accessible to the person anymore. Sometimes a person is a bit disoriented for a while after being charmed. The bigger the thing one has to forget, the longer and more dazed one might be. Some people need repeat charming or are immune to Memory Charms. Overly strong Memory Charms can screw up a memory for life. The charm can be broken, but only by a powerful wizard like Voldemort and the end result is a nonfunctioning brain, as in Bertha Jorkins' case. The incantation is Obliviate.
Muggle-Repelling Charms: These charms were used on the QWC 1994 stadium to keep Muggles away from the area. Every time a Muggle would come near the stadium, the charm would cause them to remember urgent engagements elsewhere causing them

to dash off. They have been used mainly for Quidditch pitches since the 1300s. It's a form of Repelling Spell, Muggles just happen to be what's being repelled.

Obliteration Charm: A charm used to wipe out things. Hermione used it on snowy footprints to Hagrid's cabin. The incantation is Obliviate.

Patronus Charm: This charm is very highly advanced magic, well beyond OWL standard. The charm produces the only thing that scares dementors away, a Patronus. The Patronus acts as a shield or protector and places itself between a wizard and a dementor and rendering the dementor ineffective. Most wizards can only produce noncorporeal Patronuses that look like silvery jets of gas. They have no distinct shape, but they work against dementors successfully. Pr Lupin and Dumbledore have non-corporeal Patronuses. A truly corporeal Patronus is rare and kind of fun because a wizard can command a corporeal Patronus to go after people as well as dementors, as Draco, Goyle, Crabbe and Flint who were knocked over by one can attest. Corporeal Patronuses are *very* corporeal.

The Patronus is a projection of the wizard who created it and made up of the all the positive forces dementors desire to feed on - hope, happiness, the desire to survive. But a Patronus doesn't have bad memories or feel despair, so the dementors can't hurt it or suck it into nothingness. To produce a Patronus one must be able to concentrate solely on a single very happy memory. If the memory is not strong enough or not happy enough, the charm will fail quickly or not work at all. It must be an extremely strong, extremely happy memory. What a Patronus looks like is unique to each wizard, comes from within the wizard and usually is related to a wizard's feeling about her or his father. Harry's Patronus is a huge stag. Cho's is a swan. Seamus' is a hairy thing. Hermione's is an otter. The incantation is Expecto Patronum.

Permanent Sticking Charm: This charm is used to keep things in a certain place, forever. Mrs Black used one on her portrait and another on the Black family tree tapestry so no one could remove them.

Pig Charm: A charm that should turn a person into a pig. Hagrid attempted to use it on Dudley, but the broken wand probably interfered with the execution.

Portkey Charm: Used to turn an object, any object, into a Portkey. The incantation is Portus. It is illegal for anyone to do except members of the DMT's Portkey Office.

Protean Charm: This is a mimic charm. Whatever the primary object does, the copies will do the same. Protean Charms are NEWT standard and only Hermione seems to do them so far. Hermione used this charm to create Galleons that show the date of the next DA meeting rather than a serial number on the side. When Harry changed his Galleon's numbers, all the others change as well to mimic his.

Reverse Charm: A charm to cure brooms that are reluctant to reverse. Found in Harry's Broom-Servicing Kit book.

Scourging Charm: A charm used for cleaning. Neville used it to remove frog guts from his fingernails. Scourgify is probably the incantation.

Severing Charm: This charm cuts off whatever it is directed at, rather like magical scissors. Ron used this charm to rid his dress robes of lace. It can by used to remove crup tails as well.

Shield Charm: This charm is used to cast a temporary invisible, or sometimes visible, shield in front of, oneself. It deflects most spells, causing them to rebound onto the original caster. Said to be only for minor jinx deflection, it really depends on the quality of the wizard. Voldemort used it to deflect magic done by Dumbledore. It works well against Legilimens too. The incantation is Protego.

Silencing Charm: A charm used to render a speaker voiceless. A 5th year charm, it is most frequently used by owners of fwoopers. The incantation is Silencio.

Slug Charm: A charm that causes one to vomit slugs. Ron attempted to use it on Draco. Hagrid says it's a curse and a fairly difficult one to execute, but he may be mistaken since it doesn't meet the standard of a curse.
Stunning Charm: This charm stops people or animals by Stunning them. Useful on almost any creature, multiple Stunning Charms can bring down even a dragon, or Pr McGonagall. The incantation is Stupefy.
Substantive Charm: A type of charm likely to be on the OWLs which Seamus practiced before his OWL practical exam in Charms. It probably creates an independent and real entity from thin air.
Summoning Charm: A charm used to bring something to the user. It is a 4th year charm. The incantation is Accio followed by what one wishes to summon. For example Accio Parchment would bring one a parchment.
Talon-Clipping Charm: For use on dragons so one doesn't have to get too near them.
Tickling Charm: Usually accompanied by a silver light from the wand, this charm is used to produce the sensation of tickling. Harry hit Draco with this charm. The incantation is Rictusempra.
Unbreakable Charm: This charm renders whatever it is used on unbreakable. Hermione used it on a glass jar she had Rita Skeeter (in beetle form) in so she couldn't transform and escape.

HEXES

Incantations may or may not be given. For some hexes the incantation is simply unknown.

Bat-Bogey Hex: This hex puts live bats all over the victim's face. It is Ginny's specialty. She used it on Draco to fine effect.
Head-Beating Hex: A popular one attached to Library books. When activated by a person mistreating the book in some way, the book beats the person about the head. This curse is no respecter of persons, even Dumbledore's been beat up by a book. It may also cause the book to follow, continually beating, the offender.
Horn Tongue Hex: Harry read about it in preparing to deal with dragons in TT Task 1. He decided they didn't need another weapon.
Hurling Hex: A hex that causes a wizard to be thrown from her or his broom or other object. Pr Quirrell used it on Harry's Nimbus 2000.
Impediment Hex: A hex that stops almost anyone dead by tripping or otherwise impeding her or his progress.
Instant Scalping Hex: It instantly removes all of the hair on the victim's head.
Knee Reversal Hex: It causes one's knees to bend backwards, like bird legs.
Pepper Breath Hex: It causes one's breath to become fiery.
Stinging Hex: A hex that produces a scorchlike mark on the victim it's directed against. Harry accidentally did it to Pr Snape.
Twitchy Ears Hex: It causes one's ears to twitch so they look like they are wiggling violently.

JINXES

Incantations may or may not be given. For some jinxes the incantation is simply unknown.

Anti-Disapparation Jinx: This jinx keeps people from Disapparating. Dumbledore used it on the Death Eaters that raided the MoM.
Impediment Jinx: This jinx stops things by tripping them. Similar to Impediment Hex, but less painful.
Jelly-Legs Jinx: This jinx turns one's legs to jelly so one wobble as one walks. This jinx was used on Neville. It's also said to be a curse.
Jelly-Legs Jinx + Furnuculus Curse: This jinx-curse combination causes one to sprout tentacles all over one's face and get knocked out. The combo was used on Draco.
Leek Jinx: This jinx causes leeks to sprout out of one's ears. It was used on a Slytherin and a Gryffindor before a big game between the 2 teams. Given that leeks are a Welsh national emblem, it seems obvious that this is another indication Godric was Welsh, and that would make the leek a Gryffindor symbol as well.
Sneak Jinx: Created by Hermione, this jinx is activated by a person ratting out other people's doings. It causes the word SNEAK to be spelled out in purple pustules across the offender's cheeks and nose so everyone knows what happened. Hermione put this jinx on the DA club membership parchment and Marietta later activated it. It is apparently very difficult to cure as Madam Pomfrey couldn't. Presumably Marietta will have to get specialist treatment at St Mungo's. Some have called this a hex, but one doubts Hermione would be so vengeful as to forever scar someone that way, even if she or he was a sneak.
Trip Jinx: This jinx causes one to trip and fall over. Draco used it on Harry as he tried to escape the DA roundup.

SPELLS

Incantations may or may not be given. For some spells the incantation is simply unknown.

Anti-Cheating Spells: These spells are used on new quills before they're used for exams, OWLs and NEWTs.
Conjuring Spells: This is an unknown spell. It comes up in 5th year Charms. Presumable it is a form of Summoning Charm.
Cross-Species Switching Spells: A form of Transforming Spell. Used to turn one species into another, eg, a rabbit into a bird.
Enlarging Spell: This spell makes things enlarge so that they can hold more than normal without any change to their appearance. Arthur used it on the inside of a sedan car so that it seated 10 comfortably.
Extinguishing Spells: This spell is supposed to put out the fire of the dragon, if used by multiple wizards simultaneously. Dragon handlers like Charlie Weasley stood by at the TT ready to intervene with this spell in case any of the dragons got out of hand.
Four-Point Spell: This spell allows one to make a wand point North like a compass needle. Harry used it in TT Task 3 to get around the maze.
Invisibility Spell: A spell that makes something invisible. It is used very cleverly on the Headless Hats Fred and George created.
Repelling Spells: These spells repel anything one's wand is pointed at.
Shock Spells: These spells are used as a form of treatment given at St Mungo's for the mentally ill. Similar to the old shock therapy that was used widely in the 1950s and seems to be making a comeback among Muggles.

Stealth Sensoring Spells: These spells detect suspicious activity and report it to their creator somehow. Pr Umbridge used them on her DADA office door, all around the doorway, after the nifflers got in. They do not indicate who did the suspicious activity, just that it happened.

Switching Spells: These spells change one thing into another. They are learned in 4th year Transfiguration. They are on the OWL written exam in Transfiguration.

Transforming Spells: Used in Cross-Species Switches. Turning a rabbit into a hawk would be an example of Cross-Species Switches. It's 5th year Transfiguration work.

Vanishing Spells: These spells make thing disappear. Making live animals disappear is 5th year Transfiguration work. The more complex the animal (kitten v. snail), the more difficult it is to make the spell work. Evanesco is a Vanishing Spell that Pr Snape is very fond of using.

CURSES

Incantations may or may not be given. For some curses the incantation is simply unknown.

Avada Kedavra Curse: One of the Unforgivable Curses, it causes instant death. Avada Kedavra is the incantation. Usually the curse is accompanied by a bright flash of green light and a rushing sound like something flying fast through the air, perhaps the sound of rushing death. There is no countercurse and no magical way of blocking it, however one can always duck or try to get a phoenix to swallow the curse whole. This curse requires very powerful magic behind it to make it work. One must truly want the intended victim dead, and possibly enjoy seeing them die. Only powerful wizards can make this curse work. Use of this curse on any human being results in an automatic life sentence at Azkaban.

Babbling Curse: It makes one babble nonstop. Pr Lockhart supposedly cured someone of it in Transylvania, but that in itself makes it doubtful.

Conjuctivitus Curse: A curse that causes Conjunctivitis. It's recommend for use against a dragon's eyes since they are its weakest point. Viktor Krum used it during TT Task 1.

Cruciatus Curse: This is one of the Unforgivable Curses. It produces a torture of terrible pain in the entire body or a specific portion thereof. If used long enough it can drive a person permanently insane. The Longbottoms were victims of this curse. One must be a powerful wizard that likes torture and wants to see the intended victim tortured to get the curse to work. Lack of intent causes a lesser effect for a shorter period of time. Use of this curse on any being results in an automatic life sentence at Azkaban. The incantation is Crucio. Harry used this curse on Bellatrix Lestrange, very ineffectively. Technically he should go to jail for it, but given Bellatrix was an escaped Death Eater, in the MoM, with Voldemort, one doubts the MoM will be pressing any charges.

Curse of the Bogies: Unknown beyond the name. Pr Quirrell taught the 1st year DADA students about it in 1991. Possibly it produces a specter to worry and harass a victim.

Entrail-Expelling Curse: A medical and therapeutic curse invented by Healer Urquhart Rackharrow in the 15th century. One assumes the actual entrails are not expelled, but only the contents thereof.

Furnuculus Curse: This curse makes a person break out in boils. Harry accidentally hit Goyle with it making his nose break out in boils.

Hair-Loss Curse: The victim's hair falls out, probably permanently. Pr Viridian wrote about this one.
Impediment Curse: This curse slows down or obstructs anything that it's directed.
Imperius Curse: One of the Unforgivable Curses. It puts a person under the total control of another. It can be fought but it takes real strength of will and character thus not everyone can do it. Only a powerful wizard who really enjoys controlling people could use it. Use of this curse on any human being results in an automatic life sentence at Azkaban. The incantation is Imperio. Barty Sr used it illegally on Barty Jr. Voldemort used it on Barty Sr and tried to use it on Harry. Lucius Malfoy used it on Sturgis Podmore and Broderick Bode. For a curse that's supposed to work, it has a tremendous ultimate failure rate. Eventually everyone seems to break free of it. But for short-term use, it does the business.
Leg Locker Curse: This curse causes one's legs to stick together so one can only bunny hop. Draco used it on Neville. The incantation is Locomotor Mortis.
Petrification: also to be Petrified. To cause complete and total petrification, a deathlike state. One is not really dead, but frozen. Looking into a basilisk's eyes indirectly, such as with a mirror or through a camera eyepiece, causes this state. It takes Dark magic of the most advanced kind to cause Petrifications like this. Because of the severity of the condition produced, the Dark magic aspect, and the fact the magic is of an advanced nature, I've put it in the Curses section.
Reductor Curse: This curse reduces anything to dust, including the planet Pluto. It also allows one to blast through solid objects. Parvati is quite good at this curse.
Thief's Curse: A curse that activates if one reads a book too long without paying for it. It has very unpleasant consequences one cannot describe here.
Tongue-Tying Curse: Pr Viridian wrote about it. It involves the victim's tongue being tied up in knots so she or he can't speak.
Transmogrifian Torture: To transmogrify is to change or alter the appearance into a grotesque or humorous form. Obviously it can leave one dead and possibly it is a painful process. But likely more humiliating than "torturous." It's mentioned by Lockhart as a possible cause of Mrs Norris' petrification, which says something about the way she looks. Because torture is involved, it's a curse.
The Unforgivable Curses: The Avada Kedavra Curse, Cruciatus Curse, Imperius Curse are the three Unforgivable Curses. Using any one of them results in an automatic life sentence in Azkaban. In order for them to work completely one must be a powerful wizard, truly want to use the curse and truly enjoy seeing its effect. One must want to murder (torture or enslave) and enjoy murdering (torturing or enslaving) a victim for the Avada Kedavra (Cruciatus or Imperius) Curse to work. If the feeling is half-hearted on the part of the wizard doing the curse, the results will be lackluster.

POTIONS

This section includes all potions that are made from scratch. Manufactured potions appear in the Magical Products section which follows.

Aging Potion: A potion that makes one older. It can make one a few months or many years older. Several Hogwarts' students tried to use it to get their names accepted to the TT.
Babbling Beverage: A potion that makes one shout nonsense.

Befuddlement Draught: A potion that inflames the brain and results in a desire to act recklessly or exhibit hot headedness. Components may include sneezewort, lovage, or scurvy-grass.

Blood-Replenishing Potion: A potion that replenishes lost blood in the body. Arthur had to take it after getting a snakebite that wouldn't stop bleeding.

Boil Curative: A very simple 1st year potion that cures boils. Components include nettles, snake fangs and horned slugs. Acid green smoke and loud hissing emits from the cauldron when the potion is made correctly. Somehow having boils don't seem so bad, comparatively speaking, if the cure is drinking Boil Curative.

Burn Curative: An orange paste good for even 3rd degree burns a dragon might give a person. It was used on Cedric by Madam Pomfrey.

Calming Draught: A potion frequently used by Madam Pomfrey on stressed out 5th and 7th years. It gets a lot of use the last couple months before OWLs and NEWTs.

Confusing Concoction: A potion that makes one confused. The 3rd years were expected to able to make it for their Potions final exam.

Confusing Draught: A potion that inflames the brain and results in a desire to act recklessly or exhibit hot headedness. Components may include sneezewort, lovage, or scurvy-grass.

Cursed Potion: This potion, made of snake venom and unicorn blood among other things, gave Voldemort back a semblance of a child's body. But due to the use of unicorn blood, it curses those who drink it to live a half-life, meaning either life is cut short or the quality thereof is diminished.

Deflating Draft: This potion reverses the effects of Swelling Solution.

Draught of Living Death: A sleeping potion made with asphodel and wormwood. It makes one appear dead, which could be a bad thing depending on where one parked one's body after taking the draught.

Draught of Peace: A potion to calm anxiety and soothe agitation. If done badly one can put a person into a permanent coma. Components include moonstone and hellebore. It is learned in the 5th year and is often on the Potions OWL.

Elixir of Life: Not really a potion so much as a secretion that comes from the Sorcerer's Stone. One may have to make a potion, or elixir, with the secretion in it.

Forgetfulness Potion: It makes one forget things.

Gregory's Unctuous Unction: A potion that persuades its drinker that the giver is their very best friend. Gregory the Smarmy invented it.

Hair-Raising Potion: It probably makes one's hair stand on end. It's a 3rd year potion.

Healing Potion: This potion is purple, stings when applied and smokes in the wound. It seems to sterilize rather than heal a poisonous wound, such as a dragon claw cut.

Invigorating Draught: A potion learned in the 5th year. It gives one extra energy and vigor.

Love Potion: This potion exists but is banned at Hogwarts. It makes the drinker fall in love, usually with the first person she or he sees.

Mandrake Restorative Draught: A powerful potion that can undo the effects of most poisons and spells. It was used to treat the Petrified students, cat and ghost in May 1993. It contains stewed mandrake roots.

Pepperup Potion: A potion for people with colds or flu or who are generally worn out or run down. It works instantly, though it does leave the drinker with smoke coming out of their ears for several hours afterwards. Madam Pomfrey uses a lot of this potion.

The Harry Potter Companion

Photographic Developer Potion: Unlike the regular kind of developer, this one makes the pictures move, even between pictures and to some extent take on the personality of the person. It doesn't allow the photographed person to speak.

Polyjuice Potion: A complicated potion that allows one to turn into somebody else for 1 hour. It takes about a month to make because fluxweed has to be picked at the full moon and the lacewings need stewing for 21 days. A recipe for this potion can be found in Library's Restricted Section in the book *Moste Potente Potions*. Components include a bit of the person one wants to turn into, lacewing flies, leeches, fluxweed, knotgrass, bicorn horn, and the skin of a boomslang snake.

It gives off black smoke and becomes a thick, dark brown, mudlike gloop when ready. The last thing added is the bit of the person one wishes to turn into. The potion then turns a color. Essence of Millicent's cat is a sick yellow, essence of Goyle is a khaki color, essence of Crabbe is a dark murky brown. It is very unpleasant to take. It makes one's insides writhe, causes nausea, and the sensation of bodily melting. Despite the fact Pr Snape never seems to teach it, it turns up on the OWL written exam in Potions.

Interesting things about the potion include that if one dies looking like someone else, one stays looking that way. This happened to Mrs Crouch Sr after she died. The potion can be used continuously for a year without any ill effect. Barty Jr was Moody for 10 months and was still Barty Jr at the end. And, as long as one drinks the potion every hour, one can remain another person indefinitely. The only drawback of the potion is using a nonhuman bit. It seems to cause an incomplete transformation that subsequently changes a person's looks semi-permanently. Hermione's use of a cat hair had serious consequences that took several weeks of intensive therapy in the Hospital wing to sort out.

Rebirthing Potion: A potion which allows a wizard to be reborn. Components include a huge stone cauldron, water, a bone of the person's father, the blood of the person's enemy and the flesh of the person's servant. Apparently one can use "damaged goods" as Peter sacrificed his right hand with a missing index finger for Voldemort to be reborn and Voldemort was reborn perfectly complete (but for a conscience) despite it.

Scintillation Solution: Madam Nettles can whip up one that makes her life of the party. It makes one scintillating. Kwikspell teaches this potion.

Shrinking Solution: A potion which causes things to shrink. It is a 3rd year potion. Components include daisy roots, shrivelfigs, caterpillar, rat spleen and leech juice.

Sleeping Draft: A potion that makes one sleep.

Sleeping Draught: A sleeping potion Charlie used on the dragons in the TT. Sleeping Drafts and Sleeping Potions are not all the same thing. Draught is for animals. Draft is for sleep, Potion is for instant, dreamless sleep.

Sleeping Potion: This potion produces an almost instant dreamless sleep. It's purple.

Strengthening Solution: A potion for strengthening a person physically. It takes about 4 days to make. Components include salamander blood, pomegranate juice and griffin claw. It is a 5th year potion.

Swelling Solution: A potion that causes anything it's applied to to swell up magnificently. It is a 2nd year potion.

Truth Potion: Truth Potion. It makes the drinker tell the truth, but exact effects are unknown.

Wit-Sharpening Potion: A potion to make one more clever, its components include scarab beetles, ginger roots and armadillo bile. It is a 4th year potion.

Wolfsbane Potion: A potion of recent discovery (pre-1992) that allows a werewolf to keep possession of her or his mind after transforming so she or he can just curl up quietly in a room till transforming back into a human being. The potion smokes quite a lot and is rendered useless by the addition of sugar. It must be taken in the week before the full moon to be effective. Pr Snape made it by the cauldron full for Pr Lupin so it must have some ability to store for a bit before using or one needs to drink a lot of it. It is a very complicated and difficult to make potion. There aren't many wizards that have the skill to make this potion according to Pr Lupin, but Pr Snape as a Potions Master does. Obviously an over-the-cauldron product is a few years off yet.

Veritaserum: A potion that forces one to tell truth even against one's will. It is so powerful that 3 drops will have a person spilling her or his guts, apparently unasked. It is a serum-based potion. It is clear but has a distinctively peppery taste so wizards should be aware of what it is, after they taste it. It takes a full moon cycle to mature, so it takes at least 28 days or more to make, but Pr Snape keeps a bottle ready at all times. The MoM has guidelines about how it can be used, which is odd because the Imperius Curse has the same effect and it's illegal. Oh well.

MAGICAL PRODUCTS

Magical products are commonly used powders, potions or preparations that are manufactured and sold in the wizarding community. More mechanical magical devices, such as a Quick-Quotes Quill, are under the heading Magical Devices.

Anti-Jinx Varnish: Used on Cleansweep 11 broomsticks, it makes the broom resistant to jinxing.

Baruffio's Brain Elixir: A potion that is reputed to make one smarter, give one better concentration and keep one more alert that is usually used by students taking exams. Eddie Carmichael was selling it to 5th years for 12G a pint in 1996, till it was confiscated by Hermione.

Doxycide: A black liquid aerosol solution used to immobilize doxies. One needs to wear a mask over one's nose and mouth to use it because it will apparently affect humans. After the doxies are immobilized one can just throw them and their eggs out as the anesthesia's effects lasts several hours.

Dr. Ubbly's Oblivious Unction: A salve used on Ron for the brain-attack injuries he sustained. It was supposed to wipe out the brain's thoughts. Madam Pomfrey thought it was working quite well.

Fleetwood's High-Finish Handle Polish: Harry got this with his Broom-Servicing Kit. It's wood polish.

Flesh-Eating Slug Repellent: A preparation used to get rid of Flesh-Eating Slugs. Hagrid bought some in Knockturn Alley to protect his cabbages. It is unclear if the slugs are carnivores and the cabbages flesh. But I prefer not to think about it.

Grow-Your-Own-Warts Kit: An item Harry found in a Christmas cracker. Its purpose is self-explanatory. Possibly warts are fashionable or just a fun accessory.

Honeydukes' Chocolate: While it is just candy in one sense, chocolate has long been considered a medicinal in many cultures and Honeydukes' product gets a special mention because of its wide use and great effectiveness in undoing the effects of a dementor encounter.

Mrs. Skower's All-Purpose Magical Mess Remover: A cleaning potion that Filch likes. Its slogan is: No Pain, No Stain. This company was one of the sponsors for QWC 1994. Filch tried the potion on the message left in the corridor where Mrs Norris was found Petrified, but it didn't do a thing because it was some type of Dark magic.

Skele-Gro: A potion that regrows bones over a 8hr period. It steams prolifically and, although it works, the process it induces is quite painful. Madam Pomfrey used it to regrow 33 of Harry's arm bones after Pr Lockhart deboned him.
Sleekeazy's Hair Potion: A potion that makes kinky, curly, flyaway or otherwise unruly hair flat, sleek and perfectly manageable. Hermione used it on her hair for the Yule Ball, but said it was too much trouble to use every day.
Spellotape: A magical tape for binding up magical broken things such as snapped wands.
Wartcap Powder: A powder that will cause a crusty tough brown layer to form on one's skin wherever it's dusted. Some got on Sirius' hand as he was cleaning out 12 Grimmauld Place. Fred and George are experimenting with it.

A Few of Filch's Banned Products

The following are items that are probably on Filch's list. Given there are 437 items on Filch's list this should not be considered exhaustive.

Belch Powder: A powder that when ingested causes belching. A joke item.
Bulbadox Powder: A powder that causes one to break out in boils anywhere the powder touches. A joke item Fred and George used on Kenneth Towler in their 5th year.
Dr. Filibuster's Fabulous Wet-Start, No-Heat Fireworks: Fireworks that are not hot, will work when wet and last at least 30 minutes. They are perfectly safe to use indoors and will not set fire to anything. Fred and George Weasley are very fond of this product.
Dungbombs: A small ball-shaped bomb that releases smoke and stench when broken open. They are more smoke than stink, but very annoying all the same. A favorite device of Fred and George.
Ever-Bashing Boomerangs: They don't just bring down their victims, they proceed to bash them into submission afterwards.
Fanged Frisbees: A rather aggressive frisbee with fangs. Difficult to use without artful catching skills. They were used indoors and out till they were banned by Filch.
Frog Spawn Soap: It's not actually soap, so one gets frog spawn all over one's intimate person.
Garroting Gas: An odorless colorless gas that once set off will garrote to death (murder) anything that walks through it. It is something Fred and George like.
Hiccup Sweets: Eat the sweet and get a severe case of hiccups.
Nose-Biting Teacups: If one drinks from the cup it bites one's nose.
Screaming Yo-Yos: Yo-yos that scream while being used, though it's unclear what they scream, if anything.
Stinkpellets: Similar to Dungbombs but with the emphasis on stench. A joke item Fred really likes that was banned by Filch.
Whizzing Worms: A joke item. They have an unknown function. Given the word whizzing, possibly they are worms that fly and make a whizzing sound or worms that excrete copious quantities of liquid.

Weasleys' Wizarding Wheezes' Products

This section contains only products the Weasley twins make and sell.

Blood Blisterpod: A Skiving Snackbox sweet. The sickness is the purple end of the bicolored sweet. It makes one bleed prolifically from any orifice. Katie Bell was given one accidentally and ended up in the Hospital. The opposite end stops the bleeding.

Canary Creams: It turns the consumer into a large canary for a short time. One molts about a minute after eating it and returns to normal. It's supposedly a hex-operated candy though it fails to meet hex criteria. They cost 7S each.

Extendable Ears: They are very long flesh-colored strings that allow one to listen in on people standing some distance away or even in a different place. One end of the string goes into the ear and the other will wiggle, snake and even crawl under a door to listen in unnoticed. Molly tried to trash them all without success.

Fainting Fancies: A Skiving Snackbox sweet. They cause one to slump over unconscious. The cure is the purple end. The use of this candy requires an assistant to administer the cure, and someone that knows the diffrence between the purple end of a Fainting Fancy and the purple end of a Blood Blisterpod.

Fake Wands: A device that appears to be a wand and actually can be used briefly before turning into something else. They squawk or squeak and become rubber chickens, tin parrots, rubber mice or rubber haddocks. Ludo paid 5G for a fake chicken wand it so delighted him.

Fever Fudge: A Skiving Snackbox sweet. The illness end will elevate one's temperature. It had the side effect of putting massive pus-filled boils on one's bottom while it was in development, but this difficulty was overcome by using murtlap essence in the product.

Headless Hats: A hat that makes the wearer's head invisible while they are wearing the hat. The hat however remains visible. It has a pink fluffy feather on it. Remove the hat and the head appears again.

Nosebleed Nougats: A Skiving Snackbox sweet. Similar to the Blood Blisterpods in effect. They cause one to bleed out. As of 1996 there was no antidote. But Fred and George continue to work on it.

The Portable Swamp: A very fine product which creates a huge swamp that requires a punt to cross it. Fred and George first used it to turn a 5th-floor section of the east corridor near Gregory the Smarmy into a swamp as a diversion so Harry could use the Floo Network for a floo call. Pr Flitwick later cleared up all but a small patch under a window, that is now roped off, because it was such good magic he wanted to leave some as an example. An honorary E level NEWT in Charms really ought to have been awarded to the twins for it.

Puking Pastilles: A Skiving Snackbox sweet. The orange end induces projectile vomiting. The purple end makes one stop – if one can get it down and keep it down.

Skiving Snackboxes: Fred and George's line of double-ended color-coded sweets that make one ill enough to be dismissed from class (skiving off a class is getting out of or skipping a class), and then cures one the minute one is excused. Puking Pastilles, Fainting Fancies and Nosebleed Nougats are some of the candies in the Snackboxes. But there is ongoing product development for this line. The twins took a few doxies and some Wartcap Powder from Sirius' house to experiment with for some new candies.

Ton-Tongue Toffee: A candy invention of Fred and George that causes one's tongue to grow continuously and rather quickly while turning it purple and slimy. It uses an Engorgement Charm. Dudley ate one and his tongue got 4' long before the Dursleys let Arthur shrink it.

Weasleys' Wildfire Whiz-Bangs: Fireworks of a spectacularly noisy, fast-moving, startlingly magical variety. They include sparklers that write rude words, Catherine's wheels that roll around, rockets and more. They all just keep going and getting stronger as they go. Stunning them only makes it worse. Vanishing them makes them multiply by 10. They ended up all over Hogwarts when Fred and George set some off as a diversion for Harry to use the Floo Network for a floo call. The Whiz-Bangs come in 2 sizes: the Basic Blaze box for 5G, and the Deflagration Deluxe box for 20G.

Catherine Wheels: A large wheel with spikes projecting from the rim. St Catherine was martyred on one in 307 AD, hence the name. It was used throughout the Dark Ages as a torture device. The fireworks are wheels with projecting firework spikes. In the case of the Whiz-Bangs they move around as well as rotate.

WIZARDING FOOD AND CANDY PRODUCTS

These are consumable items made by wizards for wizards that are not a part of Fred and George's product line. They are ranked as products because they seem to be for showy effect first and actual eating a distant second.

Acid Pops: A Honeydukes' Special Effects sweet. Fred gave Ron one when he was 7 and it burnt a hole through his tongue.

Butterbeer: It is a mildly alcoholic beverage which can be served cold or hot and foaming. It comes in a corked bottle. At the Hog's Head its 2S a bottle. It is not strong for people, probably less than 5% alcohol, which is why children at age 13 are drinking it, but it is too strong for house-elves, especially in the quantities that Winky drinks it.

Chocolate Frogs: A candy that comes with Famous Witches and Wizards Trading Cards which feature wizard's photos on them. Agrippa and Ptolemy are the most difficult to acquire and Ron, who has over 500 cards, doesn't have either. Collecting and trading cards is a hobby with many young wizards. Ernie, Hannah, Ron and Harry all collect them. Harry started his collection with 9 cards including one of Dumbledore. Signs are often left on noticeboards in the common rooms from students that want to trade cards.

Bertie Bott's Every Flavor Beans: Similar to jelly beans except they can be any flavor. Chocolate, peppermint marshmallow, marmalade, spinach, liver and tripe are just a few. Dumbledore ate one that was vomit flavored and it put him off them for years. He gave them a second chance in 1992 but it was ear wax flavored. A booger flavored one was once eaten by George. Most kids love them and they're one of Harry's favorite candies. Harry and Ron have had beans the flavor of sprouts, toast, coconut, baked bean, strawberry, curry, grass, coffee, sardine and a funny grey one that was pepper, while on the train to Hogwarts in 1991.

Blood-Flavored Lollipops: It is a Honeydukes' Unusual Tastes item designed with vampires in mind.

Cauldron Cakes: A popular snack food on the Hogwarts Express. Probably similar to a chocolate cupcake.

Chocoballs: A Honeydukes' confection. A large chocolate ball that's more candy than effect. Particularly popular for its strawberry mouse and clotted cream filling. Its magical qualities are unknown.

Cockroach Clusters: A popular delicacy in many countries, but a Honeydukes' Unusual Tastes item. Possibly for ogres and maybe goblins.

Drooble's Best Blowing Gum: A Honeydukes' Special Effects sweet. This gum creates bluebell-colored bubbles that leave one's mouth and float around. The gum

manufactures enough bubbles to fill an entire room. The bubbles cause further fun, or irritation, by often refusing to pop for days.
Exploding Bonbons: A Honeydukes' Special Effects sweet. They explode, probably in the mouth, but have no untoward effects.
Fizzing Whizbees: A popular magical sweet that contains billywig. See FB for interesting details on billywigs and what ingesting them can do to a person.
Fudge Flies: This was Scabbers favorite sweet. One expects they actually fly.
Ginger Newts: McGonagall's favorite cookie. She keeps a tin full on her office desk. Probably newt-shaped ginger snaps that really move about like newts.
Ice Mice: A Honeydukes' Special Effects sweet. They make one's teeth chatter and squeak very loudly. It's a candy Pr Flitwick gave Harry so he must like them himself.
Jelly Slugs: A hot item at Honeydukes. Rather like gummy bears, but slugs, and they wiggle and move around. One hopes they don't crawl around leaving a trail of jelly to be licked off various surfaces.
Levitating Sherbet Balls: A Honeydukes' Special Effects sweet. They make one levitate a few inches above the ground when one sucks on them.
Licorice Wands: Presumably like licorice sticks but shaped like wands. Possibly they can do a spell or two like Fred and George's Fake Wands.
Pepper Imps: A Honeydukes' Special Effects sweet. A tiny black sweet Ron and Hermione brought some back for Harry on their first outing to Hogwarts. They make one smoke at the mouth and breathe fire.
Peppermint Cream Toads: A Honeydukes' Special Effects sweet. They are actually hop around, but only when in the consumer's stomach.
Pumpkin Pasties: Difficult to say what they are. Probably not a sweet but a meat and vegetable or vegetarian pasty that's heavy on the pumpkin. See Cornish Pasty in the Recipes section in Part II.
Sugar Quills: A Honeydukes' Special Effects sweet. It's a quill made of spun sugar. Similar to a candy cane in that one can suck on it. It's designed so that one can eat sweets in class without drawing attention to oneself.
Toothflossing Stringmints: A Honeydukes' Special Effects sweet. Hermione bought some for her dentist parents as a Christmas gift. They are strange and splintery.

MAGICAL BEASTS

This section contains the names of all known magical beasts, but information only on the beasts that have appeared or been described in the series proper. For full, and sometimes astonishingly graphic, information on undescribed Beasts, see Newt Scamander's *Fantastic Beasts and Where to Find Them*. In addition to those creatures normally thought of as Beasts, are beings who wish to be classified as Beasts and creatures whose existence may not be fictional but simply lacking in proof.

Some creatures in this list are considered to be Dark creatures. A Dark creature is any beast that is out to do a person intentional mischief. Banshees, boggarts, hinkypunks, grindylows, kappas, pogrebins and red caps would all be considered Dark creatures. Werewolves are both beast and being, but are considered Dark only in beast form when not taking suppressive potion therapy. Dementors and the like are not Dark creatures, but Dark magical beings. Magical beings may be Dark or not, but they are still Beings as defined by the MoM. Therefore they are listed in the Other Magical Beings section in Part V. Frankly I refuse to label any Being-classified individual. As Harry proved one can choose to fight the worst elements of one's nature, this makes Dark a preference, not an unalterable condition.

The Harry Potter Companion

Abraxan: See Winged Horses.

Acromantula: A large spider with 8 eyes as well as 8 legs that is capable of human speech. It's unclear if the 8 eyes are grouped like a fly, 2 eyestalks with 4 eyes apiece, or 8 individual eyes on 8 eyestalks. They live can live 50 years or more and their habitat is easily recognizable from the giant dome-shaped web they spin and secure directly to the ground rather like a pup tent. Usually acromantulas are all blacke and have thick black hair covering their entire body and legs, but they may get grey a few hairs when old. There are no white, brown, or other colored or patterned acromantulas.

They use poisoned pincers to kill prey but also to speak and make clicking noises, like a telegraph, to communicate to other spiders that they are excited or angry. The species as a whole is little studied but human-spider interactions are rare. Despite films like *Eight-Legged Freaks* or books like *The Hobbit*, these spiders are not man eaters. Acromantulas are content to stay in their forests and nibble on the creatures therein, deer, birds or even each other. It is only when human encroachment on spider habit occurs that dangerous encounters and death result. Even then, most solitary spiders will not tackle human prey. Only a large group of spiders feels secure enough to make the effort.

The eggs are Class A Non-Tradable Goods but Hagrid illegally hatched one at Hogwarts anyway in the 1940s. Aragog, the resulting hatchling, and Mosag his wife have since produced an entire colony of acromantulas in the Forbidden Forest. Some smaller infant acromantuals or part-acromantulas have taken up residence in the castle itself, but seem to prey only on typical spider food: insects. Strange facts about acromantulas include refusing to say the word basiliks and carrying prey in their forelegs rather than with their pincers. One only hopes Dumbledore can convince Hogwarts' acromantual population to join his side against Voldemort as they would be very effective. One doubts even giants could survive an acromantula attack if numerous spiders were involved.

Aragog: A huge spider that lives in an enormous spider-cleared hollow in the Forbidden Forest under a misty dome-shaped spiderweb. He is the size of a small elephant, but not as dangerous since he is old, blind and arthritic. He moves very slowly and is probably fed by his kids these days. He has some grey hairs, scattered through his his body and legs, but on the whole his coat is black. He seems to have cataracts as each of his eyes is milky white and tends to wander vaguely. He has a rather ugly head, but he still managed to find a mate, so looks aren't everything.

Aragog can speak, in English as well as spider, and probably learned from Hagrid. Hagrid is Aragog's only human friend and he would never hurt Hagrid or Fang, but anyone else, even friends of Hagrid, are fair game for Aragog's children. Aragog says he came from a distant land but he likely got that information from Hagrid since he was in the egg when a traveler gave him to Hagrid. After hatching in 1942, Hagrid fed him on tablescraps and, because he likes dark and quiet places, he lived hidden in a cupboard in the dungeons (now Pr Snape's personal store cupboard). Aragog knew about the basilisk at Hogwarts, as spiders and basilisks have always been enemies and spiders have sixth sense when it comes to basiliks. When the basilisk was released in 42/43, Aragog could sense is moving about Hogwarts and pleaded with Hagrid to be let go, but it wasn't until June 13, 1943 that Hagrid was forced to oblige him.

Hagrid, when he found out that Tom Riddle was trying to frame Aragog for being the monster of the Chamber of Secrets, helped him escape into the Forbidden Forest. Despite the fact everyone seemed to believe that Aragog was guilty, no one from the MoM's Committee for the Disposal of Dangerous Creatures went into the forest to try and find and kill him. Years later it was Hagrid that managed to find Aragog a wife, Mosag, and they have since had many 100s of children all of whom seem to thrive in the Forbidden Forest. Some of the smaller ones went to live in the castle but left as soon as the basilisk stirred in 1992.

Mosag: An acromantula and the wife of Aragog. She was illegaly acquired by Hagrid for Aragog and now has many children living in the Forbidden Forest. Aragog and Mosag's children are the size of cart horses, so slightly smaller than Aragog himself and possibly only part-acromantuals. They have large low-slung hairy bodies with black legs, gleaming eyes and shiny black razor-sharp pincers. It's unknown if she is alive. Usually female spiders kill their mate soon after mating, so it's very unusual that Aragog is still alive. He could not have killed her or there would have been no children. Perhaps she is under the domed web and doesn't like human visitors but for Hagrid.

Aquavirus Maggots: A magical creature Luna's father believes the MoM is breeding. Probably an extrapolation based on small bits of information he's heard about the Brain Room.

Ashwinder: see FB.

Auguery: see FB

Banshee: It appears as a skeletally thin woman usually with floorlength black hair, corpselike greenish skin and the ability to release an unearthly, long, wailing shriek. Traditionally seeing one or hearing one wail meant death was on its way to someone in the family. The name is from the Gaelic, Ben (woman) Jee (god), meaning goddess. In this context it's understood to mean goddess of death. It is said to be found only in Celtic lands, particularly Ireland, which is why Seamus fears them most of all. Pr Lupin says they are a creature rather than spectral.

The Bandon Banshee: Supposedly defeated by Lockhart, but of course it wasn't. It was however a real Banshee and defeated, just not by Lockhart.

Basilisk: A snake of unknown heritage but said to be from chicken's egg that was brooded over by a toad. It has solid green skin as vivid and bright as a tree python. The snake's head is blunt, like a viper or python, but the body is thick as tree trunk, like an anaconda. Its large eyes are yellow and bulbous. If male it's said to have a red roosterlike crest. It can grow to over 20' long and has thin 1' long saberlike poisonous fangs. Its venom is extremely effective and if even one fang sinks into a person they will die within a minute or two. A basilisk may make a loud explosive spitting noise when upset. Its voice, for those Parselmouths that can hear it, is cold and said to chill one's very bone marrow.

The basilisk has no defensive mechanisms beyond its look and its venom. Looking indirectly into its eyes will cause Petrification and but directly will kill a person instantly. Its eyes can produce lasting scorch marks on stone, Petrify or kill animals as well people and even burn camera film but don't affect phoenixes. Once past the look and its bite, its scaly skin is easy to penetrate. The basilisk doesn't seem to mind the cold, as most snakes do, and operates with ease in the dead of winter when most snakes are hibernating. Though it did hibernate for most of its lifespan. The venom seems neurotoxic, like a pit viper but at 20' it must be a python x viper cross of some type.

The monster of the Chamber of Secrets, in service to the Heir of Slytherin, Tom Riddle, was a basilisk called the Serpent of Slytherin. Salazar Slytherin put it there in c 900 AD probably as an egg. Since basilisks live a long time, up to several 100 years normally, Salazar's heir had plenty of time appear. The basilisk was able to leave the Chamber of Secrets via the pipework when called by the Heir of Slytherin and emerged from a sink in Moaning Myrtle's bathroom. It appeared repeatedly in 42/43 and 92/93 but only killed one person was ever killed. Slytherin's basilisk was defeated by Fawkes, the Sorting Hat and Harry on May 29, 1993. It died at the incredibly ripe old age of 1,085 years old, not from age itself but from being stabbed through the brain by Godric's old sword.

Harry hears the basilisk speak 3 times:
1 Lockhart's office
2 Dungeons, after attacking Mrs Norris
3 Staircase, before attacking Hermione and Penelope

8 victims of the basilisk:
1 Hagrid's rooster, 1st week of Sep 1992 (actually killed by Ginny)
2 Mrs Norris, 2nd floor corridor, Oct 31
3 Colin Creevey, on the marble stairs, Nov
4 Hagrid's 2nd rooster, 3rd week of Dec (actually killed by Ginny)
5 & 6 Sir Nick and Justin Finch-Fletchley, 2nd Floor corridor, 3rd week of Dec
7 & 8 Hermione and Penelope Clearwater, near Library, Apr 1993

Bicorn: A 2-horned animal often mistaken by Muggles for a common billygoat. Its horn is used in Polyjuice Potion.

Billywig: see FB.

Blast-Ended Skrewt: Something Hagrid created, breaking the Experimental Breeding Ban. He later recouped his position by letting the TT use the remaining skrewt in Task 3. Skrewts, now thankfully extinct, were the result of a fire crab-manticore cross. The result was not pretty. They appeared to be pale slimy deformed lobsters minus the shell. They had legs sticking out in odd places and smelt strongly of rotting fish upon hatching. They hatched about 6" long in size and were immediately capable of shooting sparks out their back ends with a small gaseous sound. The blast propelled them forward several inches. It was believed that the males had the scorpionlike giant tail stingers which they can arch over their backs and the females had suckers on their stomachs.

They had no discernible head, which made feeding rather difficult, and it was unknown what skrewts ate, but they grew swiftly all the same. Larger skrewts were very aggressive though only toward their own species. At 2 months they were 3' long and began killing each other. At 3 months they were well over 3' long, very strong and had developed a thick, shiny, greyish armor. They start to look like a scorpion-crab cross, but with no eyes or head, as they got bigger. A single gaseous emission from the backend allowed them to drag a 14-year-old several yards on her or his stomach. By 4 months they were almost 6' long, had powerful legs on which they scuttled about and were capable of shooting jets of fiery sparks from their posterior end. At 10 months they were 10' long and looked a lot like a giant scorpion.

Blibering Humdinger: A magical creature Luna believes in. It probably doesn't exist.

Blood-Sucking Bugbears: Possibly a bearlike creature that sucks blood. Hagrid thought one might be responsible for his dead roosters in 92/93. They live in the Forbidden Forest. Bugbears are normally spectral, but without more information about them, no definitive state of being can be determined.

Boggart: A shape-shifter that likes dark enclosed places, like cabinets under sinks, closets, armoires, desk drawers or gaps beneath beds. They tend to cause what they inhabit to wobble or bang and so are noticeably trying to warn wizards off long before actually appearing. It can take whatever form it thinks will frighten a person most but it is thought unable to assume a form till it actually sees a victim. It can become confused when dealing with groups thus making confusion is the best weapon to use against it.

A boggart can be forced to shift shapes so many times so quick in succession that it can't go on. At that point it explodes into tiny whips of smoke. Whether this smoke is caused by the death of the boggart or merely its disappearance to another location is unknown. One would like to think the boggart simply removed to another locale but there is no evidence for this. As a Dark creature, it was a DADA topic in 93/94 under Pr Lupin and students were exposed to an actual boggart to practice getting rid of it. The following list shows what fears were revealed by the encounters.

Shapes/fears:
Neville - Pr Snape
Parvati - mummies
Seamus - banshee
Lavender? - rat
Unknown - rattlesnake
Unknown - a single bloody eyeball
Dean - a severed hand creeping on the floor
Ron - acromantula spider
Lupin - moon (losing control of himself); cockroaches
Harry - dementors (his fear is itself fear)
Hermione - Pr McGonagall saying she failed everything.

A strange fact about the boggart is that it actually becomes whatever it is it becomes. In Harry's case when it became a dementor, it had all the dementor's powers and was able to suck happiness out of Harry and force him to hear his mother's voice. This is extremely fascinating as most shape-shifters can only take on the appearance of a thing, not become the thing itself with all the virtues and powers there of. One would have to say it's a very good thing Harry didn't fear Voldemort or the results of his lessons might have been truly deadly.

Bowtruckle: aka tree gaurdians. These beasts are usually only found in trees with wand-quality wood (wand-trees). Small pixie-ish creatures, they have strange, flat bark-covered faces with glittering brown eyes and produce a high-pitched chattering when upset or excited. They look like living wood, much like the old Ents only smaller and more flexible. They are generally brown and knobbly, but one assumes the come in a variety of colors such as trees do.

Bowtruckles have pliable arms and legs but it is the 2 sharp, pointed, twiglike fingers at end of each arm that most unwary individuals tend to encounter as bowtruckles will attempt to gouge out the eyes of anyone threatening their tree. Raising an axe or torch to a tree or even just kicking it or shouting near it can constitute a threat. They like wood lice, which are considered a delicacy, and can be distracted or appeased by these if for any reason a wizard needs to do something to the tree they inhabit. The Care of Magical Creatures OWL practical exam included a demonstration of the correct way to handle a bowtruckle.

Bundimun: see FB

Centaur: Centaurs are the smartest (and most difficult) of creatures inhabiting the Forbidden Forest. Hagrid feels they have a lot of influence in the Forbidden Forest, but how exactly or by what means is unknown. A number of centaur herds occupy different areas within the forest, but how many herds and centaurs are in the forest in total isn't unknown as sending anthropologists to study them would be dangerous and offensive. There is a herd of around 50 (probably a quarter of which is female and half foals) in the forest that is (or was) Firenze's group. All the centaurs that Harry has met have been half-man, half-horse. Are they half-woman, half-horse centaurs as well? Male centaurs speak of foals, so they must have children. However male centaurs insult other centaurs by calling them common horses so one would assume centaurs don't form relations with horses, mules, etc. One therefore must assume female centaurs exist but prefer not have contact with anyone outside their herd.

Centaurs live in the wild, refuse clothing (at least males do) and prefer to live away from all humans, wizard and Muggle. They consider themselves an ancient people, which is true since they have been around several 1,000 years at least, and as a whole far more intelligent than humans. They don't recognize MoM law or wizards' self-proclaimed superiority. Prior to Mar 1996 the centaurs of the Forbidden Forest were kindly disposed towards Hagrid and would show up to talk with him if he needed them. But in Mar 1996 Hagrid broke centaur law by saving a centaur that was condemned to death, Firenze, and at that point centaurs decided to forgo all contact with humans (and pro-wizard centaurs) and claim the Forbidden Forest for their own. They are now so upset that these normally gentle beings will even attack wizards wandering into their territories.

Centaurs are willing and able to defend themselves, their territories and their herd with deadly force if necessary as they are all trained in the art of crossbow archery. They carry crossbows and arrows with them at all times when they feel endangered. On the whole, centaurs just want to be left in peace, are not violent unless provoked and prefer to spend their time in the study and practice of divination and astronomy. They are deep thinkers and know many things (or think they do) which the stars reveal to them, but they don't say much. This silence probably comes from their tendency to look at stars for decades before deciding what's going on, or will be going on, in the world. They tend to speak very cryptically when asked directly for information and are quite secretive at the best of times.

There is heavy disagreement among centaurs as to whether or not they should have contact with humans now that Voldemort is back. The head of the Firenze's herd, as well as the majority of its members, don't want to get involved in the war to come between Voldemort and Harry which they see as a human war and not concerning them. In some respects they cannot get involved as centaurs take vows never to interfere with the course they see written in the stars. Stars may prove wrong down the road, but centaurs never put a hoof in to make the change that proves them wrong. Since centaur herds are not a democracy, the male head of the herd makes the decisions and the rest are expected to follow his will. Those who don't agree may risk being kicked to death. Obviously, centaur law can obviously be a bit harsh.

For all the beast rehtoric they put out, centaurs call themselves a people, as in people group, not herd, as in animals. Centaur culture is a hierarchy with a male centaur always at the top. Law is laid down by the head centaur and there is no democratic discussion about changing a law. The culture differs greatly from horse culture in that the male head of the herd doesn't chase off other males in an attempt to form a harem of females and juveniles. It may be that each male centaur has a female mate, though this is unclear. Children are refered to as foals, so there is clearly an equine mindset, however calling a centaur a donkey or mule is an insult. Would a centaur marry a horse? Difficult to say. Clearly they don't think of horses as beneath them, since they are half-horse themselves, but they also feel themselves a distinct culture and may not be allowed to marry outside of their own kind. Finally British centaurs all appear to be White, though this may be due to the fact that centaurs don't travel outside their established territories. Thus African or Asian centaurs might exist, they just don't turn up in Britain.

The named centaurs are:

Bane: He is a wild-looking White man with black hair, a black beard and a black horse body. He is the leader of a small subgroup within Magorian's herd. This group included at one time Firenze and Ronan. Dominating, angry and proud, Bane feels centaurs have been mistreated by the MoM and that the MoM has no business dictating to them. He doesn't think it's a centaur's job to be looking after people in anyway, no matter what the circumstances - this includes young children about to be murdered. He doesn't want to be involved in what is essentially not a centaur's fight (the Voldemort v. Harry war).

Bane reminded Firenze that of the vow he took not to work against the future as told by the stars. He follows he norms and dictates of his herd, meaning he intends to stick to his own vow not to act. On the other hand, Bane all but provoked a war with humans (wizards) on his own after he lost his temper and carried Pr Umbridge off. Granted, he has been provoked. Pr Umbridge had attacked the centaurs. But she was a MoM official still at that point. One hopes Dumbledore's interventions can keep the MoM from going after Bane as a "dangerous" creature. Bane's name would indicate he's the herd's problem centuar, but his parents might have given him the name Bane of Wizards, thus Bane is nickname and a problem to others.

Firenze: He is a younger centaur, younger than Bane or Ronan anyway, and has more liberal views on centaur-human interactions. He is a White man with white-blonde hair, astonishingly blue eyes that are said to be like pale sapphires (which is quite difficult to understand as sapphires are dark blue, never pale) but probably actually like blue topaz and a palomino body. His name is the Italian name of the city the English call Florence, so he might be half-Italian stallion, or his maybe his parents liked art which Florence is justly famous form.

He is very atypical for a centaur personality-wise, very forward looking and modern compared to the rest of his herd, so his name, which is synonymous rennaisance and a new way of looking at the world, is quite appropriate. When he first saw Harry in the forest, he knew exactly who he was and directly told Harry he was in great danger. He then went even further astray and allowed Harry to ride on his back, so he could take Harry to safety. Firenze not only broke centaur secrecy, humiliated his species and interfered with destiny, he then told his fellow centaurs he'd side with humans if he had to in order to pit himself against Voldemort.

It is this sort of flagrantly politically incorrect and unrepentant behavior that eventually gets Firenze in trouble his herd. In 1996 Firenze finally went too far somehow, we don't know how exactly, but it was so glaring a breach of centaur law that he was sentenced to be kicked to death by the others in his herd for it. Hagrid saved Firenze and ended up joining Hogwarts's teaching staff in place of the sacked Sybill Trelawney. He takes this job because he can't risk staying in the forest or even going too near it. So he lives and teaches Divination in Classroom 11 on the ground floor of Hogwarts. The room was enchanted by Dumbledore to resemble his forest and seems to be magically expanded to the size of a forest as well.

Firenze as a teacher is painfully honest about centaur divination. He says it takes years to learn, years to figure out what the skies are saying and even then they have been read incorrectly before, even by centaurs. Hardy encouraging. But on matters concerning centaurs themselves he makes it quite clear to his students that centaurs are neither toys for wizards' amusement nor the servants of wizards. Students for their part respect Firenze and his teaching. It's unclear, now Dumbledore is in charge of Hogwarts again who will teach Divination. Clearly Sybill must be rehired but it is not as clear that Firenze is safe to return to the forest. The centaurs might have let

The Harry Potter Companion

Dumbledore save Pr Umbridge but the verdict of death still hangs over Firenze's head and, judicially, he must die if he goes back to the forest.

Magorian: He is a White man with long black hair, high cheekbones and a chestnut body. He seems to always carry his rather large crossbow and quiver full of arrows. He is the head of the herd Bane, Firenze and Ronan belong to. He sees Firenze as complete disgrace and worthy of death. In 95/96 he was extremely upset with Hagrid for intervening on Firenze's behalf and disrupting the law of the centaurs. He called what Firenze was doing at Hogwarts selling the centaurs' knowledge and secrets to humans. He was disgusted that a centaur would chose to serve humans.

Magorian does however have a sense of justice and doesn't approve of murdering the young or innocent, even if they happen to be humans and wizards. This attitude later allowed Harry and Hermione to get away from the centaurs without too much incident, once. But Magorian has no patience for humans who take advantage of centaurs for their own ends (or destructive giants tearing up the ancient trees by the score for the sheer pleasure of destruction) and eventually Harry and Hermione overstepped his patience. In trying to escape Pr Umbridge and they attempted to use they centaurs to get rid of her. Magorian got wind of this and decided they were fair game. Harry and Hermione might have talked their way out of the situation if Pr Umbridge hadn't shot her mouth off, overstepped her authority and started arresting centaurs.

Magorian and his centaurs very justly carried off Pr Umbridge to a fate unknown and would have taken Harry and Hermione as well, if they hadn't been stopped by Grawp. Magorian realized they had bigger problems at that point and attacked Grawp, leaving Harry and Hermione free to go about their business in the forest. Although Grawp got a nice grouping of arrows in the face, giant blood prevailed and Grawp survived completely unharmed. What happened to the centaurs is unknown. Doubtless Grawp will be an ongoing issue between Dumbledore and the centaurs for some time to come as Hagrid has no intention of getting rid of his half-brother and MoM laws (giants are supposed to be in exile Abroad) mean nothing to him when it comes to family.

Ronan: A White man with red hair and a red beard, he has a chestnut body with a long reddish tail. He supports Firenze's pro-human position, but refuses to break rank with Bane or the rest of the herd over it. He has a gloomy voice and an equally morose outlook on the world. He says throughout time it has always been the innocent that are the first victims in war. He would probably like to help Harry against Voldemort but hasn't the courage to leave his herd. He was friendly to Hagrid and obliquely tried to help or warn him in happier times, but had to stop after the incident with Firenze. He is a peacemaker by nature and willing to have relations with humans, but since his herd turned anti-human, he feels he must follow the rules of his herd. No doubt more so after seeing Firenze almost kicked to death.

Chimera: A very dangerous Greek creature made up of 3 various animal: lion, goat and serpent. It has the head of a lion, the body of a goat and the tail of a reptile or snake. Said to be a fire breathing shegoat, and being bitten one usually results in death. It is thankfully rare and best left to experts. A chimera was instrumental in the death of veteran risk-taker "Dangerous" Dai Llewellyn. The eggs are Class A Non-Tradable Goods.

Chizpurfle: see FB.

Clabbert: see FB.

Cockatrice: Since no one would dare use a basilisk in a TT, this is likely to be a chicken hatched from a serpent's egg, making it large, evil, extremely dangerous

creature with a killer bite. One went on a rampage in 1792 at the TT and since snakes can't rampage, it seems to confirm the fact it's a chicken. The incident shut down the competition until 1994, when there was a vain attempt restart the TT.
Crumple-Horned Snorkack: Possibly from Sweden. A magical creature Luna believes in. It probably doesn't exist.
Crup: An animal that 5th years cover in Care of Magical Creatures. It is not a dog, but looks like a Jack Russell terrier. It has a forked tail, one fork of which is usually removed so the animal can blend in. This docking is usually done when a puppy. Crups are monitored by the DRCMC, partially so they don't accidentally fall into human hands.
Demiguise: see FB.
Diricawl: see FB.
Double-Ended Newt: A newt with 2 heads, 1 at either end of its body. It may not be magical, but it seems to be since one was taken to the Magical Menagerie for care.
Doxy: Small creatures, like fairies, that have a humanoid form. Doxies have a body and 4 arms, all covered in thick black hair. A fully grown doxy has shiny whirring beetlelike wings and tiny poisonous needle-sharp teeth. One needs to keep a bottle of antidote on hand when planning to deal with doxies. Doxies will gnaw through curtains and other items made of fabric. They seem to prefer nesting in curtains. The drawing room curtains of Sirius' house was loaded with them. Doxies lay small black eggs. Doxies can be easily immobilized and removed using Doxycide (see Magical Products).
Dragons: Dragons range in size but can be upwards of 50' tall and shoot fire up to their body length out of their mouth or nose, depending on the variety, with Hungarian Horntails the most adept at long-range fire projection. Most dragons have a deafening, earsplitting roar they use when angry or upset which will alert a wizard to danger if they were previously under the impression the had encountered a friendly dragon. Running is advised in such situations as dragons are extremely difficult to kill and fairly lazy. In addition to their size, fire breathing abilities and spike-ridden bodies, their hides are thick and imbued with ancient and powerful magic which makes them virtually unkillable (which is also why dragon hide is valuable for gloves and other protective garments).

Only the most powerful spells launched by the most powerful wizards can penetrate a dragon's scales. Usually 6 or more wizards using a Stunning Spell together are required to do the job. The most vulnerable point on a dragon are its eyes, the skin is thin in that area (but the eyes themselves are very keen). Conjuctivitus Curses are recommended in otherwise unresolvable situations. Dragons are a protected species - unless one is threatened with imminent death by one - and most dragons are confined to reservations where they can be kept from harm, or harming others. There they can be studied or observed by wizards without interference to their natural behaviors. Dragon reserves are generally established by the various national MoMs where dragons are naturally found. Some are Unplottable, others have Muggle-Repelling Charms on them.

Dragons are reptiles and as such lay eggs rather than give birth to live young. The female usually lays an entire clutch of rather large eggs, the color of which varies with the variety. The eggs are then bathed in a constant flame heat, which the mother provides, until hatching. In the absence of a mother dragon, baby dragon care can be very difficult for wizards to preform as hatchlings are dangerous from birth and need things like buckets of chicken blood and brandy every half hour to get them properly started. In addition, hatchlings grow very fast. After 1 week, they can grow to 3 times the size they were when hatched and start breathing fire. By 1 month they will be eating crates of rats and require 4 brooms to lift. Beyond a month one faces the real danger of become accidentally burned, bitten, crushed or slashed to death. Even professional dragon handlers, like Charlie Weasley, can get hurt in such situations.

Thankfully the keeping and breeding of dragons was outlawed by Warlock's Convention of 1709 and simultaneously adopted by the ICW. The eggs are a Class A Non-Tradable Goods, though unscrupulous wizards can find them on the black market. It's illegal to keep dragons as pets because they're highly visible to Muggles, untamable and dangerous. Four types of dragon were used in TT Task 1. Hagrid owned a fifth type of dragon he hatched from an illegal egg he acquired via gambling. These 5 will be discussed. There are 10 known breeds of dragon, see FB for copious detail on all dragons and their unique behaviors.

Types of Dragons
Chinese Fireball: A red dragon with an golden fringe around its face made up of fine gold spikes. It gets the name "fireball" from the mushroom-shaped fire clouds it shoots. It comes from China.

Common Welsh Green: A smooth-scaled green dragon that is smaller than a Horntail. Considered to be the most "gentle" of dragons, this breed was responsible for the Ilfracombe Incident of 1932. It comes from Wales.

Hungarian Horntail: A gigantic black dragon that is more like a lizard than most dragons. It is scaly and sinewy with leathery black wings like a small aircraft and a spiked tail it uses as a weapon. It has vertical slit pupils set in yellow eyes that bulge when it's angry. It can shoot fire 40' or more from its mouth. The females lay huge granite grey or cement color eggs. It was the worst and most difficult of the 4 breeds used for the TT. It comes from Hungary.

Norwegian Ridgeback: A very rare, very aggressive breed of dragon. It is jet black with huge spiny wings and orange eyes that tend to bulge. It is distinguishable by horns on the head, a long snout with wide nostrils and very poisonous pointed fangs. The females lay huge black eggs. It comes from Norway.

Norbert: A Norwegian Ridgeback dragon. Norbert was secretly hatched by Hagrid in 1992. Hagrid kept Norbert at his house for about 4 weeks till he became almost too big to handle. At that point Ron helped Hagrid send Norbert to Romania and the dragon reserve where Charlie works. It took 4 of Charlie's friends to haul him away on broomsticks in a crate slung between them.

Swedish Short Snout: A silver blue dragon with a short snout and long pointed horns. It is one of the hottest flamed (temperature wise) dragons. It was one of the TT dragons and gave Cedric a nasty burn.

Other Dragon species include:
Antipodean Opaleye: see FB.
Hebridean Black: see FB.
Peruvian Vipertooth: see FB.
Romanian Longhorn: see FB.
Ukrainian Ironbelly: see FB.

Useful Dragon Parts
Dragon Blood: The blood is the color of the dragon. The blood has 12 different magical uses. Dumbledore discovered all of them. One of them is healing. It also is good for lessening pain and swelling. Hagrid used it on a black-eye once.

Dragon Claw: Powdered claw gives the consumer a brain a boost. It makes one cunning for a few hours. Harold Dingle was selling it during Harry's OWLs. Dragon claw is known to work, but Harold's powder was not actually dragon claw.

Dragon Heartstrings: These are used as wand cores. Rare and acquirable only after a dragon is dead, these are probably how reserves keep money incoming.

Dragon Hide: aka dragon skin. It is very thick and imbued with protective and magical properties. It is great for gloves, aprons or armor. Dumbledore sent a roll of it with Hagrid and Olympia to present to the Gurg of the giants. It was given to Gurg Golgomath.

Dragon Horn: It has magical properties.

Dragon Liver: It has magical properties.

Dragon Steak: When raw it has the color of the dragon from which it was taken. Hagrid used a steak that was green-tinged, thus from a Welsh Green.

Dugbog: see FB.

Edam: Apparently it's a large creature that is known for gleaming when excited. Ludo's excited face was describes as resembling the Edam. No reference can be found in Scamander. One presumes it is not a cheese in this context.

Erlking: see FB.

Erumpent: see FB.

Fairy: A humanoid creature with wings. It also glows softly. Fairies don't mind sitting around looking pretty or being admired, so they can be used decoratively. Pr Flitwick uses them as Christmas lights in his classroom every year. They were also used in the grotto created for the Yule Ball.

Flesh-Eating Slugs: Hagrid buys Flesh-Eating Slug repellent in Knockturn Alley, to save the school cabbages. It is unclear if the cabbages are made of actual flesh or the slugs are just settling for the cabbages in lieu of flesh.

Fire Crab: It looks like a giant tortoise with a jewel-encrusted shell. However, it can be dangerous as it shoots flames from its posterior when it feels threatened. The blast-ended skrewts inherited this feature from the fire crabs. The Magical Menagerie had one in the front window. Feeding and cleaning a fire crab without getting seriously burned was on the Care of Magical Creatures OWL practical exam.

Flobberworm: A thick brown worm, approximately 10" in length. They have no teeth. It is herbivorous, and prefers shredded lettuce but can die if given too much. It exudes a mucus sometimes used in potions, but which potions is unknown. Hagrid spent many Care of Magical Creatures classes on this exceedingly unremarkable creature during the 93/94 school year.

Fwooper: see FB.

Fluffy: A fierce 3-headed dog of uncertain breeding, about 10' tall. It sees very well with its crazed rolling eyes and its sense of smell with its 3 twitchy quivering noses is excellent. It has thunderous growls and hot smelly breath with exudes from its drooling mouths. Particulary disgusting are slippery ropes of saliva which hangs from its yellowed fangs. Fluffy is immediately put to sleep by music, even very badly played music. Hagrid owns Fluffy. He bought him from a Greek man he met in the pub and subsequently loaned him to Dumbledore to guard the trapdoor leading to the Sorcerer's Stone in 91/92. Harry defeated Fluffy by flute playing. Where Fluffy is now is anyone's guess.

Ghoul: The Weasleys have one in the attic. He seems to prefer to remain unseen and make his presence known by throwing pipes, screaming and making general noise when it's too quiet. He lives directly above Ron's room in the attic of the Burrow. Ghouls are generally considered harmless but a murderous ghoul was found in an upstairs toilet in Sirius' house. Apparently ghouls come in male and female.

The Harry Potter Companion

Chameleon Ghouls: They are a subspecies which can disguise themselves by transforming into something relevant to their environment. At Hogwarts the seem to like being suits of armor.
Glumbumble: see FB.
Gnome: Considered a common garden pest, the gnome is a small leathery looking creatures with an overly large head for its body, that is knobby, bald and resembles a potato. They are barely 10" high, have horny little feet and razor-sharp teeth. Gnomes talk, squeal and occasionally kick if one tries to pick them up. Crookshanks loves chasing gnomes at the Burrow and the gnomes seem to enjoy it too. Arthur is easy on them because he thinks they're amusing. So, the gnomes naturally love it at the Burrow and creep back into the yard through the hedges after every degnomeing.

Degnomeing involves grabbing a gnome by the ankles, swinging it around over one's head then releasing it and letting it fly at least 20-50'. If a gnome becomes dizzy enough, it can't find its way back to its former home. However if a gnome senses one's heart is not really in the job they'll put up a struggle, which may include kicking and biting. They generally are not too bright. Though they live in holes in the ground, they always come out to see what's happening the moment they hear a degnomeing going on instead of staying put. Gnomes, after being made homeless in a group, tend to walk in a line, their little shoulders hunched.
Graphorn: See FB.
Griffin: An animal that is part bird, part lion. It has the head and wings of a bird (usually an eagle) with the body of a lion. Its powdered claw is used in Strengthening Solution.
Grindylow: A cadaverous light green water creature with fangs. It has green teeth and small sharp horns on its head. It prefers living in tall weeds underwater. It uses its long fingers and powerful grip, to try and drown unwary swimmers. However, its fingers are spindly and brittle and their grip is easy to break if one puts up determined resistance. They can be found in the Lake at Hogwarts among stands of weeds. The Merpeople like to keep them as pets, usually they are tied to a stake in the front yard and lurk behind the weeds like a watch dog. Pr Lupin used to keep one in a tank in his office to use in his DADA classes in 93/94. One presumes they are saltwater creatures only.
Heliopaths: Supposedly spirits of fire, they are said to be very tall, made of flames or exuding flames from their body, rather like the balrog. These creatures gallop across the ground, so they may be horselike, and burn everything in front of them, though not intentionally. It simply happens. Luna claims Fudge has an army of them. Fudge would probably like an army of them, but evidence suggests they are fictional creatures.
Hinkypunks: A little one-legged creature that looks like it's made up of wisps of smoke. They are very small and rather frail and harmless looking but they live murder (and possibly then eat) human beings. They lure their victims, usually travelers unfamilar with their boggy homeland, into the bogs with a lantern (probably a lumious appendage) that dangles from their hand. Their intent is to drown the victim. Pr Lupin used to keep one in a small glass box to show his DADA classes in 93/94.
Hippocampus: see FB.
Hippogriff: A beast with the head, front legs and wings of a giant eagle and the body, back legs and tail of a horse. They all have steel color beaks and large brilliant orange eyes but they come in a wide variety of coat colors: dark grey, bronze, pinkish roan, chestnut and black to name just a few. In the distant past (pre-1300 AD), hippogriffs were often used for long-distance travel by wizards because brooms were uncomfortable and unreliable. Hippogriffs remain popular for travel today, especially among those who cannot Apparate over long distances. In recent years hippogriffs have

also been raised just for their beauty alone. Hippogriffs are easy to handle once their trust is gained, small enough to be kept indoors, and eat an easily obtainable diet of worms, rats, chickens or just about any insect or meaty creature. Hagrid taught on hippogriffs in 3rd year Care of Magical Creatures class.

Hippogriffs can be tamed and make fine pets but one must be exceedingly careful when handling hippogriffs as they are highly sensitive creatures and can react badly to rough treatment. It will, if verbally insulted, lash out with its very sharp, but not poisonous, talons in revenge. Hagrid had leather collars with long chains around the necks of his hippogriffs to control them, but even so one slashed Draco. The chains were dual purpose and could also be attached to the collars like reins so one could then easily guide the hippogriffs in flight. The secret to befriending a hippogriff is to show it respect. One must always wait for the hippogriff to make the first move. Keeping eye contact without blinking is also a good idea and proves one is trustworthy and unafraid. One may walk toward it, and bow, but only if it bows back one may touch it. If it doesn't, one must get away quickly as it will likely lash out.

Hippogriffs bow by bending their front knees, more like squatting as the joints go backwards, if they are willing to let the person ride them. To ride a hippogriff, one msut mount it as it bows and seat oneself behind the wing joints. The 24' wings (12' on either side) will beat and eventually the beast will become airborne. They are not very easy to ride but they fly silently like owls and are able to carry 2 even 3 people at a time which makes them an excellent stealthy means of transport. Today fewer people ride hippogriffs than in the past and it's the many hippogriff fanciers and breeders that really keep the species alive, however, all wizards love and appreciate hippogriffs and most have a fancy hippogriff calendar hanging about somewhere in their home or office.

Buckbeak: aka Beaky. A grey hippogriff Harry first rode in his first Care of Magical Creatures class. He fits on the bed in Hagrid's cabin if his wings are folded tight and particularly likes crunchy rats and ferrets. Draco called him an ugly brute and he responded by slashing Draco's right arm open. This admittedly long deep gash sparked a trial in which the MoM decided he was dangerous and needed to be executed, Buckbeak not Draco. Buckbeak, with the help of Harry, Hermione and Dumbledore, escaped with Sirius Black. Sirius flew him to a tropical hide out, Java or there abouts, and back to Britain. Eventually Buckbeak ended up stashed in Mrs Black's old room at 12 Grimmauld Place in 95/96. Since Sirius died it's unclear what will happen to him. He is still under the legal threat of death.

Horklump: see FB.
Imp: see FB.
Jarvey: see FB.
Jobberknoll: see FB.
Kappa: Creepy water-dwelling creatures that look like scaly monkeys with webbed hands. They like to strangle people who unwittingly wade into their pools. Pr Snape says it is more commonly found in Mongolia, but Scamander puts it more in Japan. Given that Mongolia barely has any water, one would agree tend to agree with Scamander. Such a gross error with such a common creature is probably why Pr Snape keeps getting passed over for the DADA position.
Kelpie: A water-dwelling creature that can take any form but most frequently appears as horse. It eats people who try to ride it. But as long as one avoids riding it, one is safe and the kelpie harmless. One lives in Hagrid's well and he likes it there. Pr Lockhart once thought it was there because Hagrid didn't know how to get rid of it.

THE HARRY POTTER COMPANION

Knarl: A small spiny creature that looks amazingly like a hedgehog. They are highly suspicious in nature and this is usually how one distinguishes them. If one tries to offer a knarl any type of food, it feel threatened and go berserk. The 5th years covered it in Care of Magical Creatures. It was on the practical exam OWL for Care of Magical Creatures.

Knarl Quills: Dung got a bag full of quills for Fred and George for 6S. Why they would be illegal is possibly because of the type of magical effects they can produce. Just what those are, is unknown.

Kneazle: A catlike creature covered in 5th year Care of Magical Creatures. Newt Scamander has 3 of them. Crookshanks may be part Kneazle and has a typical Kneazle personality: highly intelligent, a good judge of character and devoted to those he loves.

Leprechaun: Very tiny bearded men (and only men, no women) who can fly without the benefit of wings. They prefer the outdoors, particularly wooded areas. At QWC 1994 they wore red vests and carried minute lamps of green or gold. They are the Irish national team's mascots, and the mascot of the Kenmare Kestrels (Seamus' team). They are popular for their amazing displays of formation flying and ability to put on a light show. Only from Ireland, they can produce realistic gold in various Galleonlike forms but it vanishes after a few hours. They have a very good sense of humor.

Lethifold: see FB.

Lobalug: see FB.

Mackled Malaclaw: see FB. One is sure Fred and George will make a sweet out of this one's venom sometime soon.

Manticore: A dangerous Greek beast with a man's head, a lion's body and a scorpion's tail. A manticore was once convicted of a crime but the sentence was vacated because no one wanted to go near the beast to carry it out. The blast-ended skrewts were half manticore.

Merpeople: They live in the Lake at Hogwarts, but they can live anywhere there's salt water. Their village is near a rock painting of them chasing a giant squid. The giant squid and sharks are their only natural enemies. Merpeople enjoy rock painting, carving, beading, spear making and singing. They speak Mermish, which often sounds loud and screechy above the water. They don't know any magic but are afraid of wands which they know can do magic. When Harry pointed his wand at them, they all backed away from it.

Merpeople live in a variety of dwellings. Some choose caves, others crude dwellings of stone stained with algae which have dark windows. Some houses have gardens of weeds and a pet grindylows tied to a stake outside the door, some are in the village packed close together and lining the village square. Most merpeople seem to like living in a village, probably because it offers more protection - safety in numbers. In the village square in the Lake is a crude stone carving of a giant genderless merperson. This may be an important historic merperson, a warning device to scare away the squid and sharks away or just a place marker to help other merpeople find their town.

Merpeople have greyish skin, yellow eyes and let their dark green hair grow long and wild. They have gills, webbed hands and powerful fish tails of silver. Their teeth are yellow and broken and their voices harsh and croaky. Generally the men are tall, about 7' head to tail, and have long green beards. They carry spears and seem to do all the defensive work as well as the hunting. Men wear chokers, some of shark's teeth, while women wear thick ropes of pebbles. Merpeople appear to have female leaders but governing may be a job open to both genders.

Merchieftainess Murcus: She is the very wild and ferocious-looking head of the merpeople in Hogwarts' Lake. She told Dumbledore why Harry was delayed during TT Task 2. Her voice is rather screechy.
Moke: see FB.
Mooncalf: see FB.
Murtlap: Murtlaps are valued for the tentacled growths they have. A healing solution can be made from the strained and pickled tentacles. It produces a yellow liquid good for soothing skin problems such as cuts and boils. Murtlap essence is a popular medicinal in many wizards' medicine cabinets.
Nargles: Said to be nasty creatures that inhabit mistletoe, they are possibly fictional creatures. Luna believes in them.
Niffler: They are fluffy black creatures similar to moles except they have long snouts. The niffler's front paws are flat like spades and used for digging, which they do with great skill and efficiency. They're not accustomed to light or sunshine and look politely puzzled when above ground. They're natural habitat is undergound and they are usually found in mines because they like things that sparkle, like gold but anything sparkling will due, and are useful as treasure detectors. They are able to plunge into and swim through soil like it's water and will spit up any found sparkling items (silver, gold, coins, jewelry) into their owner's hands.

They should never be used as house pets because despite their love of darkness, they can see somewhat in the light and will scamper around tearing up everything in sight in a quest for sparkling items. Pr Umbridge had a niffler completely rifle her office on 2 separate occasions, thanks to Lee Jordan. One can't wear watches or jewelry around them or they'll try and bite them off. The resulting experience is quite painful as they have very strong teeth and little regard for useful anatomy like hands or throats. Otherwise, they are quite cuddly.
Nogtail: see FB.
Nundu: see FB.
Occamy: see FB.
Phoenix: The phoenix is a heavy, swan-size, scarlet bird with a long (about 3'), glittering, golden tail, a long sharp gold beak and gleaming gold talons. They have beady black eyes and large wings with glossy feathers that emit a soft gold glow. Phoenixes can make highly faithful pets but they are not for everyone. They are very difficult to tame and will but rarely become to any one wizard. Once they do, however, they remain with that individual and faithful to that individual for life, which can be 100+ years. This bird lives for a very long time by self-immolating and being reborn from the ashes whenever it become too elderly to go on. A bird will repeat this strange and rather painful process many times during its lifespan often causing it to outlive its owner.

A Burning Day is the day on which this fiery rebirthing process occurs. Just before a bird burns it will look like a decrepit half-plucked turkey, make strange gagging noises and have a dull cast to its eyes. Finally its most magical part, its tailfeathers, which are often used as wand cores, will fall out. At this point it will burst into flames and become a fireball. It gives a final loud shriek and appears to turn into ashes on the floor, however, amidst the burning embers and ash will be found a tiny featherless baby bird with wrinkled skin. The resulting very ugly bird will have the old bird's memory, but need to grow up all over again, which takes under a year. Most of the time however, they are very handsome with wonderful red and gold plumage (Gryffindor colors).

THE HARRY POTTER COMPANION

Among the many virtues of this amazing bird is that it can carry immensely heavy loads (600lb with its tailfeathers alone), its thick, pearly tears can heal any wound, and it can even swallow the Avada Kedavra curse and survive by bursting into flame and reincarnating again. The song of the phoenix is eerie, even unearthly and causes one's whole body to vibrate. The spine-tingling music makes good people take courage and grow stronger, but bad people to lose heart. These birds are capable of appearing (Apparates) and disappearing (Disapparates) with a burst of flame. In the spot where it appears, flames erupt first then the bird shows up a few seconds later. Even a single feather has this same power and anything touching the bird, or a single feather of it, can Apparate and Disapparate with it. They feel warm to the touch (like a fire), are very gentle by nature and extremely sympathetic to those who are loyal to their owner.

Fawkes: A phoenix belonging to Dumbledore that was born sometime before 1992. He sits on a golden perch beside the door of Dumbledore's office often swishing his long tail. When the door opens, he is blocked from the visitor's view. He is extremely intelligent and very loyal to Dumbledore. He sits on Dumbledore's shoulders or knees now and then. He will help anyone loyal to his master and in 92/93 brought Harry the Sorting Hat and blinded the basilisk to help him against Tom Riddle. Apparently though a basilisk's gaze can Petrify or kill a common cat, it doesn't work on other powerfully magical beasts like phoenixes.

Pixies: Found in Cornwall. They are humanoid in form with pointed faces but are electric blue, about 8" high and fly very, very fast despite the fact they have no wings. They have shrill.voices similar to parakeets. Normally very active, when caged they remain calm as long as they are kept in the dark. They are very intelligent and quite excitable. Whey caged they will chatter, rocket around, rattle cage bars and make bizarre faces at people.

Pixies are very destructive. They will, given the chance, reek havoc on anyone or anything around them. They have an excellent, rather wicked sense of humor, somewhat along the lines of Peeves. When released indoors most will immediately attempt to head for the outdoors but many prefer to spray ink all over people, shred books and tear pictures from walls before departing back to the wild. They tend to stay out of reach, with their tongues stuck out, when people trying to catch them. They can fly so fast few can catch them and their velocity can carry them right through glass windows unharmed. They are very strong, only 2 were able to easily hoist Neville up by the ears to the chandelier of the DADA classroom, and enjoy dancing. Freezing Charms seem to control them. They were a DADA subject in 92/93 under Pr Lockhart.

Pimply: see FB.

Pogrebin: see FB.

Porlock: These gaurdian creatures are similar bowtruckles, but tend to horses instead of tres. These are creatures covered in 5th year Care of Magical Creatures class.

Puffskein: For anyone who watches Star Trek, they will immediately recognize this creature as Tribblelike. They are funny, custard-colored furballs that hum loudly. Ron had one till the Weasley twins killed it by using it for Bludger practice. A nest of dead ones was in the drawing room of Sirius' house. They make great family pets and are very popular with wizarding children.

Quintaped: see FB.

Ramora: see FB.

Rat: According to the owner of the Magical Menagerie there are magical rats, and judging from the lot in her shop which skip rope, understand English and appear interested in what goes on around them, one would have to say it's true. These rats seem super intelligent, but what actual magical powers they can possess are unknown.

Red Cap: A nasty little goblinlike creature that lurks wherever blood has been shed, usually in dungeons or potholes in battlefields. It will bludgeon to death any lost wanderers. A subject covered by Pr Lupin in DADA during 93/94. Not to be confused with members of the British Army, some of whom are called Red Caps and are similar to Green Berets.
Re'em: see FB.
Runespoor: see FB.
Salamander: aka Fire Salamander. Salamanders are small lizards that live in and love fire flames. Brilliant orange in color when in a fire, they will run around on burning logs very happily for many hours. Hagrid taught on them in Care of Magical Creatures. Fred and George stole one and fed it a firework once and, either by choice or design, it went up the floo as quickly as possible. Salamanders can get scale rot but it's easily treatable.
Salamander Blood: It's used in Strengthening Solutions.
Sea Serpent: see FB.
Shrake: see FB.
Snidget: aka the golden snidget. A very rare and protected species of bird with rotating wing joints. The Golden Snitch was designed to mimic the snidget's size and coloration as well as its ability to fly fast, elude capture and change directions instantly. Severe penalties are attached to snidget capture, use or injury.
Sphinx: Of Egyptian origins, this beast has a female human head with almond-shaped eyes and the body of an oversized lion. It has a deep hoarse voice, is intelligent and delights in creating puzzles or riddles which it tries people who try to pass her. Answer a sphinx correctly and she moves aside, wrongly and she attacks but remain silent and she allows one to walk away.
Streeler: Snails that can change colors. They were at the Magical Menagerie. See FB.
Tebo: see FB.
Thestral: see Winged Horses.
Troll: While trolls walk upright and are able to be taught a few simple words they are not intelligent. The have no magical powers in their own right and are simply very strong. There are 3 different types of troll with mountain trolls reputed to be the stupidest. The smartest trolls can be trained to be rather surly security trolls who will walk about brandishing their clubs, talking in grunts and leering at people. Dumbledore hired a few to guard the Fat Lady in early 1994. All male trolls wear clothes, at least pants and sometimes shirts. As with goblins and centaurs, we've never seen a female troll and what they wear or do, remains mystery.

The average male mountain troll stands up to 12' tall, is about as wide and is extremely heavy. It will have a small bald head that looks like a coconut on top of its gigantic lumpy boulderlike body. It has short legs that are thick as oaks and huge flat horny feet but exceedingly long arms which will tend to drag on the floor. The troll has long ears which it waggles when trying to make up its tiny mind, has a tendency to slouch as it lumbers about and looks stupid partly because of its ugly snout. It has lumpy grey gluelike boogers, speaks in low grunts, shuffles when it walks and usually carries a huge wooden club.

A troll can become berserk when it hears shouting or echoes because such things are disorienting to its small mind. Like giants, a troll will roar deafeningly when upset, try to simply life by killing an offending party and is very hard to kill because of its thick dull granite-grey skin. Trolls are very tough making them difficult even to Stun. Indeed, a troll will not even notice when things that kill a normal person are thrown at it. A troll has at least 1 defensive weapon besides strength and toughness, an incredibly strong foul body odor that wafts for several yards around it. The smell is a mix of everyone's worst nightmares well-worn socks and uncleaned toilets. This factor warns most wizards of a troll's approach long before it's sighted and allows them to flee to safety thus avoiding needless confrontations. Two other types of troll exists, forest and river. See FB for details on these varieties.

Umgubular Slashkilter: A probably fictional creature that Luna claims Fudge has as a weapon against those who oppose him.

Unicorn: This is a bright, gleaming white, beautiful horse with a long single horn coming out of its forehead and a pearly white manes. They have golden hooves, long slender legs and are very fast. Unicorns are pure creatures and harming one invokes the ultimate penalty – the cursed life. Luckily harming them is difficult. They so fast even a werewolf couldn't catch one, and are powerful magical creatures in their own right. Unicorns are though of as defenseless creatures but will use their teeth, hooves and even horn to defend themselves – as Mr Ollivander, who was almost gored by a stallion's horn once, will be the first to admit.

At least one herd lives in the Forbidden Forest, but they are shy creatures and don't seek out human contact so they are rarely seen. They are considered by some to be rather unintelligent but may just be misunderstood. They prefer a woman's touch and are become skittish around men or boys. Foals are born golden and then turn silver at 2 years. At 4 years they (apparently both males and females) will grow white horns. At 7 years they will be fully grown and completely white. Like most horses, they like sugar lumps and eat a diet of grass or hay. Unicorns were a very popular study in Care of Magical Creatures during 94/95 and were on the OWL practical exam for Care of Magical Creatures.

Unicorn Horn: Horns are used in potions.

Unicorn Tail: Tailhairs are used in potions and single ones are used for wand cores.

Unicorn Blood: It is silvery-blue and will keep the consumer of it alive even if on the verge of death, but at a very high price. Such people will live a half life, and be forever cursed from the moment they touch the blood to their lips. No sane wizard would ever kill a unicorn. But someone insane, with nothing left to lose, would commit such a crime, and Voldemort did. In 91/92, he killed 2 unicorns in 1 week.

Veela: This beast can take the form of a woman, but in reality has a sharp, cruel beak, the head of a bird and long scaly wings protruding from its shoulders. When veela get upset they revert to their true form. As women their skin shines moon-bright and they have long white-gold or slivery hair. They have the power to entrance men with their dancing but have no effect on women. They will only dance to music, when there is no music they stop immediately dancing and, luckily, they seem to produce no music of their own.

The faster they dance, the more agitated men become. Men may become so infatuated with them they start lying about themselves. Harry almost jumped from the Top Box at QWC 1994 without realizing it while seeing them dance. They don't seem to want to hurt men, it just happens. The Bulgarian team brought 100 to QWC 1994 as mascots and to influence the male referee. Veelas are able to conjure a handful of fire at will and, failing to win over the referee with dancing, they set fire to his broom. It's not known if veela talk, they don't seem to, and it may be the combination of beauty, silence and controllability that got to Fleur's grandfather, who married a veela.

Surprisingly veelas can and will marry and mate with wizards, Fleur's grandmother is one example. But it remains to be seen what specific traits are passed on to children of such unions, such as daughters being able to throw handfuls handfuls of fire or having bird parts. Given veela are defined as Beasts and not Beings, it's surprising the French MoM allowed a wizard to marry one. It's technically like marrying a goat. It's unknown if such marriages endure beyond a few years, though Fleur's grandfather's did. Certainly there must be a decided lack of actual relationship, not to mention veela as Beasts are generally owned rather than married. How exactly a man would present a veela wife socially without looking ridiculous in the extreme is a bit perplexing.

Werewolf: See the Werewolves section in Part V.

Winged Horse: There a 4 breeds of winged horses of which only 2 are germane, the abraxan and the thestral. For granian and aethonan horses see FB.

Abraxan: These are huge amazingly powerful winged palominos with fiery red eyes. Madam Maxime uses 12 to pull her coach and also breeds them to keep a supply on hand. They require forceful handling and drink only single malt whiskey (which may account for the red eyes). Given the eyes and the food, it seems possible these animals might spit fire, but that has never been stated.

Thestral: A rare, black, winged horse with a skeletal and reptilian appearance. They are considered unlucky by many because they can only be seen by those who have witnessed the death of another human being, live and in person. The fact they can be seen by some people and not others proves they are visible all the time, but certain individuals are blind to them. It is when the person changes the horse is seen so the fault lies in the person not the thestral. Thestrals aren't invisble, people are blind to them.

Hogwarts' Thestrals: The thestrals in the Forbidden Forest were bred by Hagrid from an initial herd of 1 stallion and 5 mares. There are over 200 now. Used to pull Hogwarts' carriages for student tranport, Dumbledore also uses the thestrals but only for extended journeys, probably in excess of 500 miles, when he doesn't want to Apparate. Though whether this means he rides one on they pull a flying carriage is unclear.

A short list of people who see thestrals and the people they saw die follows:
Hagrid: unknown? Perhaps his father.
Harry: Cedric. Harry obviously didn't see either of his parents die. Possibly Harry's crib was behind a screen blocking his actual view of his parents' death and only saw the green light.

What is weird about Harry's case is that he saw Ced's death, but didn't see the thestrals pulling the carriage from Hogwarts to the station at the end of the year (1995), though he did see the carriages themselves. It was not until 2 months later at Hogsmeade Station he saw the thestrals. There may be a delay period between the actual death and the ability to see thestrals. Hermione, Ginny and Ron, who saw Sirius die, do not remark that they saw the thestrals leaving Hogwarts in 1996 either, though they certainly rode the carriages to the station. Hermione specifically wanted to see thestrals and still didn't comment. Either she didn't see them due to the delay factor or she was being kind to Harry. One rather thinks the former.
Luna: her mom.
Neville: his grandfather Longbottom.
Unknown Slytherin (in Harry's year): unknown?
Dumbledore: unknown. At his advanced age, and having lived through both World Wars and Voldemort's first attempt to rise to power, one would assume he's seen many, many people die.

Hogwarts' thestrals are black reptilian horses with long black manes and tails. They are skin and bones, but lack muscle flesh. Every bone is visible beneath their clinging coats. Large black leathery bat-type wings wing grow out from each wither and they have an odd shrieking cry. Their head and neck are dragonish, probably Norwegian ridgeback, in appearance. Their eyes that have white staring pupils which give them a sinister and eerie look. They like the smell of meat and prefer to eat fresh meat but really anything will do, even garbage. They will sometimes go for wild owls, but Hagrid's trained them not touch Hogwarts' owls. They are attracted to the smell of blood and don't mind giant blood either. They prefer the dark woods as the deep forest is their natural habitat.

Thestrals are quite harmless, and very useful. They never get lost, have an amazing sense of direction and can go wherever they're told. Say the place (eg, the MoM) and they will take one there even if they have never been there before. Like hippogriffs, they are very intelligent, seem to understand English very well and will only bite at someone if really annoyed. They are ridden with one's legs behind the wing joints. Unlike hippogriffs, they blast up into the air at a steep angle on take off and one needs a very good grip on them to avoid sliding off their bony rumps. They do however land very smoothly and gracefully.

Thestrals are extremely fast can make it from Hogwarts to London about twice as fast as the Hogwarts Express. Figuring a 600 mile journey at 60 mph on the Express, that puts thestral travel at about 120+ mph. They are faithful to their riders and content to hang around in an area and wait for their rider to return as long they have something to eat. Flying is after all hungry work. How exactly Dumbledore got the 6 thestrals home from the MoM in Jun 1996 is a mystery. They might have flow back on their own, given they have a great sense of direction. But enough people in England have seen death to make that untenable. Maybe he Disillusioned them temporarily.

Tenebrus: He is the favorite thestral of Hagrid. Tenebrus was the first thestral born in the Forbidden Forest. He's a large stallion. It isn't clear how old Tenebrus is but given the size of the herd and the fact he was firstborn he must be about 15-20 years old which implies thestrals live a long time.

Wood Lice: They are brown and look a bit like brown rice kernels. Bowtruckles love to eat them. They are not to be confused with pill bugs which some Muggles refer to as wood lice.

Yeti: The ICW has as special task force that keeps an eye on the yeti situation in Tibet. Lockhart claimed contact with a yeti, but this is doubtful at best.

DISEASES

So far just the one has come up.

Scale Rot: A disease that dragons, salamanders, possibly thestrals, and other reptiles can get. It can be cured in salamanders by rubbing chili powder on the affected area. How one does this with dragons is unknown.

ANIMALS: NON-MAGICAL

This section contains information on non-magical animals, birds, fish, insects, mammals and reptiles, in this order. Pets like Hedwig, Pigwidgeon or Crookshanks can be found under their species, eg, Cats would include Crookshanks. Scabbers is here as well because so much of his time was spent as a rat. Secondary information on animals, such as diseases, cures and associated services, are also in the species section. For instance, Owl Post would be in the Owl section. For magical beasts, such as dragons or centaurs, see the Magical Beasts section.

BIRDS

Chicken: Molly keeps some free-range brown chickens at the Burrow. Hagrid keeps some in a chicken coop. Hagrid had 2 roosters killed in 92/93, by Ginny.

Eagle: A 30-41" carnivorous bird with a very impressive wingspan of about 6.5 feet, large talons and a very sharp beak. They come in several varieties (golden, bald, brown, steppes) and are found in most parts of the world. Eagle feathers are used for writing quills. Hermione buys them as gifts for Harry, who seems to prefer them. The eagle is the symbol mascot of Ravenclaw House and appears on their banner. They prefer to nest on high cliffs or the tops of trees so this may explain why Ravenclaw has a tower for its student lodgings.

Flamingo: A large pink tropical bird. Hannah Abbot Transfigured one ferret into a whole flock of these birds during her OWL practical.

Owl: Owls are generally used to deliver letters, messages or parcels. The first owl Harry saw used for postal delivery came out of Hagrid's pocket. First years are allowed to bring an owl to Hogwarts if they wish, but the school has many owls any student may use. *The Daily Prophet* is delivered by owls which carry pouches on their legs for collecting the 5K-per-day fee. Owls most often carry letters and papers in their beaks while larger items, scrolls, packages, a leg of ham, may require the use of feet and at times more owls. Harry's Nimbus 2000 was delivered by 6 screech owls. Letters may be tied to an owl's leg, but this is less common.

Owls can be Apparated by a wizard for instant arrival but this is not good for the owl, who ends up looking dazed and ruffled. However, in an emergency situation Apparating an owl is sometimes the only option. Most wizards are content with the pace of owl delivery and owls are terribly clever and find the addressee no matter where they are, even if they're 1,000s of miles away and never met the person. Owl use is pretty simple and even the Dursleys have used owl delivery. They use Hedwig to send a Christmas present to Harry every year. Probably it's the only way for them to send presents to Hogwarts, but still, its hard to imagine them using an owl or sending Harry a present at all. Probably Petunia does it, but loathes even looking at an owl. As for Vernon, he probably goes into another room till it's gone.

Because owls prefer to be out at night, usually to hunt for food such as mice or frogs, and then sleep in the day, mail delivery at Hogwarts is during breakfast. An owl will circle the tables until spotting its owner then drop letters and packages into her or his lap and fly off to the school Owlery for some sleep. Some owls will land and have a bite of toast before departing. Owls are quite competitive (or maybe just tired) so if more than one has a delivery to make to the same person, the owls will jockey around trying to be the priority owl. Owls have a wide variety of personalities, they can be kind, ditzy, tired, proud, nagging, nasty, elegant or annoying. Most owls seem to be devoted to their owners and one can think of few Muggle falconers that could give their owls the sort of latitude wizards do without having their owl desert them.

Owls are popular, even trendy, in the wizarding world. Most wizards have at least one owl in the family. A personal owl is status indeed. Draco owns an eagle owl of undetermined origins. Hagrid gave Harry a Artic snowy owl, Hedwig, for a birthday gift. Ron was given a very tiny owl (probably a scops) as a gift from Sirius. Even Hermione wanted an owl, but fell in love with Crookshanks on the way to purchase one. There are several varieties of owl used by wizards, some native to Britain, some not. Some care needs be used with non-native owls lest Muggles spot them. However, most owls have excellent hearing, fly noiselessly due to a specially serrated leading edge to their feathers, and have good eyesight, contrary to popular belief. They can

The Harry Potter Companion

disappear before a Muggle even knows they were there (unless they vocalize). At need they can be amazingly agile fliers and can even fold their wings during midflight to negotiate a tight space and make an escape.

Owls range in size and weight within their species and in some species the females are consistently larger than the males (a phenomenon call sexual dimorphism). Owls can bring down very large prey, if they are large themselves. The eagle owl can bring down a fawn if it were starving and no other smaller prey were available. Most owls, however, prefer more manageable meals, rodents, insects, frogs and the like, which helps keep the environment in balance. Few people would knowingly shoot an owl today, but people are still a threat to owls. The greatest danger to owls is eating something that may have been poisoned, such as a rat that ate poison (as part of a human being's vermin control plan) or water filled with chemical run off not intended for consumption but still lying in open spaces where owls can drink of it.

Owl Order: It's similar to mail order just with owls. Some wizarding companies sell by owl-order. Hermione used an owl-order company to get a gift for Harry's 13th birthday. Sirius used one to get Harry a Firebolt. Weasleys' Wizarding Wheezes started out an owl-order business. Since owls are very intelligent and will go wherever told, and even find people even without any address at all, it's a lot better than mail order. An owl will track a customer down, no matter what, and one doesn't even have to pay extra postage for the service.

Owl Treats: Ron gives them to Pig to shut him up. They are so large, for Pig, that they sometimes cause him to choke or get his beak stuck together.

Barn Owl: aka Tyro alba. There are many species of barn owl found in Europe and America. Gran Longbottom appears to own a barn owl which invariably brings Neville things he's forgotten at home or the occasional Howler. *The Daily Prophet* is often times delivered by this type of owl. It's a medium-size owl with relatively long legs and a distinctive heart-shaped facial disk. Very variable in coloration depending on race, but generally reddish with grey undertones and a white face. Females tend to be generally darker and more heavily marked than males. Their diet consists mainly of small mammals, especially rodents, but also small birds, reptiles, frogs and sometimes insects. They are 11-17" and 6.5-14oz and found throughout Europe. They would not be out of place to the Muggle observer in Britain. It is not an endangered species.

Brown Owl: aka Brown Wood Owl or Strix leptogrammica. Sirius used this type of owl quite often. Probably because it was easily available when he was in hiding in the tropics, he brought one home. They are a medium to large owl, with no ear tufts and dark eyes and have a dark brown crown. The facial disk can be whitish or light red with dark rings around the eyes. They are quite impressive looking. They are 14-21" and 17-24oz and enjoy small mammals, birds and reptiles. Found in the forest jungles of Sumatra, Sri Lanka, the Malay Peninsula and Borneo (all very good tropical hiding places for Sirius), they would be out of place to the Muggle observer in Britain. However it take an avid birdwatcher to spot it. The average person would call it a mutant barn owl and walk away. It is not an endangered species.

Eagle Owl: aka Bubo bubo bubo. It's at the top of the owl food chain and is both the largest and most aggressive of all owls. It is a very large owl with prominent ear tufts and vivid orange eyes. Its coloring is variable throughout its range. Generally it is buff-brown and heavily marked with black, with a greyish facial disk. It's quite distinctive in appearance. The latest DNA evidence suggests that the snowy owl is very closely related to the eagle owls. They are 23-29" and 52-147oz and eat mainly mammals, from shrews up to foxes and even young deer. It will also hunt a wide range of birds, reptiles and amphibians. It is generally found in Western Europe and would not be out of place to the Muggle observer in Britain. It is not an endangered species.

(Unknown) Eagle Owl: This owl belongs to Draco. It brings him sweets from home every day. Probably a Mackenzie's Eagle Owl, an African owl and the largest most aggressive bird of a large and aggressive species.

Great Grey Owl: aka Strix nebulosa. It is the largest owl the Post Office in Hogsmeade uses. Errol is probably this type of owl. A very beautiful rather large grey or greyish owl with small yellow eyes. They are 23-27" and 28-59.5oz and eat mainly small mammals, particularly rodents, but also birds, frogs and beetles. They are found in Northern Europe and would not seem out of place to the Muggle observer in Britain. It is not an endangered species.

Errol: Probably a great grey owl. He is the Weasley's family owl. He is old, bleary eyed, and tends to collapse upon delivering mail. Hedwig and another owl had to physically help him complete a delivery once. He's a bit clumsy too. He fell in Hermione's milk jug spraying her with milk and feathers while bringing a Howler for Ron. He resembles a large grey molting feather duster. His perch is just inside the back door of the kitchen at the Burrow, but when he flops off his perch from exhaustion, he is placed on the draining board. After delivering food to Harry from Molly, he had to rest 5 days before starting the return journey home. He is annoyed by Pigwidgeon, so Pig is generally kept upstairs away from him when Ron is home.

Scops Owl: aka Otus scops scops. This is the smallest owl the Post Office in Hogsmeade uses. It is only for local deliveries. It is a small, grey or buff, eared owl with small yellow eyes. About 6-8" and 2-4.5oz , it eats mainly insects and other invertebrates but also small lizards, frogs and small mammals. These owls have a low, short, piping whistle that repeats at 2-3 second intervals. It is generally found in Western Europe and would not be out of place to the Muggle observer in Britain. It is not an endangered species.

Pigwidgeon: aka Pig. Probably a scops owl. He is a small grey feathery tennis-ball-size owl. He fits in the palm of Ron's hand. He has plenty of pluck and was eager for a job delivering mail when Sirius found him, so Sirius sent him to Ron in Jun 1994. Ron was glad to have Pig as a replacement for Scabbers, but he makes rude comments about him all the same. He likes to nibble Ron's fingers in what he believe is an affectionate way but it actually hurts. Ron loves him all the same.

He's a very happy little owl. He whizzes around excitedly when he gets an opportunity to do a delivery. Ginny named Pigwidgeon, Pig for short. Luna thinks he's sweet. Hedwig thinks he's undignified but doesn't mind sharing quarters with him. Hermes and Errol don't want to be in the same room with him because they feel he's so annoying, and they're right. Pig will, it must be said, hop up and down or zoom around excitedly, twittering, in his small cage (or the room, if loose) when there is any sort of activity going on around him.

Screech Owl: aka Otus Kennicottii. Often the owl of choice at the MoM for letters traveling outside of the building. A lovely small to medium owl with small ear tufts and large yellow eyes. They are generally grey, but can be reddish in color, with a whitish face. Despite the name, they're call is actually a double trill, with the first trill being shorter in length and rising then falling in pitch. They are 8-9" and 4.5-8.75oz and will eat insects, small mammals, birds, reptiles and amphibians. They are common to North America and would be out of place to the Muggle observer in Britain, however it would have to be spotted by an avid birdwatcher. The average person would call it a scops owl and walk away. It is not an endangered species.

The Harry Potter Companion

Hermes: A handsome screech owl that was given to Percy as a gift from Molly and Arthur for being made a Prefect in 91/92. Hermes hangs out in the kitchen of the Burrow with Errol when Percy's at home. He too is annoyed by Pig. Since Percy moved to his own place in summer 1995, Hermes hasn't been back to the Burrow.

Snowy Owl: aka Nyctea scandiaca. This is the type of owl that Harry owns. These are large, pure white owls with black markings. The females are more heavily marked than males. They have very small ear tufts, often not visible, and yellow eyes. Unlike most owls they will hunt during day and almost continuously. This comes from the fact that they are generally found in the polar regions where they day can be 23 hours long and the temperatures keep any kill frozen till they wish to eat it. However they can go up to 40 days without food because of stored body fat. The latest DNA evidence suggests that the Snowy Owl is very closely related to the Eagle Owl. They are 20-26" and 24.5-103oz with a wingspan of 4.5-5'. Their diet is mainly mammals especially lemmings, hares and also birds up to the size of ducks. They would be out of place to any Muggle observer in Britain, necessitating some caution in its use as a mail carrier. It is not an endangered species.

Hedwig: She is a large snowy owl with amber eyes (this is unusual as they generally have yellow eyes). She was an 11th birthday present to Harry from Hagrid. Her name is from the book *A History Of Magic*, but who exactly in wizarding history she is named after and why that witch was so famous as to turn up in a book on the history of magic we don't know. Hedwig is very proud and demands respect from any and all but particularly Harry. She hates being treated badly or carelessly. She snubbed Harry for a long while, and even turned her back on him when he came to the Owlery, after the multiple indignities culminating in ejection from the flying Ford Anglia in 92/93.

She is very intelligent and rather sensitive but devoted to Harry. She will go around to his friends, and even the Dursleys, without him knowing, to make sure he gets birthday and Christmas presents. She goes to the Great Hall every morning, with or without mail to deliver, so Harry doesn't feel left out of getting owls. She enjoys nibbling Harry's ear or fingers and having toast or cornflakes with him at breakfast in the Great Hall. She generally sits on Harry's knee or his shoulder. She takes her job as a mail owl very seriously – mabye a bit too seriously. Instead of tossing Harry's mail into his lap, Hedwig lands on the table and puts them on Harry's plate.

She gets very angry and jealous when Harry uses another owl and has been known to cuff Harry in the head with her wing when he upsets her or start clicking her beak disapprovingly at him. She hoots loudly when she's bored. She doesn't mind Errol and lets him recoup in her cage for a few days when he comes to the Dursley's house. She hangs out with Errol at the Burrow and doesn't mind Pig, though she doesn't think Pig is very dignified, especially for a mail owl. She tends to sit on top of wardrobes when indoors and away from her cage because she likes looking down on things. At Hogwarts, she spends her time in the school Owlery sleeping in the day generally, and hunting at night.

She hates being padlocked in her cage with just water, which occasionally happens at the Dursley's but she doesn't mind the cage itself. She prefers sit on top of her cage at night and look out the back window at the yard when Harry is home so she can go out and catch her own food when she spots something in the garden (which the Dursleys must love). During the day, she likes to sleep in her cage with her head under her wing. She will eat toast and cornflakes, prefers mice and frogs, but loathes soggy vegetables from cold canned soup.

Tawny Owl: aka Strix aluco. A medium-size grey-brown owl with no ear tufts, dark eyes and a stocky appearance. It looks like it's been lightly dusted with snow about the eyes. The Hogwarts' school owls are many and varied, but usually tawnys. Hogwarts' owls are also rather self-important looking. They are 14-18" and 13-23oz and enjoy a wide variety of prey including small mammals, frogs, birds, insects, earthworms and even fish. Found throughout Europe, they would not be out of place to the Muggle observer in Britain. It is not an endangered species.

Parakeet: A small 4" colorful bird usually kept as a pet. Also call budgies and budgerigars.

Bungy: A waterskiing parakeet who lives at the Five Feathers in Barnsley, Gloucester in England. He was "interviewed" by Mary Dorkins for the 7pm news in the summer of 1995.

Parrot: Many various species exist from several continents. They are usually colorful fun-loving birds that can live quite a long time and even learn to speak. Dudley had a parrot of unknown variety but traded it for an air gun sometime prior to Jul 1991. The parrot was probably very grateful.

Peacock: They are interesting birds in their own right and have incorrigible personalities. They like newly planted flowers just a little too much to have around a smaller garden and can be a bit hard on dogs because they like to tease them, but despite all this peacock ownership has continued to flourish over the years. Peacocks have always been considered a rather ostentatious statement of wealth. One particular wizarding individual had some in front of the tent she or he occupied at the QWC 1994. The tailfeathers of this bird is used for making fancy writing quills. They fall out once a year of their own accord in the fall, so no harm is done the birds in the collection of this product. Notably Pr Lockhart uses such a quill for all his autographs and book signings. It's also his personal quill of choice.

Pheasant: A large colorful (male) or brown (female) bird of the grassy woodlands and forests. Very spectacular in startled flight, especially in pairs, across a lonely New Zealand road, in late afternoon, when they are inches from the nose of an unsuspecting walker. It is about the size of a large turkey with an impressive wingspan. They are edible and Hagrid usually has some hanging from his rafters. These come from the Forbidden Forest. Their feathers are also used for fancy writing quills and Hermione has at least one.

Raven: They are very intelligent, rather large, black, birds occasionally used in Charms class for their wonderful noisiness. Ravens were once thought by the Celts to carry souls to heaven since they were always found around dead bodies.

Swan: Large (50-70") elegant, water-loving birds, they often mate for life and are very devote to their families. They come in black and white depending on the species. Cho's Patronus in a swan, which says good things about how she thinks of her father.

Vulture: A large carrion-eating bird. There is a stuffed one on Gran Longbottom's hat. They seem to be a fashion statement that only the most stylish can pull off well. Needless to say Pr Snape refused to wear the one he pulled from a Christmas cracker but Dumbledore put it on at once.

FISH

Eel: Eel eyes are used in potions, such as the cure for Spattergroit. The remainder is quite tasty and the skin can make excellent wallets.

Giant Squid: A very elusive and rare creature that we know exists, but not much else about it. They are deep sea creatures and seem to be about 100' long. Tentacles 40' long have been found around Chile and New Zealand and from them a size was estimated, but no one knows for certain how big they can get. No living squid has ever been photographed or even seen. There is one that lives in the Hogwarts' Lake (which must be connected to the sea somehow), but the merpeople treat it as a deadly enemy. It's very friendly and helpful to students. It will swim with them or put them back into their boats if they fall out and it doesn't mind being touched or eating the odd bit of toast thrown to it. We don't know enough about giant squids to know if it's behavior could be called magical.

Haddock: Some of Fred and George's Fake Wands turn into rubber haddocks. These are small fish related to the common Atlantic cod and considered good for eating.

Lionfish: Its spines are used in potions. Found in the tropics of the Pacific, it's an usually brilliantly striped and barred fish. It is a member of the scorpion fish family and has venomous dorsal spines.

Puffer Fish: Its eyes are used in potions. It's also a poisonous fish that kills many people each year, mostly in Japan where it is considered a great delicacy and something *real* men eat.

INSECTS

Beetle: They are used for turning into buttons in Transfiguration class. Or, if one is Fred or George, for putting in people's soup. Black beetle eyes are used in potions.

Dung Beetle: A beetle that rolls balls of dung in which to lay eggs and on which its larvae will feed. Something Harry would like to turn Dursleys into.

Scarab Beetle: These beetles were once held scared in Egypt as a talisman and a symbol of resurrection. They are stout bodied with lamallate antennae. They are used in Wit-Sharpening Potion.

Dragonfly: A long glittering winged insect found near water. It's what Pr Trelawney looks like.

Earwig: An insect in the flowers Hagrid sent to Harry while he was recovering from a broomstick fall. They have many-jointed antennae and large pincers at the end of their bodies.

Lacewing Fly: They are used in Polyjuice potions. A netwinged insect with long antennae and brilliant eyes.

Spider: Amazing web-spinning 8-legged creatures. They are all over the place at Hogwarts until 92/93 when they were seen fleeing the site of the Petrifications. It's unknown if they left for good. As the basilisk, their mortal enemy, is dead, it is likely they have all trundled back. They are sometimes used in potions. Ron is very afraid of spiders of any size or variety because of a childhood prank Fred and George played on him, made worse by a trip to Aragog's place in 92/93, and will avoid them at any cost.

Black Spider: A type of aggressive spider sold in Knockturn Alley. Undoubtedly it has Dark Arts applications.

Tarantula: A very large attractive spider found in the western US and Mexico. Lee Jordan had one he took to school in 91/92.

MAMMALS

Armadillo: A small, burrowing, nocturnal animal with a body and head covered in bony plates of armor. They curl up when attacked, much like a pill bug. Found only in the warmer parts of the Americas, Texans used to think of them as tasty. Its bile used in Wit-Sharpening Potion.

Badger: The symbol and mascot of Hufflepuff House. Something some rather advanced 4th years were turning each other into in 92/93 Transfiguration class. A dead one was once mistakenly worn as toupee by Uric the Oddball. They are valued for their pelt which is usually black with white accents. In life they are very aggressive and quite good at digging. Severe injuries, even death, can result from being attacked by a badger. They like to be underground and usually construct burrows there. This may explain why Hufflepuff House is underground.

Bat: A small winged mammal with sharp claws used for hang onto rocks inside caves. It prefers to come out only at night, usually in large numbers, to look for prey. They have excellent sensory abilities including echo location, infrared and night vision. Generally harmless, one is not advised to spend any length of time in a bat cave as breathing the guano can cause blood poisoning and death. Bat spleen is used in various potions.

Fruit Bat: Something Harry would like to turn Dursleys into. These large European bats prefer warm climates and diet of fruit. They are also called flying foxes in some areas.

Barny: A fruit bat. The mascot of the Butterbeer company and the Ballycastle Bats. He does Butterbeer commercials in his free time. Apparently he talks, which makes him something more than just a fruit bat.

Vampire Bat: These South American bats are the only bats that are blood sucking. They subsist on blood and are dangerous to humans and animals only because they carry diseases like rabies. A very frightening en mass release from under a Chaser's robes during QWC 1473 created a new foul. It's unclear how long he had them under his robes before their release but one hopes wizards have better, less extremely painful, cures for rabies than Muggles.

Beaver: Found in the Forbidden Forest, Hagrid hunts them for their skins. They are water-dwelling creatures that enjoy building, mostly dams, with logs they have gnawed down with their amazingly tough teeth.

Boar: Hagrid hunts these very dangerous often tusked hogs in the Forbidden Forest. Hence his owning Fang, the boarhound. Wild boar can be found in many varieties around the world. None of them are friendly. Some can grow to 6' at the top of the shoulder. And in the past, a few have even killed the people hunting them with their tremendous tusks.

Cat: They can be taken to school by 1st year students. They are not kept in cages, even at the train station on the platform. Hermione wisely keeps Crookshanks in a wicker basket when boarding or leaving the train. Cats may freely roam the interior or grounds of the castle, and even go into the Forbidden Forest. Kittens, as complex mammals, are used in Transfiguration by advanced students to practice Vanishing Spells.

Crookshanks: An enormous thick, fluffy ginger cat. He is a bit bowlegged and his face is grumpy, ugly and oddly squashed looking (possibly he's part Persian). He has big yellow eyes, an inscrutable stare and a long bottlebrush tail. Hermione thinks he's gorgeous. Hermione acquired him from the Magical Menagerie in Aug 1993 with money her parents had given her to buy herself an early birthday. He must have cost under 10G, as that was all she had left when she went into the shop. He'd been in the shop for a long time and was already fully grown. No one else had wanted him so that's probably why he was so cheap.

Hermione carries him around in a wicker basket with leather straps when traveling, but lets him out to roam at every opportunity. She gives him complete freedom at Hogwarts, or when she's visiting at the Burrow or Headquarters. He's a very well-behaved cat. Most of the time he sleeps in a chair in the common room in Gryffindor tower, but he likes to get out and about if there's mischief around. He is very good at catching things, like spiders, which he eats, or illegal Animagi, both good and bad. He loves chasing gnomes, Snitches and wizard's chess pieces, but just for fun and not to eat. He may look like a ginger cushion, but he's all cat. He always flicks the end of his bushy tail before he pounces, is an excellent jumper and, despite his bulk, very light on his feet.

Hermione dresses him up for Christmas with a collar of tinsel, but he looks very grumpy about it. He likes Harry and often sits on his lap or tries to get him to scratch his ears. He's a very brave and intelligent cat. He immediately knew Scabbers was a bad person in disguise and tried to pounce on him. Failing to kill him, Crookshanks continued to spit and hiss at Scabbers every time he was nearby. He recognized Sirius as a good person in disguise and did everything he could to help him. He stole the passwords from Neville, took Sirius' order for the Firebolt to the Hogsmeade post office, tried to kill Scabbers in Ron's dorm room and even planted himself in the line of fire (on Sirius' chest) when Harry was about to kill him.

Crookshanks was a great friend to Sirius and took every opportunity to sit on his lap. It seemed that he liked Sirius even more than Hermione and whenever they were all together, he always preferred to be on or near Sirius. Perhaps he has a sense that Sirius' life would be cut short and was trying to show him love and affection to try make up for all the bad things that had happened to him. His loyalty to Sirius was certainly profound, a kneazle trait, and it would seem that Crookshanks has some kneazle blood based on his immediately negative reaction to Scabbers (Peter Pettigrew), the fact that he was from a magical animal shop, not a Muggle pet shop, and perhaps his tail (though it is difficult to interpret what bottlebrush means, whether the whole tail is thick and furry, or just the tip end). If the tip end of his tail were the only part fluffed up, as true bottlebrushes look, it would further confirm he's part kneazle. Regardless of looks though, he does have a kneazle personality.

Mr. Paws: A deceased cat of Mrs Figg's. She was always showing Harry pictures of her dead cats before he knew she was a Squib.

Mr Tibbles: aka Tibbles. Mrs Figg's current cat. He was watching Harry, on Arabella's request, from under a car near the Dursley's house in summer 1995. Obviously a very smart cat, he ran to get Arabella when he saw Harry walk off on his own. It would seem to imply the Mrs Figg is a little magical, if she can command a cat.

Mrs Norris: aka My Sweet. She is a scrawny, skeletal, dust colored (grey) cat with bulging eyes just like Filch's, except they are yellow and lamplike. She has a high-pitched voice and mewls (cries weakly) rather than yowls. Her excellent sense of smell can find a person even if she or his can't be seen under an Invisibility Cloak. She patrols the school corridors alone, but break a rule or put a toe out of line in front of her and she whisks off for Filch, who appears 2 seconds later. Many students' over the years have harbored as their dearest ambition giving her a good kick. She follows Hagrid around whenever he comes up to the castle because apparently Filch doesn't like Hagrid, possibly because he knows Hagrid to be a half-giant. She's Filch's deputy, advance scout and all around friend. Filch calls her with a chirupping sound. She is definitely cat and not kneazle, but the fact Filch can command a pure cat makes him much more a wizard than even Dumbledore.

Snowy: A deceased cat of Mrs Figg's. She was always showing Harry pictures of her dead cats before he discovered she was a Squib.

Tufty: A deceased cat of Mrs Figg's. She was always showing Harry pictures of her dead cats before he discovered she was a Squib.

(Unknown) Cat: Millicent Bulstrode has a black cat with yellow eyes that she takes to school with her.

Cow: The Hogwarts Express passes several fields with cows as it goes North.

Deer: There are deer in the Forbidden Forest, at least there were till 1995 when Hagrid brought Grawp home and Grawp began eating them all. Prongs, Harry's Patronus, is a stag probably because his father, James, used to turn into a stag.

Dog: Dogs are popular with Muggles and wizards. Marge has 12, Hagrid has one (Fang), and Sirius could become one (Snuffles). The Dursley's nextdoor neighbor have a dog, so even posh Privet Dr has them, and the MoM keeps some working dogs for magical purposes, though where in the building is unknown.

Albino Bloodhound: A dozen of them are kept by the Pest Sub-Division of the DRCMC for removing Nogtails from farms. There is nothing actually magical about them.

Fang: A very big black boarhound belonging to Hagrid. Fang wears a collar and sometimes a leash but Hagrid usually let's him run free. Fang can usually be seen loping along at Hagrid's heels as he strides the grounds. Hagrid says that no harm can come to one in the Forbidden Forest if one is with him or with Fang. But Fang is basically a cowardly dog and tends to run from any type of danger. He has a basket with a blanket in Hagrid's house and hides under the blanket when afraid.

To be fair though, Fang has his share of reasons to bail at the first sign of trouble. Norbert bit Fang on the tail once but there was no lasting kink put in his tail. He deserted Harry in the forest, but only because he was face to face with Voldemort. He avoided making a fuss when the roosters died because Ginny was a friend and possessed by Tom Riddle, a double-whammy situation. He wouldn't go after Sirius in any way because, like Crookshanks, he likely knew a good person in dog form when he saw one. During the year of the TT there were skrewts, then dragons, abraxans and Death Eaters stumping about so keeping his head down was really the wisest thing to do.

When push came to shove however, and Hagrid himself was in danger, it was Fang that defended him, and got hit with a Stunning Spell in Hagrid's defense, while Hagrid's supposed "friends" Harry, Ron and Hermione stood on a rooftop watching but doing absolutely nothing to help. Still Fang didn't hold that against them. He likes Harry, Ron, Hermione and Dumbledore and drools over them whenever they visit. Fang drools a lot, has long teeth and a booming bark, but he is quite friendly and licks people's ears as a greeting when he likes the individual. Favorite things include being scratched him behind the ears and peeing on a sycamore tree near Hagrid's house.

Ripper: Marge Dursley's favorite dog, 1 of 12 bulldogs she owns and breeds. He is the one that usually travels with her everywhere she goes. He is an old and evil-tempered thing and once treed Harry for many hours after he accidentally stepped on his tail. Marge usually carries Ripper around by hand and so spoils him that he drinks tea out of her saucer, which horrifies Petunia.

Donkey: An insult among centaurs. Bane accused Firenze of acting like one, once. Given donkeys durability and adaptability to change, which Firenze certainly exhibits but his herd does not, hardly an insult.

Ferret: Found in the Forbidden Forest similar to stoats except Hagrid doesn't seem to eat them. Ferrets are traditionally used for hunting rats. Draco was Transfigured into white one in 93/94 and bounced unceremoniously around the Entrance Hall by Barty Jr (Moody) as a punishment. Given Barty Jr had a passion for punishing disloyal or unpunished Death Eaters, it probably didn't take much cause to get him to abuse the son of Lucius Malfoy. The fact that no one though this behavior odd shows that the real Moody could easily have done the same thing. Hannah Abbot had to Transfigure one on her OWL practical exam, see Flamingo.

THE HARRY POTTER COMPANION

Fox: A small, reddish doglike carnivore that is reputed to be very sly and crafty. They live in the Forbidden Forrest. Hagrid thought they might be responsible for his dead roosters in 92/93. Gran Longbottom's scarf is fox fur. Lavender's rabbit was killed by a fox. The Headless Hunt, one assumes, hunts spectral foxes, which were alive once.

Goat: A creature whose ability to eat anything, give milk and make wool has made it popular to own for centuries. They are nimble-footed and related to sheep, though generally more vocal and outgoing. The beozar is from the goat's stomach. Giants eat goats, the Hog's Head smells of them and Aberforth was prosecuted for performing illegal charms on one. It's seems safe to say, goats are popular in the wizarding world.

Gorilla: A large black Great Ape. Harry saw one that resembled Dudley at the Zoo. Given troll's looks, they are probably related to the gorilla.

Horse: To date only magical horses have had any mention but this is not to say horses aren't used by wizards. Numerous ghost horses carry the wizarding ghosts of the Headless Hunt riders and the Headless Polo teams. How exactly one acquires a ghost horse is sketchy, but that these were once real horses is unquestionable.

Lion: Symbol and mascot of Gryffindor. Luna once magically put a roaring lion head on her hat to show support for Gryffindor during a Quidditch match. This large, carnivorous feline is also the national symbol of Bulgaria and on the Bulgarian flag.

Mouse: There are lots of mice in Hogwarts castle. Probably they escaped from Transfiguration classes long ago and formed a little colony. There are certainly many mouseholes in the castle walls and lots of room for them to set up house. They are always running around in the building walls, which given the number of cats around to pick them off on assumes there must be 1,000s of them.

Mouse, White: Hagrid carries white mice around in his pocket. The Christmas crackers at Hogwarts usually have white mice in them, among other things.

Mole: Usually found in the Forbidden Forest, Hagrid uses their skins, which are black and furry, to make vests and coats. They are small, burrowing creatures and spend most of their time underground, hence the fact they have poor eyesight.

Mule: An insult among centaurs. Bane accused Firenze of acting like one. Stubbornness is a well-known mule trait. The fact Firenze's stubborn determination to fight Voldemort at the expense of his life, makes him mulish indeed. But hardly an insult.

Otter: A semi-aquatic, carnivorous, very endangered mammal. It's basically a waterborn weasel with stronger teeth and claws, webbed feet, a big tail and a beautiful dark brown waterproof skin. Clowning, social, loving and agile (in the water), the otter is Hermione's Patronus, which says very kind things about how she thinks of her father.

Polecat: Polecat means a lot of things to a lot of people. It could be a large carnivorous wildcat (in the US), a ferret (in some European countries), or a skunk (in various US and British places). They can be found in the Forbidden Forest whatever they are and during QWC 1473, a Chaser transfigured into one much to the dismay of the opposing team. One presumes the opposing team would be more afraid of an airborne wildcat than an airborne ferret, but an airborne skunk could be quite nasty too.

Porcupine: A small nocturnal animal whose body is covered in sharp spiny quills as a protective device. Its quills are used in a potion to cure boils.

Rabbit: They are used for turning into slippers by 2nd year Transfiguration students. Hagrid hunts them in the Forbidden Forest and makes gloves out of them.

Binky: Lavender Brown's baby rabbit. It was killed by a fox and she heard about it on Oct 16 1992, as Pr Trelawney predicted.

Raccoon: Used in 6th year Transfiguration. A small furry bearlike creature that is usually grey with a black mask around its eyes making it look like a bandit. They are very agile climbers and excellent at getting into trashcans, attics and stormdrains.

Rat: Common rats are only supposed to live about 3 years. Norbert and Buckbeak are both fond of a good crunchy rat.

Rat Spleen: This is used in Shrinking Solution.

Rat Tails: These are also found in some potions.

Rat Tonic: It comes in a small red bottle. Ron bought some at the Magical Menagerie in Diagon Alley when Scabbers became ill in the summer of 1993.

Scabbers: aka Peter Pettigrew or Wormtail. The Weasley's had him 12 years till he was found to be not a rat but an Animagus on the Dark side. As Scabbers, he joined the Weasley family in 1982. Percy had him for 6 and took him to school for another 5 years. Ron inherited him and took him to school (though they weren't on the list of approved pets for 1st year students) for 3 more years, until he was exposed as Peter Pettigrew. Ron loved Scabbers despite the rude things he tended to say about him or the fact that he was used goods. Ron used to carry him around in a pocket of his robes. Scabbers was a common greyish-black rat. Fat with tiny bulging black eyes, he had a tattered left ear and was missing the index finger of his right front paw. Fudge Flies were, and probably still are, his favorite sweet.

He liked to sleep on Harry's pillows or at the bottom of Ron's bed. Useless for anything but chewing sheets or snoozing in a patch of sun, he seemed to get on well with everyone when he was awake, except those who would hurt Ron. He had sharp little teeth, and sank them into Goyle's knuckle on the Hogwarts Express in Sep 1991 when Goyle attempted to steal a Chocolate Frog from Ron. So, there is some streak of loyalty in Peter, somewhere. He started losing weight in Jul 1993 while in Egypt, after learning that Sirius Black was out of Azkaban. Upon returning to Hogwarts in the fall he had to deal with Crookshanks and Sirius trying to kill him multiple times. He finally faked his own death and escaped to a kitchen cupboard in Hagrid's cabin.

However, in Jun 1994 his clever plan unraveled when Remus and Sirius, more talented wizards, magicking him back into human form again. He'd been a rat to avoid the wrath of Sirius who would have exposed him, not to avoid angry Death Eaters after Voldemort disappeared after using his information about the Potters. Given the deep secrecy Voldemort operated in one assumes Peter was passing information directly to Voldemort rather than through anyone. This would mean, none of the Death Eaters knew of his existence, let alone his name. So if Peter was in hiding, it was only from Sirius. Once Peter had cut off his finger and faked his death there was no going back despite the fact Sirius was captured. Why he didn't go Abroad as a rat and start a new life as a man is a bit of mystery though.

Sabertooth Tiger: What Molly looks like when angry. A thankfully extinct species of extremely large carnivorous tiger with saber-size teeth.

Stoat: Hagrid hunts them in the Forbidden Forest and uses them for sandwiches. Rather like ferrets, but tastier. They are broadly considered weasels, and usually have a brown coat and black-tipped tail.

REPTILES

Crocodile: The heart used in potions. They are a much threatened, misunderstood and mistreated species. One hopes only hearts from naturally deceased crocs are being used or Steve Irwin would surely have something to say about this practice.

The Harry Potter Companion

Frog: Many frogs live in the pond at the Burrow. Frog brains are used in potions. It's unclear which variety is being used. There are 1,000s.
Frog Spawn: A popular and useful wizarding item. Lily used to bring it home from school. Ron had an aquarium tank full of it one summer. The Burrow seems to have a pond full. It can be purchased at any wizarding grocery store.
Bullfrog: They are used in Charms for their noisiness.
Leech: They are used in potions. Polyjuice Potion requires leeches. Generally found in tropical climates in ponds or rivers, they are blood sucking and have many medicinal properties.
Lizard: Unknown species. Harry saw them at the Zoo.
Horned Toad: Despite the name, they are small harmless insectivorous lizards with hornlike spines. They are found in the western US and Mexico and used in many potions.
Newt: A semi-aquatic salamander. The tail is used to bring its carrier protection.
Horned Slug: They are use in a potion for curing boils.
Snail: They are used in intermediate Transfiguration because, as non-complex invertebrates, they are simple to vanish.
Snake: The fangs are used in a potion for curing boils. The snake is the mascot and symbol of Slytherin House.
Nagini: Voldemort's very large female snake of unknown species. It's about 12' long, with a diamond patterned tail but not body and an ugly triangular head. It would seem to be an Albanian snake but the size, fact it would eat a person and markings suggest it's a python, which are not found in Albania. The head shape, hematoxic venom and area of origin would suggest it's a viper, but they don't come 12' long and diamond patterned. The name Nagini, suggests it's part of the *Naja* or cobra group of snake, but again, cobras don't exist in Albania. For a while Voldemort lived off a potion containing Nagini's venom - which as a hematoxin is a good trick in itself.

When Voldemort moved out of the forest to England he had Nagini brought with him. More of necessity than kindness, but he does seem to love his snake. The snake ratted out Frank Bryce, and possibly ate a potion of him after Voldemort killed him. Later she turned up in Little Hangleton and was promised a bite of Harry, but luckily never got it. On the surface it would seem that Nagini was Apparated into the MoM, bit Arthur Weasley, and then Disapparated back to Voldemort in Dec 1995. And this could be so as Voldemort appears to be able to allow his mind to inhabit Nagini's body (which is how Harry ended up there as well), though when his mind leaves her body, Nagini survives because unlike true possession, he's only using legilimency on her.

On the other hand, it may be that Voldemort himself can become a snake at will and thus Apparate and Disapparate wherever he pleases, including in and out of the MoM. Thus Harry's mind was in the snake's mind because Voldemort was the snake. At this point there is really no way to prove either theory. Nagini's venom (or Voldemort's depending on what the real truth is about the snake that was in the MoM) is an anticoagulant. Anyone bitten can't heal but will continue to bleed until they die, unless the get immediate medical attention. Voldemort's desire to bite Dumbledore (as Harry experienced it) would seem to indicate Voldemort was the snake. But again there's no way to be sure. For now one must presume the snake was Nagini till proven otherwise.

It is interesting to note however that if Voldemort can indeed become a snake, through either natural talent or magical ability, Harry would be able to turn into a snake as well from inheriting this natural talent or magical ability through the failed curse that links him to Voldemort. It is possible this talent will crop up visibly in Harry

236

during 6th year Transfiguration, when students learn to turn others into animals (the way Barty Jr Transfigured Draco into a ferret). As of yet Harry has never tried to Transfigure anyone, let alone himself, and doesn't know much about the process. Realization that he is able to become an Animagus, naturally or through magical talent, may take help. Just as being a Parselmouth didn't manifest fully till someone else (Pr Snape) diagnosed it and another (Ron) explained its use to him, being an Animagus may take this sort of assistance to give Harry the confidence to fully manifest as one. Of course, he may not turn into a snake, he may turn into something else entirely. The talent he inherited permits the transformation; his personality will determine what he turns into.

Boa Constrictor: A glistening brown, very long and large, snake with beady eyes, who was bored of people coming and tapping on his window. It was a zoo-bred snake with plans to go to Brazil. Harry first spoke Parseltongue with this snake and then accidentally freed him. Hopefully he has found his way to South America by now.

Boomslang: A type of African treesnake which is extremely dangerous. It is quite poisonous and a bite from this snake will kill a person in 1-3 days. Victims die of internal bleeding. Its skin is used in potions, like Polyjuice Potion.

Cobra: A highly poisonous Indian or African snake. One of the most deadly on earth. Generally not aggressive unless provoked, cobras blind their victims by spitting in their eyes. The Zebra-Striped Cobras of Africa are notoriously dangerous as they have highly toxic venom they can spit a long way for a long time. There are many subspecies of cobra of which the Hooded Cobra is the most well known. Harry saw one at the Zoo.

Python: Very large, long and dangerous South American snake. Harry saw one at the Zoo. They have thick bodies and are capable of crushing a man to death, then swallowing him whole. The can get to be 33' long though a 64' was once recorded caught and killed in the early 19th century.

Toad: First year students can bring them to school as a pet but they are considered old fashioned and those who do may be laughed at. One may even lose one's toad if the Potions Master gets ideas about testing poison antidotes.

Toad Liver: It is used to cure Spattergroit.

Warty Toad: A very attractive type of toad that looks like it has 1,000s of tiny pustules all over its skin. Something Harry would like to turn the Dursleys into.

Trevor: A toad of unknown species. He belongs to Neville Longbottom, but is always trying to escape from him - perhaps from fear of being accidentally squashed. Trevor was given to Neville by his Great Uncle Algie in Sep 1991 and was still alive in 95/96 school year. He seem to be quite large and is possible an African toad which can live up to 20 years.

Tortoise: Similar to a turtle but a tortoise dwells strictly on land and usually liked to burrow into the ground. Dudley had one but threw it through the roof of the greenhouse in Jul 1991, during a fit of temper.

Worm: They are something Buckbeak, being part bird, eats. However most eagles, it should be noted, would never eat a worm unless desperate. They much prefer catching salmon, rabbit, rats and the like.

Caterpillar: Small wormlike creatures, they are used in Shrinking Solution.

Tubeworm: They are used in potions. Harry occasionally has to stay behind after Potions and clean their remains off of desks.

Plants: Magical or Used in Magic

Because most common non-magical plants have magical applications or uses, wand-trees for instance, and some plants are very magical yet are still plants, the Whomping Willow, it seemed reasonable to combine all plants into one section. Obviously there are at least 1,000 magical herbs and fungi, but for reasons of space only the pertinent plants can be listed.

Abyssinian Shrivelfigs: Something Harry pruned in Greenhouse 3 in in his 2nd year of Herbology.

Aconite: It is also called monkshood or wolfsbane. It all parts of it are deadly poison. The term wolfsbane came from the Greek's use of the plant to kill wolves, by dipping arrowtips in aconite. In medieval times it got the name monkshood, from the shape of the flower it produces, the upper sepal of which hoods the rest of the flower.

Alihotsy: A plant whose leaves produce hysteria when eaten. Glumble treacle is the antidote.

Apple: The Weasleys have a field surrounded apple trees that the boys use for Quidditch playing.

Ash: A tree whose wood was used for early broom handles, usually unvarnished - ouch!- and today is used to make Firebolt broom handles. Ash is a native of Britain but grows throughout Europe and America. There are many types of ash tree. Manna ash produces a sweet edible substance, mountain ash berries can be made into cider or jelly and prickly ash bark was once chewed to cure toothaches. It is a tall as well as deep-rooted tree, and the Vikings considered Ash the monarch of trees with its roots in hell and its branches reaching the heavens. It is associated with rebirth.

Asphodel: A plant used in potions. In Ancient times they were planted near tombs, and the flowers were regarded to be the form of food preferred by the dead. In Persia, glue was made from the bulbs, which were first dried then pulverized. When mixed with cold water, the powder swells and forms a strong glue.

Beech: A tree used for making wands. A beech tree may grow tall very (140') and wide (21'), especially on chalky and sandy soil.. They have a soft, smooth grey bark, and from early spring to autumn their bright leaves change from one vibrant color to another. The beech produces nuts which may be feed to most grazing animals and an oil that can be used for cooking, much like butter. During WWI, Germans attempted to use the leaves as a substitute for tobacco among soldiers; they were handily rejected.

Belladonna: The essence is used in potions. Harry uses up a lot of it. Every part of the plant is a deadly poison to humans and some animals. According to old legends, the plant is tended by the devil in his free time, and only on one night of the year, Walpurgis, when he is preparing for the witches' sabbath, can it be destroyed. Far less legendary is tradition that King Duncan I of Scotland and the soldiers of Macbeth poisoned a whole army of invading Danes by mixed alcoholic beverages with an infusion of Belladonna and giving them to the Danes during a truce meeting. Suspecting nothing as the Danes were honorable people, they drank up, passed out and were murdered in their sleep by the Scots.

Birch: Twigs from this tree are used to make aerodynamic tails for Firebolts. Birch has had a variety of uses over time. The bark was used for writing paper, the trees themselves for boats and roofing and an oil can be made of it for preparing leather. Rods for beating unruly children are well-known to come from this tree and making threaten wands. A beer, wine, spirit and vinegar can be prepared from it. Birch Wine is made from the thin, sugar sap of the tree, collected from incisions made in the trees in

March. Honey, cloves and lemon zest are added to the sap then the whole batch is fermented with yeast. About 16 to 18 gallons of sap can be tapped from a tree without doing harm.

Bouncing Bulbs: Something Harry as a 4th year repots in Herbology. They wiggle around and will hit the unwary in the face.

Bubotubers: A 4th year Herbology plant. It is a giant sluglike plant that sticks up vertically out of the ground. The ugly thick black plants squirm about and have a number of large shiny liquid-filled swellings than can be popped like zits. The thick yellowish-green liquid smells of gasoline. In 4th year Herbology, Harry had to collect the pus in bottles wearing dragon-hide gloves because undiluted pus can do funny things to skin if it comes in direct contact with it. Hermione had her fingers swell up with boils from getting some undiluted bubotuber pus on them. The collected pus was given to Madam Pomfrey who uses it medicinally. There is no effective antidote to the pus. Hermione had to go around with bad fingers for a bit.

Chili Peppers: A chili pepper powder of uncertain variety is used for curing scale rot in salamanders and probably dragons too but I don't know if anyone has ever gotten close enough to a dragon with scale rot to try it.

Chinese Chomping Cabbage: In 5th year Herbology, Hermione spent some time diagraming one. One hopes that it is from China and chomps, rather than it prefers to chomp on those who are Chinese.

Daisy: The roots are used in Shrinking Solution. This wizard usage is probably where Muggles developed the popular superstition that daisy roots boiled in milk and given to animals will cause them to stop growing.

Devil's Snare: A 1st year Herbology plant. It likes the dark and damp, but hates light and heat. It has tendrils that twist and snake around any person that comes near it. The harder a person fights it, the faster and tighter it winds around its victim. A devil's snare was below Fluffy's trapdoor. Hermione defeated it with bluebell flames. When hit with the flames it lost its grip and cringed, then unraveled and took to wriggling and flailing. Broderick Bode was murdered by a devil's snare, probably sent to him by Lucius Malfoy.

Dittany: A plant of the mint family. One might use it in a potion. It is listed in *One Thousand Magical Herbs and Fungi.*

Ebony: A hardwood tree whose lovely black wood is used for making wands.

Fanged Geraniums: They have fangs and bite. Harry faced this plant during his Herbology OWL practical exam, and was bitten.

Flitterbloom: It looks similar to devil's snare. Supposedly this was the plant sent to Broderick Bode.

Flutterby Bush: A quivering plant 4th years in Herbology must prune.

Fluxweed: A plant used in Polyjuice Potion. It is sensitive to the moon's cycle.

Gillyweed: A slimy, grayish-green plant that looks like rat tails. It has a rubbery slimy taste similar to calimari. Pr Snape's keep some in the private store cupboard in his office. Dobby stole some from Pr Snape to give to Harry to help him with TT Task 2. When eaten it allows the consumer to breathe underwater for up to an hour by growing gills in her or his neck. It also causes one's feet to elongate like flippers and one's hands and feet will become webbed. All of these effects reverse when the hour passes.

Ginger: The roots are used in Wit-Sharpening Potion. This plant has long been known by the Chinese for adding zing to people.

Hazel: Twigs of this tree were used as early broom tails, with mixed results. This tree has long been thought to possess mystical powers, such as the ability to ward off any evil. Hazel has astringent properties, which are healing and soothing.

Hellebore: The syrup made from this plant is used in the Draught of Peace. There are several varieties, all of which are poisonous. Long ago people used to bless their cattle with this plant to keep them from evil spells. It was dug up with certain mystical and religious rites because it was noticed to stay green and flower in December, thus acquiring the name Christherb. In an old French tale, a sorcerer, to make himself invisible when passing through an enemy's camp, scattered powdered Hellebore in the air, as he walked. Certainly if it didn't knock the enemy out and kill them they were probably too busy vomiting and washing their eyes out (it burns anything it touches) to be able to chase or even see him.

Holly: A tree used for making wands. It usually grows to a height of 30-40' with a 2' trunk. The wood is hard, compact and even except towards the center of very old trees. It is beautifully white, and can be brought to a very high polish. An evergreen, anciently considered to represent long life or immortality. Its use as Christmas decorations derives partly from a Roman custom of sending boughs, accompanied by gifts, to friends during Saturnalia and partly from the Druids, who decorated their huts with evergreens, including Holly, during winter as a home for forest-dwelling spirits.

Honeysuckle: The Burrow has this fragrant vine growing in its backyard.

Honking Daffodils: Pr Sprout grows some somewhere, whether in the flowerbeds or the greenhouses is unknown. They are daffodils that actually honk. Whether like a car horn or a goose is probably down to variety.

Hornbeam: A tree used for making wands. A member of the birch family, it has extremely hard white wood.

Hydrangea: Petunia has one at the front of the house under the living room window that Harry hides under occasionally to hear the news.

Knotgrass: It is used in Polyjuice Potion. Shakespeare in his *Midsummer Night's Dream* writes of this plant as "the hindering Knotgrass,"and is thinking of a then commonly held belief that this plant could hinder the growth of children and animals if eaten.

Leaping Toadstools: A fungus Herbology 2nd years repot in Greenhouse 3.

Lovage: A plant Harry reads about for 5th year Potions. It is used in the Confusing and Befuddlement Draughts. It may produce hot headedness or cause a person to behave in a reckless manner. Lovage was primarily used as a drug plant in the 14th century, though it was never an "official" cure for any specific disease. It's use as a medicinal was probably due to its aromatic odor, produced when dried leaves are made into a tea. It

Mahogany: An expensive imported dark hardwood tree. Nimbus 2000 broom handles are made of it.

Mallowsweet: It is burned, along with sage, by centaurs for divination. The smoke and flame shapes are read and interpreted. Mallows in times past have been eaten by Greeks during times of famine. When boiled first then fried with onions and butter, the roots are said to be quite tasty. The Romans considered them a great delicacy and have been said to plant them everywhere they went, much like the did for many varieties of grapes which were used in Italy for winemaking.

Mandrakes: aka mandragora. It is a powerful restorative for returning people who have been Transfigured or cursed to their original state. It is an essential part of most magical antidotes. It was used to restore the basilisk's victims to health, though how Madam Pomfrey got Nearly Headless Nick to drink it is a bit of a mystery. One presumes she did a spell to make it rot and then pored it through his open mouth as that is how ghosts eat. Given that many human cures don't work on animals, it's surprising Mrs Norris could take it. But she did and, sadly, was restored to her usual well-hated self.

If mandrake is grown from seed one will need to repot it a couple of times before it is ready for use. It takes about a 9 months to become full grown. A mandrake begins life as a small seedling with purplish green leaves. When pulled up by the tufty leaves, a small muddy root that looks like an extremely ugly baby pops out. The root has pale green mottled skin and likely scream as loudly as possible. The cry of an adult mandrake will kill any person that hears it. However a baby mandrake's cry is less powerful and, while its cry can't kill, it can knock a person out for several hours. Wearing earmuffs is sufficient protection when dealing with baby mandrakes. Still, baby mandrakes are dangerous and don't like coming out of the earth. Lacking a cry that can kill, they can still squirm and kick, have small sharp fists they like to flail at offending persons and gnashing teeth.

The plants must be transferred to a larger pot and covered with with dark damp dragon dung compost until only the leaves show. In the winter, they might need to be dug up and have socks and scarves put on them to keep them warm and growing but this is a job only for an Herbology specialist, like Pr Sprout. Within 6 months the mandrakes will become moody and secretive, meaning they are fast leaving childhood. When their acne clears up they should be repotted a 3rd time. They will sometimes throw loud and raucous parties at this stage. The moment they start moving into each others' pots, they're considered fully mature and ready to be cut up and stewed.

Maple: A tree used for making wands. Known for it's very hard beautiful golden wood and ability to produce a sweet syrup.

Mimbulus mimbletonia: Neville was given one in summer 1995 by his Uncle Algie who had brought it from Assyria. A small grey cactuslike plant covered in boils rather than spines, that pulsates slightly and looks like a diseased internal organ (probably a liver). They are extremely rare plant and one assumes they are a native Assyrian plant. It has an amazing defensive mechanism that activates when it's poked. A thick stinking liquid (known as Stinksap) squirts out from every boil at a shocking velocity. Jets project about 6-8' without difficulty. The dark green slimy liquid smells like rancid manure. With care, in about a year, it will grow a great deal and start to make odd crooning noises when gently touched.

Mistletoe: Dobby hung some at Christmas in the Room of Requirement. Druids particularly loved his plant and thought them a protection from evil and witchcraft. When a mistletoe fell to the ground they believed something terrible would happen to the nation. Luna claims this plant is often infested with nargles and implies one should probably not get too close to it. Shakespeare calls it 'the baleful Mistletoe,' an allusion to the Scandinavian legend that Balder, the god of peace, was slain with an arrow made of mistletoe. Balder was restored to life, eventually, and mistletoe was given into the care of the goddess of love, who commanded everyone who passed under mistletoe should receive a kiss, to show the branch had become an symbol of love not of hate. It is technically a semi-parasitic shrub and with so much bad press, it is likely to continue to be viewed with doubt by wizards.

Monkshood: It is also called wolfsbane or aconite. See Aconite.

Nettle: It is used in potions for curing boils. One can also make wine or tea out of it. There are over 500 varieties of nettle and while the sting of a nettle may be aggravating (it can be cured by rubbing the afffected area with rosemary, mint or sage leaves), the good it can do outweighs the bad by miles. Romans first brought nettle to Britain to rub on their chaffed or sore bits. In the 16th and 17th century nettle was used to make cloth in Scotland. People still eat it today to help with their digestion in nettle soup or nettle pudding. Nettle beer can be made as well as nettle wine. Nettle can make green or yellow die, be fed to live stock and even pressed to make an oil used for lighting.

Oak: A nice hardwood used for making wands. Box and ebony are harder, ash and yew tougher, but the English oak best combines both qualities. One tree may yield thousands of acorns, the carefully prepared ground powder of which many Native Americans used for making bread. In addition the bark produces a purple die, the leaves have medicinal properties and the wood makes excellent ships, charcoal and furniture that will last 1,000 years - really.

Oak, Spanish: A tree whose wood is used for making Cleansweep 11 broom handles. Usually the wood is very dark as well as hard, dense and heavy.

Orchid: To test Fleur's wand before the TT, Mr Ollivander made an orchid stem out of it.

Peony: The Burrow has a peony bush. A large colorful shrub that produces fragrant many petaled flowers the size of roses. They are a Chinese plant and much associated with spring, opulence and riches.

Pomegranate: The juice of the fruit of this tree is used in Strengthening Solution. It also produces a red stain that's impossible to get out of clothing.

Privet: Used for making attractive evergreen hedges that afford privacy from neighbors and protection from strong winds. It can grow about 12' tall. Despite the name, Privet Dr doesn't seem to have any.

Rose: Petunia and Molly both have many rosebushes at their homes.

Rosewood: A nice tropical hardwood that usually has a purplish streaked pattern. It is used for making wands as well as attractive decorative inlays on fine furniture. It can be used for small articles or furnishings, but one rarely sees anything large made of rosewood.

Sage: It is burned with mallowsweet by centaurs for divination. The smoke and flame shapes are then read and interpreted. Sage has however long been used for culinary and medicinal purposes as well. Sage tea was so popular in China once it was preferred to all native varieties.

Screechsnap: It is a 5th year Herbology plant. Seedlings of this plant don't like to be overfertilized and wriggle and squeak if one puts too much dragon dung on them. It will apparently screech and snap at people when fully grown.

Scurvy-Grass: A plant Harry reads about for 5th year Potions. It is used in Confusing and Befuddlement Draughts and may make a person temperamental, short-tempered, rash or reckless.

Sneezewort: A plant Harry reads about for 5th year Potions. It is used in Confusing and Befuddlement Draughts and may make a person rash or reckless.

Sycamore: Fang's favorite tree to urinate on. It grows on the edge of the Forbidden Forest near Hagrid's house.

Venomous Tentacula: A dangerous spiky, dark red plant found in Greenhouse 3. One must be careful of when it's teething or one could get eaten. Just slap it and it will draw back its feelers which tend to inch around sneakily.

Venomous Tentacula Seeds: They look like shriveled black pods and are a Class C Non-Tradeable Substance. Dung got some seeds for Fred and George to experiment with for 10G.

Wand-Trees: Trees with wood of a quality that can be used for wandmaking. Bowtruckles are usually found in such trees.

Willow: A tree used for making wands. The willow has long been known as the witches' tree and Robert Graves suggests the words witch, wicker and wicked all derive from "willow." A witches' broom is traditionally made with an ash handle and birch twigs bound with willow.

Willow has also known as one of the best water-divining woods and this association with finding underground water led to willow wands being used as a protection on journeys into the underworld and the unconscious. The willow's underworld associations led it to be connected to grief and death and the willow is often thought of as the tree of grief or sorrows because of its long "weeping" branches. By wearing a piece of willow, one indicates to others that one is in mourning or grief and by association, been a victim of misfortune. And yet for all the negative press the willow has had, it is a very useful plant.

The White Willow or *Salix alba* produces salicin, which converts to salicylic acid when ingested. Salicylic acid from willow bark is the natural drug which aspirin, the synthetic version, has displaced. Willow bark is known to reduce fever and relieve pain. Water-loving willow on riverbanks are deeply rooted into the ground and prevent the collapse of the banks during floods. When a willow branch or twig breaks off, it will take root easily grow into a new tree, without any attention. The willow has many magical uses besides broomsticks. It is useful for any ritual associated with the moon, for charms of fascination, and for binding magical or sacred objects. In Celtic legend it is associated with poets and it has always been known as the tree of dreaming and enchantment.

Whomping Willow: An valuable exotic plant not native to Britain. The one planted at Hogwarts is an ancient tree planted after Molly's time there. It was brought to Hogwarts fully grown from somewhere else for the benefit of Remus Lupin and planted just before his 1st year. It has gnarled boughs, thick branches, and knobby twigs at the end of its branches. It has a somewhat flexible trunk which can bend almost double. It was planted to guard the entrance to the tunnel to the Shrieking Shack.

The tree is very violent. If anyone approaches it, it will begin to wildly swing its branches at the offending person. It will hit, crush, mangle and otherwise destroy anything the comes near it. The Ford Anglia was severely abused by this tree. Students were forbidden near the tree after the Davey Gudgeon incident in the 1960s or 1970s. Apparently he was playing a game, popular till then, that involved trying to touch the trunk. The willow can be deactivated only by pressing a knot on one of its roots, which usually requires a pole to reach.

Wolfsbane: It is also called aconite or monkshood. See Aconite. One hopes it is *not* in Wolfsbane Potion.

Wormwood: It is used in potions. Considered by many a purgative (for getting rid of internal parasites). Its high tannins make it quite bitter tasting. It was also once an ingredient used in a love potion which says something about love.

Yew: A tree used for making wands. Yew can grow 40-50' and is often planted in graveyards as it is a symbol of death and immortality. The leaves, seeds and fruit are very poisonous and cattle have died eating bits of the tree. Historically the Druids considered the yew sacred and temples were often built near stands of yew.

Stones: Magical or Used in Magic

If it is considered or called a stone by those using it, it's in this section.

Beozar: A gallstone from a goat's stomach. Said to be used in potions that cure poisoning victims, it will cure most but not all poisons. Anciently, rich and powerful people used to carry them around and drop them into their goblet before drinking out of it to avoid being poisoned. Though, being a nicer person would probably have been an easier way to avoid death.

Diamond (Yellow): It is most likely, given all the other fabled gemstones belong to other Houses, that the diamond is Hufflepuff's stone. Diamonds come in yellow, the House color, and are renowned for their toughness, as are badgers, the House mascot. Many kings owned them because the stones were thought to make people invincible, particularly in battle. Despite this association with war the stone is considered to represent peace. Owners of this stone are imbued with the ability to understand Truth capital T, and therefore they are said to release that of the Divine that is within every soul. This is a stone of transformation through hard work, as a diamond is the most difficult of all stones to perfect, and would well suit the Hufflepuffs whose abilities shine - with a little elbow greased applied to them.

Emerald: This stone represents Slytherin. Emerald is green beryl. During the period in which Salazar lived and worked, the emerald was considered the mark of the Elect (those chosen by God) and those who held fast to their faith. This stone ideally represents members of Slytherin House who think of themselves as chosen and hold to their ancient faith (in pure blood). Bearers of emeralds are said to be gifted with farsightedness, which Salazar certainly was, and good health, which he also must have had, being the only founder to produce an heir.

Moonstone: A pale white stone with iridescent qualities. When ground up, it's used in the Draught of Peace. Many of the stones have a blue or white glow when exposed to moonlight. This stone has been revered for centuries in India and is said to bring harmony and good fortune to marriages and love relationships. Asian tradition credits moonstone with giving its bearer deep spiritual understanding, much as Western gem lore credits the sapphire with this ability.

Ruby: This stone represents Gryffindor. Ruby is a type of corundum, as is sapphire, making Ravenclaw and Gryffindor twins in this respect. At the time Godric chose this stone to represent his house, the ruby was considered the sign of devotion to duty and the symbol of freedom, charity and dignity - all very knightly qualities. Regard for the rules is associated with this stone, which may be how Hermione was Sorted to Gryffindor. Rubeus is the Latin name for the ruby, and may be why Hagrid was Sorted to Gryffindor. July is the birth month of this stone, which may be part of the reason Harry was Sorted to Gryffindor.

The gold coronation ring of the English kings contains a large, tablet-cut ruby engraved with the figure of St. George's cross, and ruby was called by ancient Hindus ratnaraj or the king of precious stones, implying the ruby has long had royal connections. Rubies worn as talismans were said to warn their owners against danger and disaster by growing darker when threat was near. It was said to cure blood diseases and stop bleeding, a very good thing if one is in battle frequently. And, according to legend, rubies were an ancient symbolize of courage and bravery and no doubt why Godric's sword is encrusted with them.

Although rubies are closely associated with love and said to bring love to their owners, it doesn't appear Godric had any romantic attachments during his life. However, rubies are associated with good health, particularly the heart and blood, and said to chase off the spirits of the dead and evil spirits not contained in hell. So Godric may have enjoyed good health for a very long time and averted many an attack by Salazar during his life a result of owning rubies. Too, he might have been in love in a courtly love way. Courtly love was very common for knights. It compelled a knight to be forever true even if he or his lady married, or were already married to other people, as was often the case. Courtly love forbid anything but distant adoration of the beloved.

Sapphire: This stone represents Ravenclaw. Sapphire is blue corundum, while ruby is red corundum. This makes Ravenclaw a type of twin to Gryffindor. It may be that Rowena and Godric were closer in thoughts and ideals to each other than the 2 other founders and in both of them choosing corundum they were expressing that relationship. Or, more likely, Godric had a "courtly love" relationship with her, and chose the ruby after she chose the sapphire to express his devotion to her. Sapphires have long been held to make their bearers wiser and more intelligent than others. The stone is said to bring one closer to God and clear the way for the outworking of one's divine destiny. Charlemagne, who lived during the same period as the founders, wore a talisman of a huge sapphire set in gold and surrounded by emeralds, pearls and rubies. He felt the sapphire imparted to him heavenly virtues, being the stone of heaven, and reflecting on his reign, it appears to have been true in his case.

Sorcerer's Stone: aka You-Know-What, or the Philosopher's Stone. A blood-red substance which may or may not be stone that was about 2" long. Property of Nicolas Flamel, creator of the stone. It transformed any metal into gold and produced the Elixir of Life, which would keep one alive and healthy indefinitely as long as one continued to drink it. Kept initially at Gringotts, in Vault 713, all by itself, it appeared to be just a small dirty package wrapped in brown paper. On Jul 31, 1991 it was moved to Hogwarts, behind the door at the end of the right-hand corridor on the 3rd floor, and protected by 7 enchantments created by Hagrid, Pr Sprout, Pr Flitwick, Pr McGonagall, Pr Quirrell, Pr Snape and Dumbledore. See schematic N for details.

Dumbledore never thought the stone was a very good thing. He feels infinite life and unlimited wealth can't really make a person happy but this is probably because Dumbledore has never been really ill and really poor. Voldemort believed that the Elixir of Life would allow him to create a body of his own, that it would bring him back to full strength and power and, with the stone's elixir, he would never die. Given Voldemort's ability to create unusual potions to suit his need, this might have been possible. However in Jun 1993, shortly after Voldemort unsuccessfully attempted to steal the stone a second time, Dumbledore convinced his old friend Nicolas Flamel and his wife Perenelle that the stone should be destroyed. The Flamels died peacefully shortly after the stone was destroyed and Voldemort's theories remained untested.

The Sorcerer's Stone and Its 7 Protections: In order of encounter: Fluffy (Hagrid), devil's snare (Sprout), winged keys (Flitwick), wizard's chess (McGonagall), troll (Quirrell), seven potions (Snape), Mirror of Erised (Dumbledore).

The Sorcerer's Stone and the 7 Potions: Pr Snape's protection for the stone was 7 potion bottles of different shapes, sizes, colors, all in a line on a table. A poem gave clues as to which potion to take to get through either the purple fire blocking the door back to the troll room or the black fire blocking the door to the mirror's room. The poem is actually a logic puzzle. The answer looking at bottles from left to right is as follows.

    1 largest bottle, poison
    2 Nettle wine
    3 smallest bottle, allows one to go forward
    4 poison
    5 poison
    6 Nettle wine
    7 round bottle, allows one to go back.

The 7 choices say a lot about Pr Snape. Death, drunkenness or victory. Failing to make the right choice, one can die via being poisoned or get tanked on nettle wine. Considering his potionmaking talents he could have chosen, in addition the correct potions, several nonlethal potions such as a potion to make the drinker fall unconscious until she or his is found by someone. He could have stopped a thief without killing them. All the other teachers used traps that were survivable. Pr Snape condemns everyone that fails his challenge to death or at best drunkenness. It really makes one wonder what he thinks about in the wee in hours of the night, and how much he drinks when he thinks.

MAGICAL GADGETS, GIZMOS AND DEVICES

This section includes all magical devices except those used for transporting wizards or involving a person's image, such as photo.

Age Line: An age line knows how old a person is and can be set at any age. It is not fooled by Aging Potions or other magical means of falsifying one's age and will not allow anyone under the age (over the age, or, no the age) it has been set at to cross it. Dumbledore used this meand to protect the Goblet of Fire from underage entrants. He traced on the floor a thin gold line 10' in diameter around the cup. It would not let anyone under 17 past it. The Weasley twins attempted to cross the age line and were bodily hurled out of the circle. They landed 10' back from the line, on the floor, after which a loud pop resounded and they sprouted identical long white beards. Miss Fawcett and Mr Stebbins suffered similar fates.

Anti-Burglar Buzzer: A device on the Bluebottle Broom. It probably causes the broom to buzz (vibrate) so it can't be ridden.

Black Quill, Dolores Umbridge's: A long thin magical black quill with an unusually sharp point. As one writes with it, it cuts whatever is being written into the back of one's hand. The words come out on the parchment in red, because it's the author's blood. The hand will heal over almost at once, but the more one writes, the less likely it is that the cuts will heal. Dolores used it as torture device. It could be a seriously bad Dark Arts object, or it could just be an average wizarding quill used occasionally for contracts that need to be signed in blood. One would think it's the latter.

Candles: At Hogwarts the candles seem to turn on when people touch them. Hermione was sitting in the dark in the Gryffindor common room and suddenly a light flickered on without benefit of any means to do so. She had to have touched the candle to activate it because she didn't have her wand or strike a match. Given everyone has candles on their desk (and never carry matches), even in the Library and teacher's offices, they must only use touch-activated candles, never gas. Candles also appear have the ability to levitate on their own, without anyone continually pointing a wand at them, as well as being drip-free, which is a big plus when they are floating over one's head.

Clock, Dumbledore's: A common gold pocket watch on the outside but inside, instead of hands and numbers, it has tiny planets moving around the edge. Obviously one would have to be quite good at astronomy to be able use it for telling time as Dumbledore does.

Clock, Molly's Grandfather: A tall grandfather clock belonging to Molly, it stands in the living room at the Burrow. It doesn't have numbers on the face, it has writing instead. The writing on the face includes things like mortal peril; home; school; work; traveling; lost; prison; and the other things it says are unknown. Mortal peril is at the

12 o'clock position but one hopes rarely used despite its prominence. It has a golden hand for each of the 9 members of the Weasley family with an individual name being engraved on each hand. The longest hand is Arthur Weasley's. The hands point to what the individuals are doing, where they are or what condition they are in.

Clocks, Molly's Kitchen: Molly has a clock in the kitchen, in a corner opposite the door with one hand (for herself only) and instead of numbers it has reminders. Stops for this clock's hand includes: time to feed the chickens; you're late; and time to make tea. This clock is strictly a housewitch's helper.

Cribbage's Wizarding Crackers: aka Wizard Crackers. A traditional part of every British Christmas is pulling apart a cracker, a large cylinder stuffed with toys or confetti and so forth then wrapped with foil and tied at each end. One person takes one end and another person the other. Both pull till it cracks apart with a blast like a cannon and enough variously colored smoke to engulf a table full of people. The insides are exploded out, showering the pullers with gifts. Hogwarts uses loads of them every Christmas during the feast. They always have lots of neat things in them: funny hats, wizard chess sets, white mice, a pack of non-explodable, luminous balloons, a Grow-Your-Own-Warts Kit or other fun things. Students are allowed to keep all the things in the crackers which is nice if a student can't get home for Christmas or doesn't have a home to go to.

Dark Detectors: A whole genre of devices that are used primarily to detect Dark wizards or Dark activity. But most have a multiplicity of applications. The following are considered Dark Detectors: the Sneakascope, the Secrecy Sensor and the Foe-Glass. Moody has a large collection of them. Of course, if one is a Dark wizard, a Foe-Glass would show when Aurors were near. A Secrecy Sensor likewise would pick up anything anyone was trying to conceal, not just Dark Arts things. A Sneakascope picks up on any sneaky behavior, not just Dark wizards' doings, which is why it's useless at Hogwarts where students are always up to something.

The Dark Mark, Airborne: The symbol of Voldemort. A huge gaseous skull made of emerald-colored stars with a serpent protruding from its mouth like a tongue. It is shot off into the sky and rises, green and glittery, in an haze of greenish smoke. Voldemort and his Death Eaters used to set off the Dark Mark whenever they killed someone. During Voldemort's initial rise to power wizards would come home and see the Dark Mark over their homes knowing it meant one or all inside were dead. Oddly though, it scared away the Death Eaters when it was shot off at QWC 1994. Apparently Death Eaters who pleaded Imperius Curse to the MoM and got off scot free while loyal Death Eaters went to prison weren't too keen to see Voldemort return. Perhaps they thought Voldemort was back and killing off disloyal Death Eaters - a very reasonable thought.

The Dark Mark, Physical: All true Death Eaters bear a Dark Mark brand (the skull and snake) on their inner left forearms. Peter Pettigrew, Igor Karkoff, Lucius Malfoy and Pr Snape, to name a few, all have the Dark Mark. Apparently the brand grows clearer and brighter the closer and or stronger Voldemort is. When he was a vapor in Albania it was hardly visible, but when he was reborn it turned red and clearly visible. The brand is normally russet like a burn mark, but it turns black when Voldemort wants the Death Eaters to appear immediately. Possibly it also burns, as most wizards wear long-sleeve robes and would never see it had turned black unless some sensation indicated to them they needed to look at it.

In theory the Death Eaters Apparate to wherever Voldemort is, though how they know where he is is a bit difficult to explain. Possibly the brand is part homing device and takes them to within a few feet of wherever the activated mark is currently. When Voldemort presses the brand on any Death Eaters arm with his finger, it causes the

Death Eater pain, then the Dark Mark turns jet black. Voldemort himself apparently doesn't have a brand. The Dark Mark is also a means by which Death Eaters can distinguishing one another without exposing their faces or giving names. Though most of the hardcore Death Eaters seem to know each other from school, and Lucius Malfoy knew everyone who raided the MoM with him, despite the masks.

Detachable Cribbing Cuffs: These are detachable robe sleeve cuffs which one can write notes on to crib off of during an exam. They are banned from the examination hall at Hogwarts. Given the cuffs at Hogwarts are black, the writing must appear in a faint but lighter, possibly luminous, color.

Dream Instrument, Dumbledore's: A fragile silver instrument Dumbledore has in his office, just tap it gently with the tip of a wand and it tinkles to life making rhythmic clinking noises. It produces small puffs of colored smoke from a tiny silver tube at the top. The smoke then turns into what one has dreamed about. Give it another tap and the instruments stops and the smoke disperses. In Harry's case the smoke was pale green and turned into a serpent. When Dumbledore asked the smoke a question, the smoke responded by recomposing itself to form another visual answer.

It's hard to say if the machine looks at dreams or into souls. What the machine detected was a) the snake Harry had been and b) that Harry and Voldemort had merged into a single entity (for a millisecond) during that snake moment, then split back into two distinct parts. Given that Harry and Voldemort had actually mentally merged during the time Voldemort attempted to kill Arthur and then split apart again, it would seem Harry's "dream" wasn't a dream but reality. This in turn would mean Dumbledore's machine doesn't do dream analysis. Harry might believe it analyzed dreams, but this doesn't seem so. One hopes Dervish and Banges doesn't sell a lot of these if this turns out to be the case.

Enchanted Icicles: Icicles that never melt. A popular wizarding Christmas decoration.

Enchanted Mist: An average looking mist that will hover above the ground on a single spot without moving. A person stepping into this mist will stay connected to the ground, but otherwise feel flipped upside-down and as if she or he is about to fall off the planet into an endless sky above. Upon taking one foot off the ground though, the person immediately falls out of the mist and into a normal reality.

Enchanted Snow: Snow which is warm and dry. This can either fall continually without causing a wet floor indoors or can be heaped around like drifts on the carpet without ever melting. Sirius really liked to used this at Christmas time.

Enchanted Windows: The MoM uses enchanted windows in all its underground offices and corridors. The weather is determined by Magical Maintenance but usually reflects what is going on outside, above ground.

Exploding Dustbins: Moody used his trashcans as an alarm system to alert him to Dark wizard intruders. Obviously they work since they went off when Barty Jr came to call. Unfortunately his projectile garbage shooting, noise-maker dustbins had started life as Muggle trashcans and it's not legal to charm Muggle objects. However, such incidents are only a caution from the Misuse of Muggle Artifacts Office if one gets caught with some.

Figurines: Figurines, like wizarding photos, are imbued with all the attributes of whatever or whoever the figurine resembles. In the case of the Hungarian Horntail, the figurine stretched its wings and barred its fangs at Harry. At night it yawns, curls up on Harry's bedstand and goes to sleep just as a real dragon would do. It's unclear if it shoots fire, has poison fangs and roars as well, but it probably does. Famous Quidditch players' figurines are a particular area of collecting and one with a wide following. Quidditch player figurines reflect the personality of the players, they strut around, sometimes waving, just like their real life counterparts. The figurines can't talk, they just walk around. Ron bought a figurine of Victor Krum at the QWC 1994. It scowled and walked around duck footed with its shoulders rounded just the way the real Krum does. Ron dismembered it after finding out Hermione was dating Krum.

Flags, QWC 1994 Memorabilia: These flags played the national anthem of whatever country they represented whenever they were waved.

Foe-Glass: A mirror that shows one's enemies as shadowy figures moving inside of the mirror if they are far away from owner of the glass. They come into focus when they come nearer, about 25' or so. It shows their faces if they are about 12' away. Barty Jr (Moody) had this Dark Detector in his office.

Galaxy Dome: It shows a working, and current, model of the planets and sun suspended in space in a globe and is generally used for astrology purposes. Pr Trelawney has one she keeps under her chair. It cuts down on having to figure out where the planets are at any given moment.

The Goblet of Fire: It's a large rough-hewn wooden cup filled to the brim with magical, dancing, blue-white flames. It is kept in a large, wooden, jewel-encrusted magical chest that looks very old and probably dates back to the 11th century. Tap the chest 3 times and it will creak slowly open. The Goblet is only used for the TT and only ignites at the start of each TT. It was used as an impartial judge to select the champions for the TT on Halloween 1994. Placing one's name in the Goblet constituted a magical binding contract, so one couldn't change one's mind once selected without magical consequences.

The Goblet was put on the sorting stool in the Entrance Hall with an Age Line drawn around it. Would-be contestants put a slip of parchment with their name and school on it into the Goblet. It turned briefly red and emitted sparks when a parchment was entered. The Goblet then considered all the names for about 12 hours and later spit back the 3 worthy champions for the TT. With each name spit up, the flames turned red, sparks flew out, a flame shot up and then a parchment came out with the flame. After all the names were popped out, the Goblet were out. It will not light itself again until the next TT and apparently cannot be tricked into relighting.

Goblin-Made Indestructible Helmet: This is a gift that Dumbledore had Hagrid and Olympia take to Gurg of the giants. They gave it to Golgomath as a 1st gift. As giants tend to get into a lot of fights, such a helmet was an excellent gift.

The Golden Egg: A device used in the TT to give a clue about Task 2. The outside had a groove all the way around it so it could open in half. It was hollow and empty inside but made a horrible loud screechy wailing noise when opened anywhere but underwater - the sound is the merpeople singing. See the TT section in Part II for more information.

Gringotts' High-Security Vaults: These underground vaults are heavily guarded by dragons and other magical means as well as being located deep under Gringotts. The vaults only respond to a goblin's touch and any non-goblin touching the vault will fall through the door and not be found till the goblins made their once a decade check of all the vaults.

Gubraithian Fire: An everlasting magical fire that can be put on whatever one chooses to use as the object. Dumbledore made a branch with Gubraithian Fire on it for Hagrid and Olympia to take to the Gurg of the giants. It was the 1st gift they offered Karkus.

Hand of Glory: A Dark object. It is a withered hand which when a candlestick is put in will give light only to the holder. Borgin and Burkes sells it as the best friend of thieves and plunderers. Needless to say Draco was very interested in it.

The Harry Potter Companion

Hall of Prophecy Orbs: A small (hardly larger than a walnut or Snitch) spun glass ball containing a prophecy given in the past. Each prophecy is set on a shelf with a label, a small yellowing slip of paper recording the initials of who gave the prophecy, who received the prophecy and who or what the prophecy is about. If the prophecy has not yet come to pass the orb containing it will appear to have white pearly swirling stuff in it. The orbs go dark after the prophecy it contains is either fulfilled or perhaps past beyond happening (expired, the person it's about died, etc). Once the prophecy has been released from its orb, intentionally or not, it is gone forever.

Only the person (or persons) the prophecy is about can remove it from its shelf without harm. All others attempting to take it down will go mad, as Broderick Bode did. The orbs don't appear to have corks so they can't be opened while on the shelf. One seems to have to smash them open, or perhaps there is magical way of unsealing them known only by the DoM. Once opened an image of the person giving prophesying and an image of the person hearing it form from the pearly white stuff within the orb. An audible as well as visual reenactment of the prophecy then takes place. Although no one was sure that Harry was the person the prophecy stored in the orb was about till after he got the scar, the fact he could take the prophecy down proves it was about him. Ironically, as the prophecy was also about Voldemort, he too could have taken it down off the shelf if he'd simply done it himself.

Hats, QWC 1994 Memorabilia: Ireland's hats had dancing shamrocks on them. Given Bulgaria has a lion on its flag, they probably had miniature dancing lions on their hats.

Homework Planner: Hermione gets these from a shop in Diagon Alley. They verbally encourage people to study every time their opened. Ron and Harry find them particularly annoying and rather abusive

Hogwarts' Acceptance Letters: They seem to be magical. They know exactly where as recipient is, down to where they sleep, and they keep coming until they reach that person's hand. After 3 tries, they multiply by $3 = 3$, then by $4 = 12$, then by $2 = 24$, by $2 = 48$ and by $2 = 96$. They don't take no for an answer no matter how hard one tries to discourage them.

What happened to Harry's letters:

Jul 24 - Tues - 1 letter, found by Harry, burned by Vernon, addressed to Harry in the cupboard under the stairs.

Jul 25 - Weds - 1 letter, found by Dudley, confiscated by Vernon, addressed to Harry in the smallest bedroom.

Jul 26 - Thurs - 3 letters, torn up by Vernon.

Jul 27 - Fri - 12 letters, all burned by Vernon.

Jul 28 - Sat - 24 letters, handed to Petunia, which she shredded in her food processor.

Jul 29 - Sun - 30 - 40+ letters came out of kitchen fireplace and Vernon took the entire family on a road trip to try and escape them.

Jul 30 - Monday - 100 letters appeared at front desk addressed to Harry in Room 17, but Vernon bolted with the family again.

Jul 31 - Tues - Hagrid appeared just after midnight to hand deliver the letter to Harry on the floor.

Howler: A scarlet red enveloped letter that expresses a loud, angry message by amplifying the sender's voice 100x. It will start to smoke then burst into flames and expel its message before crumbling into ashes if not opened immediately. Even if one does open it immediately the message still yells at the recipient and the envelope still smokes at the corners, bursts into flames and curls into ashes. It's a lose-lose situation and a very public humiliation to get one. Mrs Weasley sent one to Ron for stealing the flying Ford Anglia. Gran Longbottom sent Neville one for writing down his passwords and letting Sirius Black get them. Dumbledore sent Petunia one for allowing Vernon to try and throw Harry out. Howlers are only sent in anger, never in praise or love.

Ink, Varicolor: Harry bought a magical ink in Diagon Alley that changed color as a person wrote with it.

Invisibility Cloak: They make the wearer invisible to everyone but extremely powerful magical people like Dumbledore or extremely powerful magical objects like Moody's glass eyeball. Animals also cannot see the wearer, but the wizard is still solid and can be bumped into, still has an odor that might be smelled and still might make a sound that can be heard. The cloak is made of a fluid silvery grey, gleaming, shiny material. It feels rahter liquid, like water woven into cloth. They are very rare imported items and difficult to get as well as expensive.

Harry has 1 that was his father's. Moody had 2 till Sturgis Podmore got arrested wearing his best one. Like anything, there are a variety of different quality Invisibility Cloaks on the market. What's really odd about this garment is that one can see it when it's not covering a person. It would seem that a living being has to wear it in order for the invisibility function to kick in. This may be related to the origins of the material used to make the cloak. See Demiguise in Scamander's FB for more fascinating information on this topic.

Lunascope: A device which shows one all the doings of the moon. It eliminates the need for messing with moon charts. The word scope at the end implies one would look through it or into it and see some type of moon.

Open-All Knife: Sirius gave a penknife to Harry that had multiple attachments he claimes would allow it to open any lock and undo any knot. However, when Harry used the knife in the MoM to try and open a sealed room containing love, the blade melted. So it doesn't open all, but it still opens some things. The damaged blade was just one of many attachments so the knife still has some use left. Where Sirius got it is a mystery.

Magical Chains: In Courtroom 10. They chain a convicted prisoner who is giving testimony or someone that is very dangerous during their hearing. They don't normally work on people accused but not convicted of a crime. The turn gold before they chain someone, but rattle around ominously if they detect an unsavory character.

Magical Contracts: Once entered into cannot be broken without serious consequences. One has no idea what consequence could have been worse for Harry than facing a dragon, seeing all his friends in peril, nearly drowning, witnessing Cedric's death, doing battle with Voldemort and numerous Death Eaters, but they must be very serious if they can top all that.

Magical Eye, Moody's: It's a large round electric blue magical eye that sees through everything including Invisibility Cloaks, stone walls and the back of Moody's own head. In magical eyes the pupil contracts as it focuses in on something, not according to light and dark like a normal eye. One should get 360 degree visibility with a magical eye as long as it is clean. One can clean a magical eye in common tap water. Moody claims his eye hasn't worked right since Barty Jr wore it for 10 months. That may be paranoia talking, or it may be true. He says it keeps sticking and perhaps it is a bit warped from being worn by a another wizard or Barty Jr adjusted it in some way to aid himself in using it but it's ridiculous to believe Barty did anything to it as part of a plan to hurt Moody once it was returned to him because Barty never planned on letting Moody go alive, let alone give him back his eye. Time will tell what's up with eye, if anything.

THE HARRY POTTER COMPANION

Magical Fire: A magical fire is any fire to which a magical substance has been added. Unicorn hair, Floo Powder, boomslang skin and any other magical substance could create a magical fire. If a wizard was really desperate, her or his wand could even be burned.

Magical Trunk, Moody's: This is an average looking trunk barring the fact it has 7 key holes. Each keyhole opens a different type of trunk. The 7 keyholes mean there are 7 different types of trunks inside Moody's trunk. Trunk 1 has a mass of spell books. Trunk 2 has Sneakoscopes, parchment and quills, and an Invisibility Cloak. Trunks 3-6's contents are unknown. Trunk 7 has been magically enlarged into be an underground room 10' deep. Moody was locked in Trunk 7 and controlled by Imperius Curse by Barty Jr for 10 months.

The Marauder's Map: A large, square, very worn piece of parchment. Touch it with a wand, say "I solemnly swear that I am up to no good" and thin spidery ink lines will run all over the pages and turn it into a map of Hogwarts castle and grounds. "Messrs. Moony, Wormtail, Padfoot, and Prongs Purveyors of Aids to Magical Mischief Makers are proud to present The Marauder's Map" in large green curly words will appear at the top. Given the heading, it would seem that James and his friends once planned to open a joke shop of their own. This map was created by James, Sirius, Remus, and Peter (Prongs, Padfoot, Moony, Wormtail respectively) during their school days, probably in their 6th or 7th year. Filch confiscated it during James' time at Hogwarts, Fred and George later stole it from Filch's Confiscated and Highly Dangerous cabinet and years later they gave it to Harry.

On the map a small dot, representing each person on the grounds or in the castle, will appear labeled with the individual's name. It shows them moving about as long as they stay within the boundaries delineated by the map. One can tell exactly what they are doing and even exactly what they are saying. Harry saw Peeves bouncing a ball and later little cartoon bubbles appearing with the words written in them when people were talking. Once one has finished using the map merely tap it again and say "Mischief managed" and all the writing disappears.

It is a very intelligent map. It knows who is holding it or speaking to it. It is endowed with the various personalities and knowledge of its creators at the time they made the map and when addressed verbally it will write back as its individual creators would have. The map knew Pr Snape and responded to him as James, Sirius, Peter and Remus would have, including making abusive remarks about Pr Snape's looks, his past and the fact that he now teaches at Hogwarts. The map can also answer questions when asked by people it likes. Harry asked it how to open the statue of the witch on the 3rd floor and it showed him the word of command. It is likely, since the map can think for itself and one can't see where its brain is, Arthur would classify this as a Dark object.

Mirror, Leaky Cauldron: This mirror commented on Harry's looks but was kind and actually very supportive. It sounded like an old grandmother. Mirror's probably reflect their maker's personalities - no pun intended. Possibly it was made by kindly older lady.

Mirror, Molly's: This mirror is located in the kitchen above the hearth at the Burrow. This mirror tends to makes harsh comments about how people look. It told Harry off for not tucking in his shirt.

Mirror of Erised: Erised is Desire, backwards. It is a magnificent mirror about 10-12' tall and set in an ornate gold frame that rests on a stand comprised of 2 clawed feet. The inscription carved around the top (and written backwards) reads: I show not your face but your heart's desire. It was originally located in an old classroom on the 4th floor. In it, Harry saw all his lost family. Ron saw himself as Head Boy, Captain of

Quidditch team and winner of the House Cup. Dumbledore saw thick woolly socks, he claims. It shows the deepest and most desperate desires of the onlooker's heart. The problem with the mirror is that people tend to become obsessed with it. Their desire keeps them coming back to see possibilities but they waste their time looking instead of doing and miss out on their real life and making the possiblities reality.

The mirror, claims Dumbledore, gives neither knowledge or truth but this is incorrect. The mirror does give truth and knowledge. It tells a person a truth about themselves and self-knowldege is the most helpful of all. Ron had a bad feeling about the mirror after his first use of it and rightly considered it a probable Dark object. This seems to be true since Harry started to become obsessed with the mirror after only 2 visits and others in the past had starved to death in front of it or been driven insane by it. The mirror was moved after Harry's 3rd visit, by Dumbledore, so it could become the last protection for the Sorcerer's Stone. Dumbledore came up with idea to enchant it so that only someone that wanted to find stone, but not use it, would be able to get it. Those with other designs would be frustrated by the mirror, only able to see themselves creating gold or drinking the Elixir of Life.

Mirrors, Sirius': Two small, square 2-way mirrors. If one looks into one of the pair of mirrors and calls the name of the person with the other mirror, they will be able to carry on a 2-way visual conversation. Sirius and James used them during separate detentions while they were at Hogwarts. Sirius gave one to Harry, but he never used it, then Sirius died and Harry broke his. It may still work, but one shudders to think who might have the other one at this point. Possibly Kreacher could have taken the 2nd mirror to Narcissa, who might have given it to Voldemort, which could be a very dangerous situation for Harry. Although why Voldemort would want the mirror when he and Harry are already attached at the brain is hard to fathom.

Models, QWC 1994 Memorabilia, Miniature Firebolt: They are working models and do whatever the real one does. In the case of the Firebolt model, it really flies. It may not fly at 150 mph but it flies.

Non-Explodable, Luminous Balloons: They come in Wizard Crackers. Almost certainly they are on Flich's list of banned items. They probably glow in the dark and make themselves irritating in numerous ways, such as not exploding.

Omnioculars: They look like brass binoculars but have various extra dials and knobs that allow magical functions to be used. They can replay action, show it in slow motion, or even flash a play-by-play breakdown of the action with notations. They cost 10G each. Harry got 3 pair: one for himself, one for Ron and one for Hermione at QWC 1994. The replay knob is on the left side. There is a speed dial somewhere, probably on the bottom. The slow motion dial is on the right. The play-by-play button is on the top and will show the game in slow motion with purple writing telling the names of various plays.

Platform 9 3/4 Entrance: The entrance to the platform is a magical gateway. One must to walk straight at the steel barrier between Muggle Platforms 9 and 10 at King's Cross Station. One can't stop or one will crash into it, or be scared or it won't work. The portal is likely a sensor and can pick up on fear or hesitation, both of which only a Muggle would have headed for a wall at some speed. If one is nervous, it's best to run, rather than walk, into the barrier. Upon reaching the opposite side, if one turns around, one will see a wrought-iron archway with the words Platform Nine and Three-Quarters on it. One is now on Platform 9 3/4.

The exact nature of the archway is a bit sketchy. It doesn't seem to be a portal, ie, taking one to another place altogether since the train leaves King's Cross. It may be a gateway into an expanded area; a place within the barrier itself on which an Expanding

Charm has been used. A physical train does leave King's Cross, but it seems to travel on a set of rails all its own, which implies it must be in a corridor of space alongside a normal reality (what is seen out the windows). We know the train is visible to Muggles and wizards since Harry and Ron saw it from 1,000' up in the air but why doesn't it attract the attention of Muggle steam engine enthusiasts? Granted, the train only runs a 6 times a year, and only to and from school (since the name is Hogwarts Express, not Hogsmeade Express), and only students or staff are allowed to ride on it, but the schedule is regular and Muggle train lovers would surely flock to see it, see it pass and want to know more about it, like its route and destinations.

Pensive: A magical item belonging to Dumbledore that is kept in a closed cupboard in his office. It is a shallow stone basin with runes and symbols carved all around its edge. It holds excess thoughts and memories. To siphon off a thought into the Pensive, one touches one's wand tip to one's temple and pulls. A silvery strand of thought should appear attached to the end of the wand. Eventually it will snap free from the temple and can be put it in the Pensive.

When adding a thought to the Pensive, one sees it in the basin for a moment. Harry saw himself in the basin once because he was what Dumbledore was thinking of in the thought he'd extracted. Usually a Pensive holds thoughts in the form of bright silvery white light moving ceaselessly inside itself since the substance of thoughts is neither liquid nor gas. The surface can ruffle like water beneath wind, but without any wind on it. It seems a bit misty above the surface, like clouds hovering over water.

Excess thoughts are stored in the Pensive so one can examine them at leisure or, less usual, hide them from others. The Pensive makes it easier to spot patterns and links. To review a thought or memory prod the contents of the basin with a wand. The cloudy substance will separate then the contents of the basin will swirl very fast until it becomes smooth and transparent. At that point one should be able to see a memory. Alternatively one can swirl the Pensive like a prospector panning for gold when one wants to exam thoughts or look for some pattern or link between thoughts.

If one touches a memory or thought in the Pensive, one will fall into the memory and view everything from the perspective of the person whose memory it is. It is an unpleasant experience like falling through something ice-cold and black, like being sucked into a dark, solid whirlpool. When one comes out again, one feels as if one is somersaulting out of the basin. And of course, while a Pensive can be helpful, it has pitfalls. It shows what someone remembers, but that's not necessarily the truth of a situation. Memories and thoughts suffer from accuracy problems. Pr Snape's memories showed Harry a version of the truth about his father, not truth itself.

It is probable that the Pensive was originally the property of founder Helga Hufflepuff. Helga is a Germanic name, the runes carved around the Pensive's edge are also Germanic. The runes flourished around the time Helga lived and worked at Hogwarts. It is likely that of the 3 founders that stayed on at Hogwarts, each stayed until they died and therefore each left a number of personal possessions in care of the school. These things would most likely be left in the Head's office and be inherited by each Head along with the office. This theory gains credence when one considers Godric left his sword behind. It makes one wonder what thing Rowena might have left behind.

Put-Outer: It resembles an old-fashioned, 1940s era, silver flip-top cigarette lighter. This device allows the holder to remove the light from a streetlamp, into the lighter. Just pop it open, hold it up, give it 1 click and the light goes into the Put-Outer. When finished, just pop it open, hold it up, click it again and the lighter will send a small ball of light back to the street lamp, restoring it to working order. Dumbledore owns the

Put-Outer and he seems to be the only person who has one as he has on occasion loaned this device out. It must be a high-capacity energy storage device because Dumbledore turned out 12 of the 14 street lights on Privet Dr without any problems. That's a lot of wattage to hold in one's hand without being electrocuted, especially when one is storing that energy in a metal device and wizards are notoriously electrically challenged.

Quick-Quotes Quill: It is a long, acid green writing quill that takes dictation but instead of writing exactly what one says, it writes exactly as the owner would phrase it. In Rita Skeeter's case, her Quick-Quotes Quill has a habit of expanding on truth with copious amounts of truly nasty or inflammatory lies. In order to make it work a person must suck on the tip for a moment. After that one can set it to a parchment where it will balance in midair on its point until someone starts talking. It will jot down everything it hears they way the owner of the quill would. Harry and Ron really would have benefited from having one in History of Magic but it might have just written "this is boring" over and over again.

Remembrall: Alarge marble-size glass ball full of white smoke which turns scarlet red when the owner forgets to do something. Neville had one, but he lost it. They are banned from the examination hall at Hogwarts.

Revealer: It looks like a bright red eraser, but is supposed to reveal any hidden writing when rubbed on magically hidden words. Hermione has one she bought in Diagon Alley. She tried it on Tom Riddle's Diary but it didn't work.

Rosettes, QWC 1994 Memorabilia: Small luminous rosettes that shout all the names of a team's players. Ireland's were green and Bulgaria's were probably red. The charm used on them does eventually wear off, usually within a couple of months. As the charm fades, the shouting gets higher pitched and some of the names are forgotten.

Scarves, QWC 1994 Memorabilia: Bulgaria's flag is comprised of white, green and red horizontal bars with a lion rampant in the upper left corner. The Bulgarian supporters' scarves had lions on them that really roared. Since Luna was at QWC 1994, perhaps that's where she got her idea for the roaring Gryffindor lion hat.

Secrecy Sensor: It is a long thin golden piece of metal that looks either like a straight rod or squiggly television aerial. It vibrates when it detects concealment or lies. It generally hums slightly when it is turned on. Eric, the security wizard at the MoM, uses one like a metal detector wand on wizards that pass into the MoM. Barty Jr (Moody) had one of these Dark Detectors in his office.

Secret-Keeper: See Fidelius Charm. Generally a Secret-Keeper has some piece of secret information hidden in their soul. It is said that the information cannot be known or discovered unless personally revealed by the Secret-Keeper to a person, but it begs the question, what if someone knew prior to the information being concealed? Does the person just forget they knew? If Dumbledore and Sirius were told where the Potters were going to hide before they went into hiding, and they must have been since both Sirius and Hagrid, sent by Dumbledore, showed up at Godric's Hollow without being told by Peter, they clearly didn't forget the information just because the Fidelius Charm was performed. So the charm does have a few pitfalls.

Self-Correcting Ink: This ink that will correct one's answers as well as one's spelling, sort of like the grammar and spell check functions of a Microsoft word processing system. It is banned from the examination hall at Hogwarts.

Self-Shuffling Cards: A deck of playing cards that shuffles itself. Ron has some in his room at the Burrow.

Sneakascope: A large glass top that stands balanced on its point, perfectly still, when all is well. It lights up, spins wildly and lets out a piercing whistle when there is

THE HARRY POTTER COMPANION

someone untrustworthy around. Barty Jr (Moody) had one of these Dark Detectors in his office. It was cracked but it still worked. It was extra sensitive and picked up Dark activity for a mile around.

Pocket Sneakascope: Just like a standard-size Sneakascope but smaller, it looks like a small glass spinning top. Harry has one from Egypt that Ron gave him for a 13th birthday present. Harry usually keeps it in a sock. It works very well and detected Scabbers as a sneak right away.

The Sorting Hat: It looks like a traditional 17th-century pointed wizard's hat which is odd because originally it was Godric Gryffindor's and he lived in the 10th century when hats were decidedly different. That aside, all 4 of the founders put their considerable brains in it so it could do the sorting of the students into the 4 different Houses. The hat remains in Dumbledore's (Godric's old) office on a shelf behind his desk most of the year and hears pretty much everything that happens at Hogwarts. Taking into account what it's heard over the year, it composes an original song that it sings at the start of the new school term. Occasionally the song is warning rather than intellectual or comic as the hat is honor bound to give the school warnings when it feels it's needed.

Nearly Headless Nick said the Sorting Hat had warned the school several times before the 1995 warning but its advice was always the same: stand together and be strong from within. The had encourages everyone to pull together as a student of Hogwarts, rather than a student from an individual House. True unity has yet to make an appearance however as most of the Slytherins seem quite content to see Hogwarts destroyed and Dumbledore sacked as Headmaster. And too, it must be said, none of the other 3 Houses' students actually ever reach out the branch of friendship toward the Slytherins, so the situation is not exactly 100% the Slytherin students' fault.

At the beginning of each term the hat is brought out and placed on a 4-legged stool (or 3-legged stool). The hat is very old (over 1,000 years), patched, frayed, faded, grubby, shabby, tattered, extremely dirty and black. A rip near the brim opens wide like a mouth allowing it to speak. The new students come in, and line up facing the other students, not the teachers at the High Table. The hat sings a song, the students applaud as the hat bows and the Sorting begins. Pr McGonagall reads the new students' names alphabetically from a roll of parchment. Students remove their own hat and place the Sorting Hat on their head then sit on the stool while the hat sifts through all their thoughts and decides where to put them. Sometimes it can take almost a full minute to decide. Eventually the hat shouts out which House the student belongs to and that House's table cheers.

The Sorting Hat will never force a person to go to a House, but it will mention the best House for her or him before sending that individual to the 2nd best House. In Harry the hat saw courage, intelligence, talent and a desire to prove himself. The hat said Harry could be great and Slytherin could help him achieve that end, but Harry rejected Slytherin so the hat sent him to Gryffindor instead. Since there is a part of Voldemort (who was a Slytherin) in Harry, it's not surprising the hat thought of sending Harry to Slytherin. Hermione was almost sent to Ravenclaw, she is after all the smartest witch of her age, but in the end the hat sent her to Gryffindor. Given all the Weasleys seem to end up in Gryffindor, it's not surprising Ron shows the family traits of extreme courage and valor and was Sorted to Gryffindor without any hesitation.

The Sorting Hat can be a little snide (Salazar) and superior (Godric) sometimes, but ultimately he's always helpful (Helga) and gives a correct answer (Rowena). Besides being a spectacular Legilimens, the hat is capable of other types of magic as well. When the Sorting Hat was brought to Harry by Fawkes in the Chamber of Secrets and

Harry put on the hat and asked it for help, the Sorting Hat contracted and the Sword of Gryffindor fell out on his head. Whether what happened means the hat can produce any object from Dumbledore's office or any object at all remains to be seen. It would be quite shocking to see the hat produce all 4 founders, or a body of its own to sit on. But one assumes anything is possible since all the wisdom of the founders is in the hat. This makes the hat more magical, more wise and more powerful, than any magical object or person in existence.

Statue, Hump-backed One-eyed Witch: This statue is located on the 3rd floor, with a classroom is just to the left of her. This statue is the opening to a secret passageway that leads from Hogwarts to Honeydukes' cellar. One must go through the statue's hump, down a stone slide to reach the earthen tunnel with an uneven floor. The tunnel twists and turns like a warren and after a long walk (probably about an 1 hour) ends in a flight of several 100 uneven stone steps going up to a trapdoor. The door leads one through the cellar floorboards of Honeydukes.

Suits of Armor: They give wheezy laughs at people who fall through trick steps on the staircases, sing holiday songs but only know half the words (which would be perfectly normal since they probably spoke Saxon or Gaelic), glow from inside at Christmas (who doesn't?) and move around whenever they feel like it. At Hogwarts there are many suits of armor and they all seem to have some personality, perhaps those of their previous wizarding owners. One assumes most knightly wizards wanted to leave a bit of themselves behind and so enchanted their armor to have their personalities hang around and guard the castle.

The Sword of Gryffindor: Godric Gryffindor's silver sword is set with egg-size rubies (his House's stone) on its handle. It has Godric Gryffindor engraved on it just below the hilt, which is unusual because in circa 900 AD a man would have engraved the name of the sword, not himself on it, and possibly some magical inscriptions as well. Even the Muggles of this era did this sort of thing, so surely Godric would have. Given the founding over was 1,000 years ago, it's probably a broadsword or claymore-type sword some 5-6' in length. It is unknown if it has any magical powers, but it probably does having belonged to Godric. It is kept in a glass case next to the Sorting Hat on a shelf behind Dumbledore's desk.

Talisman: While a talisman is primarily to attract good fortune and ward off ill fortune, amulets are strictly protective devices. During the basilisk attacks, there was a brisk trade in talismans among the students. Neville Longbottom 3 different items, including a newt tail, all of which were reputed to be talismans. Since Neville was not Petrified, something must have worked, thought probably it wasn't the newt tail, which obviously proved fatal to the newt.

Tents, Perkins': Arthur borrowed 2 magical tents from Perkins to use at QWC 1994. They were magically enhanced and expanded inside while on the outside they looked like regular Muggle tents. These tents were quite conservative magically speaking, as compared to others at QWC 1994. The boys' tent was inside a fully furnished 3-room flat inside, complete with bathroom, kitchen and the pungent smell of cats. The girls' tent was slightly smaller, being a 2-room flat.

Time-Turner: The MoM has an entire collection of Time-Turners (or did till Harry and the DA busted them up in Jun 1996) and strictly regulates their use. Pr McGonagall got 1 from the MoM for Hermione to use in 93/94 to take classes that occurred simultaneously. They seem to come in all sizes, but Hermione's was a tiny sparkling hourglass hanging from a long gold chain and worn as pendant. She was not allowed to tell anyone she had a Time-Turner or use it for any purpose other than going to classes but in the end she did both. For every turn back, she went back 1 hour in time. Presumably the reverse is also true, that one can go forward in time by turning the hourglass forward.

MoM law requires that one doesn't change the timeline when using a Time-Turner. However, the biggest danger seem to be running into a past or future self, believing it to be a Dark Magic doppleganger, and killing oneself accidentally. Hermione and Harry used Hermione's Time-Turner, with Dumbledore's collusion, to go back in time to save Buckbeak and Sirius. They did alter the timeline, rather severely, but the MoM obviously couldn't tell what happened so they must not be able to track the actual use of Time-Turners. In some respects the timeline righted itself 2 years later when Sirius was killed. All that remains is for Buckbeak to die and it's back to normal. Sometimes, one just can't outrun one's fate.

Unplottable: Unplottable means that due to various magical interventions an area cannot be seen, located, charted or even found on a map by Muggles. This means is used to hide or protect wizarding places and magical creatures' habitats when other devices fail. Quintapeds are protected by virtue of the MoM making their habitat Unplottable. See FB.

Vanishing Cabinet: It looks like a regular cabinet but anything one puts into it is supposed to vanish for good. There is one at Hogwarts on the 1st floor and Filch used it to try and get rid of Peeves, but it either doesn't work on poltergeists or this particular cabinet is limited in where it can send someone. As the person vanished seems to always reappear somewhere within Hogwarts when this cabinet is used, this limitation must be due to various protective enchantments to keep students from vanishing off the grounds. Vanishing in this manner seems to leave one slightly confused. Montague ended up stuck in a 4th floor toilet very confused after being put in the cabinet. But it might just have been from being stuck in a toilet for a couple days that confused him.

Wand Scale, MoM: This scale looks like a brass baby scale but actually is more of a scanner capable of reading a wand's history. It is used by Security at the MoM for all visiting wizards. A wand is placed on the scale, the scale vibrates momentarily then a slot at the bottom spits out the pertinent details including the type wood, core substance and size of the wand, and how long the wand has been in use.

Winged Keys: Pr Flitwick's created these as a protection for the Sorcerer's Stone. Going from the devil's snare under Fluffy, down a sloping stone corridor with trickling water on walls, one ended up in a brilliantly lit chamber with a high arched ceiling. The room was filled with large flock of small winged jewel-bright keys all fluttering and swirling around the ceiling of the room. Broomsticks were left leaned against the wall opposite the entrance to the room so one could try to catch the right key - a big old-fashioned silver one with a bent, bright blue wing – and get out the door leading to the next challenge.

WIZARDING TRANSPORT

Except for broomsticks, which are in the Brooms and Quidditch section in Part I, and Apparition, which is in the Learned Magical Talents section, all other means of wizarding transport are listed here.

Beauxbatons' Coach: The school has a flying powder-blue carriage the size of a large house pulled by 12 very big, winged palomino horses (abraxans). The carriage has the Beauxbatons crest painted on its doors: 2 crossed gold wands, each emitting 3 gold stars. It has a set of gold steps, which must be real gold covering titanium to bear the weight of Olympia standing on them. This coach brought Olympia Maxime and 12 of her best 17-year-old students to Hogwarts for the TT in 1994. She and her students lived, ate, studied and slept entirely in the coach while at Hogwarts. The coach was parked about 200 yards from Hagrid's frontdoor and a makeshift paddock was put up beside the coach for the abraxans. Hagrid cared for the horses, which require forceful handling and live on single malt whisky. Luckily they were in Scotland where single malt whisky is easy to find, though very expensive to buy in bulk quantities such as these horses must have needed during their 10-month stay.

Durmstrang's Ship: The Durmstrangs have a huge old black sailing ship that resembles a skeletal-looking resurrected wreck. Its black sails were always unfurled, despite the fact they were docked and it got very windy. The portholes looked like misty eyes. It appeared from the midst of a whirlpool in the Lake at Hogwarts, so it's probably a safe bet that Durmstrang is near the sea or other large body of water if they have a sailing ship. This ship brought Igor Karkoff and 12 of his best 17-year-old students to Hogwarts for the TT. He and his students lived, ate, studied and slept entirely in the ship while at Hogwarts. After Karkoff fled it was admitted that he always made the students sail the ship while he remained safely tucked up in his cabin and that this was a source of much student displeasure.

Floo Powder: A glittering magical powder that when thrown into a hearth fire creates an emerald green flamed magical fire that allows one to travel on the Floo Network. A small pinch thrown into the flames causes the fire to roar up and turn emerald green. The fire will then rise even higher and at that point it is ready to use for floo travel (traveling from hearth to hearth). After stepping into the flames, clearly state the place of arrival. There is a certain technique to floo travel. Keeping elbows tucked in and eyes shut is advisable. Fidgeting can cause a person to fall out at the wrong hearth. One mustn't panic and get out too early, but one must be sure to get out at the right grate.

Standing in the magical fire, it feels like there's a warm breeze all around one's body. One then feels as though one is being sucked down a giant drain and one's entire body starts to spin very fast in a whirl of green flames. Suddenly one feels as if cold hands are slapping one's face, at which point one has probably missed the intended hearth of arrival (which would have been where the warm air stopped) and one will fall out somewhere unexpectedly down the line. Harry's first attempt at using Floo Powder in the summer of 1992 dumped him in Knockturn Alley due to poor enunciation. But he did make it back to the Burrow via Floo Network, so it's obviously something one can get the hang of using very quickly.

Floo Powder can also be used for person to person calls. Throw the powder in the fire and say the person's name. They will hear their name in their own hearth and a head will generally turn up in the fire in response. Pr Snape called Pr Lupin this way. This is a rather difficult way to converse as one is required to kneel on the hearth with one's head in the flames for the duration of the call. To send a head somewhere for a chat, one must stick just one's head in the magical fire and state where one wishes one's head to appear, eg, Number 12 Grimmauld Place, the Burrow, Gryffindor common room, Pr Snape's Office, etc, and the head travels through the floo network to the appropriate hearth.

Floo calls are fairly uncomfortable. The same spinning and sensations one has for floo travel bodily, one has for just one's head. The head that appears in the flames is one's actual head. Molly gave Amos Diggory a piece of toast while Amos' head was in the flames and he was able to eat it. Singular body parts can also be put into the flames. If a head is in the flames and another person puts a hand in, the hand could potentially grab hold of the head and pull it back to hand's originating fire. Pr Umbridge tried to do this. For obvious reasons, only a fireplace with a floo can be used. One can't simply

The Harry Potter Companion

throw Floo Powder on a campfire. Finally, always, *always* wait for the high-intensity, magical, emerald-green flames before sticking any body part into the hearth.

Flying Carpets: Carpets were banned only in the latter part of the 20th century. They are now defined as a Muggle Artifact by the Registry of Proscribed Charmable Objects which means Britain cannot import them. The embargo on new flying carpets doesn't stop anyone flying old ones that are already in the country, but discretion in their use is advised.

Axmister: This is an older type of flying carpet, manufactured in the late 19th century. It could seat 12. Barty Crouch Sr's grandfather had one which he remembered fondly.

The Flying Ford Anglia: A magically enhanced rusty old Ford Anglia auto built sometime between 1959 and 1967. The Anglia came in 105E (sedan), De Lux (sedan with all the options) and Estate (station wagon) models. It unclear whether Arthur had the 105E or the De Lux. But it must be one of the 2, since only they have trunks. Arthur's car had an expandable interior that fit 8 people, 2 owls and 1 rat comfortably and a trunk that was also expandable and could easily accommodate 6 trunks.

The car responds to voice commands as well as traditional driving methods. On the dashboard it has a compass and in the glove box were a fat pack of toffees until Ron and Harry ate them all. The Invisibility Booster (a tiny silver button on dash) allowed daytime travel and flight without alerting Muggles. However, this feature was not perfected and frequently cut in and out with a pop before dying completely on Ron while in flight. When it worked, one couldn't even see oneself. Arthur Weasley enchanted the car to fly, but by law cars are on the Registry of Proscribed Muggle Objects, which Arthur's office oversees, so he did know better.

It was first flown by Fred to Harry's house in Aug 1992 to break him out of his prison-cell room. It was then flown by Ron from King's Cross Station to Hogwarts in Sep 1992. The car abandoned Ron and Harry upon landing and being hit by the Whomping Willow. It opted to run wild in the Forbidden Forest. It can sometimes be seen windshield wipers waving freely, horn honking, lights ablaze, crashing through the forest getting scraped and muddy. It is however a faithful car and in order to saved Ron, Harry and Fang from Aragog's hollow even lost a side mirror whipping past a tree. It then returned to its happy life in the forest where it remains to this day running on Arthur's excellent magic.

Gringotts' Carts: They are rather like roller coaster carts and take goblins and customers to the underground vaults far below London. The carts come when whistled for and know where a goblin is going without even being told. They have no steering mechanism and only 1 speed but they can gather speed as they go downhill. It is not Hagrid's favorite way to travel.

Hogwarts Boats: A fleet of about 40 wooden boats sits at the side of the Lake opposite Hogwarts castle. Each boat holds four 1st years or just Hagrid. Hagrid and the fleet of 1st years take boats across the Lake to the castle in the beginning of the year and back to the station at the end of the year. Making this journey to and fro probably activates an enchantment for the students' protection while they're at Hogwarts. The boats are voice activated so that when Hagrid says "forward" all the little boats, sail glidingly across the glass-smooth Lake.

In going toward the cliff where the castle stands, they pass through a curtain of ivy, which hides a wide opening in the cliff face on which Hogwarts sits, and are carried along by a current through a dark tunnel directly underneath the castle to arrive at an underground harbor with a rocky pebble-strew shore. Here they leave the boats and climb up a passage cut in the rock face up to a smooth lawn right in the shadow of the castle. Crossing the lawn and going up a flight of stone steps, they arrive at the castle's huge oak frontdoors to be greeted by Pr McGonagall.

Hogwarts Express: A scarlet steam engine that takes students London's King's Cross Station to Hogsmeade station and back again at the beginning and end of each year. As the name implies it is only for Hogwarts use on those days it carries students to and from school. It also runs at the beginning and end of Christmas vacation and Easter vacation. Though some other train (or the same train renamed) may connect London and Hogsmeade during the rest of the year, it doesn't seem to be so. The Knight Bus appears to be the main form of group wizard travel.

The Express is an old-fashioned Victorian steam locomotive which pulls about 17 carriages (figuring 1,000 students, sitting in full 6 seat compartments, 10 compartments to a carriage). To ride the train one must have a ticket. Harry got his 1st ticket from Hagrid, but one can buy them on Platform 9 3/4. There is a male conductor on the train who will come by to collect tickets during the journey, though passengers rarely seem to see him. The train leaves promptly at 11am and the engineer blows a whistle call just before leaving so people know that they need to board immediately because it's pulling out.

Prefects have their own carriage, usually the first carriage of the Express, where the sit and talk about the new year, duties and so forth. The train has toilets located in certain carriages, not every carriage has them. Compartments appear to hold 6 people and their luggage and owls in overhead racks. There are candlelit lanterns above the luggage racks that light up by themselves on dark days or in the evening. Compartment doors are glass paneled and slide open into the corridor of the carriage which is also lit with candle lanterns on dark days or in the evening. Compartments have a second door with a sash window that opens directly onto the platform. At the both ends of each carriage there is a door to get on or off, or go on to another carriage.

A lunch witch comes along between 12 and 1 pm with a trolley full of food for sale to those who didn't pack a lunch. She regularly carries: Bertie Bott's Every Flavor Beans, Drooble's Best Blowing Gum, Chocolate Frogs, Pumpkin Pasties, Cauldron Cakes, Licorice Wands and ice cold pumpkin juice. It's approximately a 10-hour nonstop journey, so having food available is important. The train arrives at Hogwarts after dark, at around 9 pm. When the Express pulls into the Hogsmeade village station's tiny platform, students are in northern Scotland. Students get off, leaving their luggage on the train as it will be taken to the school separately, but taking animals other than owls with them. Hagrid is usually is at platform to collect 1st years and take them down the steep narrow path through the woods and around the bend to the edge of the Lake and the boats. All other students cross trough the small station house and take the thestral-drawn carriages.

Hogwarts' Stagecoaches: The coaches, probably late Victorian in style, have tiny windows and smell faintly of mold and straw. Over a hundred drawn by thestrals are said to come for 2nd to 7th year students at the Hogsmeade station. But at 4 persons to a coach, it's more along the lines of over 200, at least 216 coaches by my calculation, and as many thestrals. Only students who have witnessed a human death can see thestrals. Apparently the death must be a full view of a human death for which one is personally present in order to count. Viewing a death on TV, or in nature among animals, like a hawk seizing a dove, doesn't count. Hermione wished she could see thestrals and one supposes since she, Ginny and Ron witnessed Sirius' death at the MoM (Neville, Luna and Harry had already seen death), she and the others will now be able to do so.

The Knight Bus: A triple-decker bus painted a violent purple, it has gold lettering on the windshield declaring it to be "The Knight Bus." It is emergency transport for stranded wizards. Just stick out a wand or wand hand and it appears with a deafening bang, blinding headlights and threateningly huge wheels. It Apparates and Disapparates through out England, Wales, Scotland and Cornwall. It can take one anywhere on the island, but it can't take one to Ireland or the Continent, because it can't cross over water.

The driver, Ernie Prang, sits in an armchair and doesn't pay much attention to the road. The conductor, Stan Shunpike, sits in an armchair next to him and makes sure everyone buys a ticket. Stan is also the supplier of extra goods and services. It costs 11S each for tickets, no matter where one wants to go. Additional costs are only for goods: for 2S one gets hot chocolate, for 4S one gets a hot waterbottle and a toothbrush in the color of one's choice as well.

The bus has wood paneled walls and candles in brackets attached to them. In the morning, it has mismatched chairs grouped haphazardly around the curtained windows. Because nothing is nailed down, it all tends to slide or fall over when the bus moves. At night the bus has several brass bedsteads with feather bed mattresses standing by the curtained windows. Candles burn in brackets beside each bed. One's trunk and things are shoved under the bed.

Harry has traveled a couple of times on the bus. Ron has been on it once and swears he'll never do it again. Madam Marsh seems to be a regular Knight Bus rider. The bus is said to be for emergency situations, stranded wizards and the like (maybe one's broom crapped out or one is underage to Apparate or too elderly to use a broom or Apparate with confidence), but it also appears to be regular bus service many people use just because it's convenient.

Motorcycle, Sirius Black's: A flying motorcycle. It flies vertically up when the engine is started or down when the engine is shut off. Sirius owned it before he was sent to prison. Sirius arrived at Godric's Hollow just after Hagrid and loaned it to him to take Harry to Dumbledore after Hagrid refused to let him keep Harry. Hagrid planned to take it back to Sirius even though Sirius said he wouldn't be needing it anymore. It's unclear what happened to it. One assumes Hagrid has it still. Clearly if one isn't allowed to enchant a car to fly, a flying motorcycle can't be that much different in the eyes of the MoM's law enforcement wizards. However, Sirius was always a bit on the edge and enjoyed doing risky things just for the heck of it. So perhaps, the fact it was illegal made it cool to have and cooler to ride.

Portkey: Any object that is charmed to take anyone that touches it to a designated place is a Portkey. If the Portkey is touch again, it returns one to where one originated from. Portkeys can take multiple people from one location to another as long as everyone touches it at the same time. A Portkey can be any object, but is usually a common one that Muggles aren't likely to notice or unlikely to pick up if they do notice, such as an old soda can or dirty shoe.

Portkey travel is not a lot of fun. One feels as if one has been hooked by the navel and yanked through a swirl of color and wind. After banging into everyone else using the key, one lands with a great deal of force, rather abruptly, and usually ends up on one's knees. The MoM used time-activated Portkeys to assist in bringing people to QWC 1994. All Portkey are supposed to be set up by the MoM to prevent travel accidents. However, though setting up an illegal or unauthorized Portkey can get one in trouble, it's a common problem because there's no way to monitor the use of the word Portus.

HARRY'S SCAR

Hagrid says Harry's scar is a mark resulting from where a powerful curse touched him, but that's what the scar is, not what it does. Harry's scar does a number of things, some within Harry's control, some beyond it. Harry believes that when his scar hurts it is a warning that means danger is coming because Voldemort is near. But Harry spent the 91/92 school year in class with Voldemort (in Pr Quirrell's head) twice a week and every day, 3 times a day, as he sat at the High Table, and not only was he never bothered by his scar, he never had so much as a bad dream. The scar hurting therefore cannot mean Voldemort is near. Does it mean Harry is in danger?

It is Dumbledore that offers an opinion, or puts into Harry's mind the idea, that the scar hurting might be a warning indicating danger. But Dumbledore is not inclined to share the truth with Harry most of the time, so what he says, while never a lie, might be a misleading truth. Harry was not in danger seeing Frank Bryce killed, but his scar hurt all the same. Harry was in danger in a sense; he was in Voldemort's mind. But this isn't the sort of danger Harry was led to believe his scar indicated. Dumbledore's theory has validity at a very basic level. So, while Dumbledore didn't lie to Harry, he certainly bent the truth and intentionally misled Harry.

What then is the root cause of the scar's ongoing reactions? To come even close to understanding, it is necessary to examine all the times Harry's scar has hurt, burned, prickled, burst, etc, in relation to Voldemort's proximity and activities. A chronology of events therefore follows, with discussion interspersed and some conclusions offered at the end. The scar seems to have 3 main applications, though there may be more. Since the 3 application don't conflict, it seem reasonable that the scar serves all 3 purposes. Harry's theory that the scar indicates Voldemort's proximity and Dumbledore's theory that it indicates Harry's level of danger, however, are not among the 3.

Prior to Attending Hogwarts
Harry says that while he was living in the cupboard under the stairs, before Jul 31, 1991, that when he thinks about his parents' death, he remembers a binding green flash of light and gets a burning pain on his forehead.

At this point in time Voldemort is Albania, nowhere near Harry and certainly not actively endangering him in any way. Simply by Harry thinking about a past event he can barely remember but witnessed, he can trigger his scar into activity. Thus when Harry witnesses an atrocity Voldemort has committed, his scar goes off. Later events seem to bear this witness theory out. (witness theory)

Harry in 91/92
Harry feels his scar go active when Pr Snape looks him directly in the eyes at the Start of Term Feast.

This is a complex situation and at least 2 explanations are possible. Pr Snape, as a Legilimens, can actively use his thoughts as a weapon. He may be projecting his hatred for James toward Harry and Harry, having no occlumency skills, may sense that hatred. On the other hand, Pr Snape is seated beside Pr Quirrell who has Voldemort in the back of his head. Voldemort must surely have known Harry was starting the school because Pr Quirrell knew it. Since the back of Pr Quirrell's turban is turned toward Harry at the same moment Pr Snape is looking at Harry, it is possible that Voldemort is also looking at Harry and releasing an extremely angry thought which Harry, sharing Voldemort's mind, picks up on.

One would tend to think the second explanation was the truth as it foreshadows Harry's mindlink to Voldemort. (mindlink theory)

After seeing Voldemort in the forest drinking unicorn blood and having Voldemort stare at him then start advancing toward him, Harry's scar goes active in a way he had never experienced before.

This case splits 3 ways, all of which seem valid. When Harry witnesses an atrocity Voldemort has committed, his scar goes off. It is possible Harry's scar became active because he saw the innocent but murdered unicorn. (witness theory)

The pain gets worse as Voldemort stares at him. This seems to be a case of Voldemort projecting hatred, which Harry picks up on because their minds are linked. (mindlink theory)

Finally the scar hurts intensely as Voldemort approaches. Essentially being 1 person split in 2 halves (Harry and Voldemort), close proximity may be like trying to force opposite magnets together. Later events in the MoM in Jun 1996 seem to bear this out. Harry says, when grabbed by Voldemort, they are united in pain. So Voldemort also feels pain when too near Harry. (magnet theory)

From the encounter with Voldemort in the forest onward Harry's scar continually feels like a stabbing pain.

The scar can't hurt because of proximity, which has already been ruled out. It can't be an indicator of danger because Voldemort isn't after Harry at this point, he's after the Sorcerer's Stone. However, Harry could be picking up on Voldemort's intense emotions. The unicorn blood has strengthened Voldemort, in turn making his emotions stronger. This case probably therefore falls under the mindlink theory.

Harry's worst case of scar pain comes when being touched by Voldemort (via Pr Quirrell). When Voldemort (via Quirrell) touches Harry, he feels a needle sharp pain in his scar which builds till he feels like his head would split in two. It is a terrible pain which builds in his head, blinds him and causes him to faint.

Lily's love protects Harry from Voldemort's hatred. Two opposing forces naturally repel each other. The more Voldemort hates Harry, the more painful it is to be touched by him. The fact Harry continually uses the phrase "splitting in two" is indicative of a literal splitting in two, which Dumbledore's Dream Instrument seemed to indicated a well. This event falls under the magnet theory.

Harry in 92/93
Harry meets with Voldemort, as Tom Riddle, in the Chamber of Secrets, and nothing happens. Tom is corporeal enough to hold a wand, but makes the basilisk go after Harry and never physically touches Harry.

What's particularly interesting here is that Tom Riddle has no effect on Harry's scar at all. The witness theory doesn't apply as there is nothing to witness. The magnet theory doesn't apply because Tom never attempts to touch Harry. The mindlink theory doesn't apply because Voldemort's spirit isn't fully in Tom's body at the time Harry confronts him, though Voldemort's spirit has begun to merge with Tom Riddle body by that time (indicated by the red eyes and the fact Tom never tries to touch Harry).

Harry in 93/94

Harry's scar is quite for another year. Since Voldemort is in Albania during this time it would seem to indicate that he has to be within about 600 miles of Harry to have any effect on him. Albania is about 1,500 miles from Britain as the crow flies.

Harry 94/95
Harry, looking through Voldemort's eyes, hears Voldemort at Riddle House planning to kill him, sees Voldemort use the Avada Kedavra to murder Frank Bryce and wakes up with his scar activated.

In this instance, Voldemort is within about 500 miles of Harry, actively plotting against him, and it would seem everything fits the proximity and danger theories, but it is neither of these are why Harry's scar hurts. Harry's scar goes off because he is A) sharing Voldemort's head (mindlink) and B) having to stand a silent and impotent witness to Voldemort carrying out a truly evil act (witness).

Harry's scar burns so badly his eyes water, when he ends up in Voldemort's head and sees Peter Pettigrew get Cruciatus Cursed by Voldemort as a punishment.

Harry is in Voldemort's head (mindlink) and seeing him commit an atrocity (witness). Harry ends up in Voldemort's head when he is about to do something really awful but unable to stop him doing it. Harry is like Voldemort's gagged conscience being forced witness to the atrocities Voldemort commits.

Harry's scar acts up like never before when he looks at Peter who is carrying Voldemort around in the Little Hangleton graveyard.

At first glance this is a throw back to the danger and the proximity theories. But Voldemort was being carried away from Harry, the only one he was thinking of killing was Cedric. So the danger and proximity theories are a total wash. Examining the events closely, Harry feels terrible pain just before Voldemort tells Peter to kill Ced. It is as if Harry is in Voldemort's mind and knows what is coming (mindlink). Then, directly after the Avada Kedavra is released but before Cedric falls dead, Harry's scar reaches its most excruciating and Harry retches. He is again made the silent witness to another's death (witness).

Voldemort presses the Dark Mark on Peter's arm to call the Death Eaters, it causes Harry's scar to burn.

Harry's scar acts up when Voldemort causes harm to another and Harry bares witness to this act (witness).

When Voldemort, after being reborn by the use of Harry's blood, either looks directly at or physically touches Harry, the scar activates with a terrible intensity.

At this point all of Voldemort's hatred is directed at Harry. Voldemort's hatred, now unobstructed by Lily's love charm, is something Harry experiences fully and totally as a result of their mindlink. That Harry's scar goes off when he is physically touched by Voldemort would indicate the magnet theory.

The effect of Voldemort using Harry's blood for his rebirth is two-fold, he can now touch Harry, which he knows and was the main purpose of using Harry in the first place, but it also subjects him to Lily's charm which he doesn't know and didn't count on. Now Voldemort has love in his veins. This becomes apparent later when Harry thinks a loving thought and Voldemort is so effected he has to release Harry and flee.

When Voldemort uses the Cruciatus Curse on Harry, Harry feels his head is splitting along his scar.

The scar is Harry's weakest point, physically, and so is naturally effected. No theory is needed to explain they why of it. Obviously Voldemort was unaffected by Harry's pain or he wouldn't have tortured him for amusement. He must also thinks nothing will happen to him if Harry dies or he wouldn't be so quick to kill him. However, the fact Harry feels his head is splitting along his scar seems to indicate that that part of Voldemort which is in Harry is trying to separate itself from Harry and return to Voldemort.

Harry in 95/96
In this particular year, Harry's scar virtually takes on a life of its own. The theory that is offered by Dumbledore is that Harry's scar picks up on Voldemort when he is near and having a very strong surge of murderous hatred. This sounds good, but it's one of Dumbledore's usual partial truths. Harry picks up on Voldemort because of the mindlink. Murderous emotion draws Harry because of the witness aspect. Voldemort plans to murder, Harry ends up in his head as witness if Voldemort is within 600 miles of him.

During the summer of 1995, Harry begins to "dream" about walking down a long corridor finishing in a dead end and locked door, which often causes his scar to prickle.

Harry thinks he is dreaming, but is actually in Voldemort mind while Voldemort is obsessively thinking about the prophecy in the DoM. Harry's scar is activated by the mindlink, which is more apparent when Harry is asleep.

When Harry thinks about, talks to, looks at or listens to Dumbledore the scar goes active.

Harry's scar hurts around Dumbledore because Voldemort hates Dumbledore and Voldemort is in Harry's mind at a subconscious level. This hatred for Dumbledore is an indication that Voldemort is taking control of Harry. Harry's mind and personality have been pulled toward Voldemort's mind and personality. This is not surprising as Voldemort has been in Harry's mind since the 1st time they met and Harry tried to deny having the Sorcerer's Stone. Voldemort instantly knew it was a lie. How did he know? He was in Harry's head (and since he never used the word Legilimens, it wasn't because of his legilimency skills). (mindlink)

When Harry is thinking about all the Weasleys dead his scar suddenly acts up. It continues prickly through the night as he dreams about the corridor with the terminus of a locked door again.

In this case, it is presumed coincidental, that Voldemort is furious at time when Harry just happens to be contemplating all the Weasleys dead and Voldemort goes on to obsess about the DoM which Harry also picks up on. But initially, it may have to do with Harry's own strong emotions about being a silent witness to murder. Just as Harry's strong emotion caused by thinking about his parents' murders made his scar hurt, so too his strong emotion about being witness to the Weasleys' death by Voldemort, via the boggart, may have activated his scar. (witness, mindlink)

When Harry touches Pr Umbridge's hand, his scar activates again.

It is presumed coincidental again, because Voldemort happens to be having a happy moment. But it also likely that Harry might be picking up Pr Umbridge's evil nature and or thoughts of mortally harming him. After all, Dolores did send dementors after him to Kiss him and if Voldemort is such an expert Legilimens maybe Harry is too and simply doesn't know it yet. (mindlink)

Whenever Harry dreams about the long corridor and locked door, his scar prickles or hurts.
All this is related to Harry's mindlink to Voldemort.

Just after Quidditch practice in October, Harry's scar starts to really sear.
Harry feels it's because Voldemort is really angry that something is not happening fast enough. It is rather creepy that Harry not only know what emotion Voldemort is feeling, he knows exactly why Voldemort is feeling it. The mindlink connection between Harry must be getting very strong if he can read Voldemort's mind without even trying, but as Dumbledore's machine later indicates, they are the same in essence, just in different bodies.

When Harry sees, through being in Voldemort's mind and thus Nagini's as well, Nagini bite Arthur at the MoM near the door to the DoM, his scar goes off.
Harry is no longer witness to Voldemort's acts, Harry becomes Voldemort. That Harry is sucked into Voldemort vortex, and not vice-versa, is particularly scary and shows that Voldemort is truly the stronger of the 2, at least for the moment. If Harry doesn't find a way to break free of the mindlink, or become the stronger of the pair, he's going to become Voldemort.

After seeing Arthur get bitten by Nagini, when Harry finally looks into Dumbledore's eyes as he grips the Portkey to Grimmauld Place, Harry's scar goes painful and he suddenly consumed with a desire to bite Dumbledore.
Later, Dumbledore says he saw Voldemort looking at him from Harry's eyes in that moment. Thus confirming Harry's own personality is losing ground to Voldemort's. While a mindlink is not possession, it is certainly so strongly influential it is only just shy of possession.

Harry's scar hurts as he continues to dream about the corridor, and of something he wants beyond a black door.
The scar hurts because Harry's mind is in Voldemort's. The fact that Harry can't block himself from entering Voldemort's mind or Voldemort entering his, is partially because they share the same mind. Occlumency can't work to save Harry, not because Harry is inept or Pr Snape is the wrong person to be teaching him, but because Harry's mind is Voldemort's mind. Occlumency can only block an outsider from invading Harry's thoughts. It can't stop another part of his mind talking to itself, even if the 2 halves are in separate bodies. If Harry's skills were more developed, Voldemort's mind would be like an open book to him. (mindlink)

Harry scar cuts loose again when Voldemort realizes where in the MoM the corridor the door to the DoM actually is.
Harry senses Voldemort's happiness, maybe. Voldemort originally sent Nagini, with his mind inside her, to have a look around the MoM to find the DoM, but had to back her off once she bit Arthur. He may not have known he had found the door until

Harry relived his memory of seeing the right door. The difficulty in this scenario is, did Harry realize because Voldemort did, or did Voldemort realize because Harry did, or was it a simultaneous, instantaneous realization because both parts of the same mind so to speak were working on the same problem at the same time? Hard to say. In any case it was mindlink that caused the scar to activate.

Just after Harry and Voldemort realize where the door to the DoM is, Harry gets glared at by Pr Snape and the scar activates strongly again and remains active for several hours culminating in Harry waking up laughing because Voldemort is so happy.

It would seem from later events, that once Voldemort knew where the DoM entrance was, he immediately got in touch with the dementors and had his Death Eaters released so they could act on his behalf. Harry in this case would have been picking up on Voldemort's emotions via mindlink and it would have nothing to do with Pr Snape. On the other hand, if at this point Voldemort's hatred for Dumbledore is becoming Harry's as well, there is nothing to say that Voldemort's hatred for Pr Snape, who is a traitor to his cause, isn't also becoming Harry's as well via the mindlink.

Harry gets his scar activated when he ends up in Voldemort's head, and starts living through him. After interviewing Rookwood, he looks in a mirror, realizes he's in Voldemort's head and worse, Voldemort realizes Harry's in his head.

As Harry says, he was Voldemort at that time, just as he was Voldemort in Nagini previously. The mindlink is slowly overpowering Harry. At this point, Voldemort apparently realizes what is happening and, in realizing, starts to take even more advantage of and more care with the connection he has with Harry.

When Dumbledore touches Harry, before going on the lam, the scar again activates and Harry again is "possessed" by Voldemort and his hatred for Dumbledore.

It would seem that it is not only when Harry is in Voldemort's mind that his scar hurts. When Voldemort is in Harry's mind it also causes he scar to hurt. (mindlink)

From this point on, whenever Harry dreams about the DoM and the Hall of Prophecy, his scar hurts.

This pain is all because Harry's mindlink and being in Voldemort's mind.

At last Voldemort lets Harry into his mind and shows him Sirius being tortured at the DoM, in the Hall of Prophecy, and Harry's scar hurts.

Harry's scar hurts from being in Voldemort's mind but probably also from having to witness Sirius' torture – even though, as in the case of the Weasleys, it's not real.

After the prophecy is broken, Voldemort becomes enraged about this and his rage is passed on to Harry causing his scar to go searing till his eyes ran with tears.

Voldemort is in the very room, but invisible, and Harry's scar doesn't hurt from that. It hurts from the mindlink.

Harry's scar burst open when Voldemort in the form of snake constricts around Harry.

Harry claims he and Voldemort are bound together by pain. Implying that Voldemort felt pain in the attempt to crush Harry to death. The magnet theory. At the same time, Voldemort is possessing Harry in the sense that he can use Harry's body, speak through Harry's mouth, even though Harry is fully conscious of what is happening to him. Voldemort is only dispossessed of Harry's body when Harry feels the emotion of love, for his now dead godfather Sirius Black. Voldemort cannot endure the emotion of love and immediately vanishes.

So what does all this say about Harry's scar? It seems to say that Harry and Voldemort are reverse twins, two parts of one person. As such, each mind has almost total access to other mind through the mindlink as they are within say 600 miles of each other and no magical barriers impede (such as being skilled in occlumency). Harry is apparently Voldemort's conscience (or good side) and is drawn to Voldemort only when he is about to murder someone. He has no power over Voldemort to stop his actions, and thus ends up witness to the atrocities Voldemort commits. Physically Harry and Voldemort are magnetic opposites and repel or cause each other pain whenever they touch each other.

Because Voldemort's skill as a wizard is more developed, he has tended to come off the dominant personality. Yet it would appear the curse Voldemort used to try and kill Harry blended them which means Harry must have exactly equal abilities to Voldemort, although they are not developed. They are equal parts of the same person, but over the past 15 years they have developed independent personalities and skills. Harry developed to be a good wizard, Voldemort continued on the Dark path. Voldemort's learning and skill are great, Harry never knew he had skill and remains underdeveloped by comparison. But Harry has an additional power, love, that Voldemort doesn't have. With this power, Harry can kill Voldemort.

From Sybill's prophecy, it would seem that neither Voldemort nor Harry can live while the other survives. Given they are both alive and living and surviving, on the surface this would seem a false statement. Perhaps it would be more accurate to say at a certain point in time, it is going to prove impossible for both Harry and Voldemort to continue to exist in the same world. The steadily growing mindlink between them is only going to get stronger as Harry get older and Voldemort stronger. The only way to break the link is for one to kill the other. But the prophecy states is that only one can kill the other and live. If Dumbledore kills Voldemort, Harry will probably die. This is why Dumbledore said he wouldn't kill Voldemort and used no deadly magic against him at the MoM in Jun 1996.

It is Harry that has to do the actual killing of Voldemort, perhaps in a magical way, perhaps in a Muggle way. The prophecy seems to specify death "by the hand of" implying use of Muggle method. Dumbledore stopped Voldemort in the MoM, not by magically cursing him as in traditional duels, but by drowning him under a sheet of water. Since there is now more that enough human to Voldemort to be killed, perhaps every magical precaution he took to avoid death, will prove only capable of preventing a magical death. If Voldemort could be smothered by water, he could certainly not survive the immediate death beheading with a sword could bring. It will be interesting to see the end he ultimately meets, and what happens to Harry when he meets it.

PORTRAITS ETC.

Because portraits, photos, statues and tapestries are all representations of real people, alive once in the recent or the distant past, their names are also listed in the Magical Beings section. However, it seemed fitting, given the unique ways in which they interact with the living and the fact that they are not themselves alive in any meaningful way, that they should be in a category of their own. Some of the following individuals have connections to Hogwarts, some do not. Where biographical information is known, it is given. Locations likewise are given where they are known. The entries are alphabetical by last name, if the last names is known, by first name if only that is known, or by description and gender (male, female) if nothing else is known.

PORTRAITS

Portraits have feelings, motives, access to information, the ability to make choices and the ability to talk, eat and drink. The living can interact with a portrait as they would the person themselves. People in portraits are able to move freely to between other portraits of themselves even if they are separated by great distances. Portraits can also cross through other neighboring portraits. Important institutions are likely to have many portraits of important figures. Beyond being decorative, they can be helpful. Dumbledore keeps 12 previous Headmasters and Headmistress of Hogwarts in his study to consult with. Each of the 12 has portraits else where that allows Dumbledore to have a wide sphere of influence if ever he needs it. All that being said, portraits are in the end just canvas and paint. Destroying a portrait does not destroy a living thing.

Mrs Black: d 1985. She was the pureblood mother of Sirius and Regulus Black. She rejected her son Sirius when, at age 16, he ran away from home in a final rejection his parents and their pureblood philosophy. Supposedly she was heartbroken over Sirius because he was a such a disappointment. She grew to utterly hate him and finally swore he was no son of hers. She was an avid believer in pureblood philosophy and a supporter of Voldemort till her favorite son Regulus was murdered on Voldemort's orders in 1980. Her husband died at an unknown point after Regulus but before herself and she lived at 12 Grimmauld Place, London with her house-elf Kreacher for the remainder of her life.

A life-size, tromp d'oie portrait of Mrs Black, painted sometime in the last years of her life, is in the front hallway of her London residence located between two moth-eaten velvet curtains. Upon first glance it seems one is actually looking out a window behind which is an old woman in a black cap screaming as though she's being tortured. It's a very realistic and very unpleasant portrait. She is usually drooling and rolling her eyes. She has yellowing skin (possibly from liver disease) and she brandishes her clawlike hands (possibly from arthritis) at people as if threatening to rip their faces. Unfortunately the portrait is affixed to the wall with a Permanent Sticking Charm.

Usually the curtains are pulled over the portrait to keep it quite. Should any noise occur, it goes off like a rocket. The curtains fly apart and Mrs Black begins to scream uncomplimentary things about nonpurebloods, which in turn sets off the other portraits in the hallway, who also begin screaming. Once the curtains are forced closed, usually requiring 2 men to do it, she goes quiet again. One hates to think that Sirius' mother was that deranged but paintings always give a fair representation of what the person was like in life. Let us hope she went as crazy as she appears in the very last years of her life rather than when Sirius was a child.

Sir Cadogan: A large painting beside another large painting of a large, angry looking wolfhound. Harry, Hermione and Ron originally found Sir Cadogan on a 6th floor corridor at Hogwarts. He's quite helpful most of the time. He led them up a nearby staircase to the 7th floor of and the North Tower right to the spot where the ladder to Divination class is put down by Pr Trelawney. When the Fat Lady was removed for repairs, he spent almost 2 terms guarding Gryffindor Tower's entrance. He bravely volunteered for the job, but got it because he was the only volunteer. He spent half his time challenging people to duels and the rest thinking up complicated passwords which he changed frequently (sometimes twice a day). After letting Sirius Black into Gryffindor Tower, because he had the passwords, Sir Cadogan was fired. He is currently back on his lonely landing on the 6th floor.

Sir Cadogan loves the knightly life filled with parties, quests and daring deeds. He uses words like knave, villain, scurvy braggart and rogue. He threw a Christmas party in his painting, inviting a few monks, his pony and several previous Headmasters of Hogwarts; copious amounts of mead were served. He is a short squat knight in a suit of armor and has a fat dapple grey pony, from which he keeps getting thrown into the grass. He's a bit fight happy and only too willing to brandish his overly large sword at any and all. His sword is a bit heavy for him, as is his armor, and he keeps falling down as he tries to threaten people. He is more comical than threatening but his heart is good.

Madame Elfrida Clagg: A witch who became Chieftainess of the Wizards' Council in the 14th-century. She attempted to define being, with disastrous results, but is best remembered for her conservation efforts and forever changing the face of Quidditch. As a leading figure in wizarding history, she has portraits in many places. Her portrait is on the 8th level of the MoM. Everard saw Arthur being taken up from the 9th level from her portrait. Due to the lack of any codified ways of spelling in the Middle Ages occasionally her name is spelled Cragg.

Dilys Derwent: Following a brilliant career as head Healer at St Mungo's, 1722-1741, she became a celebrated Headmistress at Hogwarts, 1741-1768. She is an elderly witch with long silver ringlets whose portrait resides next to Everard's in Dumbledore's office. The background of her portrait is a dark curtain with a handsome leather chair in the foreground.

Armando Dippet: A former Headmaster at Hogwarts, he was Head in 42/43 when Chamber of Secrets was initially opened by Tom Riddle and Dumbledore was a Transfiguration teacher on his staff. In 1943 he was a wizened, frail-looking man and bald but for a few wisps of white hair. Dumbledore convinced Armando to keep Hagrid on and train him as Gamekeeper after Hagrid was expelled. When he died or retired is unknown. His portrait is currently in Dumbledore's office. He is very supportive of Dumbledore.

Everard (Unknown): Everard is a former celebrated Headmaster at Hogwarts whose portrait resides in Dumbledore's office. A sallow-faced wizard with short black bangs, he has another portrait in the MoM. He raised the alarm and made sure Arthur was saved by the right people, ie, other members of the OoP in Dec 1995, when Arthur was bitten by Nagini.

The Fat Lady: She is a very fat woman in a pink silk dress in the oil painting that guards the entrance to Gryffindor Tower located at the end of a corridor on the 7th floor of the castle. She likes to dress up for Christmas and has been known to wear a tinsel hairband during the season. Her painting covers a hole in the wall that is raised a few feet up off the floor. There is a noticeboard on the wall beside her picture so students from other Houses can post messages. The painting swings forward to open.

The Fat Lady has been serving as a guard for Gryffindor since at least the 1940s and probably earlier. She makes up the passwords for Gryffindors and is usually very good at her job as guard but she can get a bit surly and unreliable. She chewed Molly out for being out till 4am with a boy (Arthur) once. She sometimes goes visiting in other paintings or falls asleep before every student of the House is in for the night. She gossips with Vi, her best friend and the resident gossip. And she sometimes gets drunk. She was found tipsy one Christmas evening after she and Vi consumed a few boxes of chocolate liqueurs in her portrait. The telltale wrappers were found at the bottom of her frame.

However, she did refuse entry to Sirius Black during the Halloween Feast, 1993, at great personal risk, so she's there when it counts. She had her portrait slashed for her trouble. Great chunks of it were torn away and she was so frightened and ashamed she ran off through a 4th floor landscape which had trees she could hide behind and finally hid in a map of Argyllshire on the 2nd floor. She was expertly restored and returned to her post, with the security trolls for back up, for the rest of the 93/94 year.

(Unknown) Fortescue: A former well-respected Headmaster, his portrait resides in Dumbledore's office. He is a corpulent, red-nosed wizard who sits in a thronelike chair. He gets riled up about other portraits, ie, Phineas, when they refuse to help Dumbledore. He refers to such behavior as dereliction of duty and insubordination and has been known brandished his fists at offending portraits. He thinks its dull when Dumbledore's not around. He told Harry that Dumbledore thinks very highly him. It is difficult to tell when he was Headmaster, but it was back when the MoM did not cut deals with petty criminals, so it must have been at least circa 1800 or earlier.

Phineas Nigellus: He has 2 portraits. One is in Dumbledore's office, because Phineas was a former Headmaster, and the other is in the house at 12 Grimmauld Place, because Phineas was the Great-Great-Grandfather of Sirius Black. See schematic T. He went to Hogwarts and was a Slytherin. He says about those of his House, Slytherin, that they are brave but not to the point of folly and given a choice they will always save their own lives. He disagrees with Dumbledore on many points, but admires him for his style. On the other hand he thinks Sirius, his own family, is completely worthless.

He was the least popular Headmaster Hogwarts ever had, probably because he loathed being a teacher. He felt, and still feels, that it was impossible to teach chlidren because they were so convinced they were right about. Which may be true, but a good teacher is supposed to be able to work around such difficulties. At Headquarters his picture was in Ron and Harry's bedroom. He was never in the frame but just outside it spying and or sniggering. He turned up visibly only once, to tell Harry off, which he rather enjoyed, and give him a message from Dumbledore.

Phineas is a clever looking wizard with a pointed beard. He was painted wearing Slytherin colors of green and sliver. He has thin black eyebrows and one presumes black hair. He strokes his pointed beard when he thinks or is stalling. He has a sly bored reedy voice, wears silk gloves and slopes as he walks. He doesn't really ever want to help Dumbledore but he's honor bound to help another Head. He was probably Head around 1860-1880.

(Unknown) Female Headmaster: Her portrait is in Dumbledore's office. She is a gimlet-eyed witch with an unusually thick wand that looked like a birch rod. She threatened to "persuade" Phineas when he stalled on helping Dumbledore.

(Unknown) Mermaid: Her portrait hangs in the Prefects' bathroom. She has long blond hair and sits on a rock. She's usually asleep on her rock at night.

Urquhart Rackharrow: b 1612-d 1697. A portrait in the Dai Llewellyn Ward at St Mungo's. He is a rather vicious looking wizard. He was a Healer and the inventor of the Entrail-Expelling Curse. He is probably Scottish given his name.

Violet: aka Vi. She is a pale, wizened witch and a friend of the Fat Lady's. Her portrait hangs in the chamber off the Great Hall behind the High Table where the champions for the TT met. She likes to gossip with other pictures and with students. She is fond of chocolate liqueurs and got tipsy on them with the Fat Lady one Christmas. She's apparently a bit of flirt as well. She winked at Bill from her frame when he came to meet Harry before Task 3 of the TT.

PHOTOS

All wizard photos are alive in some manner and reflect a person's personality as it is, if that person is currently living, or as it was at the time the picture was taken, if the person is long dead. Percy's image walked out of an old family photo after he started quarreling with his family. Harry parents wave cheerfully at him from their wedding day photos. Photos, unlike portraits, lack the ability to talk. The photos are usually black and white but can be color. They are taken with a normal camera and film but the reason they move is magical developing potion. The process must be fairly simple over all as Colin Creevey was making wizard photos at age 11.

Obviously some of the wizards discussed here were long dead before the photographic process was developed and there is no possibility of using a photo from life. One presumes a number of these are "artists' renderings" turned into paintings which were then photographed. Also, some of the following are photos might be of tapestries, statuary or other more solid art forms created in a wizard's lifetime and perhaps even capable of posing and preening for her or his photo. Of course, as with portraits that are painted, no matter how real a photo seems, it's still a photo and can be torn up without regrets.

Agrippa: b 1486-d1535 He's on the Chocolate Frogs' Famous Witches and Wizards Trading Cards. Probably Heinrich Cornelius Agrippa von Nettesheim, German mystic and alchemist. Agrippa of Nettesheim was born of a once-noble family near Cologne, and studied both medicine and law there, apparently without taking a degree. Agrippa argued, in *De Occulta Philosophia*, against the persecution of witches, and ended up in jail. A woodcut of him probably survives.

Circe: c 1000 BC. On the Chocolate Frogs' Famous Witches and Wizards Trading Cards. She was a famous ancient Greek sorceress with a gift for Transfiguration. Circe, the daughter of Helios, lived on an island called Aeaea, near Italy, to which she lured sailors then changed them into various animals, pigs being a particular favorite. One would assume a statue of her survives.

Cliodna the Druidess: c 300 AD. On the Chocolate Frogs' Famous Witches and Wizards Trading Cards. Presumably Irish. Cliodna was the most beautiful woman in the world in her time. She traveled in the company of 3 magical birds who sang so sweetly that the sick fell into healing dreams. One would think a tapestry or brooch bearing her likeness survives.

Alberic Grunnion: b 1803-d 1882. On the Chocolate Frogs' Famous Witches and Wizards Trading Cards. A powerful Visigoth wizard whose life shows up in the mythic poem *Song of the Nibelungen*. The poem was later the basis for Wagner's Ring Cycle operas in which Alberic is said to be a powerful Dwarf wizard. He makes a ring from gold that he has found and places a thief's curse on it. The ring, much like Tolkien's ring, is the source of much trouble and tribulation. Alberic is also reputed by some to be the inventor of the Dungbomb.

Hengist of Woodcroft: On the Chocolate Frogs' Famous Witches and Wizards Trading Cards. He was a 5th-century Jute and invader of Britain. He helped King Vortigern defeat the Scottish Picts. Later, he founded the county of Kent. Exactly how he was magical was unknown, but he defeated the very magical Pitcs, so we must assume Hengist was very magically powerful in his own right. A tapestry may survive of him.

Merlin: c 500 AD. On the Chocolate Frogs' Famous Witches and Wizards Trading Cards. Probably Britain's most famous Dark Age wizard. A great friend to King Arthur and archenemy of Morgana. He spent most of his time helping Arthur keep his kingdom together, although all of Arthur's most magical items and experiences, oddly, had nothing to do with Merlin. A tapestry of him may survive.

Morgana: c 500 AD. On the Chocolate Frogs' Famous Witches and Wizards Trading Cards. Called Morgana Le Fey, she was a great witch and believed to be part fairy (fey is French for fairy). She was rather fond of causing trouble for King Arthur in hopes her own son would inherit Camelot when Arthur died. A tapestry of her may survive.

Paracelsus: b 1493. On the Chocolate Frogs' Famous Witches and Wizards Trading Cards. Probably an alchemist named Auroleus Phillipus Theophrastus Bombastus von Hohenheim, who was also known as Paracelsus. Despite the Greek name, he was a German wizard. A portrait of him may survive.

Ptolemy: On the Chocolate Frogs' Famous Witches and Wizards Trading Cards. A famous family of ancient Egyptian wizard kings, who were actually Greek, but were given Egypt in a power-sharing agreement. One would venture to say, in the absence of any other compelling evidence, Claudius Ptolemy, born in 85 AD, who was an astronomer and geographer is likely the Ptolemy pictured. Doubtless several statues and tomb paintings survive of him.

STATUES

It would seem that at least some statues are imbued with the power to imitate their owner. Most wizards are probably not magically powerful enough to use the medium of stone to embody their personality. Statues can move and talk, depending on the magic used on them. See the section on Sculpture in Part I for more detail.

Boris the Bewildered: Located by the Prefects' Bathroom on the 5th floor is the statue of Boris the Bewildered. The statue shows him lost looking, wearing the wrong gloves on each hand. No doubt his magical talents preoccupied him most of the time.

Gregory the Smarmy: Located in the East wing just in front of an entrance to one of the secret passageways out of the school. Reputedly the famous inventor of Gregory's Unctuous Unction in the Middle Ages.

Hump-backed One-eyed Witch: Possibly Gunhilda of Gorsemoor who fits the description. She was reputed to be a Healer in the 16th century. Located on the 3rd floor, a classroom is just to the left of her. This statue is the opening to a secret passageway that leads from Hogwarts to Honeydukes. One must go through the statue's hump, down a stone slide to an underground tunnel that evenutally leads to a trapdoor in the cellar of Honeydukes.

Lachlan the Lanky: Probably Scottish. He stands on the 7th floor between the stairs leading down to the 6th floor and the Fat Lady's portrait.

Paracelsus: His bust stands halfway down the corridor leading from the Gryffindor Common Room to the shortest route to the Owlery. See the Photo section.

(Unknown) Wizard: He is a Medieval wizard. His bust mumbles to itself in Latin and is located near the DADA office.

Wilfred the Wistful: His statue is somewhere near the Owlery. There is no way to determine which Wilfred this is, but given wizards tendency to give their children individual names, it is possibly Wilfred Elphick, 1112-1199. See FB.

TAPESTRY

Wizarding tapestries are similar to photos in that they are alive and actively reflecting a person's personality but cannot talk. On the other hand they are more like portraits in that that they are actively interested in what's going on around them and move around to neighboring tapestries for a better look.

Barnabas the Barmy: He has a tapestry on the 7th floor of Hogwarts near the Room of Requirement. It shows him being clubbed by trolls. He had attempted to train trolls to do ballet with limited results. One assumes the clubbing was due to clash of personalities, not the result of poor teaching methods used by Barnabas or lack of talent by the trolls.

PART IV. BIOGRAPHY: WIZARDS ABBOT-RAVENCLAW

ALPHABETICAL LISTING OF WIZARDS A-RA

THE FOLLOWING SECTION CONTAINS an alphabetical list of all relevant wizards. Some have only a first name or last name, others no name. As far as possible they are listed in the most appropriate and logical place. Thus Tom is in the T section, Mr Fortescue in the F section, and St Mungo's Welcome Witch is in the S section. Those called by titles, such as Barnabas the Barmy are under their first name, in this case B for Barnabas rather than Barmy.

Information for those persons featured in portraits, photos, statues, busts, or tapestries has been put in Part III in a separate division called Portraits Etc. Their names are entered in this list because they were, at one point, real people and it seems logical that some readers might look for them here first. Thus the Fat Lady has an entry here, though information pertaining to her is in the aforementioned section.

A ? has been used with some dates to indicate uncertainty. While it would be preferable that all students that start Hogwarts finish, as Cedric Diggory proved, not all do. Therefore a date projected in the future if all goes well is given, but a ? reminds the reader it is not a certainty.

Hannah Abbot: b 1980. A Hufflepuff, 1991-1998? She started Hogwarts in 91/92. She is a pink-faced blonde who wears her hair in pigtails. She has been a good friend of Ernie and Justin since arriving at Hogwarts. They are trio similar to Harry, Ron and Hermione, whom they are usually also always on friendly terms with. She and Ernie collect and occasionally trade Chocolate Frog cards. She was one of the first

Hufflepuffs to believe Harry was the Heir of Slytherin in 92/93. In 93/94 she thought Sirius could turn into a flowering shrub.

In 94/95 she wore a Support Cedric Diggory badge during the TT until Cedric told his House to tone down the rancor. In 95/96 Both Hannah and Ernie became Prefects. In Oct 1995 they both joined the DA. She had the dubious distinction of being the first to break during the 95/96 OWLs year. She began crying in Herbology one day in Apr 1996, confessed herself too stupid to take her exams and had to be given a Calming Draught by Madam Pomfrey. Her fears were slightly justified when she later Transfigured a single ferret into a flock of flamingos on the OWL practical in Transfiguration.

Euan Abercrombie: b 1984. A Gryffindor, 1995-2002? He started Hogwarts in 95/96. He is a small boy with very prominent ears. Possibly a *Daily Prophet* reader from the way he initially reacted to Harry.

Stewart Ackerley: b 1983. A Ravenclaw, 1994-2001? He started Hogwarts in 94/95.

Agnes (Unknown): A woman whose head is covered in cat fur. She seems to be a long-term resident of the ward. She was in the Janus Thickey Ward with Lockhart in Dec 1995. She barks instead of talking or meowing. She has a son that comes to visit her.

Agrippa: See Portraits Etc., Photo section.

Archie (Unknown): A stubborn old wizard who wore a long flowery nightgown in order to blend in with Muggles at QWC 1994. He later refused to put on pants when confronted by Obliviators because he said he liked a healthy breeze around his privates.

(Unknown) Auror: A witch working with the MoM as an Auror, she started prior to 1992. She has an eye patch covering one eye, which one is unknown. One assumes she lost the eye on the job.

(Unknown) Avery: b 1954. A Slytherin, 1966-1973. He was part of a gang of Slytherins who nearly all turned out to be Death Eaters. He started Hogwarts in 66/67. See Note 1 at the end of this section. He got out of trouble in 1981 by claiming Imperius Curse. However, he rejoined the Death Eaters when Voldemort called him via the Dark Mark to Little Hangleton in Jun 1995. He was then minorly Crucio Cursed by Voldemort. Part of the failed raid on the MoM, he was put in Azkaban as of Jun 1996.

Malcolm Baddock: b 1983. A Slytherin, 1994-2001? He started Hogwarts in 94/95.

Ludovic Bagman: aka Ludo. Brother of Otto. See schematic S. He played Beater for the Wimbourne Wasps and England in the 1980s, and is thought by many to have been the best the Wasps, or England, ever had. While Ludo was playing with the Wasp, they won the League 3 times. He was then a tall, fit, lean, muscular man with an unbroken nose and round blue eyes. In 81/82, while playing for England, he ended up on trial for being a Voldemort supporter. His trial was sometime after Karkoff's ratting out some other Death Eaters.

Augustus Rookwood, a friend of Ludo's dad, had asked him for information. Ludo gave it to him thinking he might get a MoM job after finishing his Quidditch career and trying to ingratiate himself. He never thought Rookwood was working as a spy for Voldemort, especially as Rookwood was with the MoM. Ludo was tried by Barty Crouch Sr, who firmly believed he was guilty. Moody on the other hand believed Ludo was just stupid by nature. The case confirmed Moody's suspicions rather than Barty Sr's. Ludo was acquitted because his trial followed a Saturday when he had played very well for England against Turkey. The verdict went to a vote and no would convict him. Mr Crouch continued to believe that Ludo should have been jailed.

Ludo went on playing League Quidditch for a while and after retiring went to work for the MoM. He eventually, prior to 1994, became the enthusiastic Head of the DMGS. By 94/95, Ludo was a powerfully built man that has gone slightly to seed. He had round baby-blue eyes, short blonde hair and a rosy complexion. He looked like an overgrown schoolboy with his round rosy face, large belly and squashed nose. Ludo was clean shaven and had a springy walk, but was out of shape and puffed when he walked too far. He had a schoolboy's sense of humor and loved Fred and George's fake wands.

He came to QWC 1994, wearing his now too tight in the stomach black and yellow Wasps robes, which are horizontally striped robes with a wasp picture across the chest. He went around with a quill and notebook taking bets on QWC 1994 prior to the start of the game. He acted as commentator for the game as well as playing host to foreign dignitaries from Bulgaria and prominent British wizards he'd invited himself. He bet rather too much on the game, lost all his own money and got in trouble with goblins after he lost some of theirs as well. He paid Fred and George's winnings, and probably others, in leprechaun gold.

He hoped to make all the money back by betting on Harry to win the TT by himself. He was commentator for all 3 TT tasks and wore his old Wasp robes to the TT Task 1. At the Yule Ball wore robes of bright purple with large yellow stars. By TT Task 2 the goblins were hounding him for their money. Eventually, after Task 3, he had to flee the country because Harry didn't win the TT alone, which Ludo had bet on him doing, but with Cedric. The matter with the goblins was never resolved and Ludo, left his job and fled Abroad. The goblins who were after Ludo expected the MoM to pay his losses but the MoM didn't and this event has now soured the goblins on the MoM and probably on helping the MoM against Voldemort. Swearing: good lord, Damn.

Mr Bagman: Otto and Ludo's father. He worked at the MoM and was a friend of Augustus Rookwood's.

Otto Bagman: Brother of Ludo. He got in trouble over a lawnmower with magical powers. Arthur smoothed it over, so Ludo gave him Top Box QWC 1994 tickets.

Millicent Bagnold: She was the Minister of Magic before Fudge. She saw the MoM through the 1st rise of Voldemort and the reconstruction afterwards. She probably left office at the end of 1990.

Bathilda Bagshot: c 1900? Author of *A History of Magic,* Hogwarts' textbook for History of Magic. Her book was published by Little Red Books, 1947.

(Unknown) Banges: Co-owner of magical instrument shop in Hogsmeade. Gender unknown.

Barnabas the Barmy: See Portraits Etc., Tapestry section.

Wizard Barrufio: This wizard said S instead of F during an incantation for some reason and found himself on the floor with a buffalo on his chest. Used as an example by Pr Flitwick as an example to students to encourage the proper pronunciation of magical words, it is probably the wizard equivalent of an urban legend. There are very few incantaions where the subsititution of a single letter would result in a spell that actually works. He is also the inventor of Barrufio's Brain Elixir. He may or may not be alive today.

Ali Bashir: He is an exporter of flying carpets and believes there is a niche market for a family vehicle in Britain. He was upset by the embargo Arthur put on flying carpets and, according to Barty Sr at QWC 1994, wanted to talk to Arthur about it. Around Christmas 1994, Ali was caught trying to smuggle a consignment of flying carpets into UK. He is probably in Azkaban.

Basil (Unknown): He works for the MoM (Portkey Office probably) and is a friend of Arthur's. When Harry met him in Aug 1994, he was a tired and grumpy looking wizard working the Portkeys at QWC 1994 with another wizard. He was wearing a kilt and poncho, which may explain the grumpiness. His job was collecting up the used Portkeys and putting them in box where they couldn't be rehandled. He also had a list with people's campsites written on it.

Katie Bell: b 1978. A Gryffindor, 1989-1996. She started Hogwarts in 89/90. She was Chaser for the House team. During Ron's first practice as Keeper in 95/96, he hit her in the face with the Quaffle, giving her a nosebleed. Fred accidentally gave her the wrong end of a Nosebleed Nougat and eventually the practice had to be called off because she continued losing blood at an alarming rate. She was in the DA from the start in Oct 1995.

Aunt Elladora Black: This witch started the Black family tradition of beheading house-elves who were judged too old to to be useful, ie, carry tea trays.

Mrs Black: See Portraits Etc., Portrait section.

Mr Black: d circa 1984. Sirius and Regulus' father. He put every security measure known to wizardkind on his house. It's unknown why he did this but he seems to have been a heavy collector of Dark Arts items and may have been afraid of a MoM raid. He and his wife suffered from pureblood mania and hated Sirius because he wasn't a pureblood believer. They thought that being a Black was like being royal and Mr Black had a large gold ring with the Black family crest on it (which Sirius threw out).

He and his wife were supporters of Voldemort's plan to purify the wizarding race, get rid of Muggle borns and have purebloods in charge. However, they got cold feet when they learned more about Voldemort's methods. They were proud of Regulus for becoming a Death Eater and this action made Regulus the family's favorite son. One assumes after Regulus died their fervor for the cause was further dampened. It is unknown how Mr Black died. It may or may not have been natural causes. One assumes something caused Mrs Black to snap and if it wasn't Sirius' desertion, Regulus' murder or Sirius' imprisonment, it must have been Mr Black's death.

Regulus Black: b 1957-d 1980. Sirius' younger brother. Probably a Slytherin, 1968-1975. He started Hogwarts in 68/69. He was drawn into his parents' beliefs about purebloods and as a result was considered a much better son in their eyes and the in the eyes of the Black family in general. He became a Death Eater, but got in too deep, panicked over what he was being asked to do, and tried to back out. He was murdered by Voldemort, or on his orders. Since deserters from Voldemort's cause are murdered, and Death Eaters know this, one wonders what he was being asked to do that giving up his own life seemed a better alternative. He was probably asked to murder his father and refused to do it.

Sirius Black: aka Snuffles. b 1955-d 1996. Eldest son of Mr and Mrs Black, older brother of Regulus. He went to Hogwarts and started in the same year as James Potter, Peter Pettigrew and Remus Lupin, 66/67. It isn't clear what House he was in, probably Slytherin, 1966-1973. Both Sirius and James were exceptionally bright, troublemakers and very popular with the student body. So inseparable were they that one would have thought they were brothers. Co-ring leader with James of the gang of 4 at Hogwarts, his favorite target was Severus Snape, who was also in his same year. He loved torturing Severus or seeing him tortured (by James) because he considered Severus a nosy weirdo and into the Dark Arts.

Taller than Severus with rather long black hair falling in his blue eyes, he usually looked bored and haughty. Sirius possessed a casual elegance that made him sought after by the girls, though he always seemed to be more interested in spending time in the company of his male friends and never got involved with any girl during or after school. He was very handsome and full of laughter during this period of his life. He and James were the best at school in whatever they did and being highly intelligent, they had a lot of free time on their hands to get up to no good. For instance, after befriending Lupin in his first year, he and James set out to become unregistered Animagi in order to accompany Lupin in his wolf state on romps around the Forbidden Forest and Hogsmeade, despite the danger they posed to others.

He succeeded in his 3rd year (as did James), and found he was able to turn into a enormous, jet black dog with pale (one assumes blue) gleaming eyes and inch-long teeth. Often compared to a bear in this form, he was a very big, wide, hulking figure that was remarkably hairy, extremely strong and yet stealthy and quiet. He always used to want it to be full moon so he could romp around with Lupin and James, and later Peter. He took to calling his friends by their nicknames, particularly James whom he called Prongs, and began to exhibit doglike traits, in particular his laugh became barklike. No one seemed to notice they'd become Animagi, despite their not to careful use of their gifts and they went on having adventures until graduation and perhaps even afterwards.

At 15 Sirius, by his own admission, had spent too much time in detention, usually with James, to ever be made a Prefect. At 16, he hated his family so much that ran away from home and was burned off the Black family tapestry by Mrs Black. He never went home again and camped out at Mr and Mrs Potter's during holidays and summer vacations where they treated him like a second son. During his 6th year as Hogwarts, he intentionally tried to get Severus killed or bitten by Remus in wolf form, but wasn't expelled for it. At 17 he got his own place after his Uncle Alphard died and left him a large amount of gold as an inheritance. After that he looked after himself but was always welcome at the Potter's house for Sunday lunch. He became a member of the OoP after graduating and gave himself a new image by cutting his hair short.

Sirius had an ongoing quirk concerning his hair. He wore it long till he graduated, then cut it short, as if cutting off his hair was leaving his old life behind. After he left prison and came to a sense of himself, he cut his hair short again. After a year out of prison, his hair was long again because he was living on the run which must have been difficult and depressing. He cut his hair shortly after he moved home to work with the OoP, but found himself housebound, fell into a depression and let his hair grow long again. Because Sirius never talked about his haircuts, it is difficult to say exactly why he did what he did and it will forever remain a mystery.

Speculating, one would have to say Sirius suffered from periods of deep depression brought on on by confinement or confining circumstances and when these moods were particularly dark, he neglected his appearance and let his hair get long. When the depression left him, he cut his hair. A further thought to consider is the English expression "he has a black dog with him" meaning, the person one is speaking of is depressed. Given his Animagus form, Sirius always had a black dog with him or in him in some sense and may have always had a personality prone to fits of depression, which would be unsurprising given his upbringing. Since his mother suffer from insanity, possibly from all the inbreeding between purebloods, and it is possible Sirius' depressions were a mild form of inherited mental illness.

Going back to Sirius' post-Hogwarts years, after graduating it's unclear what he did to support himself financially before being falsely arrested. He may have been left enough money by his uncle that he didn't have to work and could devote himself to the OoP, but this is doubtful. Sirius was best man at James' wedding and later made Harry's godfather, which means Sirius was at the time a Christian of some description, probably Catholic or Anglican. In drawing up a will, Lily and James appointed Sirius as Harry's guardian in case anything every happened to them (which means the Dursley's were never meant to be taking care of Harry). When Dumbledore became worried someone close to the Potters was a double agent, the Potters decided to make Sirius their Secret-Keeper and into hiding.

Sirius had agreed to help Lily and James, but before he could become their Secret-Keeper Peter Pettigrew suggested to Sirius that Voldemort would certainly suspect him, as a very talented wizard and friend of the Potter's, of being the Potter's Secret-Keeper, but he would never suspect someone as talentless as himself. Sirius sense of the crafty kicked in and he liked the plan immediately and convinced the Potters to use Peter Pettigrew as their Secret-Keeper but continue to let everyone believe he was actually the Secret-Keeper. Part of what caused Sirius to use this plan was the fact Sirius believed Remus was the spy (and vice versa). Sirius knew Remus would never suspect Peter of being the Potter's Secret-Keeper and he was right. A week after the Fidelius Charm was performed, using Peter, the Potters were dead and everyone, including Remus, thought Sirius had betrayed them to Voldemort.

After the murders, Sirius showed up at the Potter's house and wanted to take Harry into his care, but Hagrid, who was already there and holding Harry, said Dumbledore wanted Harry and Sirius made no further objections. Sirius gave Hagrid his huge flying motorcycle to take Harry to Dumbledore and decided to go after Peter Pettigrew and exact revenge. He found Peter on a busy street packed with Christmas shoppers and attempted to confront him but Peter blew up a huge area of the street, and 12 Muggles with it, and escaped as a rat down the drain leaving Sirius to be jailed for the murders of 13 people (including Peter). Sirius was sent to Azkaban by Barty Sr, without a trial, and for the next 12 years, he lived in a small barred top-security cell with 2 dementors outside his door day and night. Prior to this time his brother Regulus died. His parents were still alive by never visited him. Eventually his father and then his mother died and he inherited all of his parents' wealth, in the absence of any other living relation who knew where the house was and how to get into it without setting off some trap.

Sirius never went insane in prison as others did because he was able to hold on to a single unhappy thought, that he was innocent. As an unhappy thought, it couldn't be sucked out of him. When prison got to be too much he'd turn into a dog. However, because his emotions as a dog were less complex, or dementors can't read animal emotions at all, it was thought by the dementors that he was losing his mind. In the summer of 1993, after seeing a picture of Peter (as Scabbers) in the newspaper and realizing Peter was at Hogwarts with Harry, he became obsessed with escaping, killing Peter and confessing to Harry what had happened to his parents. Sirius knew from being in the OoP that eventually Voldemort would return and when he did, Peter would kill Harry. He slipped past the dementors as a dog, squeezing through the bars because he was skinny, and swam back to the mainland.

At this point, after escaping Azkaban he retained vestiges of his former good looks but his face looked sunken and gaunt and was surrounded by matted, elbow-length, tangled hair. His skin was waxy white and his eyes were sunk in deep in their dark sockets. His skin stretched tight over his bones giving his head a skull like appearance. His teeth were yellow, his hands clawlike, and his voice hoarse from lack of use. In short, he looked a lot like his mom. He was still taller than Severus, in fairly good physical condition and magically still very powerful. He wore his filthy grey prison robes for lack of having any others and an unwillingness to steal any and draw attention to himself one supposes.

In his dog form (aka Snuffles), he traveled to Hogwarts, lived in the Forbidden Forest and repeatedly tried to get into Gryffindor Tower throughout 93/94, without success. He slashed the Fat Lady when he wouldn't let her in. He formed a friendship with Crookshanks and, despite his criminal status, he managed to get a Firebolt for Harry through mail order using Harry's name but his own vault number and Crookshanks as a delivery agent. This begs 2 questions, 1) why didn't he buy himself some new robes and 2) why didn't the goblins report activity on an escaped criminal's account? But there are no answers to either. After having Crookshanks steal the passwords to Gryffindor Tower, he attempted to break into the Tower to kill Peter who hung out in Ron's bed, but Peters as Scabbers had by then vanished, seeking refuge at Hagrid's. Sirius escaped again, and waited another opportunity.

Eventually Sirius exposed Peter to Harry and Remus, cleared his name with Dumbledore and escaped on Buckbeak to freedom in the tropics, possibly Java. He stayed there for several months, corresponding with Harry and Dumbledore, but after hearing Harry had been involuntarily entered into the TT, he returned to Britain. He stayed in a cave in the mountain that overshadows Hogsmeade and continued to watch over Harry. At this point in time, only Remus, Peter, Dumbledore, Harry, Ron and Hermione knew about Sirius being an Animagus. So, passing for a lovable stray, Sirius scrounged around Hogsmeade for food and old discarded *Daily Prophet* newspapers. Eating mostly rats, as he couldn't steal too much food without drawing attention to himself, he had Harry send him food. He went to visit him one Hogsmeade weekend and he was still wearing the ragged grey prison robes he had when he left Azkaban. His black hair was longer, untidy and matted again and he was very thin.

After watching over Harry throughout 94/95, he went home to 12 Grimmauld Place which he had given Dumbledore permission to use as the OoP's Headquarters back in 1993 and where Remus had been living since losing his job at about the same time. Although Remus could come and go and go, Sirius was housebound because he was still a wanted man in the MoM's eyes. This was unfortunate because Sirius was one of the few that believed Voldemort was back (and actually used Voldemort's name). By the summer of 1995, when Harry arrived at Grimmauld Place, Sirius' hair was once again short and clean but his eyes still had a deadened, slightly haunted look. He didn't like being home because it brought back bad memories, especially of his mother whom he loathed. In addition he had Pr Snape, whom he viewed as suspect and probably a traitor, traipsing though on Order business and rubbing Sirius' nose in the fact he was housebound.

As if this was not enough, Sirius also had to deal with Molly who disapproved of his treatment of Harry and Kreacher, his mother's house-elf, who hated him. He told Harry he judged a man by how he treats his inferiors not his equals, but then went right on abusing Kreacher physically and verbally, till Kreacher eventually left and betrayed him into Lucius Malfoy's hands. Ah well, the good advice we give, we rarely take ourselves. Despite, or perhaps because of, his being housebound and having a 10,000G reward on his head, he went to see Harry off on the Hogwarts Express in his dog form. Which brings up an interesting point. Peter, though supposedly a loyal Death Eater, never tells Voldemort about Sirius being an Animagus, which shows some rather latent loyalty toward his old friend. It is Lucius Malfoy who discovers the truth, seeing Snuffles on the platform. He subsequently tells Voldemort and the Death Eaters and Bellatrix in Jun 1996 refers to Sirius as "the Animagus Black."

But I digress. By Dec 1995, Sirius, tired of being stuck in the house, became depressed and started to neglect his appearance. His hair grew long again and began landing in his eyes, he was a bit unshaven and he'd begun drinking and apparently sleeping lot. Things picked up briefly when all the Weasleys, Harry and Hermione stayed over Christmas with him. He got into the swing of things, decorating and singing carols such as *God Rest You, Merrye Hippogriffs*. But it is around this time he accidentally set Kreacher free, who immediately began plotting against him with his youngest cousin Narcissa. A few months later, he was "killed" by his 1st cousin Bellatrix Black Lestrange in the MoM during the Jun 1996. After being hit by a Stunning Spell and falling through the curtain of the arch in the Death Chamber. Dumbledore said he was dead, so we must assume he is.

Sirius had a lot of doglike qualities. He gnawed on bones in a very doglike way, had a short barklike laugh, growled and snarled when angry, tended toward shagginess, was an indiscriminate eater, liked being outside or with people he loved and enjoyed chasing his tail or cats, except Crookshanks to whom he was very devoted. As a human he had a habit of balancing his chair on its back 2 legs. Dumbledore described him as a brave, clever, energetic man. He tried on the whole to be a good godfather, though Molly might have disagreed. He thought of Harry more as a substitute for James than a child he was supposed to look after. He was loyal, proud and protective of Harry, but he could go a bit moody and short-tempered if anyone, especially Harry, tried to curb his risk-taking nature. However, given his long confinement and the many risky adventures he'd had over a lifetime - that had always turned out alright - risk-taking probably seemed more important to him than being further confined to a "safe" life inside the walls of his mother's home.

Miles Bletchley: b 1978. A Slytherin, 1990?-1997? Keeper for the House team since 91/92 season. Given that one must be in one's 2nd year to be on a House team, and he's still playing in the 95/96 season, he must have started Hogwarts either in 89/90 or 88/89. If it was 88/89, he graduated Jun 1996. If it was 89/90, he's got another year to play.

(Unknown) Blotts: Co-owner of a bookstore in Diagon Alley. Gender unknown.

Stubby Boardman: Lead singer of the popular singing group The Hobgoblins, he retired in 1980 after being hit by a turnip during a Church Hall concert in Little Norton. Doris Purkiss claimed he was really Sirius Black in the Sep 1995 edition of *The Quibbler*.

Bob (Unknown): He is a large, bearded wizard that works at the MoM. He is with the DRCMC, in the Ban on Experimental Breeding section. He knows Arthur.

Broderick Bode: b 1947-d Jan 6, 1996 at age 49. He was an Unspeakable with the DoM. A sallow-skinned wizard with a mournful face, unfaltering gaze and sepulchral voice, he ended up in St Mungo's before Christmas 1995 due to Lucius Malfoy trying to make him remove an orb from the Hall of Prophecy while under the Imperius Curse. He ended up in Ward 49, the Janus Thickey Ward, completely insane and thinking he was a teapot. He was visited by a very stooped old wizard with a hearing trumpet and shuffling gate which may have been his father, or possibly a Transfigured Lucius Malfoy checking up on his progress. Broderick was making a slow recovery and was starting to talk, when for Christmas he was sent a flitterbloom, actually a devil's snare, and it strangled him a few weeks later.

(Unknown) Bole: b 1976. A Slytherin, 1988-1995. He started Hogwarts in 87/88. He played Beater, for the House team until graduating in Jun 1995.

Pierre Bonaccord: French. He was the 1st Supreme Mugwump of the ICW in 1692. His appointment was initially contested by the warlocks of Liechtenstein because of intended anti-troll hunting and assorted troll rights legislation.

Madam Amelia Susan Bones: Sister of Edgar Bones and an unknown brother who is Susan's father. Aunt of Susan Bones. Head of the DMLE since c 1983 when Barty Sr got shifted to Head the DIMC. As a judge she is fair, honest and will hear a person out. She has a broad, square jaw, very short grey hair and wears a monocle. She is forbidding looking, has a booming voice and thick eyebrows. She should have privately questioned Harry and decided on the matter of Harry's underage magic charges, without more than a few people knowing about it, but she was clearly persuaded by Fudge to try Harry by a Full Court instead on Aug 12, 1995. She was quite interested in Harry's corporeal Patronus at the trial and later even told Susan about it being a stag.

Edgar Bones: Brother of Amelia Bones and uncle of Susan Bones. He was a great wizard, one of the best of the age, and was in the original OoP 1970-1980. He and his wife and children were killed on Voldemort's orders c 1980 by one of the Death Eaters that later was an Azkaban escapee in Jan 1996.

Susan Bones: b 1980. A Hufflepuff, 1991-1998? She started Hogwarts in 91/92. Her father is the brother of Edgar and Amelia Susan. Susan was named after her aunt. Her aunt is Head of the DMLE and talks to Susan about the various goings on in her department, which is how Susan found out about Harry's corporeal Patronus being a stag. She became a DA member in Oct 1995. Her uncle Edgar and his family were killed by a Death Eater but no one at school knew this till it came out in the paper Jan 1996, when the murderer escaped Azkaban. She achieved a rather gruesome notoriety, similar to Harry's, and was afterward able to sympathize with Harry. In Jun 1996 she came to Harry's aid on the Express when Draco tried to jump him. She wears her hair in a long braid down her back. See schematic S.

Terry Boot: b 1980. A Ravenclaw, 1991-1998? He started Hogwarts in 91/92. He attended the Dueling Club and, in Oct 1995, joined the DA with his friend Michael Corner. He came to Harry's aid on the Express when Draco tried to jump him.

Mr Borgin: Co-owner of Borgin and Burkes in Knockturn Alley, he is a purveyor of Dark Arts goods who buys as well as sells things, not all of which are legal to possess. He is a stooped man with pince-nez glasses and greasy hair that he wears pushed back from his face. His voice is as oily as his hair, but he's only oily to a customer's face. If anyone shows the least interest in something he scurries toward them and becomes fawning and informative. He'd rather sell items than buy them and haggles with the customers trying to sell him things.

Lucius visited him in Aug 1992, to unload some Dark Arts poisons and other illegal items, but Mr Borgin knew he hadn't been sold a half of the Dark Arts stuff that was, at that time, hidden in the Malfoy's manor. He was expected to pick up the goods he'd bought from Lucius at the Malfoy's manor so Lucius wouldn't risk getting caught with them on him. He knows Lucius well, and Draco, probably because Dark Arts retailers all know each other. He privately despises the family though it's not clear why other than Lucius' superiority complex, treacherous nature and general cheapness.

Boris the Bewildered: See Portraits Etc., Statue section.

Bertie Bott: b 1835-? Inventor of Every Flavor Beans, probably in the late 1800s. See Note A on the Comprehensive timeline for why these dates are correct.

Bozo (Unknown): A *Daily Prophet* photographer. He is a short, paunchy, irritable-looking man. He can usually be found dancing around taking photos with a large black camera that emits puffs of purple smoke with every flash used. He worked the Lockhart signing at Flourish and Blotts and with Rita Skeeter on the TT.

(Unknown) Bradley: A Ravenclaw, he played Chaser on the House team in 95/96. It is unknown what year he is.

Eleanor Branstone: b 1983. A Hufflepuff, 1994-2001? She started Hogwarts in 94/95.

ACASCIAS RIPHOUSE

Mandy Brocklehurst: b 1980. A Ravenclaw, 1991-1998? She started Hogwarts in 91/92.

Lavender Brown: b 1980. A Gryffindor, 1991-1998? She started Hogwarts in 91/92. Her best friend is Parvati Patil. Her favorite teacher is Pr Trelawney, whom she treats with great respect, since she predicted the death of her pet rabbit Binky in 1993. She used to spend her lunchtimes with Pr Trelawney and Parvati in the North Tower until Sybill was sacked in Mar 1996. Her least favorite teacher is Hagrid, probably because she got burned by a skrewt. Lavender attended the Yule Ball with Seamus Finnegan in 1994, despite the fact he thinks her best friend is prettier. She initially believed the smear campaign *The Daily Prophet* ran about Harry in the summer of 1995, but was returned to reason by her roommate, Hermione. She joined the DA in Oct 1995.

Millicent Bulstrode: b 1980. A Slytherin, 1991-1998? She started Hogwarts in 91/92. A large, square girl who is a lot bigger than Harry. She has a heavy jaw that juts out, probably due to an overbite, and makes her look aggressive. Harry thinks she's so ugly she could be a hag. She was a member of the 92/93 Dueling Club, during which she found a wand just not personal enough when beating someone up and actually wrestled Hermione into a headlock once. She was a member of the Inquisitorial Squad in 95/96. She has black hair and a black cat with yellow eyes that she brings to school.

K. Bundy: A student at Hogwarts in the 1990s. Fond of Quidditch. Gender, House and year are unknown.

(Unknown) Burkes: Co-owner of a Dark Arts store in Knockturn Alley. Gender unknown.

Sir Cadogan: See Portraits Etc. Portrait section.

S. Capper: A student at Hogwarts in the 1990s. Gender, House and year unknown. Fond of Quidditch.

Eddie Carmichael: b 1979. A Ravenclaw, 1990-1997? He started Hogwarts 90/91. He racked up 9 O level OWLs in 94/95 and peddled in 95/96 mental aids to 5th year students, particular Baruffio's Brain Elixir for 12G a pint. Ron and Harry tried to buy some but Hermione confiscated it all and poured it down a toilet.

Owen Cauldwell: b 1983. A Hufflepuff, 1994-2001? He started Hogwarts in 94/95.

(Unknown) Chambers: A Ravenclaw. She or he is a Chaser on the House team in 95/96. Year, House and gender is unknown.

Cho Chang: b 1979. A Ravenclaw, 1990-1997? She started Hogwarts in 90/91. She is probably of Korean descent, Cho being a Korean name but Chang can be Chinese. She is quite small, about a head shorter than Harry at age 13, and extremely pretty. She usually wears her long, shiny black hair loose, even during Quidditch. She is very popular and almost always surrounded by a group of girlfriends. Beginning in 93/94, she played Seeker on the House team. She supposedly had injuries that prevented her playing prior to 93/94, but she's made every game that Harry's had to play against Ravenclaw so she must have made a full recovery. Although most of her team rides Cleansweep 7 broom, she rides a Comet 260. She is a very good Seeker and a great lover of professional Qudditch. She was at QWC 1994 and has been an avid supporter of the Tutshill Tornados since she was 6.

She was Cedric Diggory's girlfriend for about 6 months in 94/95 and the relationship only ended when Cedric died. She took his death quite hard and tried dating Harry in 95/96 as a way of keeping Cedric's memory alive but it didn't work out. She became a member of the DA in Oct 1995 and was responsible for her friend Marietta Edgecombe joining as well. Her Patronus is a swan. She is still on friendly terms with Harry though she seems to blow hot and cold where he's concerned. This is perhaps because Harry is rather too forceful in pointing up the obvious, Cedric is dead

and Marietta is a rat while Cho prefers to tread lightly over such matters. She started dating Michael Corner in Jun 1996.
Mrs Chang: Cho's mother. Sep 7 is Mrs Chang's birthday.
Circe: See Portraits Etc., Photo section
Madame Elfrida Clagg: aka Elfrida Cragg. See Portraits Etc., Portraits section.
Penelope Clearwater: aka Penny. b 1976. A Ravenclaw, 1987-1994. She started Hogwarts in 87/88. She became a Prefect in 91/92 and in that year stayed for Christmas and began meeting Percy all over the school in secret for romantic assignations. In 92/93 she was Petrified for a short time. She gambles and once bet Percy 10G on a Quidditch match in 93/94, which indicates she's rich as well. She has long curly hair of unknown color. It's unknown if, since she graduated, she is still romantically involved with Percy.
Cliodna the Druidess: See Portraits Etc., Photo section
(Unknown) Connolly: A male, Irish national team Beater in QWC 1994.
Michael Corner: b 1979. A Ravenclaw, 1991-1998? He perhaps started Hogwarts in 90/91. He is dark haired and a friend of Terry Boot. He met Ginny at the Yule Ball and started dating her at the end of the 94/95 year. He joined the DA in Oct 1995. Ginny dumped him in 1996 after he got sulky when his House lost a match to Gryffindor. He started going out with Cho in Jun 1996.
Mr Crabbe: b 1955. A Slytherin, 1967-1974. He started Hogwarts 67/68. See Note 1. A Death Eater. Father of Vincent Crabbe. He showed up in Little Hangleton when Voldemort activated the Dark Mark in Jun 1995. Like his son, he's large and rather slow witted. He was part of the failed raided the MoM during which he got his head stuck into bell jar of time in the DoM and had it regress to the state of a baby's head. He went to prison Jun 1996.
Vincent Crabbe: b 1979. A Slytherin, 1991-1998? He started Hogwarts in 91/92. He is the son of a Death Eater and the henchman of Draco Malfoy. Taller than Gregory Goyle, he is thick set and looks extremely mean. He is a big kid with a punchbowl haircut and a thick neck. He has a big mouth, huge flat feet and big fists at the end of long gorilla arms. He holds his arms stiffly when he walks. He tends to rub or crack his knuckles in a menacing way. He is slow rather on the uptake, but brighter than Goyle by a fraction.

Draco picked him to be his second in the wizard's duel that never happened, in 1991, so he must like Crabbe slightly better than Goyle. It is Crabbe that tries to pick up Draco when he's been turned into a ferret in 1994, not Goyle. And it is Crabbe that supports Draco in his lies about Hagrid by claiming to have been bitten by a flobberworm (it has no teeth) in 1995. He went to the Yule Ball in 1994 stag, wearing green robes that made him look like a moss-colored boulder. He became a Beater for the House team in 95/96 and during his first match hit a Bludger at Harry's back after the whistle had been blown to end the game.
Elfrida Cragg: See Elfrida Clagg.
Colin Creevey: b 1981. A Gryffindor, 1992-1999? Brother of Dennis. He started Hogwarts in 92/93. He is a very small, mousy haired boy with lots of pluck. His entire body is about as thick as Crabbe's neck yet he sticks up for himself and his fellow Gryffindors even against Draco and his henchmen. Like Harry, he'd never seen Quidditch before Hogwarts. Colin is Muggle born, the son of a milkman, and, like Harry, was very surprised to get a letter to Hogwarts. In his first year, he spent a lot of time following Harry about saying hi 6-7 times a day, rather like a very talkative shadow, and photographing everything is sight. He lugged a Muggle camera

everywhere he went so he could make wizarding photos, white-bordered black and whites, to send home to his dad.

He's a true papparazzi, always inappropriately taking photos, but it probably saved his life in the case of the basilisk attack. He was Petrified after Mrs Norris in Nov 1992. He was found on the marble staircase with grapes in hand (for Harry who was in the Hospital) by Pr McGonagall. He was taken to hospital still holding his camera to his eye, having tried to take a photo of the basilisk. His brother was accepted to Hogwarts in 94/95 and they've been the classic double act even since. In 94/95 he and Dennis tried to fix the Potter Stinks badges, in 95/96 they hung out together in Hogsmeade and at school, and in Oct 1995 they joined the DA in Oct 1995, where Colin mastered the Impediment Jinx after only 3 sessions.

Dennis Creevey: b 1983. A Gryffindor, 1994-2001? Brother of Colin. He started Hogwarts in 94/95. He has mousy hair and is very small like his brother. He fell in the lake on his first crossing but the giant squid pulled him out of the water and put him back in his boat. He thought it was an awesome experience. He is very enthusiastic and outgoing like his brother. He also seems to shadow his brother, like Colin did Harry. Shorter even than Colin, he needed to stand on his seat in the Great Hall just to be able to see the Goblet of Fire, making him something like 3' tall or shorter.

The brothers Creevey seem to like each other's company, or perhaps only they can stand long periods of time with each other. During Dennis' 1st year he and Colin spent their time together trying to cook the Potter Stinks badges to say something more flattering, with little success. He somehow got permission to go with 3rd year Colin to Hogsmeade (probably due to hags) despite the fact he was only a 2nd year. He joined the DA in Oct 1995, with Colin. Curious, inventive, outgoing and blessed with boundless enthusiasm and pluck there's a good chance the Creevey boys will go very far in the wizarding world.

(Unknown) Croaker: A Unspeakable in the DoM since before 94/95, he worked with Broderick Bode.

Doris Crockford: An old woman who drinks sherry and smokes a long pipe. She first met Harry at Leaky Cauldron in 1991. She knew who he was and was so excited to see him she repeatedly came up to him just to shake his hand.

Bartemius Crouch Sr: aka Barty. c 1930-1995. A great wizard from one of the oldest pureblood families, he was powerfully magical but sadly power hungry as well and definitely not a good person. Originally the Head of the DMLE before Madam Bones, during Voldemort's initial rise, c 1970-1983, he became obsessed with catching Dark Wizards. He descended to the level of the Death Eaters in his cruel and ruthless methods and this appalled some, but many others supported his "fight fire with fire" policy. He was adamantly against the Dark side, but it was under Barty Sr that the Aurors were given the power to kill, rather than just capture, and many people were sent to Azkaban without a trial, Sirius among them.

He was tipped for the Minister of Magic job after Voldemort vanished but then his son, Barty Jr, was found to be a Death Eater. Anything that tarnished his reputation and jeopardized his chances of being Minister of Magic he got rid of, including his son, and he used his son's trial to publicly disown him, in front of his wife, rather than hear his side of things. After his son went to prison, Barty Sr and his wife made a deathbed visit to their son and sprang him from prison by subsituting Mrs Crouch for Barty Jr. Shortly after this his wife died, in Barty Jr's place at Azkaban, but he never even went back for the body. People turned against him after his son "died" because they reckoned he probably never liked his son and thus drove him to turn to the Dark side.

THE HARRY POTTER COMPANION

Given public sentiment, there was no way he could become Minister of Magic, and his continuing as Head of the DMLE was out of the question. He was given a lateral "promotion" and made Head of the DIMC, c 1984. Barty Sr spoke over 200 languages including Mermish and Gobbledegook and Troll, so it was a logical appointment. Things went well for a time, until Bertha Jorkins, who worked with him in the DIMC, discovered he was secretly keeping Barty Jr at home. Barty Sr put an overly strong Memory Charm on her and, although he damaged Bertha's memory, he felt no pity for her (St Mungo's probably could have helped her get some function back, but he was too scared of what she might remember). He then transferred her out of his department hoping that would be the end of it and for a decade or so it was.

Barty Sr was still heading the DIMC in 1994 when Percy got a job there. At the time Harry met him in Aug 1994, Barty Sr was around 60 with wrinkled skin. He was a stiff upright elderly man with short grey hair (that was originally dark), an exactingly straight part and a toothbrush mustache (think Hitler gone grey). He spoke with a curt voice and was not very good with names. He called Percy "Weatherby." Along with Ludo, the Head of the DMGS, whom he despised and thought of as a Death Eater gone uncaught and unpunished, he helped to organize both QWC 1994 and the TT. In part no doubt because Ludo didn't speak Bulgarian, or even Gobbledegook despite his constant interactions with goblins. Barty Sr's office organized the Portkeys and probably the campsites for QWC 1994.

During QWC 1994, Barty Jr escaped the grasp of Winky, Barty Sr's house-elf. Barty punished Winky by giving her clothes, which fired her, but the greater ill was that he'd finally lost control of his son. Barty Jr managed to escape him completely and ultimately had his revenge when one night, with Voldemort, he called on his father and had him put under the Imperius Curse. Barty Sr attended the selection of the champions for the TT, under Voldemort's Imperius Curse, but no one noticed anything was wrong. Despite the fact he was already displaying signs of being cursed, such as having a skull-like appearance. He looked eerie and ill with circles under his eyes and had a thin papery look to his wrinkled skin. In Nov 1994, he went missing altogether but Percy believed he was ill and just sending in instructions by owl, discounting the fact Barty Sr had never taken a day off work in the past.

After Christmas, other officials at the MoM began to think Barty Sr was missing and that Percy was covering it up because he liked being in charge so much. The MoM started looking for Barty Sr only to find his house deserted. In May 1995, Barty Sr broke free of the Imperius Curse and made his way to Hogwarts to try and confess to Dumbledore what was happening but he was caught by his son on the grounds, taken into the Forbidden Forest and murdered. Barty Jr Transfigured his father's body into a bone and buried in the forest where it was never to be found. He was doubtless replaced at the DIMC but it's unknown who took the job.

Mrs Bartemius Crouch Sr: c 1940-d 1983. She loved Barty Sr and Barty Jr equally and their dislike of each other helped send her to an early grave. She sat next to her husband during the trial of her son but fainted when her husband publicly declared he had no son. She was frail and wispy looking at the trial. She was wasting away (probably of cancer or TB brought on by stress), rather like her son in prison, and decided since she was dying already she had nothing left to lose. She made her husband, who loved her greatly, promise to help her spring her son from Azkaban. They went on deathbed visit to their son about 1 year after he was incarcerated and she exchanged places with him, using Polyjuice Potion. She died in Azkaban for her son and was buried, still in his likeness, outside the prison wall. Her death was then publicly staged by her husband.

288

ACASCIAS RIPHOUSE

Bartemius Crouch Jr: aka Barty Jr. c 1963-Jun 24, 1995. Although Barty Jr is not dead, he is now worse then dead, so a death date is given. When he was young he had straw-color hair and freckled milk white skin. He was average in height, quite thin and rather nervous looking. He was extremely bright and got 12 OWLs. When he was about 19, in 1982, he was caught with a group of Death Eaters who'd managed to avoid Azkaban initially by creative lying to the MoM about being under the Imperius Curse. This group was trying to find Voldemort and return him to power by torturing the Longbottoms into telling them where Voldemort was.

No one knew Barty Jr to be a Death Eater for certain and he seems not to have had the Dark Mark which all Death Eaters have. He claimed to be innocent, just in the wrong place wrong time, but after a trial everyone voted him guilty. (In point of fact he was actually guilty.) He was sent to Azkaban by his father and looked sickly when brought to prison so no one was surprised when he supposedly died a year after he arrived. In reality he was sprung from prison by his mother, using Polyjuice Potion, and his father assisted by putting him under the Imperius Curse and taking him home to live with him. He was nursed back to health by Winky, the house-elf, kept subdued by use of the Imperius Curse by his father and forced to wear an Invisibility Cloak 24/7. He had not been out of the house for years before QWC 1994, which Winky convinced Barty Sr to allow Barty Jr to attend as a reward for good behavior.

At QWC 1994, Barty Jr stole Harry's wand out of his backpocket while in the Top Box, later shot up the Dark Mark, one supposes in hopes of letting Voldemort know he was around or else scaring the Death Eaters who were never caught, then escaped and somehow found Voldemort or was found by him. He became part of a plot to get Harry for Voldemort's rebirthing. He called himself Voldemort's most faithful servant and proved it by kidnapping Alastor Moody, using Polyjuice Potion to become Moody and then taking his place as DADA instructor for the next 10 months at Hogwarts. For 94/95 he was Moody. Probably acting in all respects as Moody would have, which is scary.

Just like a normal teacher, he took role every day and taught DADA, just as Dumbledore instructed him to, despite or perhaps because it was against MoM educational rulings. Barty Jr was an excellent person to be teaching DADA classes on the Unforgivable Curses with which he had such and intimate knowledge of using and defeating and he was well liked and respected by all the students and most teachers, Pr Snape being a notable exception. During his time a Hogwarts he stole boomslang skin from Pr Snape's office for making the Polyjuice Potion and when caught said he was ordered to search it and topped it off by claiming Auror's privilege. It is odd that Dumbledore didn't guess that he wasn't working with the real Moody, having known him at least 3 decades, but Barty Jr was likely a very good Occlumens as well as a good actor.

Barty Jr's only real job at Hogwarts was to get Harry into the TT and to the TT Cup that he'd made into a Portkey, which would take Harry to Voldemort in Little Hangleton where Voldemort could use Harry's blood for rebirthing. He managed to get Harry in the TT and spent the best part of the year coaching Harry through the various TT tasks, surreptitiously. One does also wonder why Barty Jr didn't just hand Harry a Portkey sometime during the year rather than go to such elaborate lengths as entering Harry in the TT. But that aside, Barty Jr's motives for not going to Little Hangleton when the Dark Mark was activated and Harry already gone are even more obscure. Perhaps he was supposed to stay at Hogwarts, undercover.

he was still a Death Eater to the core.

Unfortunately, his plans for Harry went badly astray and, after going to the length of murdering is own father (because he'd suffered indignity at his hands) to hide his identity, he blows his own cover and gives himself away by obsessing about what Voldemort did to the other Death Eaters when he should have been making an escape. But, if there is one thing Barty Jr hates its Death Eaters that walked free, because he didn't, and he wanted gory details. Sadly he doesn't even get that satisfaction. Before Harry say anthing, Barty Jr was captured by Dumbledore, who wanted Barty Jr alive to prove Voldemort was back. But, shortly after his capture, Barty Jr received the Dementor's Kiss, apparently without Fudge's direct order,however Fudge said he didn't believe Barty Jr about Voldemort because anyway because Barty Jr was a raving madman. Swearing: Merlin's beard.

Roger Davies: b 1978. A Ravenclaw, 1989-1996. He was Captain of House team and played Chaser until graduating. He'd been Captain since at least 93/94. One assumes he played on the team well before that. He attended the Yule Ball with Fleur Delacour in Dec 1994. He asked Cho Chang out in early 1996 but she turned him down. He recovered rather quickly and was dating a pretty blonde a couple weeks later and even took her to Madam Puddifoot's on Valentine's Day where he kissed her, in front of Cho and a host of others. He graduated Jun 1996.

(Unknown) Dawlish: An Auror with MoM in 1996, he joined the force before 1992 at least. He is a tough-looking wizard with very short wiry hair. He went to Hogwarts sometime during Dumbledore's administration and refused to cross wands with him when Fudge tried to order him to arrest Dumbledore in 1996.

Caradoc Dearborn: d 1980. He was in the original OoP. He vanished 6 months after the photo Moody showed Harry was taken (sometime before 1981) and his body was never found.

Death Eater (Unknown): Escapee 1: b 1952. A Slytherin, 1963-1970. He started Hogwarts in 63/64. A wizard that escaped from Azkaban Jan 1996. A Death Eater, but his name and crime are unknown. We'll probably hear more about him later since he was one of only 6 Death Eaters not captured at the MoM Jun 1996.

Death Eater (Unknown): Escapee 2: b 1955. A Slytherin, 1967-1974. He started Hogwarts 67/68. See Note 1. A wizard that escaped from Azkaban Jan 1996. A Death Eater, but his name and crime are unknown. We'll probably hear more about him later since he was one of only 6 Death Eaters not captured at the MoM Jun 1996.

Fleur Delacour: b 1976. French. Sister of Gabrielle. A Beauxbatons student. She was the Beauxbatons' champion in the TT. She is part veela, her grandmother was one, which makes her a part-human creature. She has a long sheet of silvery blonde hair that is almost waist-length, large deep-blue eyes and very white, even teeth. She speaks with a heavy French accent, is always shaking her hair and generally sweeps rather than walks. She usually looks haughty and unruffled and most boys have an inexplicable attraction to her.

She did well in Task 1, though she got her skirts burned. She wore silver-grey satin robes to the Yule Ball in Dec 1994, which she attended with Roger Davies. She completely failed Task 2 after she was attacked by grindylows and Harry had to rescue Gabrielle. This act endeared Harry and Ron to Fleur and after Task 2 they became friends. Her mother and little sister came to the TT Task 3. Either she has no father or he couldn't attend. It was just before Task 3 that she met Bill Weasley and developed an instant infatuation for him. After surviving the TT and graduating Beauxbatons, she got a job at Gringotts' London branch to improve her English. As of summer 1995 Bill returned to the London branch and she started dating Bill, who also was giving her English lessons. She doesn't seem in any way involved in the OoP.

Gabrielle Delacour: b 1986. French. Younger sister of Fleur. She has the same silvery hair that Fleur has, probably as a result of being part veela. She served at Fleur's hostage in TT Task 2, but was ultimately rescued by Harry after her sister had to abandon the task. She was no more than 8 at the time.

Mrs Delacour: French. She came over from France to see Fleur compete in TT Task 3. It's not to clear if Fleur's dad was busy working or no longer alive. It is unknown if Mrs Delacour is the half-veela or her husband. One would assume it is only women than can be veela and that veela only produce more veela, making Mrs Delacour the half-veela.

Derek (Unknown): A Hogwarts student. He stayed over the Christmas break in 1993, but it's not clear what year or house he is in. In 1993 he isn't a 1st or 5th year, a Slytherin or a Gryffindor.

(Unknown) Derrick: b 1977. A Slytherin, 1988-1995. He started Hogwarts in 88/89. He was a Beater on the House team till he graduated in 94/95.

(Unknown) Dervish: Co-owner of a magical instrument shop in Hogsmeade. Gender unknown.

Dilys Derwent: See Portraits Etc., Portrait section.

Dedalus Diggle: A tiny old wizard with a wide smile and a squeaky voice. He usually wears a violet top hat and violet cloak and tends to be excitable. Pr McGonagall says he's never had much sense but he seems decent enough. He once bowed to Harry while he was out shopping with aunt and cousin, before Harry knew he was a wizard. He lives in Kent and is presumed to have set off shooting stars there the day after Voldemort disappeared in 1981. Dedalus bumped into, and hugged, Vernon around the middle then spoke to him as he was walking out the frontdoor of Grunnings to go home Nov 1, 1981.

He met Harry formally at the Leaky Cauldron in Jul 1991 and was delighted that Harry remembered him from various passings by. He seems to be have been a part of the ongoing task force of OoP members that secretly, casually checked up on Harry till 1995. He always seemed to see Harry when Petunia took him out of the Little Whinging area and stayed close by till he was spotted or they returned home. He was part of the original OoP and lived to be a still active member. He was part of Harry's escort to Headquarters in 1995. Given the death rate for early Order members, he must be a pretty impressive wizard.

Amos Diggory: Father of Cedric. There is a Mrs Diggory as well. He works in the DRCMC. He found Winky with Harry's wand at QWC 1994 and immediately overreacted. His reactions are more knee-jerk than rational but he's a good guy. He warned Arthur to get over to Moody's to keep Moody from prison. The Diggorys live in the Ottery St Catchpole area. He has a scrubby brown beard and is not very aware of the Muggle world. He says Please-men = Policemen. He was a bit of a braggart about his son, before he was killed. He was devastated by Cedric's death in the TT in 1995.

Cedric Diggory: aka Ced, Pretty-Boy Diggory. b 1978-d Jun 1995. A Hufflepuff, 1989-1995. He started Hogwarts in 89/90. He was doted on by his father, Amos, a friend of Arthur's from the MoM where they both work, and his family also lives in the Ottery St Catchpole area. He became Captain and Seeker of the House team in 93/94. He was much bigger than the average Seeker, but an excellent one nonetheless. He was tall, extremely handsome and thought of as the strong silent type. He had a straight nose, dark hair and grey eyes. A really nice person, he was also an excellent hardworking student, a good and loyal friend and valued fair play. He was made a Prefect in 93/94. He entered the TT in Oct 1993 and was selected to represent Hogwarts. He cooperated with Harry throughout the TT and at the end of Task 3 agreed to a joint victory with him. He was subsequently murdered at the graveyard in Little Hangleton by Peter Pettigrew, with the Avada Kedavra Curse, on Voldemort's orders. Harry was able to bring his body back to his parents.

Mrs Diggory: Wife of Amos. Mother of Cedric. She came to Hogwarts to collect her son's body in 1995 and thanked Harry for bringing back his body. She told Harry he could keep the TT prize money and seemed to be better able to handle Ced's death than her husband on the whole.

(Unknown) Dimitrov: A Bulgarian Chaser in QWC 1994. Presumably male, from the -ov ending.

Harold Dingle: House and year unknown, but probably an older Gryffindor. He is a student in 95/96. He seems to be the chief black market connection at Hogwarts, peddling powdered dragon claw and firewhisky among other things.

Armando Dippet: See Portraits Etc., Portrait section.

Emma Dobbs: b 1982. House unknown, 1994-2001? She started Hogwarts in 94/95.

Elphias Doge: An original and still active member of the OoP. He is a wheezy-voiced, silver-haired wizard that was part of Harry's escort to Headquarters in 1995. He used to wear a stupid hat in 1970s (it was the 1970s, who didn't?).

Antonin Dolohov: b 1953. A Slytherin 1964-1971. He started Hogwarts in 64/65. See Note 1. A Death Eater of the worst strip, he tortured Muggles and anti-Voldemort wizards just for fun. He was caught shortly after Karkoff. Karkoff didn't know this and attempted to rat him out, so he was doubly damned. He has a long pale twisted face. Antonin was Escapee 8 in the Jan 1996 Azkaban breakout. He was in for the murders of Gideon and Fabian Prewett. He was part of failed raid on MoM. He is back at Azkaban as of Jun 1996.

J. Dorny: A Quidditch-loving student at Hogwarts in the 1990s. House, gender and year unknown.

(Unknown) Drooble: Inventor of a special blowing gum. Gender unknown.

Aberforth Dumbledore: Brother of Albus. It unknown if he's the older or younger brother, but one presumes the younger. It is likely he was born c 1917. A strange man according to Moody, who is very strange himself, so Aberforth must be spectacularly odd. He was prosecuted for practicing inappropriate charms on a goat years ago and the story ran in all the papers, according to Albus. Given the British wizards only seem to have 1 paper, he was either in Muggle or international wizarding papers as well, meaning his crime was spectacular in nature.

Despite the press, Aberforth didn't go into hiding and apparenty carried on as if nothing had happened, head held high. Albus is not entirely sure Aberforth can read so this can't be considered bravery although he must be fairly brave since he was an original OoP member and probably a current one as well. Possibly Aberforth is the barman at the Hog's Head, which smells of goat, and whose barman vaguely reminds Harry of Albus. Given that someone caught Voldemort's spy and chucked him out after hearing only half the prophecy Sybill gave Dumbledore in 1979, it would have to be someone that owned the bar and was loyal to Dumbledore. Only Aberforth seems to fit the bill.

Albus Percival Wulfric Brian Dumbledore: Brother of Aberforth. See schematics S and Zc. It unknown if he's the older or younger brother, but one would think older since when Albus formed the OoP, Aberforth joined and a younger brother following the lead of an older brother is more common than the reverse. Born circa 1915, see Comprehensive Timeline for why, he may be Muggle born, given his love for Muggles, but one suspects he is from a wizarding family for 2 reasons. One, Lucius Malfoy hates Albus for loving Muggles and not being a Muggle born. Since being a nonpureblood is the greater evil in Lucius' eyes, Lucius would surely have harped on that point more than any other, but he doesn't. Two, Albus states he tried a Bertie Bott Every Flavor Bean in his youth, which he wouldn't have done if he were raised in a Muggle family.

He attended Hogwarts and started in 26/27. A Gryffindor, 1926-1933, it is unclear if he ever played Quidditch, was made a Prefect or became Head Boy. As student he was known for his style rather than his brains but that is not to imply he was stupid. He was very magically gifted and Madam Marchbanks, who conducted his OWLs and NEWTs, said he did things with a wand that no one had ever seen before. He was then, and is still, well-known for his wand "twiddling" and his unusual wand movements. By the time Albus graduated, It seems certain he was in the top of his class, especially in Transfiguration, and his love for Muggle sweets was well established. He probably was also a Puddlemere United supporter, a chamber music lover and a tenpin bowling player by then as well.

We can't be sure what Albus did after graduating Hogwarts, but given the advanced nature of his abilities, he probably pursued studies on his own or under the tutelage of a mentor since wizarding universities don't seem to exist. After a number of years, maybe as much as a decade, he was hired to teach at Hogwarts. By the 42/43 school year, we find him teaching Transfiguration and he seems to have been there some length of time. He distrusted Tom Riddle and when Hagrid was expelled, he went to Headmaster Armando Dippet and got Hagrid placed as trainee Gamekeeper. From that point on he watched Tom Riddle very closely, probably having realized he was the Heir of Slytherin as well as a 2-faced liar and a bad seed.

Albus left Hogwarts after the 44/45 school year ended, and Tom Riddle graduated, and seems to have kept tabs on Tom even as he went on with his own life. Later in 1945 he defeated the Dark wizard Grindelwald, which from the name, could possibly have been a Swiss wizard helping Hitler stay in power. He most likely got the scar above his left knee in dueling with Grindelwald and his Order of Merlin, 1st class for defeating this Dark wizard. After 1945, he seems to have given in to his love of tinkering, invention and gadgetry, and spent the next years, in collaboration with Devonshire lad Nicolas Flamel in the study of alchemy.

Alchemy is not an easy subject, and he likely spent the next 20 years (1946-1965) engaged in this difficult and fascinating work. It is probably during this period that he discovered the 12 uses for dragon's blood. One assumes Albus lived off his savings from teaching, an inheritance and the revenue off several patents relating to his inventing. As his fame increased during this 20-year period that he became involved in politics, probably out of a hope to effect change in the wizarding world. Ultimately he ended up Grand Sorcerer (probably of the legislative body of the MoM), Chief Warlock of the Wizengamot and Supreme Mugwump of the ICW, not to mention got his picture on Chocolate Frogs trading cards. Eventually he was offered the post of Headmaster of Hogwarts when Armando Dippet retired (or died).

From things that Lupin has said, Dumbledore became Headmaster of Hogwarts c 1965 and immediately began to reform the school's policies. He permitted werewolves to study at Hogwarts, which had been banned prior to Albus' rule, he hired Hagrid to Gamekeeper *and* Keeper of Keys when Mr Ogg retired, and developed the OoP in 1970 to fight Voldemort. As Head he tried to cultivate unity among all wizards (not just purebloods) and train his students to defend themselves against the Dark Arts. He recruited several former students into the OoP, including Lily, James, Sirius, Remus and Lupin in 1973. He fought an uphill battle with little hope in sight until, in Dec

1979, he met Sybill Trelawney at the Three Broomsticks and heard her give a prophecy about the birth of a child that could defeat Voldemort.

Albus learned from Sybill that at the end of Jul 1980, this child would be to parents who had 3 times escaped or defeated Voldemort. Since few couples met these criteria, by Jan or Feb, he would have learned that Alice Longbottom and Lily Potter were pregnant and expecting to deliver at the end of Jul, thus offering two candidates for the prophecy to rest on. When Harry was born in 1980, Dumbledore and the Potters put him down for Hogwarts immediately. Also during 1980 Severus Snape decided to switch loyalties and become a double agent for Albus and it was through Severus that Albus learned someone close to the Potters was passing information about them to Voldemort since around Oct 1980. Albus volunteered to be the Potter's Secret-Keeper so they could go into hiding, but they rejected his offer and said they would use Sirius, not telling anyone, even Albus, that at the last minute they used Peter Pettigrew instead or Sirius.

After James and Lily died a week later, in Oct 1981, he knew by the scar on Harry's forehead that Harry was the person that Sybill had prophesied about and that he would only be able to live under an enduring blood-bought protection as long as Petunia, Lily's last blood relative, cared for him. So, Albus took Harry from Sirius, his rightful guardian, and left him with Petunia to seal the charm Lily created by dying for Harry. Part of why he took Harry from Sirius was because he believed Sirius to be a Death Eater, something he continued to believe until 1993. Albus knew that Harry would suffer at the Dursleys, but he also knew he would be safe. He set Mrs Figg and other members of the OoP to watch over Harry as he grew up, and went back to his work at Hogwarts.

Shortly after this, Albus vouched for Severus' change of loyalties to the MoM and hired him on as Potions Master at Hogwarts to provide him a safe haven. For the next 10 years, Albus remained at Hogwarts. In 1990 there was an attempt to make him Minister of Magic, and thus head of the MoM when Millicent Bagnold retired, but he refused the honor. He knew from Sybill's prophecy that Voldemort wasn't finished yet and wanted the next generation of wizards ready to fight him whenever he eventually resurfaced. Albus also kept his job as Head to protect Hogwarts itself, which for some unknown reason Voldemort desires to have as his own. Eventually Harry showed up at Hogwarts in 1991, somewhat the worse for wear having lived with the Dursleys, but in no way magically diminished.

When Harry started Hogwarts, Albus knew that someday Harry would have to destroy Voldemort, if and when he showed up, or be destroyed by him, so he did everything he could to prepare Harry to fight Voldemort - without telling him. This secrecy had many repercussions, most of which were truly heinous. Albus came to really love Harry and care that he might be killed, not for the world's sake, but for his own, thus impairing his own judgement. The downside for Harry in not immediately being told his fate is that he spent the first 5 years at school never knowing what was actually going and thus constantly throwing himself into dangers that might well have been avoided. These dangers grew steadily worse until the last person in the world Harry would see dead, Sirius, was murdered before his eyes directly because Albus refused to tell Harry what was going on and why.

In 91/92, because Albus kept Harry in the dark, Harry needlessly confronted Voldemort without knowing who he was or how to fight him. In 92/93, because Albus didn't tell Harry the history of Voldemort, Harry didn't realize who Tom Riddle is or what his motives might be and again was almost killed. In 93/94, because Albus never told Harry his family's history, Harry doesn't realize who Sirius Black is or what a danger he might be (back when people thought him dangerous). In 94/95, Albus never tells Harry his brain might be connected to Voldemort's, and takes no precautions to prevent it, so that by 95/96 its too late to protect Harry and Sirius dies needlessly. Albus told Harry in Jun 1995, that everything he's done has been to try and spare Harry additional grief and difficulty because he loves him, but clearly love like Albus' is about nearly as dangerous to Harry as Voldemort's hatred.

But I digress. In 91/92, Albus does what he can to protect Harry, without telling him why, and eventually it is Albus that saves Harry and the stone from Voldemort in the underground chamber. In 92/93, Albus is sacked after the Heir of Slytherin goes on a rampage, but gets his job back and Lucius Malfoy sacked, thanks to Harry defeating the basilisk and uncovering Lucius' plot. In 93/94, Albus learns the truth of Peter, Remus and Sirius and Sirius loans Albus the house at Grimmauld Place to use as the Headquarters of the OoP and lets his old friend Remus live there. In 94/95, the disastrous TT happens. Albus tells the world Voldemort is back and reactivates the Order. He sends Hagrid and Olympia to ask help of the giants Abroad, without success. In 95/96 Albus gets slandered by the MoM and eventually loses his job, but is saved by Voldemort's appearance in the MoM, proving he has been right all along in saying Voldemort is in Britain, alive and corporeal. For now, the MoM and Albus are on the same side.

Albus started life auburn haired but is now completely silver haired. His hair and beard are very shiny and waistlength. He tends to throw his beard over his shoulder when he eats to keep it out of the way. He has a thick silver mustache and eyebrows, his nose is long and crooked, as though broken at least a couple times (possibly from Quidditch), and he wears gold half-moon glasses that sit halfway down his nose. He has bright sparkly twinkling light-blue eyes and a searching look from them is like being x-rayed. His face has lines and wrinkles, but it is a strong ancient face that no one thinks of as old. When he gets in a cold fury, which is rare, he is positively scary even to those who know him well. He has a deep voice, which can be quite chilling when sent in a Howler. He habitually puts his long fingertips together and looks over them when he's thinking. He has a scar above his left knee hat's a perfect map of the London Underground. He is tall (6'5"-6'7"), thin and very old. When he's tired, he looks old, but usually he is filled with such great energy that he seems young.

Albus is quite fond of purple things and whenever he magicks something up from thin air, it tends to be purple. He has a purple floorlength cape, deep purple robes scattered with silvery stars and a matching hat, and a magnificently embroidered purple and gold dressing gown he wears over a snowy white nightshirt. At night he might be seen wandering around in a long woolly dressing gown and nightcap. He has a few sets of long robes: green, deep green with stars and moons embroidered on them and midnight blue. He likes the traditional 17th-century wizard look: high-heeled, buckled boots, cloak and a pointy hat. He always wears a hat, probably matching. Other clothing quirks include: wearing earmuffs when it's cold and wishing people would give him thick woolly socks for Christmas rather than more books.

Albus seems to really like pork (chipolatas are pork) and given a choice, he'll choose pork chops as he did at the Yule Ball in 1994. He has a thing for sweets and for dessert likes custard tarts. He prefers Muggle sweets to wizard-made ones because in his youth he once had one of Bertie Bott's Every Flavor Beans that was vomit flavored. Lemon drops are a Muggle candy favorite, though Peppermint Humbugs are a close second. He always uses a candy as the password to his quarters in Godric's old tower. He loves hot chocolate and always finds that a large steaming hot chocolate cheers him up. He can usually be found coming downstairs in the middle of the night for one.

People think Albus is a bit crazy, even if they like him. He's a good person, a genius and the best wizard in the world today, however, he is undeniably quirky. He cries when the school song is sung. He doesn't lie, but he sometimes refuses to answer or answers in a misleading fashion. He loves jokes, has a great sense of humor, which tends to be very dry humor at times, and most often pokes fun at people with excessive niceness. He reads Muggle newspapers and likes Muggle borns. He likes animals, wants equality for all magical creatures, part-humans and the like, and feels that wizards have for too long dominated and oppressed others. He is totally anti-dementor and doesn't think anyone should be thrown to the dementors, let alone Kissed by them. He never felt the MoM should be aligned with dementors, didn't trust them to stay loyal with Voldemort offering them greater opportunity and in the end he was right on both counts.

Albus has collected all sorts of wacky gadgets and instruments, speaks Mermish, and loves pulling crackers and wearing silly hats at Christmas Feast. He doesn't mind sitting on the floor or a bit of furniture like a desk but he doesn't use a broomstick, and will use thestrals for long journeys when he doesn't want to Apparate. He stands up when a lady enters the room, blushes when complimented by women and has managed to tame a phoenix, Fawkes. He has narrow, loopy, rather messy writing, corresponds with anyone that writes him and he is always willing to help out by sharing his expertise and wisdom. He is in short, the last of a dying breed, a true gentleman.

Albus almost always has a very good relationship with his teachers, barring those forced on him by the MoM. He's hired some teachers himself (Trelawney, Snape, Hagrid) and some he's inherited (Binns, McGonagall and others) but they all seem to love and respect him even if they aren't members of the OoP. He calls all the teachers by their first names and while all the teachers call each other by their first name when in private, only Pr McGonagall seems to call Albus by his first name. As a Head Albus is surprisingly humble and will even admit when he is wrong, with grace, before his students. Although when students do wrong, such as fly a Ford Anglia to school, he will write their parents. He is in charge of hiring teachers and annually writes the advertisement for a new DADA teacher.

He has powers that are very great but he is too noble to use them in evil manners. He can become invisible without a cloak. He can see through Invisibility Cloaks. He Apparates and Disapparates in total silence. He can draw a chair with his wand and it will appear, usually a squashy chintz armchair which he prefers. He reputedly knows more or less everything that goes on at the school and even when he's not there, he senses when there is trouble and he needs to be there, and usually shows up just in time. Granted he didn't know 3 students became Animagi and ran around monthly with a werewolf but that's fairly minor. Some might say, he didn't notice Pr Quirrell had Voldemort in his head or that Barty Jr was passing for Moody, but this is unfair.

Although Albus is a sufficient Legilimens, Voldemort is a master Legilimens and Occlumens. Doubtless Voldemort was able to block Albus' ability to discern the truth from Pr Quirrell. Barty Jr, a very powerful Dark wizard, was also able to block the fact he was passing for Moody. In the case of Pr Lockhart, Albus said he was impaled upon his own sword after he had the Memory Charm backfire on him. This implies that Albus knew all along that Lockhart was a fraud, and how he went about perpetrating that fraud - Memory Charms. The fact no one else would teach DADA in 92/93 is the reason he was hired. Dumbledore gave him a chance to change, that he didn't take it wasn't of great concern. Dumbledore is always willing to give people a 2nd chance: Pr Snape, Lupin, Moody, Hagrid, Dobby and Winky to name but a few. By and large, people make the most of the chance Albus gives them. The few who don't, do so to their own detriment.

Albus doesn't however give everyone a second chance. Or even a first chance. He kept watch on Tom Riddle as a student before he opened the Chamber of Secrets. When Tom left school, Albus left and watched him. After Voldemort had become a vapor, still Albus watched him through an international, spy network he set up and kept continually running via the many foreign wizards that are in the OoP. Yes, Albus had good reason to watch Tom, later Voldemort, but one wonders if all that watching didn't provoke Tom into the man/thing he's become. Does it really help an abused and abandoned orphan to be put under surveillance by his teachers? No, it just makes him or her paranoid, which is exactly what happened to Tom. Albus pushes Tom's buttons and vice versa. Even today Voldemort is paranoid about Albus. Admittedly Albus' power is great and he is considered the finest wizard of his age, but Voldemort survived death itself. Why should he fear Albus? Paranoia.

Albus is out to get Tom and always has been from what Albus himself says. So why should Voldemort want to take Hogwarts, Albus' school? Probably to get the thing he loves (Hogwarts had treated Tom well), away from the person he hates (Albus). Albus for his part hardly makes the situation any less volatile. Albus calls Voldemort by name (or Tom), keeps telling others to do the same, which further irritates Voldemort and heads and is the Secret-Keeper for an international, covert, organization trying to capture Tom. To top it off, Albus would like to capture Voldemort alive *only* because he thinks that will be safer for Harry. It isn't clear, after all, what would happen to Harry if Voldemort were to be killed. Albus is a good person, but like Harry, he often creates a really bad situation by acting unnecessarily on limited information.

B. Dunstan: A Quidditch-loving student at Hogwarts in the 1990s. House, gender and year unknown.

Madam Edgecombe: She works in the DMT's Floo Network office. She helped police the Hogwarts' fires under Pr Umbridge's regime in 95/96. Marietta is her daughter.

Marietta Edgecombe: b 1978. A Ravenclaw, 1990-1997? She started Hogwarts in 90/91. Daughter of Madam Edgecombe. She has curly reddish-blonde hair and is a good friend of Cho Chang. She joined the DA because Cho wanted her to. Eventually she tried to rat out the DA and ended up with SNEAK across her nose and cheeks in purple pustules of an enduring variety. She was given a Memory Charm by Kingsley Shacklebolt to keep her from ratting out the DA completely. She now doesn't recall any of the meetings but as of Jun 1996 she still had the pustules.

Elfric the Eager: Apparently a little too eager for change, he headed an uprising.

Emric the Evil: He got a mention in 1st year History of Magic, but no details are available. Clearly, he was evil.

Everard (Unknown): See Portraits Etc., Portrait section.

(Unknown) Eeylops: Owner of an owl emporium in Diagon Alley, where Hedwig came from. Gender unknown.

The Fat Lady: See Portraits Etc., Portrait section.

S. Fawcett: A Ravenclaw, years unknown. Her family is from Ottery St Catchpole. She was a member of the Dueling club in 92/93. She and her close friend Mr Stebbins tried to cross the Age Line to enter their names in the Goblet of Fire in Oct 1994 and ended up with beards. She attended the Yule Ball in Dec 1994 and was caught with Mr Stebbins in the bushes by Pr Snape. She is quite an incorrigible.

Mr and Mrs Fawcett: Miss Fawcett's parents. A family that live near Ottery St Catchpole.

The Harry Potter Companion

Benjy Fenwick: d circa 1981. Original OoP member. He was killed and only bits of him were found.

Female Headmaster (Unknown): See Portraits Etc., Portrait section.

Mrs Arabella Doreen Figg: A neighbor of the Dursleys. Her Muggle husband is apparently dead and has been so since prior to 1981. She keeps Harry anytime Petunia goes out. Harry usually stays with her every year when it's Dudley's birthday and the Dursleys go out as they don't trust him in the house. It is said she took care of Harry when the Dursleys went on vacation, implying as a child he spent extended time at her house.

Harry originally thinks of her as the mad old woman 2 streets away on Wisteria Walk who can often be seen walking up and down the street going to buy canned cat food at the corner shop. Harry initially hates Mrs Figg and her house because, although she lets him watch TV and gives him stale chocolate cake, the whole place smells of cabbage and he was always made to look at photos of all the cats she's ever owned, including now dead ones. Her collection of cats include: Tibbles (aka Mr Tibbles), Snowy, Mr. Paws and Tufty. Her home has mismatched chairs with crocheted covers and the strong smell of cats.

In reality, Arabella is a Squib, a member of the original OoP, and has been watching Harry for years for Dumbledore. She purposely made visits to her house a bit hellish so he wouldn't tell the Dursleys he was enjoying himself and thus be banned from coming to see her. But her work has not been easy. She broke her leg tripping over a cat in Jun 1991 (she is now less fond of cats) and couldn't take Harry on Dudley's 11th birthday. Later, in Jul, while still on crutches, she was knocked over by Dudley on his racing bike. In the summer of 1995, she began inviting Harry to tea every time she saw him while Harry tried to avoid her because he though she was weird. Admittedly, she talks to herself, wears her grizzled grey hair in a hairnet and walks around in public in tartan carpet slippers. But she's as normal as Harry.

Other members of the Order stayed at her house on a rotating shift basis during this summer to watch over Harry. On the night of the dementor attack, Dung was supposed to be standing guard during the evening but had left his post. After the dementor attack happened, and Harry saved himself and Dudley, Arabella had to blow her cover and take Harry and Dudley home. When Dung returned, long after he could be of use, he was beaten on the head with a string shopping bag full of catfood cans. In Aug 1995 she testified that dementors had been in Little Whinging. Possibly she couldn't see dementors and lied for Harry at his trial but she did certainly feel their presence. Swearing: Good Lord.

Argus Filch: Hogwarts' Caretaker. He's a Squib and embittered toward students that can do magic he can't. He was taking the Kwikspell Course in 92/93 to improve his abilities, but embarrassed about it and considering he's been at it a few years, it doesn't seem to be helping him much. He is considered by students to be more of an irritation than Peeves and they all hate him. Usually he wears a brown coat and possibly a thick tartan scarf, but on special occasions, like Christmas Feast, he wears a very old and rather moldy looking tailcoat. At night he wears an old flannel dressing gown.

He calls Hagrid an oaf and has Mrs Norris follow him whenever he comes to the castle. Harry and Ron have been on his bad side since their first morning, because Filch found them trying to force the door to the out of bounds corridor on the 3rd floor and wouldn't believe they were just lost. The only thing Filch cares about is Mrs Norris. When Mrs Norris was Petrified, he cried dry, racking sobs and took to skulking around the corridors red-eyed, giving out detentions for breathing loudly or looking happy. He even set up a chair to sit and guard the scene of the crime and in off hours waited for the criminal to return. Luckily she was restored to health by Mandrake Restorative Potion.

Argus is a bit of a sadist and thinks it's a pity that the old punishments died out. He would like to hang students by their ankles from the ceiling for a few days and has got dungeon chains in his office behind the desk. He keeps them well oiled in case they are every needed. He threatens and lectures students, and curses when enraged. He tends to leer nastily at people and thinks hard work and pain are the best teachers. He is always begging Dumbledore to allow him to whip students and owns a horsewhip just in case. He liked Pr Umbridge, because she gave him permission to torture students (Approval for Whipping) and was willing to get rid of Peeves for good. He was sad to see her go and Albus return.

He wages a one man war against the use of magic in the corridors between classes. He has an extended list of objects forbidden in the castle which ran to 437 items in 94/95 and was available for consultation in his office. Another aspect of his job is to check out students as they go to Hogsmeade to make sure no one leaves without permission. He stands inside the frontdoors of the Entrance Hall and checks off names against a long list as they leave the castle. Other duties include cleaning everything in the castle, including scrubbing the pictures and oiling and polishing the armor, and one assumes changing candles, repairing damage to the castle itself, broken windows and the like, and vermin control.

He has bulging, pale, lamplike eyes (as does his cat Mrs Norris). His voice is soft and greasy. He has a pouchy face, sunken veined pouchy cheeks and a tic in one cheek. His jowls quiver when he gets upset and his eyes pop alarmingly. His nose is bulbous, his hair thin grey, and his hands are knobbly. He has rheumatism in his back that doesn't allow him to bow too low and is so out of shape that he wheezes when he runs. He hobbles around generally, but when he runs it's flat footed with Mrs Norris racing alongside. He has an excellent knowledge of the school's secret passageways, short cuts and hiding places. He knows the school better than anyone (except the Weasley twins), and can pop up as suddenly as any ghost out of the darkness. He knows about 4 of the 7 passageways out of Hogwarts, but not the ones to the Shrieking Shack, Honeydukes', or the caved in one.

Kudos though for the most creative swearing, including: dung, great sizzling dragon bogies, frog brains, rat intestines.

Justin Finch-Fletchley: b 1979. A Hufflepuff, 1991-1998? A curly haired Muggle-born boy who was down for Eton originally. His mother was slightly disappointed by his chosing to go to Hogwarts, but changed her mind after reading Lockhart's books. His mother is now glad he chose Hogwarts. He started Hogwarts in 91/92 and quickly became friends with Ernie and Hannah. He is cheerful, outgoing and good mannered. He likes Harry, Ron and Hermione. Justin was a member of the Dueling Club in 92/93 and was unfortunately the target of the snake Draco released. He was Petrified, with Nearly Headless Nick, in Dec 1992 and joined the DA in Oct 1995.

Mrs Finnigan: Mum of Seamus. A witch who kept her wizarding skills from husband till after they were married, giving her spouse a unpleasant shock. She is sandy haired and an avid supporter of her national Quidditch team. She attended QWC 1994 with her son and had a shamrock-covered tent. Her Muggle husband didn't attend with her, which makes one wonder if he refuses to participate in her magical activities.

Seamus Finnigan: Irish. b 1979. A Gryffindor, 1991-1998? He started Hogwarts in 91/92. It took the Sorting Hat almost a minute to figure out where to put him. Possibly because he is such a hard worker Hufflepuff was considered. He is a half-wizard and half-Muggle. He's a sandy haired boy and a good friend of Dean Thomas and Neville.

He's also a roommate of Harry and Ron. He wears button up pajamas and keeps a poster of the Kenmare Kestrels by his bed. He supports the Kenmare Kestrels and possibly he plays the harp as Kestrel supporters are known for this. He claims to have spent his childhood zooming around on a broomstick in the Irish countryside but has yet to apply to the House team. He plays wizard's chess and owns a rather willful set that he loaned Harry once in 1991.

In 92/93 DADA he faced his worst fear, a banshee. He almost cracked under the strain of classwork during the Easter holidays in 93/94. He attended QWC 1994 with his mother and Dean Thomas and later pinned an Ireland rosette to his headboard when he returned to school for 94/95. The rosette's magic started to wear off after a couple month so it shouted only some of the players names in a feeble and exhausted way, but this was surely a relief to his roommates. His mother didn't want him to return to school in 95/96 because she believed *The Daily Prophet* reports about Harry being insane and glory-seeking and Dumbledore being senile. He fought with Harry over the issue for several month time but eventually they reconciled. He was very briefly a member of the DA in 1996.

Nicolas Flamel: b 1327-d 1992. Husband of Perenelle. He died at age 665. An alchemist, opera lover and the only known maker of a Sorcerer's Stone, he enjoyed leading a quiet life in Devon with his wife. He allowed Dumbledore to partner with him in his alchemy experiments when Dumbledore was younger and they became good friends as a result. When the stone was destroyed, he no longer had Elixir of Life which had sustained he and his wife and died. For them death was like going to bed after an extremely long day, according to Dumbledore. They didn't fear death but thought of it as the next great adventure.

Perenelle Flamel: b 1334-d 1992. She died at age 658. Wife of Nicolas Flamel. She lived in Devon, surviving off the Elixir of Life from the Sorcerer's Stone. Probably the world's longest surviving marriage, God bless her!

Mundungus Fletcher: aka Dung. He joined the original OoP and is very loyal to Dumbledore who once helped him out of a tight spot. What that tight spot was is unknown, but probably has something to do with Aberforth, goats and the Hog's Head. An old dealer in questionable things to wizards and Muggles alike, he is useful to the Order because he operates in a world where information about illegal activities is more prevalent and thus he hears things more upright citizens never would. He knows all the crooks, because he's a thief himself.

He was banned from the Hog's Head by the barman in 1975, probably for theft. He tried to hex Arthur Weasley when his back was turned during a MoM raid in Aug 1992. He put in a spurious claim for a ruined 12-bedroom tent with en suite jacuzzi after the Death Eater incident at QWC 1994 when he found out people were getting compensation from MoM for losses caused by lax security at the QWC 1994 (Dung however was sleeping under a cloak propped up on sticks). He was supposed to be keeping an eye on Harry, while staying at Mrs Figgs' home, on a shift basis, in the summer of 1995, but instead went off to see about some stolen cauldrons. Harry got attacked and had to defend himself for which Dung was of course quite sorry but the cauldrons were a deal he just couldn't pass up and apparently couldn't wait.

The strong smell of drink and stale tobacco lingers about him. He is squat, unshaven and wears a long tattered overcoat. He has short bandy legs, long straggley ginger hair and bloodshot baggy eyes that give him a basset hound look. He has grubby hands, his hair is long, matted and hangs over his eyes, and when he lays down he looks like a pile of rags that has a grunting snore. He smokes a grimy black pipe that makes greenish smoke so thick it obscures him in seconds. Probably a good smokescreen for when one of his operations goes bad. The smoke is quite smelly too, an acrid smell like burning socks. He drinks wine, to excess.

When he's stolen things, he tends to hide them in his overcoat which becomes oddly lumpy in unlikely places. He got Fred and George some illegal Venomous Tentacula seeds so he's obviously a fairly good sneak thief. He has the mind of a thief and is always looking at things and wondering about their value - like Sirius' silver goblets. He and Sirius tended to get along well and Sirius even let him stash some stolen goods at his house once, but Molly doesn't approve of him at all. Arthur doesn't seem to mind him probably because the members of the OoP are few in number at best. Dung seems more information than action as far as the OoP goes, but that's probably best. He is loyal enough, but more than slightly unreliable. Swearing: blimey.

Marcus Flint: b 1975. A Slytherin, 1986-1994. He started Hogwarts in 86/87. He was Captain and Chaser for the House team which is very unusual for someone that is big or male. He never played fairly. He's very brutal, very big (larger than Wood) and rather stupid looking, which is accurate enough because he failed to graduate on time. He had to repeat his final year, graduating in 93/94.

Pr (Unknown) Flitwick: Teacher of Charms. Head of Ravenclaw. He was a dueling champion when he was young probably in the 1920s. He was the Charms teacher when James and Severus were in school doing OWLs. He is a old man, praobably 70ish, with a shock of white hair and so tiny he has to stand on a pile of books to see over his desk. He sits at the High Table on a stack of cushions and when sitting in a chair at the Three Broomsticks, his feet dangle a foot from the ground. His voice is more of a squeak and he squeals when horrified. He embarrasses easily and buries his head in his hands when he's embarrassed. He starts each class by taking role. He gave such an excited squeak at Harry's name the 1st day that he toppled out of sight.

In 91/92 he made Trevor fly around the room as a demo. In 92/93 Ron's wand hit him between the eyes creating a large throbbing green boil but he wasn't a bit upset. In 93/94 he taught the frontdoors to recognize Sirius Black. He usually decorates his classroom for Christmas, with fairies, and gives up trying to teach class the last week before Christmas vacation, which is nice. He just lets students play games instead. His favorite drink is cherry syrup and soda with ice and an umbrella. He is also fond of Ice Mice, telling jokes and a good bit of magic. He left a bit of Fred and George's Portable Swamp, because it was such good magic (and possibly as a memorial to them). He is a really kind easy-going teacher. He doesn't seem to be involved in the Order.

Florence (Unknown): In Hogwarts around the time Bertha Jorkins was at Hogwarts. She was seen (by Bertha) kissing a boy behind the greenhouses. Bertha later mentioned this to the boy and got well and truly hexed for it.

Mr (Unknown) Flourish: Flourish and Blotts, Manager and co-owner. He was bitten 5 times in 1 day by *The Monster Book of Monsters*, despite the fact he wore very thick gloves and used a large walking stick to extract books from the cage they were in. He understandably refused to stock the *Monster Book* again. It was the store's worst disaster since 200 copies of the very expensive *Invisible Book of Invisibility* went missing. He keeps a small corner at the back of the shop devoted to fortune-telling, but he warns customers off the book with the Grim on it.

Florean Fortescue: He is the owner of Florean Fortescue's Ice Cream Parlor, a Diagon Alley ice cream shop with outdoor seating. Florean knows a great deal about Medieval witch burnings and helped Harry with his homework one summer, as well as giving him free ice cream sundaes every half hour. Probably a relation to the portrait of the same last name.

(Unknown) Fortescue: See Portraits Etc., Portraits section.

Vicky Frobisher: A Gryffindor. In 95/96 she is a 2nd year or above, but her exact year is unknown. She is involved in many school societies and tried out for Keeper but fell out of consideration after she said she'd blow off training if it clashed with her Charms Club meetings.

Cornelius Oswald Fudge: Fudge started with the MoM probably in the 1960s and by 1981 he was Junior Minister of the DMAC. In this capacity, he was the first to arrive on the scene of Sirius Black's capture and being of sensitive nature, still dreams about the crime scene. He and his wife used to go to concerts with Mr and Mrs Barty Crouch Sr and Barty Jr, so apparently he likes music and sucking up to political heavyweights. Eventually the sucking up paid off and he ended up Minister of Magic in 1991. In the beginning, he daily asked Dumbledore for advice about running the MoM, which Dumbledore didn't mind because Fudge was a bungler but he had a good heart and tried hard. Unfortunately, Cornelius grew increasingly ambitious and paranoid about his position over the years.

At last began to feel threatened by Dumbledore's magical power and popularity and was easily swayed by special interest groups, like Lucius Malfoy and his money. In 92/93 he bowed to pressure from Lucius and removed Hagrid to Azkaban for 2 months without proof Hagrid committed a crime. In 93/94, he was convinced that Voldemort was alive, but wasn't worried about it because he presumed Voldemort was alone, friendless and noncorporeal. But in 94/95, when he replaced Barty Sr (and Percy) as the 5th panel judge for TT Task 3 and discovered Voldemort was alive, after Harry came back from dueling with Voldemort, he refused to believe Voldemort was alive, corporeal and in Britain with Death Eaters.

Blinded by love of his office, he insisted Barty Jr wasn't acting on Voldemort's orders but was just an isolated madman. He knew that if were Voldemort truly alive and back to finish his work it would more likely make Dumbledore and Harry heroes than himself. He subsequently forced *The Daily Prophet* not to mention Cedric's death in the TT and tried to take over public opinion via the paper. In Jun 1995 he began a smear campaign to discredit both Harry and Dumbledore and even tried to have them both of them chucked out of Hogwarts. He hired Percy as his personal assistant to unwittingly spy on the Weasleys and Dumbledore but the plan backfired and Percy broke with his family to side with the MoM.

Unfortunately for the wizarding populace, Fudge is not just vain and stupid, he's prejudiced as well. During his administration, he's puts emphasis on the pureblood philosophy and bills that are prejudiced against giants, half-humans of any kind, and nonpurebloods exponentially proliferate and pass with his approval. Part-human creatures, especially werewolves, suffer terribly under his bigoted administration. This was not wholly unexpected as he had chosen an even bigger bigot than himself, Dolores Umbridge, to be Senior Undersecretary to the Minister and reinforce his own narrow bigoted views.

In 95/96 he became so paranoid he tried to take over Hogwarts because he thought Dumbledore was out to overthrow him and make himself Minister of Magic. He kept students from learning any defensive or offensive magic in DADA classes for fear of Dumbledore's forming a private army. Obstinate, blustering, pompous and angry, it is only in Jun 1996, when Voldemort breaks into the MoM's offices with 12 Death Eaters, Fudge's personal friend Lucius Malfoy among them, and seriously trashes the place in front of host of witnesses, including himself and other MoM employees, that Fudge admits he was wrong about everything and agrees to work with Dumbledore.

Fudge is a plump-faced, portly little man with generally rumpled grey hair. He wears a pinstriped suit, scarlet tie, long black cloak and pointed purple boots. He has a lime green bowler hat he seems very fond of. He also has a long pinstriped cloak with silver fastenings that he wears with a bottle-green suit. He drinks Red Currant Rum, owns a gold pocketwatch and rocks back and forth on his feet like a house-elf when upset. He's a pajamas and slippers man at night and seems to always have an Auror or 2 guarding him. Swearing: My God!

Mrs Fudge: She apparently likes going to hear live music. She and her husband went with Mr and Mrs Crouch Sr and their son to a concert once when Barty Jr was a teen. But she doesn't like sports and wasn't allocated a seat up in the Top Box when Fudge was conducting QWC 1994.

(Unknown) Gambol: Co-owner of a joke shop in Diagon Alley. Gender unknown.

Anthony Goldstein: b 1980. A Ravenclaw, 1991-1998? He started Hogwarts in 91/92. He became a Prefect in 95/96 and a member of the DA in Oct 1995.

Miranda Goshawk: b 1921. Author of *The Standard Book of Spells (Grade 1),The Standard Book of Spells (Grade 2) The Standard Book of Spells (Grade 3), The Standard Book of Spells (Grade 4), The Standard Book of Spells (Grade 5) The Standard Book of Spells (Grade 6) The Standard Book of Spells (Grade 7)*. The Hogwarts' textbooks for Charms class.

Gregory Goyle: b 1979. A Slytherin, 1991-1998? He started Hogwarts in 91/92. He became a Beater on the House team in 95/96. A henchman of Draco, he is tall, thick-set, and looks extremely mean. Almost as stupid as he is mean, he still always manages to pass his exams. Like his co-goon Crabbe, he has the ability to crack his knuckles in a menacing fashion and is greedy for food to the point of stuffing down 4 helpings of trifle and a chocolate cupcake in one meal. He was attacked by Scabbers for trying to take a Chocolate Frog from Ron in 1991.

He attended the 1994 Yule Ball stag, wearing green robes that made him look like a moss-colored boulder. He usually has a bewildered look when asked questions by teachers because he's a bit slow on the uptake. In 95/96 he tried to steal the leprechaun gold, not realizing it was fake. Goyle hates writing because he's not very good at it and doing lines is the worst punishment in his book. Though not as well liked as Crabbe by Draco, Draco did pick Goyle to be the one to help pretend to be a dementor. Draco stood on Goyle's shoulders. This implies Goyle is probably a bit taller than Crabbe.

Goyle is a big person with wide shoulders, a broad back and a chest like a barrel, and a thick neck. Harry turned into Goyle for an hour on Christmas 1992 after drinking Polyjuice Potion, and nearly ripped all his clothes. Goyle has small, dull, deep set eyes, a low grunt of a voice, and thick wrists. He is a foot taller than Harry. He has short stiff bristly hair that hangs down to his eyebrows. He has big feet, long gorilla like arms, knuckles like bolts and thick fingers with broad nails. He seems to exist solely to do Draco's bidding. His father is a Death Eater.

Mr Goyle: b 1956. His first year at Hogwarts is 67/68. He is Gregory Goyle's dad. See Note 1. He showed up in Little Hangleton when Voldemort activated the Dark Mark. He is very large, like his son. He was not a part of the MoM raid in Jun 1996 and is one of 6 Death Eaters not in jail.

Hermione Granger: aka Little Miss Perfect; Miss Prissy, Hermy, Little Miss Question-All and Herm-own-ninny. She is Muggle born, the daughter of 2 dentists, and arguably the cleverest witch of her age. Born in Sep 1980, she was let into Hogwarts a year early because of her smarts. She was surprised and pleased to get letter from Hogwarts and started studies in 91/92. A Gryffindor, 1991-1998? - though the Sorting Hat did think about putting her in Ravenclaw at first. She is particularly interested in Transfiguration and good at at anything book-learned but a bit leery of subjects one can't learn from a book, like flying.

The Harry Potter Companion

Her first few months at Hogwarts were difficult as she was very concerned about rules being kept and losing House points. Being killed, to her, was not as bad as being expelled. This attitude helped her get along with Percy Weasley but won her few real friends. She tried to make the acquaintance of Ron and Harry, but was rebuffed by Ron, who pointed up she had no friends because she was so interfering (in the best interest of the persons involved, of course). She became friends with Harry and Ron when, against her nature, she lied to Pr McGonagall about the mountain troll attack, Halloween 1991. She relaxed about rule breaking, realized she's too smart to be thrown out after getting 112% on her 1st year Charms final, and became a much nicer person.

She is tops in everything but DADA and good at everything but wizard's chess. She loves books, will buy or borrow extra ones for light reading and can usually be found in the Library. She's very good at Transfiguration, can do advanced charms and even whip up Polyjuice Potion in a bathroom stall. She thrives on complex work which she does well because she's careful, thinks things through and does everything step by step. She is the voice of reason and logic, and this is usually a help to Harry and Ron who seem to lack these qualities. Conjuring up portable waterproof fires is her specialty and she can even produce a bright bluebell-color fire which can be carried around in jam jars without smothering from lack of air.

She helps Harry and Ron with homework by reading it over and correcting it, but doesn't let them cheat by copying off her own homework. She draws up study schedules and color codes her notes and nags Ron and Harry to do same 10 weeks out from exams but will do it for them if they ignore her. She is a bit high strung when it comes to finals and usually chides herself for not starting to prepare 14 weeks out from exams. By exam time she always starts driving Harry and Ron nuts though they try to ignore her. She tends to talk fast and snap at people when she's under stress. When hurt, she retreats to the Library, Hagrid's or the girls' bathroom. She has very neat writing and a bossy sort of voice.

She is always the first to raise a hand and answer questions in class and usually sounds like she swallowed a textbook. She repeatedly reads and brings to school with her other things *Hogwarts, A History*, which she uses to answer almost every question anyone has about Hogwarts. She is an overachiever and will write 2 whole rolls of parchment more than asked for on homework assignments, which is rather hard on teachers who have 1,000 other students. She is a know-it-all, but hates when that is pointed up to her, especially by Pr Snape, during a class. When given the opportunity to take electives in her 3rd year, 93/94, she took 5 rather than the usual 2. After that proved too much, she dropped only 2, and continued to take 3.

Though she is very booksmart, she is very brave as well and tends to keep her head in really bad situations. This allows her makes connections others don't. For instance, only she saw the trapdoor Fluffy was guarding, rather than panicked. Over the course of only 2 years, 91/92-92/93, of knowing Ron and Harry, she became so good at the arts of flattery, trickery and out right lying, she suggested the use of Polyjuice Potion to interrogate Draco, tricked Pr Lockhart, whom she idolized, into give her a note for use of Restricted Section book *Moste Potente Potions*, stole the required ingredients from Pr Snape's office and even put Sleeping Draught in 2 plump chocolate cupcakes for Goyle and Crabbe. By the end of 92/93, she ripped a page from an old library book!

She is definitely the smartest one of the trio. She was the only one to figure out it was a basilisk in the pipes in 92/93, realize Pr Lupin was a werewolf in 93/94, discover Rita Skeeter was an Animagus in 94/95, and understand that Voldemort was playing on Harry's need to save people to get him to the MoM in 95/96. Also the most progressive and political of the trio, she became acquainted with house-elves in 1992, realized that

Hogwarts had them in Sep 1994 and, not being one to see injustice and pass over it, she immediately established SPEW, with herself as president, to change the way house-elves are treated. In 1995 she learned to knit and started trying to leave hats and socks around that house-elves might accidentally pick up during their nightly cleaning of Gryffindor Tower and be, she presumes, accidentally set free. Which is kind if not a bit, well, stupid.

Unfortunately, Hermione doesn't really seem to have done her research on house-elves, because it is only when the master of the house (in Hogwarts' case this would be Dumbledore) personally gives them a piece of clothing by hand, that the elf is free. If this were not the case, how could house-elves possibly do a family's laundry without being set free? Clearly as house-elves prefer their presence to be unknown, factual information about them might be difficult to acquire. She really needs to have a sit down with Dobby. But at least she genuinely cares about the plight of the house-elves which is more than many other wizards can say.

In Aug 1993, as a birthday present from her parents, Hermione, on her way to buy an owl to take to school as a pet, ended up buying a cat instead, the fluffy ginger cushion known as Crookshanks. In Dec of that year, she ratted out Harry and his Firebolt, rightly thinking the broom he come from Sirius but wrongly thinking it was booby-trapped, causing a temporary rift in the trio. In 1994, she went with Viktor Krum to the Yule Ball, though she admitted she didn't find him good looking, and fought with Ron about it afterwards. In this year she also able to force Rita Skeeter to keep her quill to herself for a whole year, or be ratted out as an Animagus. She probably went to visit Viktor in Bulgaria in the summer of 1995 but it can't be serious if at the end of Jul 1995 she was back in Britain hanging out with Ron.

She and Ron were made Prefects in 95/96. She is always bickering with Ron but well aware that he really likes her. She continued to keep in touch with Viktor via letters throughout 95/96 and Ron continued to be quite jealous of her relationship with Viktor, but Hermione stood on tiptoe to kiss Ron's cheek (he is quite a bit taller than she) just before his first match as Keeper, proving a bit of her affection for him at last. During this year Hermione suggested Harry organize the DA to fight against Pr Umbridge, created the jinxed parchment all the DA members signed which later led to Marietta's unfortunate pustules and discovered her Patronus is a rather cute, playful otter.

Hermione usually spends her Christmas and Easter vacations with Ron and Harry and summers with her parents. On Hogsmeade weekends the 3 of them usually go into town together, and eventually end up at the Three Broomsticks where she drinks something that has a paper umbrella and a cherry in it. No visit would be complete without a trip to the stationary store, and she usually picks up some quills at Schrivenshaft's before heading back. In thinking about her future, Hermione has said she would like to do something worthwhile with her life like advance SPEW to the next level, but she was part of the group of DA members who exposed Voldemort and the Death Eaters at the MoM in Jun 1996 and it remains to be seen if she, or anyone, will out last being on Voldemort's naughty rather than nice list.

Hermione has long bushy brown hair, brown eyes and tans well. After her vacation in France, she had very brown skin. When she's determined to do something she gets a very formidable steely glint in her eye rather like Pr McGonagall. Until Nov 1994 she had braces, but after being hit by Draco's buckteeth curse, she ended up in the Hospital wing and Madame Pomfrey shrank her front teeth to a better than normal state and straighten the rest so she didn't need braces anymore. She has no problem walking around in her black robes and wearing just a watch, but she is very attractive when dressed up. She wore robes of a floaty periwinkle blue material, with her hair slicked back in a French twist type knot at the back of her head to the Yule Ball. People didn't recognize her she looked so different, but she thinks it's too much work to slick up her hair and dress up every day. She wears a pink bathrobe at night.

(Unknown) Gregorovitch: A wandmaker probably located in Russia or Bulgaria. Mr Ollivander knows his work. He is know for his unusual wand styling.

Gregory the Smarmy: See Portraits Etc., Statue section.

Daphne Greengrass: b 1980. Unknown House, 1991-1998? She started Hogwarts in 91/92.

Grindelwald: A Dark wizard defeated in 1945 by Dumbledore. From the name, he could possibly be a Swiss wizard, who was probably helping Hitler stay in power. Grindelwald is the name of a town and a valley in the Bern Canton of Switzerland.

Pr Wilhelmina Grubbly-Plank: She is a substitute teacher that takes over for Hagrid in the Care of Magical Creatures class when he's absent. She is brisk, likes punctuality and smokes a pipe. She has a brisk voice, a prominent chin and a rather severe haircut. Her hair is grey. Like Madam Hooch, she's a bit manly in her mannerisms, but there are no conclusions that can be drawn from this. She is very good at treating animals and treated Hedwig when her wing was injured. She took 1st years across the Lake in 95/96, as Hagrid was away till later in the year. She teaches age-appropriate lessons that most students seem to really appreciate.

Alberic Grunnion: See Portraits Etc., Photo section.

Godric Gryffindor: c 900. A founder of Hogwarts school. Said to be bold and from wild moor. From all indications he was a Welshman who remained a bachelor all his life, which was not uncommon (monks, Knights Templar, monarchs) for those dedicated to a worthy cause which marriage might jeopardize. He took only the bravest, most chivalrous students because he was looking for knightly virtues, implying he was one himself. It was Godric that fell out with Salazar instigating and wholly causing the breakup of the founders. Godric's original office is now the Head's office, where Dumbledore lives and works. Godric's hat became the Sorting Hat (it was his idea to create it) and his sword still sits on a shelf in his old office. It was his sword that defeated Salazar's basilisk, so even in death, these 2 keep feuding. He might have had a thing for Rowena Ravenclaw, given he chose the ruby for his stone and she a sapphire, but it appears to have been a courtly love situation. One presumes that Godric was the DADA teacher in his time.

Davy Gudgeon: A boy attending Hogwarts at the time when Lupin was there, the late 1960s or early 1970s. He used to play a then-popular game of trying to get near enough the Whomping Willow to touch the trunk. He almost lost an eye.

Gladys Gudgeon: A huge fan of Pr Lockhart. She requested a signed picture in 1992 and has been writing to Pr Lockhart weekly since he was put in St Mungo's.

Mr Hagrid: Rubeus Hagrid's dad. He has the same crinkled black eyes as Hagrid. A very tiny little wizard who married the giantess Fridwulfa. The marriage lasted about 5 years (1927-1932), which was long-term commitment for a giantess. Fridwulfa left him, breaking his heart, and he never remarried but he was happy being a dedicated dad. Hagrid, at age 6, used to put him up on his shoulder or the dresser when he was angry with him and it made his dad laugh so he was probably a very kind person with a good sense of humor. He died during Hagrid's 2nd year 41/42 at Hogwarts, thankfully before Hagrid was expelled.

Rubeus Hagrid: aka Hagrid. b 1929. Gryffindor, 1940-1943. Rubeus is Latin for ruby, the stone of of choice at Gryffindor. He is a part-human. His father was a wizard and his mother, Fridwulfa, a giantess. His mother abandoned the family when he was 3 years old. He had a half-brother by his mother, a full giant named Grawp, but he did not know of him or meet him until the summer of 1995. Hagrid attended Hogwarts from 40/41 to 42/43. In his school days, he was in trouble every week, but he was wrongly expelled in his 3rd year, on Jun 13, 1943, for supposedly opening the Chamber of Secrets and allowing its monster (supposedly his pet spider Aragog) to kill a Muggle-born student (Moaning Myrtle).

His wand was snapped in half and he was forbidden to used magic from that point on. However he kept the pieces of the wand and does do small amounts of relatively innocuous magic with them from time to time. Dumbledore went to bat for Hagrid with then Headmaster Armando Dippet and Hagrid, at age 13, was allowed to remain as the trainee Gamekeeper under Mr Ogg. Eventually he took over as Gamekeeper and Keeper of Keys (it is unknown what he holds the keys to exactly) sometime later. Hagrid has since become a beloved fixture to most students and a memorable part of their Hogwarts' experience.

He joined the original OoP in 1970 and continues to be an active member. Dumbledore trusts Hagrid wholeheartedly and put him in charge of collecting Harry from Godric's Hollow to Little Whinging in 1981. He borrowed Sirius Black's flying motorcycle for the job, and probably still has it. He howled when Harry had to be given over to the Dursleys. He had no contact with Harry again till he was sent all the way to Hut-on-the-Rock, The Sea to make sure Harry had received his Hogwarts' acceptance letter in Jul 1991. It was through Hagrid that Harry had his first knowledge of his parents, their true cause of death and the wizarding world.

Hagrid is very good-hearted and did his best to welcome Harry to Hogwarts. He befriended Harry, Ron and Hermione and has since dragged them into many misadventures. In the first year, his monster fixation, particularly for dragons, cropped up. He hatched a dragon in his home, which bit Ron and got Harry and Hermione detentions. In 92/93 he ended up in Azkaban for 2 months, as a suspect for opening the Chamber of Secrets, again, and sent Harry and Ron into Aragog's hollow where they almost got eaten. In 93/94 Hagrid became a teacher at Hogwarts, as well as Gamekeeper and Keeper of Keys. His subject is Care of Magical Creatures, an elective course. Hermione and Harry had to save Buckbeak from execution in 93/94, narrowly avoiding being kissed by dementors. (Oddly, he is allowed to teach even though he isn't a fully qualified teacher and never finished his 3rd year in school.) He continues to get in trouble for using dangerous but interesting creatures, which almost always injure students, and occasionally illegally bred creatures for the next 2 years.

In 94/95 Hagrid created blast-ended skrewts, illegally and met and fell in love with another half-giant, Olympia Maxime, the Head of Beauxbatons. In the summer of 1995 Dumbledore sent them as his emissaries to the giants Abroad. It is during this trip he discovered Grawp, his half-brother. He brought him back to Britain, against his will, to save him from other giants who beat up on him, and in direct violation of MoM law. He then asked Harry and Hermione to go deep into the Forbidden Forest and talk to Grawp now and then, at which point Hermione nearly had a breakdown. Surprisingly, keeping an illegal giant was not what almost got him arrested in 95/96. Instead, he was the victim of Pr Umbridge's gross bigotry against half-giants.

Although Hagrid told Harry there is nothing he wouldn't put up with to keep his family together, one does wonder if the fact that Grawp is a fairly ugly, dangerous and violent creature, adds any additional reasons for which Hagrid wanting to keep him. The centaurs certainly don't want the giant in their forest and have already attacked Grawp once, to no avail. It remains to be seen if there will be a happy ending for

THE HARRY POTTER COMPANION

Grawp and Hagrid. See Other Magical Beings, Giants, in Part V for information on Fridwulfa and Grawp.

Hagrid and Magic: Considering Hagrid is teaching, one would think he'd be at least allowed A) to get himself a new wand, and B) to take classes and finish school (since he was wrongly terminated from his studies in 1943). But neither seems to have happened and lets face it, Hagrid in a Potions class? Pr Snape would either die or voluntarily rejoin Voldemort for real. Oddly too, Lucius Malfoy has never complained that an unqualified teacher is teaching his son. No one seems to care Hagrid has less than a secondary school education in any and all magical subjects, not just the one he is teaching.

After his wand was snapped, Hagrid hid the pieces in the shaft of a pink, flowery umbrella with a spearlike point which he keeps it in his coat when he travels or leaned up against the side of his cabin when he's home. It tends to exude flashes of light and make a sound like a firecracker exploding when used because it is a broken wand. Strictly speaking he's not allowed to do any magic unless given permission by Dumbledore. Though this is a bit odd as he is an overage out-of-school wizard and they can do anything they want.

Hagrid used his wand legally to get to Hut-on-the-Rock to give Harry his letter, and to put a protective charm on his hen house. He used it illegally to make a fire to cook with, motor the rowboat back to shore, give Dudley a pig's tail (though he did intend him to become a pig) and put an Engorgement Charm on his Halloween pumpkins. His wand came from Ollivanders. It's 16", oak and rather bendy (which is a good trick with oak). The core substance is unknown but one would tend to guess dragon heartstring and it is difficult to see Hagrid using anything that doesn't have a monster involved.

Hagrid Swearing: Ruddy hell, Gawd.

Hagrid's looks: Hagrid is twice as big as normal man (11'+), and five times as wide (5'+). He takes up 2 seats on a Muggle train. He is fierce and wild looking with a big head of long shaggy black hair. His tangled bushy hair is like wire and if he tries to comb it there will usually be broken comb teeth left in his hair. His beard is large, bushy and tangled. His bristly black hair hides his mouth so well that one can only tell he's smiling when his beard twitches. His eyes are like glinting black beetles under bushy eyebrows. He has huge feet and hands and very muscular arms.

He wears a black moleskin overcoat, a black moleskin coat with numerous big pockets in which he keeps a wide variety of things, a black moleskin vest and leather boots. When cold and wet, he wears rabbit fur gloves and beaverskin boots. He carries a large, sometimes very dirty, spotted handkerchief. He has a thick black traveling cloak and a haversack big enough to stick a child in which he uses when he travels. In winter one might find him wearing a woolly balaclava. For special occasions he has a gigantic hairy brown suit with a horrible yellow and orange checked tie and uses some kind of axle grease to slick down his hair into two bunchy ponytails. On one fancy occasion he wore a flower like an oversized artichoke in his boutonniere and a particularly awful eau de cologne.

Things one might find in Hagrid's inner and outer pockets: a large sticky homemade chocolate cake with Happy Birthday Harry in green icing on it, a copper kettle, a squashy package of a dozen sausages, a poker, a teapot, chipped mugs, a bottle of amber liquid (possibly beer), a live slightly ruffled owl, a bit of parchment and a long quill, a couple of doormice, some moldy dog biscuits, bunches of keys, slug pellets, balls of string, peppermint humbugs, teabags, strange-looking coins (wizard money), knitting needles and yellow yarn.

Hagrid the Man: Surprisingly, no one knew Hagrid was a half-giant till Jan 1995 when a disturbing article by Rita Skeeter ran in *The Daily Prophet*. People merely thought he'd had an Engorgement Charm or Skele-Grow accident. Apparently wizards will think of any magical excuse, rather than go for the most likely nonmagical answer. As a part-giant, besides being large, he ages very slowly, is so tough that spells don't effect him and is so incredibly strong he can easily bend metal with his bare hands. He doesn't seem to know his own strength and a pat from him can send one over the table or down on one's knees. When he blows his nose it sounds like a foghorn, 4 pints of mulled mead is a average-size drink and Harry must take 3 steps for every one of Hagrid's.

Hagrid is a simple honest rustic woodsman, with manners to match. He speaks with a powerful cockney accent, can't spell Voldemort, or anything else for that matter, and his writing is very untidy, scrawling scribble but he's the bravest person Harry knows. He is decent, kindly and loves Harry. While Harry was in the hospital, he sent to all Lily and James Potter's old school friends asking for wizard photos of them which he put together in a handsome leather-covered book and gave to Harry so he could see his mother and father smiling and waving at him and be comforted. He swore he'd never drink again after he accidentally precipitated Harry's first encounter with Voldemort, but of course he did. As Pr McGonagall observes, his heart is in the right place but he can be careless.

He would do anything for Dumbledore and will not hear anything bad said of him and Dumbledore in turn would trust Hagrid with his life. He says a scar is what one gets when a powerful evil curse touches one, which might say something about Dumbledore's left knee scar. He calls the Malfoys rotten to the core, folks with bad blood, and they don't like much like him either. Lucius and Draco are forever trying to get rid of him. He likes Harry and Ron and frequently has Harry, Ron and Hermione over for tea in the afternoons or during holiday vacations. He refuses to join SPEW on grounds the house-elves are happy and Hermione just doesn't understand them. He can obviously see the thestrals since he's trained a herd of them, but whose death he has seen is unknown.

Hagrid is easy to get information out of, especially through trickery or flattery, and so trusting and easy going that he is easily manipulated. He plays cards for money or objects in the Hog's Head, Hogmeade's seedy village pub, and sometimes gets in trouble because he drinks too much and then talks about things he shouldn't. He is on a first name basis with the bartender at the Leaky Cauldron and doesn't even have to say what he wants because Tom remembers Hagrid's usual drink (though anyone who drinks 4 pints of anything in one clip is bound to be remembered by a bartender). He is a poor cook but doesn't know it because as a half-giant he is strong enough to eat the fudge and other things he makes badly without problems. He is fond of large chocolate and raspberry ice creams topped with chopped nuts, hamburgers and baking tea treats. He likes to knit, darns his own socks and is fond of the color yellow.

In the winter one might see Hagrid defrosting broomsticks before the Quidditch match, bringing in the Christmas fir trees or turning red from drinking lots of wine at the Christmas Feast. In the spring one might see him outside his house with binoculars watching the Quidditch matches or maybe in the stands with Gryffindor friends. In the summer one might see him sitting in an armchair outside his house, trousers and sleeves rolled up, shelling peas into a large bowl. In fall one might find him hunting pheasant, stoat or boar in the Forbidden Forest with his boarhound Fang. Nothing if the forest ever hurts Hagrid, an even Aragog remains his friend.

Hagrid has lived all his life in the wizarding world. He thinks being made to live as a Muggle is the worst possible punishment, and this is after having been to Azkaban for 2 months. He doesn't know how to use Muggle money or other common Muggle things. He is a subscription reader of *The Daily Prophet,* gets cartsick at Gringotts and is allergic to cats (which is why he bought Harry an owl). He uses the word dead a lot, as in dead useful, one of his favorite phrases. Hagrid is the the one who first took Harry to Diagon Alley, though Harry had to help him with the trains, tickets, turnstiles and the like, gave Harry his first ticket for the Hogwarts Express and was the first person ever to give him a birthday present and cake or an invite to tea.

Warty Harris: A purveyor of toads that Dung has dealing with occasionally.

Hengist of Woodcroft: See Portraits Etc., Photo section

Terence Higgs: A Slytherin. He was the House Seeker 91/92. It's not clear what year he started. Draco was made Seeker in 92/93 because of brooms Lucius Malfoy gave the team to let Draco play. There is no indication Higgs graduated and it would be a typically Slytherin thing to stab someone, in this case Higgs, in the back for personal gain.

Hog's Head, Barman: He is a tall thin man that was rather grumpy looking when Harry met him. He is fairly old and has a great deal of long grey hair and a beard. He looked vaguely familiar to Harry. Possibly he is Dumbledore's brother Aberforth. If not they seem to share a love a goats at any rate.

Hogwarts Express, Conductor: A man on the Hogwarts Express that takes people's tickets and announces when the train is coming to a specific stop. He walks through the train calling out the passing town names and time till arrival, like the old-fashioned conductors used to do.

Hogwarts Express, Lunch Lady: A smiling dimpled witch of undetermined age. She sells students food, candy and drinks from a trolley.

Hogwarts Express, Ticket Inspector: At Platform 9 3/4, he sells people tickets on the day everyone is leaving, and on the day they come back he signals them when it's appropriate to walk through the ticket barrier into the Muggle side of King's Cross Station.

Mr Honeydukes: A bald wizard with an enormous backside. Co-owner of Honeydukes in Hogsmeade.

Mrs Honeydukes: A witch who handles sales at the candy shop. Co-owner of Honeydukes in Hogsmeade.

Madam Hooch: Teacher of Flying and Quidditch at Hogwarts. She learned to fly on the now discontinued Silver Arrows, but given that a broom will fly for 50 years or more and most of the Hogwarts' brooms are old, it would be inappropriate to assume she's as old as a Silver Arrow. Passionate about Quidditch and racing brooms, she and Pr Flitwick stripped down Harry's Firebolt in 93/94. She's tough and kind of a jock but she truly cares about her students. She has short grey hair and yellow eyes like a hawk. She has a silver whistle, barks commands and referees almost all of the Quidditch matches.

Geoffrey Hooper: A Gryffindor. He was at least a 2nd year in 95/96 but it's unknown exactly what year he started Hogwarts. He tried out for Keeper but was reject because Angelina thought he was a real whiner.

Mafalda Hopkirk: She works at the Improper Use of Magic Office, MoM. It must be an office that's open 24/7 because she sent Harry a warning Jul 31, 1992 and another Aug 3, 1995 both at very late hours, between 9 and 10pm. Given she sent Harry the letter saying he had to attend a disciplinary hearing, one presumes she's the Head of the office.

ACASCIAS RIPHOUSE

Mr Hornsby: Olive's brother. Myrtle attended his wedding.
Olive Hornsby: She attended Hogwarts in the 1940s around the same time Myrtle did and used to tease Myrtle relentlessly about her glasses. Exact years and House unknown. She found Myrtle dead in the bathroom and remembered it to her dying day, probably mostly because after Myrtle died she, in revenge, haunted Olive for years. Myrtle followed Olive all around the school and after graduation stalked Olive in general, including going to with Olive to her brother's wedding. Eventually Olive went to the MoM to stop Myrtle stalking her and Myrtle was then confined to Hogwarts.
Helga Hufflepuff: c 900. A sweet and extremely talented witch, from valley broad. Possibly of Germanic and Irish decent. She took the hardest working of the students. If one had to guess, and one does, she was probably teacher of Charms. She also is probably the one that left the rune-carved Pensive in the Head's office. She seems to have never married, which was common among women of that period who wanted to do something important with their life other than be chattel and die in childbirth.

She seems to have had some affinity for Salazar rather than Rowena or Godric. Both Helga and Salazar picked underground dwelling animals as their mascots, both have non-British first names, implying one parent was foreign, and both Houses are underground near each other as opposed to the two towers the Rowena and Godric chose. This is not to say anything romantic was going on, just to point out it more likely Salazar and Helga were friends who initially teamed up with Rowena and Godric who were friends, probably through Rowena and Helga's friendship.
(Unknown) Hump-backed One-eyed Witch: See Portraits Etc., Statue section.
Inigo Imago: Author of *The Dream Oracle*. Probably an Italian warlock from the -o ending which most Italian male names have (Guido, Roberto, Georgio, etc).
(Unknown) Ivanova: A Bulgarian Chaser at QWC 1994. Given the -va ending name, she's probably a witch, though Ludo specifically says "he."
(Unknown) Japes: Co-owner of a joke shop in Diagon Alley. Gender unknown.
Joey Jenkins: Chudley Cannons Beater in 95/96.
Arsenius Jigger: Author of *Magical Drafts and Potions*. A Hogwarts' textbook for Potions years 1-5.
Angelina Johnson: b Oct 24, 1977. A Gryffindor, 1989-1996. She started Hogwarts in 89/90. She is a tall, Black girl who wears her hair in numerous long small braids. She put her name in the Goblet of Fire, legally, but sadly wasn't selected. She went to the Yule Ball with Fred Dec 1994. Chaser for the House team, she became Captain as well after Wood graduated in 94/95. Like Wood, she was Quidditch crazy and carried a whistle. She joined the DA in Oct 1995. She graduated in 95/96.
Hestia Jones: A pink-cheeked, black-haired witch. She became a new member of the OoP in 95/96. She was part of Harry's escort to Headquarters in the summer of 1995.
Lee Jordan: b 1977. A Gryffindor, 1989-1996. He started Hogwarts in 89/90. He is the best friend of the Weasley twins and shares their sense of humor and love of adventure. The 2nd week of school in 91/92, he found a the secret passage out of school behind the statue of Gregory the Smarmy, which twins found in the first week – great minds think alike. He was the somewhat biased commentator for all Quidditch games, being always pro-Gryffindor and usually going off track until brought back to reality by Pr McGonagall. He wanted to date Angelina Johnson during their school days but he could never get anywhere with her. He is a tall boy with dreadlocks (but is never said to be Black) and has a pet tarantula he keeps in a box that he got in 1991. He joined the DA in Oct 1995. He graduated in 95/96, after harassing Pr Umbridge to the best of his ability with nifflers, and is possibly now in business with the Weasley twins.

Bertha Jorkins: b 1951. House unknown, 1963-1970. She was a few years ahead of Sirius, starting in 63/64, but most of her school years were under Dumbledore's administration since he became Head in 65/66. She was a bit stupid but had an excellent memory for gossip. She never forgot what she heard or saw, but she also never knew when to shut up about it. This always got her in trouble. She was a plump child and got severely hexed at 16 years old, in 68/69, for telling schoolmate Florence's boyfriend she'd seen them kissing. She continued to be a very nosy idiot with no brains after graduating and throughout the early 1980s while working for DMLE under Barty Crouch Sr.

Finally c 1985 she had occasion to visit Barty Sr's home and realized Barty Jr was alive, escaped and living with his father. Barty Sr put a overly strong Memory Charm on her causing her memory to be permanently damaged. She was then shifted from the DMLE to another department, then shunted around the various MoM departments, till she ended up working for Ludo in the DMGS sometime before 1994, probably c 1992. She remained there until, while on vacation visiting relations in Albania in the summer of 1994, she had the misfortune to run into yet another supposedly dead wizard, Peter Pettigrew. Peter unfortunately knew who she was, from school days, and where she worked, from living in the Weasley house as a rat and listening to Arthur talk about her.

Peter captured her and took her to Voldemort, who was living in a forest as a snake. Voldemort broke the memory charm (no doubt via torture) and extracted the information about Barty Jr being out, Moody teaching at Hogwarts, and the upcoming QWC and TT. Then because her brain was mush and he couldn't inhabit her or use her in any other way, Voldemort killed her. No one looked for her even after she went missing because Ludo said she had a poor sense of direction, a memory like a leaky cauldron and had gotten lost for months on end plenty of times before. Even after she'd been missing for over a month, Ludo still didn't send anyone to look for her. Finally Fudge became personally involved and a search was started in Dec 1994. She was never found.

(Unknown) Jugson: b 1952. A Slytherin 1964-1971. He started Hogwarts in 64/65. Probably Escapee 5: the wizard escaped from Azkaban Jan 1996. His crime is unknown. He was returned to prison Jun 1996 after being caught in the failed raid on MoM. See Note 1.

Igor Karkoff: b 1954. He started as a student at Hogwarts with Snape in 66/67. A Slytherin, 1966-1973. Formerly a Death Eater during Voldemort's initial rise to power, he was arrested after Voldemort's fall and put in Azkaban. However in 1982 he started naming other Death Eaters and the MoM let him out. He left Britain, in fear for his life due to uncaught loyal Death Eaters, and became Head of a school called Durmstrang, located in Russia or Bulgaria, that is for purebloods only and where they teach the Dark Arts. He only speaks English so all the students had to be bilingual. He is a pureblood himself and Lucius once thought of sending Draco to Igor's school. As Head of Durmstrang he turned up at Hogwarts for the TT with 12 students, Krum among them. Dumbledore welcomed him back to Hogwarts.

He had truly completely repented his old ways and panicked when the Dark Mark was activated in Jun 1995. He had no desire to rejoin Voldemort's ranks and bolted for parts unknown, though Voldemort said in Little Hangleton that he would find Igor and punish him. It remains to be seen if that means death or forcing Igor to reenlist in the Death Eaters. His disappearance was a small loss to students who really didn't care for him. He didn't steer the ship that transported everyone to Hogwarts but stayed in his cabin and let the students to all the work. He was only ever nice to Viktor. Everyone else was a 2nd-class being.

He is tall and thin and affects superiority and elegance like Lucius Malfoy. He had dark hair in 1982, but he's since gone sleek and silver-white. He keeps it cut short and wears a goatee that finishes in a small curl on his otherwise noticably weak chin. He curls his beard when he's nervous or preening. His teeth are rather yellow and his ice blue eyes are cold and shrewd. He has steely smile and a fruity unctuous voice. He wears a sleek silver fur cape and is always clutching at his furs and accusing others of treachery, corruption and double dealing. He is more than a bit paranoid but this probably comes from knowing he betrayed Voldemort and loyal Death Eaters are looking for him.

He is a friend of Lucius Malfoy and Severus Snape, both of whom were Death Eaters. He asked Severus for advice when the Dark Mark grew clearer, but Severus couldn't really help him without blowing his cover. As for Lucius, he's hardly reformed and it would seem odd the Lucius thought of sending Draco to a school where the Head was a truly reformed Death Eater. But in the eyes of the MoM Lucius is also a truly reformed Death Eater. Lucius had no hard feelings about Igor naming a few names to get out of Azkaban (since his wasn't one of them) and probably thought Igor just as loyal a Death Eaters as himself (if one can call Lucius loyal at all). Slytherins, after all, always save their own necks and that was all Igor was doing. If it happened to be at the expense of another Death Eater, that was unfortunate, but . . . .

Pr Kettleburn: He was the teacher of Care of Magical Creatures at Hogwarts till Jun 1993. He retired so he could enjoy more time with his remaining limbs. He lost either 1 or 2 limbs.

Kevin (Unknown): b circa 1992. Son of Mr and Mrs (Unknown). A tiny 2-year-old wizard that used his father's wand at QWC 1994 to enlarge a slug.

Kevin's MoM: She accidentally stepped on Kevin's enlarged slug. She seemed unimpressed Kevin could to magic at age 2.

Andrew Kirke: A Gryffindor. He became a Beater on the House team in 95/96, replacing Fred after the ban was imposed. He's at least a 2nd year, but what year is unknown.

Mr and Mrs Krum: Both of Viktor's parents have dark hair and are Bulgarian. His father has a hooked nose, which Viktor inherited. They must be purebloods since they sent Viktor to Durmstrang, which only takes purebloods.

Viktor Krum: aka Vicky. b 1975. A pureblood. He was a Durmstrang student still, at age 18, probably because he had to take a year off to play on the Bulgarian national team and was making it up in 94/95. He was Bulgaria's brilliant Seeker in QWC 1994, and caught the Snitch though his team didn't win the game. His face was on a poster that was plastered all over the outside of Bulgarians' tents during QWC 1994. He attended Durmstrang, or did until 94/95, when Karkoff bolted and he graduated rather underskilled anyway.

He is tall, very skinny and has dark hair. He has sallow skin, thick heavy black eyebrows growing over his dark eyes and a large curved (formerly broken) nose. He looks like an overgrown bird of prey, which is nice if one likes that look , but even Hermione admits he's not much to look at. On the ground he is not very coordinated and walks duck footed (splayed feet) with distinctly rounded, almost hunched, shoulders. He is usually slouching as he walks. He has a rather grumpy surly face and tends to scowl or look like he's brooding. He tends to be a bit antisocial but only because he doesn't at all like being famous.

THE HARRY POTTER COMPANION

During the TT he was always standing by himself not talking, looking moody or surly. He skulked away from photo ops, being very camera shy. He spent most of his time at Hogwarts in the Library where A) no one would talk to him, and B) he could look at Hermione. For a while he went up there every day while trying to pluck up the courage to talk to her. He has a strong Bulgarian accent but speaks excellent English. He calls Hermione, Herm-own-ninny, but she doesn't seem to mind. He took her to the Yule Ball and she was later his hostage during Task 2, implying he deeply cared about her more than anyone else. After the task he invited her to visit him in Bulgaria over the summer (1995).

He looked wary almost frightened as though he expected Dumbledore to say something harsh when looking at him at the Leaving Feast in Jun 1995. But it was never indicated why Viktor should look way. He'd done nothing wrong. He didn't like Karkoff, didn't know Voldemort and had nothing to do with Cedric's death. Perhaps he was just being hypersensitive, coming from a school that is known for teaching Dark Arts and yet still having failed to throw off an Imperius Curse when the chips were down. Or perhaps Viktor has a few secrets of his own that Dumbledore's keen mind has picked up on.

Viktor is completely smitten with Hermione and, whether she went to Bulgaria or not, they were corresponding throughout 95/96. Hermione may simply be keeping the lines of communication open since the Order needs all the foreign members it can get and what exactly she writes to Viktor has never been admitted to be romantic in nature. Viktor told Hermione that Harry knew how to do things (magically speaking) that he didn't know even in his final year, like how to throw off an Imperius Curse. But Viktor is a very nice person once one gets to know him and a spectacular Quidditch player. He is probably, since graduating, playing for a League team somewhere and that doesn't require one to be able to Transfigure oneself correctly.

Lachlan the Lanky: See Portraits Etc., Statue section.

Leaky Cauldron, Dishwasher: A young man who went to QWC 1994 and after seeing some Veelas said he worked with the Committee for the Disposal of Dangerous Creatures to impress them.

Bellatrix Black Lestrange: b 1952. A Slytherin, 1963-1970. She started Hogwarts in 63/64. Married to Rodolphus Lestrange, older sister of Narcissa Black Malfoy and Andromeda Black Tonks, she is a 1st cousin of Sirius Black. She has thick shining dark (one assumes black) hair and heavily hooded eyes. She is tall and has a very imperial manner that never fails her, but she is a deluded fanatic when it comes to Voldemort. She said at her trial in 1982 that she, her husband, brother-in-law and Barty Crouch Jr were the only faithful ones because they tried to find Voldemort - by torturing the Longbottoms. Voldemort, she believes, plans to honor them all beyond their dreams when Azkaban is broken into. Later events however proved otherwise.

She was in Azkaban from 1982 to Jan 1996. But Sirius hadn't seen her since he was 15, despite the fact they were in the same prison for 12 years. She was an avid pureblood enthusiast and Death Eater and claimed to have learned the Dark Arts from Voldemort himself, which is saying something if true but her performance in the MoM cast doubt on that. She was Escapee 10: the only witch to escape from Azkaban in the Jan 1996 break out. She retained a vestiges of her great good looks, but now has a harsh voice, a thin mouth and a gaunt skull. If she wasn't crazy before she went to prison, it must have done the trick because she's really nuts now. She was part of the raid on the MoM in Jun 1996 and killed Sirius during it without any remorse.

After the MoM raid failed, she was the only one to escape from the MoM. Voldemort took her with him from the MoM by magical means. One severely doubts

ACASCIAS RIPHOUSE

Voldemort saved her out of pity since she had to beg to get him to do it and he didn't do squat to save Rodolphus and Rastaban. One also doubts that Voldemort's rescue of Bellatrix was so much the presumed "honor" he was going to give her as a necessity given Dumbledore had just captured 11 of his Death Eaters and he was now down to just 5, with her 6. He obviously needed all the loyal help he could get. One the plus side, with Lucius in prison, Bellatrix can step into his shoes as leader of the Death Eaters and she at least is truly loyal.

Rastaban Lestrange: b 1956. A Slytherin, 1967-1974. He started Hogwarts 67/68. See Note 1. A thick set man, he went to prison with Barty Jr, brother Rodolphus and sister-in-law Bellatrix for the torture of the Longbottoms in 1982. He was Escapee 6: in the Jan 1996 break out from Azkaban. He believes that Voldemort plans to honor them beyond their dreams, but so far he's only been used and abandoned. He was returned to prison Jun 1996 after the failed raid at the MoM.

Rodolphus Lestrange: b 1952. A Slytherin, 1963-1970. He started Hogwarts in 63/64. A former Hogwarts student, he was part of a gang of Slytherins who nearly all turned out to be Death Eaters. He went to prison with Barty Jr, brother Rastaban and wife Bellatrix for the torture of the Longbottoms in 1982. He believes that Voldemort plans to honor them beyond their dreams, but so far he's only been used and abandoned. He was Death Eater Escapee 7: that escaped from Azkaban in Jan 1996 by was returned to prison Jun 1996, after the failed raid at the MoM.

(Unknown) Levski: A Bulgarian team Chaser in QWC 1994. Gender unknown.

"Dangerous" Dia Llewellyn: Probably the most famous Quidditch player ever. He played for the Caerphilly Catapults, till he was attacked by chimera in Greece. The "Dangerous" Dia Llewellyn Ward at St Mungo's, which specializes in creature bites, is named after him.

Gilderoy Lockhart: b circa 1960. Former DADA teacher at Hogwarts in 92/93. He's particularly known for his smile of big white gleaming teeth and winning *Witch Weekly's* Most Charming Smile Award, 5 years in a row (1987-1991). Author of numerous books including *Gilderoy Lockhart's Guide to Household Pests, Magical Me, Break with a Banshee, Gadding with Ghouls, Holiday with Hags, Travels with Trolls, Voyages with Vampires, Wanderings with Werewolves,* and *Year with the Yeti.* He always has big photos of himself beaming at people from the covers of his books, which are all very expensive.

Harry first met him at Flourish and Blotts doing a book signing. He uses a large peacock quill and has an enormous loopy signature. All the ladies like him, including Hermione and Molly, but middle-age witches make up the bulk of admirers. Very good looking with wavy blonde hair and bright blue eyes, he winks cheekily at people from all his photographs. He usually wears forget-me-not blue robes that exactly match his eyes and a matching pointed wizard's hat set at a jaunty angle. He has a large assortment of colored robes and matching hats: turquoise, jade green, aquamarine, palest mauve, midnight-blue, forget-me-not blue, deep plum, lurid pink. He has an entire trunk just for clothes, and a second for his books and photos of himself. Favorite platitudes include: Fame is a fickle friend and celebrity is as celebrity does.

He has an Order of Merlin, 3rd class and is an Honorary Member of the Dark Force Defense League but he probably got the Order of Merlin for giving money and the Honorary Member implies he doesn't actually do anything with the Dark Force Defense League. He is a total publicity hound and needs to be the center of attention at all times. He is outgoing to the point of obnoxiousness and rubbed all the teachers (and most of the students) the wrong way. He can show all of his large white teeth even

The Harry Potter Companion

when he isn't smiling and strides around confidently except when caught out in a lie, at which point, without his smile, his chin looks weak and he seems a bit feeble.

He has traveled all over the world, but only to listen to other people's stories. He then puts a Memory Charm on them so they forget what they have done, allowing him to write about their deeds and claim credit for them. In point of fact, he is a terrible coward, knows nothing about DADA and can barely use a wand let alone a defend against the Dark Arts. He got the DADA teaching position because he was the only person willing to take it. Dumbledore was well aware of what Lockhart was doing, but hired him anyway since he needed the help. Lockhart might have mended his ways, but for some reason, greed probably, chose not too.

Things he made his class learn: His favorite color (lilac - *Year of the Yeti*), his secret ambition (rid the world of evil and market his own range of hair-care potions) and what would be his ideal birthday gift (*Year with a Yeti* - chapter 12, harmony between all magical and nonmagical peoples or Ogden's Old Firewhisky). He started a Dueling Club, with Pr Snape as an assistant, and nearly got himself killed. The club doesn't seem to have survived his sudden departure to St Mungo's. He ended up in St Mungo's after he attempted to flee rather than face the basilisk. When Ron and Harry forced the issue, he tried to escape by jumping Ron for his wand and trying to completely Obliviate Ron and Harry's memory. Unfortunately, he was using Ron's bad wand and ended up erasing his own memory completely. However, he seems to be a better person without any memory and is now brainless yet pleasant and refreshingly honest about himself.

Since losing his mind he has been living on the 4th floor of St Mungo's in the locked Janus Thickey Ward. Harry, Ron and Hermione found him there in Dec 1995. He is usually wearing a long lilac dressing gown and carrying his battered peacock feather quill in his pocket. He is steadily improving according to his Healer and can do childish cursive writing now. He never gets any visitors but Gladys Gudgeon writes weekly. He is kept in a closed ward because he's a danger to himself; he doesn't know who he is and tends to wander off and forget how to get back. He's still a bit self-centered and thinks everyone wants his autograph, though he doesn't know why they want it, but Healer Strout thinks his doing autographs will eventually improve his memory. Swearing: Great Scott.

Alice Longbottom: Probably born c 1940 since she had graduated school and the Auror Training program and been a respected Auror for a while before dying. Wife of Frank Longbottom, mother of Neville, daughter-in-law to Gran Longbottom. A pureblood and an original OoP member, she was formerly a highly gifted witch and an Auror. She was Cruciatus Cursed to insanity by the 3 Lestranges and Barty Crouch Jr in 1982. She has since been in the Janus Thickey Ward in St Mungo's and will probably never recover. She had a round friendly face, exactly like Neville's, when she was young and healthy. She now looks thin and worn with overly large eyes and hair that is white, wispy and dead looking. She is completely insane and keeps giving Neville Drooble's Best Blowing Gum wrappers, which he always keeps, whenever he visits.

Algie Longbottom: aka Uncle Algie. Probably born c 1920. Neville's Great Uncle, husband of Enid. He is the brother of Gran Longbottom's deceased husband and the uncle of Frank. He is a pureblood. Responsible for discovering Neville's magical abilities when he was 8, by dropping him from an upstairs window, he bought Neville his toad when he finally got accepted into Hogwarts. He must be something of a traveler since he brought a Mimbulus mimbletonia back from Assyria for Neville in 1995.

ACASCIAS RIPHOUSE

Enid Longbottom: aka Auntie Enid. Probably born c 1920. Neville's Great Aunt, wife of Algie Longbottom. She is the maker of an excellent meringue.

Frank Longbottom: Probably born c 1930. The pureblood son of Gran Longbottom, husband of Alice, father of Neville. He was a very talented warlock, a respected Auror and an original OoP member. He and his wife were very popular in the wizarding community and had escaped or defeated Voldemort 3 times previous to his vanishing in 1981. He was Cruciatus Cursed to insanity by the 3 Lestranges and Barty Crouch Jr in 1982 because they thought he had information on Voldemort's whereabouts and were hoping to restore him to power. His wife Alice suffered the same fate though it is unknown if the cursing was simultaneous or one had to watch the other suffer first. He has since been in the Janus Thickey Ward in St Mungo's and will probably never recover. He appears to be catatonic. Neville visits during holidays, but neither he nor Alice recognize him.

Gran Longbottom: Probably born c 1910. A pureblood, like her husband, she is Frank's mother, Alice's mother-in-law, Algie's sister-in-law and Neville's grandmother. She uses a barn or tawny owl usually to send Neville his forgotten things or a Howler, such as for letting Sirius Black steal the Gryffindor passwords. Gran is not afraid to say what she thinks and point blank admitted she believed Harry and Dumbledore about Voldemort being back when all the MoM was against them and it was not even in her best interests to believe such a story. She says she always knew that Voldemort would be back, and this despite the fact she's not an OoP member. She likes Harry and Hermione, and thinks the Weasleys are fine people.

She is a formidable, elderly witch with a bony nose and shriveled clawlike hands who has taken care of Neville since 1982, when his parents were incapacitated. She cried with happiness when it was discover that Neville was magical. She doesn't think Neville is as talented as her son Frank was - but then she's been making Neville use his father's wand all these years instead of getting him one of his own. She always wears a tall hat topped with a stuffed vulture, a long green lace-trimmed dress, a moth-eaten fox-fur scarf and a big red handbag. When Neville tried to think of something scary as something he wasn't afraid of, he pictured Pr Snape, dressed as he Gran. So he must really find her kindly and loving, despite her appearance. She is a friend of Griselda Marchbanks.

Neville Longbottom: b at the end of Jul 1980. A Gryffindor, 1991-1998? He started Hogwarts in 91/92. See schematic S. His parents, Frank and Alice, were tortured to insanity by Death Eaters Barty Jr, and the 3 Lestranges, in 1982, and currently reside in St Mungo's Janus Thickey Ward. His grandmother (his father's mother) has raised him since 1982. He has a Great Uncle Algie and a Great Aunt Enid, his grandfather's brother and sister-in-law, whom he sees often. He and Algie get along quite well considering Algie dropped him off the Blackpool Pier and out of window but they do seem to share a love of reptiles and botany and Algie seems to be Neville's main father figure.

Neville is from a pureblood family but his magic skills have never been too good, nor too apparent. It took until age 8 for anything magical about him to appear. But he is a Gryffindor, so he must be the classic diamond in the rough and one expects to see some really amazing magical talents show up in him yet. Neville is to accidents what Peeves is to chaos. Well over 30 are recorded, running from the mundane (repeatedly losing Trevor, the toad his Great Uncle Algie bought him) to the truly ridiculous (melting 6 cauldrons in 5 years of Potions). He was never allowed near a broomstick before Hogwarts because of this tendency, but made it through Flying classes all the same.

He is terrified of Pr Snape and does horribly in Potions, but he loves Herbology and is extremely good at it. Neville was given a very rare Mimbulus mimbletonia by his Great Uncle Algie in summer 1995 and it has thrived in Neville's care. Neville is a roommate of Harry, Ron, Dean and Seamus. He snores loudly and has fluffy toed slippers. He is the last person one would expect to join the DA, but he joined in Oct 1995 and turned out to be alarming quick to improve under Harry's able instruction. He probably wanted to learn to fight because of what happened to his parents, and it is likely that all these years his talent has been held back merely by lack of confidence and using his father's wand. One expects he'll do even better magic in 96/97 with his own wand.

Neville sees the thestrals because he saw his grandfather (Grandad Longbottom, Gran's husband) die at some point after being adopted by him and Gran. He is an only child and Gran takes him to see his parents every Christmas, though they don't recognize him. He keeps all the Drooble's Best Blowing Gum wrappers his mother gives him, though what he does with them is unknown. Like his mother, he has a round pink friendly owlish face. He started out on the little side (needing a leg up through the entrance to Gryffindor Tower) and rather heavy set, yet he's gotten taller, if not thinner, since then. He started school suffering from low self-esteem, was overly sensitive, fearful and tended to tears, but he's grown up a lot in a short time.

All the Gryffindors try to build him up and he tries to be braver and stand up to more people as time passes. At one point he even got into a fistfight with Crabbe *and* Goyle. Neville loves his friends and can't bear to see them hurt (probably because of what happened to his parents). He's afraid of the Bloody Baron and nearly when into shock when Barty Jr (Moody) Cruciatus Cursed a spider in front of him. Yet he is a Gryffindor through and through. When push comes to shove, he refused to let his fears hold him back and insisted on going with Harry and his DA friends to the MoM and taking on the Death Eaters in Jun 1996. One hopes Neville will realize over the summer, if he can take on Death Eaters and hold his own, he can certainly stop being afraid of Pr Snape.

Luna Lovegood: aka Loony Lovegood. b 1981. A Ravenclaw, 1992-1999? She started Hogwarts in 92/93. Her father is editor of *The Quibbler,* her mother died in a tragic accident when she was 9. She comes from the Ottery St Catchpole region. Luna has straggley, waistlength dirty-blonde hair, very pale eyebrows and protruding eyes that make her look perpetually surprised. She's quite a nice person but distinctly odd and rather dottiness.

When Harry first met her, she was wearing a necklace of Butterbeer caps and had her wand tucked behind her left ear for safe keeping (probably a habit she got from watching her father stick an editorial red quill behind his ear all the time). She doesn't seem to blink much, habitually stares at people with her pale silvery eyes (like Mr Ollivander) and speaks in a dreamy manner. She doesn't like dancing, laughs too hard too long at jokes and believes the articles her father prints in *The Quibbler,* none of which enhances her in the eyes of fellow students.

Luna sees the thestrals because of witnessing her mother's death. She rides sidesaddle and has a unique fashion sense – wearing such things as orange radish-shape earrings and her hair in a knot on top of her head. She drinks gillywater which contains a cocktail onion on a stick for extra kick. At Quidditch matches she wears a live eagle on her head to support Ravenclaw or a roaring lion head to support Gryffindor. She is not offended by others' rudeness toward her, mostly because she is above it all in her own stratosphere, but she can be quite rude to others without seeming to notice they are offended. She tells Ron what a bad date Padma thought he was and Hagrid's closest friends what a lousy teacher all the Ravenclaws think he is.

In 95/96 Luna was the first person to say publicly that she believed Harry about Voldemort's return. However, she only seems to believe in things as long as there's no proof at all which hardly helped Harry's cause. She seems to be completely unflappable. People steal her clothes and books because she's odd, but she always gets it back the end of term and doesn't worry about it. She is captured by the Inquisitorial Squad, but she doesn't even seem to notice. She is the least scared of all the DA members during the fracas with the Death Eaters in the MoM in Jun 1996, though not even a Gryffindor.

Luna pulled her weight, and Ginny's and Ron's, during the MoM raid, and proved she's got the magical talent to go the distance. Undoubtedly she's different, but as a Ravenclaw she must be extremely smart, and as the only non-Gryffindor member of the DA team that went to MoM, she must at least as brave as she is smart which is really saying something. Finally, it is Luna's firm belief in the afterlife that bolsters Harry's own and thus comforts Harry when he is grieving for Sirius. Luna has the compassion of a Hufflepuff, the brains of a Ravenclaw and the courage of a Gryffindor. Harry could use a lot more friends with her combination of gifts and talents.

Mr Lovegood: aka Daddy. The widowed father of Luna, he lives alone near Ottery St Catchpole. His only child is Luna. Editor of *The Quibbler*. He is supportive of any anti-MoM action. He ran Harry's interview, as told by Rita Skeeter, in his monthly magazine and set the British wizarding world on its ear in 1996. He seems to be of the 1960s radical anti-government hippy persuasion, but has a large readership so many wizards must share at least some of his views.

Mrs Lovegood: d circa 1990. She was a quite extraordinary witch that liked to do experiments with spells. She was killed by an experimental spell gone bad when Luna was 9. Her death was rather horrible and Luna saw it all but what the spell was or how it went wrong is unknown.

Aidan Lynch: Irish team Seeker in QWC 1994.

Morag MacDougal: b 1979. House unknown, 1991-1998?

Ernie Macmillan: b 1979. A Hufflepuff, 1991-1998? He started Hogwarts in 91/92. He can trace his pureblood heritage back 9 generations, but that apparently hasn't helped his magical abilities if he's a Hufflepuff. A stout boy with pudgy hands, he can be a bit pompous and self-important. He is rather the self-designated leader of his year, and has been since her arrived. He tends to be reactionary. When the Chamber of Secrets was opened and the snake Harry spoke to appeared to go after his friend Justin in Dueling Club, he immediately assumed the Heir of Slytherin must be Harry. But all in all his heart is good

He is best friends with Hannah Abbott and Justin Finch-Fletchley. He and Hannah became Prefects in 95/96 and share a love of trading Chocolate Frog cards. He was at QWC 1994. He was a member of the Dueling Club and the DA in Oct 1995. In 95/96 he almost fell apart studying for OWLs and went around interrogating others about their study habits. He would compare how many hours he studied a day to how many others were doing. His average was 8 hours day, but on weekends it was 10 – a true Hufflepuff.

Walden Macnair: b 1953. A Slytherin 1965-1972. He started Hogwarts in 65/66. See Note 1. A Death Eater that managed to talk his way out of being arrested after Voldemort's fall in 1981, he subsequently found work with the MoM as an executioner for the Committee for the Disposal of Dangerous Creatures. Killing things made use of his natural talents as well as his personal inclinations. A tall strapping man with a thin black mustache, he kept an axe in his belt as his means of choice. He is an old friend of Lucius and like him, showed up the moment Voldemort activated the Dark Mark in Little Hangleton in Jun 1995. He was one of 2 Death Eaters sent to the giants Abroad in the summer of 1995. He succeeded in persuading the majority to join Voldemort. Hermione stabbed Walden in the eye with her wand in Jun 1996 during the MoM raid and this may or may not have caused permanent damage. He was caught and sent to Azkaban in Jun 1996.

Laura Madley: b 1982. A Hufflepuff, 1994-2001? She started Hogwarts in 94/95.

Draco Malfoy: b 1980. A Slytherin, 1991-1998? He started Hogwarts in 91/92, though his father considered sending him to purebloods-only, Dark-Arts-teaching Durmstrang. Son of Lucius Malfoy and Narcissa Black Malfoy, he is living proof that two wrongs not only don't make a right, they can make an even bigger wrong. In looks he strongly resembles his father, having the same pale pointed face, silver white hair, cold grey eyes and sneer as his father. He has a thin mouth, which he gets from his mother, but thankfully not her expression. His family is rolling in gold and he has the best of everything, including a large manor house with (until 1993) a house-elf.

He affects superiority by always seeming bored and using a cool, drawling voice. He is always bragging, complaining or making arrogant remarks about things or people. He thinks he is better than others because he is a pureblood. His family has always been in Slytherin and he believes in the pureblood doctrine himself. He hates Harry for being famous, Ron for being poor and Hermione for Muggle born. But in reality his own inadequacies are all too glaring. He gets poor grades, his father publicly insults him when not ignoring him and he's a coward. He has to go around with henchmen, Crabbe and Goyle, to look important. He can't fly well enough to get on the Quidditch team and has to have his father buy the whole team brooms to get a spot. He challenges Harry to wizard's duel in 91/92 but never shows up and instead rats on him to try and get him caught by Filch. He's afraid of the Forbidden Forest because he thinks it has werewolves and runs screaming at the first sign of trouble (which granted was real trouble). It's hard to believe he's a Death Eater's son.

He's an only child, yet when he first appears, he's alone. His father is next door buying his books, his mother is up the street looking at wands. If he didn't go home at Christmas and get sweets and cakes from home every day from his mother, one would wonder if he had parents at all. He seems to create trouble just so he can be the center of attention for a moment, such as when he pretended to be a dementor in 94/93. Though it must be admitted he seems to act out mainly to get his father's attention, the situation with Buckbeak being a case in point. His mother seems to really love him and sends him sweets by owl every day, which he opens gloatingly at the Slytherin table but doesn't share. He owns an eagle owl that usually lands on his shoulder every day, and since there is not a larger meaner owl available, one might think he was showing off or making a statement of some sort.

For all Draco's faults, he's really just a typical Slytherin – sly, self-centered and ambitious. Unfortunately he's not very bright. He does well in Potions class because Pr Snape favors him and always makes a point of praising him in public. In other classes he is put to shame by Hermione or Harry. He plays up to people that can be of advantage to him, such as when he told Pr Snape he would tell his father to put his name forward for Headmaster, but he is always ready to stab a person, even a member of his House, in the back to get a little further up the food chain. It seems plain that Pr Snape is using Draco to get information about Lucius and perhaps cultivating with an eye to turning him into an unwitting Order double agent, but Draco is oblivious to this.

Draco doesn't think much of Dumbledore, other than he's a Muggle lover and ipso facto a terrible wizard. He calls Harry and Ron, Potty and Weasel. Yet for all this charm, Draco managed to get a date and went to the Yule Ball with Pansy in Dec 1994. He wore high-collared, black velvet robes that made him look like a vicar. He was made a Prefect with Pansy in 95/96 and later they both became members of the Inquisitorial Squad. He is a terrible Prefect and abuses his power with regularity. On the plus side, he is somewhat poetically inclined and wrote the lyrics to *Weasley Is Our King*, a rather useful dual action (Slytherin and Gryffindor) Quidditch anthem.

As of Jun 1996 his father was put in jail and he made threats against Harry, but this isn't the lose-lose situation one might think. It was unremarked but, technically Narcissa is an accomplice in a conspiracy to murder, breaking and entering the MoM and treason, and should be in jail as well. Tragic as losing both parents might be for Draco, and he did seem genuinely upset about his father's imprisonment, he is now in control of the Malfoy money and goods at the tender age of 16. If his parents don't get out, and he might make sure they don't by ratting them out, it's all his to do with as he wishes. Swears: God, My God.

Lucius Malfoy: b 1953. A Slytherin, 1965-1972. He started Hogwarts in 65/66. Father of Draco, husband of Narcissa Black Malfoy. He got sucked into the pureblood doctrine at an early age, probably more because he saw opportunity in it than any actual belief in the philosophy. He graduated school and became a Death Eater, rising to the point of being chief Death Eater and someone Voldemort entrusted with precious Dark Arts items like Tom Riddle's Diary. He married another pureblood with decided Voldemort leanings, and had a son, Draco, in 1980. When Voldemort disappeared in 1981, Lucius was one of the first to abandon ship and claim he was bewitched into following Voldemort.

He wriggled off the hook with the MoM, doubtless because he was rich, and made a few well-placed and highly public donations to the MoM but many people didn't believed his act and Arthur in particular thought Lucius never needed an excuse to go to the Dark side. Despite his past, Lucius was able to continue greasing palms, till he ended up on the Hogwarts' Board of Governors sometime prior to 1991. This made life rather difficult for Dumbledore as Lucius hates him, supposedly for letting nonpurebloods into the school but probably really for having set up the OoP and worked against Voldemort during his first rise to power. Although Lucius knows Dumbledore and most of the teachers from his own years at Hogwarts, he refuses to admit there is nothing wrong with the people or education there.

During 91/92, Lucius is unusually quite, but doubtless heard all about Voldemort's return via Pr Quirrell. As Dumbledore said everyone in the school knew what happened with Harry and the Sorcerer's Stone, it would be ridiculous to think Draco didn't or didn't pass such information on to his father. Therefore, Lucius, covering his own backside, needed to make some pretense at loyalty to Voldemort and started plotting for 92/93 at a minimum in Jul 1992, but probably well before. In the summer of 92 he purchased Slytherin House Quidditch team Nimbus 2001 racing brooms so Draco could become Seeker. But this was more to glorify Slytherin and the Malfoy name than anything to do with loving Draco, whom he spends money on but feels free to totally humiliate in public.

The purchase of the brooms does little for the team however, as Quidditch was canceled due to basilisk attacks. This of course was also the work Lucius. Although he'd rather let other people do his dirty work, he's not above doing it himself. He stuck Tom Riddle's Diary in Ginny's second-hand Transfiguration school book in a blatant attempt to get her disgraced for killing Muggles and by association get Arthur and his

Muggle Protection Act disgraced. And, if it had the added effect of sacking Dumbledore and engratiating him to Voldemort, all the better. His plan didn't work and ultimately got him kicked off the Board and lost him his house-elf, Dobby, in Jun 1993, but all this didn't deter him any.

The following year he made a complaint to the MoM after Draco got cut by Buckbeak, forced it to trial and demanded an execution. And, not even above using his own son, also lied to Draco, telling him that Sirius Black worked for Voldemort. Lucius as leader of the Death Eaters, knew that Sirius wasn't a Death Eater. He went to school with Sirius and knew that Sirius had always been solidly against pureblood philosophy and Voldemort. One can only speculate that Lucius hated Sirius for being a pureblood working against Voldemort with Dumbledore's OoP and wanted him further punished for helping to bring about Voldemort's downfall.

Lucius continued to spread the gold around to become friends with influential people at MoM, mainly so he could later have laws he didn't like delayed, but in the summer of 1994, after giving money to St Mungo's, Fudge brought him and his wife and son as guests to the Top Box at QWC 1994. Apparently Lucius is much more interested in sports like Muggle-killing and after the game he and several other former Death Eaters were responsible for the Roberts, a Muggle family running a campsite at QWC 1994, being assaulted. He has no qualms about doing things like this because he believes all Muggles should be got rid of, as well as pureblood wizards, like Arthur Weasley, who mix with Muggles. He referred to Arthur being kind to Mr and Mrs Granger as a wizard sinking to the lowest level.

While Voldemort was out of power, Lucius kept to the old ways, he just put a happy face on it by giving generously (or wore a mask). He never bothered to look for Voldemort, despite being the top man among the Death Eaters and probably didn't care to. However he immediately showed up when the Dark Mark activated in Little Hangleton in Jun 1995. Voldemort knows enough to call him "my slippery friend" but welcomed him back into the fold without cursing him in any way. One supposes that Voldemort understands Lucius is really loyal only to himself but finds him useful all the same. It must be admitted, Lucius is very intelligent, truly crafty and artful in the extreme. Besides which, he agrees with Voldemort that the bloodlines are important than anything else and Muggles should be got rid of. Definitely there is common, albeit bloody, ground.

Lucius usually wears a black traveling cloak and affects an air of gentlemanly unconcern or studied politeness. He has the same pale pointed face and cold pale grey eyes, the same sneer and lazy manner of speaking as Draco. He is right handed, drums his finger when impatient and curls his lip or flares his long nostrils when he's angry. He is rather cold, remote and emotionless and never seems to really like or care about anyone or anything but Malfoy purebloods taking over the world. He associates with the top people at the MoM including Fudge and Dolores Umbridge, both of whom lean toward the belief that bloodlines are important and both of whom he knows well, but they can't be considered friends. Lucius has followers and underlings, not friends.

The Malfoy name commands respect, not least because everyone knows Lucius is a powerful wizard with few scruples. He has a mansion in Wiltshire with house-elf, Dobby (or did till until he accidentally freed him in May 1993), is very wealthy and presumably doesn't work for a living. He is deep into the Dark Arts, to the point of having a secret chamber under his drawing room where he stashes a horde of illegal Dark Arts items, or did till Arthur raided his house in 1992, though it's probably restocked by now. He affects to be a gentleman, and made Mr Borgin come and pick up the items Lucius sold him (because he didn't want to get caught with the goods on him) but he haggled with Mr. Borgin when selling his Dark Arts goods, which is very vulgar and not at all gentlemanly.

In Jun 1996, Lucius got a little overzealous on Voldemort's behalf and got caught raiding the MoM with several notorious convicted Death Eaters and even Voldemort, who put in a brief but memorable appearance. He was sent to Azkaban as a Death Eater, one assumes he had a trial, but maybe that is still ahead of him. It remains to be seen how Lucius will wriggle out of jail. Imperius Curse seems a bit tired, but without dementors guarding the prison, he could likely escape quite easily using his skill as a wizard and with the help of the other Death Eaters. In any event, he was definitely outed to the MoM and there seems no way back. Swearing: good lord.

Narcissa Black Malfoy: b 1956. A Slytherin 1968-1975. He started Hogwarts in 68/68. See Note 1. Wife of Lucius Malfoy, mother of Draco, 1st cousin of Sirius Black, and youngest sister of Bellatrix Black Lestrange and Andromeda Black Tonks. She is tall, slim, blonde and might have be pretty if she didn't always look like she smelled something rotten all the time. She wanted Draco to go to school closer to home rather than Durmstrang and seems to dote on him. She sends him sweets and cakes by owl, every day. She probably loves Draco more than Lucius, at least she seems to. Draco for his part is rather embarrassed by her and her usual facial expression.

She may not be a branded Death Eater, but she believes in Voldemort's cause and it is Narcissa's doings that lands Lucius in jail and gets Sirius killed because it is to Narcissa that Kreacher goes after being thrown out by Sirius. She uses Kreacher to get Harry to the MoM for Voldemort in Jun 1996, which in turn brings Sirius. It is unknown if she has been sent to prison for her part in the raid. Certainly she was instrumental in luring Harry there to help Voldemort get the prophecy and legally she is a conspirator to in the break in, attacking the MoM which is treason and the murder of Sirius Black. But the MoM may pity the family and allow her to go free to "care" for Draco.

Madam Malkin: She is a squat, smiling witch who is usually dressed all in mauve. She is owner of Madam Malkin's Robes for All Occasions in Diagon Alley.

Griselda Marchbanks: aka Pr Marchbanks. b circa 1900. She was an Elder with the Wizengamot, but resigned in protest when the Hogwarts High Inquisitor legislation went through. Because she protested, *The Daily Prophet*, under pressure from Fudge, tried to link her to subversive goblin groups. She is a member of the Wizarding Examinations Authority and a long-time friend of Gran Longbottom. Draco claims his family knows her, but Neville disputes this. She examined Dumbledore in Transfiguration and Charms during his NEWTS (c 1933), did Draco's Charms OWL practical and Harry's Potions OWL practical, Divination OWL practical and Astronomy OWL practical in 1996. She is a tiny, stooped witch with a very lined face. She is also a little deaf, but she is close to if not over 100 years old.

Madam Marsh: An elderly witch who often rides on the Knight Bus. She left the bus at Abergavenny, Wales in 1993. She was on it again in Jan 1996 when Harry, Ron and Hermione rode it back to school.

Madame Olympia Maxime: French. She is the Head of Beauxbatons Academy of Magic. She has a strong French accent. She showed up at Hogwarts for the TT in 94/95. She is as tall as Hagrid (somewhere around 10-12 feet) and is even more unnaturally large, leaning more toward the giant side in looks. Dumbledore barely has to bend to kiss her hand. She is so tall her head touches the chandelier. She has olive skin and a handsome face with large, black, liquid eyes and a beaky nose. She wears her black hair in a knob at the back of her neck. She is usually dressed in black satin and wears a gleaming opal necklace and matching rings on her fingers. She wears a silk shawl when it's cold or at night. To the Yule Ball wore flowing gown (not robes or a hat) of lavender silk.

She is half-giant and half-human like Hagrid, but lies about it because of the way people feel about giants. Initially she denies she's a half-giant even to Hagrid, but eventually she admits it. She accompanied Hagrid on the embassy to the giants Abroad in the summer of 1995 where she proved herself fiery and fearless. Once roused to anger, she is a tiger and does remarkably fast spellwork. Among other talents, Olympia is an excellent dancer, doesn't complain about roughing it and is extremely tough, brave and kind, just like Hagrid. She breeds abraxan horses and has a large power blue coach pulled by 12 of them. She and Hagrid will likely keep in touch.

Kirley McCormack: He is from Portree, Scotland and lead guitarist with the Weird Sisters.

Natalie McDonald: b 1982. A Gryffindor, 1994-2001? She started Hogwarts in 94/95.

Minerva McGonagall: Scottish. Born probably c 1925. She is the current member of the OoP and one assumes she was with the Order in the 1970s as well, given her long stay at Hogwarts and the fact she saw Harry off to the Dursleys in 1981. She is the Head of Gryffindor House and Professor of Transfiguration at Hogwarts since 1956. Minerva is also Deputy Headmistress and as such is responsible for sending out acceptance letters and booklists, managing the Sorting Ceremony, gathering a list of of those staying for Christmas and filling in as acting Head whenever Dumbledore is suspended or absent.

She is a registered Animagus able to turn into a tabby cat with markings around her eyes when a cat that look just like her square glasses when she's in human form. She usually turns into a cat and back with a slight popping noise. She demos her ability to 3rd year classes during which she usually teaches on Animagi and rags on Pr Trelawney. She is tall, severe looking and has black hair that she wears in a tight bun. She has a very stern face, beady eyes and usually wears emerald green cloaks and robes. She is strict, clever and not someone to cross. A smile or "very good" from her is high praise and "that was excellent" is the highest praise she can offer.

Though she rarely smiles, she is a kind, tender person with a good heart and can choke up with suppressed tears in public at a moment's notice. Very sensibly, she usually carries a lace handkerchief. She has long pointed nose and tends to look sternly down over her glasses at people when angry. Her lips go thin and white, her thin nostrils that flare and a cold fury creeps into in her voice when she's very angry. She has a muscle that twitches in her cheek when she's extremely angry (such as Valentines Day, 1993). She can contract her eyebrows to look positively hawklike, but at least this is an option and not a perpetual state of affairs as with Viktor Krum.

Although she usually wears green robes, at the Yule Ball she wore robes of red tartan, probably of her family's sept, and a rather ugly wreath of thistles (Scotland's national floral emblem) around the brim of her hat. At night she wears a tartan dressing gown and hairnet. She also has a tartan bathrobe, carpet bag and cookie tin. She's extremely fond of tartan. Currently she uses a walking stick (as a result of being Stunned multiple times by Pr Umbridge and her cronies). Whether that will be a permanently used item is hard to say. Luckily her study is on the 1st floor of Hogwarts.

She can spot trouble quicker than any teacher in school even if its in Gryffindor Tower in the middle of the night, so perhaps she has a good relationship with the portraits around the school. She gives her classes a talking to the moment they sit down in their first class, brooks no messing around and has a gift for keeping her class quiet without effort like Pr Snape, her former pupil. She seems to have a good relationship with Pr Snape, a sort of friendly rivalry over the Quidditch Cup, which she likes to put in her study where he can see it when he drops in. She likes to see her House win at Quidditch and feels embarrassed when her House gets creamed.

She was very fond of the Potters, who were both her students. James was in her House and on her House team, so she has been Gryffindor's Head since at least c 1965. It's unknown if she herself or Lily were in Gryffindor. She is kindly disposed toward most students, no matter their House, and almost all the other teachers at Hogwarts, though she thinks Divination is a very imprecise branch of magic and has no patience for Sybil Trelawney, whom she generally manages to ridicule at those times the two find themselves thrown together. This is interesting since both women have lived at the school for a long time, seem to have no other family but the school and Sybill has proved her usefulness, and that of Divination, to the Order.

Like Dumbledore, she is not above having fun, at appropriate times, and has been known to wear a lopsided top hat and blush and giggle when kissed by Hagrid at the Christmas Feast. She owns a purple microphone, drinks gillywater and prefers her chairs straight backed and wooden. She is probably Dumbledore's most trusted friend at Hogwarts. An interesting thing worth thinking on occurred when Ginny was taken by Tom Riddle into the Chamber of Secrets and the school was about to shut down. Pr McGonagall says it is the end of Hogwarts and Dumbledore always said . . . . But she doesn't finish. What Dumbledore has always said what about the end of Hogwarts remains unknown. Obviously Dumbledore has been talking about how Hogwarts would meet its end, and apparently attacks on students, the Chamber of Secrets and Tom Riddle are all involved.

Marlene McKinnon: An original OoP member. She was killed 2 weeks after Moody's photo was taken (prior to 1981) probably c 1980. Voldemort killed her and her whole family, or at least ordered the hit. They were considered to be some of the best wizards and witches of the age.

Dorcas Meadowes: An original OoP member. Voldemort killed her personally c 1980, so she must have done him some real damage at one time.

Uncle Alphard Melifula: d 1973. Sirius' rich uncle, Mrs Black's brother. He died and left Sirius a lot of gold when Sirius was about 17. This act caused Mrs Black to burn him off the Black family tapestry.

Arminta Meliflua: Mrs Black's and Alphard's cousin. She tried to force a bill through the MoM's legislature that would have made Muggle-hunting legal. Obviously she was very involved in wizarding politics as well as devoted to the pureblood philosophy.

Merlin: See Portraits Etc., Photo section.

Eloise Midgen: b 1979. A Hufflepuff, 1991-1998? In 94/95 she tried to curse her acne off and ended up having to go to Madam Pomfrey to get her nose put back on. Her acne was loads better by Christmas 1994 and Hermione says that she's really nice but Ron insists her nose is off-center and wanted nothing to do with her. It is unclear what year she is in. Since Hermione knows her and wanted Ron to take her to the Yule Ball, one presumes they are all in the same year.

Cuthbert Mockridge: He is the Head of Goblin Liaison Office since some time prior to 1994.

(Unknown) Montague: A Slytherin. He has been Chaser on the House team that we know of since 93/94 but may have been a Chaser since 92/93. He became Captain in 95/96 and was on the Inquisitorial Squad in 95/96. He is built like Dudley, with massive forearms like hairy hams. He ended up trapped in a toilet after being put in the Vanishing Cabinet by Fred and George in 1996. It is not clear what year he is in.

Alastor "Mad-Eye" Moody: Scottish. B circa 1930. An original and current OoP member, he is also a retired Auror. He was one of the best Aurors the MoM ever had but he suffered a lot for it. Though the DMLE went to seed under Crouch Sr, Moody kept his personal integrity and never killed if he could help it. He brought people in alive whenever possible and never descended to the level of the Death Eaters or Crouch Sr. People now think he's a bit of a joke because of his "constant vigilance" and his going off over the smallest thing, but he's made many enemies over his long career and truly needs to be watchful. The bulk of his foes are family members of those he's caught and put away. Half the people in Azkaban are said to be there because of him, either because he arrested them or presented evidence against them. His biggest fear is an assassination attempt and so it should be.

Arthur knows Moody from the OoP during the 1970s and from the MoM in the 1980s. During Voldemort's first rise to power, Moody was after Lucius Malfoy and believed him to be a Death Eater, but never caught him. He caught Karkoff when he was a Death Eater, after 6 months of pursing him, and put him Azkaban for a time. Moody was a great wizard in his time and has been a friend of Dumbledore's since at least the 1970s which is why Dumbledore wanted him to come teach at Hogwarts in the DADA slot in 93/94. However Moody was kidnapped by Barty Crouch Jr, right before he was to take office. Amos Diggory and Arthur Weasley unwittingly helped his assailant by getting him out of his dustbin dilemma with a lesser, non-jail term, punishment. Eventually he was rescued, but he got very twitchy after his 10-month stay in the trunk - who wouldn't?

Moody is terribly battlescared from his work, with a badly scarred face and hands. Over time, Moody lost various body parts doing his job. He lost a leg and some teeth sometime before 1981. He lost a large chunk of his nose in 1982. He lost an eye sometime after 1982. He has a lopsided gash of mouth and his face looks like weathered wood and is covered in scars. One eye is small dark and beady, the other large, round and a vivid electric blue. The blue eye moves ceaselessly without blinking and moves up and down and side to side independent of the dark eye. It even looks out the back of his head. It sees through wood, stone, Invisibility Cloaks, everything. The blue eye is white where a normal eye would be white and seems to be made of glass. It can move around at a very high speed which sometimes makes people looking at him feel a bit sick.

Moody has a mane of long dark grizzled grey hair. Replacing his a portion of his leg is a carved wooden leg ending in a clawed foot. For those who care, it appears to be his right leg that's missing. A number of missing teeth are visible but only when he yawns. His face looks even more peculiar when he's smiling. His hands are clawlike and gnarled and he usually walks with the help of a long staff. He told Harry he should never put his wand in his back pocket because wizards had lost buttocks that way. It would seem he speaks from experience and one would guess from his walk his right buttock is missing. He has a low growling voice and uses the Scottish word "laddie" a lot. He wears a nightshirt to bed. He eats with his pocket knife and drinks from a hip flask to avoid assassination. His table manners are a bit graphic but as person he's really nice.

He was part of Harry escort to Headquarters in the summer of 1995. Usually he wears a voluminous old traveling cloak when he's in public and when he's among Muggles he wears a bowler hat to cover his magical eye but it only makes him look more suspicious. He escorted Harry to King's Cross Station looking very odd indeed. He has 2 Invisibility Cloaks, but Podmore got arrested with his best 1. The Order was using it for watching the door to the DoM in 95/96. He came to the rescue of the MoM in early Jun 1996 and later that month he came to Harry's rescue, by threatening the

Dursleys, specifically Vernon, with social embarrassment if they didn't treat Harry better. Swears: damn it.

(Unknown) Moon: b 1980. House unknown, 1991-1998? He or she started Hogwarts in 91/92.

(Unknown) Moran: A female Irish Chaser in QWC 1994.

Morgana: See Portraits Etc., Photo section

(Unknown) Mortlake: A warlock taken away for questioning by the Committee on Experimental Charms in Aug 1992 for extremely odd ferrets.

Hassan Mostafa: Egypt. Chairwizard of the International Association of Quidditch. A small, skinny wizard, he is completely bald but has a large mustache. Considered the finest referee around, he's the Pier Luigi of the wizarding world. He was the referee for QWC 1994 and wore robes of pure gold and a silver whistle for the game. The veela set fire to his broom with a handful of fire and later he was kicked in the shins by a mediwizard when he went ga-ga over the veela but he stuck it out and made it through the game unpredjudiced despite all this.

(Unknown) Mulciber: b 1951. A Slytherin, 1962-1969. He started Hogwarts in 62/63. See Note 1. A Death Eater, he was caught prior to Karkoff ratting him out in 1982. He was an Imperius Curse specialist and forced many people to do many horrible things before he was nabbed. He was Escapee 4 in the breakout from Azkaban Jan 1996. He ended up back in Azkaban Jun 1996 after the failed MoM raid.

(Unknown) Mullet: A female Irish Chaser in QWC 1994.

Eric Munch: A security guard at the MoM. He caught Sturgis Podmore trespassing, trying to force his way through a door in or to the DoM. He is badly shaven and usually can be found reading *The Daily Prophet*.

Madam Z. Nettles: A witch who can be scintillating and who likes Kwikspell. From Topsham.

Phineas Nigellus: See Portraits Etc., Portraits section.

Mr Nott: b 1950. A Slytherin, 1962-1969. He started Hogwarts in 62/63. See Note 1. The father of Theodore Nott. He is a Death Eater, but was never caught for it. He showed up when Voldemort activated the Dark Mark in Little Hangleton in Jun 1995. He is a stooped figure and so possibly he's a bit elderly. He was part of the failed raid on the MoM and finally ended up in Azkaban Jun 1996.

Theodore Nott: b 1979. A Slytherin, 1991-1998? He started Hogwarts in 91/92. He is a weedy looking boy and a friend of Draco, Crabbe and Goyle.

Mr Oblonsk: The Bulgarian Minister of Magic in 1994. He attended QWC 1994 and wore splendid black velvet robes trimmed in gold. He does speak English but pretended not to because it amused him to watch Fudge struggle.

Tiberius Ogden: He was an Elder of the Wizengamot, but resigned in protest when the Hogwarts High Inquisitor legislation went through. He told Pr Tofty that Harry could do a corporeal Patronus.

Mr. Ogg: He was the Gamekeeper at Hogwarts before Hagrid. Molly remembered him. Hagrid was a trainee under him from 1943 till he retired.

Mr. Ollivander: An old man with a soft voice and wide pale eyes that shine like moons especially in his rather gloomy shop. He has creepy silvery, misty eyes and long, white fingers. He remembers every wand he sells and all the people that buy them. He sold Lily, James, Hagrid, Harry and Voldemort their wands. He believes that wands choose the wizard they wish to work for. He measures a customer first, then pulls wands. The more wands he pulls for someone, the happier he gets because he

The Harry Potter Companion

likes tricky customers. He's a bit formal and bows as one leaves his shop. He conducted the Wand Weighing at the TT in 1994.

Mr Ollivander is a wandmaker, meaning he collects the wood and the core materials himself, then crafts the wands. He never uses veela hair because it makes wands temperamental but he uses just about everything else. His styling of wands is quite unique in that he likes his wands with some bit of flexibilty. As wood is viritually inflexible, he must add some magic of his own to his wands or use a unique varnish on them. Bendy oak, pliable mahogany or flexible willow are pairs of words that don't go together in the Muggle world. He also seems to have a fondness for short wands. 14" is a big wand and 16" is a rarity and only used for part-giants. The average wand is around 10" give or take an inch. Granted, smaller wands are easier to hide and easier to carry around, but they are a far cry from ancient wizards staffs which were 6' and thick. One assumes over time wandmaking techniques allowed for smaller, but just as powerful wands.

Paracelsus: See Portraits Etc., Photo and Statue sections.

Pansy Parkinson: b 1980. A Slytherin, 1991-1998? She started Hogwarts in 91/92. She is a very mean, hard person. She is pug faced and thicker than a concussed troll. A complete cow according to Hermione. She is the very nasty leader of a gang of Slytherin girls. Not surprisingly she was Draco's date to the Yule Ball in Dec 1994 and wore very frilly pale pink robes. She became a Prefect in 95/96 and later part of the Inquisitorial Squad. Given Draco's embarrassment about his mother's rather ugly face, it's odd that he would date Pansy. Perhaps as Sirius says, choices are few if one is only going to marry a pureblood.

Padma Patil: b 1979. A Ravenclaw, 1991-1998? She started Hogwarts in 91/92. Possibly of Indian descent. She has a twin sister, in Gryffindor, though it is unclear if they are twins, identical twins or superidentical twins. Padma and Parvati, according to Seamus, are the 2 best looking girls in their year. She has dark eyes and dark hair. She was Ron's date for the Yule Ball in Dec 1994 and wore bright turquoise robes. She was not too enthused about going with Ron and went off with a Beauxbatons boy when Ron wouldn't dance with her. She later became a Prefect in 95/96 and joined the DA in Oct 1995.

Parvati Patil: b 1979. A Gryffindor, 1991-1998? She started Hogwarts in 91/92. Possibly of Indian descent. She has a twin sister, in Ravenclaw. Padma and Parvati, according to Seamus, are the 2 best looking girls in their year. She has dark eyes and dark hair. She is the best friend of Lavender Brown. Her favorite teacher was Pr Trelawney and she used to spend lunchtimes with Pr Trelawney, and Lavender, in the North Tower till Firenze came along. Parvati has the makings of a true Seer, but this is according to Pr Trelawney whose judgment is a little suspect.

She likes dressing up and put a butterfly in her hair for the arrival of the Beauxbatons and Durmstrangs, though Pr McGonagall later made her take it out. Harry's date for the Yule Ball in Dec 1994, she was very pretty in robes of shocking pink with her hair in a long dark plait braided with gold and wearing gold bracelets on both wrists. She got her sister to go with Ron. Harry didn't know how to dance, so Parvati led Harry. She later went off with a boy from Beauxbatons because Harry wasn't a very good date. Up until that time Parvati had a small a crush on Harry, which Lavender knew about.

She was very cool to Harry after the Yule Ball because he was such a jerk and she started seeing a Beauxbatons' boy the next Hogsmeade weekend. Despite the bad date, she joined the DA in Oct 1995. She became fearsome at the Reductor Curse - so good she reduced the table carrying all the Sneakoscopes in the Room of Requirement to dust. She doesn't like Hagrid as a teacher and though she likes Pr Trelawney, she developed a thing for Firenze in 95/96 when Sybill was replace by him. Given centaurs don't think much of humans, it seems unlikely she will ever be able to attract his romantic attentions.

Arnold Peasegood: aka Arnie. An Obliviator, with an Accidental Magic Reversal Squad since sometime prior to 1994.

(Unknown) Penfriend: Bill's penfreind from Brazil. He sent Bill a cursed hat because Bill truthfully claimed his family couldn't afford to send him on exchange trip.

(Unknown) Perkins: An timid-looking old warlock that works under Arthur in the Misuse of Muggle Artifacts Office. It's only the 2 of them in the office. Perkins doesn't camp much himself these days because of lumbago, but he loaned his 2 tents to Arthur for QWC 1994. Perkins is a stooped wizard with fluffy white hair.

Sally-Anne Perks: b 1979. House unknown, 1991-1998? She started Hogwarts in 91/92.

Peter Pettigrew: aka Wormtail, Scabbers. b 1955. Hogwarts, 1966-1973. He started Hogwarts in 66/67. See Note 1. House unknown, but probably Hufflepuff since he worked so hard to become an Animagus. Peter always liked big friends that could protect him because he was, and remains, relatively weak and talentless. He was always hopeless at dueling. When he was young he was small with mousy hair and a pointed nose. He chewed his fingernails, scuffed the ground with his toes and was generally anxious looking. Not very bright, he cribbed off neighbors during OWLs. Pr McGonagall was often sharp with him. He deeply admired Sirius and hero worshiped James but he did have some talent of his own since he learned to become an illegal Animagus (rat) after 5 years of trying.

He was a friend of James, Sirius and Remus and after graduating he joined the original OoP with them. As time passed however, he was leaned on by Voldemort and started passing on information to him (c 1980) for about year before the Potter were murdered. He eventually became a Death Eater, complete with the Dark Mark, and turned on his friends completely. He suggested to Sirius that he and not Sirius become the Potter's Secret-Keeper, arguing that Voldemort would be sure to come after Sirius with his great talents, but never would he suspect someone as weak as himself.

So Peter became the Potter's Secret-Keeper and betrayed them a week after they confided in him. Sirius went after him and confronted him, but Peter shot off a massive curse, killing 12 Muggles, and escaped as a rat down the exposed sewer line after leaving a heap of bloodstained robes and a finger of his own to convince people he was dead. He was posthumously awarded the Order of Merlin, 1st class for dying. His mother, who was then alive, accepted it for him. Sirius went to Azkaban for supposedly killing him and the Muggles.

About a year after he became a rat, he came into the possession of the Weasley family. He was Percy's rat for about 9 years, then he became Ron's for another 3 years. Many supposed he'd been hiding from Voldemort's supporters all that time because he had given Voldemort the information that, when used, all but finished him off, but he was really hiding from Sirius. After he learned Sirius had escaped Azkaban and was headed to Hogwarts, he faked his death again, this time pinning the blame on Crookshanks. Eventually he was found and forced back into human form by Remus and Sirius.

It's said the longer one remains an animal the more like it one becomes and possibly eventually one can't get back to one's original state, however Remus and Sirius seemed to think otherwise. In the end Peter's becoming human again was due to Sirius and Remus magicking him back to himself because Peter refused to. He was by this time a very short man, hardly taller than Harry at 13, with thin colorless grey unkempt hair and a large bald spot on top of his head. He had a shrunken appearance as if he had been fat once and grubby skin. His face was ratlike with a very pointed nose and very small, watery eyes. Even his voice was squeaky. His right hand was missing its index finger.

Peter managed to escape again, and vanished off to Albania in Jun 1994. By consulting with the rats of Albania, he found Voldemort in a forest. He met Bertha Jorkins on his way to find Voldemort, and brought her along with him as a present/peace offering. He helped Voldemort get back to the UK where he took care of him at Riddle House (Aug 18-25, 1994). Not a very good servant, Peter does whatever Voldemort tells him, but often not well. He lost Barty Sr and got tortured for it, though not to death or insanity as Voldemort would have had no one to rely on at that point. Peter's loyalty to Voldemort is further compromised as he owes a Blood Debt to Harry. He even tried to dissuade Voldemort from using Harry for his rebirth (and then killing him) after he learned of Voldemort's plan.

In the end Peter went along with Voldemort's plan, killed Cedric and even cut off his right hand for Voldemort to be reborn, but there was at least some pang of conscience first. In return for his cooperation, Peter was given a molten silver hand, like a dazzling glove, that is incredibly strong and can crush a twig into powder as if he was merely snapping his fingers. As of 95/96 Peter is a short, balding man with graying hair and a pointed nose, who wheezes when he exerts himself and wears a long black cloak. He claims that he isn't really bad, just weak, and this is probably true, but when one lets one's weakness keep one from doing what is right, one truly is bad. Neville is weak, but he fights his weakness. Harry has Voldemort in his very brain, but he fights against that influence. To be weak is not a sin, not to at least strive to be stronger is.

Madam Irma Pince: Hogwarts' Librarian. A thin irritable woman who looks like an underfed vulture, but this is all probably due to the fact that she is the only librarian the school has and is in charge of almost a million books and 1,000 students using them. She has been known to add unusual jinxes to books in her care, well beyond the usual library spells. When Dumbledore doodled in *Theories of Transubstantial Transfiguration*, the book beat him fiercely around the head. She demands heavy fines for damaging book, particularly for ripping out pages or dropping books in the bath. She checks notes from teachers authorizing Restricted Section book use by holding them up to light to try and detect forgery. She alone can go into the Restricted Section to get out books without incident.

Madam Pince tends to stalk when angry, brandishes her feather duster at students and gives reproving looks to loud or rowdy students. She can usually be found dusting her book or polishing those with gilded covers but she sometimes also prowls the Library menacingly breathing down the necks of people that touch her books. She has one shoe that squeaks, so forwarned is forarmed,. and can be quite scary when her shriveled face contorts with rage. Her preferred protective spell involves objects, ink bottles, books, bookbags, etc, whacking someone on or about the head and chasing after someone whacking them on or about the head. Clearly wizards must have very strong skulls.

Sturgis Podmore: b 1957. A member of the OoP since the 1970s, Sturgis is a square-jawed wizard with thick straw-colored hair. He was put under the Imperius Curse of Lucius Malfoy and forced to try to enter the top-security door into the DoM in Sep 1995. He was caught and arrested for trespassing by Eric Munch and sent to Azkaban for 6 months. Hopefully he was let out in Mar or Apr 1996, though he wasn't at the raid on the MoM in Jun of that year.

(Unknown) Poliakoff: He is 1 of 12 Durmstrang students that accompanied Karkoff to the TT in 93/94. He got reprimanded for letting food dribble down the front of his robes. He was at least 17 years old in 1993.

Madam Poppy Pomfrey: She is Hogwarts' school nurse and runs the Hospital wing. She is very skilled at healing, rather strict, but a kind woman who has only the best interest of her patients in mind. She doesn't say anything about students maladies and seems to have a "don't ask, don't tell" policy. She won't pursue a student's story if it starts to go a bit fishy or ask too many questions about how student might have ended up with the symptoms she or he presents with.

She can mend any injury, even reattach a nose, but Hermione's Sneak Jinx proved too much for her skills. She was however able to fix Harry's broken bones almost instantly, or could have if Pr Lockhart hadn't deboned him. She was however able to regrow the 33 bones over the course of a single night. She usually has a very good relationship with the staff, even Filch, but she definitely didn't care for Pr Lockhart at all because he was incompetent to give medical treatment but tried to mend Harry's broken arm anyway.

She has an office at the end of the Hospital ward with a door on it so she can keep an eye on her charges. She will allow hospitalized students to receive and eat stacks of candy, cakes and sweets, bottles of pumpkin juice and piles of cards, books or homework, but will confiscate unhygienic items such as toilet seats. She is very protective of her patients and after Hermione and Penelope were Petrified in 92/93, she closed the ward and locked the doors. She was afraid whatever was Petrifying people would come back to finish her patients off. She was at the scene of each task during the TT in case champions needed care, but she definitely didn't approve of the event itself. She feels that sports are inherently dangerous and doesn't care for them. When the dementors were around she used boulder-size chocolate lumps she had to break with a small hammer for the patients.

She has quarters right off the Hospital ward and at night she can be found bustling around wearing a nightdress and a cardigan. She brings patients meals on trays and administers various regimes throughout the day and night. She normally allows visitors if it doesn't intrude on her therapies for that patient but will tackle even Fudge even she feels a visitor is not best for her charge. As a patient, one can hear people in the corridor by the main doors from the hospital beds. She takes care of staff as well as students but each year it's the students that cause her to goes through a lot of bubotuber pus (for acne treatment). She tut-tut-tuts at people when upset, which is not as irritating as Umbridge's hem, hem, since Poppy is a genuinely nice person who cares for her patients. She has been at Hogwarts probably since sometime after 1973 because she doesn't seem to know about Remus or the Whomping Willow. She told Dumbledore she liked his earmuffs and made him blush.

Roddy Ponter: He bet Ludo Bagman Bulgaria would be the first to score in QWC 1994.

Harry James Potter: aka The Boy Who Lived, Potty, Scarhead, Patronus Potter. b Jul 31, 1980. A Gryffindor, 1991-1998? He started Hogwarts in 91/92. See schematic R for a family tree. He is half-blood. His mother was a Muggle born and his father a pureblood. He is the son of Lily Evans Potter and James Potter, nephew of Petunia Evans Dursley and cousin of Dudley Dursley. Sirius Black was his godfather. He has no other known living relations but he must have some if his father was a pureblood and all purebloods are interrelated.

It was prophetically foretold by Sybill Trelawney (1979) that Harry must kill Voldemort, or vice versa. Voldemort got wind of this and throughout 1980 plotted to destroy the Potters. Finally on Halloween Oct 31, 1981, Voldemort tried to preemptively kill Harry and his father at his home in Godric's Hollow. Both his parents died but Harry survived, with a scar over his right eye, and became famous throughout the wizarding world for a) surviving the death curse of Voldemort and b) ridding the world (temporarily) of Voldemort. However, it was due to this death curse that Harry and Voldemort's lives became inextricably linked from that point on. Their very essences became one in a way that is both profound and terrible, but neither knew it at the time, and, from the time of the failed curse, they went their separate ways for the next 11 years. They are essentially 1 person, in 2 bodies, until one kills the other.

During Harry's early life, ages 1-10, there were abundant signs he was magical, but his aunt and uncle tried to ignore them. He could make magical things happen when he was angry or scared, but they were always beyond his control to instigate or stop. Usually Harry simply lost control and what happened as a result was more or less out of his hands. After these type of episodes, the Dursleys generally punished him by locking him in his cupboard and not feeding him though this did little to change Harry. He did however learn to pick the cupboard doorlook and sneak out for food while Dursleys were asleep so perhaps not a total loss as an experience.

Early Indications of being magical:
Harry tried to jump behind some big trash cans, and suddenly found himself sitting on the chimney on the roof of the school kitchens
(punished: locked in the cupboard).
Turned a teacher's wig blue
(unknown if punished).
Grew full head of hair in one night
(punished: 1 week in cupboard).
Shrunk an old brown sweater with orange fluff balls on it, that was originally his cousin's, till it was hand-puppet size
(not punished).
Made a glass barrier disappear at the Zoo and released a boa constrictor
(punished: over 1 week in the cupboard).

Harry and the Dursleys: Harry has lived with the Dursleys since he was orphaned because he has to. It is the only place that he will be protected from Voldemort (but not dangers like dementors or Dudley). As long as he is living with Petunia, Lily's blood relation, the charm Lily created by dying for him will remain effective. It would seem that he must spend at least 4 weeks, including his birthday, at her house, and receive a Christmas present every year from her for him to be considered "family" in the eyes of the charm. He has no memory of parents at all, and initially has no photographs of them and is forbidden by the Dursleys to discuss them. He grew up thinking his parents were killed in a car crash as all he recalls of their death is a blinding flash of green and a high cold cruel laugh (Voldemort's).

Harry's early life (age 1-10) was primary school with his cousin, the cupboard and Mrs Figg's living room. He had no friends, received no mail and wasn't even allowed a library card. At school, he was ostracized by classmates because his cousin's gang hated him and no one wanted to get on the bad side of the gang. At home was hated and feared for being magical. In public, sometimes odd-looking strangers seemed to know him but they always vanished when he tried to get a closer look or Petunia would panic and drag him away from them. A typical day for Harry was waking to Petunia's shrill voice, the first thing he heard in the morning, dressing in his spider-ridden cupboard and being told at breakfast by Vernon to get a hair cut (Harry usually gets a haircut every week, but it doesn't help as his hair is very uncooperative and does what it wants). He then went to school and got ignored or beat up, came home to do homework and spend more time in the cupboard, then went to sleep.

Three rules Harry developed for living a quiet life with the Dursleys were: 1) don't ask questions 2) never talk about anything acting in some manner it wouldn't normally, even if it's a dream or a cartoon, and 3) never let anything strange be seen to happen around yourself. Even with these rules, life with the Dursleys is hellish. Things finally came to a head on Dudley's 11th birthday, Jun 24, 1991, when Harry was taken to the Zoo with the Dursleys and Piers Polkiss. Although it was the first real outing of his life and he wanted nothing to go wrong, Rule 3 went by the boards at the reptile house when he spoke to boa constrictor then accidentally vanished the tank's glass barrier.

He was punished for a couple weeks in the cupboard, but eventually got out. During the remainder of the summer holiday, he spent all possible time out of house wandering around trying to avoid Dudley's gang. He was looking forward to attending Stonewall High, the local public secondary school, in the fall of 1991, where at last he'd be free to make friends and didn't know his name has been down for Hogwarts since he was born, but on Jul 24, 1991, a week before his 11th birthday, an acceptance letter from Hogwarts arrived. The Dursleys recognized the letter, destroyed it in a panic and gave Harry his cousin's 2nd bedroom, the smallest bedroom of the house. It took only 1 trip to move all his possessions but there were already in the room several items such as clock (which he manages to repair), a large parrot cage (which Hedwig can hang out in as opposed to her travel cage) and shelves of books in pristine condition.

After a week of trying to get the letter to Harry in conventional and unconventional ways, Harry was at last given his Hogwarts' letter by Hagrid while at Hut-on-the-Rock, on Jul 31, his birthday. It's from Hagrid finally that he finds out his parents belonged to a different world, as does he, and that the Dursleys knew about everything and kept from him. He was relieved to discover he's a wizard and can go to Hogwarts but justly angry with his aunt and uncle. Before Harry could begin to dwell on what's happened, Hagrid whisked him off to London by rowboat then train to get the many school supplies he will need for the coming year. At the Leaky Cauldron he was introduced to Pr Quirrell, without his turban, then was shown by Hagrid how to enter Diagon Alley and how to get to Gringotts Wizarding Bank.

Harry discovered his parents left him a substantial amount of money and wisely decided not to tell the Dursleys about it. He bought school supplies including a right-handed 11" wand of holly with a phoenix tailfeather core and made the acquaintance of Draco while buying robes. It is in Diagon Alley, Harry was give Hedwig as a birthday present from Hagrid, his first real present since going to live with the Dursleys. After an eventful day, Hagrid escorted Harry part way home and gave him a ticket for the Hogwarts Express. Harry, upon returning to the Dursleys, is subsequently ignored for the rest of the summer. The Dursleys drove him to King's Cross Station on Sep 1, only because they're going to London anyway, but they must have been really glad to get rid of him since it's a 3.25 hour trip to reach King's Cross Station from Little Whinging. Once there Harry is dumped with his possessions between Platform 9 and 10, and left to find his own way to the train.

Harry 91/92: Harry first met Molly, Ginny, Fred, George, Percy and Ron Weasley at King's Cross Station between Platform 9 and 10. After hearing Molly use the word Muggle and seeing her boys with trunks and an owl, he asked her for help on how to get through the barrier. On the train he sat in a compartment with Ron and during the ride to Hogwarts he was introduced to many aspects of the wizarding world, including Chocolate Frog wizard photo trading cards on which he sees Albus Dumbledore for the first time. Draco, along with Crabbe and Goyle, turn up to introduce themselves, but after Draco insults Ron, Harry decides to hate the trio in perpetuity. Hermione Granger and Neville Longbottom also turn up, but Harry's reaction to them is less severe, especially as they all end up in Gryffindor together.

Harry was sorted into Gryffindor, his father's old House, and discovered in the 1st week he'd inherited is father's flying skills as well. A natural-born flyer with the light speedy build of a Seeker and the ability to focus so totally on small things (Snitch, Rememberall) that he sees them moving in slow motion, Pr McGonagall quickly got Dumbledore to bend the "no 1st years on House Quidditch teams" rule for Gryffindor and Harry became the youngest House player in a century. Pr McGonagall bought Harry a "state of the art" racing broom, the Nimbus 2000, apparently with her own money, she's so determined to get the Quidditch Cup back from Pr Snape, and Harry began secretly practicing with Oliver Wood right away.

It takes Harry less than week to decide he hates Filch and Pr Snape, who seem to hate him for no reason or at least reasons he has yet to discover, and History of Magic because it's so incredibly boring. He, and all Gryffindor 1st years, had Friday afternoons off which he put to good use either practicing Quidditch or visiting with Hagrid. Harry and Ron became friends with Hermione on Halloween 1991 through the mountain troll incident, which was a good thing for Harry because he desperately needed someone of her intelligence in his circle. Harry's blessed with great courage, wizarding talent and the ability to see the big picture (saving the world really is more important that passing exams) but Harry's blindspot is lack of wisdom. Like Sir Cadogan, he usually develops the wrong take on a situation then does something unnecessary making the situation worse.

Harry is fond of treacle tart, good at Quidditch and gets good grades, but he likes having adventures the way Sirius liked risk-taking - just a little more than he should. It was Harry's opinion that the Sorcerer's Stone was in danger and had to be saved when in fact Dumbledore's clever use of the Mirror had completely stumped Voldemort and if Harry hadn't shown up, he'd never have gotten it at all. However, Harry, Ron and Hermione did go to rescue the Sorcerer's Stone. Harry got the stone but then found himself in a struggle with Pr Quirrell (Voldemort) and nearly died. He was saved by the appearance of Dumbledore, as was the stone, and ended up in hospital wing in a coma for 3 days while Voldemort disappeared back to Albania.

On the plus side, Harry's defeat of Voldemort, with help of Ron, Hermione, and Neville, won Gryffindor the House Cup in 1992 (though did however lose the 1992 Quidditch Cup, again). On the minus side, even after all this, Dumbledore still refused to tell Harry why Voldemort wanted to kill him in the first place. However Dumbledore does admit to Harry that Voldemort, using Pr Quirrell's body, was unable to touch him because he couldn't stand the love which Lily imbued Harry's very skin with by dying for him. Harry discovers Voldemort cannot endure love of any kind, a tidbit that will serve Harry well in years to come – whenever he actually considers it.

Harry Potter 92/93: Harry spent most of the summer cut off from his friends, thanks to Dobby, the Malfoy's house-elf, who stopped all Harry's mail, in a misguided attempt to make him think he'd been abandoned so he'd decide not to return to Hogwarts. When that doesn't work out, Dobby turned to plan B, and got Harry in trouble with the MoM, trying to prevent him from returning to Hogwarts by ticking the Dursleys off, breaking magical law and getting him expelled. When the Dursleys discovered Harry couldn't do magic out of school, they locked all Harry's school things in the cupboard under the stairs, even though he has homework assigned over the school holidays, and Vernon vowed Harry would never to return to Hogwarts.

ACASCIAS RIPHOUSE

To make good on his threat, Vernon then proceeded to turn Harry's room into a solitary confinement cell, complete with bars on both windows and a cat flap in the door for sliding in horrible food 3 times a day. Luckily the Weasley's catch wind of Harry's predicament and Ron and the Weasley twins break him out and take him to the Burrow, where he spends the rest of the summer. Harry had his first experience traveling by Floo Powder from the Burrow to Diagon Alley or nearly. He broke his glasses, yet again, and ended a few stops down the line in Knockturn Alley Dark Arts shop. Needless to say Floo Powder did not become his favorite way to travel. Hagrid, who was also in the alley, and shepherded him back to Diagon Alley, the decent side of the shopping district, where he rejoined the Weasleys. At Flourish and Blotts he discovered, to his complete horror, that Gilderoy Lockhart was hired as the new DADA teacher.

On Sep 1, Harry and Ron failed to get through the barrier at King's Cross Station because Dobby had blocked it, causing them to miss the train. They are "forced" to fly the Ford Anglia to Hogwarts and, after a disagreeable landing in the Whomping Willow, finally make it back to school in 1 piece, though Arthur's car ran off into the Forbidden Forest. Almost immediately Harry had to deal with the basilisk, having heard it speaking in the walls during his very first week. A couple months later, after Nearly Headless Nick's Deathday Party, he encountered the voice of the basilisk again and followed it upstairs to find a Petrified Mrs Norris and the writing on the wall saying the Chamber is open. This unfortunate discovery sets people to thinking he may be the Heir of Slytherin.

Shortly after this incident Harry's streak of bad luck continued when Dobby set a rogue Bludger to attack him in another vain attempt to try and force him to leave Hogwarts. But Dobby's new plan also fails and Harry survives the attempt with a broken arm, which Lockhart tries to fix, but ends up completely deboning. After this things took another turn for the worst when Harry joined the Dueling Club and it came out that he was a Parselmouth which confirms many students' suspicions that he is the Heir of Slytherin. Harry is actually only a Parselmouth because some of Voldemort's powers were transferred to him when he was struck with the curse as a baby, but none of his classmates know this. Harry believing that Draco was the real culprit, then attempted to prove it by taking Polyjuice Potion and turning into Goyle for an hour to question Draco. Sadly, the exercise proved pointless as Draco was for a change truly innocent.

Harry eventually found Tom Riddle's Diary in Moaning Myrtle's bathroom and began to try and figure out how it worked. The Diary's enchantments drew him, making him feel the book was an old friend he wanted to open up to, and Harry finally communicated with Riddle, who was up to his own game, but as usual because of Dumbledore, Harry hadn't a clue he was in danger. Harry was shown a version of what happened the last time the Chamber was opened by Riddle and swallowed it hook, line and sinker. Alas, before Harry was able to do much more with the Diary, his room was rifled and the diary stolen back by Ginny. Harry, checking out the events the Diary showed him, attempted to consult with Hagrid, but before Hagrid could be much help, he is taken into custody. Hagrid was able to give Harry only 1 clue to help prove he is innocent, so naturally Harry and Ron had to follow it up. They ended up in Aragog's hollow, discovered Hagrid was innocent of opening the Chamber in 42/43 and barely escaped with their lives. Aragog's children are defeated with the help of the feral Ford Anglia.

Events progressed until Hermione was Petrified and the school threatened to close for good. Before giving up on the school, Harry decided to visit the Petrified Hermione and discovered she had solved the riddle of the monster of the Chamber, it was a basilisk. Harry quickly realized the serpent must be coming through Moaning Myrtle's bathroom and after Ginny was taken by Tom Riddle, Harry and Ron went after her down the pipework with a very reluctant Pr Lockhart, the DADA instructor. Pr Lockhart tried to overpower them and Obliviate their memories but Ron's wand backfired and Obliviated his own memory. Ron became trapped behind some debris after the tunnel collapsed and Harry was then forced to go on alone. Harry discovered the Chamber of Secrets, found Ginny and met Tom Riddle, whom Harry had no idea was out to kill him.

Tom revealed to Harry that he was trying to become mortal by sucking Ginny's life out of her. Harry, shocked and horrifed, immediately set out to stop Tom. Harry defeated the basilisk, with the help of Fawkes and the Sorting Hat, and stabbed Tom Riddle's diary with a basilisk fang so he would be destroyed (at least for now). Harry then followed up these triumphs but getting Dobby set free and Lucius Malfoy sacked as a school governor. Harry was rewarded with a Special Services to the School award. From this adventure Harry realized that though he had obtained some of Voldemort's traits and powers, he was not like Tom Riddle because he chose not to be put in Slytherin. He resisted his worst potential nature and the House that might have encouraged it.

Harry 93/94: Harry kept in touch with his friends over the summer and all went well till Aunt Marge arrived. After enduring almost a week of her constant ill-mannered remarks about his parents, Harry blew her up - accidentally. He reckoned he had become an outcast and a fugitive in the magical world as a result and ran away from home. While wandering around he saw the Grim (actually Sirius) but, before more could come of it, he was picked up by the Knight Bus. He was dropped at the Leaky Cauldron, where he met with Fudge who told him everything was ok as far as his magical slip-up with Aunt Marge. Fudge warned him to stay at the Leaky Cauldron for the remainder of his vacation and to only go into Diagon Alley only in the day time. So, for the next few weeks, Harry had a great time wandering in Diagon Alley and living at the Leaky Cauldron.

Harry, as a 3rd year student student now, added 2 electives to his schedule, Divination and Care of Magical Creatures. In picking up his Divination textbook in the Flourish and Blotts' Fortune-Telling he realized he has seen the Grim, just before he was picked up by the Knight Bus. But Harry had more than the Grim to worry about and later the Weasleys let slip that Sirius Black was after him. On the Express to Hogwarts, he had his first encounter with a dementor and Pr Lupin, the new DADA teacher. Harry's reaction to the dementor was swift and hard, he collapsed. With the help of chocolate, he was back on his feet by the time he arrived at school. At the feast he received another shock: Hagrid had been made the new Care of Magical Creatures class teacher.

Classes began and almost immediately Harry found Divination ridiculous and was sorry he had chosen it. It hardly helped that Sybill was always predicting his death and seeing the Grim in his teacup. Hagrid's class, while more thrilling than Divination, was a little too thrilling and though Harry mastered Buckbeak the hippogriff, Draco was slashed by the same for insulting the very proud and intelligent creature. Pr Lupin, however, struck a happy medium beween the 2 classes and taught a very practical, safe and exciting DADA class that put him on just about everybody's good side, except Pr Snape's. This year Harry also has the opportunity to go into Hogsmeade, but with Sirius Black after him, and no permission slip, Dumbledore won't allow him to leave the grounds.

ACASCIAS RIPHOUSE

Harry, forbidden to go to Hogsmeade on the first outing of the year, has an interesting time anyway and spent afternoon with Lupin, who promised to give him Patronus lessons to get rid of future dementors he may meet. Later Harry's problems with Sirius proved more pressing as Sirius attempted to get into Gryffindor Tower to attack Harry (people suppose, but actually to get at Peter [Scabbers]). The Fat Lady luckily defended her post and Sirius wasn't let through. The Fat Lady went in for repairs and Sir Cadogan was brought in to replace her, but still Harry wasn't as concerned about Sirius as he the dementors. His fears seemed unjustifed when during a Quidditch match, he saw what he thought was the Grim again while, but it is the 100 dementors that simultaneously rushed onto the field below him that caused him to fall off his broom about 50'. Luckily his fall was broken by Dumbledore, who happened to be there watching. Harry ended up in the Hospital and worse, discovered his Nimbus had drifted over to the Whomping Willow and got smashed to bits.

Although Harry was not supposed to leave the grounds, Fred and George gave him the Marauder's Map and he couldn't help but use it. He ended up at the Three Broomsticks and overheard that Sirius and his father were great friends in their youth at Hogwarts and how Sirius was even James best man at his wedding, but later Sirius betrayed his parents to their death. Harry was greatly angered and surprised by these revelations but doesn't really do anything about them except stew. Over the Christmas holidays Harry found out about Buckbeak having to face a trial for slashing Draco and promised to help Hagrid form a defense but Harry never really fulfills his word. On Christmas Harry received an anonymous present, a Firebolt, that was actually from Sirius and things look up until Hermione rats Harry out. The broom was then confiscated for intense inspection by Pr Flitwick and Madam Hooch and was almost thrown off the House team for being broomless.

After the holidays, Harry began his private anti-dementor lessons with Pr Lupin and all did not go well. Harry finally got his broom back, somewhat salvaging his relationship with Hermione, but about this same time Neville's passwords were stolen by Crookshanks for Sirius and Scabbers (Peter) faked his death as a rat. Harry won the next Quidditch match against Ravenclaw even though he had to contend with his growing attraction for Cho Chang and Draco's lame attempt at sabotage by going on the pitch dressed as a dementor but best of all, the Patronus lesson paid off, and Harry was at last able to produce an amazing corporeal stag-shape Patronus that trampled Draco and his cronies. All was well that night until, after the celebrations died down, Ron woke to find Sirius standing by his bed, holding a large knife.

Sir Cadogan was hastily replaced by the Fat Lady and some security trolls, but Harry, who still refused to admit he could be in danger, snuck off to Hogsmeade the next Hogsmeade weekend once again. However, this time he was spotted by Draco and nearly caught by Pr Snape. Pr Lupin rescued him but subsequently took his map. The final Quidditch match rolled around and Harry helped Gryffindor smash Slytherin and take the Quidditch Cup but final exams did not go as well. Harry's Divination exam turned frightening when Sybill nodded off and gave yet another real prophecy about Voldemort. She warned Harry that Voldemort would be getting his servant back. Harry took this to mean Sirius (but she meant Peter). Before he could make much sense of her words, Buckbeak lost his appeal and got axed, Ron got dragged off by Snuffles and Harry and Hermione ended up in the Shrieking Shack.

The truth finally comes out that Peter was the one that betrayed Harry's parents, Sirius was innocent of all that he was accused of and Harry's godfather, Scabbers was really a man and Lupin was really a werewolf that had also been a friend of James' at school. On the way back to Hogwarts castle to let Dumbledore in on all the news,

THE HARRY POTTER COMPANION

things went seriously astray. Lupin turned wolf and Sirius turned dog to try and head him off before he harmed anyone, however Sirius was outed and he, Harry and Hermione became surrounded by dementors near the Lake. Then, from the far side of the Lake, a huge Patronus appeared and saved them all. Harry, Ron and Hermione were found and taken to the Hospital and Sirius was locked in Pr Flitwick's office. Harry told Dumbledore the truth of things and Dumbledore allowed Harry and Hermione to use the Time-Turner to go back in time to make things right.

Harry and Hermione saved Buckbeak, themselves at the Lake, and then Sirius by letting him escape on Buckbeak and in the process Harry discovered he was the really powerful wizard that saved himself, Hermione and Sirius from across the Lake by producing a huge corporeal Patronus.. His Patronus is a stag the size of a horse, bright like the moon and able to scare off 100 dementors. He named his Patronus Prongs, after his father's Animagus form. Harry finally got his Hogsmeade form signed, by Sirius, which was good enough for Dumbledore, and Harry was able to get better treatment from the Dursleys by telling them he had a mass murderer for a godfather and that his godfather was very interested in his welfare.

Harry 94/95: For the entire summer, Harry and Dumbledore corresponded with Sirius, who had gone into hiding somewhere in the tropics. Near the end of summer Harry received his first look at Voldemort's doings from inside Voldemort's brain. He saw Voldemort murder Frank Bryce, but when he woke up, other than his scar hurting, he didn't give the "dream" too much credence. He was invited to QWC 1994 by the Weasleys, who made the fatal error of picking Harry up via the Floo Network, further deteriorating the Dursleys' opinion of wizards in general and Harry in particular. Harry and his friends Portkeyed to QWC 1994 where Harry met Ludo and Barty Sr and became acquainted with the Dark Mark.

Harry's wand was stolen by Barty Jr and later used to send up the Dark Mark. Harry got his wand back and spent the remainder of the summer with the Weasleys. Once at school Harry met Barty Jr (pretending to be Moody) and learned about the Unforgivable Curses. Harry was entered into the TT by Barty Jr, and was thus forced by magical contract to compete. Harry managed to outwit the dragon in Task 1, get Ron back as a friend, save Ron in Task 2, survive another foray into Voldemort's mind during which he witnessed the torture of Peter Pettigrew, get through a dance at the Yule Ball with Parvati, ride out Rita Skeeter's ridiculously stupid stories about him and even a peek into Dumbledore's Pensive where he peruses Albus' memories of several Death Eater's trials conducted under Barty Sr, but then came Task 3.

During Task 3 he ended up in Little Hangleton, in Voldemort's hands and was forced to give blood to allow Voldemort to be reborn. To his lasting regret, his blood enabled Voldemort to get around Lily's charm and touch him. Voldemort thought using Harry's blooe would make him stronger because of the protection Lily put on Harry, but in reality, though he has yet to discover it, it just gave Harry a means of defeating him. Harry was then forced into a duel with Voldemort, to prove to the Death Eaters that Harry was nothing special, however quite the reverse was proved. Harry and Voldemort's wands locked and it was Harry's will that proved the stronger and Voldemort's wand that ended up regurgitating shadows of the more powerful spells it had done. A crowd of people, all killed by Voldemort's wand, appeared and started encouraging Harry but discouraging Voldemort.

Harry survived the duel, out ran the Death Eaters, and, with Cedric's body, managed to grab the Portkey and get back to Hogwarts. He was immediately taken to the castle, by Barty Jr, and grilled for the grizzly details of how Voldemort punished the Death Eaters. Dumbledore appeared on the scene during this interrogation and finally Barty Jr was unmasked as an impostor and confessed to a litany of ills. But, because Fudge could not face the fact Voldemort was back, the truth was buried by the MoM. A month went by and Dumbledore finally ended the term by telling the students that Voldemort was back. The MoM started a smear campaign against Harry and Dumbledore in response. On the Express home, Harry gave Fred and George his 1,000G winnings from the TT so they could start their joke shop. More information on the TT, its history, and events connected with it, is in the Triwizard Tournament section in part II.

Harry 95/96: Harry spent the summer reading *The Daily Prophet* and listening to the 7pm Muggle news to try and pick up on anything Voldemort might have been doing but all to no avail. Meanwhile, Harry started to experience rather severe personality shifts due to his growing mental, spiritual and now physical connection with Voldemort. He was not consciously aware of this connection and neither was Voldemort, but it was there all the same, and clearly Voldemort's personality was the dominate of the pair. Harry, in a foul humor, tried to pick a fight with Dudley one night on the way home from a park but before things could come to a head, they were trapped in an alley by 2 dementors (sent by the MoM's Dolores Umbridge) to suck the soul out of Harry and stop all the trouble he'd been causing. Harry defended himself and was taken home by Mrs Figg, whom he discovered is a Squib, and part of a large group of people who have been watching him 24/7 since 1981.

Harry received a passle of letters telling him he's basically in trouble with everyone. The MoM was upset because he used underage magic, magic in front of Muggles and magic out of school and Dumbledore was upset because he wanted to leave the house for good and all. Harry quickly realized how serious things were when Petunia received an Howler (from Dumbledore) and overrode Vernon's decision to throw him out though Harry was already willing to leave. Harry subsequently stayed in his room till a few days later, when Harry was taken from Privet Dr by members of the OoP including Lupin, Tonks, Moody, Diggle, Shacklebolt, Doge, Vance, Podmore and Jones. He was removed to Sirius and 12 Grimmauld Place, London, the Headquarters of the Order where he discovered all but Percy of the Weasleys were in the Order, and that Sirius and Pr Snape were also members.

Harry's immediate reaction was to have a fit of anger about not being kept informed about things by his friends but was not told that at this point that this was because Dumbledore was aware there could be a connection between Harry and Voldemort and was purposely keeping him in the dark. At this point Harry's mind had begun looking into Voldemort's obsessive thoughts about breaking into the Hall of Prophecy to get at the orb containing Sybill's prophecy. Harry began dreaming about the doorway to the DoM, but didn't know what it was, or that it was actually Voldemort's thoughts he was seeing. While at Headquarters, he discovered Sirius' family history, met Mrs Black's portrait and tried to find out more about what the Order was doing (but couldn't). However, he had enough of his own problems to deal wil and on Aug 12 he faced a Full Court for his use of underage magic.

He was only just saved from prosecution by Dumbledore and Mrs Figg then was returned to Grimmauld Place for the remainder of the summer. The day before he was to return to Hogwarts, Harry received another blow when he discovered that Ron and Hermione were made Prefects while he had been passed over. On the train to Hogwarts Harry met Luna Lovegood and learned about *The Quibbler*. When he arrived at school, Harry found out he could see thestrals (because of witnessing Cedric's death, so he obviously didn't actually see his parents die) as could Neville and Luna. Harry discovered that Dolores Umbridge, who had been at his trial, was the new DADA teacher. Many students felt that Harry was cracked because of all the bad press he'd gotten and, even Seamus had words with Harry, but this changed after confronted Pr Umbridge over Voldemort's return in DADA class and received a week's detention. Neville, Ron, Luna, Ernie and Hermione all supported Harry and declared they believed him.

This confontation began for Harry a series of negative encounters with Pr Umbridge that eventually culminated at the end of the 1st a Quidditch match of the season with Harry being thrown off the House team and told he was banned for life by Pr Umbridge. Things got worse when the MoM, out to take over Hogwarts, installed Pr Umbridge as Hogwarts High Inquisitor and stopped students from learning any practical defensive magic. Harry in response rebelled and started a secret, highly practical DADA club called Dumbledore's Army (the DA for short). Almost 30 people joined and, with the help of Dobby, they began to meet weekly in the Room of Requirement where, just before Christmas, Harry received his first kiss from Cho.

Before vacation started, Harry again entered Voldemort's mind and saw, while in Nagini (or possibly Voldemort was the snake), himself bite Arthur, who was guarding the door to the DoM. Arthur was subsequently saved by Harry waking up and telling all this to Dumbledore, who made sure Arthur was found and sent to St Mungo's. Harry and the Weasleys then removed to Grimmauld Place for Christmas to be near Arthur. At this point, Voldemort realized Harry was having a wander through his thoughts and cooked up a way to use them against him, with the help of Narcissa Black Malfoy and Kreacher. Dumbledore informed Pr Snape that he was to give occlumency lessons to Harry in order to prevent just such a plot as Voldemort's but the lessons backfired and opened Harry's mind the point that he began pick up on all the Voldemort felt, putting him right where Voldemort wanted him.

Harry dated Cho, once, on Feb 14, and whatever attraction there might have been ended within a few hours due to Harry's lack of dating skills and Cho's unresolved grief over Cedric. He moved on quickly and the same day gave his story about Little Hangleton to Rita Skeeter and Luna's dad, who printed it in *The Quibbler* in the Mar issue. The DA was eventaully ratted out by a friend of Cho's, further worsening her relationship with Harry, and Dumbledore was forced to go on the lam. Harry continued to study occlumency as hard as he could but it seemed only to make him weaker and less able to defend his mind. One night while Pr Snape was called away, Harry has a peek in his Pensive found out some unpleasant things about his father, Pr Snape caught him and forthwith refused to give any more lessons. Harry floo phoned Sirius and Remus to find out if any he saw in the Pensive was true and received a bit of a nasty shock: while his dad might have grown out of being a prat, he had been as Pr Snape remembered him.

Later in the year, Harry had some career advice from Pr McGonagall, who promised to help him become an Auror if it was the last thing she did just to spite Pr Umbridge and Hagrid took Harry and Hermione to meet Grawp, his half-brother, and made them promise to come and talk to him if he got sacked. By the time Harry tok his OWLs, during which Hagrid went on the lam and Pr McGonagall was injured and sent to St Mungo's, he was practically Voldemort's 24/7 aerial. During his OWL in History, Harry had what he thought was another peek into Voldemort's mind. It involved Sirius being tortured at the Hall of Prophecy. He tried to find Sirius, but Kreacher tricked him in to thinking he was out of the house and at the MoM. He and 5 DA members went to the MoM, where he discovered the truth - Voldemort only lured him there to get the prophecy orb.

ACASCIAS RIPHOUSE

Harry, Luna, Ron, Hermione, Neville and Ginny fought 12 Death Eaters until the Order showed up to rescue them. Despite winning the battle, Sirius dies, and only 11 of the Death Eaters, including Lucius Malfoy and Mr Crabbe, are captured. But, Voldemort was finally exposed to the MoM and Dumbledore at last told Harry about why he'd been avoiding him, so good things came of a bad situation. Harry was told about the lost prophecy in which Sybill informed Dumbledore that a child born at the end of Jul to parents who had escaped or defeated Voldemort 3 times and marked by Voldemort would have the power to defeat Voldemort. Dumbledore also revealed to Harry that he was that person the prophecy speaks of, that either he must die at Voldemort's hands or vice versa.

Dumbledore told Harry that Voldemort accidentally gave Harry a share of his powers when he scarred him, but the real power Harry has is love (the same power that melted Sirius' knife in the door to the chamber holding "love" at the DoM). It is with this force that Harry can defeat Voldemort and in fact he has already used it against him effectively since Harry's mere thought of Sirius, whom he loved, caused Voldemort to flee the MoM. Harry was, understandably, not too whipped up about all this information, but was glad that he at least now knew the truth - for the first time in 5 - and was at last able to make informed choices. Swearing: damn.

Harry's Looks: He looks like his father, except for his eyes which are like his mother's in shape and color, almond shaped and startlingly green eyes. At age 11, he was small and skinny for his age and, though he didn't look it, very fast and good at sports. He has a thin face, knobbly knees and uncontrollably untidy thick jet-black hair that sticks up in the back and in all manner of weird direction like his father's. He wears bangs which Petunia tries to use to cover his scar but Harry's hair is very uncooperative. He has a very thin lighting shape scar on his forehead over his right eye from when Voldemort attempted to kill him by curse, which most people recognize him by immediately. The scar is the only thing he likes about his appearance so his hair always shapes itself in such a way as to reveal it.

He possibly has a crooked nose since he has been repeatedly punched in it over his lifetime with Dudley. He wears broken glasses held together with copious amounts of scotch tape but which he can magically repair when he's in school and allowed to use magic. All his clothes are his cousin's hand-me-downs and very baggy. He's 4 times smaller than Dudley and looks perpetually scruffy, which his neighbors on Privet Dr don't appreciate. He has running shoes that are falling apart and ripped jeans. By the time he reaches Hogwarts he is wearing a watch, so he must have bought himself one before school.

When he's home, he keeps a chart and puts X's on the days as they pass because he so longs to be back at Hogwarts where people like him and think he's normal. He keeps his school trunk, which is large and wooden, at the end of his bed. At night he wears pajamas, slippers and a dressing gown. He always puts his glasses on the bedstand before he goes to sleep and usually keeps his Hungarian horntail figurine there as well. Harry generally writes with an eagle-feather quill using red ink. He has a leather bag for coins, which is possible the biting one Hagrid gave him and which may be moke. He has dark bottle green dress robes in the style of his school robes that Molly bought for him because she felt the color would bring out his eyes.

James Potter: Father of Harry James Potter, husband of Lily Evans Potter. b 1955. A Gryffindor, 1966-1973. He started Hogwarts in 66/67. He was an only child and quite the bag of tricks, though less so than Sirius. Occupation unknown, but he left Harry a lot of money in a vault at Gringotts. Though from a pureblood family, he never held with the pureblood philosophy. He bought his 11" wand at Ollivanders and favored a pliable mahogany which had a little more power than usual that was excellent for Transfiguration. He was an excellent Quidditch player and a Quidditch Cup winner. He was Captain for his House team, and although it is never said what his position was, he might have played several. It seems from the fact that he was always toting a Snitch around in 5th year that he was mostly a Seeker.

Though he never was made a Prefect, he did manage to become Head Boy anyway. He was close to Dumbledore and owned an Invisibility Cloak, which he left with Dumbledore who kept it for Harry. James used it mainly for sneaking off to the kitchens to steal food. During his school years he was a friend of Lupin's and became an illegal Animagus, a stag (Sirius named him Prongs), to accompany him on his monthly romps. He was the best friend of Sirius and they stuck together like brothers. When Sirius ran away from home at 16, he camped out at James' parents house during all his vacations. James and Sirius, who was the more dominate of the two, headed up a gang of 4 at school which included Lupin, a Prefect, and Pettigrew, who hero worshiped James.

James was sort of jerk (prat) in school. He rumpled his hair intentionally to look like he'd just come off a broomstick. He stole a Snitch so he could be seen playing with it and admired for his skill and reflexes. He lived for admiration and attention according to Pr Snape, who seems to have been right. Pr Snape said he was so arrogant that criticism simply bounced off him and that too seems true. Only Sirius, whom James called Padfoot, could call James on his ridiculous behavior and be paid mind - eventually. Sirius said an aspect of risk always made things all the more fun to do for James. At 15 James is smitten with L.E. (Lily Evans), but she refuses date him because she rightfully thought him a jerk. He would hex people in the halls if he didn't like them, mostly Severus because he and Severus hated each other.

James hated Severus just for existing, because Severus was slightly weird and heavily into the Dark Arts. They were both students at Hogwarts, in the same year, but at different houses. He saved Severus' life after Sirius had told him how to get into the Shrieking Shack - knowing Lupin was there in wolf form ready to bite or even kill him. Severus didn't appreciate being in debt to James and despite the fact they were both in the Order, at least at the end, he never found opportunity to do James a good turn and pay him back. Because James and Sirius were the best at school in whatever they did, it left a lot of free time in which James did things, nasty things, just to alleviate Sirius' boredom. In one instance he humiliated Snape by flipping him upside down and removing his underpants for all to see by the Lake while on a break in between OWL exams.

Eventually James became less of a prat, in his 7th year, and started dating Lily. After graduating they both joined the original OoP and in time got married. It is unknown what James did for a living but as a creator of the Marauder's Map, he might of had a joke shop. Just over a year after Harry was born, Lily and James planned to go into hiding and made Peter Pettigrew their Secret-Keeper not knowing that he'd been passing information to Voldemort for over a year. A week after performing the Fidelius Charm, Lily and James were murdered by Voldemort at his home in Godric's Hollow Oct 31, 1981. He, and Lily, put up a fight against Voldemort to protect Harry, but Lily was killed, then James, one assumes of his wounds after partially being hit by a death curse (there is much debate on James' death all we know for certain is he died after Lily). Their deaths were not in vain however as they allowed Harry to survive Voldemort's death curse.

It is assumed that James' parents were dead before Harry was orphaned since Harry seems to have no blood relatives except Petunia and Dudley. Though as James was a pureblood, there should be some wizarding relations, 2nd cousins and so forth. The Potters certainly seemed to have been alive during James' school years and, according to Sirius, afterwards for a time since Sirius would go to lunch on Sundays there. It's not clear what happened to them, or when. Sirius does say that Voldemort wanted to kill the last of the Potters which implies Voldemort had a desire to kill the whole Potter line off. Voldemort may have killed James parents, thus prompting James to take his family into hiding.

James was a tall thin man with black hair that was very untidy and stuck up in the back like Harry's does. He also wore glasses (for distance, like Harry does). He had hazel eyes and a nose slightly longer than Harry's. He had the same thin face, mouth and eyebrows Harry does. At 15, James stood almost exactly the same height as Harry at 15, give or take an inch so perhaps Harry wasn't quite as stunted at 11 as he thought, he might merely come from a thin family that grows tall very slowly.

Lily Evans Potter: b 1955. House unknown, 1966-1973. She started Hogwarts in 66/67. Sister of Petunia Evans Dursley, wife of James Potter, mother of Harry James Potter. Occupation unknown. She was Muggle born and had 1 Muggle sister. She bought her wand at Ollivanders: 10.25" made of willow, it was swishy and nice for charm work. She attended Hogwarts and was probably a Ravenclaw (but possibly she was a Gryffindor). She was close to Dumbledore and after graduation became a member of the OoP. She was a talented witch and very pretty, with startling green almond-shaped eyes (like Harry's) and thick dark red hair.

She was in the same year as James Potter and Severus Snape. She was made Head Girl in her final year, but it's unknown if she was ever a Prefect. One rather assumes she was since she was balling James out in their 5th year for abusing Severus and didn't go away till Severus insisted he didn't want her help. She wasn't too fond of James and didn't start dating him till 7th year when he cleaned up his act and stopped being such an arrogant bully. Lily brought James home to meet her family, including Petunia one day. They were married some time after graduation, c 1975. Lily and James knew how Petunia and Vernon felt about them and wizards in general and seems to have met only at the Evan's funerals though Lily obviously sent a birth announcement to Petunia and Vernon since they knew about Harry.

She gave birth to Harry Jul 31, 1980, but even before that point Dumbledore must have realized that there was a possibility that he might be the child Sybill foretold as being born at the end of Jul to parents that 3 times defeated or escaped Voldemort. How exactly she and James defeated Voldemort or what sort of situation they were in that they needed to escape him is unknown. She had not spoken to Petunia in several years before her death but Lily seems to have had no problems relating to her parents. The Evans were supportive of her being a witch and appear to have liked Lily slightly more than Petunia. One presume that Mr and Mrs Evans died sometime after Lily graduated but way before Harry was orphaned as Harry didn't end up with them.

Dumbledore discovered that someone close to the Potters were betraying them (through Severus) and had been doing so for almost a year and advised the Potters to go into hiding. They took Dumbledore's advice but were betrayed by their Secret-Keeper, Peter Pettigrew. She was murdered at her home in Godric's Hollow on Oct. 31, 1981 by Voldemort. Voldemort said he had no desire to kill Lily, only James and Harry, because apparently he was after blood-born "Potters" in general. She gave her life to protect Harry thus activating a charm that would remain with him the rest of his life. It is Lily's charm and it's protection that Voldemort wanted for himself and why 13 years later he used Harry's blood for his rebirth. The Potters are always called Lily and James, never James and Lily. Why? This is unknown. Possibly wizarding custom, but it doesn't seem so.

As an aside, one does have to wonder why Petunia says she saw Lily doing magic (Transfiguration to be exact) on her vacations. This is very illegal. One might add that the only other person doing illegal magic on their school vacations at this time is Severus Snape. He also fails to get reported, warned or sanctioned. While Severus's case might be explainable, Lily's is not. Why doesn't she get caught? Is the underage magic detection system not up and running in this time period? Did Severus get his father to cover up Lily's magic, turn off the detectors at her house? Did Severus tell her how to get around the system because of some attachment he might have had for her in their early years at Hogwarts? It's difficult to say. The fact that only Lily of all the Prefects, attempted to cross James, the most popular student, to save Severus, the least popular student, implies that she was either super conscientious or at one time, before Severus got into the pureblood philosophy, they were close friends.

Mr and Mrs Potter: James' parents. They adopted Sirius as a second son and welcomed him into their home during school holidays after he ran away from his parents at 16. It's not clear what happened to them, or when. Sirius continued to go there for Sunday lunch after graduating Hogwarts in 1973. It is assumed that James parents were at his wedding but dead before Harry was orphaned since Harry seems to have no blood relatives except Petunia and Dudley by 1981. Sirius does say that Voldemort wanted to kill the last of the Potters (Harry) which implies Voldemort had a desire to kill the whole Potter line off. Voldemort may have killed James' parents, prompting James to take his family into hiding.

Ernie Prang: aka Ern. Driver of the Knight Bus. He is an elderly wizard with an owlish face and very thick glasses. He's not a very good driver but he doesn't hit anything as most objects, even whole houses, will jump out of his way. He may or may not be the only but driver, but he always seems to be driving it, both day and night.

The Prewetts: This entire family was killed by Voldemort, or on his orders. They were considered some of the best wizards of the age. Fabian and Gideon were among those the Prewetts killed.

Fabian Prewett: Original OoP member. It took 5 Death Eaters to kill him and his brother Gideon. They fought heroically but were ultimately killed by Antonin Dolohov.

Gideon Prewett: Original OoP member. It took 5 Death Eaters to kill him and his brother Fabian. They fought heroically but were ultimately killed by Antonin Dolohov.

Apollyon Pringle: He was the Caretaker of Hogwarts in Molly's day. Apparently he gave Arthur scars for life after hexing him for being out late with Molly during their time at school.

Graham Pritchard: b 1982. A Slytherin, 1994-2001? He started Hogwarts in 94/95.

D. J. Prod: A warlock living in Didsbury who likes Kwikspell.

Ptolemy: See Portraits Etc., Photo section.

Adrian Pucey: A Slytherin. He was on the House team as a Chaser 91/92 and 92/93, then a Keeper 93/94, then a Chaser 95/96. He had to have started Hogwarts in 90/91 or earlier to be on the team in 91/92, but which is unknown.

Madam Puddifoot: A very stout woman with a shiny black bun, she is owner of Madam Puddifoot's Coffee Shop in Hogsmeade, a popular location for young couples on Hogsmeade weekends. She works the tables herself.

Doris Purkiss: She lives at 18 Acanthia Way, Little Norton. She is quoted in the Sep 1995 *The Quibbler* as saying Sirius Black is a false name for Stubby Boardman.

Augustus Pye: Trainee Healer of the "Dangerous" Dia Llewellyn Ward at St Mungo's, under Healer Hippocrates Smethwyck. It was his idea to try Muggle stitches on Arthur's snakebite, with unfortunate results.

(Unknown) Quigley: Irish Beater in QWC 1994. Gender unknown.

Orla Quirke: b 1983. A Ravenclaw, 1994-2001? She started Hogwarts in 94/95.

Professor Quirrell: d 1992. A teacher of DADA at Hogwarts in 91/92 and for some years prior to that. A pale young man presumably with blonde hair at the start. He was usually nervous and trembling and stuttered with fear. Hagrid said he had a brilliant mind and was fine while he was simply studying books but he took a year off to get first-hand experience, had a negative encounter with vampires in the Black Forest then a hag and when he returned, he was a changed man. In actuality what Pr Quirrell met that changed him was Voldemort in the forests of Albania.

Voldemort converted Pr Quirrell to his own sick way of thinking, there is no good and evil only power and those too weak to seek it, then sent Pr Quirrell back to Hogwarts to wait for a suitable opportunity. That opportunity came when Pr Quirrell found out the Sorcerer's Stone was going to be taken to Gringotts for protection in 1991. Voldemort wanted Pr Quirrell to bring the stone back to Albania but things didn't go quite as expected. On Jul 31, 1991, the day Pr Quirrell met Harry at the Leaky Cauldron and claimed he was going to pick up a book about vampires, he was actually going to Gringotts at some point that evening to try and steal the Sorcerer's Stone. He got into Gringotts and the high-security vault the stone had been in, but found it had already been removed.

Pr Quirrell returned to Albania with the bad news and due to this failure, and apparently others over the years, Voldemort decided to keep a closer watch on him by sharing his head. One presumes that it was Pr Quirrell that got Voldemort his wand and gave it to him when he went back to Albania to tell him the bad news about not being able to get the stone. As a professor of DADA at the most respected school in Britain, Pr Quirrell would doubtless be trusted with such a Dark collectible as the wand that had formerly been Voldemort's. The MoM would have found it in Godric's Hollow among the rubble of the Potter's house and likely put it in a museum as proof Voldemort was gone. After a number of years, 10 or so, it went off display and was put in the basement among other off-display treasures and thus available for Pr Quirrell to "borrow" for show-and-tell.

Pr Quirrell began wearing the large purple turban at start of term 91/92 (after he apparently shaved his head and Voldemort became resident in it) and started to smell very peculiar, though what that smell was is unknown. He was a good actor (stuttering and shaking) but a poor liar (he turned pink when Seamus questioned him about the zombie). He pretended to be scared of everything, including his students and his subject, but in truth he feared nothing but Voldemort's punishments (which is odd because they shared the same body and what could Voldemort really do that wouldn't hurt himself as well?). Pr Quirrell was quite a powerful Dark wizard in his own right, and, though he considered himself weak because he sometimes found it hard to follow Voldemort's instructions, all this actually showed was that he still had a conscience.

After the Christmas holidays he began to grow paler and thinner, as Voldemort was sharing his brain and feeding off his body strength (he really did encounter a vampire in the truest sense when he met Voldemort). He tried to kill Harry by jinxing his broomstick, doubtless on Voldemort's orders, but Pr Snape stepped in and saved Harry. Pr Snape suspected Pr Quirrell of trying to steal the stone (probably for his own benefit though, not Voldemort's) and tried to get him to drop the matter and leave the stone alone, but it didn't work. Well, how could it with Voldemort in his brain? Eventually

The Harry Potter Companion

Pr Quirrell made his move for the stone but Harry was able to defeat him with help from Hermione, Ron, Dumbledore and his mother's love charm.

Pr Quirrell, sharing his soul and body with Voldemort, was affected by Lily's charm and could not physically touch Harry without being burned by Lily's love, or Voldemort's hatred, depending on how one looks at it. Voldemort departed Pr Quirrell's body and in doing so Pr Quirrell died of wounds inflicted by Harry, who had grabbed Pr Quirrell's face with both hands, to keep from getting cursed to death and parboiled Pr Quirrell's brains. By all accounts Pr Quirrell was a good DADA teacher, played the harp fairly well and had a way with trolls. His loss kicked off the great series of DADA teachers at Hogwarts. He was known to swear under pressure but how exactly isn't known.

Urquhart Rackharrow: See Portraits Etc., Portraits section

Rowena Ravenclaw: c 900. She was 1 of Hogwarts 4 founders. She was fair and clever, the most intelligent of the 4. She decided to take only the smartest students. The Sorting Hat said she was from a glen, so possibly of Scottish decent given her name and area. One would guess, given her brains, she was the school's Transfiguration teacher. Like Helga, she seems to have remained single for life, as most intelligent woman with plans for their life had to do at that time to escape being chattel or dying from childbirth. Since she and Godric share gem stones and tower locations and British names, it is likely they were closer to each other than the other 2 founders. Rowena was probably friends with Helga, who introduced her (and Godric) to Salazar.

Note 1: Although "a gang" of Slytherins were involved, this gang was initially spread across several years. Rodolphus has a brother Rastaban, making a gap between their births. Bellatrix, who became a Death Eater with her husband, was part of the gang, and she is older than Andromeda her sister, who is older than Narcissa, who married Lucius Malfoy, who was a known part of the gang. Immediately, this creates a spread of years as the Lestrange brother and the Black sisters were not born in the same year.

We know too, from Sirius' statement, that although he names some Death Eaters as part of a gang of Slytherins who almost all became Death Eaters, he is only naming *part* of the gang. There were others he didn't name. Add to this a list of known Death Eaters and factor in that Voldemort seems to have exclusively targeted young Slytherins to gather to his cause during his first rise to power and one develops a certain picture of how the gang of Slytherins that became Death Eaters came to be.

In the following list Death Eaters 1 and 2 are those escaped from Azkaban in Jan 1996, whose names we do not know as they were not part of the MoM raid, and remain at large as of Jun 1996. Some non-Death Eaters are thrown in the list as comparison markers. Death Eaters are separated by a backslash rather than a comma to distinguish them. Obviously the list presupposes everyone went to Hogwarts which in the case of some persons listed can't be proved.

Start	Year of Birth	Graduated
62/63	Sep 50-Aug 51	68/69
		Rookwood/Mulciber/Nott
63/64	Sep 51-Aug 52	69/70
Bertha,Rita		Bellatrix/Rodolphus/Death Eater 1
64/65	Sep 52-Aug 53	70/71
		Wilkes/Rosier/Jugson/Dolohov

346

65/66   Sep 53-Aug 54   71/72
Andromeda   Lucius/Macnair
At this time Albus became the Head of Hogwarts.

66/67   Sep 54-Aug 55   72/73
Sirius, James, Remus   Peter/Severus/Avery/Igor

67/68   Sep 55-Aug 56   73/74
                          Rastaban/Crabbe/Goyle/Death Eater 2

68/69   Sep 56-Aug 57   74/75
                          Regulus/Narcissa/Travers

WHAT YEAR?

The following chart is a quick reference to birth years, and Hogwarts start and graduation years. This is the author's opinion based on copious research. A few names are given in years where familiar faces crop up. It is not an exhaustive listing.

Start	Birth Year	Graduated
55/56	Sep 43-Aug 44	61/62 Arthur & Molly
56/57	Sep 44-Aug 45	62/63
57/58	Sep 45-Aug 46	63/64
58/59	Sep 46-Aug 47	64/65
59/60	Sep 47-Aug 48	65/66
60/61	Sep 48-Aug 49	66/67
61/62	Sep 49-Aug 50	67/68
62/63	Sep 50-Aug 51	68/69 Rookwood, Nott
63/64	Sep 51-Aug 52	69/70 Bella, Rodolphus
64/65	Sep 52-Aug 53	70/71 Jugson, Dolohov
65/66	Sep 53-Aug 54	71/72 Lucius, Macnair
66/67	Sep 54-Aug 55	72/73 Severus, Sirius
67/68	Sep 55-Aug 56	73/74 Rastaban, Crabbe
68/69	Sep 56-Aug 57	74/75 Narcissa, Travers
69/70	Sep 57-Aug 58	75/76
70/71	Sep 58-Aug 59	76/77

.
.
.

81/82	Sep 68-Aug 70	87/88 Bill
82/83	Sep 70-Aug 71	88/89
83/84	Sep 71-Aug 72	89/90 Charlie
84/85	Sep 71-Aug 73	90/91
85/86	Sep 72-Aug 74	91/92
86/87	Sep 74-Aug 75	92/93 Marcus
87/88	Sep 75-Aug 76	93/94 Percy, Oliver
88/89	Sep 76-Aug 77	94/95 Derrick, Bole

89/90	Sep 77-Aug 78	95/96 Fred, George
90/91	Sep 78-Aug 79	96/97 Cho, Cedric
91/92	Sep 79-Aug 80	97/98 Harry, Ron, Hermione
92/93	Sep 80-Aug 81	98/99 Ginny, Colin, Luna
93/94	Sep 81-Aug 82	99/00
94/95	Sep 82-Aug 83	00/01 Dennis
95/96	Sep 83-Aug 84	01/02 Euan, Rose
96/97	Sep 84-Aug 85	02/03
97/98	Sep 85-Aug 86	03/04

First Name Please!

The following is listing of individuals by their first name. Sections are wizards, giants and other beings, and Muggles. Repeated names will be in bold. Clearly wizards favor names starting with A.

Aberforth Dumbledore
Adalbert Waffling
Adrian Pucey
Agatha Timms
Agnes
Agrippa
Aidan Lynch
Alastor Moody
Alberic Grunnion
Albus Dumbledore
Ali Bashir
Alicia Spinnet
Alice Longbottom
Algie Longbottom
Alphard Melifula
Amelia Bones
Amos Diggory
Andrew Kirke
Andromeda Black Tonks
Angelina Johnson
Anthony Goldstein
Antonin Dolohov
Apollyon Pringle
Arabella Figg
Archie
Argus Filch
Armando Dippet
Arminta Melifula
Arnold Peasegood
Arsenius Jigger
Arthur Weasley
Augustus Rookwood
Augustus Pye

Augustus Worme
Barnabas the Barmy
Barry Ryan
Bartemius Crouch Sr
Bartemius Crouch Jr
Basil
Bathilda Bagshot
Bellatrix Black Lestrange
Benjy Fenwick
Bertie Bott
Bertha Jorkins
Bilius Weasley
Bill Weasley
Blaise Zabini
Bob
Boris the Bewildered
Bozo
Broderick Bode
C. Warrington
Caradoc Dearborn
Cassandra Trelawney
Cassandra Vablatsky
Cedric Diggory
Celestina Warbeck
Charlie Weasley
Cho Chang
Colin Creevey
Cornelius Fudge
Cuthbert Mockridge
D. J. Prod
Dai Llewellyn
Davey Gudgeon
Dean Thomas
Dedalus Diggle
Dennis Creevey
Derek
Derrick
Dilys Derwent
Dolores Umbridge
Dorcas Meadowes
Doris Crockford
Doris Purkiss
Draco Malfoy
Eddie Charmichael
Edgar Bones
Elladora Black
Elfric the Eager
Elfrida Clagg (Cragg)
Eloise Midgen
Elphias Doge

Emeric Swich
Emma Dobbs
Emmeline Vance
Emric the Evil
Enid Longbottom
Eric Munch
Ernie Macmillan
Ernie Prang
Euan Abercrombie
Evan Rosier
Everard
Fabian Prewett
Fleur Delacour
Florean Fortescue
Florence
Frank Longbottom
Fred Weasley
Gabrielle Delacour
Geoffrey Hooper
George Weasley
Gideon Prewett
Gilbert Wimple
Gilderoy Lockhart
Ginny Weasley
Gladys Gudgeon
Godric Gryffindor
Graham Pritchard
Gregory Goyle
Gregory the Smarmy
Grindelwald
Griselda Marchbanks
Hannah Abbot
Harold Dingle
Harry Potter
Hassan Mostafa
Helga Hufflepuff
Hengist of Woodcroft
Hermione Granger
Hestia Jones
Hippocrates Smethwyck
Igor Karkoff
Inigo Imago
J. Dorny
Jack Sloper
James Potter
Janus Thickey
Joey Jenkins
Justin Finch-Fletchley
K. Bundy
Katie Bell

Kenneth Towler
Kennilworthy Whisp
Kevin Whitby
Kevin
Kingsley Shacklebolt
Lachlan the Lanky
Ladislaw Zamojski
Laura Madley
Lavender Brown
Lee Jordan
Lily Evans Potter
Lisa Turpin
Lucius Malfoy
Ludovic Bagman
Luna Lovegood
Mafalda Hopkirk
Malcolm Baddock
Mandy Brocklehurst
Marcus Flint
Marietta Edgecombe
Marlene McKinnon
Merlin
Michael Corner
Miles Bletchley
Millicent Bagnold
Millicent Bulstrode
Minerva McGonagall
Miranda Goshawk
Miriam Strout
Molly Weasley
Morgana
Mundungus Fletcher
Narcissa Black Malfoy
Natalie McDonald
Neville Longbottom
Newton Scamander
Nicolas Flamel
Nymphadora Tonks
Olive Hornsby
Oliver Wood
Olympia Maxime
Orla Quirke
Otto Bagman
Owen Cauldwell
Padma Patil
Pansy Parkinson
Paracelsus
Parvati Patil
Patricia Stimpson
Penelope Clearwater

Percy Weasley
Perenelle Flamel
Peter Pettigrew
Phineas Nigellus
Phyllida Spore
Pierre Bonaccord
Poppy Pomfrey
Porpentina Scamander
Quentin Trimble
Rastaban Lestrange
Rubeus Hagrid
Regulus Black
Rita Skeeter
Roddy Ponter
Rodolphus Lestrange
Roger Davies
Ron Weasley
Rose Zeller
Rowena Ravenclaw
S. Capper
S. Fawcett
Salazar Slytherin
Sally-Anne Perks
Seamus Finnigan
Severus Snape
Sirius Black
Stan Shunpike
Stewart Ackerley
Stubby Boardman
Sturgis Podmore
Susan Bones
Sybill Trelawney
Ted Tonks
Terence Higgs
Theodore Nott
Tiberius Ogden
Tom
Tom Marvolo Riddle Jr
Uric the Oddball
Urquhart Rackharrow
Veronica Smethley
Vicky Frobisher
Viktor Krum
Vincent Crabbe
Vindictus Viridian
Violet
Walden Macnair
Warty Harris
Wendelin the Weird
Wilbert Slinkhard

Wilfred the Wistful
Wilhelm Wigworthy
Wilhelmina Grubbly-Plank
Will
Willy Widdershins
Wizard Baruffio
Z. Nettles
Zacharias Smith

Giants and Other Beings
Bodrod the Bearded
Sir Patrick Delaney-Podmore
Dobby
Fridwulfa Hagrid
Golgomath
Grawp
Griphook
Karkus
Kreacher
Myrtle
Sir **Nicholas** de Mimsy-Porpington
Ragnok
Remus Lupin
Urg the Unclean
Wheezey
Winky

Muggles
Angus Fleet
Dennis
Dot
Dudley Dursley
Frank Bryce
Gordon
Hetty Bayliss
Humberto
Jim McGuffin
Malcolm
Marge Dursley
Mark Evans
Mary Dorkins
Petunia Evans Dursley
Piers Polkiss
Ted
Tom Riddle Sr
Vernon Dursley

PART V. BIOGRAPHY: WIZARDS RIDDLE-ZONKO AND ALL OTHER BEINGS

ALPHABETICAL LISTING OF WIZARDS RI-Z

Mrs Tom Riddle Sr: d 1927. (Miss Unknown Marvolo). A witch from the village of Little Hangleton. Probably a pureblood, definitely a descent of Salazar Slytherin. She was Tom Riddle Jr's (Voldemort's) mom. She fell in love with Tom Riddle Sr (a Muggle) but he abandoned her after discovering she was a witch. One presumes they were married but perhaps not. After giving birth to Tom Jr in relative secrecy, she lived long enough to give her son his father's name, Tom Riddle, then died of complications. It's not clear why she let her son go to an orphanage. Her relations may have been dead, Tom Riddle Sr would not have wanted Tom Jr. But still, there must have been a wizard orphanage somewhere.

Tom Marvolo Riddle Jr: aka Lord Voldemort, the Dark Lord (a title he ripped off from reading *Lord of Rings* in the 1960s), You-Know-Who, and He-Who-Must-Not-Be-Named. b 1927. A Slytherin, 1938-1945. He is a half-blood. His father was Muggle and his mother a witch. His grandfather was a wizard named Marvolo, but it's unclear if that's was a first or last name. One presumes it's a last name given the time in which he was born and the penchant people of the age had for using the mother's surname as a middle name. Tom is the last blood descendent of Salazar Slytherin and like Salazar, he's a Parselmouth. See schematic R.

His mother was abandoned by his father when he found out she was a witch. It is unclear if Tom Sr was married to her or even knew about the child. For all we know, Tom Jr may be illegitimate. His mother gave birth to him in 1927, but she died of complications shortly after naming him Tom Riddle after his father and Marvolo after his grandfather. Tom Jr was put in a Muggle orphanage where he remained, unadopted, until circa age 15 when he got permission to live at Hogwarts. One presumes that Tom either had no living wizard relations on the Marvolo side to take him, or they didn't want him because he was a Mudblood.

Tom started Hogwarts in 1938, at age 11. He bought his 1st wand at Ollivanders: 13.5" of yew. It is a powerful wand with a phoenix tailfeather core, and a very powerful wand in the wrong hands, which his unfortunately were. The same phoenix, Fawkes, gave only one other tailfeather and it ended up in Harry Potter's wand. All this begs the question, how did Tom know about Diagon Alley and where did he get Galleons to pay for his wand, if he had no wizarding relations? Perhaps someone was sent for him, as in Harry's case, and his mother left him money. Though if she died at his birth, and no one knew about him, how did his name get put down for Hogwarts? Perhaps Salazar magicked the rolls so any relation of his would automatically appear on the list at birth.

Tom is the Heir of Slytherin, despite being a half-blood, but how did he discover this? No one knew about his Slytherin connection but his mother, who was dead, and he had no contact with Slytherin relations, who didn't exist, or knowledge about Slytherin, before he arrived at Hogwarts. One can only presume he was sorted into Slytherin, wondered why since he wasn't a pureblood and to find out became an expert in genealogy during his first year at Hogwarts. Once he realized there was a connection Slytherin, he must have become obsessed with finding out all he could about Slytherin.

In doing the research he must have come across information about the Chamber, because it took him 5 years to uncover everything he needed to know about the Chamber of Secrets. How did he know he was a Parselmouth? It might be something he discovered accidentally or found out about when he was researching Slytherin. Why would he look for a Chamber? Because, apparently, in discovering he was a Slytherin descendent, he became obsessed with purging the world of Mudbloods, which Slytherin didn't like, and Muggles, which he didn't care for because his father had abandoned his mother and himself.

Tom was a handsome boy, tall with black hair and very white skin. He was a brilliant student, at the time the best ever. He was considered to be poor but brilliant, parentless but brave, and a model student. As a 5th year student in 42/43, he became a Prefect and wore a silver Prefect's badge. He opened the Chamber of Secrets in 42/43 and set the Serpent of Slytherin on Muggle borns, killing Myrtle. Rather incredibly, despite another student's death, he went to Headmaster Armando Dippet and asked if he could stay the summer. Usually Tom was returned to the Muggle orphanage during summer holidays, but as a Prefect he thought he would be allowed to stay. Armando said, he'd have agreed under normal circumstances but since Myrtle had been killed, he couldn't even consider it, and anyway the school was probably going to close because of the killing.

After Tom found all this out, on Jun 13, 1943, he immediately got Hagrid blamed (and expelled) for opening the Chamber and Aragog pegged for Myrtle's death. He closed the Chamber so the school would stay open and he could remain at Hogwarts. Tom got a Special Services to the School Award in 1943, a burnished gold shield still in the Trophy Room on the 3rd floor, for catching the individual (Hagrid) that opened the Chamber and ending and the attacks by the monster (Aragog) of the Chamber. He also got permission to stay at the school over summer holidays from then on and, though Armando Dippet trusted him completely, Dumbledore always watched him, most particularly after he got Hagrid expelled. This pushed Tom's paranoia button, and set him forever against Dumbledore.

Apparently Tom planned to record his opening of the Chamber of Secrets for posterity and, when the Chamber scheme failed, his frustrations mounted and he sat around devising a new way to kill Mudbloods. He created his infamous Diary in 1943 as way to come back and finish the work he started, but also as a means of becoming a real person for second time, sort of a backup plan to destroy the world in case the first one failed. The Diary was eventually entrusted to his chief Death Eater, Lucius Malfoy, many years later. It's unclear if the success of the Diary would have meant 2 Tom Riddles wandering around, but certain facts indicate the "spirit" Voldemort was being gathered into the Tom Riddle produced by the Diary and would have left just one young corporeal person with a really old evil mind.

The school year 43/44 passed without event but Tom got permission to leave the school for 1 day during the summer (1994), and spent it traveling to Little Hangleton, home of his father. He murdered his paternal grandparents, Mr and Mrs Riddle, and his father, Tom Riddle Sr and caught the evening train back to Hogwarts. He was always good at research, so he probably bent his mind to finding his father after he got hooked on killing Muggles in 42/43. What Muggles would have deserved death more in his mind? Interestingly he didn't bend his efforts to find his distant wizarding family. Perhaps he realized by then, having boned up at Hogwarts, that they were all pureblood enthusiasts, even the non-Slytherins, and he wouldn't be accepted by them.

As a teen Tom slouched as he walked, furrowed his brow when he was upset and bit his lip when he was nervous. He had long fingers and habitually twirled his wand when he was bored. In 44/45 he became a Head Boy and got a medal for Magical Merit (for an unknown reason). After graduating in Jun 1945, he traveled the world learning all he could about the Dark Arts and making himself immortal and all powerful. Dumbledore, who also left at the same time, and traveled, knew what he was up to, as he told Harry that Tom consorted with the worst of the magical world. Tom underwent many dangerous magical transformations and was barely recognizable as Tom Riddle when he reappeared as Lord Voldemort. Tom's new name and title is an anagram he'd cooked up in 1943. "I am Lord Voldemort" rearranges into "Tom Marvolo Riddle."

Voldemort, is probably based the French/Latin: Vol from Vola meaning palm of hand, de meaning of, morte meaning death, ie, Lord Hand of Death, which is quite impressive. It may however be from another Latin word that means fly, making his name Lord Flies from Death, (which sounds cowardly) but one hopes it's not Scandinavian making it Lord Mouse of Death. It's rather odd he kept his Muggle father's name in his new name at all since he hated him so much, but one expects that "I am Lord D'Lover " really isn't the sort of name one would use to take over the world. At any rate, from 1970 to 1981, he worked on destroying the MoM, murdering Mudbloods and Muggles and trying to take over the world using mainly oppressed beings and beasts as his foot soldiers.

As Tom started acquiring followers, some joined because they were afraid to stand up to him and others just because they wanted a share of his power. Once he became very powerful, his following representing a large percentage of wizards, he began taking over by killing those that stood up to him. The years of his rise to power were marked with Muggle and magical disappearances. Dumbledore and the Order of Phoenix worked tirelessly to stop him, but they were outnumbered 20 to 1 making at least about 400-500 Death Eaters and proving how popular Voldemort's view were in the wizarding community. Dumbledore was really the only person Tom feared, because he was and is the more powerful wizard of the 2. Only Hogwarts was safe, because Tom didn't dare try to take it while Dumbledore was there.

As Lord Voldemort he killed some of the best wizards of the age, including the McKinnons, the Bones, the Prewetts, and most of those in the OoP. No one ever lived after he decided to kill them and many feared to come home and see the Dark Mark floating above their house. He became progressively more powerful and more paranoid, and after hearing a bit of Sybill's prophecy in 1979, started focusing in on Potters as a threat to his immortality and power. On Oct 31, 1981, he attacked the Potters at Godric's Hollow. He didn't to want to kill Lily, as she was not a blood Potter, but she forced him to kill her to activate a charm on Harry's life. Tom, rather stupidly, didn't consider that might happen. He went ahead and tried to Avada Kedavra curse Harry but it backfired and nearly destroyed him, not to mention the entire house.

After that night, Tom disappeared and was considered to have lost his powers and been too weak to carry on. No one really thought him dead, just not able to carry on. Tom had done many experimental and questionable Dark Arts practices on his quest to become immortal or at least immune to death between 1945 and 1970. The steps he took seem to have worked. He remained alive, but as mere vapor whose only talent left was to possess creatures or people. He escaped to Albania where he took up residence in a deep forest and languished in obscurity, inhabiting snakes and eating creatures in the forest. Possibly there was not enough left of the human being to die at that point. But not being truly alive again, unfortunately he couldn't be truly killed. He remained there for some time until Pr Quirrell blundered into his area.

Don't ask how, maybe Pr Quirrell was a closet Parselmouth, but he struck up a conversation with Tom and became a convert. When this possibly happened we don't know. According to Hagrid, Pr Quirrell had taught at the school for a while, taken a year off to do vampire research, and, when he came back he was a changed man. It was implied that he had been in that condition for some tim before 1991. Tom waited for an opportunity to arise that would enable him to get his body and his life back and eventually, through Pr Quirrell, he heard about the Sorcerer's Stone. At that point Tom tried having Pr Quirrell snatch the stone from Gringotts but when Pr Quirrell returned to Tom in the forest in Aug 1991 with the bad news that he didn't get it, Tom took matters into his own hands.

Tom inhabited Pr Quirrell's body, specifically his head, and back they both went to Hogwarts. At this point it would appear some unquantified weirdness takes place, but this is actually not the case. One might ask, how can Dumbledore not realize he has Voldemort in the school and teaching DADA no less? Remember, Tom is an expert in occlumency, he can fool Dumbledore into not realizing he's there. And what about Pr Snape, why doesn't Tom get him to help Pr Quirrell? Obviously because Tom is an expert at legilimency and he's probably has figured out from the fact that Dumbledore vouched for Pr Snape at his trial and subsequently hired him to teach at Hogwarts, that Pr Snape was a mole and a double agent.

Even if Tom wasn't a Legilimens, he's not completely stupid, though his actions may indicate otherwise most of the time. He surely must have asked Pr Quirrell what all his Death Eaters were doing now and what had happened between the time of his departure and the time he met with Pr Quirrell. It would be plain to even a nonmagical person that Pr Snape had switched sides and Tom would be fool to ever trust him again, other than letting back into the fold just to use him by feeding him false information or kill him. Lucius Malfoy is another story altogether, Tom knows Lucius is a slippery individual, but he also knows Lucius is loyal to the cause as long as it serves him well in return. And Tom has no problem with that arrangement, but he can't appear less than all powerful to Lucius.

So back at Hogwarts, Pr Quirrell toes the line and looks for ways to get to the stone, which is fairly easy as he was asked to protect it and knows all about what is protecting it. When Tom and Pr Quirrell at last reach the Mirror of Erised they can't get the stone until Harry obligingly arrives and gets it out for them. Tom sees into Harry's mind and knows he has the stone in his pocket. At that time Tom appeared as a face in the back of Quirrell's bald head. The face was terrible, livid chalk white, and had wide, mad, glaring red eyes and slits for nostrils like a snake. He still has a high cold voice and cackles when he laughs. No matter what Tom was able to manifest as, he couldn't do it all without a body. When Tom (Pr Quirrell) touched Harry his hands became red, raw, shiny and blistered as if he'd touched acid or fire. Pr Quirrell being virtually allergic to Harry due to Tom living in his body and Lily's active charm, screamed the minute Harry gabbed his head in return.

Tom fled Pr Quirrell's body, killing Pr Quirrell, and went back to Albania as a vapor again. He was stronger than he had been, due to the sharing of Pr Quirrell's body for a year and drinking unicorn blood, repeatedly, but he was still a vapor. Tom didn't care that Pr Quirrell died because he doesn't care about anyone but himself. He doubtless thought Quirrell deserved it as Tom is very hard on those how let him down and does not forgive mistakes easily. He discards followers without mercy or second thoughts and punishes erring followers in obscene and awful ways. One wonders why he is so terribly popular.

By trying to kill Harry to get the stone, Tom may have got Quirrell killed, but he really only hurt himself. Tom and Harry are linked through Tom's failed curse. Just because one ultimately has to kill the other, doesn't mean the one that does the killing won't suffer for it. No one really knows what will happen when one of the pair dies. But Tom continues, quite imprudently, to try and kill Harry despite this fact. Dumbledore has already said he wants to take Tom alive, probably in order to spare Harry. Dumbledore feels that if Tom keeps being thwarted he might never return to power. Since this route insures that Harry survives, Dumbledore would be quite content for things to go that way.

Actually, Dumbledore has little to worry about as Tom tends to be his own worst enemy and constantly sets himself up to be thwarted if not killed. Tom's second attempt to get a real body failed as badly as the first. Lucius Malfoy started the ball rolling, perhaps more because he wanted to thwart Arthur's Muggle Protection Act bill than any desire to see Tom back, but perhaps once he realized Tom was still around, Draco surely would have told him about events at Hogwarts in 91/92 as the whole school knew what Harry had done, he thought he'd better make an effort to show some loyalty. Lucius put Tom Riddle's Diary into Ginny Weasley's possession and Ginny, not knowing what it was, began to be drawn by the spells on it that make it seem like an old friend and started pouring out her soul, literally, to Tom Riddle.

Tom needed a soul to become fully alive again and could get it if a person confided enough of themselves to the Diary. He grew stronger on a diet of Ginny's deepest fears and darkest secrets, till he was more powerful than she and able to control her, without her realizing it at first and then without her being able to stop him. Oddly enough though, when she didn't have the Diary in her possession, he wasn't able to possess her. When Ginny finally put enough of herself into the Diary, Tom was able to start pouring his secrets and his soul back into her. Through Ginny he opened the Chamber of Secrets, killed Hagrid's roosters, daubed the messages on the wall and set the Serpent of Slytherin on the school's Mudbloods and even a Squib's cat. Rather unsuccessfully one might add since not one of them actually died. Or perhaps it was Tom's plan all along simply to use the Diary to lure Harry to himself and pump him for information.

Later Tom was able to release himself from the Diary into reality as a slightly blurry image. When Harry first saw him, he was strangely blurred around the edges and Tom admitted he could only be fully real after he'd sucked all the life out of Ginny. Tom became clearer and more alive as Ginny became weaker and her life drained into him. He claimed he was very anxious to meet Harry as Harry represented a key to his past, present and future. Tom seemed to know, probably because he was already plugged into the spirit of Voldemort in Albania, that he would eventually become Lord Voldemort. He pumped Harry for information on what happened to him in the future and Harry, quite stupidly, gave it to him. Through Harry the current Voldemort in Albania was able to discover how Lily's death acted a powerful countercharm to his curse, which allowed Harry to survive and all but destroyed his past self. This revelation, Tom mistakenly felt, showed him that Harry was no great wizard to be contended with.

It is at this point that Tom looked at Harry with an odd red gleam in his hungry eyes. Given that redness was a part of the currently in Albania Voldemort's eyes, it would seem that the 2, the image and the spirit, were connected in some way and the image was drawing not only Ginny's life but Voldemort's spirit into itself simultaneously. Voldemort's noncorporeal self had to be in Riddle's image because it was only through this conversation with Harry that the vaporous Voldemort could have learned how Harry survived. Since, a few years later Voldemort brought this whole event up, Harry surviving by Lily's charm, it is clear that Voldemort's spirit was connected to the image of Tom Riddle that Harry conversed with.

But Tom Riddle was not to be a second time. Harry, with the help of Fawkes, the Sorting Hat and Godric's Sword of Gryffindor (which may or may not be magical), defeated the basilisk and, with a poisoned fang of the basilisk, stabbed the Diary and destroyed it and Tom Riddle's second self. Riddle fell in death throws and vanished, at least for now. The real Tom remained a frustrated vapor in Albania inhabiting animals (preferably snakes) because inhabiting other living things was the only power left to him. A year passed 93/94, and though it seems nothing much happened in Albania, it was during this time that Peter Pettigrew, the man whose information got Tom turned into a spirit in the first place, was exposed as Scabbers. Once exposed, Peter had no where to run to but back to Tom. So, in the summer of 1994, Peter, by consulting with the rats of Albania, attempted to find Tom. Along the way Peter met Bertha Jorkins and brought her along as a present to Tom, whom he finally found in a creepy forest.

It's unclear exactly what happened next, but apparently Tom, with Peter's help to make a magical potion comprised of a mixture of unicorn blood, Nagini's venom and other things, was returned to an semi-human form. He resembled a deformed humand being, something like a crouched child. He was ugly, slimy, hairless and scaly looking. His skin was dark, raw and reddish black. He had arms and legs, but they were thin and feeble to the point of being almost useless to him. He was helpless and had to be carried around, but he could still hold a wand and do magic. His face was flat and snakelike with gleaming red eyes, apparently a lasting feature. He continued using snake venom to stay alive - apparently Nagini was a snake he befriended in the forest and became a sort of really evil pet. Peter had milk Nagini for venom and though it's unclear how much venom Tom had to drink to stay alive, it seems Tom needed feeding quite often.

At this point Tom managed to get his wand back. Possibly after Pr Quirrell managed to get the wand and bring it to Tom when he couldn't get the stone from Gringotts thinking better something than nothing, Tom buried it in his old hiding place in Albania, just in case. The way he created the Diary just in case. Tom perhaps thought once he had a new body, via the Sorcerer's Stone, he'd then slip out of Britain back to Albania, get his wand, secretly gather his old Death Eaters to him and quietly draw up his plans in seclusion till he was ready to move out against Britain's MoM and wizarding community, which he seems to particularly hate as opposed to any other MoM or wizarding community.

Whatever the case, with his new body and old wand, Tom was able to break Barty Sr's Memory Charm and question Bertha. Knowing Tom, this process involved copious use of the Cruciatus Curse. Bertha revealed to him news of the upcoming QWC 1994, the TT at Hogwarts, Moody teaching DADA and Barty Crouch Jr being out of Azkaban and secretly living at Barty Sr's house under the care of Winky. After questioning, Bertha's body and brain were useless and, since Tom couldn't posses her in that state, he killed her with his usual Unforgivable death curse. She was probably then buried in the forest by Peter after being nibbled on by Nagini. With the information Bertha provided, Tom sets his sights on Harry.

Tom decided he needed to become fully human in form again and since, with the particular rebirthing method he planned to use, he required the use of a wizarding enemy's blood, he opted to Harry's blood for the lingering protection Lily's charm would offer him (obviously he heard every word Harry said to Riddle in the Chamber of Secrets or he wouldn't know this fact), but also because he would then be able to touch Harry and kill him, proving to his Death Eaters that Harry was nothing more than lucky in surviving the death curse of 1981. He returned to England, to his father's house, killed Frank Bryce with the Avada Kedavra curse and waited out QWC 1994 to set his plan his motion.

After Barty Jr freed himself, he fortuitously found Tom. Tom went to the Barty Sr's house and placed him under the Imperius Curse and Barty Jr was drafted to replace Moody and get Harry to Little Hangleton graveyard via touching the TT Cup which would act as a Portkey. All went well till Tom was actually reborn. If he thought rebirth would help his looks, he was dead wrong. He was reborn as a thin man with chalky white skin, livid scarlet eyes with cat slit pupils, a flat nose with slits like a snake and no lips. Possibly after living on snake venom and inhabiting snakes for so long a time, it had an adverse effect on his gene structure, not to mention the highly dicey potion he used for rebirth which included Peter's maimed and ratlike hand.

Instead of quitting while he's ahead, he continued with his plan prove to his Death Eaters that Harry was nothing special and forced Harry to duel with him. Priori Incantatem set in, Harry proved himself stronger than Tom, and Tom's wand ended up regurgitating its former spells. Numerous old enemies appeared and did all in their power to aid Harry and thwart Tom. Harry subsequently escaped both Tom and the Death Eaters leaving all highly humiliated. Knowing Tom doesn't forgive or forget and makes people pay their debts in pain, a lot of suffering probably ensued for the not-really-at-fault Death Eaters. Needless to say Tom vowed to get everyone who pushed his buttons: Harry, who magically bested him, Severus, who outwitted and betrayed him, and Igor, who abandoned him.

Newly corporeal, Tom set out to once again build up his army. He contacted the giants in exile Abroad, who helped him during his previous attempt to destroy the MoM, and the dementors, who were his natural allies since he could give them a steady supply of victims. Besides recruiting Dark creatures, who flocked to him because of the way the MoM has oppressed them over the years, Tom actively used tricks, jinxes and blackmail to acquire wizards to his burgeoning flock. Tom is well practiced at operating in secrecy and doesn't mind bullying others, using his legilimency skills to figure out how to get at people or bewitching people with the forbidden Imperius Curse. Around this time, Tom also decided to try and get his hands on the entire prophecy Sybill gave in 1979, which happened to be stored in the MoM.

Things went badly with the plan to get the prophecy until Dec 1995 when Tom discovered that he could share Harry's mind when Harry's mind was relaxed and vulnerable - asleep. Tom immediately set out to use this mindlink to get Harry to go to the MoM and take down the prophecy orb for him. In Jan 1996, Tom was able to get the dementors to let 10 Death Eaters escape Azkaban so that he might use them to meet Harry at the MoM and wrench from him the prophecy that tells how he might be destroyed. Over the course of 6 months, Tom worked on Harry's mind. Eventually he was able to convince Harry that he had Sirius in the Hall of Prophecy and was torturing him to get the prophecy orb down. Tom played on Harry's need to save people, and won. Harry showed up to rescue Sirius but instead found himself surrounded by Death Eaters. To Tom's disappointment, Harry escaped the Death Eaters, again.

Tom showed up in the MoM himself for reasons not entirely clear since he knew the prophecy had been smashed by Neville and there really was no logical reason for him to expose himself by appearing. Ok, maybe he was just angry enough to want to kill Harry for smashing the prophecy, but was that worth exposing himself to the MoM officials as alive and well and in Britain when no one at the MoM believed he was back? No. So for reasons that are totally unfathomable, Tom duels with Dumbledore in front of Aurors and Fudge instead of leaving. He vowed to kill Dumbledore, before the Aurors showed up, but failed. Then things get even weirder.

Tom inhabits Harry and tries to get Dumbledore to kill him. Since Tom has no idea what is in Sybill's prophecy except that his defeat or death has something to do with someone that's a Potter, why on earth would he wrap himself around Harry Potter and ask Dumbledore to kill him? By far, it is the stupidest thing Tom has ever done in a very long line of really stupid things. Before much can come of the situation, Harry's scar splits open and in thinking he will see Sirius again in death, a person Harry loves, Tom is exposed to a loving though, an emotion that is too strong for him and one that he cannot endure, and immediately vacates Harry's body.

Tom did take Bellatrix Black Lestrange with him, but that was more necessity than courtesy. He left the other 11 Death Eaters in the hands of the MoM. He himself lingered just long enough for the MoM to fill with people who all saw him. At the time Tom appeared as a tall, thin man wearing a black hooded cloak. He had his usual high, cold voice and terrible white snakelike face with pitiless slit pupil eyes of scarlet. Everyone recognized him. Thus he completely blew his cover and gave credence to Dumbledore's and Harry's continued claims. Tom, with Bellatrix, Apparated out of the MoM; he seems to be able to Apparate and Disapparate silently as well as become invisible at will, all much like Dumbledore. No one was able to follow him, though the hunt was officially on at that point. All in all, a very weird night.

Although Tom's curse formed a link between himself and Harry, Harry so far has the weaker mind. Tom's legilimency and occlumency skills work on Harry, but Harry's don't work at all, yet. Tom finds it easy to access Harry's mind and Harry picks up and acts on Tom's emotions like an aerial but can't access Tom's mind at will or make Tom subject to his emotions. They do however seem to share one trait. Harry becomes ill and says he is bound together with Tom by pain in that moment when Tom inhabits him. So it would seem Tom does feel some pain inhabiting Harry, though obviously no where near what Harry experiences or can take. Harry has only has power Tom does not, the ability to feel love, and love is stronger than all Tom's powers. At the point Harry feels love, Tom is forced to leave him, whether that's because love pains Tom physically or simply renders him powerless is unknown.

Since Lily's love saved Harry, through her charm love will always save Harry. Since Tom's curse formed a link between his mind and Harry's, he can be influenced by Harry mentally thinking of love. Tom made things worse for himself when he used Harry's blood to get a body. Tom will now always be physically, as well as mentally, affected by Harry feeling love. Dumbledore has intimated to Harry that love is Harry's greatest weapon against Tom, but as yet Harry has never had the presence of mind to actively shield himself with love and attack Tom with love. Dumbledore also says that Tom's greatest weakness it that he has failed to understand there are fates worse than death and this provides Harry an area of attack to use his weapon against. Since Tom fears death, and Harry doesn't, Harry will always have the advantage in face-to-face combat.

A final interesting point to consider is Harry's blurting out that Voldemort is a half-blood to all the Death Eaters. Bellatrix immediately reacts negatively to this statement and calls him a liar. Lucius Malfoy on the other hand says nothing. Lucius knows Voldemort is Tom Riddle. We know this because Draco in 1991 knew Voldemort had been a Slytherin. He says to Harry at Madam Malkins that You-know-how was a Slytherin. How would Draco know that unless he knew that Voldemort was also Tom Riddle, the name Voldemort used in school? And where would he find this information out unless from his father? How many other Death Eaters might know the truth is open to speculation. Perhaps none.

Augustus Rookwood: b 1950. A Slytherin, 1962-1969. He started Hogwarts in 62/63. See Note 1, Part IV. During the time of Voldemort's 1st rise to power he was an Unspeakable at the MoM and a friend of Ludo Bagman's father, who also worked at the MoM. Augustus told Voldemort about the prophecy being stored in the Hall of Prophecy but, before anything could be done about it acquiring it, he was ratted out by Igor Karkoff in 1982 as a spy and went to prison. Augustus implicated Ludo Bagman, who was found to have been passing information to Augustus, but it didn't help Augustus get out of Azkaban. He was Escapee 9: from Azkaban Jan 1996. He is a pockmarked man with greasy hair. Along with 11 other Death Eaters, he broke into the MoM in Jun 1996. He was caught and sent back to Azkaban.

Evan Rosier: b 1953. A Slytherin 1964-1971. He started Hogwarts in 64/65. See Note 1, Part IV. He was named by Sirius as part of a gang of Slytherins who nearly all turned out to be Death Eaters. He was killed by Aurors in early 1982. Igor Karkoff tried to rat him out later in 1982, but didn't know he was dead. He's the one that took the chunk out of Moody's nose.

Madam Rosmerta: The attractive owner of the Three Broomsticks in Hogsmeade. A curvy sort of woman with a pretty face, she usually wears sparkly turquoise high heels. She sold Dumbledore 800 barrels of mulled mead for the Yule Ball in 1994. She has probably lived at the Three Broomsticks all her life since she served Sirius drinks when he was in Hogwarts, over 20 years ago. She is the only one who reserved doubts about Sirius' guilt. She liked Sirius and James because they used to make her laugh.

Barry Ryan: Irish team Keeper at QWC 1994.

St Mungo's, Welcome Witch: A plump blonde witch who is rude to people in need.

Mrs Scamander: Mother of Newt Scamander. A breeder of fancy hippogriffs.

Newton "Newt" Artemis Fido Scamander: b 1897. The "Steve Irwin, Crocodile Hunter" of the magical world. He attended Hogwarts 1908-1915, worked with the

MoM after graduating and later became the author of *Fantastic Beasts and Where to Find Them* which has been a Hogwarts' textbook for Magizoology and a Care of Magical Creatures supplemental text since it first appeared in 1927. He is retired and currently lives in Dorset.

Porpentina Scamander: The wife of Newt Scamander.

(Unknown) Scrimgeour: A male wizard at the ministry that kept asking Tonks and Kingsley funny questions in 95/96. It's not clear if he was trying to sound them out to see if they were loyal or if he had some other motive.

(Unknown) Scrivenshaft: Owner of a quill shop in Hogsmeade. Gender unknown.

Second Cousin (Unknown): This cousin is Molly's. He's a Squib who became an accountant. Molly never talks about him, according to Ron. But she must or he wouldn't know about him.

Kingsley Shacklebolt: An Auror with the MoM. He is a tall, bald, Black wizard with a calm, deep, slow voice and wears a single gold hoop earing. He's a new member of the OoP and was part of Harry's escort to Headquarters in 1995. He was in charge of the hunt for Sirius and kept feeding the MoM information that he was in Tibet. He says firelegs = firearms. He didn't tell anyone at the MoM he supported Dumbledore because would have lost his job, but outed himself by showing up with Dumbledore to duel with the Death Eaters in Jun 1996.

Stan Shunpike: b circa 1974. He's about 18 or 19 in 1993 when Harry meets him. He is the conductor of the Knight Bus. Possibly there are other conductors but he always seems to work with Ernie. He wears a purple uniform and sits in an armchair beside the driver. His job seems to be jumping out and announcing the bus when it stops, welcoming new arrivals and getting them settled, and taking care of the extras the bus offers. He's thin with large protruding, jug ears and a number of pimples. He tends to be a little rude and throws baggage out after people that depart the bus before slamming the doors shut. He's a bit star-struck and likes famous people, even if they are considered dangerous and deluded. He was at QWC 1994 and when he saw the veelas he claimed he was about to become the Minister of Magic.

Pr (Unknown) Sinistra: She teaches in the Astronomy Dept. Considering she only works nights and is only seen inside the castle during the day, one wonders if she might not be a vampire.

Rita Skeeter: b 1951. She has been a writer for *The Daily Prophet* and *The Quibbler*. When writing for *The Daily Prophet* she was working freelance as a special correspondent. Her main talent is turning any story into a lurid scandal, even if she has to lie to do it. She is an illegal Animagus and becomes a beetle with markings around her antenna that are exactly the same as her jeweled glasses. Up until May 1994, when Hermione caught her in a jar, she gathered her stories by turning into a beetle and eavesdropping. Hermione said she wouldn't turn her to the MoM in if she stopped writing for a year. Rita kept this bargain and later was rewarded by becoming the author of Harry's version of Voldemort's return in Little Hangleton for *The Quibbler*. She probably didn't mind making the MoM look bad in the process as her chief job at *The Daily Prophet* seemed to be just that.

Her pen describes her as blonde, attractive and 43 (in 1994). She has been a journalist since at least 1982, as she covered Ludo's trial. When in the money, she keeps her hair set in elaborate and oddly rigid curls that contrast strangely with her heavy-jawed face. She has 3 gold teeth one can see when she smiles widely and heavily penciled brows. She has a very strong grip, thick fingers and large mannish hands with 2" long painted (crimson or shocking pink) nails. She wears jeweled spectacles all the time and carries a clasped crocodile skin handbag with an acid green Quick-Quotes Quill and parchment in it.

She is one tough cookie. She has a piercing stare, drinks firewhisky and wipes her mouth on the back of her hand, a very bug-like habit. She interviewed Harry for the TT in a broomcloset, so apparently she likes the dark bug-type spaces as well. She has magenta, acid green, banana-yellow robes and a thick magenta cloak with a furry purple collar. She was unemployed from May 1995-May 1996. Apparently she can't do anything but write. During this time she wore her hair lank and unkempt around her face, her scarlet nails were chipped and some of the false jewels were missing from her winged glasses. Let's hope she has better times now she can "write" again.

Mrs Skower: Inventor of an All-Purpose Magical Mess Remover that bears her name.

(Unknown) Sleakeazy: Creator of a line of a hair straightening products Hermione uses when she dresses up.

Wilbert Slinkhard: Author of *Defensive Magical Theory*. Hogwarts' DADA textbook under Pr Umbridge.

Jack Sloper: A Gryffindor. Beater for the House team, he replaced George 95/96 after he was banned from Quidditch. Jack is at least a 2nd year in 95/96, but what year he is in is unknown.

Salazar Slytherin: c 900. He is 1 of the 4 original founders. He prized pure blood, resourcefulness, determination and intelligence. The Sorting Hat said he was shrewd, ambitious, and basically power hungry. Possibly he's of English (Fen Country) and or Spanish or Portuguese descent. Slytherin House has snake for its mascot symbol, because Salazar spoke Parseltongue. Slytherin wanted magic kept magic within all-magical families because he thought people of Muggle parentage were inherently untrustworthy and this is mainly why Slytherin House accepts primarily pureblood students.

Although Hogwarts was built in an era when magic was much feared by the common Muggle and wizards suffered great persecution, instead of pulling together over time, disagreements sprang up between the founders, ie, Salazar and Godric Gryffindor, started alas by Godric. Finally, Godric and Salazar had a serious argument and Salazar left. However, he had built a secret and hidden chamber under the castle, the Chamber of Secrets, and put a basilisk in it. He then sealed it shut and magicked up so that none but his own true heir could unseal it and release the basilisk to purge the school of all unworthy (in his opinion) to study magic. The basilisk could only be controlled by an heir that speaks Parselmouth, an apparently rare and genetically inherited talent.

He is the only one of the founders known to have left the school and the only one known to marry. This of course adds substantial weight to the "married people are usually evil" theory. Although one doubts Salazar was so much evil as pushed beyond his limit of patience by Godric, who was "out to get him." It is unknown where Salazar went upon leaving or who he married. One presumes he married a pureblood. He and his wife had at least one child whose descendants carried on to the present. Tom Riddle is the last blood relative of Salazar, so, unless he has a child, the Slytherins will end with him.

He seems to have been a closer friend to Helga Hufflepuff than any of the other founders since they both have underground-dwelling mascots. As Head of Slytherin House he doubtless had lodgings underground near Slytherin House underground, especially as he spent his free time undergound creating the Chamber of Secrets and, one presumes, trying to hide several million tons of displaced dirt. He was probably the

Potions Master during his time at Hogwarts and, given his dealings with a basilisk, possibly he taught a little Magizoology or Care of Magical Creatures as well.

Snakes are not social animals, which may say something about Salazar, but they aren't territorial either so diverse snakes living in groups are often found if den sites are rare. Another interesting facet of snake behavior, and probably Slytherin's House, would be most species are found in 50:50 gender ratios. In short, Salazar would have been socially progressive, even for a wizard, in accepting students of all races and an equal number of male and female students. The other 3 founders probably didn't accept either, social norms being what they were in 900 AD. Salazar however, had a certain disregard for the rules, according to Dumbledore, and this would certainly have included social rules.

(Unknown) Slytherin: A student that started Hogwarts in 91/92. Described as a stringy Slytherin boy. In Care of Magical Creatures class, he was able to see the thestrals. Nothing more is known. He is possibly Theodore Nott, who fits the bill well and is described as weedy.

Veronica Smethley: A Lockhart fan who wanted a signed photo of him in late 1992.

Hippocrates Smethwyck: aka Healer Smethwyck. Healer in charge of the "Dangerous" Dia Llewellyn Ward at St Mungo's. He treated Arthur for snakebite in Dec 1995. He is mentoring Healer trainee Augustus Pye.

Zacharias Smith: A Hufflepuff. He probably started Hogwarts in 90/91, but we don't know for sure. He is tall, skinny, and blonde and has an aggressive face with an upturned nose. He joined the DA in Oct 1995. He is a Chaser on the House team in 95/96. Swearing: Good Lord.

Mr Snape: Father of Severus. It is unknown if he is alive or dead. One would assume he's alive given Pr Snape's age, but he may have been murdered by his wife or son. Mr Snape is a tall, pureblood man with a hook-nosed man. He is verbally, and probably physically, abusive to his wife. For some reason he seems never to have been prosecuted for mistreating his wife and it would appear that his son was able to get away with performing minor bits of underage magic without getting taken in for it. This leads one to believe that Mr Snape works or worked in the Improper Use of Magic Office and would explain how Severus came to have a blinding hatred for people who seem to live "above the law."

It is possible, given Mr Snape's disposition, that he abused his son as well. This seems likely given Severus spent his vacations as a teen in his room (away from his fathers sight) killing flies (imagining they were his father). Such a home life would have made it very easy for Severus to join Voldemort, who also had father issues, and then kill off his father in order to become a Death Eater. Given Pr Snape's superb potion making skills, it would not have been that difficult for him to poison his father and get away with it and certainly if Mr Snape's co-workers were aware of his abusiveness, they may not have been inclined to investigate his death all that closely.

Mrs Snape: Mother of Severus. She is or was a pureblood. The victim of verbally, and probably physically, abusive husband, she cowers when he shouts. She is probably still alive if Mr Snape hasn't killed her. One hopes she has left her husband since Pr Snape left home, as divorce seems undoable in the wizarding world. On the other hand, if Mr Snape was where Severus learned all his hexes, it may be than Mrs Snape may be where Severus learned the Dark Arts, particularly potions, and she may have poisoned her husband without getting caught for it.

Severus Snape: aka Snivellus, Snively. b 1954. A Slytherin, 1966-1973. He started Hogwarts in 66/67. The son of pureblood parents, he ended up getting sucked into the pureblood philosophy in his teens. He was in the same year as James and Sirius but

The Harry Potter Companion

never part of the "in crowd." His home was particularly abusive because of his father, who was verbally and possibly physically abusive to his mother, though his mother gets a share of the blame for not a) picking up a frying pan and beating the crap out her husband or b) having him arrested and put in Azkaban.

Severus was a scrawny boy who was terrified of his father and not surprisingly grew into a greasy haired teen who spent a lot of time alone in his dark room shooting down innocent flies with his wand. The latter does bring up the issue of his using illegal underage, out-of-school magic and yet never being nabbed for it. It implies his father worked for the Improper Use of Magic Office. This could explain where Severus got his burning anger for those that live above the law and how he could he delved so deep in the Dark Arts without being questioned about it. One assumes if he was self-taught in the Dark Arts, out of anger toward his father, or learned it all from watching his father or mother.

At any rate, he arrived at Hogwarts knowing loads about Dark Arts. Sirius described him as a little oddball and the entire student body knew Severus was up to his eyes in Dark Arts. He certainly knew more curses when he arrived than the 7th years did. This in itself made him unpopular but then he added to his unpopularity by following around the 2 most popular students, James and Sirius, trying to catch them rule-breaking so he could get them expelled. In other words, he was acting the part of a twisted policeman - shades of his father. Severus was particularly jealous of James' popularity, magical talent and prowess on the Quidditch field, according to Sirius and Remus, and felt James was allowed to live above the rules because of these things.

He was always poking his nose into other people's business, mostly James' and Sirius', and, after about 5 years of this, Sirius finally got so sick of Severus' behavior (they were probably both in Slytherin House in the same year, making the course of avoidance difficult) that he allowed Severus to "accidentally" find out how to stop the Whomping Willow and open the tunnel to the Shrieking Shack when Remus happened to be in it. The idea was to trick Severus into approaching Remus while he was a wolf to get him killed or at least bitten. James, Remus and Peter had nothing to do with Sirius' plan, but James found out about it and saved Severus, at great risk to himself, for which Severus was eternally resentful, being put in James' debt.

Severus never lost an opportunity to hex James, even after James saved his neck, and James and in turn never lost an opportunity to hex him back. Lily once tried to step in and help Severus when James got incredibly abusive during 5th year OWLs but he rejected her help because she was a Mudblood, proving he was then already a part of the pureblood believerhood operating at Hogwarts. During his 5th year he had long, greasy hair, round shoulders and walked in a spiderlike manner. He was very angular in build and only slightly shorter than Sirius. He was in short, the type of person that was easy to laugh at or make fun of. Eventually he hooked up with Lucius Malfoy and became a part of a gang of Slytherins who nearly all became Death Eaters.

Clever, talented and zealous, he was certainly a good addition to the Death Eater squad, but he remained anal about rule keeping and jealous of those whose fame let them live above the law into adulthood. This jealousy is probably what eventually turned him against Voldemort whose power and fame certainly had him living above the law. He joined Dumbledore's OoP some time before Voldemort's downfall, in 1979 or 1980 since Dumbledore knew about Voldemort being give information about the Potters for a year before their deaths. At the time, Severus was likely trying to repay the debt he owed James by saving him and his family or Lily for extending friendship to him once long ago. However, despite his efforts, Lily and James were murdered.

ACASCIAS RIPHOUSE

Severus continued to appear to be acting in Voldemort's service to those he knew were Death Eaters, but firmly remained a double agent for Dumbledore. It's unclear if Severus held a job during his Death Eaters years, but he probably did. After Oct 31, 1981, when Voldemort vanished, Dumbledore vouched for his reformed nature and he was hired by Dumbledore as the Potions Master of Hogwarts probably in that same year or early 1982 – after all, what does an out of work Death Eater do? He had applied for the ever-open DADA position but was turned down, probably for lack of DADA knowledge. He's been teaching at Hogwarts ever since and continues to apply for the DADA position regularly but never gets it.

Well known for being a Death Eater and Lucius Malfoy's lapdog, he was ratted out by Igor Karkoff in 1982. However he'd already been cleared by the Council of Magical Law and vouched for by Dumbledore, Head of the Wizengamot, who said that Severus had proved himself to him. No doubt his work against Voldemort proved him to be truly converted. Although, he is still very afraid of Moody, and one wonders why that would be if Severus were really on the straight and narrow. Perhaps he was hiding something illegal, being fond of the Dark Arts. One also wonders why is he always magically sealing his classroom, as it is in one of the dark quiet dungeons (were Aragog used to live), and his office just off the classroom. One assumes Snape's lodgings are underground in the dungeons and magically sealed as well.

Severus seems cold and distant to everyone and Harry describes his eyes as cold and empty, like looking into dark tunnels, but this would probably be an unfair assessment. Since turning on Voldemort he has had to constantly hone and perfect his skills as an Occlumens. Even after Voldemort turned into a vapor, he was still alive and Dumbledore always knew he would be back and thus he would need Severus to continue to appear to be a Death Eater. That being the case, until Voldemort is truly destroyed, Severus cannot afford to let his guard down or get close to anyone who might jeopardize the control he constantly exercises over his mind. As he said himself, strong emotions disrupt occlumency. He can't allow himself to any, which is probably why when he does have one, it's unusually strong and he goes quite out of control. This also explains why he is unattached.

When Severus first looked into Harry's eyes at the feast in Sep 1991, Harry's scar burned with a sharp, hot, shooting pain. Given that most of the scar burning incidents are associated with Voldemort in some way and at the time we know that Voldemort was living in Pr Quirrell's head, it was probably just coincidental that it happened at that moment in time. On the other hand, given Severus' skills at getting into people's minds and the fact Harry is the very image of his father, it's not inconceivable that Harry might have picked up on Severus' all-consuming hatred for James and by extension Harry himself. Severus refers to Harry as the famous Potter and Ron as his sidekick Weasley however, though he hates Harry and would like to see him expelled, he doesn't want Harry dead and did save Harry's life on one occasion.

Dumbledore's take on Severus is that yes, he hated James, but he owed him. He feels Severus saved Harry's life to repay his debt to James, and so that when the debt was cleared he could to hate Harry freely. As Dumbledore knows Severus best, one has to assume this is true. But there may be other reasons of which he was not aware. It is after all easier to hate someone and keep up one's guard than love them and do the same. He may feel he owes Lily a debt as well. One cannot say for certain, that Severus removed the scene of his 5th year humiliation from his thoughts to the Pensive to hide them from Harry because he was embarrassed by what happened to himself. After all, why not let Harry see what a jerk his father was? He may have hid hid the thought because Lily's attempt to save him was also bound up in it and he didn't want

Harry to see that. Often people hide their best memories as well as their worst. In after years he may have reflected on the fact it was Lily that tried to save him from James, not his Slytherin friends.

As a teacher, Severus always favors his house. Slytherins get special treatment even when they do badly in his classes. He takes role at start of class and has a gift for keeping class silent without effort like Pr McGonagall. He loves his craft - potions, and is extremely good at it. He calls other forms of magic a foolish and a little wand waving. He calls potionmaking a subtle science and an exact art. He appreciates the beauty of a simmering cauldron and the power a potion has to bewitch and ensnare. He claims that one can create fame and glory, and even stop death. But if this were true, would he still be a Potions Master? Certainly Severus is decidedly lacking in fame, glory or immortality.

Severus is in personality a typical Slytherin, smart, subtle, sly and self-centered. He criticizes everyone but Draco, who he seems to like and favor, but is probably sucking up to get information out of. He likes hardly any of the students and is always taking points from non-Slytherins, though not excessively. He thinks most of his pupils are idiots and in return, most non-Slytherin students are scared of him and dislike or hate him. He tends to sweep or prowl around in a his long, black, hooded cloak watching and making snide remarks about the students in his classes. He snarls at people who make mistakes and removes the contents of their cauldrons with a wave of his wand.

He's usually in a bad temper and can be very cruel, bitterly sarcastic and extraordinarily unpleasant. But one wonders whether he's that evil or just playing a part to hilt. He does seem the type to be evil, but he spends breaks in the 2nd floor staffroom, in a low armchair, eats at the High Table and makes conversation with other teachers, so he's not nasty to anyone except students. He has a good rapport with Pr McGonagall, his former Transfiguration teacher, and Dumbledore, both of whom are also OoP members. He had issues with most of the DADA teachers, but there was always good reason. His relations with other teachers are usually cordial, though he did have a bit of tiff with Pr Sprout when she was asked to make the Mandrake Restorative. He felt he was being overlooked as Potions Master and carped about it.

He seems to have an instinct about trickery, in students or teachers, and knows it when he sees it. It was Severus that felt the troll was a diversion and went to check on the Sorcerer's Stone. It was Severus that understood Pr Quirrell was hexing Harry during the Quidditch match and stopped him. Oddly though, Severus didn't report Pr Quirrell when he knew what was happening, instead he took him out to the woods and told him to think about his loyalties and warned him he was making a bad enemy if he kept on the path he was on. He tried to bring Pr Quirrell back from the Dark side rather than rat him out to Dumbledore, despite the fact that Severus is loyal to and trusted by Dumbledore. Perhaps like Harry, Severus enjoy saving people or like Dumbledore is willing to give them a second chance.

Severus is always the first to find someone acting illegally, especially if it's Harry. Severus was first to find Harry and Ron after the events at the Whomping Willow. He was first to suspect Harry was doing something nefarious at the witch's statue that leads to Honeydukes. He was the first to make a shrewd guess that Harry was probably a Parselmouth and intentionally had Draco set a snake on Harry to prove it. And the list goes on and on. It has to be said however that Severus is more than a little paranoid and many times no one is doing anything shady. However his attitude of paranoia is justified given the course of his life. What's less justified is how petty he can be. He sometimes keeps Harry back after Potions and makes him clean up and scrape tubeworms off the desks. He refused to believe the truth about Sirius just because he hated him so much. And, after Sirius escaped and he lost his Order of Merlin, 2nd, possibly 1st class, he ratted out Lupin, whom he also loathed, as a werewolf to his students just so he'd have to leave.

Only once has Dumbledore let Severus substitute teach the DADA class, for Lupin, and it was a disaster. One would presume the reason Dumbledore doesn't give him the job is A) Dumbledore needs people trained in defense against not use of Dark Arts, B) no student would be able to learn from Severus given they hate him so much, and C) Severus is not as knowledgeable about his subject as he claims, the "kappa lives in Mongolia" error being a case in point. But Severus has other useful talents, spying on Voldemort not the least of them. He is a superb Occlumens and though the occlumency lessons was ordered by Dumbledore to give Harry didn't work, it was for reasons had nothing to do with A, B or C above, though Dumbledore agreed it was a mistake to let him teach Harry.

Severus has a dangerous job, finding out what Voldemort is saying to the Death Eaters and reporting it back to Dumbledore without getting killed, that is made slightly less dangerous by living at Hogwarts where there are many enchantments that can protect him, not to mention the one person Voldemort is afraid of, Dumbledore. To all intents and purposes, Severus has tried to appear to Voldemort as a mole in Dumbledore's service but Voldemort is not fooled and said so in Little Hangleton. Voldemort feels Severus has left his ranks forever and plans to kill him for it. Since 1995, Severus has been in much more danger than he realizes and probably only still alive so Voldemort can feed him false information that will be relayed back to Dumbledore. But Severus takes pride in being a spy, and that has perhaps blinded him to the reality of his situation and will prove his undoing.

Severus in 1995 is slightly less tall than Sirius, but still quite tall. He has cold black eyes and greasy shoulder-length black hair. He is thin with very sallow skin and his fingers look long and yellow. His face is thin to the point of looking gaunt with lines etched on it. He has a hooked, overly (abnormally some have said) large nose and long nostrils. His teeth are yellowish and uneven and he usually wears a slight sneer achieved by curling just the upper lip of his thin mouth. Occasionally he bares his teeth or even spits on the ground. He has the Dark Mark on his left inner forearm. He has spiky scrawled writing and usually uses black ink. His voice is cold and soft. He rants and shouts only rarely, as usually when he's angry he speaks softly, in barely more than a whisper or hiss. His definition of a weak person is someone who wears their heart on their sleeve, can't control their emotions or wallows in sad memories and words. This explains a lot about his life.

Severus always wears long-sleeved black robes (which cover the dark mark) and owns a billowing black traveling cloak. He walks briskly with robes fluttering or billowing most of the time. Pr Quirrell thought he swooped around like a bat. But Severus has a second walk, which can be describe best by the word prowling, that he uses in class or when sneaking around. Severus seems to like the color grey, in addition to the color black. When he was a student, he wore grey undergarments. At night, now he's grown up, he wears a long grey nightshirt. Given his level of paranoia, he may not let the house-eves do his washing and may prefer to do it himself, throwing the blacks in with the whites in 1 load and thus the whites achieve a permanent mellow grey tone. Swearing: damn.

Alicia Spinnet: b 1978. A Gryffindor 1989-1996. She started Hogwarts in 89/90. She was a reserve Chaser for the House team in 90/91, moving up to Chaser in 91/92-95/96. She joined the DA in Oct 1995. She graduated in Jun 1996.

Phyllida Spore: Author of *One Thousand Magical Herbs and Fungi*. Hogwarts' textbook for use in Potions and Herbology.

Pr (Unknown) Sprout: Teacher of Herbology. Head of Hufflepuff. She is a dumpy, squat, little witch with grey flyway hair and wears her patched hat slightly askew. She usually has a large amount of earth or dragon on her robes and under her fingernails. In winter or when dealing with mandrakes, she wears pink earmuffs. She is generally quite a cheerful person. She carries large greenhouse keys on her belt and there are at least 3 greenhouses in her care. Her preferred type of fertilizer is dragon dung (Hebridean Black probably). She's serious about her plants and a very a knowledgeable teacher. She is environmentally conscious and teaches all her students to compost.

Most of what is grown in the greenhouses is used at the school, either in potions or for medicinal purposes. She herself is a very good potionmaker, though Pr Snape is loathe to admit it. In 92/93 she ended up with her arm in bandages from treating the Whomping Willow, after the flying Ford Anglia incident, and when it was later suggested she make the Mandrake Restorative Draught, she almost got her another arm broken, by Pr Snape. In 94/95 she told Barty Jr (Moody) that Neville was really good at Herbology, which he is, and consoled the Diggorys after Cedric, one of her House's students, was killed by Voldemort in Little Hangleton.

Mr (Unknown) Stebbins: b 1954. House unknown, 1966-1973. He started Hogwarts in 66/67. He was in school with Lily and James. His son is currently a Hufflepuff so perhaps he was too.

(Unknown) Stebbins: A Hufflepuff. His year is unknown. He and Ms Fawcett seem to be very close. They both tried to cross the Age Line together to enter the TT in Oct 1994, and ended up with beards. He took Ms Fawcett to the Yule Ball where they were caught together in the bushes by Pr Snape. One assumes they graduated in Jun 1996, but there is no proof of this.

Patricia Stimpson: b 1977. A Gryffindor, 1989-1996. She started Hogwarts in 89/90. She kept fainting during her 5th year because of all the extra work she had to do to prepare for the OWLs.

Miriam Strout: Healer at St Mungo's. In 95/96 she was working on the Janus Thickey Ward. She is a motherly looking woman who wears a tinsel wreath in her hair at Christmas. She's a bit careless though. She left the locked door at the far end of the corridor unlocked to get presents and Lockhart slipped out then she missed the fact the plant by Bode's bed was devil's snare. She is obviously not deterred by working with the really spell damaged and she's good at actual healing. She was curing Bode before he died and Lockhart is also improving, unfortunately for the rest of the world.

Mr (Unknown) Summerby: A Hufflepuff. He was House Seeker in 95/96. It's unknown what year he is.

Mr (Unknown) Summers: A Hufflepuff. He is student in 94/95. What year he started Hogwarts is unknown.

Emeric Swich: Author of *A Beginners' Guide to Transfiguration*, Hogwarts' textbook for Transfiguration class, years 1-3.

Janus Thickey: He faked his death in 1973 but was found by his wife and children sometime later not far away, living with the landlady of a pub. Mrs Thickey did him some irreparable spell damage and today the ward for the incurably spell injured at St Mungo's is named after him.

Dean Thomas: 1979. A Gryffindor, 1991-1998? He is Muggle born. He started Hogwarts in 91/92. He is very tall, even taller than Ron, and Black. He is the best friend of Seamus and a roommate of Harry's. He draws very well and created a lion on a Quidditch banner in 91/92 and offered to forge a signature on Harry's Hogsmeade permission slip in 93/94. He really likes soccer, particularly West Ham, and has a nonmagical West Ham poster by his bed at school. He fought with Ron about which was a better sport soccer or Quidditch and has pajamas that are West Ham colors, claret red and sky blue.

In 93/94 he hoped Hogwarts would get a vampire for a DADA teacher next year, having had so much fun with the werewolf teacher. In the summer of 1994, Dean went with Seamus and Mrs Finnigan to QWC 1994. In 94/95 when he got back to school, he tacked up a poster of Viktor Krum over his bedtable with the West Ham poster next to it. In 94/95 he got his hand blasted by a skrewt and, after Harry survived Task 1 of the TT, he put up new banners depicting Harry zooming around the Horntail on his Firebolt and a few that depicted Cedric with his head on fire. He joined the DA in Oct 1995 and eventually got Seamus to join as well. In Jun 1996 he started dating Ginny Weasley.

Agatha Timms: She put up half her shares in her eel farm that QWC 1994 would be a long match. That was one bet Bagman didn't have to pay up on.

Pr (Unknown) Tofty: He is with the Wizarding Examination Authority. He is the very oldest (100+), baldest examiner and He has extremely veined and knotty hands. He wears pince-nez glasses. Tiberius Ogden is a friend of his and told him Harry could do a Patronus. He did Harry's OWL practical in Charms, Astronomy and DADA. He gave Harry an extra point on his DADA OWL practical for producing a corporeal Patronus that galloped the length of the room.

Tom (Unknown): The elderly, slightly stooped, owner and bartender of the Leaky Cauldron. He is quite bald and wizened and toothless (apparently wizards don't wear dentures or have a cure for tooth loss). He wears an apron when he works and a nightshirt when he goes to bed. Tom has at least 1 employee, a young man that is a dishwasher. Tom knows Hagrid as a regular customer and is on friendly terms with most of the wizarding world. He's a very nice host. He snaps his fingers and the fires light. He bows courteously to customers when he leaves the room.

In 1991 Tom cried at the sight of Harry and welcomed him back, implying he'd been in as a baby with his parents. In Aug 1993, Harry stayed at the Leaky Cauldron for a few weeks and Tom watched over him to make sure he stayed in Diagon Alley and came back to the inn before nightfall. He woke Harry each morning with a grin and tea. It's unclear how long Tom has owned the Leaky Cauldron. He may have inherited it from his parents as the pub-inn has a long and famous history. Swearing : Good Lord, bless my soul.

Andromeda Black Tonks: b 1954. A Slytherin 1965-1972. She started Hogwarts in 65/66. She is a pureblood, and the middle sister of Bellatrix and Narcissa. She was Sirius' very favorite 1st cousin. She is Tonks' mother and the wife of Muggle-born wizard Ted Tonks. She was burned off the Black tapestry by Mrs Black for marrying a nonpureblood. Apparently she's also a bit of a fool according to Tonks.

Nymphadora Tonks: aka Tonks. An Auror. She is the youngest Auror working today. She is the daughter of Sirius 1st cousin Andromeda and Muggle born, thus a she's a Mudblood. However she was burned off the Black family tapestry for becoming an Auror, rather than being born. She is a half-blood as her pureblood mother, Andromeda Black, married a Muggle-born wizard, Ted Tonks. She says some pretty harsh things about her parents, calling her mom a fool and her dad a slob. It seems like she's most upset about her name.

At school, she was never a Prefect apparently because she couldn't control herself. One presumes that the school she went to was Hogwarts, but it's never stated. She went on to Auror training (3 years), and got top marks in Concealment and Disguise but nearly failed Stealth and Tracking because of her unrelenting clumsiness. She qualified in Aug 1994. She thinks Moody is a bit over the top, but then she hasn't been an Auror that long. She rides a Comet 260. She was not in the OoP last time, she was too young (under 17).

She is a current member of the OoP and was part of Harry's escort to Headquarters. She did not admit she worked with Dumbledore at work or she would have lost her job, but it sort of came out in Jun 1996 when she was severely injured from dueling with Death Eaters with Dumbledore. She is probably 21 years old when Harry meets her in Aug 1995. Her favorite word is "Wotcher" and no matter what form she is in, she is still terribly clumsy. She is a metamorphmagus, so describing her actual look is a bit dicey. She seems to always have a pale heart-shaped face, dark twinkling eyes, and, when herself, short spiky hair of a bubble gum pink color.

Ted Tonks: A Muggle-born wizard. Husband of Andromeda Black Tonks. Father of Nymphadora "Tonks" Tonks. Apparently he's a bit of slob, according to Tonks.

Kenneth Towler: b 1977. A Gryffindor, 1989-1996. He was in the same year as George and Fred, starting Hogwarts in 89/90. He broke out in boils during his 5th year because they put Bulbadox Powder in his pajamas.

(Unknown) Travers: b 1957. A Slytherin 1968-1975. He started Hogwarts in 68/68. See Note 1, section IV. He helped murder the McKinnons. He was caught prior to being ratted out by Karkoff in 1982. He was probably Escapee 3 from Azkaban Jan 1996. He was not a part of the MoM raid and is the one of 6 Death Eaters still on the loose.

Cassandra Trelawney: Sybill's Great-Great-Grandmother. A noted Seer in her time, probably well over 100 years ago.

Sybill P. Trelawney: She is the Great-Great-Grandaughter of noted Seer Cassandra Trelawney. She has been teaching Divination and living in the North Tower at Hogwarts since 1979. She was hired by Dumbledore because she gave a real prophecy about the fall of Voldemort and he figured she was too valuable to be left out of his care. She does have an actual Gift but it rarely manifests. When it does, she never remembers it happening or consequently the prophecy she gave during the trance. Before she gives a real prophecy she goes rigid, her eyes become unfocused and her mouth sags. Her eyes then start to roll like she's having some sort of seizure and she speaks in a harsh voice unlike her own but she may typically "put on" a voice.

Sybill is very thin and usually wears a tragic expression. She wears large glasses which magnify her eyes several times and innumerable chains and strings of glittering beads hung around her thin neck and arms. She wears long emerald earrings, clinking bangles and her long fingers seem encrusted with rings. She is always draped in a gauzy spangled shawl and carries a small self-embroidered handkerchief. She doesn't eat with the other teachers, but she joined them at the Christmas Feast, 1993, wearing a green sequined dress and looking like an oversized glittering dragonfly. She has a soft misty dreamy voice, that can become very normal sounding when she gets peeved, say at Pr McGonagall. Pr McGonagall is her most vocal critic.

During class she sits in an large wingback armchair in front of the fire. She has a habit of predicting bad things, even death, for her students. She predicts the death of a student every year - but they never die. She constantly told Harry he was going to die. Then Pr Umbridge sacked her and Harry's interview came out in *The Quibbler* and she suddenly said Harry would live to an old age, have lots of children, and be Minister of Magic someday. She is Parvati and Lavender's favorite teacher. She feels students have the Gift or they don't and grades and tests don't really matter. She's probably right. For all the flack about being a fraud she puts up with, she is right about 90% of the time if one looks closely at each prediction. She doesn't have a gift for predicting death, but everything else she's pretty good at. It may take some time to unfold, but it happens.

She drinks when upset, cooking sherry most likely, and quite a lot of it. She does needlework as a hobby embroidery on hankies, mostly. She was sacked by Pr Umbridge in 1996 and is currently still sacked. Firenze the centaur is teaching her classes, but it's difficult to say what will happen in 96/97 since Firenze can't go back to the forest. Perhaps if Pr Sinistra retires he can teach Astronomy, though he would doubtless be uncomfortable on top of the Astronomy Tower. Perhaps Dumbledore can placate the centaurs so that he can return home without getting killed. Dumbledore did go into the forest to rescue Pr Umbridge, he may have had words about Firenze as well. Or, Hogwarts might end up with 2 divination teachers, which they do need, mathematically speaking, given the number of students.

Quentin Trimble: Author of *The Dark Forces: A Guide to Self-Protection,* Hogwarts' textbook for DADA in the 91/92.

(Unknown) Troy: Irish Chaser in QWC 1994.

Lisa Turpin: b 1979. A Ravenclaw, 1991-1998? She started Hogwarts in 91/92.

Dr (Unknown) Ubbly: Inventor of Dr Ubbly's Oblivious Unction. Unknown if male or female.

Madam Dolores Jane Umbridge: She was a Hogwarts' student once, but her House and years are unknown. Originally Senior Undersecretary to the Minister of Magic in the 1990s. She is a sadist, a bigot and hopefully now a prisoner. She drafted anti-werewolf legislation in 1993, which after it was passed proved extremely detrimental to werewolves trying to earn a living. In 1994 she campaigned to have merpeople rounded up and tagged. In 1995 she started in on half-giants. She loathes part-humans, half-breeds, half-humans, etc. She did very illegal things behind Fudge's back because she felt everyone, including Fudge, talked about problems but didn't do anything about them. She used her position to order dementors to attack and Kiss Harry to get rid of him in Aug 1995 because he was proving problematic to the MoM.

She was appointed the new DADA teacher for 95/96, by the MoM since Dumbledore couldn't find a replacement (and for whatever reason decided he didn't want to teach it himself, which he well probably could have). She was there primarily to spy for Fudge and wanted students to spy on each other and the teachers as well. She later became Hogwarts High Inquisitor. As High Inquisitor she inspected other teachers and sacked those she found unfit to teach such as Hagrid and Sybill. She finally became Head of Hogwarts after Dumbledore went on the lam in 1996. She tried to use the illegal Cruciatus Curse on Harry. She hasn't seen death and can't see thestrals, but has been carried off by centaurs in the Forbidden Forest. She was saved by Dumbledore. Currently she is either on the run, or in prison for attempting to use dementors inappropriately.

She wears rather odd clothing. To the Start of Term Feast she wore a fluffy pink cardigan over her robes and a matching headband. Luckily her clothes were overshadowed by her rudeness to Dumbledore when she stood up and made a speech. She wears luridly flowered robes in her off hours and most surfaces in her office is covered in similar materials. She has a flowered bag in which she keeps pink parchment, quills and a clipboard. She takes her handbag everywhere and must have something in it she's afraid someone will find or just really weird. She uses pink parchment notepaper. In winter she wears a green tweed cloak and matching hat with earflaps. She frequently wears her pink cardigan with a black velvet hair ribbon and bow on top of her head.

She is short, barely reaching Hagrid's navel (so about 5'), with pallid skin. She looks like a large pale toad, squat with almost no neck, a broad, flabby face and a very wide, slack mouth. Her eyes are large, round, pouchy and slightly bulging. She has stubby fingered hands with loads of ugly old rings on them. She has short curly mousey-brown hair. She speaks in a high-pitched simpering rather breathy, fluttery and girlish voice (till someone ticks her off) and a silvery laugh. She makes a ridiculous hem, hem noise when she wants to interrupt people and apparently collects plates with Technicolor kittens on them.

Uric the Oddball: Mentioned in History class. A very strange, bald wizard who was interested in magical animals. He conducted experiments with augereys, imagined himself to be a ghost once and is responsible for the wrongful silencing of the fwooper. He is remembered best for wearing a live badger as toupee while giving his fwooper report to the Wizards' Council. Since he was speaking to the Wizard's Council, he is a medieval wizard dating from pre-1300 AD.

Cassandra Vablatsky: Author of *Unfogging the Future*, the textbook for Hogwarts' Divination classes.

Emmeline Vance: A stately looking witch who wears an emerald-green shawl. An original and ongoing member of the OoP. She was part of Harry's escort to Headquarters in Aug 1995.

Pr (Unknown) Vector: A witch who teaches Arithmancy. A subject Hermione has great respect for.

Violet (Unknown): See Portraits Etc., Portraits section.

Pr Vindictus Viridian: Author of *Curses and Countercurses: bewitch your friends and befuddle your enemies with the latest revenges: hair loss, jelly legs, tongue tying and much, much more by Prof. Vindictus Viridian.* A book that really interested Harry. He saw it in Flourish and Blotts in Jul 1991.

Voldemort: See Riddle, Tom Marvolo Riddle Jr.

(Unknown) Volkov: A male, Bulgarian Beater in QWC 1994.

(Unknown) Vulchanov: Bulgarian Beater in QWC 1994. Probably male, because of the -ov ending to the name.

Adalbert Waffling: Author of *Magical Theory*. Hogwarts' textbook for Magical Theory classes in year 1 and 2. After that it's probably a supplemental text for Transfiguration and Charms.

Celestina Warbeck: A popular singing sorceress first heard by Harry on the Weasley's kitchen radio at the Burrow on the Witching Hour radio program. She recorded the Puddlemere United anthem to raise funds for St Mungo's Hospital for Magical Maladies and Injuries.

C. Warrington: b 1977, Sep or Oct. A Slytherin, 1989-1996? His first year was 89/90. He entered his name in the Goblet of Fire but was rejected. He was on the House team as a Chaser in 93/94, 94/95 and 95/96. He is quite big and looks like a sloth so perhaps rather hairy, bright eyed and dark haired.

Arthur Weasley: b 1943. A Gryffindor, 1955-1962. His first year was 55/56. He still has scars from where Mr Pringle hexed him for staying out late with Molly and this is probably his most memorable school experience. Husband of Molly. Father of Bill, Charlie, Percy, Fred and George, Ron and Ginny. Resident of Ottery St Catchpole. He is tall, thin, freckled and going bald, though he has some traces of red hair left. His ears go red under pressure or stress, and when he's angry or lying. He is very good natured, easy going and curious. He wears horn-rimmed glasses and long green robes that are usually dusty or travel-worn and shabby.

ACASCIAS RIPHOUSE

The Weasleys are an old pureblood wizarding family but none of them hold the pureblood doctrine. Arthur is a long-time friend of and believer in Dumbledore and the work of the Order. Arthur has been a member of the OoP since the 1970s and was one of the first to rejoin in 1995. Arthur's "day job" is working at the MoM as Head of the Misuse of Muggle Artifacts Office. Arthur doesn't make much money, but he loves his work and he and his family are very happy. He has a good sense of humor and enjoys his children's antics, but he has a healthy respect for Molly and her temper. As a pastime He loves to tinker with (read illegally charm) Muggle technology in a little shed on his property and is responsible for creating the flying Ford Anglia.

In 91/92, Arthur and Molly visited Charlie in Romania at Christmas. Arthur didn't meet up with Harry during that year, but he was surely told about him by Ron and certainly knew of him from working with the Order. In Aug 1992 when Ron, Fred and George brought Harry to the Burrow. Arthur who had been working nights for the MoM, raiding locations that were thought to contain bewitched Muggle items, was out when Harry arrived. Arthur was delighted to find Harry staying at the Burrow when he came home one morning and, for the duration of Harry's stay, he always had Harry sit next to him at the dinner table so he could ask questions about life with Muggles, and Harry could explain how things like plugs and the postal service work.

Arthur was part of 9 raids the night Harry arrived, and old Mundungus Fletcher's place was among those raided. Despite both of them having belonged to the Order in the past, and currently, Dung tried to hex Arthur when his back was turned. This did not however damage their relationship. Later in the summer of 1992, on a family trip to Diagon Alley before the start of 92/93 school year, he discovered the Grangers at Gringotts exchanging some Muggle money for Galleons and immediately took a shine to them. He almost asked the Grangers how a bus stop worked, after they told him that's how they'd gotten to Diagon Alley, in 1991, but Molly stopped him before he could cross the bounds of good taste.

He invited the Drs Granger to the Leaky Cauldron and later on while they were all book shopping in Flourish and Blotts, they met up with Lucius Malfoy. An ugly scene ensued as Lucius called Arthur a disgrace to the name wizard for loving Muggles and associating with the Grangers and Arthur responded by physically attacking Lucius. A slug-fest ensued. Arthur was getting the best of Lucius when the fight was broken up by Hagrid who was passing by. Arthur definitely has a bit a temper, which is probably where Ron gets his fiery nature from, but unlike Ron, he has to be seriously provoked to lose it. Age has probably tempered him some.

Arthur's interest in Muggle things extends to cars. He acquired an old Ford Anglia and claimed to just wanted to see how the car worked but actually he enchanted it to fly. There's a loophole in the law, which he wrote, that says as long as he wasn't intending to fly the car, the fact that car could fly isn't a crime. It was this car that Fred, George and Ron used to rescue Harry and this car that Ron and Harry flew to Scotland on Sep 1, 1992. The MoM wasn't too happy with Arthur, since many Muggles spotted the car flying, and he faced an inquiry at work. Eventually around Christmas 1992, he was fined the large sum of 50G for bewitching the car. However, this steep fine didn't quell his Muggle obsession any and he continues to be fascinated by how Muggles get along without magic.

He drafted a new Muggle Protection Act, a more stringent legal means to protect Muggles from magicals during this same time period, and was working to get it passed in 92/93, much against Lucius' will. Ironically though, his best support came from Lucius. Though Arthur's favorite sayings about magical objects is never trust anything that can think for itself if you can't see where it keeps it's brain, Ginny got involved

375

with Tom Riddle's Diary anyway, which in turn caused Muggle-born students to be Petrified, thus proving the need for more Muggle protection. The summer after Ginny had her adventure with Tom, in Jul 1993, Arthur won the annual *The Daily Prophet* Grand Prize Galleon Drawing. With the 700G prize money, he took the entire family to visit Bill in Egypt.

It was being photographed during this trip with Scabbers for a front page story in *The Daily Prophet* that set off all the events of 93/94. Sirius Black escaped after seeing the picture and in it Peter Pettigrew, in rat form. Arthur tried to warn Harry about Sirius Black just before he returned to school, because he felt Harry had a right to know about Sirius, but was relieved to discover at the train station Harry already knew Sirius wanted to kill him that and thus he didn't have to cross Molly to tell Harry. For the rest of the year one doesn't hear much of Arthur. Though at some point Dumbledore told Arthur that Sirius was not a Death Eater and therefore still a part of the Order since they end up working together shortly afterwards.

Arthur may love Muggles, but in Aug 1994 he set Muggle-magical relations back a step after he blew up the Dursley's fireplace in an effort to pick up Harry to take him to QWC 1994, and then tried to magically repair Dudley's tongue after he'd eaten one of Fred and George's Ton-Tongue Toffees. Despite these minor goofs, and the fact he tends to get Muggle words wrong quite frequently: escapators = escalators; pumbles = plumbers; fellytone = telephone; eclectic = electric, eckeltricity = electricity, Arthur is more Muggle aware than most magicals and really desires to help and understand Muggles. This is why he pumps Harry and the Grangers for information, collects plugs and batteries, and thinks a set of screwdrivers are such a marvelous Christmas gift.

Arthur received 10 Top Box tickets to QWC 1994 from Ludo after smoothing over Otto Bagman's lawnmower problems and so, in Aug 1994, he was able to take his children, and Harry and Hermione, to the event in style. After arriving at the campsite by Portkey, he tried harder than most wizards to observe Anti-Muggle Security and blend in with Muggles, by not doing magic and wearing a golfing sweater, very old jeans that were a bit too big and a thick leather belt. Like his Muggle vocabulary, his Muggle fashion sense could use some work. At QWC 1994, he bet Bagman 1G that Ireland would win, but probably never got his money. Arthur can only afford to bet small amounts since his pay at the MoM is less than sufficient and Molly would not approve of large-sum gambling.

Later that summer, when Moody was in trouble for the dustbins, he was able to sort things out with the policemen by modifying their memories and with the MoM by cautioning Moody instead of letting the Improper Use of Magic Office arrest him. Unfortunately it wasn't Moody but Barty Jr he saved, setting off Harry's 94/95 troubles. Still despite the occasional snafu, Arthur is justly proud of his work and doesn't take promotions because he likes it where he is, even if it is just him and Perkins in a cramped office. By the summer of 1995, Arthur was active in the OoP again, as was Molly this time, despite a real risk of losing his job if his was found to be supporting or consorting with Dumbledore. He joined the rotating guard that was set up to protect the DoM and Sybill's prophecy regarding Voldemort.

Things went well until one night just before Christmas. While wearing an Invisibility Cloak, Arthur nodded off and was attacked by Nagini (Voldemort). Arthur was rescued by the portraits and rushed to St Mungo's where he remained in the "Dangerous" Dai Llewellyn Ward over Christmas. After many attempts by Healers to cure him, including a bout with Muggle stitches, Arthur at last recovered and was sent back to Headquarters. He continued with the Order, trying privately to convince people Voldemort was back and trying to get them to help Dumbledore. One supposes his task was less difficult after the raid on the MoM in Jun 1996. Unlike Moody, Tonks and Kingsley, his association with Dumbledore is still secret. Swearing: Good lord. Damn.

Bilius Weasley: Brother of Arthur. Uncle of Ron. He died 24 hours after seeing a Grim, sometime prior to summer 1993.

Bill Weasley: b 1969. A Gryffindor, 1981-1988. He is the oldest child of Arthur and Molly. In his youth he had a Brazilian penfreind and wanted him to visit on an exchange trip but Bill couldn't afford it. The penpal was offended and sent him a cursed hat that made his ears shrivel up. Still Bill had dreams of visiting far-flung places. He went to Hogwarts starting in 81/82. He got 12 OWLs and was made Head Boy in his last year 87/88. After graduating he built on his love of adventure and travel and became a Curse Breaker for Gringotts, working in the tombs of Egypt. Rita Skeeter called him a long haired pillock while doing an interview with all the Gringotts' Charm Breakers (aka Curse Breakers) but it didn't matter to him. Molly and Arthur visited at him in Egypt during Christmas 1992.

Bill is the cool one in the family. He is tall, has long red hair he wears in a ponytail and like all the Weasley kids he has freckles. He wears a fang earring in one ear (which one is unknown). The earring is new as of Summer 1994. He wears tshirts, jeans and leather boots of dragon hide. All in all he looks like he belongs at a rock concert. Bill is a chess player and, like Ron, doesn't like Pr Snape, but he has to work with him for the sake of the Order. He became a member of the OoP in 1995 and applied for a desk job at Gringotts' London office so he could come home and work with the Order. He misses the tombs but he's met and started dating Fleur Delacour who also works at Gringotts' London office, so that's a bit of compensation. Swearing: damn.

Charlie Weasley: b 1972. A Gryffindor, 1983-1990. He is the 2nd oldest of Arthur and Molly's children. He started Hogwarts in 83/84. He was Captain of House team and an extremely good Seeker despite being short and stocky. It is said he could have played for England if he'd wanted but he didn't want to. Although great on a broom, he did have take his Apparition Test twice. He missed the first time by several miles. After graduating in 89/90 he went to study dragons at a reserve in Romania. Arthur and Molly went to visit him at Christmas in 1991. He returned to Hogwarts as a dragon handler for the 1st task of the TT Nov 1994. He joined the OoP in 1995 but stayed in Romania trying to make contacts on his days off and recruit foreign wizards into the Order.

Like all the Weasleys, Charlie has red hair and freckles. He takes after his mother and is shorter and more stocky than Billy, Percy or Ron who take after their dad. He has a broad good-natured face, which is weather beaten and freckled to the point of appearing tan. He has muscular arms, one of which has a burn on it from the wild dragons in Romania and he also has burns, blisters and calluses on his large hands. Like all the Weasley kids, he wears jeans, tshirts and Muggle shoes. Charlie has sewing skills and can often be found darning his fireproof balaclava. He also snores.

Fred and George Weasley: b Apr 1978. Gryffindors, 1989-1996. They are superidentical twins and even Molly can't tell them apart. They are the 4th and 5th born of Arthur and Molly's children. It seems that Fred is the older twin. They are very kindly, but they do love practical jokes and can get a little out of hand. Their sense of humor is decidedly quirky and their constant dream throughout their schooldays was opening a joke shop. To this end they began inventing candies and tricks even before they hit the doors of Hogwarts.

They started Hogwarts in 89/90 and both became Beaters for the House team in 90/91, playing till 95/96 when they were banned from playing. Typical twins, they both have gold wristwatches and ride Cleansweep 5s. They both wanted to join the

The Harry Potter Companion

OoP in early 1995 but weren't allowed to because they weren't out of school, though they were of age. They both got good marks and everyone thought they were both really funny. They both spent a lot of time trying to go into the Forbidden Forest, and being stopped by Hagrid.

As superidentical twins they are impossible to tell apart. They have the same flaming red hair and are identical to the last freckle. They take after their mother, being shorter and stockier than Bill, Percy or Ron. They both are quite outgoing and usually sit with other people conversing loudly. They both have catlike moves, a practiced stealth to their walk and feel there are some Muggle skills worth knowing, lock picking for one. Despite the fact they both lost lots of points for Gryffindor over the years, they were still well liked, probably because they think everything is a joke and like to make light of serious matters to lessen tension. They were also likely popular for sneaking into the kitchens or Honeydukes for sweets during Gryffindor celebrations.

In 91/92 they got punished for bewitching several snowballs to follow Quirrell and bounce off the back of his turban, stole Percy's Prefect badge and tried to send a toilet seat to Harry while he was in hospital. In 92/93 they flew the Ford Anglia to Harry's house, took turns covering themselves with fur or boils and jumping out at Ginny from behind statues to cheer her up, and walked around announcing "The Heir of Slytherin is coming" when Harry was in real disgrace and feared by rest of the school. In 93/94 they made Percy's Head Boy badge say Bighead Boy, gave the Marauder's Map to Harry so he could visit Hogsmeade despite Sirius being after him and got only 3 OWLs a piece. In 94/95 Fred let Ton-Tongue Toffees fall out of his pocket, so Dudley would eat one, both whipped up aging potion to try and fool the Goblet of Fire and were given 1,000G by Harry, Harry's TT winnings, to help them get their joke shop started.

In 95/96 they bought illegal seeds from Dung, stole doxies and Wartcap Powder from Sirius' house for the Skiving Snackboxes and didn't want to go back for their 7th year, since they were 17. But Molly made them go back so, rather than actually study, they did marketing research and product development for their joke shop. They were given a lifetime ban on Quidditch playing by Umbridge, became members of the DA in Oct 1995 and eventually, after reeking havoc on Pr Umbridge, quit school mid-term and opened a joke shop in Diagon Alley. They turned out to have a very successful business and in a few short weeks were walking around in gaudy expensive green dragon-skin jackets (Common Welsh Green presumably). It was not said if they had joined the Order, though they may have. Dumbledore would of course welcome such actively sneaky, risk-taking characters.

Between the pair of them, Fred seems the more dominate twin so he may be the eldest of the pair. Fred seems to instigate, and while George shares Fred's nature and enjoys all the adventures they get into, he's more of a follower. Fred likes to be the center of attention more than George. Fred does the demo puking, George holds the bucket. Fred drives the flying car, George picks the locks. George chooses the less showy more secretive route. But George does have a short temper, can be very snide and is much less easy going than Fred, perhaps because he knows he has to keep himself in check. George will burst out angrily at team mates. In a fury he hit a Bludger at Pr Snape. Later he beat up Draco for insulting his family. And George is the one that takes the most pleasure in causing Pr Umbridge suffering.

None of this is to say George, or Fred, is a bad person. He and Fred are both decent, inventive and fun loving. They both have problems and conflicts with their mother. One merely points out, George is always mentioned 2nd of the pair, is a lot more physically expressive of his anger than Fred and very clearly has a quite different personality. Anyone having had superidentical twins as friends knows how different twins can be. For all that is said, they are different people, and even superidentical twins are usually noticeably different to those who know them well, one always being very subtly of a thinner, very slightly taller, build than the other. Fred swearing: dammit. George: he swears, but it's unrecorded, probably for a good reason.

Ginny Weasley: b 1981. A Gryffindor, 1992-1999. She is the youngest child and only daughter of Arthur and Molly. She is a great cat lover, wears a long night dress, and her Bat-Bogey Hexes are amazingly powerful. She really wanted to go with her brothers to Hogwarts in 1991 but was too young, so she cried and ran after the train at the station. In 91/92 she was a small girl with bright brown eyes, flaming red hair and freckles. She normally never shuts up but after developing a crush on Harry she became shy, clumsy and blushing around him from 1992 until about 1995.

She was accepted to Hogwarts in 92/93. She got all her robes and school things second-hand on a shopping trip to Diagon Alley, during which time she came into possession of Tom Riddle's Diary thanks to Lucius Malfoy. She quickly discovered how the Diary worked and started to tell it how her brothers teased her, how embarrassed she was to go to school in second-hand robes and how she didn't think Harry would ever like her. Her first year was very memorable as she became possessed by Tim Riddle, killed 2 of Hagrid's roosters and repeatedly opened the Chamber of Secrets and let the basilisk out. Her adventure culminated in being kidnapped by Tom Riddle. She survived, and was quite embarrassed, but Dumbledore admitted Tom had tricked better, older wizards and saw no reason to expel her.

She remains small with a long mane of red hair at 14. She thinks anything's possible if one has enough nerve, a philosophy she originally acquired from hanging around Fred and George, but embraces wholeheartedly. She became a good broomstick flyer from secretly breaking into the Weasley brothers' brooms and flying them since she was 6, so obviously she practiced what she preaches. She became the replacement Seeker on the House team in 95/96 after Harry was banned. She'd rather be a Chaser than Seeker and will likely try for the Chaser position in 96/97, where she'll have a good shot at becoming one since all 3 Chaser slots will be open, she's an excellent player and Harry, as eldest team member, will likely end up Captain, and if not him, Ron as 2nd oldest team member.

By 1995 Ginny was no longer interested in Harry and stopped being quiet or clumsy around him. She dated Michael Corner from early 1995 and they both joined the DA in Oct 1995 but she broke up with him toward about Apr 1996. She started dating Dean Thomas at the end of the year. Around the same time, Jun 1996, she got involved in helping Harry outwits Pr Umbridge and the Inquisitorial Squad, flew a thestral and had her shot at taking on Death Eaters during the MoM raid where she was amazingly effective. She knows Luna, though they are in different Houses and is the one that introduced Harry to her. She thinks Luna is alright, and should do since she saved her life at the MoM. Swearing: oh damn.

Grandfather (Unknown) Weasley: Ron was given his old chess set. He died sometime prior to 1991.

Molly Weasley: b 1944. A Gryffindor, 1955-1962. She started Hogwarts in 55/56 and says they planted the Whomping Willow after her time at Hogwarts. Wife of Arthur. Mother of Charlie, Bill, Percy, Fred and George, Ronald and Ginny. She is a pureblood, but has a male 2nd cousin who is a Squib and became an accountant. is a housewitch in Ottery St Catchpole and couldn't join the OoP the first time round, though Arthur did. She became a member of the OoP in 1995. She is plump and shorter than Ron at 12 years old, has red hair, freckles and a kind face.

She is the essence of motherliness and very tender hearted. She is loved by all her children and the boys used to lean out the train's window just so she could kiss them goodbye. She always holds Ginny's hand as she walks about station or when shopping. She developed an instant deep sympathy for Harry, because of his being an orphan but has no awe for his ridding the world of Voldemort in 1981 as others do. She immediately embraced him as another son and a part of her family. Out of her deep compassion for Harry, she sent him food and a sweater the very first Christmas after they meet in passing at the station.

She carries a remarkable handbag which seems to hold a lot of stuff. She keeps a handkerchief, a large clothes brush, and sandwiches for 5 in it. She always makes sandwiches for the train ride, but Ron implies her cooking isn't that great because she doesn't have much time to cook with so many kids to look after. She looks remarkably like a sabertoothed tiger when angry, her eyes flash and she swells up magnificently. She can shout for a long time, loudly, when upset and be very physical, for instance poking a finger in one's chest and yelling till she's hoarse. One must cut her off before she hits her stride yelling or she can yell for hours. All her sons are taller than she but they cower when her rage breaks and is directed toward them.

She says she never had any trouble with Bill, Charlie or Percy, when they were at school but she received lots of owls about things Fred and George did and Ron is getting a bit wild as well. She's a very decent, rather traditional woman, and expects her children to be upright and law abiding. If that requires sending periodic Howlers to remind them of their duty, so be it. She doesn't allow her children into Knockturn Alley and uses terms like "scarlet woman" to describe a girl dating 2 boys at the same time. She is happily married but owns a copy of *Gilderoy Lockhart's Guide to Household Pests,* as well as all his other books, and blushes at the suggestion she may be sweet on him.

At home she wears a flowered apron usually with her wand sticking out of the pocket. She has robes of varying degrees of shabbiness, a quilted purple dressing gown and bedroom slippers. She knits sweaters and socks for her family. She would like a house-elf for ironing and makes tea whenever people are upset. She writes on purple parchment for letters. She is very poor, at one point there was only a very small pile of silver Sickles and 1G in her vault, but she never fusses or complains about it. She and Arthur are very happy and she has learned to make ends meet despite her meager budget. She gets on very well with Hermione and Ginny and told them she once made a love potion when she was young. She can get quite giggly over girl talk, but she frets and worries over Harry.

She fusses over the state of Harry's socks and tries to force 4th helpings on him at every meal whenever he visits. She thinks of Harry as her own child and hugs him before he gets on the Hogwarts Express. She was very upset Harry got entered in the TT and came to Task 3 as Harry's family, with Bill, to see he was alright. By summer 1995 she was looking paler and thinner because of severe worry about her family being killed by Voldemort. She said she even dreamed about it. She doesn't approve of Dung or Sirius, even though they are also in the Order, and she felt Sirius was trying to make Harry into a substitute for James rather than looking after his interests as a guardian should, and told him so loudly and repeatedly. She for her part is a little overly protective of Harry.

Molly's great sympathy for Harry and her desire to take care of him probably springs from the fact that he is an orphan and in some sense she considers herself as one as well. She did have one parent die in her childhood, and the remaining parent remarried to an uncle of Sirius' making her his cousin. See schematic T. It is possible that sometime after the marrige her remaining parent also died, leaving her in the care of a step-parent, who was doubtless kind to her, but still making her technically an orphan. This would also explain why she seems to have no parents and is so afraid her family will die that she even dreams about it. For her, seeing her family dead would be reliving a past full of unimaginable grief and sorrow.

She wanted all her children to work at the MoM, but Bill opted for Gringotts. Charlie and Percy work at the MoM, but Charlie is overseas and she hasn't spoken to Percy since the summer of 1995. After he disowned the family, she attempted to reconcile with him by going to his apartment but he would not receive her and later returned the Christmas sweater she sent. He failed to even visit his father in the hospital on Christmas Day. She failed to get Fred and George through school, let alone posted at the MoM, but since they are happy and prospering, she accepts their choice of career. Given Ron wants to be an Auror, a very dangerous but certainly MoM post, she'll probably consider it a mixed blessing. As for Ginny, she seems a little more likely end up on a professional Quidditch team.

Percy Ingnatius Weasley: b 1975. A Gryffindor, 1987-1994. He started Hogwarts in 87/88. He became a Prefect in his 5th year and for making Prefect got an owl, Hermes, and a set of new robes from his parents. He wore the shiny silver badge, with a P on it for Prefect, pinned to his sweater vest even before school started. He wears horn-rimmed glasses, has red hair and freckles and is tall and thin like Arthur. He has neat hair and usually looks superior, smug or pompous. The back of his neck turns red when he argues or gets embarrassed. He started out a decent but rather uptight person with no sense of humor but over time has been mislead by his own ambition - to become Minister of Magic - and become a total prat. Signs of this trend started at Hogwarts.

In 91/92 Fred and George had to practically force him to have Christmas Feast with family, rather than the other Prefects with whom he normally sits. He achieved 12 OWLs, the maximum possible, and was a very good student, if not a very good person. He was very uptight about rules being kept but only so that no one blew his chance to become Head Boy. Only Hermione got along with him. He had a set of Gobstones, so he might played with school club and this is perhaps how he hooked up with Ravenclaw Prefect, Penelope Clearwater. He spent summer 1992 shut up in his room writing love letters to Penelope and only coming out for meals. He continued to wear his Prefect badge on his sweater vest for some weeks before school started.

He was very ambitious and by 92/93, he had his future all planned out. He wanted to ultimately become Minister of Magic and saw being Head Boy a step in that direction. He was still a Prefect, so when any Gryffindor misbehaved, he would get hugely upset, overreact like Molly and sometimes even threaten to take points from his own House. His greatest threat to his brothers was that he'd write Molly about what they're doing. In 93/94, Percy finally got his wish and became Head Boy. He was so proud of himself that in Aug, while on still on vacation and staying at the Leaky Cauldron, he became formal toward everyone, changed for dinner and wore his Head Boy badge so everyone could see it.

After graduation, in summer 1994, he got a job with the DIMC under Barty Crouch Sr. He sucked up to Barty Sr, who couldn't even remember his name and considered him over-enthusiastic, but it paid off and he got elevated to personal assistant to Barty Sr. Percy was left in charge while Barty Sr was at Hogwarts for the Halloween Feast and later became virtually Head of the DIMC after Barty Sr stopped coming to the office and started sending in owls with instructions instead. Percy told people Barty Sr hadn't been well since the QWC 1994 and needed a rest instead of investigating to see if anything was wrong. He attended the Yule Ball in place of Barty Sr, in brand new navy blue dress robes, attended the 1st and 2nd tasks of the TT and continued running the office, saying Barty Sr was taking well deserved time off at Christmas and afterward.

Percy was far too happy being in charge to look squarely at the facts of the situation, but eventually it caught up with him and he got in trouble for not realizing his boss must be missing or dead and he wasn't allowed to judge the 3rd task, let alone run the DIMC. After an inquiry at work that proved Percy should have realized Barty Sr was mad and told someone, his career was unaffected. He ended up getting promoted to Junior Assistant to the Minister of Magic in summer 1995. At this point Percy fell out with Arthur, who pointed out that Fudge probably only promoted Percy to use him as a spy against the Weasley family and Dumbledore. Percy was so offended he moved out of the Burrow into a flat in London and broke all contact with his family. He even walked out of the family photos.

Percy viewed his father as someone with a bad reputation that could jeopardize his career and became loyal only to the MoM and his own ambition. He even warned Ron not to associate with Harry, whom he called a crackpot, dangerous and possibly violent. In his new job, he followed Fudge everywhere he went, taking notes and was even Court Scribe at Harry's trial. When Molly attempted to see him, he closed his door in her face. When she sent him a Christmas sweater, he returned it. It remains to be seen, now that the MoM has seen the error of its ways and admitted Voldemort is alive and Harry and Dumbledore were right, what will happen between Percy and his parents. Obviously he was in the wrong and should make a move toward reconciliation but seems unlikely he wants to be reconciled to his family since he didn't show up to meet Ron at King's Cross in Jun 1996 with the rest of his family.

Ron Weasley: aka Ronnie, Ronald, Weasel King. b 1980. A Gryffindor, 1991-1998? He is the 6th born, and the youngest son of Arthur and Molly. He started Hogwarts in 91/92. He is the best friend and roommate of Harry whom he met on their 1st train to Hogwarts and bonded with over their mutual poverty. He takes after Arthur, Bill and Percy and at 11 he is almost as tall as the twins, who are 13, but shorter than Goyle and Crabbe. By 13 he is as tall as the twins, who are 15. And at 15 he is taller by a good deal than the twins, who are 17. He is thin and gangling with big hands and feet and has flaming red hair, freckles and a long nose. Currently he's long and lanky and much taller and thinner than Fred, George or Charlie. He is the second tallest person in school, Dean Thomas being the tallest.

Ron is an avid supporter of the Chudley Cannons and thinks Quidditch is the best game in the world. With infinite money, he says he would buy a Quidditch team (yes, they have owners). He is an excellent wizard's chess player and has a very old, battered chess set, that like everything else he owns, was someone else's first, in this case his grandfather's. Ron knows his men really well so he has no trouble getting them to do what he wants and particularly likes playing Hermione because she's so bad at it. He had an old Shooting Star, which he never brought to school because it was easily outstripped by passing butterflies. He has had an extreme phobia about spiders ever since he was 3 and Fred turned his teddy bear into a large spider at an unexpected moment.

Ron is much taller than Harry or Hermione, right handed and can use a hairpin to pick locks. He snores, says fellytone = telephone and knows nothing of the Muggle world, despite his father's work or tinkerings with Muggle technology. Ron always gets a thick handknit, maroon, letterless, sweater for Christmas from Molly. He wears maroon socks too and usually gets a pair at Christmas. Maroon clashes horribly with his hair, but his mother seems to think the contrast is nice. He wears maroon and paisley pajamas, which are too short for his legs and leave several inches of of ankle showing. Dumbledore is Ron's hero and he's very impressed by him, but Ron still thinks he's crazy. He has a watch and rather untidy scrawl for handwriting. When he gets mad, embarrassed, under stress or is lying, his ears go pink, then red. Occasionally he blushes severely, which must be an interesting sight given his copper hair and maroon sweater.

When Ron first met Harry on the train to Hogwarts, he complained that he never gets anything new and this is an ongoing gripe in his life. He has Bill's old robes, Charlie's old wand and Percy's old rat (even though rats weren't on the list of approved animals to bring to Hogwarts). He hates being poor, and worse he's obviously poor. His robes are ofetn too short - one can see his sneakers underneath. He has no money for the lunch cart on the Express and must eat the corned beef sandwiches he brought but despises. He hates being born the last son as well. Since all his brothers are older they all achieve things first. Even if Ron then accomplishes something to rival their achievements, it's nothing special because they've done it before him. It is probably this reason that causes Ron to occasionally resent Harry for his celebrity. It's also probably what keeps him going on all the adventures Harry gets into because, in addition to being fun, they present opportunities to do something unique - like dueling with Death Eaters - that will make him stand out from his brothers.

In 91/92 he volunteered himself to be Harry's 2nd in a wizard's duel, against Draco, whom Ron also hates, but it never happened. He and Harry became friends with Hermione by defeating the mountain troll together on Halloween 1991. In the Mirror of Erised Ron sees himself as Head Boy and Captain of House team holding the Quidditch Cup. Because he's always been overshadowed by brothers, he wants to see himself alone and the best of the lot. He helped Hagrid with Norbert but ended up in Hospital after his hand was cut by Norbert's poisonous fangs while him feeding rats. He accompanied Harry on the quest to save the Sorcerer's Stone and defeated Pr McGonagall's chess set. He proved he is willing and able to take a hit or be sacrificed for good of others, but also that he's terribly brave and gallant.

In 92/93 Ron gained some celebrity of his own by borrowing his father's flying Ford Anglia and following the Express to Hogwarts, from a couple thousand feet up. He broke his wand landing in the Whomping Willow, and for the rest of the year it was held together by only a few splinters and Spellotape and was constantly doing weird things. Ron has a temper that is very quick to flare up, but especially quick to rise when it comes to people hurting Hermione. When Hermione, was called a Mudblood by Draco, Ron retaliated on her behalf and told Draco to eat slugs. Unfortunately his wand backfired and it was Ron that ended up vomiting slugs, for about 12 hours. It was thanks to Ron and his wand that Pr Lockhart finally got his just deserts and ended up in St Mungo's.

In 93/94 Ron sent Harry his first birthday card in Jul 1993. Ron's parents took the entire family to Egypt to visit Bill and while there he got very freckled from all the sun. After returning home, he got a new wand suited just to him. He elected to take Care of Magical Creatures and Divination in his 3rd year, but his first Divination class was a disaster. He decided he was just going to make up homework all year and surprisingly, got away with it. During the course of this year Ron discovered Scabbers was actually a person, Peter Pettigrew. He was horrified at the revelation and disowned him immediately. He received a replacement pet, a small owl, from Sirius Black in Jun 1994. He named the owl Pig, short for Pigwidgeon.

During Aug 1994, he brought Harry and Hermione with him and his family to QWC 1994. For 94/95 Ron was given a shabby set of dress robes with lace cuffs and collar and adding insult to injury, Ron believed Harry had entered himself in the TT by some magical means and failed to tell Ron purposely. Ron lost his temper and snubbed Harry for a long while, hanging out with Fred and George instead. Harry reciprocated this resentment rather intensely and at one point things got so bad Harry hit Ron in the forehead with a Potter Really Stinks badge just because Ron expressed concern for him. Eventually after TT Task 1 Ron realized that someone must be trying to kill Harry by forcing him to compete in the TT, as Harry had always maintained, and patched their relationship up.

At Christmas that year, Ron gave Dobby his mom's maroon Christmas sweater to go with his tea cozy (which is either maroon or knit or both) and took Padma Patil to the Yule Ball only to discover Hermione is going with Viktor Krum. Ron had a fit of jealousy about Hermione's date but was too embarrassed to admit he liked her, so nothing more was said. He continued to be jealous long after the Yule Ball but Hermione continued to befriend Viktor all the same. She knew about Ron's interest in her, chose not to act on it. However in the summer of 1995, Hermione chose to stay with Ron and OoP at Headquarters rather than her family. It's never said when she arrived there, perhaps immediately after summer holidays started, but why is Hermione there? She isn't a Weasley and she's not a part of the Order. Did Ron invite her? Does Dumbledore think it best to protect her as a friend of Harry's? Difficult to say. Perhaps Ron just wants her there and she want to be there with him.

Before returning to Hogwarts, Ron received new pajamas because he'd grown 6 inches and was finally bought some decent dress robes by Fred and George, at Harry's secret request. By this time Ron now needs to crouch under the Invisibility Cloak to prevent his feet showing. He was made a Prefect (oddly, the Prefect badges are gold with a lion now, rather than silver as Percy's was) and his parents gave him a Cleansweep 11 for becoming Prefect, despite the fact he has an old cauldron, Charlie's, that's rusting through. With the new broom, he became Gryffindor's new Keeper, replacing the now graduated Wood, and inherited Wood's old robes.

Throughout 95/96 he was still very much infatuated with Hermione and jealous of her penpal relationship with Viktor but Hermione refused to stop writing and has never said whether her letters are romantic rather OoP related. However, just before his 1st game as Keeper, Hermione gave him a kiss on the cheek for luck rather proving she does really care about him. Sadly, he's so dazed with fear he hardly noticed. For a long while, he was not a very good Keeper and lost Gryffindor a couple games thus further dispiriting himself and his team mates. Draco even wrote a nasty song about Ron's skills to further intimidate him and for a while, it worked. At the final game of the season, Ron found his stride and due to his excellent keeping, Gryffindor won the Quidditch Cup.

As if this is not enough acclaim, Ron, joined the DA in Oct 1995 and in Jun 1996 found himself, along with Harry, Hermione, Ginny, Luna and Neville, holding his own against 12 Death Eaters at the MoM and winning 50 points for Gryffindor as a result. During the fight Ron was attacked by a brain, but according to Madame Pomfrey has since recovered. He is now certainly not on Draco's good side, since he was partly responsible for Lucius being jailed, but he has finally won the sort of acclaim he always dreamed of. Swearing: Blimey, damn it, Thank God.

Wendelin the Weird: She enjoyed being burned so much she allowed herself to be caught and burned 47 times, in various disguises, during the 14th century.

Kennilworthy Whisp: Renowned Quidditch expert and author of *Quidditch Through the Ages* and other Quidditch related books. He lives in Nottinghamshire but is willing to follow his favorite team wherever they go. He is a vegetarian who enjoys cooking, backgammon and has a large collection of vintage broomsticks.

Kevin Whitby: b 1982. A Hufflepuff, 1994-2001? He started Hogwarts in 94/95.

Willy Widdershins: Responsible for the regurgitating toilets in summer 1995. He was knocked unconscious by an exploding toilet at the scene of his crime and arrested in Dec 1995. He was let off by the MoM because of information he had about Harry's DA club but was caught again, selling biting doorknobs to Muggles, a short time later and sent to prison.

Wilhelm Wigworthy: Author of *Home Life and Social Habits of British Muggles*. Published by Little Red Books, 1987. It explains all about Muggle life and is the Muggle Studies textbook at Hogwarts.

Wilfred the Wistful: See Portraits Etc., Statues section.

(Unknown) Wilkes: b 1952. A Slytherin 1964-1971. He started Hogwarts in 64/65. A Slytherin of unknown year. See Note 1, Part IV. He was part of a gang of Slytherins who nearly all turned out to be Death Eaters in the 1970s. He was killed by Aurors in 1981.

Will (Unknown): A not very intelligent purveyor of stolen toads.

(Unknown) Williamson: A scarlet-robed man with a ponytail who works at the MoM and saw Voldemort there in Jun 1996. He is an Auror.

Gilbert Wimple: He's with the Committee on Experimental Charms. In 1995, he had horns which Arthur said he'd had for awhile now.

(Unknown) Wizard: He was on the Committee for the Destruction of Dangerous Creatures in 1994. An ancient wizard with a reedy voice.

(Unknown) Wizard: He works for the MoM with Basil in the Portkey Office. He was at QWC with a gold watch making sure the arrivals came in on time or perhaps the watch was Protean Charmed and is what activated the time-activated Portkeys. He was on the day, tired and grumpy looking, but he was wearing the thing-high galoshes with a tweed suit in Aug.

Oliver Wood: b 1975. A Gryffindor, 1987-1994. He started Hogwarts in 87/88 and graduated in Jun 1994. He was Captain and Keeper of House team. He is tall, burly and obsessive about Quidditch. He desperately wanted to win the Quidditch Cup before graduating, which he did, and worked the House team in rain, snow, dark and crack of dawn. Slightly manic, he always urged his team to eat breakfast before a game, but never did himself, and always gave the exact same a pregame pep talk. He was and is a real jock; his eyes gleam with crazed enthusiasm whenever he talks about Quidditch and he once spent a whole summer devising a new training program for the House team. He is however a very nice person too. His Captain and Keeper skills got him signed to Puddlemere United's reserve team summer 1994. He saw Harry at QWC 1994.

Augustus Worme: The owner of Obscurus Books. He commissioned Newt Scamander to write a book on magical creatures in 1918.

Blaise Zabini: b 1979. A Slytherin, 1991-1998? He started Hogwarts in 91/92.

Ladislaw Zamojski: Poland's top Chaser in 1995.

Rose Zeller: b 1983. A Hufflepuff, 1995-2002? She started Hogwarts in 95/96.

(Unknown) Zograf: The Bulgarian Keeper in QWC 1994. Unknown if male or female.

(**Unknown**) **Zonko:** This wizard has a joke shop in Hogsmeade. Unknown if male or female.

OTHER MAGICAL BEINGS

In this section are goblins, giants, house-elves, hags, ogres, vampires, zombies and specific individuals belonging to these classifications of Beings. Thus Winky and Griphook are here. Werewolves have been moved to a separate section specifically devoted to them, because as both Being and Beast, they deserve a separate category. Remus Lupin can be found there.

Dementor: These creatures are among the foulest and most horrible things on Earth. They are said to infest only the darkest filthiest places, but it's not clear what that means. Does it mean physically dark and filthy? Morally dark and filthy? Spiritually dark and filthy? Hard to say. What we do know is that dementors glory in decay and despair.

Dementors are usually cloaked figures that stand about 10' tall (one presumes only the dwarf ones boarded the Hogwarts Express or they wouldn't have been able to stand up in the carriages), they glide silently rather than walk and they keep their faces hidden under their hoods at all times but for when they lower their hoods to give someone the Dementor's Kiss. Dementors are blind and there is thin grey scabbed skin stretched over the empty sockets where the eyes should be. Their skin glistens and is slimy looking, like something dead that has decayed or rotted in water.

They sense emotions, what people are thinking or feeling, and are not fooled by tricks, disguises or even Invisibility Cloaks. However they are fooled by Animagi and Polyjuice Potions. They have putrid cold breath and instead of a mouth, there is a gaping, formless hole, through which they suck in air in long rattling breaths and speak. Fudge says he talked to them and they told him Sirius was talking in his sleep, so they speak. Their hands are strong, clammy, and scabbed and their touch feels icy. Their very presence brings intense bone-chilling cold to those around them.

When dementors are around, both wizards and Muggles can feel them, though only wizards, and possibly Squibs, can see them. The presence of a dementor makes people feel as if they were doused with ice cold water, then like they are being sucked under the water and drown in cold. Finally they will start to relive all the worst moments of their lives. People say they feel as if they will never be happy again and in some respects dementors can be said to cause a type of depression. Another aspect of dementor presence is darkness, utter and total darkness. Muggles and wizards experience that sensation that the world goes suddenly dark. If out of doors, the sky and all that's in it vanish, sun, stars and moon. Victims feel as though they have gone blind. At the same time, all surrounding sounds, cars, birds, etc, will be cut off as well. To be deaf and blind to anything but one's own most horrible thoughts is the work of dementors.

If one should manage to scare dementors off, with a Patronus, they will swoop away like bats, which implies a sort of flying ability rather than any Appartating ability. How exactly they travel is unknown as is whether they sleep, have a social structure, or can reproduce. Chocolate, a very ancient cure dating back to Aztec times, and perhaps dementors are South American, is the recommend medicinal after a dementor encounter. Dementors were used by the MoM as guards for the prison of Azkaban up until 1996. They were effective as guards because they drained peace, hope and happiness out of the air around them neutralizing most resistance. They drown prisoners in their own despair. Shortly after this process starts a prisoner either goes insane or loses the will to live, stops eating and dies.

The more of them there are, the more difficult it becomes to resist their effect – so it is said. But it seems from observation that dementors are A) not as effective as has been claimed and B) work only on people that have had bad things happen to them, in essence victimizing the victims of society. The dementors are supposed to drain a wizard of her or his powers, as well as sanity, if left with them too long, but Sirius was sane when he escaped and powerful too. All the Death Eaters that escaped in Jan 1996 were not only sane, they were still incredibly powerful, as the destruction at the MoM Jun 1996 proved. These supposed dementor effects are probably wishful thinking on the part of Fudge.

Going to victimization, Sirius was the classic lucky rich kid. What did he have to feel bad about? In Azkaban he said he stayed sane because he would obsess about James and Lily being betrayed by Peter and killed by Voldemort. In other words, this really was the only "bad" thing that happened to him. Instead of reliving all his bad moments, he only relived 1, because he'd only had one really bad thing happen. He didn't hang on to the thought, it was the only thought the dementors left him with. Ditto Harry. When dementors boarded the train, despite the fact Harry was sitting with Lupin (who'd had loads of really bad stuff happen to him), Ron, Hermione, Neville (who also had loads of really bad stuff happen to him) and Ginny, only Harry reacted to the dementor because his stuff was extremely bad. And in every subsequent dementor encounter Harry had, he only had one experience – his parents death.

So do people relive *every* bad thing that happened to them? Probably not. First of all most people don't have more than 1 really bad event in their life and of those that do, the event rarely caused them deadly despair (ie, they wanted to or tried to commit suicide). The majority of folks, like Neville, Lupin, Ron, Hermione and Ginny, simply experience fear in the presence of dementors that isn't attached to any bad memory or event from the past. This then means that only people who have already been victimzed in some way, witnessed a murder, been raped, etc, can be victimized by dementors. The average Death Eater who got a cheap thrill out of murdering isn't going to relieve the murder because that would be a good thought. Dudley doesn't think back to the horrific things he's done to others, on the horrific thing that was done to him.

What is most repugnant about this situation is that the MoM apparently believes that simply punishing someone in a way likely to induce death is an answer to criminal activity. Even those for the death penalty do not impose it on every criminal regardless of the crime. Hagrid, who wasn't even convicted of a crime, spent 2 months there and might easily have suffered an ill fate, but the MoM didn't care. And the situation is compounded by the fact there is no rehabilitaion program. One is sent to Azkaban and that's that. Even if the sentence is short – Sturgis Podmore, 6 months – there is no attempt to discuss what happened, to understand, help or reform the prisoner. Though one expects this is in keeping with wizarding medicine which appears to deny almost all mental or physical conditions and therefore expects everyone to be without underlying psychological or physical ailments of a Muggle variety that may have precipitated a "crime." The number of paranoid-schizophrenics wrongly held as Death Eaters at Azkaban must be mind boggling. But I digress.

Dementors need people, alive, to satisfy their hunger. They need to be able to suck every good feeling or happy memory out of victims. Considering they are always sucking the happiness out of people, one would think they would eventually become happier creatures. But this doesn't seem to be so. They will feed on a person long enough to reduce her or him to something like itself, soulless and evil. They knew they had more to gain by serving Voldemort as in the past, during his last rise to power, they had joined his team and he had given them an endless supply of victims to feed off. The MoM didn't offer them much scope for their talents, and they were basically left with 200 persons and no promise of more once they were gone. So they revolted and went to join Voldemort in Jun 1996

One wouldn't suspect it but dementors have feelings. They were angry when Sirius broke out of Azkaban on their watch, they were frustrated at being locked out of Hogwarts, and they were attracted to all the happy feelings of a large crowd of students at a Quidditch match. This is quite a bit of emotional range for something considered souless and evil. The lifespan of a dementor is unknown. Possibly they don't even die, just rot away from lack of feeding. Some of the ones that left Azkaban and went over to Voldemort's side may have served him the first time he tried to grab power. Certainly dementors have no concept of right or wrong or loyalty. They just want to eat and live, like most beings and ultimately whomever gives them victims that supply the positive energy that happy emotions provide, gains their attentions.

It is unknown if dementors have gender, date, marry or reproduce. They are classified as Beings and not Spirits (or Beasts), so they probably reproduce somehow. That they are unattractive in human eyes doesn't mean that every Being views them with distaste. Hags are also considered unattractive in human eyes, but Beings none the less. Perhaps there's some dementor-hag connection. The social structure of dementors is nebulous. It would seem it's every dementor for itself, but they all acted in a group at Azkaban and Fudge spoke to a leader of sorts there. If they have a leader, it's not clear how that dementor is chosen to lead. Is it elected or does it just fight its way to the top? We may never know.

The Dementor's Kiss: The very worst, ultimate punishment in the wizarding world, the loss of one's soul. Dementors have a gapping hole of a mouth which they clamp onto the mouth of a victim and via which they are are able to suck the victim's soul out. When the soul is gone the victim has no sense of self anymore, no memory, no emotions, no nothing. She or he simply lives and exists as an empty shell of a person. One can never recover from a Dementor's Kiss, it's utter destruction. Dementors like sucking the soul out of people because for them it's a feast of emotions.

The MoM orders it done only to criminals it finds an extreme threat. It was ordered in the case of Sirius Black, but never happened. Barty Crouch Jr got the Dementor's Kiss without it being order because he'd escaped the dementors' care and made them look bad and they were pissed off. Dolores Umbridge illegally ordered the dementors to give Harry the Dementor's Kiss, but he managed to fight them off. Dumbledore feels this is a punishment that should never be used but failed to say just what he thought would be a good alternative, though he indicated he wanted to subject Voldemort to a fate worse than death. The Kiss is certainly is a form of death, far worse than outright execution because the body lingers on, for awhile, like a mindless corpse.

The Dementor's Kiss is a bit of a conundrum. Why would a dementor kill off the very thing it needs to survive? If a person has no emotions at all, it has nothing to live off. Soul removal could possibly be like one huge binge of emotion for a dementor but in the long-term picture, it's self-defeating. What would dementors live on if they sucked out everyone's soul? It is also unclear what exactly they do with the extracted soul. They may hold it within themselves, they certainly can't destroy it because souls are indestructible. Technically souls aren't really something anyone but God has ultimate power over. One would presume when a dementor dies, the souls it sucked out are finally released to go to their netherworld destination but I'd prefer not to speculate further because it's just too creepy.

Dwarf: This species obviously exists since Pr Lockhart hired 12 of them to deliver musical Valentines on Feb 14, 1993. Dwarfs are grim and surly looking, though that might just have appeared that way because they were made to dress as Cupids. They are short in stature (generally under 4'8"), very tough and quite aggressive. They play the harp and sing pretty well, though in an edgy, "you'd better listen" sort of way. One expects from the way they barged into classes and elbowed people out of their way to deliver Valentines they wouldn't have done the event if they weren't hard up for cash. They even kicked people in the shins or seized them by the ankles to get them to listen to them sing. Dumbledore has yet to mention enlisting them into his Order, but dwarfs are well reputed for being men and women at arms and he would do better with 400 dwarfs than 12 giants - though enlisting both groups would be even better.

Giant: The majority of giants are dangerous, lazy and like destroying things. They are almost extinct due to warring among themselves in the 19th century. In the 1970s, when they were already dying out, they joined Voldemort because he offered them rights and freedoms that had been denied them under they MoMs. They were responsible for mass Muggle-killings and the Aurors then killed a good number of them, but when Voldemort was defeated, the remainder left Britain under a MoM agreement and have not been seen since. The wizards agreed to let them go Abroad but confined them to a small area, despite the group being composed of different and warring tribes of giants.

There were a few surviving British giants when they departed for the far North, somewhere in northern Russia it would seem, but giants aren't made to live in groups or in tightly confined areas and soon the hostilities began. They felt they had to live in a group for protection after being exiled by the wizards to such a remote and inhospitable area but while in these close quarters, the men began to fight each other and the women began to fight each other so their numbers continued to dwindle. They usually prefer to live in the mountains for the most part and the giants Abroad do occasionally kill Muggles that wander into their mountainous territory but the MoM's cover it up and it's usually put down to climbing accidents.

It's unclear if giants ever marry within their own social milieu. Given the independent nature of giants, it would be safe to say what marriages do exist but for various reasons are short lived, like Karkus'. They don't seem to know what long-term commitment is and when they're bored of a marriage they just leave, leaving behind children as well sometimes. Giants will obviously marry outside their species if Mr Hagrid, a human wizard, was married to a full giantess but this type of union is highly atypical as giants don't like magic as a rule, particularly when used against them, and fear wizards in general. Full giants cannot do magic and rely on their natural toughness to protect them. They are very hard to Stun and, like trolls, magic just bounces right off of them.

Giants can live an exceedingly long time because they are so tough. Hagrid, a half-giant, is in his 60s when he delivered Harry his Hogwarts' letter, but doesn't look it and is as strong as ever he was. It's unknown exactly how long giants live, but one would think well over 100 years if they don't get killed by another giant. A pure giant is about 20' tall, 25' is the biggest they get and 16' is considered a runt. Of the 100s of different tribes around the world that once existed now only 80 giants survive in the mountains north of Minsk, by a mountain lake. Of the remaining giants currently Abroad some are hiding and some are in negotiations with Voldemort's people. Giant languages must be similar enough to each other to make living together and electing a leader achievable and some giants seem to know non-giant languages, like English.

Gurg = chief in Giant language. In dealing with a Gurg, who is always male, one must walk into his camp looking at him and no one else. After presenting a gift at his feet and making the introductions, it's best to promise to return the following day another present then leave. Repeat the following day, but this time say something about the purpose of the visit. Keep repeating. Giants don't like a lot of information at once. If strangers overload a Gurg with information he could kill them just to simplify things. Giants seem to prefer to use their hands or rocks in a fight, but one doubts they are averse to clubs and other simple weapons. Unexpected physically attacks are the greatest danger when working with giants.

Giants seem to like military clothing and weapons and one presumes that the gift of the indestructible goblin-made helmet Dumbledore sent with Hagrid and Olympia in the summer of 1995 would have suited any giant, so giant tastes must run to that sort of apparel. Hagrid and Olympia were sent to try and win the giants over to Dumbledore's side, but seemingly did not achieve this goal due to a sudden Gurg change. Hagrid and Olympia were very kind to some of the wounded giants, after the new Gurg beat them up, so it is hoped that some of them will remember their kindness and what they said and someday join Dumbledore's camp. At least 1 giant has been illegally and forcibly returned to Britain, Hagrid's little half-brother, Grawp.

Fridwulfa Hagrid: aka Mrs Hagrid. Hagrid's giantess mother. She was one of the last giants in Britain. After marrying Mr Hagrid and having Rubeus, she decided she was not the maternal sort and left. They were probably married about 5 years and Hagrid was 3 at the time. She died many years before 1995, but the exact date is unknown. She had a 2nd son by a full giant and named him Grawp. She was probably a somewhat petite giant since Hagrid is tall for a man and, as Harry pointed out, less abnormally large than Olympia while his brother is very short for a full giant, being only about 4' taller than Hagrid.

Golgomath: A giant who became Gurg after Karkus was killed. He is one of the biggest giants. He has black hair and teeth and a necklace of bones, including some human ones. He is currently in league with the Death Eaters and Voldemort as of Aug 1995.

Grawp: aka Grawpy. Hagrid's half-brother, Fridwulfa's son by an uinknown full giant father. Probably around age 20-40. Hagrid secretly brought him home from the giants' camp in the mountains because at 16' he was considered small and Hagrid felt other giants were picking on him. Hagrid spent several months in 95/96 keeping him tied up in he Forbidden Forest, trying to teach him English and civilize him. Grawp feeds himself on deer and birds' eggs. No creatures in the forest will come near him because of his aggressive behavior. He is very strong and enjoys breaking trees off at the roots for fun. The centaurs are very upset he's in the forest because he's so destructive and eventually he got a face full of arrows from them. But being a tough giant, he survived the encounter and was just fine.

He looks strangely misshapen. He has a perfectly round head and it is larger in proportion to his body than a human head to a human body. He has a round face and almost no neck. His nose is shapeless and stubby and his mouth is lopsided and full of misshapen teeth that are yellow and the small bricks. He has small hazle eyes, large fleshy ears and short tightly curled hair the color of bracken. When asleep he looks like a vast mossy boulder. When awake he is surprisingly speedy and agile. He wears a dirty brown smock of animal skins that have been crudely sewn together. He doesn't wear shoes and has enormous filthy bare feet. Whenever he is upset, he roars or takes a swipe at the offending party.

Hagrid introduced Harry and Hermione to Grwap in the hopes that they would somehow keep up his English lesson if Hagrid was suspended. Whatever Hagrid's ultimate plan, Grawp has learned to speak in halting English and become loyal to Hagrid and his friends. Grawp seems to be quite attached to Hermione, whom he calla Hermy, and saved her and Harry in the forest when the centaurs got a bit snippy. Hagrid has said he may try and find Grawp a girlfriend but if 1 giant is illegal to keep on British soil, one doubts that 2 will go over any better.

Karkus: He was the Gurg Hagrid and Olympia initially spoke to when they arrived at the giants' camp. He and his wife laid around and were fed by the other giants which apparently is a perk of the job. He particularly liked goats. He was about 22-23' tall with hide like a rhino but in the end it couldn't save him. The biggest, ugliest, laziest giant of the exiled group, he was murdered a day after Hagrid and Olympia met with him, by Golgomath, who took his place as Gurg.

Goblins: These creatures have been known for causing or being in trouble for at least the past 7 centuries if not longer. Little is known of them except the DRCMC is always hauling them up on charges, they love money and their talent at creating metal objects such as Galleons or indestructible battle helmets surpasses even the most skilled metal-charming wizards. At QWC 1994, the goblins alone sat counting their gold even while the Death Eaters were on a tear. They didn't even care about the Death Eaters moving through the camp as long as they were left alone with their gold. They are very clever and quite capable of looking out for themselves even when dealing with wizards. Goblins, like house-elves, have their own brand of magic and don't need a wand to use it effectively.

While goblins don't like the MoM wizards much because they have been denied freedoms for centuries under their rule, they wouldn't join Voldemort. The didn't join him in the 1970s because he murdered a prominent goblin family near Nottinghamshire and Bill seems to think they may just stay out of any coming conflicts too. However, as Hagrid, says never cross a goblin and the consequences of Voldemort's overt crossing of the goblins the last time may very well prove to result in them joining Dumbledore this time – not to bolster a government system the despise, but merely to get revenge. Goblins seem to stick together, and, while killing a male goblin is bad, killing a female and children seems to be the ultimate crime in their book.

As already discussed in Social Structure in Part I, females are never seen in goblin society, possibly because of their dominance. The male goblins may not know what they are going to do if Voldemort returns because while business is in the hands of male goblins, government is in the hands of females. Killing a female goblin therefore would be the ultimate act of aggression against goblins. Young goblins may be considered too vulnerable to be interacting with others until they are of age, thus are kept at home and not seen except by their parents. Therefore the killing of the young is also particularly heinous as they are completely defenseless.

Full-grown goblins are a head shorter than Harry (at age 11 and he's quite short), swarthy and have clever faces. They wear pointed hats, have dark slanting eyes and pointed beards though apparently no hair on their heads. Although short in stature, they have very long fingers and feet. Goblin English isn't always too good as they prefer to speak their own language, Gobbledegook. Currently goblins are best known for establishing, owning and running Gringotts. Individual goblins are responsible for casting all coins, Galleons, Sickles and Knuts and will put a serial number on the side of a Galleon to show what individual made it. The fact that goblins make, create and distribute money means in effect they control the wizarding economy. If they decide to close the bank, wizards have no money and could never get at it since the carts and vaults respond to goblins only.

How exactly the MoM monitors goblins, who are terribly secretive, and their businesses, is unknown and one would have to say they don't. While goblins have a generally good rapport with wizards as bankers, and even hire them to work for them and with them at the bank (Bill, Fleur), they are extremely touchy about wizard thieves and will go to great lengths to find a thief or someone who defaults on them. They sent groups of goblins after Ludo. Goblins regard the money in their care as a private matter between themselves and wizards and will not report vault activity of even known and wanted, at-large felons, like Sirius Black, which can be good if one likes privacy but bad if one is an Auror.

Bladvak: It means pickax in Gobbledegook and is the only word Ludo knows of the language. One does wonder why exactly Ludo is familiar with this word. It is perhaps because he was threatened with death by one if he defaulted.

Bodrod the Bearded: A typical goblin name among those involved in rebellions of the 18th century.

Gobbledegook: The name of the goblins' language.

Gringotts: Goblin founder of the wizarding bank. Possibly Gringott, and the bank is Gringott's but over time they've chose to drop the apostrophe.

Griphook: This male goblin escorted Hagrid to the school vault and Harry to his safe in Gringotts in 1991. He handles donation from wizards to Comic Relief UK, Harry's Books Fund.

Ragnok: A male goblin Bill works with at Gringotts that feels anti-wizard because Bagman ripped the bank off and the MoM covered it up and never made good the gold Ludo owed them.

Urg the Unclean: A typical goblin name among those involved in rebellions of the 18th century.

Hag: They are very ugly female beings who unfortunately like to eat children. They are not as adept as wizards at disguising themselves and tend to stick out in a Muggle crowd. They generally prefer to live in places like Hogsmeade where their species is known and understood. The existence of hags in Hogsmeade is one of the reasons only students age 13 up are are allowed to visit the town. At 13 they are too old to be desired edibles by hags. Hags glide rather than walk. It may be that that are related in some way to dementors. They are certainly not spectral if they are eating human children. Whether they marry or can reproduce is unknown, but one would think they are related to and possibly hook up with dementors.

House-Elf: The plural is house-elves. They are small, ugly creatures with large orblike eyes and large collapsible bat-wing type ears. They are usually found in very rich, very old wizarding families like the Malfoys (who had 1 elf), or in big old manor houses (like the Crouch's or the Black's who each had 1 elf), castles (like Hogwarts, which has 100 of them) and places similar. Average people don't have one. House-elves are enslaved to the family of their master or mistress and are inherited by a living member of the family as chattel when their original owner dies (which is why Kreacher went from Mr Black, to Mrs Black, to Sirius, [Regulus was dead, Bellatrix the firstborn sister who was in jail, Andromeda the 2nd sister was hated by Mrs Black], to Narcissa the 3rd born sister). They and any children born to them are enslaved to that same family. Clearly elves can skip a member of the family if they don't like them.

It seems house-elves have only 1 child in lifetime. A house with 1 elf, has always 1 elf, even centuries later. An elf will have a child to replace itself, but there is no house that started with 1 elf years ago and now has 30 due to marriage and natural increase. Dobby and Kreacher both speak of their mother, not their father, implying there are no lasting unions or marriages and in each case the mother preceded them at the same house. The Black family shows the generations of progeny from a single elf, one elf per generation, in stuffed heads. There are clearly male and female elves, it is true, but with the majority of house-elves living alone, it would seem, if females do reproduce themselves, and the master of the house owns the elf and her children, the birth of a male elf signals the end of house-elves in a house.

Dobby is the last elf the Malfoy family would ever have had, ditto Kreacher and the Black family. The Crouch family would have continued to have at least one more generation of elves because Winky was female. Only at Hogwarts where male and female elves continue to exist in large quantities will there always probably be more the 1 elf per female elf produced. Although no one that visits the kitchens has seen a baby elf, one is sure Hogwarts has a bundle of them stashed somewhere. In a case like Hogwarts, marriage and multiple births is possible due to the stability of life there and the generally agreeable masters (Heads). Dumbledore goes out of his way to make sure the elves are happy and well treated and in turn the elves, even Dobby, are content. Winky, with her debilitating personal issues and alcoholism, is unhappy but not because of working conditions.

Generally house-elves wear pillowcases, handkerchiefs, tea towels and the like. The Hogwarts' elves have tea towels stamped with the school seal, rather like a laundry mark. Their duties include all interior household chores. By definition, they do housework. There is much ignorance about house-elves given their innate desire for secrecy and obscurity but a house-elf can leave the house on its own, usually to do various chores (get wood, gather food, etc). Many wizards think elves can't leave their house without being ordered to or being given clothes but, as Dobby proved, an elf can do as they please, repeatedly, though they might have to punish themselves afterwards for it. A simple "out" by a master is enough to allow an elf to leave a home forever. Many wizards also think elves can't use magic without their permission, but this also is untrue. The elves have powerful magic of their own and usually won't use it except to do their own work but this is not to say they can't.

Elves, like goblins, don't need a wand to do magic, just a finger, which is why Winky, even if she had done the Dark Mark at QWC 1994, didn't need a wand to do it. Elves can even Apparate and Disapparate at will, with a loud pop, which is very advanced magic indeed. Should an elf be caught doing some magic a master didn't authorize, the elf's master can do anything she or he wants to the elf without legal repercussions, including whipping them. Some owners do insist on punishments as a general daily or weekly ritual even if no wrong has been done. Lucius Malfoy used to give his elf extra punishments for no reason, as well as daily death threats. This is quite the inequity as elves are bound to uphold the family's honor, never speak ill of them or disobey them and if one should do or say something improper, they will punish themselves very severely anyway.

House-elves are enslaved to serve a single family until they are given a piece of clothing by their master, the head of the family they serve, which sets them free. Even after being dismissed an elf will go on keeping the secrets of their master because that's part of an house-elf's enslavement. It is very difficult for an house-elf that's been dismissed to get a new position because generally whatever they have done to get fired is really heinous. Should an elf be dismissed, they usually try to hook up with another member of the same family's lineage. If a family dies out or rejects the elf altogether, they may go to the House-Elf Relocation Office at the MoM which deals with the reassignment of house-elves. The typical elf, like Winky, doesn't want to be free and most wizards want to keep elves enslaved so the system is self-perpetuating.

SPEW, the Society for the Protection of Elf Welfare, is an organization started by Hermione in 1994 to free the elves or at least get them legal entitlements like holidays, pay and safe working conditions. It currently has only 3 wizard (Ron, Treasurer; Harry, Secretary; Hermione, President) members and most elves are insulted by the organizations efforts on their behalf and hope it doesn't succeed in its stated aims. Dobby is considered an exceptional member of his species because he wants freedom. Most elves do not want to be free and see those that do as disturbed and not truly representative of their species. They like working without pay and would prefer that their presence not even be known in a house, which is considered the mark of a good house-elf.

Hogwarts' house-elves represent the largest group in any 1 dwelling in Britain. They think they have the best job in the world, but of course they work for Dumbledore, who treats them well. They hardly ever leave the kitchens but they do come out to tidy, change sheets, gather laundry, tend the fires, mop floors, put warming pans in beds, and do other housework. They are happy to be of service to students and staff and feel they have no right to be unhappy when there is work to be done and people to be served. They are never punished as Dumbledore is one of the few masters that doesn't believe in punishing elves. However the elves will still punish themselves, even Dobby, who is a paid employee. Hogwarts is probably safer from Voldemort with 100 happy house-elves around than an army of Aurors.

Most house-elves are, unsurprisingly given the law doesn't protect them from abuse, fearful of displeasing and extremely emotional. They will rock when upset and even take to drink. Elves, like people, run the gamut in personality. They can be sweet and gentle, lively and outgoing, shy and secretive, evil and crafty. Elves can lie, just not to their master. But by the same token, they can hint around at the truth if they want to. It is wise to always treat an elf with kindness because they will typically respond in kind. Dumbledore believes in treating house-elves with kindness and even took in Dobby and Winky as employees when they were down on their luck. However, kindness was not enough to save Kreacher, who was very set in his ways and living in antagonistic relationship with Sirius, both of which didn't help any.

Dobby: An house-elf originally in service to the Malfoy family until May 1993. Unlike most of his kind, Dobby understood he was enslaved and wanted to be free more than anything else. This was not surprising as he was always having to punish himself and no one thought anything about it except to remind him to do extra punishments. Lucius Malfoy in particular was very abusive to Dobby giving him death threats 5 times a day and floggings for no reason at all. When an opportunity arose to cross his master in 1992 (Dobby overheard Lucius planning to use give the Diary of Tom Riddle to one of the Weasley kids) Dobby decided to act. Dobby knew the Diary would bring Voldemort to life again, apparently something more than Lucius knew, and that Voldemort alive would be a threat to Harry. Because life in general had improved for his kind since Voldemort had vanished and Dobby didn't want to see him come to power again and therefore tried to protect Harry himself.

As he could do nothing to stop Lucius' plan for the Diary, Dobby attempted to thwart it by removing Harry from Voldemort's vicinity, Hogwarts. He made several attempts, each of which failed, and eventually Harry was forced to confront and destroy Tom Riddle. Dobby subsequently implicated Lucius Malfoy in the Tom Riddle Diary affair and Harry, in return for all Dobby's help, got Dobby set free by forcing Lucius to carelessly throw an old sock from his hand directly to Dobby's, thus giving

Dobby clothes and immediately setting him free. Dobby's initial reaction was joy but when Lucius threatened Harry, Dobby turned angry and magically knocked his former owner down a staircase. He felt no need to punish himself for this act, but after thanking Harry, he promptly vanished all the same.

Dobby began looking for work in June 1993, but didn't have any real luck till about 15 months later when he hooked up with Winky in summer 1994. After 4 more months, in Dec 1994, Dobby and Winky approached Dumbledore for work and were granted employment. Dobby allows himself to be paid only 1G a week and be given only 1 day a month off because he didn't want too much leisure and riches. He likes work better than play and is still a house-elf at heart, even if he is a bit odd. However, even after Dobby found paid work and was under Dumbledore's protection, he was still afraid to speak ill of the Malfoys, whom he calls bad Dark wizards, and then punishes himself for it.

When Harry first met Dobby, he was about 2-3' tall with enormous green eyes the size of tennis balls that bulged slightly, an ugly dark brown face and a wide toothy smile. He looked like a large ugly doll with long fingers and feet and wore a filthy ripped pillowcase that he apparently never laundered. He had a pencil-shape nose, batwing ears and a high-pitched voice. It is uncertain how old Dobby is but he seems to have been with the Malfoy family for a number of years and seems to have known and worked for Lucius all his life which probably makes him about 50 years old or more. Dobby appears and disappears with a sound like the crack of a whip, has a very strong grip and is so short he hugs Harry around the midriff (and Harry isn't that tall himself).

Dobby is a very dramatic and emotional creature, even for an elf, and wails, sobs and is in general flamboyantly expressive. He is very nimble and quick, and quite difficult to catch. He is self-punishing in the extreme, and, depending on who his master is, beats himself up quite a lot. Dobby will betray a master he doesn't like and punish himself to make up for it, but he he'll do it all the same. He admires Harry who treats him like an equal and thinks Dumbledore is the greatest Headmaster Hogwarts has ever had. The reason he had so much trouble finding a job other places was because he wanted to be paid, to the horror of other house-elves, including Winky. Dobby has ideas above his station as a house-elf according to Winky.

With steady paid employment, Dobby took up knitting, portrait painting and collecting clothes, particularly socks in his spare time. He's become a clothes horse, or is simply celebrating his freedom, and at times will wear numerous articles of the same clothing. He particularly likes to wear several hats, scarves or socks at a time. The multiple socks make him taller, and the hats at least give him the appearance of height, though it doesn't seem that Dobby is intentionally trying to be taller. He keeps all his clothes clean and well cared for and at any given time he might be spotted wearing a hat with a number of badges, a patterned tie, soccer shorts, and greatly mismatched socks, which he believes is the way socks come, in mismatched pairs.

During the Christmas season of 1995 he tied a bauble to the loop on top of his tea cozy to be seasonally festive. Whether Dobby is a Christian or not, is speculative, but he certainly celebrates Christmas. He acquired a maroon sweater and a pair of violet socks from Ron at Christmas 1995, and a pair of knobbly mustard yellow socks from Harry. He had knitted a very interesting pair of mismatched socks for Harry for a Christmas present in 1994, and painted him a portrait in 1995. Dobby does have to work for a living though and it's not all portraits and sock. He primarily works in the kitchens, but he also spends a lot of time cleaning Gryffindor Tower as no other elves will go there because of Hermione's knitting, which they feel insults them because they don't want to be free and know what she's trying to do. So, Dobby is doing all the cleaning at the Tower and taking all Hermione's SPEW knittings for himself.

Dobby is very helpful and knew just how to find the Room of Requirement after only a few weeks at Hogwarts. Something no students, even Fred and George in their 7 years there, had ever done. He is always glad to help out, especially Harry and when Dobby is happy, his ears waggle and he gives a little skip while clapping his hands together. When he's sad he gets a doleful look and becomes very apologetic. When he's being self-punishing he runs into walls, hits himself in the nose, attempts to kick himself, or beats his feet on the floor, among other things. He's been known to go to real extremes when he punishes himself, but it depends on who is his master, how cruel the person is, how badly he betrays them and how that person would normally punish him.

Obviously betraying Lucius Malfoy or Dolores Umbridge would be more heinous and have more repercussions than calling a Dumbledore a name, which he has permission to do anyway. Dobby seems to treat a paying master in the same way as a master he's enslaved to. Technically, as a free but paid employee under Pr Umbridge, Dobby could say what he please about her and not need to punish himself. He could even leave. But he either didn't feel he could or didn't know do either. Perhaps he just didn't want to leave Winky. Dobby appears to be in a friendship relationship with Winky, but he also cares for her when she goes on a bender and the other elves want nothing to do for her. As of yet, they don't seem to be a married or even dating.

Kreacher: A disgruntled, ancient, short-snouted, slightly mad, Dark-side-inclined house-elf. He formerly belonged to, and still misses, his old mistress Mrs Black, Sirius' mom. When Mrs Black died, he became the property of Sirius, the last remaining Black descendant of that branch of the family. He wandered around 12 Grimmauld Place house for about 10 years taking orders from Mrs Black's deranged portrait from the time she died, till Sirius came home in 1995. Lupin had lived there since the summer of 1993, but he couldn't order Kreacher to do anything since he wasn't technically his master.

Devoted as Kreacher was to Mrs Black and her pureblood philosophy, he hated Sirius. He felt Sirius was a Mudblood lover who had broken Mrs Black's heart. Sirius returned this hatred and said that Kreacher had always been a foul little creature, and more devoted to Mrs Black than Mr Black (to whom he actually had belonged). While Dumbledore told everyone to be kind to Kreacher, no one really did except Hermione. Much as Kreacher hated Sirius, he could not disobey a direct order from him because he was the master. Much as Sirius in turn hated and would have liked to get rid of Kreacher, he couldn't set him free because he knew too much about the Order. As a result, there was a lot of tension at Grimmauld Place for a long while and it often spilled over on guests.

Kreacher, while working for Sirius, pretended to be mad but was actually very sane and quite evil, being nice to Sirius' or a guest's face but making very abusive remarks under his breath (loudly enough so that person could hear him) about that person. His chief ambition was to have is head stuffed and mounted on the wall beside his mother's and other familial ancestors. He slept in the cupboard off the kitchen and had a den under the boiler pipes where there was only about a foot of space but it was warm. Here he had made a jumbled nest of assorted rages and smelly old blankets piled directly on the floor. Things one might have found in the nest: stale bread crusts, coins he'd saved from Sirius' trashing of the house, and silver-framed family photos with shattered glass.

During the house cleaning in summer 1995, Kreacher was always sneaking off with objects, by hiding them under his loin cloth, to his room so they couldn't be thrown out. Bellatrix's photo was his favorite saved item. He even Spellotaped up her broken glass front after rescuing her. He had also been caught hugging Mr Black's pants, he was that upset by the goings on. In Dec 1995, Sirius made the fatal mistake of telling Kreacher to "get out." Kreacher took this literally and went straight out of the house to Narcissa Black Malfoy, the youngest daughter of Mr Black's younger brother and next in the chain of Black family relations that were Dark and available. Kreacher began working as her, and thus Voldemort's, agent in Sirius' house.

Kreacher was not able to betray the secrets that Sirius had expressly forbid him to, like Order business, but he could tell anything he wasn't forbidden to. Although Kreacher had to injure himself for setting Sirius up, he didn't have to for lying to Harry about Sirius, since Harry was not his master and elves can lie to anyone not their master with impunity. It was Kreacher's efforts that end up getting Sirius killed in Jun 1996. It is unknown if he was imprisoned or executed for his part in the MoM break in and murder of Sirius. One would expect some severe punishment for him. Legally he's guilty of conspiracy to burgle the MoM, treason (to the MoM) and conspiracy to commit a murder. There could be extenuating circumstances, like a psychological need to obey Narcissa, but still, he was competent and responsible for his actions. One hopes he is not still free and hanging out with Bellatrix, though it is possible.

Kreacher wears a filthy rag tied like a loincloth around his waist and is naked but for this cloth. He is very old and his skin appears to be baggy like it's several times too big for his body. He is bald like all house-elves, but has lots of white hair growing out of his large batwing ears. He has bloodshot, watery grey eyes, and a large fleshy nose rather like a pig snout. Being quite elderly, he is hunchbacked and shuffles as he walks. He has a deep hoarse voice like a bullfrog, calls Voldemort the Dark Lord and can frequently be heard talking to himself. He's a bit creepy and disturbed and tended to wander into the bedrooms at night and stare at Sirius' guests. Given he betrayed his master, mistreated guests, stole, and committed other acts of elf treachery, as elves go, he is as abnormal as Dobby, if not more so. Dobby may have worked in a Dark wizard's house, but he never adopted what passes for Lucius' moral standard. Kreacher on the other hand went Dark, liked it and stayed that way.

Winky: Winky is a slightly smaller than Dobby, probably 2"6"-2"10". She has enormous brown eyes and a nose like a large tomato. She has a teeny, quivering, squeak of a voice. She started her career as Barty Crouch Sr's house-elf and wore a tea towel toga while working for him. She took care of Barty Jr after he escaped Azkaban with his parents' collusion and convinced Barty Sr to give Barty Jr rewards for his good behavior, like the opportunity to attend QWC 1994. She is afraid of heights and didn't watch the game, thus didn't see Barty Jr steal Harry's wand.

When the Death Eaters started assaulting Muggles just after QWC 1994, Winky was able to bind Barty Jr to herself and drag him out of their tent and into the woods by elf magic. Unfortunately he managed to break free of her, shot up the Dark Mark and escape. She was found with Harry's wand in her hand and when the wand was forced to regurgitate the last spell it had done, it was the Dark Mark, proving in many minds that she was guilty of some crime. Barty Sr went ballistic, disowned her (because she'd lost Barty Jr) and gave her clothes. Hermione was a witness to Winky's dismissal and it was this event that prompted her to set up SPEW, though Winky herself doesn't approve of the organization.

Winky knew Dobby, for how long is unknown but it indicates house-elves have a network to keep in touch with each other. This makes sense as an "only elf" in a house must get together with other elves now and then or how could they have children? After being fired, Winky hooked up with Dobby to look for work. One guesses 2 disgraced elves are better than 1 undisgraced elf was the thinking, but they were wrong. After being unemployed for about 4 months (Dobby about 19 months) they found jobs at Hogwarts around Christmas 1994. Apparently Dumbledore hired them, but would not have them a slaves so Winky is not enslaved to Hogwarts and is free to leave, just as Dobby is, the only difference is that she hates being free.

Winky refers to herself as a disgraced elf, but she says she hasn't sunk so low as to allow herself to receive pay. Still, disgrace does not suit her. Her family had a tradition of service, her mother and grandmother (but not father or grandfather) worked for the Crouch family. So she is understandably having trouble adjusting to freedom. She ashamed of being free and though she can now speak her mind, she won't, and continues to keep Barty Sr's secrets. She arrived at Hogwarts wearing a neat little blue skirt and blouse with matching blue hat with holes for ears, probably because Dobby cleaned her up for the interview with Dumbledore, but her clothes have since become stained and dirty as Winky fell into a deep depression almost as soon as she was hired.

As her depression grew, she began neglecting herself and spent her days sitting by the kitchen fire and drinking Butterbeer, which is strong for an house-elf, even if they aren't having Winky's quota of 6 bottles a day. Occasionally she passes out and the other elves, who feel she's a disgrace, cover her over with a tablecloth where she falls. Dobby cares for her because they're friends and, though he tries to help her, he isn't having much success. Dobby sometimes takes her to the Room or Requirement to get her sobered up, but it never lasts. A year after she was hired by Hogwarts, she was still drinking heavily. Her take on life is: house-elves are not supposed to have fun. It remains to be seen if she can recover from being disgraced. It's not clear if house-elves commit suicide or go in for therapy, but Winky seems headed for one or the other.

Wheezy: Little is known about this house-elf other than he is Dobby's best friend. This may be an individual Dobby met after being released from the Malfoy's service but he doesn't seem to be. Wheezy seems to be an elf Dobby has known a long time. How exactly they got to know each other or kept in touch as single, male, working house-elves is a mystery.

Ogre: An ogre is typically a hideous giant that feeds on human beings. Exact looks and eating habits vary. Some ogres, like hags, eat children, others go for goats or other livestock. All of them prefer a diet of meat and vegetarian ogres are unknown. Ogres are believed to live in Hogsmeade. At least Ron has said he's seen one at the Three Broomsticks. Ogres do come in male and female, and have children. Do they marry? It's unknown.

Skeleton: It's difficult to comment on this form of being as they seem more of a human being that is fleshless than a Spirit or Beast. What one can say is that Dumbledore hired a troupe of dancing skeletons one year for Halloween, so skeletons seem to be able to enter into agreements, do work for pay and be somewhat able dancers and choreographers. What exactly a skeleton would spend money on, beside perhaps clothing, jewelry or musical instruments, is unknown.

Vampire: These individuals start life as human beings and become vampires after being repeatedly bitten by one. They can be male or female, and of any age, but they cannot reproduce. They increase their numbers by humans voluntary (or involuntarily) allowing the same vampire, usually 1 they are in relationship with, to bite them 3 times. Once bitten thrice, the person stop aging and will have immortality as long as they avoid sun, holy water and being staked through the heart. Vampires live by drinking blood, on a daily basis, mostly human blood and this is preferred, but anything will do. Vampires can't drink their own blood because technically they don't have any. Considered a Dark creature, they are easily repelled by a simple cross or crucifix (but not other religious symbols apparently).

Generally Vampires are recognizable by their waxy white skin, nocturnal shopping habits (they do eat and drink just like other humans) and lack of reflection in a mirror. Other telltale signs would be having a coffin lined with dirt from their homeland as a piece of bedroom furniture, keeping all the window drapes closed during the day, or the ability to turn into a bat. Vampires are hearty eaters but avoid garlic, probably because of it's blood purifying affects. They can't cross running water, such as a river or stream, but many enjoy ocean or lake sailing. Pr Quirrell is said to have met some in the Black Forest, Germany, which would make sense as vampires probably seek small hidden communities in dark areas such a dense forest.

Zombie: Apparently real if no one questioned what Pr Quirrell was doing in Africa when he said he was getting rid of a zombie. A zombie is a reanimated corpse which cannot speak and has no will of its own. They tend to move very stiffly and though reanimated retain their decayed and corpselike appearance. A zombie can't be killed in traditional ways because the person is already dead. It is said that holy water is effective as is burning. In Pr Quirrell's case it is likely that he broke the magic of the individual who was activating the corpse thus causing it to become fully dead again.

WEREWOLVES

Being and Beast. Werewolves are people 29 days of each month, but on the night of the full moon, when they look at the unobscured full moon, they turn into ravenous wolves. If they can avoid looking at or exposing themselves to the moon, they don't transform. It is very painful to transform and, added to the actual physical pain, there is a lot of psychological pain caused by irrational prejudice. As very few people are willing to hire a werewolf, most are financially insolvent and practically starve. In late 1993 MoM pass anti-werewolf legislation made the average werewolf's life even more completely miserable.

Werewolves must register with the MoM Werewolf Registry in the DCRMC, in the Beast Division. There are Werewolf Support Services in the Being Division for wizards seeking help with managing they condition, information on the latest potions and therapies for Lycanthropy, and help finding one assumes, support groups, employment or tips on finding a werewolf -friendly neighborhood. Should potion therapy and isolation fail, there is a Werewolf Capture Unit, located in the Beast Division. They will capture and detain a werewolf till it can return to human form if it is proving too great a threat to the people around it or is itself threaten.

One can tell if a person is a werewolf or not by several small indications such as the nose. The 5 signs of a werewolf are features observable either in a person (if they are a werewolf) or if they are a wolf (it they're really a person):

    1) snout shape (in both human form and wolf form)
    2) pupils of the eyes (in both human form and wolf form)
    3) tufted tail (in the wolf form)
    4) unknown
    5) unknown.

Probably the last 2 signs are hair color and texture (in the human and wolf form) and a tendency to seek out humans (in the wolf form).

Werewolves are tremendously dangerous creatures due to an unfortunate bent, when a wolf, toward finding and biting (or killing) humans. Once transformed into a wolf, they have no human mind or conscience left. They will attack man, woman or child. One can only become a werewolf by being bitten by a werewolf and the werewolf does have to be in wolf form for the bite to be effective. Once bitten, the victim is immediately effected and during the next full moon, unless preventative care is taken, the victim will become a demented wolf. There is no known cure, but a recent potions research breakthrough has come up with a potion that suppresses of the worst symptoms, ie, the loss of one's human mind and the desire to kill or injure other humans.

The medical term for the werewolf condition is Lycanthropy. It would seem from Tom Riddle's comments that werewolves possibly develop relationships with wolves rather than humans and the products of such relationships are werewolf pups. Probably werewolf pups are wolves that never turn into people. They are perhaps distinguishable by physical features or vocalizations differing from wolves in general. Given the short period of time a werewolf is a wolf, and the fact they are madly seeking humans to bite during that time, the werewolf-wolf relationship seems speculative. On the other hand, if Sirius as a dog could dissuade Remus as a wolf from doing anything harmful, this proves that canine-canine relationships curb the "madness" and are possibly the best possible outcome for a werewolf.

Remus J. Lupin: b 1955. House unknown, 1966-1973. A former Hogwarts student, probably Ravenclaw, he started in 66/67. An original member of the OoP. His name implies he might have a twin brother named Romulus. He was bitten by a werewolf at the age of 6 and feared he wouldn't be allowed to go to Hogwarts, but then Dumbledore took over just before he was about to start and school policies changed. A special protected area was created, the Shrieking Shack, and a secret underground passage to it was created, guarded by the Whomping Willow, which was planted in the year Remus arrived at Hogwarts. The nurse would smuggle Remus out of the castle each month and get him into the tunnel after which he could safely transform into a wolf and return to school when the episode was over.

It was, and is, very painful to transform into a wolf, and once transformed Remus would bite and scratch himself since he couldn't get to any humans. The villagers thought the house was haunted because of all the noise Remus made and Dumbledore encouraged that rumor to the point that even Hogwarts' ghosts still avoid it. Within the first few months of going to Hogwarts Remus met and became friends with James Potter, Sirius Black and Peter Pettigrew. Though Remus tried to keep being a werewolf a secret from them, they worked it out on their own very quickly. The trio decided to become illegal Animagi so they could let Remus run free and join him on theoretically well-planed monthly adventures. It took 3 years for James and Sirius and 5 for Peter, but they all did manage to become Animagi.

As animals they were in no danger of being bitten by Remus, and as Animagi they had their human minds and could look after Remus and keep him from going after humans. Remus says he became less dangerous with company and together they would roam around the village, with James and Sirius keeping him in check because they were larger animals. Peter being smallest, as a rat, would hit the knot on the Whomping Willow and stop the tree attacking anyone. James and Sirius would then get Remus out of the tunnel. During the night they would go off the grounds of Hogwarts to Hogsmeade and one assumes the Forbidden Forest. They romped around nightly as animals, until Remus was back to human form and ready to return to Hogwarts. Once back in human form and back at school they would begin to plan their next adventure.

This went on for the next 4 years (though only 2 of which Peter was able to participate in since he was slow in becoming an Animagus) while they were all in school without anyone, including Dumbledore, discovering what they were doing. Remus was made a Prefect in his 5th year, so Dumbledore never let the fact that Remus was a werewolf stand in the way of treating him like any other student under his care, or rewarding him and honoring him for those achievements he managed on his own. He was an excellent student, a bit of bookworm really, but he knew his stuff, especially when it came to DADA. Remus personally thought Dumbledore made him a Prefect to control James and Sirius, and that may be true, but it didn't work.

In their 6th year, while Remus was a Prefect, Severus Snape realized the 4 were up to something and that it started at the Whomping Willow. Sirius intentionally let Severus find out how to open the tunnel while Remus was a wolf, hoping he'd be attacked or killed. Severus went into the tunnel but James rescued him. Dumbledore, when he found out about Severus' adventure, made him swear never to tell that Remus was a werewolf and he kept his promise for the next 13 years or so. By his own admission, Remus had some close calls, meaning he almost hurt another human being during his monthly outings. But, he also says they were the best times of his life, because he had supportive friends and he liked having monthly adventures as a wolf with his friends (pack). Remus never told Dumbledore, even confidentially, that he was getting out each month, or that his friends has become illegal Animagi and were helping him. In youth, he and his friends liked to live on the edge, but liked it a little to well and fell over it.

He remained friends with James, Peter and Sirius, all of whom joined the OoP as he did. He began to have doubts about Sirius a few months after Harry was born because he was aware someone was leaking information to Voldemort about Lily and James and thought only Sirius was that close to them and clever enough to be a spy. When Lily and James were killed, and Peter also appeared to have been killed by Sirius, whom Remus supposed was Lily and James' Secret-Keeper, and then Sirius went to prison, he basically lost the only real friends he had all the space of 48 hours (Oct 31- Nov 1). He never really made any other close friends after these events, was shunned most of his adult life and, being a registered werewolf, was for the most part unable to find paid work. Considered a Dark creature, he all but starved though he was talented, kindly, capable and intelligent.

He was hired to teach DADA at Hogwarts for 93/94, for which he was very grateful. When he arrive he carried a small battered briefcase, with peeling gold letters, that was held together with a lot of neatly knotted string and wore extremely shabby robes that had been darned in several places and were frayed at the edges. Remus was a great DADA teacher who really knew his subject as well as his remedies. He carried the universal cure-all to dementors, chocolate, with him at all times (or he may just like sweets). Pr Snape didn't appreciate having to deal with Remus on a daily basis as during their 5th year at Hogwarts together Severus was attacked by Remus' friends, in Remus' presence and, despite the fact Remus was a Prefect, he kept his nose in a book and did nothing about it.

Remus had, and still has, no grudge against Pr Snape and treated him with courtesy and respect, even friendliness. Pr Snape however was not willing to let bygones be bygones. He turned the Slytherins against Remus and actively kept an eye on him with a view to getting him sacked. Because Remus was working at Hogwarts though Pr Snape had to make Wolfsbane Potion for him every month. Wolfsbane Potion is a recent discovery which allows werewolves to keep possession of their mind when they transform. Remus would just curl up in his office, in his wolf form, and wait out the moon till it waned. Remus had to drink it in the week before the full moon for it to be effective and admitted that before the Wolfsbane Potion he really did become a monster. Surprisingly Pr Snape never tried to poison him, or made an error with the potion, like adding sugar.

At one point Pr Snape substituted for Remus during a DADA class and assigned a paper on how to recognize werewolves to expose Remus to the DADA students. When this failed, he continued poking his nose in Remus' business with an eye to finding another way to expose him. Eventually after Remus discovered the truth of Sirius and Peter, Severus attempted to capture Sirius and planned to implicate Remus as a conspirator. After Sirius escaped, causing Pr Snape to lose his opportunity to avenge himself on both of them and receive an Order of Merlin, 2nd class, he ratted out Remus as being a werewolf to the Slytherin House. Remus was instantly forced to resign and was further embarrassed by having to admit to Dumbledore that he had led 3 students into becoming illegal Animagi.

Although Remus left the school in Jun 1993, he started living at Sirius' house and working with Dumbledore on Order business so what he did in the past seems to be forgiven by Dumbledore. Which is a good thing as Remus remains one of the few that has no problem saying Voldemort. On the other hand he does call him *Lord* Voldemort, which is something only Death Eaters do, or former Death Eaters and it makes one wonder exactly what he means by it. But, that aside, Remus was glad to have a place to live, food and company because the anti-werewolf legislation drafted by Dolores Umbridge had passed in 1993 making getting another job well and truly impossible. Remus loathes Umbridge because of her treatment of part-humans and he doubtless had some overlapping time at Hogwarts with her as she was only a few years older. He had probably heard her prejudiced views even then.

Remus is usually recognizable by his clothes, which are all patched, shabby and threadbare. He has a watch but no other jewelry. He is generally pallid, tired or ill looking. He's quite young, but his light brown hair is flecked with (wolflike) grey and his face is quite youthful, but has lines on it. His eyes are alert and wary and his voice tends to be slightly hoarse. Not a popular dinner guest with most of the wizarding community because he's a werewolf, he's nonetheless a very kind, patient and fair person. He tries to listen to people and is willing to hear both sides of a story before forming an opinion. Members of the OoP form the bulk of his friends, though Sirius was his oldest and closest till his unfortunate demise.

Remus seems to eat and drink everything a normal person does, including wine and chocolate, both bad for canines, and never eats raw meat so one presumes when he's human, there's no animal left in him, unlike Animagi who seem to acquire their animal counterpart's habits. Granted Remus is wolfish in his quietness, gentleness and care for the young, but he lacks the essential wolf trait of loyalty to the pack. Remus would have deeply investigated Sirius' case and would have had to have been utterly and completely convinced that Sirius was guilty to turn on him. Oddly, Sirius, so doglike in most ways, also lacked this essential canine trait as well. Among Remus' special talents he can produce flames in his bare hand. Swears: my God.

The Waga Waga Werewolf: Supposedly this individual was cure by Lockhart with a Homorphus Charm. This is a typical Lockhart lie, as one can't cure werewolves.

THE MOON AND LYCANTHROPY

For most of the time, Lycanthropy can be contained through careful use of potions and isolation away from the full moon. Technically the full moon lasts only a few minutes (ie, the time it is 100% fully illuminated), but to the naked eye, the moon would appear to be fully illuminated for many hours or even for several nights in a row if it is clear.

The moon is 100% illuminated only on the night closest to the time of exact full moon, but on the night before and night after will appear 97-99% illuminated; most people would not notice the difference. Even 2 days from full moon when the moon is 93-97% illuminated, most people think it's full.

All that being said, it is wise to remember that most magical conditions are very specific. In this case, if a person must see a full moon to become a man-eating wolf, the transformation could only be activated during those few minutes when the moon was actually full, and fully visible to a person with Lycanthropy. Also, once activated, the transformation itself should only last the 1 night (or day) the moon is full. Even though one might wish to recuperate from the transformation for a day or so afterwards, it would be as a human being and that person would be totally unaffected by the *seemingly* full moon. Remus Lupin's case seems to bear the specific-conditions magic theory out.

On the day of his ride to Hogwarts on the Express, the weather was so foul that the full moon which occurred could not be seen and Lupin, though clearly not too well remained a man. Remus' greatest fear, as displayed through the boggart, is seeing the shining 100% full moon. He often disappeared for a only a couple of days at a time, but he would need at least 4-5 days off if the appearance of a full moon (less than 100% illumination) kept activating his condition. Also, Remus, on a full moon night, was fine inside the Shrieking Shack and was fine even outdoors as long as the moon was hidden from his view by clouds.

Given the above, Lycanthropy would probably be more manageable for Remus than one first might think. First, several full moons occurred either on weekends or holidays when no questions would be asked if he disappeared for a couple of days. Second, he was living in Scotland where sight of the moon is often obscured by cloud, fog, rain, hail, snow and other assorted weather phenomena. Third, he was able to access suppressive therapy as long as Pr Snape was willing to make the complicated Wolfsbane Potion for him. Fourth, he still had knowledge of and access to the Shrieking Shack.

The following chart gives the problem dates for British Lycanthropy sufferers. Time is given in Greenwich Mean Time (British time, using 24:00hr system). One would suspect that someone with Lycanthropy would be as likely to turn into a wolf seeing a full moon setting at 6:31am, as seeing it rising at 9 pm. Even so, very few days seem inevitably out of control or likely to arouse suspicion. As shown, there are only 4 bad days in the entire 10-month school year Lupin worked. It would seem that any werewolf who cared to could hide their condition entirely by claiming sick leave or taking long weekends a few times a year. Barring their employer checking their name with the Werewolf Registry of course.

Book 3: Harry Potter and the Prisoner of Azkaban
1993 Sep 1 02:34   Wed   It was rainy, obscured moon
1993 Sep 30 18:55   Thu   **Potentially bad day**
1993 Oct 30 12:39   Sat   It's a weekend
1993 Nov 29 06:31   Mon   **Potentially bad day**
1993 Dec 28 23:06   Tue   Christmas Vacation
1994 Jan 27 13:24   Thu   Can't see full moon
1994 Feb 26 01:17   Sat   It's a weekend
1994 Mar 27 11:11   Sun   Its a weekend
1994 Apr 25 19:46   Mon   **Potentially bad day**
1994 May 25 03:41   Wed   **Potentially bad day**

1994 Jun 23 11:35 Thu   Can't see full moon
Book 4: Harry Potter and the Goblet of Fire
1994 Jul 22 20:17 Fri
1994 Aug 21 06:48 Sun
1994 Sep 19 20:02 Mon
1994 Oct 19 12:19 Wed
1994 Nov 18 06:58 Fri
1994 Dec 18 02:17 Sun
1995 Jan 16 20:27 Mon
1995 Feb 15 12:16 Wed
1995 Mar 17 01:27 Fri
1995 Apr 15 12:09 Sat
1995 May 14 20:49 Sun
1995 Jun 13 04:05 Tue
Book 5: Harry Potter and the OoP
1995 Jul 12 10:51 Wed
1995 Aug 10 18:17 Thu
1995 Sep 9 03:38 Sat
1995 Oct 8 15:54 Sun
1995 Nov 7 07:22 Tue
1995 Dec 7 01:28 Thu
1996 Jan 5 20:52 Fri
1996 Feb 4 15:59 Sun
1996 Mar 5 09:23 Tue
1996 Apr 4 00:08 Thu
1996 May 3 11:49 Fri
1996 Jun 1 20:48 Sat
Book 6: Untitled Work?
1996 Jul 1 03:59 Mon
1996 Jul 30 10:37 Tue
1996 Aug 28 17:54 Wed
1996 Sep 27 02:52 Fri
1996 Oct 26 14:13 Sat
1996 Nov 25 04:11 Mon
1996 Dec 24 20:43 Tue
1997 Jan 23 15:12 Thu
1997 Feb 22 10:28 Sat
1997 Mar 24 04:46 Mon
1997 Apr 22 20:34 Tue
1997 May 22 09:15 Thu
1997 Jun 20 19:10 Fri
Book 7: Untitled Work ?
1997 Jul 20 03:22 Sun
1997 Aug 18 10:57 Mon
1997 Sep 16 18:52 Tue
1997 Oct 16 03:47 Thu
1997 Nov 14 14:13 Fri
1997 Dec 14 02:39 Sun
1998 Jan 12 17:26 Mon
1998 Feb 11 10:24 Wed

1998 Mar 13 04:35 Fri
1998 Apr 11 22:24 Sat
1998 May 11 14:30 Mon
1998 Jun 10 04:20 Wed
1998 Jul 9 16:02 Thu
And after:
1998 Aug 8 02:11 Sat
1998 Sep 6 11:23 Sun
1998 Oct 5 20:13 Mon
1998 Nov 4 05:19 Wed
1998 Dec 3 15:20 Thu
1999 Jan 2 02:51 Sat
1999 Jan 31 16:08 Sun
1999 Mar 2 07:00 Tue
1999 Mar 31 22:50 Wed
1999 Apr 30 14:55 Fri
1999 May 30 06:41 Sun
1999 Jun 28 21:39 Mon
1999 Jul 28 11:26 Wed
1999 Aug 26 23:49 Thu
1999 Sep 25 10:52 Sat
1999 Oct 24 21:03 Sun
1999 Nov 23 07:05 Tue
1999 Dec 22 17:33 Wed

SPIRITS

What is a spirit? Usually we think of ghosts. According to Nearly Headless Nick wizards can chose to leave an imprint of themselves on the earth to walk as ghosts where their living selves once trod, but few choose that path. Nonwizards, says Nick, don't have a choice when they die, which historical record would not agree with, but perhaps Nick has never met any nonwizard ghosts. Beyond ghosts, there are poltergeists, who are not the essence of someone dead but usually the displaced and disturbed psychic energy of young children reeking havoc in a household. Given the number of young children at Hogwarts, it's no surprise that Peeves is there, or is the great chaos maker that he is.

Broadly a spirit is a noncorporeal being. Beings may have vastly different powers, capabilities or forms they can take. Angels and demons are spirits that can appear in a wide variety of forms. God is called by the Native Americans, the Great Spirit. The genie of Arabian fame is a spirit, sometimes good, sometimes mean, and the djinn is the wholly evil counterpart of the genie, but both take human form as *The 1001 Arabian Nights* confirms. Spirits of course are not constrained to be only human or humanlike creatures. The Grim is a classic example of a death-warning spirit using the form of a dog. And some spirits may not choose a form at all, but instead choose to inhabit something that has form, for instance, Death itself as a spirit inhabits a cassock.

And what of all that armor walking about Hogwarts? It is very likely to be, if not magically imbued, the spirit of a former owner activating it, and it is certainly a spirit snickering at the odd student that gets his foot caught in the missing step. And who can really say what is causing the bust of Paracelsus to mumble to himself. Possibly magic activity on the same level as say a wizard photograph or portrait, but maybe that too may be spirit activated. However, despite wide range of spirits gliding about the world, for the purpose of this discussion we will stick to the Hogwarts-related and other relevant spirits. Subdivisions of this section include Ghosts, Ghost-Related Stuff, Poltergeists, and Assorted Spirits.

Ghosts

Hogwarts has about 20 pearly-white, shiny, misty, silver, semi-transparent ghosts. They glide around the entire school, and spend time talking to each other, students, and teachers. Some ghosts are helpful, some are not. They can't eat, but they enjoy pretending to. They allow the food to go rotten, then pass through it. The strong odor makes them feel like they ate. As taste is related almost solely to smell (if one is blindfolded and one's nose clothespinned, one wouldn't know the difference between and apple and an onion). When ghosts pass through or touch a living person, it feels like being ducked in ice cold water. It would seem that the living person has no effect on the ghost that touches or passes through, or if so, it's mild and not unpleasant, possibly a momentary sensation of a living person's body warmth.

House Ghosts are extremely interested in and dedicated to the affairs of their House. They sit at the House tables during meals or at least during feasts, follow their House's Quidditch matches assiduously and help the students of their House if they get lost, need advice or are in trouble. Given that ghosts haunt the place they lived, it would seem all the House Ghosts lived at Hogwarts Castle and attended the school in various different time periods. Of the 4 House Ghosts, we have only been introduced to 3, Nearly Headless Nick, the Bloody Baron, and the Fat Friar, and all of them are decidedly male, despite the fact 2 of the houses were started by great witches. Perhaps the Ravenclaw ghost, when it finally turns up will be a she, possibly the tall witch seen gliding around by Harrt in 1991.

Pr Binns: d 1966. Teacher of History of Magic at Hogwarts since c 1955. He fell asleep in front of the staffroom fire one evening, died, but didn't realize it and got up the next morning to teach leaving his body behind. The most exciting part of his classes are when he enters or exists the room through the blackboard. He is ancient and shriveled and looks like a wrinkled old tortoise when pursing his lips (except tortoises don't have lips). He reads from his notes in a flat drone like an old vacuum which puts most of his class to sleep. When asked about the Chamber of Secrets, he got snippy and said he dealt in facts not myth or legend. He was aggravated at being questioned about something he found preposterous, indicating he was not on staff until a good while after 1943.

He has a dry reedy voice and when he clears his throat it sounds like chalk snapping. He reads without ever looking up at the class. No one ever asks questions. When in the 92/93 Hermione did, he looked at her as though he'd never seen a student before. He was amazed anyone would interrupt and completely thrown by a show of interest by the class. He doesn't know anyone's name and calls everyone by a wrong name even after they state their name: Hermione - Miss Grant, Seamus - O'Flaherty, Parvati - Miss Pennyfeather. While most students fall asleep 5 minutes after he starts talking, and find him boring, he is knowledgeable about his subject nonetheless and very informed about what he deems "myth" as well.

The Bloody Baron: The House Ghost for Slytherin. A former student, probably in the 1500s when barons were very important, and very bloody, in Scotland. He talks in a hoarse whisper, but very rarely. He used to ride Sir Nick about Gryffindor losing the Quidditch Cup to his House so many years in a row. He is the one ghost that is able to scare Peeves into submission. When anyone has problems with Peeves they go to the Baron and he takes care of it. He put his foot down and forbid Peeves going to the Start of Term Feast in 1994. So, a rather helpful specter. A silent specter covered in sliver bloodstains, he has horrible, blank staring eyes in his gaunt face, and no one knows how his robes came to be bloodstained.

In thinking of the Scottish baron this author is best acquainted with, the baron of Morton Castle, who had a servant ripped in 2 by wild horses, over a course of a nearly 3-mile run and was later immortalized for it in poetry, of which this is but one stanza,

"Gae, fetch to me yon twa wild steeds,
Whilk gang on Knockenshaw;
And ere I either eat or drink,
To death I will him draw,

the author would prefer not to dwell how the Bloody Baron got his stains, though one doubts very much the blood came from his own veins.

Sir Patrick Delaney-Podmore: The fully decapitated ghost who is the Head of the Headless Hunt. He is a large ghost with a beard who likes to do things with his head to make people laugh, like blowing a horn while his head is under his arm or lifting his head over the crowd to see. He tends to get about by horse, ghost horse, and travels with a retinue that is the Headless Hunt. Sir Patrick refuses to let Nearly Headless Nick join the Hunt because his head is still technically attached.

He enjoys Horseback Head-Juggling, Head Hockey, and Head Polo. He loves to put a pin into the balloon that is Nearly Headless Nick's ego, sense of propriety and dignity. He upstaged Nearly Headless Nick terribly at his Deathday Party in 1992. Exactly why he was beheaded, when, where and how are all a mystery. The hunt has a long history, beheading an even longer one. One would tend to say Sir Patrick is a 17th-century ghost, based on his use of a horn but lack of dogs. That is however complete guess. See the discussion of beheading in Nick's entry for more detail on the subject of beheading.

The Fat Friar: The House Ghost for Hufflepuff. A former student, probably in c 1300 since the Franciscans didn't exist before c 1290. Apparently a Catholic, Franciscan Friar. That fact that he exists sort of proves that magical beings feel they can be Christians. He wouldn't be supporting a school House that creates wizarding people if he didn't approve of it. The Friar is a very merry ghost and quite friendly and kind hearted. He is always willing to give Peeves another chance, though he is usually overridden by the rest of the ghosts. He wanted to give Peeves a chance to attend the Start of Term Feast in 1994 but the Bloody Baron overrode him at the Ghosts' Council.

Knight with an arrow sticking out of his forehead: It's difficult to know if he is one of the 20 ghosts from around Hogwarts castle or a visiting ghost, but given he came to Nearly Headless Nick's Deathday Party and the fact there is knightly armor everywhere at Hogwarts (which seems to move and probably is inhabited by the knightly ghosts of former owners), he seems appropriate to be a Hogwarts' ghost.

Sir Nicholas de Mimsy-Porpington: aka Nearly Headless Nick. d Oct 31, 1492. He is the House Ghost for Gryffindor and resident ghost of Gryffindor Tower. He probably attended Hogwarts as a Gryffindor. Nick's decapitation involved 45 whacks with a blunt axe and it still wasn't complete. A 1/2" of skin is still connecting his head to his neck on the left side. He can pull his left ear and have his head unhinges and falls on to his left shoulder. He has never said why exactly someone tried to cut his head off or who it was that ordered it done. But it was probably done at the Tower and ordered by the ruling monarch. Much of the following discussion on decapitation applies to Sir Patrick as well, except the monarch that axed him was probably Charles I.

At the time Nick died (during the early reign of Henry VIII), decapitation with an axe in England was very rare and reserved only for aristocracy (he is a knight and qualifies as aristocracy) who had gone bad. About 150 people were beheaded in total during the use of this method of execution. He would not have been beheaded for being a wizard, but only for committing an act of treason (or very rarely a murder, only about 5 of the 150 were axed for this). Beheading was rarely done publicly except in cases of treason, but it seems from Nick's comments (he claims he was ridiculed at his beheading), he did die publicly. In public executions the head was held up by the axeman and "behold the head of a traitor" was declared. With 99% surety, one can say he was whacked for treason, which in that time period could have meant saying something impolite about a monarch, not necessarily committing what we today know as treason.

Nick wears a ruff to keep his head on, and for feasts a very large rough to be extra festive. In keeping with times in which he died, he wears tights and a dashing plumed hat on his long curly hair (which is quite strange as the fashion at that time he lived was short straight hair, long curly only coming into fashion in the 1640s) and a tunic or sometimes a doublet. He is pale as smoke, and one can see right though him but he's very human all the same. He has elegant hands and mannerisms. He is a real gentleman, or tries very hard to be one at least. He can get a bit snippy sometimes but when he takes offense, it's always for a good reason and he usually bears personal attacks with a decorum befitting his station.

In 1991, Nick said he hadn't eaten for nearly 400 years, implying he died in 1590 or later. But in 1992, he threw himself a 500th anniversary Deathday Party confirming he died in 1492. Perhaps all the years fade into each other at a certain point. He wanted his party to be a dignified affair with lots of social tone and guests include: Harry, Ron, Hermione and many ghostly guests such as the gloomy nuns, a ragged man in chains, the Fat Friar, a knight with an arrow sticking out of his forehead, Moaning Myrtle, and the Wailing Widow from Kent. The Bloody Baron was there but given a wide berth by the other ghosts who also seem afraid of him. Nick is a very popular ghost and had several hundred ghostly guests from all over Britain at his party.

Nick's biggest irritations in death are that he can't qualify for Headless Hunt and Peeves. He feels the Peeves gives the ghosts a bad name, even though Peeves isn't one. He's slightly social climbing, which is why he wants to be a part of the Headless Hunt. He wanted Harry at his Deathday Party because he's a big name and could tell Sir Patrick how impressive and frightening he thought Nick was. Even after Nick was Petrified in Dec 1992, he didn't take that as a warning and mend his ways. Petrification for Nick was similar to human Petrification. He turned all black and smoky, went rigid and was found floating horizontal 6" off the ground with an expression of shock. It is unclear how he was revived. Given he can't eat, there was no way for him to take the Mandrake antidote prepared for others by Madam Pomfrey. But maybe if it rots and just passes through his mouth that's good enough.

Nick likes to be the center of attention. He participates in formation gliding and occasionally on Halloween will reenact his beheading, though he claims no one wishes more than he his head had come off in 1 blow. Given Nick was in Gryffindor House, he's actually rather more like a Slytherin. He's ambitious, self-centered and cowardly. He is afraid of the Bloody Baron. He tells Harry that he doesn't know what's on the other side, because he was too cowardly to cross over when he died. And he refused to confront Sir Patrick when the Headless Hunt came bursting into his party causing chaos. Despite all that, he is an all around good guy who really knows how to throw a great party and will even step in and save students in trouble, though in a nonconfrontational and completely guiltless way. He did after all have Peeves push the cabinet over to distract Filch from writing up Harry. His courageous nature will show up someday; if he's a Gryffindor, it's got to be in him somewhere.

Moaning Myrtle: A Muggle-born witch whose life was noting but a misery at Hogwarts. She died in 1943 in a basilisk attack while in a bathroom on the 2nd floor. She particularly haunts the last toilet (4th of 4), down around the U-bend. A squat ghost of a girl with a glum face, half-hidden behind lank hair and thick pearly spectacles. She has small see-through eyes and a pimple on her chin which she is prone to pick at. She was in the bathroom on the day of her death because Olive Hornby teased her about her glasses but died probably of her own stupidity.

She claims she heard someone come into the bathroom and speak strange words (except Parslemouth speak in hisses, not words), looked out from her stall and saw a boy by the sink (since she did not recognize him, apparently making her the only person in school who didn't know all the Prefects). She told Tom Riddle to leave, then she looked into the eyes of the basilisk and died (meaning she was either a first year in Magizoology and didn't know enough to look away when a big snakehead appeared out of the sink or she purposely looked at the basilisk to end her life). Needless to say, Myrtle's story has a lot of flaws. It is most likely she was so unhappy at school that she intentionally, knowingly looked at the basilik's eyes. If not, she was a very stupid girl indeed.

It took several hours for someone to find her because she had no friends and no one missed her. Olive Hornby eventually was sent to find her but found her body instead. Myrtle opted to come back as a ghost because she was determined to haunt Olive for being so cruel to her during her life. Myrtle haunted Olive for years, at school and aferward, and even went to Olive's brother's wedding. Eventually Olive went to the MoM about being stalked, at which point Myrtle was forced to come back to Hogwarts to live. She seems to be confined to the grounds of Hogwarts rather than the castle itself as sometimes, due to toilet flushing, she ends up in the Lake. The merpeople always chase her away when she gets too close though. So, it would seem even in death not a lot of folks like Myrtle.

She has an abundance of feelings, even though dead. She is sulky, emotional, temperamental, hypersensitive and bossy. She is fond of thinking about death and relishes when bad things happen to others. Slightly paranoid, she always thinks people are talking behind her back. When upset she cries silver tears into a handkerchief (yes, even ghosts carry handkerchiefs) she keeps in her robes. When she has tantrums it floods the bathroom, so it's often out of order. This is hardly a loss as she wails at students as they try to urinate. It is unclear what year Myrtle was in when she died. One would tend to say at least her 2nd but perhaps she was even further along. Her mistake with the basilisk would indicated a 1st year, but her torment by Olive and her hatred for the school would suggest an older student. One would guess she was either a Hufflepuff or a Gryffindor. She was certainly not smart enough to be a Ravenclaw and as a Muggle-born unqualified to be a Slytherin.

It was in Myrtle's bathroom that Hermione whipped up the Polyjuice Potion. It was always empty because of Myrtle haunting it – the entire month it took to make the potion there was not a soul seen in the bathroom. Myrtle grew rather sweet on Harry during the 92/93 year and blushes silver when he's talking to her. She was even willing to share her toilet with Harry if he died. Ron, she's not too fond. One of her less attractive qualities includes spying on the Prefects from the bathroom taps on the 5th floor bathroom. One presumes she does this from other taps as well. However she did help Harry with his egg for TT Task 2 and pointed Harry in the right direction toward

THE HARRY POTTER COMPANION

the hostages while under the Lake during the task itself. So Myrtle may have her issues, but she's ok.

Nuns: A group of ghostly gloomy nuns attended Nearly Headless Nick's Deathday Party. Given that ghosts can apparently be free to travel or confined to a specific place, it's difficult to know if these are some of the 20 ghosts from around Hogwarts castle or visiting ghosts. One would guess if the Fat Friar is a ghost from Hogwarts, the nuns probably are as well.

Ragged man in chains: It's difficult to know if he is one of the 20 ghosts from around Hogwarts castle or a visiting ghost, but given he came to Nearly Headless Nick's Deathday Party and they have dungeons at Hogwarts, he seems appropriate to be a Hogwarts' ghost.

Ravenclaw Ghost: Probably the tall witch that drifted by Harry in 91/92. But this is never said and who she actually is, or was, is unknown.

Voldemort: See Tom Riddle's Diary in Part III and Tom Riddle. Obviously Voldemort was a spirit for a long time (13 years) and as a spirit went about inhabiting creatures (possession) for his own ends. As a spirit he inhabited Pr Quirrell's head and as a spirit he popped out of Tom's Diary. It is difficult to draw any conclusions about spirits in general from Voldemort as a spirit.

Voldemort's spirit leaving a body caused it to die, this is not normally the case in cases of possession. Exorcism might have saved Pr Quirrell, and countless others, but that is past trying now he has body again. Most spirits do not choose to inhabit snakes, have a need to kill and eat things or the ability to manifest corporeally by draining a soul out of someone living. In these respects Voldemort is unique, and rather creepy.

The Wailing Widow: A particularly distinguished guest Nearly Headless Nick invited to his Deathday Party in 1992. She is from Kent.

GHOST-RELATED STUFF

This section has information related to ghosts' lives and things that happen in their world.

Deathday Party: Obviously since ghosts aren't alive any longer, they can't celebrate birthdays. However, in keeping with the tradition, they celebrate the years they have been dead with Deathday Parties. The parties can be very elaborate, with extensive decorations, abundant food, dancing, 100s of guests and even speeches. They even include a cake, just as in a Birthday Party. It seems to be that large parties are only thrown for significant deathdays. Nearly Headless Nick had a big bash only when he turned 500 in 1992.

Ghost Animals: Since the Headless Hunt is mounted on ghost horses and chasing a ghost fox, it is clear that animals can manifest as ghost. Nearly Headless Nick would likely say this is at a wizard's discretion. It could not be at the fox's or horse's discretion, who were probably, respectively, sick of being chased or chasing in life.

The Ghosts' Council: Whenever there is something serious afoot in the spirit community at Hogwarts, the ghosts call a council meeting and talk about it. The council votes on matters with the majority carrying the day - or if the Baron has a strong opinion, whatever way the Baron decides. The Council voted Peeves couldn't attend the Start of Term Feast in 1994. Oddly they didn't get much involved while Pr Umbridge was there. Perhaps they feared being evicted by the MoM, which has that power, since she was also a high-level MoM employee.

Ghost Music: According to Harry it sounds like a 1,000 fingernails scraping on an enormous blackboard. Nearly Headless Nick had a 30-piece saw orchestra on a raised black-draped stage for his Deathday Party. There were hundreds of people drifting around a crowded dancefloor, waltzing. Apparently the more traditional music suits ghosts just fine. It is interesting to note that Nearly Headless Nick didn't play music from his own time period as the waltz became popular from 1750ish, peaked in 1900, and remains a popular dance for formal occasions. Obviously Nick is interested in dance and music that enhances the social tone and keeps up with these sort of trends.

Ghost Post: Sir Patrick sent Nearly Headless Nick a letter tell him he wasn't eligible for the Headless Hunt and other headless sports. The letter as it was received was transparent like the ghosts themselves. It rather implies there is a postal service for ghosts. I've no idea what it's actually called, so for now it's referred to as ghost post.

POLTERGEISTS

There is only 1 known to be at Hogwarts.

Peeves: aka Peevsey. The only Poltergeist resident at Hogwarts, he is everyone's worst nightmare. He is solid rather than transparent, and extremely colorful. Peeves manifests as a little man with wicked black eyes, a wide mouth an a wide malicious face. (In case this has not been apparent, like being blonde, anyone with a wide face or square-jaw is almost always a bad person.) He went to Sir Nick's Deathday Party dressed in a bright orange party hat and revolving bowtie but seems to normally wear a bell-covered hat and orange bow tie. Apparently he doesn't wear shoes, because Harry said he could see him wiggle his curly toed feet. He curses, has an evil cackle and loves to make up rude songs about people. He also enjoys making vulgar noises, sticking his tongue out at people, getting students in trouble and wrecking things.

He appears with a pop and can float in the air but doesn't seem to be able to pass through walls or doors. He can vanish from sight, but he is still there and still solid. He usually races away from the scene of his crimes so fast that he sets the armor rattling. Peeves can tell a person is around, even if that person is invisible or is under an Invisibility Cloak. He can't however see who the person is. He has a sing song voice when being annoying, and a greasy voice when being subservient. He is physically as well as verbally abusive to just about any student or Prefect. Some of the things Peeves gets up to include loosening carpets so people will trip on the stairs, alerting Filch students are doing something they shouldn't and writing nasty things on chalkboards, but this is by no means meant to be an exhaustive list.

Only the Bloody Baron can control Peeves and people who can't avoid Peeves usually go to Baron for help, in extremis. Peeves is also afraid of Dumbledore and to a lesser extent the teachers. But he doesn't give a fig about the Head Girl or Boy, Prefects, ghosts besides the Baron, students or Filch. He isn't terribly interested in anyone but himself and causing chaos. He saw Sirius Black attack the Fat Lady's portrait Oct 31, 1993, but didn't do anything that might have helped her, like call for help. On the other hand, if he's wanted to cause chaos, he obligingly will help out. He led the way in resisting Pr Umbridge after Fred and George left in 1996, though he was aided and abetted by the other teachers. He made her life a perfect horror.

ASSORTED SPIRITS

Bloodsucking Bugbears might be in this category, but we don't know enough about them to be sure.

The Grim: In England and Scotland long held to be the worst possible omen of Death. It is a huge black spectral dog with gleaming eyes. Usually when a person see it, it means their death (or the death of someone they are close to) will occur shortly. It is said to haunt churchyards but can appear anywhere. Most Grims are associated with and seem to attach themselves to certain families. Grims rarely "go away" of their own accord and some Grims have been recorded to appear to family members several centuries appart. Grims are most closely associated with families that have a military tradition. It's interesting to note that Sirius' Animagus form was a Grim. Considering he ended up in prison for 13 years, a living death, and died young, he seems to have been a Grim omen to himself.

Wood Nymphs: Fleur Delacour has said they annually serenade Beauxbatons at their Christmas Feast. They are nature-dwelling spirits who often chose to appear as young maidens. Given their fondness for trees, it is small wonder that they would show up where Christmas tress are. Naiads are water-dwelling spirits, similar to nymphs. Both have been around from ancient times, as the Greeks can attest.

MUGGLES

What is a Muggle? Muggles are completely nonmagical human beings. They are not supposed to know about the wizarding community, as the MoM doesn't want wizards being constantly harassed by Muggles who want magical solutions to their problems or a reoccurrence of the persecution of the wizards so frequent in times past. The MoM goes to great lengths to protect Muggles and memory modification seems to be the most effective way of keeping Muggles from knowing more than is good for them, but Muggles themselves assist the MoM by going to any lengths to ignore magic even if it's staring them right in the face.

The MoM works closely with the British PM on matters of mutual concern, such as the escape of dangerous magical criminals into the Muggle populace or large-scale wizarding catastrophes that Muggles have noticed (and which need a plausible explanation as they are beyond covering up). In some cases however the MoM has been less than forthcoming with the PM. During Voldemort's first attempt to seize power, the MoM never informed the PM that a powerful Dark wizard was running amok, with little deterrence from the MoM, trying to take over the wizarding world and get rid of Muggles. The MoM didn't want to appear out of control, which it was. This reticence caused many Muggles to die needlessly. If even only the PM had been made aware Muggle-killings were going on, the government might have been able to shepherd people away from potentially dangerous situations.

It is really no surprise that Muggle-wizard tension in the past caused wizards to go into hiding. But it is very surprising, in an era of toleration, how wizards cling to secrecy and by it let nonwizards die. Not wanting Muggles asking for magical solutions to life's issues seems to be just a lame excuse for wizards not to integrate into society. Wizards, as wizards well know, have no magical solutions to life's real issues. The magic they do is impossible for a Muggle to do. So what do wizards really have that a Muggle would want? Not much. Besides which, it's very little trouble for a wizard to say "no"when magic is requested and back it up with a wand. It is even less trouble for Muggles, wedded to their technology as they are, to refuse magical help.

A gun works as well as a wizard's curse. A plane is safer than a broom which one can fall off of. And can anyone seriously see a Muggle giving up a car to Apparate? Arthur is a wizard and he still wanted a car. Sirius was a wizard and he still wanted a motorcycle. The very fact the Muggles now virtually drive tanks to the market when a simple bicycle or walking would do proves Muggles not only love their technology, they are willing to destroy an entire world, environmentally speaking, in order to hang on to it. There is nothing a wizard can do, or has, that a Muggle would really be interested in doing or having.

Muggles and magicals could live side by side in an integrated world, if the MoM weren't run by people who think 100% humans with 100% pure bloodlines should have 100% of the power. How the British MoM can justify its government is beyond a reasonable wizard's comprehension. It's an autocracy of the very worst sort and why wizards put up with it is even more of a mystery. But I digress. The following list of Muggles is alphabetical, by last name or by first name if that is all that is known, or by occupation if that Muggle's name is completely unknown. For convenience, the Prime Ministers of Britain that have worked with the MoM during Harry's lifetime are listed as a group under the heading Prime Minister.

Mrs Hetty Bayliss: She is one of several people to see the flying Ford Anglia when Ron took it to Hogwarts. She spotted it in Norfolk, Sep 1, 1992, around noon, which puts the Hogwarts Express on an unusual course if it's headed North.

Frank Bryce: b 1917-d Aug 18, 1994. As a young man he left his home in Little Hangleton to serve as soldier in WWII. He had a difficult time during the war and after he was discharged in 1942 due to a bad leg injury, he preferred to lead a quiet life away from crowds and loud noises. He returned to Little Hangleton and became the Riddle's gardener. He never socialized with anyone on staff at the house and kept himself to himself. Ever since he started work for the Riddles, he'd had a key to Riddle House's kitchen backdoor hanging in his cottage by the frontdoor. He was originally arrested for the Riddle murders in the summer of 1944, because he was a loner and had a key to the house, but released because there was no evidence. Frank saw Tom Riddle Jr in the town on the day of the murders, but he didn't know who he was and no one believed him because no one else saw him.

Through the 2 changes in ownership of Riddle House after the Riddles died, Frank stayed on and continued to work on the gardens when the weather was good. The current owner paid him to look after the house and let him continue to live in a run down 2-story cottage on the Riddle House property. The cottage is very basic and has no phone. From the downstairs kitchen window, the cottage has a view of Riddle House and Frank could see if anyone was up there making mischief. In the summer of 1994, Frank was nearing 77, his stiff leg forced him to limp and use a walking stick, and he had stiff knees as well. He was very deaf in his left ear but could still hear with his right one and had a croaky voice. In Aug of that year, Voldemort returned to Riddle House. Frank saw activity in the house and went to investigate. Nagini discovered him eavesdropping and Voldemort killed him with the Avada Kedavra curse.

Mr and Mrs Creevey: Colin and Dennis' parents. Both are Muggles. He works as a milkman.

Dennis (Unknown): A member of Dudley Dursley's gang since primary school.

Mary Dorkins: She is a correspondent with the Dursleys favorite 7pm news show. She usually gets the fluff pieces. She covered Bungy's story.

Dot (Unknown): A woman living in Little Hangleton during the 1940s. She had known Frank Bryce since childhood and always thought he had a bad temper, even as a child. She thought Frank should have left town even though he was never convicted of the murders because everyone believed he was guilty. She frequents the Hanged Man pub.

THE HARRY POTTER COMPANION

Dudley Dursley: aka Ickle Dudleykins, Popkin, Popkins, Sweetums, Duddy, Diddy, Dudders, Big D, Dud, Ickle Diddykins, Dinky Diddydums. Born Jun 24, 1980. A genuinely awful person, he has been hurting Harry since the day he arrived. As a small child he would pinch and poke Harry and as he got older he hated all exercise except for punching people smaller or younger than himself and Harry Hunting. Watching Harry get bullied by Vernon was one of his favorite entertainments, so it's no surprise that Dudley started and lead a gang at primary school which Piers Polkiss, Dennis, Malcolm and Gordon were (and still are) a part of. Dudley's followers are all big and stupid but Dudley is the biggest, stupidest and most mean spirited.

Every year from age 1-10, the Dursleys took Dudley and a friend, usually Piers , out for his birthday. They would go to adventure parks, hamburger restaurants or the movies where Dudley would eat a lot of chocolate ice cream and other junk foods. Dudley never invited Harry to these celebrations and the one time Harry was forced to tag along, Dudley's 11th birthday, Dudley threw a fit. This is not surprising as his parents spoiled him terribly and usually did anything he asked or gave him anything he wanted. For his 11th birthday he receives 39 expensive birthday presents.

He insists on getting more gifts each year than the year before, despite the fact he can't seem to use them without destroying them. He receives gifts like a new computer (implying he had an old one and broke it), a 2nd TV, a bike, a video camera and a gold watch. But he's so destructive that in less than a month, several items are broken and he's hit Mrs Figg on his bike. Dudley has so much stuff that he needed 2 bedrooms. The biggest room for himself, and the smallest one for his mostly broken toys.

When Harry received his first letter from Hogwarts, he was given the Dudley's second bedroom. But giving Harry a bedroom next to Dudley's was not much of a blessing as when Dudley goes to sleep at night he lets off grunting snores that are so loud Harry can hear them through the wall. Dudley didn't like the arrangement much either. He had a tantrum and threw his pet tortoise through the greenhouse roof, it is unknown if the tortoise survived. But, since Dudley can do no wrong in his parents eyes and Petunia hates pets, one hopes the tortoise crawled off to a better home with one of the neighbors.

At this stage, Dudley's favorite Monday night TV show was The Great Humberto. His favorite foods were soda pop, cake, chocolate bars and hamburgers. If his parents did anything he doesn't like, he has a tantrum or cried till they give in. And his parents always gave in. The Dursleys allowed him to watch TV or play video games and eat all day. They even bought him a widescreen TV for the kitchen so he didn't have to miss anything going to the living room from the fridge. This of course was probably how he ended up so overweight that he needed to go on a diet by age 13.

Entering his teens, Dudley has a large pink face, not much neck and small, watery blue eyes. His thick blond hair lays smooth on his fat head and he looks remarkably like a gorilla in Harry's opinion. He looks a lot like his father, which is no compliment, and when he dresses up, he usually wears a bowtie and dinner jacket, like his father. He is about 4 times bigger than Harry, initially because he's so fat. When the Smeltings' school nurse insists Dudley go a diet, the whole family sufferws as dieting only made Dudley even more bad tempered. At the start of his diet, because he frequently breaks his own things to show how upset he is, he chucked an expensive PlayStation computer out the window.

By 14 Dudley had become hooked on low-fat snacks and had trimmed down, but he was still a considerably larger person than Harry. Unfortunately now that he's thinner he beats up even more people. His gang continues to meet into his secondary school years. Piers (Dudley's best friend and Smeltings' schoolmate), Dennis, Malcolm and

Gordon get together every day during summer breaks. Dudley's parents don't seem to care that he gets terrible grades or notice that he's a bad person and his friends are equally horrid. But he keeps them in the dark about his gang activities and they seem to believe any story he tells them.

Dudley never liked sports much, although he has had swimming lessons and rides a racing bike, but he takes up boxing in school and becomes Junior Heavyweight Inter-School Boxing Champion of the Southeast in 1995. He enjoys boxing only because it enables him to be a bigger bully and Dudley's violent streak eventually takes him from blowing up aliens on computers to vandalizing parks, smoking on corners and throwing stones at passing cars and children with his leather-jacket clad gang. He terrifies the neighbor children, beats up on 10-year-olds, and actually likes being hated and feared.

One fear Dudley has though, and shares with his parents, is the use of magic in or outside of the house by Harry. He has had several bad experiences with magic and is quite terrified of it and all people who practice it. Dudley has had a pig tail attached to his bottom, his tongue swell up and grow to 4' and nearly been Kissed by a dementor. His reasons to fear magic have only increased with age. But Dudley could stand to be afraid of something and one expects if Dudley doesn't have an epiphany of some kind soon, magical or otherwise, he'll end up in prison by 17. Hopefully, having almost been soul-sucked into a living death, he'll turn himself completely around and do something worthwhile with his life.

Petunia Evans Dursley: b 1954. She is the wife of Vernon Dursley, overly fond mother of Dudley, dreadful sister of Lily Evans Potter and awful aunt of Harry Potter. Petunia is the daughter of Muggle parents. She is thin and blonde with large pale beady eyes. She has an extremely long neck, from spying on neighbors since childhood, a thin horsey-face and is terribly bony. Her voice is shrill and she has horselike teeth and habit of grinding them loudly when upset.

She is filled with rage toward her now deceased parents and jealousy toward her now deceased sister Lily that makes her seem an overlooked older sibling. Part of her anger and fear toward Harry comes from the fact that her parents were very proud of Lily, proud to have a witch in the family, and doted on her. Petunia was understandably jealous and grew to hate her sister and see her as a freak or abnormal. She refers to Lily as "my dratted sister" and her memories of her include Lily coming home every vacation with her pockets full of frog spawn and turning teacups into rats (which implies Lily did out of school magic).

Lily brought James Potter home to her parents' house once and Petunia didn't like him at all. Petunia used to spy on her sister when she was home and at one point overheard James telling Lily about dementors and where they work - Azkaban prison. After graduating school, she married Vernon, whom she informed of Lily's wizardry. She and Vernon did everything they could to eliminate Lily from their life. But one presumes they, attended Lily's wedding, were sent Harry's birth announcement (since they knew of him) and at least saw each other at Mr and Mrs Evans' funeral or funerals.

After their last meeting, a number of years went by during which Petunia lived happily at number 4 Privet Drive in Little Whinging, Surrey without seeing or speaking to Lily. She pretended that she didn't have a sister and that the wizarding world didn't exist, and Vernon did the same. Then one night, Dumbledore left Harry on her doorstep with a note. Petunia found him as she put out the milk bottles the next day, Nov 2, 1981 and promptly screamed. Dumbledore's note explained what happened to Lily and why it was imperative that Harry stay with her. So she knew that by letting Harry stay with her, Lily's charm would be activated and Voldemort and his followers would not be able to hurt Harry while he was with her. Then a very odd thing happens.

She persuades Vernon to take Harry in with the rather foolish promise that they would stamp the magic out of him. But Petunia must have known that was impossible from living with Lily. She would also know that accidental magic is possible. As she is more afraid of social embarrassment than actual magical attack (though for Vernon, it's the other way around) and doesn't want to keep Harry, a child she both hates and fears, why does she lie to Vernon to get him to accept a Harry? Her actual motivation is unknown but presumably Dumbledore made a threat in his note because when Vernon tried to throw Harry out in 1995, she received a Howler from Dumbledore, after which she overrules Vernon and lets Harry stay. Dumbledore's Howler only reminds her of the last note he left. It would seem to confirm that "his last" was indeed a threat.

But what is the threat? Alas it is unknown. It would have to be very significant to get her to lie to Vernon and take Harry against her own will. Perhaps the threat featured severe social embarrassment. The only thing that, as Harry and Moody both later realized, works on the Dursleys effectively. Whatever it is, it works and the Dursleys take Harry in in 1981, but they continue to pretend the wizarding world doesn't exist and Harry is not a wizard. However, in spite of accepting Harry into the household for his protection, Petunia doesn't accept Harry as a person. She feels put upon for having to take Harry in and raise him, which she is actually. She pretends he doesn't exist and does everything she can to foster that illusion.

She stuffs him in a cupboard, rather than gives him a room. Though she has loads of pictures of Dudley around the house, there are none of Harry anywhere. She feeds Harry the bare minimum to keep him alive, like dinners of a wilted salad or a bread and cheese sandwich. When Dudley goes on a severe diet, she gives an underweight Harry, less food than Dudley. She even tries to kill Harry by hitting him with a soapy frying pan one day. Worst of all, she continually denies him information about himself or his parents. She never speaks of them, allows no pictures of them in the house and lies to him about his parents' death, saying they died in a car crash.

Petunia is aware enough of the wizarding community that she recognizes wizards among Muggles. Whenever she sees wizards in public, like Dedalus Diggle tipping his violet hat at Harry, she immediately leaves the area. Whether this is from fear or disgust is unknown. One presumes since she has been under watch by the OoP for Harry's entire childhood, she must have seen wizards quite regularly, to her chagrin, but she may not know good ones from bad ones. One thing we do know, she lives in constant fear of what Harry may accidentally do by magic. She tries to keep the magic in Harry contained, but sometimes it just slips out, quite publicly. She usually knows when such cases happen and punishes Harry, but he gets the benefit of the doubt and sometimes she just ignores it completely.

When the Hogwarts' letters start arriving for Harry, Petunia tries to prevent them getting through. She knows all about Hogwarts from Lily and recognizes the letters immediately. When Harry finally gets his letter and the truth comes out about Lily's and James' death, she tells Harry that James was a bad person and Lily got herself blown up. She feels no remorse about their deaths and indeed seems a little bit happy she can finally vent her spleen about the people she hated most and felt did the most to ruin her youth and her happiness once she'd finally escaped them. She and Vernon let Harry go to school just to get rid of him, make him stay there during Christmas vacation and tell neighbors he's at an institute for criminal youth.

Presumably, sharing a house together for their first 20 years or so, Petunia would be fully aware of all aspects of Hogwarts because of Lily, including that there is a no out of school magic rule but she never seems to mention it to Vernon, who must find out from a letter sent by the MoM. She also must know about Voldemort, and what his first rise to power was like, but never mentions that either, perhaps because at some level she feels sorry for Harry and knows if she told Vernon that keeping Harry would result in danger for the family, Vernon would send him to an orphanage. Petunia knows she is placing her family in great danger keeping Harry, yet she does it. Either she is not as she seems, like Mrs Figg, or Dumbledore's threat against her was massive. Given that in cases where a wizarding child is born to Muggle parents, siblings are usually also wizards (eg, the Creevey brothers), Petunia might be a witch after all.

Petunia, while she hates being gossiped about and fears anyone learning about her sister or Harry being wizards, is herself a terrible gossip hound. She is very nosy and loves really nasty gossip, even though she pretends to be above liking it at all. She listens to gossip on the news, searches for it in papers and magazines and even spies on family, friends and neighbors. She's Bertha Jorkins, with a bit more sense. She strives to live the standard cookie-cutter upper middle class lifestyle and is affluent, bigoted, ignorant and full of ridiculous affectations. She calls the living room the lounge, drinks coffee with her pinkie out and wears frilly frocks to Vernon's office parties and a salmon pink cocktail dress to dinner parties. She thinks dressing up is a part of showing the world she is better and richer than anyone else.

On the complimentary side, she is always buying bowties for Dudley and Vernon but doesn't seem to be clotheshorse herself. She dotes on them both, especially Dudley, so, one could say she's loyal to those she loves. She's a very good cook, does all her own cooking and even throws dinner parties for Vernon's clients to advance his career. She is excellent at making fancy deserts, even if Harry never gets to eat them. She strives to keep a model house, even if it is so clean it's unnatural, and does all her own cleaning. She is a bit obsessional about cleaning (she actually looks for fingerprints on walls), she would never allow anything tattered, scruffy, frayed or dirty into her house (but Harry is there) and she hates animals which she thinks are dirty (but allows Dudley a pet tortoise in the house anyway). All and all, she's a complex woman and a bit of a softie.

Marge Dursley: aka Aunt Marge, Miss Marjorie Dursley. Marge is Vernon Dursley's unmarried sister. It isn't clear whether she is an older or younger sister, but she seem older, putting her birth at c 1952. She is, incredibly, even more abusive toward Harry than Vernon though completely unaware of Harry's magical background or abilities. She lives in the country in a house with a large garden and makes her living breeding bulldogs. She rarely leaves her home because of her great love for her 12 dogs. Ripper is her favorite dog and she physically carries him everywhere she goes. She doesn't live too far away from Little Whinging and comes to visit a couple times a year, when she isn't vacationing in the Isle of Wight.

Marge often visits her brother for a week at a time and stays with them in the guest bedroom. She pays Dudley every time she hugs him, 20 pounds, and always sends him very nice birthday and Christmas presents. She believes in using the cane on children in school, because she thinks beatings affect change in 99% of people beaten, which makes one wonder if she was beaten as a child. She hates Harry and delights in humiliating him, rather like Vernon. In the past she has beaten Harry's shins with a walking stick, given him dog biscuits for Christmas and allowed her dog Ripper to tree him for almost a day after he accidentally stepped on its tail.

She believes that Harry goes to St Brutus's Secure Center for Incurably Criminal Boys and in spite of this continues to irritate him. She made the fatal mistake of insulting Harry's mother in the most vulgar manner in the summer of 1993 and as a result Harry accidentally, magically inflated her like a balloon. She was deflated and had her memory modified by 2 members of the Accidental Magic Reversal Squad, but the Petunia and Vernon remember it still. Her table manners are atrocious; she burps at the table and doesn't even apologize. She drinks, swears and uses the people around her. She makes the other Dursleys look positively civil. It is implied that Petunia is not too fond of her.

Marge is a large beefy and purple-faced woman with tiny eyes and a large jaw. She looks very much like Vernon and even has a mustache. One presume she is yet another nasty blonde given Harry's inability to met a decent blonde person, wizard or Muggle. She has shovellike hands and a very firm grip that occasionally shatters glassware. She generally wears tweed jackets and skirts and carries a walking stick, occasionally used for beating people and one assumes her dogs. She has the sensitivity of a metal pole. Marge proves everyone has at least one embarrassing relative. Swearing: damn.

Vernon Dursley: b 1954. Husband of Petunia, brother of Marge, father of Dudley, uncle of Harry Potter. He is "perfectly normal," except that his hair is blonde and his mustache is black. He has a large wide pinkish purple face, small, watery blue eyes and no neck. He has thick hair lays smooth on his fat head and his enormous walrus mustache which is bushy and blows hither and thither when he's agitated. He is big and beefy, gets easily winded and has sausagelike fingers. Veins throb in his temples and he pulls hair out of his mustache when he gets really upset. Unfortunately he gets upset very easily because hates people that are in anyway different and likes to complain about things: people at work, the council, the bank, Harry, etc.

Vernon is a creature of habit, he has a settled routine and he likes it. He reads *The Daily Mail* every morning at breakfast and tells Harry to get a haircut. The mail usually comes in morning just before breakfast 6:30am - 7:00am, so he makes Harry get it and reads that at the table as well. He has marmalade on his toast. At 8:30 he kisses Petunia and Dudley goodbye on the cheek (overlooks Harry completely) and drives his company car to work. He works for Grunnings, a drill manufacturing company about 30 minutes from his home, and is a Sales Director there. He has a window office on the 9th floor. A good day at work involves yelling at a lot of people, either in person or on the phone, having a doughnut from the bakery across the road for lunch, yelling at few more people and at 5pm starting home. When he comes home he likes to watch the 7pm news, and on Friday nights the quiz show.

Vernon is greedy, abusive, arrogant and bigoted. He always carries a briefcase and wears an expensive suit to be intimidating, throws dinner parties at which he tells racist jokes to impress big clients and judges other men by how big and expensive their cars are because he gets a new company car every 2 years. He generally wears boring ties and shiny black shoes to work and dinner jacket with a bowtie for dinner parties. He drinks wine at lunch and dinner when home and has a large brandy when upset. He is extremely affluent and can afford almost anything he wants, except a vacation home in Majorca, and everything in his house is top of the line, new or expensive.

He dotes on his son, rather sickeningly so, and tea on holidays is usually whenever Dudley comes home. He sends his son to the same private boarding school he went to as a child. He doesn't believe in using imagination and as a result is incredibly small minded. He thinks teens that listen to the news are strange and if Harry does it that he must be up to something, which says a lot about his own teenage years. It isn't known if he went to university. He seems intelligent enough, though a bad person. He owns a rifle and a sleeping bag, which means he was probably into camping and hunting animals in his youth. As an adult he believes in hanging, cheats on the watering ban during droughts and can be physically abusive.

It's unclear how long he's lived at number 4 Privet Drive in Little Whinging, Surrey. Given his parents never call, visit or send presents, it may be that Vernon inherited the house at a relatively young age, possibly even before he was married. He and Petunia seem to have lived there all their married life. He married Petunia despite her family, which implies he does have some sense of fair play. He has a good marriage, even if he is slightly afraid of Petunia. He and his wife obviously communicate well as he knows all about Lily, what she was, as well as about Hogwarts and Dumbledore. He was even willing to take Harry in, though he vowed to stamp the magic out of Harry as part of the deal (which Petunia apparently didn't tell him was impossible).

Vernon makes Harry stay the holidays at school which is probably a blessing since Vernon snores so loudly Harry can hear him down the hall and, when he's home, Vernon locks up all his school things. However, Vernon does let Harry stay the summer (Jul 1 - Aug 31) and takes him to and picks him up from King's Cross Station, over a 3 hour drive each way, even though Harry could take a train to (or from) Little Whinging to King's Cross. He and Petunia give him birthday and Christmas presents, which are awful and may only be given to keep Lily's charm activated, but they do it. Still, he hates and fears Harry because never knows when accidental magic might happen. His biggest social fear is that someone will find out there is wizardry in the family and he refers to magic or wizardry or being a wizard as "you-know-what."

It was Vernon in Aug 1992 that had bars put on Harry's windows (that were subsequently ripped off one) and a catflap in the door to shove food through. It was Vernon that forbid Harry going back to school. It was Vernon that tried to throw Harry out when dementors were after him. It is doubtful Harry will ever be accepted by Vernon Dursley, and Vernon no doubt never wants to be accepted by Harry but if Voldemort's mind in Harry's body caused Harry to want to kill Dumbledore, Harry's beloved father figure, it presents a real problem for Vernon, whom Harry detests to begin with. The fact Voldemort killed his grandparents and father, his follower Barty Jr killed his own father, and his follower Severus Snape, clearly wanted to kill his father, in the past, shows that father killings are something of theme with Voldemort.

Possibly it's something Voldemort smiles on as generally practice or may even require of people, like an initiation, to become Death Eaters (this might have been the step too far for Regulus Black). Certainly Barty Jr and Severus Snape would have had no problems offing their fathers. With Vernon always harassing Harry and Harry being a very powerful wizard who is always having magical accidents and acting on Voldemort's impulses, how hard would it be for Harry to accidentally magically kill Vernon on an impulse from Voldemort? Not very. And how could Harry fight that impulse? Not very. The one thing that gets rid of Voldemort, love, Harry doesn't feel for Vernon. Swearing: effing, ruddy hell, codswallop, for God's sake.

Mr and Mrs Evans: Parents of Lily and Petunia. They were very fond of Lily and had no issues with her being a witch, which upset Petunia greatly. They died c 1976 about a year after Petunia was married. Evans is a Welsh name and possibly the Evans were from Wales.

Mark Evans: b 1985. Unrelated to Lily or Petunia Evans. He was 10 when Dudley and his gang beat him up in Aug 1995 for cheeking Dudley.

Mr Angus Fleet: Resident of Peebles, Scotland. He is one of several Muggles to see the flying Ford Anglia when Ron drove it to Hogwarts. He is the only one that called the police.

Mrs Finch-Fletchley: She had Justin down for Eton. She was slightly disappointed by his going to Hogwarts, but since reading Lockhart's books she has realized how useful

THE HARRY POTTER COMPANION

it would be to have a fully trained wizard in the family. It's difficult to understand her conversion, given most Muggle houses don't have encounters with werewolves, banshees, gnomes and the like, how useful could Justin be?

Mr Finnigan: The father of Seamus. He didn't know till after the marriage that his wife was a witch, because she hid that from him. It was a nasty shock, but the relationship apparently survived.

Colonel Fubster: The Colonel is a neighbor of Marge Dursley. He's retired and looks after Marge's dogs when she is away. He drowned one of Marge's runts in 1992.

Gordon (Unknown): A member of Dudley's gang since primary school and a smoker.

The Great Humberto: His real name is unknown. This is the character he plays on a Monday night TV show of the same name that is one of Dudley's favorites.

Mr and Mrs Granger: The Muggle parents of Hermione Granger. In the summer of 1992 they met Mr Weasley and were taken to the Leaky Cauldron for a drink. They later had a distressing encounter with Lucius Malfoy. They are both dentists and wanted Hermione to continue with braces rather than magically fix her teeth. In 1994 magical means won out. It's not clear how they took the news. They like to spend the summer in France or other warm places and in the winter they like to ski.

Hanged Man, Pub Owner: A woman in Little Hangleton. She was sympathetic toward Frank Bryce after the 1944 murders. She knew he'd had a hard war and was willing to cut him slack.

Malcolm (Unknown): A member of Dudley's gang since primary school and a smoker.

Mr and Mrs Mason: A rich builder and his wife that the Dursleys invited to a dinner party on Harry's birthday in 1992. He's a golfer, she's deathly afraid of birds. The meal ended in disaster and the big deal Vernon was negotiating with Mr Mason for drills never closed.

Jim McGuffin: A weatherman for the 7pm news that the Dursleys always watch.

The Milkman: A male milkman that delivers milk and eggs on behalf a dairy to Dursleys. He collects the empty milk bottles left on the doorstep. He seems to come Wednesday and Saturday mornings. He handed 2 dozen eggs to Petunia (with Hogwarts' letters in them) through a window once. The Dursleys use quite an extraordinary amount of butter, milk and eggs in their daily lives.

St Mungo: A well-reputed monk and healer in the 5th century.

The Newscasters: The Dursleys love the 7pm news and watch it every night about the time they have tea. The newsanchor is Ted, the weatherman is Jim McGuffin, and Mary Dorkins is a field reporter who does fluff pieces.

Mrs Next Door: The woman who lives next to the Dursleys at either number 2 or 6. She's a married woman with problems, a daughter and a dog that got run over by Dudley's toy tank. She also likes to garden and usually has runner beans growing in the backyard vegetable patch in the summer.

Mrs Number Seven: A married woman that lives across the road from the Dursleys on Privet Dr. She can see Number 4 from behind her net curtain windows.

Mr Payne: A Muggle in charge of the second field of campsites for the QWC 1994 where the Diggorys stayed.

Mrs Polkiss: Piers' mom, poor woman. She must be fairly well off to send her son to a private boarding school.

Piers Polkiss: Dudley's best friend. A fellow classmate in primary school and is now at Smeltings with Dudley. He is a scrawny boy with a face like a rat. He's the one that usually holds people's arms behind their backs while Dudley hits them. A member of Dudley's gang since primary school, he's also a smoker. He went with Dudley on his

11th birthday trip to the Zoo, where a snake escaped and subsequently told the Dursleys that Harry had been talking to snake.

Mr (Unknown) Prentice: He lives on Wisteria Walk. Mrs Figg knows him.

Mr Prime Minister: The Prime Minister of Britain. There have been various PMs during the time frame Harry is concerned with. During Voldemort's first rise to power

Edward Heath (1970-1974),

Sir (James) Harold Wilson (1974-1976),

(Leonard) James Callaghan (1976-1979) and

Margaret Thatcher (1979-1990)

were the successive PMs. Mrs Thatcher was PM at Harry's birth and worked with MoM on the Sirius Black (Peter Pettigrew) mass murder incident.

John Major (1990 -1997) became PM just before Harry started school and worked with the MoM on the escape of Sirius Black. The final years of his administration occur just as the return of Voldemort is recognized by the MoM. Tony Blair (1997-present) was the PM during Harry's last school years. It would seem he should be involved with the MoM, or at least informed of their doings, in the final stages of the new Voldemort crisis but this remains to be seen.

Railview Hotel, Owner: A woman who tried to deliver Harry's Hogwarts' letters, over 100, but was intercepted by Vernon Dursley.

Mr & Mrs Riddle: d Jul/Aug 1944. The elderly, rich, snobbish, rude parents of Tom Riddle Sr. They were always very unpopular and no one in Little Hangleton was sad when they died. They were found dead along with Tom Riddle Sr by their maid in the drawing room of Riddle House. They were dressed in their dinner clothes. Killed by the Avada Kedavra curse of Tom Riddle Jr who was out to avenge himself on his Muggle father.

Tom Riddle Sr: d Jul/Aug 1944. Described by his son as a Muggle and a fool, Tom Sr fell in love with a witch (Unknown Marvolo) in the village of Little Hangleton, but he left her when he found out about her being a witch because he didn't like magic. He returned to his parents before Tom Riddle Jr was born. It is unknown if he was ever married to her, or if he even knew about the baby he'd fathered. Murdered by his son Tom Jr along with his parents in the drawing room of Riddle House by the Avada Kedavra curse, he was still in his dinner clothes when found by the maid. He is buried under a huge marble headstone that reads: TOM RIDDLE in the Little Hangleton churchyard. The stone was cracked in a wizard's duel in Jun 1995. His tomb was desecrated by Peter Pettigrew on behalf of Tom Jr, who wanted one of his father's bones for use in his rebirthing. Which bone is unknown, as it had turned to dust by the time it was retrieved; which was in itself highly unusual as most bodies last several hundred years in such a damp cold climate.

Riddle House, Cook: A gossipy but friendly, outgoing woman from Little Hangleton, that worked at Riddle House during WWII. She has has a fondness for sherry and frequents the Hanged Man pub. She thought Frank Bryce a bit queer and likely to have killed the Riddles on the basis that he regularly rebuffed her offers of tea and was a bit of a loner.

Riddle House, Maid: She worked at Riddle House and found the bodies of the Riddles in 1944.

The Roberts: Mr Roberts was the man in charge of the first field of campsites where Arthur and his party stayed for QWC 1994. His campsites are on a gentle slope that go up to the woods at the top of the hill. Mr Roberts is rather immune to the Memory Charm and Obliviators had to reapply it frequently. Mr Roberts, his wife, their older daughter and younger son, live in a small stone cottage, next to a gate that leads into

the campsite. He and his family were all assaulted by the Death Eaters just after QWC 1994 ended. They were saved by the opportune appearance of the Dark Mark (which must have been a first: people saved under the Dark Mark) and their were memories modified after their rescue.
Rowboat Owner: A toothless old man who let the Dursleys and Harry his rowboat to get to Hut-on-the-Rock. Kind of an evil fellow.
Ted (Unknown): The anchor for the 7pm news that the Dursley watch every night.
Mr and Mrs Thomas: Dean's parents. Their first names are unknown. They never read *The Daily Prophet*.
Yvonne (Unknown): A friend of Petunia's. She is on vacation in 1991 Majorca when Dudley has his 11th birthday.
The Zoo Director: He apologized to Dursley's for the released snake incident and gave Petunia strong, sweet tea to help her recover.
Zoo, Keeper of the Reptile House: He worked at the Zoo in the reptile house where Harry vanished the the glass from the boa's tank.

MUGGLE STUFF

Included in this section are odds and ends about Muggles that turn up and don't really fit anyplace else.

ASSORTED

Tea: A light meal that occurs between lunch and whenever one has dinner. For the Dursley's it's at 7pm, which would make dinner at 9pm. For Hagrid it's around 3pm making dinner around 5pm. Tea is usually served, along with buns or small sandwiches. Anyone interested in recipes for tea goodies can consult the Recipes section in Part II.
West Ham: aka the West Ham United Football Club. Dean' soccer team. Their colors are sky blue and claret. Supporters of this team are called Hammers, because of the crossed hammers on the teams insignia. West Ham is a suburb of London to the east of Bethnal Green. It's unknown if Dean is from that area or not.

DAYS

Bonfire Night: aka Guy Fawkes Day. Nov 5th. An annual celebration in Britain, commemorating the day a plot by Guy Fawkes to blow up the houses of Parliament was foiled (1605). People have big bonfires to burn in effigy the people they don't like, such as Guy Fawkes.
Boxing Day: Dec 26. Traditionally the day one boxes up Christmas leftovers and distributes them to the poor in one's parish or community. Today these boxes are given to one's postal worker. It's an early Victorian tradition.

GAMES

Hangman: A game Harry and Ron play in History when they aren't passed out from boredom. It involves one person choosing a word and the other person trying to guess the letter and solve the puzzle before the hanged man (a 13-part stick figure) can be drawn. For every guessed letter, right or wrong, a part of the figure is drawn. If the figure is complete before one completes the answer, one loses. See schematic U.
Tic-Tac-Toe: A game Harry and Ron play usually in their school books. It involves successfully getting 3 Xs or 3 Os in a row on a 3 space by 3 space grid. See schematic U.

Tenpins: This is a type of bowling, involving knocking down 10 bottle-shaped bowling pins 15" high with a large 27" in circumference ball. Each player can bowl 2 balls in each of 10 frames. It is one of Dumbledore's favorite pastimes. It's played outdoors with wooden pins.

Trains

InterCity 125: This is a high-speed train engine. It first came out in 1975. There are now newer, faster models in use today, but the InterCity 125s are still in wide use pulling trains all over Britain.

The Underground: This is an underground train, or subway, system that has been around since the early part of the 20th century. It services most of greater London area and connects with British Rail (the above ground trains) to take people all over Britain. It does not run on Christmas Day. People call it the Underground or the London Underground. Albus Dumbledore has a scar on his left knee that resembles a map of the Underground which he says is very useful. He got it from a very powerful curse that failed, like Harry's. He probably got in 1945 from Grindelwald, making the scar a bit outdated as a map. See schematic Zc

Part VI. Where and When

Places

This section contains wizarding and Muggle places. Subsections for wizarding locales are Diagon Alley and Environs, Hogsmeade and Other Wizarding Places which will include wizarding locales in London that are not mentioned elsewhere and Muggle towns that have a League Quidditch team, which means a substantial wizarding population as well. Subsections for Muggle locales are Little Hangleton, Little Whinging, London (including nonwizarding locales only), and Other Muggle Places. Hogwarts, being a substantial location with many sublocales within it, is listed in a separate section entirely devoted to the school in Part II. The MoM in Part I.

For the sake of those not living in Britain who probably don't know the difference between a hamlet, village (Hogsmeade), town (Little Whinging) and city (London) a short explanation follows. In Medieval times (c 900-1450) Britain ranked communities the importance the Catholic Church accorded it. People could find their way geographically by type of church a community had (or hadn't). As a rule a hamlet was a place with a very small population that didn't have a church of its own, the village had a church without a steeple and a bit larger population, the town had a steepled church and even more people, and the city had a cathedral with a bishop and the largest population.

DIAGON ALLEY AND ENVIRONS

The Apothecary: Located in Diagon Alley, most students come here every year to restock their potions kit supplies. Outside by the shop door one is likely to find a barrel of dragon dung. Please do not ask why dragon dung is medicinal, I don't know and refuse to investigate the matter. Inside it has barrels of slimy stuff on the floor; jars of herbs, dried roots and bright powders lining the walls; and bundles of feathers, strings of fangs and gnarled claws hanging from ceiling. The place has a horrible smell much like bad eggs and rotten cabbages (shades of Mrs Figg). Although basic potion ingredients can be purchased here, the shop carries a wide range of products and can meet the needs of the most discerning potionmaker. A few things one might pick up at the Apothecary would be dragon liver, unicorn horns or beetle eyes.

Borgin and Burkes: Located in Knockturn Alley, only a Dark wizard would show up here intentionally. It is the largest shop in the Knockturn Alley and a purveyor of some of the darkest and most illegal Dark Arts items available on the market (or black market). Borgin and Burkes' is a large, dimly lit shop with a cold stone hearth toward the back. There's a large black cabinet with doors on it at the back of the shop as well (possibly a Vanishing Cabinet). At the front of the shop are glass cases with a bell on the counter. Behind the counter is a back room for the employees, or possibly some sort of workshop for the creation or repair of Dark Arts items. There may be housing above the shop.

At Borgin and Burkes' they buy as well as sell Dark Arts merchandise. Doing Dark Arts is legal, up to a point, and a wizard's personal preference. It doesn't necessarily mean the wizard is a committing criminal act, though many are. That Dark Arts shops exist, but only in a very limited way, shows that few wizards go this route. Lucius Malfoy of course did and arrive at Borgin and Burkes in the summer of 1992 to sell some MoM-banned poisons. Things one might see at Borgin and Burkes' include the Hand of Glory, a bloodstained cards, a glass eye, a shelf of skulls, a hangman's rope or a murderous opal necklace. The shop decor leans to the Dark side a well with evil-looking masks on the walls, an assortment of human bones on the counter and rusty spiked instruments (probably for torture) hanging from the ceiling.

The Cauldron Shop: Located in Diagon Alley. The actual name is unknown. The sell cauldrons of all sizes and materials including copper, brass, pewter, silver and even gold. Cauldrons can be self-stirring or collapsible as well. Every student needs one, and most wizards have at least two, one for cooking and one for potionmaking. Sad things have happened when wizards have tried to get by with just one cauldron in the home. Perhaps this shop is where Peter got the stone cauldron for the rebirthing, but it given a giant stone cauldron's limited magical uses, it may have been too risky and order to place. Certainly it seems the sort of special order item that could, and probably should, attract a MoM Auror's attention.

Diagon Alley: Diagon Alley is located in central London directly behind the Leaky Cauldron. Just off Diagon Alley is Knockturn Alley. From the archway into Diagon Alley, the twisting and turning cobbled street runs further than the eye can see. Like any street, it has sidewalks, wastecans, streetlights and shops with interesting merchandise. Here a wizard can find a perfect moving model of the galaxy in a glass ball, the Firebolt racing broom or the latest in dress robes. This alleyway is the main shopping district for wizards from all over Britain. It's the place where one shops for magical supplies that are legal and on the up and up. There are no Dark Arts supplies here. The alley has many cafes with brightly colored umbrellas shading outdoor seating. Harry thinks it's a great place to just sit and wizardwatch.

THE HARRY POTTER COMPANION

Eeylops Owl Emporium: Located in Diagon Alley, it sells owls exclusively. Owls are very popular and the in-thing as pets, but they are also useful for mail delivery. Among the many breeds Eeylops carries are tawny, screech, barn, brown and snowy. Inside the shop it is dark (which owls prefer) and full of rustling sounds and flickering jewel-bright eyes. Hagrid bought Harry's birthday gift, the snowy owl Hedwig, at this shop.

Florean Fortescue's Ice Cream Parlor: Located in Diagon Alley, it is a favorite haunt of Harry's for doing homework and wizardwatching. Florean is an expert on magical history, particularly medieval magical history, and makes a mean Choco-Nut sundae.

Flourish and Blotts: Located in Diagon Alley, it's the bookstore where Hogwarts' students buy all their textbooks. It contains all manner of volume, large and leather-bound like paving slabs, small and silk-bound the size of postage stamps, invisible, full of symbols and even some with nothing at all in them. Usually the front window has golden spellbooks the size of paving slabs (3' x 3'). In summer 1993, *The Monster Book of Monsters* was in the front window, in a large iron cage, probably more because the owners were afraid of them hurting the employees or customers than anything else. The books spent their time wrestling, snapping and ripping each other apart. Only the manager, with dragon hide gloves and a poker, went near them.

The shop has several assistants in addition to the 2 owner-managers and everyone is very helpful. But one doesn't really need much help as all the sections are well laid out and easily findable. Apparently the owners don't think much of divination as they have set up the fortune-telling section in a back corner of the shop. One employee, perhaps a manager, even warned Harry off buying a divination book. That's dedication. Or maybe he didn't want to deal with a future return. Occasionally the store hosts author signings at the back of the shop. These are usually announced by a banner over the upper windows of the shop. Crowds lined up outside the shop's double doors to get in to see Gilderoy Lockhart signing copies of his autobiography, *Magical Me*, at a table here one afternoon in the summer of 1992. Sometimes, if the author is important enough, even the press shows up.

Gambol and Japes Wizarding Joke Shop: Located in Diagon Alley, Fred and George Weasley and Lee Jordan went here to stock up on various supplies such as Dr. Filibuster's Fabulous Wet-Start, No-Heat Fireworks, before heading back to school one summer. The Weasley twin's joke shop is in direct competition with this joke shop now.

Gringotts Wizarding Bank: aka Gringotts. The only known wizarding bank, and certainly the safest place in the world to keep valuable things - barring Hogwarts. Its vaults are 100s of miles under London and a virtual warren of passages, tunnels, unpassable terrain, dragons and other security measures keep treasure safe. The bank is run by goblins, who can be extremely nasty when crossed. Please note the use of the word goblin means male goblins in this entry as no female goblins work at Gringotts. Some wizards, male and female, also work at the bank, but they are the minority.

Gringotts building is made of snowy white marble building and is that tallest in Diagon Alley, towering over all the other shops. How many floors it has exactly is unknown, but probably at least 3 above the ground floor. Standing beside the bank's burnished bronze (Knut) frontdoors, wearing a uniform of scarlet and gold, is a security goblin. If one goes up the white steps, the goblin will bow. There is a second pair of doors, made of silver (Sickle) with a warning poem engraved on them. Beyond the inner doors, with a pair of bowing goblins on either side, is a vast marble hall with an uncountable number of doors (probably gold for Galleons) leading off of it.

ACASCIAS RIPHOUSE

About 100 goblins sit on high stools behind a long counter in the main hall. They can usually be found scribbling in large ledgers, weighing coins in brass scales or examining precious stones through magnifying glasses. Other goblins will be showing individuals, usually wizards, in and out of the golden doors that lead off the marble hall. Withdrawals and deposits require that one have the tiny gold key to the numbered vault one wishes to open. This key will be asked for at the counter and inspected for authenticity. High-security vaults do not have keys, but the goblins are well aware of who owns which high-security vault.

After authentication, a goblin will escort visitors through a door leading off the hall. Beyond the door is a narrow torchlit stone passageway which slopes steeply downward and has little railway tracks on its floor. A small cart like a rollercoaster cart comes when whistled for by a goblin and once everyone is seated will, without being told where to go, hurtle through a maze of passages, around tight corners, past an underground lake where huge stalactites and stalagmites grow, over a underground ravine and travel deep down into the earth where the air is cold and eye-stinging. Every now and then one might pass a burst of fire, appearing at end of a passage where a guard dragon resides.

It would be impossible to find one's way in or out of Gringotts' vault area if one was not a goblin and foolish to try. If anyone attempts to breach a high-security vault by touching the door to get it to melt away as the goblins do to, she or he would instead be sucked through the door and trapped inside the vault. As the goblins only do a sweep for trapped thieves once every 10 years it is unlikely the individual would survive till she or he was found. Only a powerful Dark wizard could break in and get out again (Pr Quirrell, Voldemort, etc). Break-ins do however upset the goblins and they will go to any lengths to find a thief so ultimately it just isn't worth attempting.

Harry's safe (smaller than the vaults) is reached through a small door in the passageway's wall. Griphook the goblin unlocked the safe door for him and green smoke billowed out when Harry first went to it. Since the green smoke was not toxic and Harry's coins appeared in perfect condition after 10 years underground, it may have been a anti-tarnish device as bronze and silver tend to go off if not polished by constant handling. Harry had inherited mounds of gold coins, columns of silver and heaps of little bronze Knuts. His wizard money could be exchanged for Muggle money if he'd wished to, but that's probably just an added reason why Harry didn't tell the Dursleys he's rich. Gringotts can convert Muggle money to wizard as well, as the Grangers discovered.

Vault 713: Dumbledore's (Hogwart's) high-security vault at Gringotts. It is where Dumbledore first kept the Sorcerer's Stone. Like all high-security vaults, it has no keyhole. The escort goblin strokes door with his finger and it melts away. It was broken into on same day Harry and Hagrid were there, Jul 31, 1991, but fortunately after Hagrid had removed the stone from the vault. Probably Dumbledore chose this vault for its easy to remember number; 713 is Harry's birthday (31.7) written backward in European date style.

The Junk Shop: Located in Diagon Alley, its real name is unknown. It's a tiny shop, full of wizarding odds and ends like broken wands, lopsided brass scales and old cloaks covered in potion stains. Percy was found here in summer 1992 reading the small book *Prefects Who Gained Power*.

Knockturn Alley: Located just off Diagon Alley near Gringotts, it is a dark narrow street devoted to trade in Dark or otherwise shady merchandise. It's where most of the not quite legal things in the wizarding community are traded. It has a dark narrow street that's the main shopping district and it's lined on either side with dingy

THE HARRY POTTER COMPANION

alleyways that have all Dark Arts shops. Considered the bad side of town, most good wizards would never go there. Hagrid goes there, but only to buy Flesh-Eating Slug Repellent for the school cabbages. Other things one might see there are shrunken heads, black spiders, poisonous candles, shabby wizards or a whole tray of human fingernails.

The Leaky Cauldron: A tiny grubby-looking London pub located on a street in a Muggle shopping district. The rear wall of the pub's back garden serves as gateway to Diagon Alley. The pub is on Charing Cross Road, residing between a big bookshop and a record store, just near a hamburger restaurant and some movie theaters. It always overlooked by Muggles, whose vision slides right over it - due to various enchantments one assumes. The Leaky Cauldron is a famous place, but what it's famous for is unknown. The interior is very dark and shabby. It is usually filled with warlocks in for an ale or whisky and arguing about ongoing magical developments or old witches up from the country for a day of shopping, sipping sherry from tiny glasses, smoking long pipes and chatting with friends. One might also see hags or dwarfs there as well.

In addition to the front pub, the Leaky Cauldron has private parlors. Just down a narrow passageway from the bar is a small parlor with a fireplace where Harry met with Fudge in the summer of 1993. From the parlor one can take the handsome narrow wooden staircase up to the inn section of the Leaky Cauldron. Harry stayed in a room with a brass 11 on the door for 3 weeks one summer (it seemed like 2 because it went so fast, but any calendar will show it was actually 3). His room had a lock on the door, a very comfortable bed, highly polished oak furniture, a fireplace, a wardrobe and a couple of windows from which he could hear buses in the Muggle street behind him and the sounds of Diagon Alley's invisible patrons below him. Every day someone came in to tidy up the room and see to the fires. Beside the bed was a mirror and a wash basin in a stand. The mirror spoke in a wheezy voice, usually about his appearance, but sometimes went off on other things as well. Generally the mirror was quite supportive.

The inn usually has many guests and plenty of rooms, at least 12, should they need to spend the night after 1 firewhisky too many. During the summer of 1993, just at the end of August, Hermione and the Weasley clan stayed at the pub. Ron and Percy had to share Room 12. The pub is a very reputable place. Prices are probably reasonable due to heavy traffic. It is owned by an old man named Tom, who also acts as the pub's host, innkeeper and bartender. He seems to have owned the inn since before 1980 and may have inherited it. A young man works there as a dishwasher. Hagrid is a regular customer and a friend of Tom's. Everyone at the pub usually recognizes Harry when he walks in, much to Harry's chagrin.

People can reach the Leaky Cauldron by Floo Network and return home from there the same way. Generally patrons use the hearth in the main section of the pub for this. Public Muggle transport does stop on the opposite side of the street and Hermione and the Grangers use the bus to get to the Leaky Cauldron. At the back of the pub is a small walled courtyard with the trashcans and weeds, the back wall of which is the gateway to Diagon Alley. Tap the brick three up and two across with the point of a wand three times and the bricks in the middle of the wall will begin to move away and form an archway into Diagon Alley. Once one passes through the archway, the arch shrinks and it instantly turns back into a solid wall.

Madam Malkin's Robes For All Occasions: Located in Diagon Alley, it is where Hogwarts' student generally get their uniforms. Madam Malkin and her witch assistants will alter the robes on the premises while one waits. Harry first met Draco Malfoy here in Jul 1991 when he ended up next to him on fitting stool while having his new robes pinned for length. Harry went back to Madam Malkin's in Aug 1993 to buys new robes, as his old ones become several inches too short in the arm and leg. There are other robe shops in Diagon Alley, including second-hand robe shops, but Gladrags Wizarding Wear is really the only other big name robe shop they compete with.

Magical Menagerie: Located in Diagon Alley, this pet shop sells all sorts of magical animals. The shop has fire crab in the front window and inside is stuffed with all manner of cage and creature. Cramped, smelly and noisy, one will find purple toads, magical black rats and white rabbits, streelers, magical cats and kneazles, puffskiens, magical snakes and ravens, and the odd double-ended newt. Run by an extremely knowledgeable witch who wears heavy black reading glasses, it is the place to go for magical animals, advice on animal care or tonics and remedies. Hermione bought Crookshanks here in Aug 1993.

Obscurus Books: Located in 18a Diagon Alley, it has been the publisher of Newt Scamander's *Fantastic Beasts and Where to Find Them* since the 1927 first edition to the present day. It is owned by Augustus Worme.

Ollivanders: Located in Diagon Alley, Ollivanders has been a aorund since 382 BC and is considered the place to go for a wand. The shop's sign has peeling gold letters and only a single wand on faded purple cushion sits in dusty front window but this doesn't deter buyers. A tiny tinkling bell on door alerts Mr Ollivander a customer is there. Mr Ollivander is a maker of wands, meaning he collects the wood and the core materials himself then crafts the wands. He is from a long line of wandmakers. Probably he has a workshop at the back of his store. It is a tiny, gloomy store with dusty air and empty but for shelves filled with 1,000s of narrow boxes of wands and one spindly chair. It feels like a very strict library, probably because any wand will work for any wizard and if a young wizard accidentally, or intentionally, grabbed a bunch of wands at one time and used them the consequences could be disastrous. There boxed wands are piled neatly right up to the ceiling of the shop. The very dust and silence seemed to tingle with secret magic to Harry. James Potter, Lily Evans, Hagrid, Ron, Cedric and Tom Riddle all bought their wands at Ollivanders.

Wands Harry tried before finding the right fit:
9" beechwood with a dragon heartstring core that was nice and flexible.
7" maple with a phoenix feather core that was quite whippy.
8.5" ebony with a unicorn hair core that was springy.
And lots more, till Harry finally found the perfect wand, 11" holly with a phoenix feather core that was nice and supple.

Wands may vary in price, but 7 Galleons was what Harry paid for his wand (about $50 US).

Quality Quidditch Supplies: Located in Diagon Alley beside an ink and parchment store, this shops sells brooms, robes and all related Quidditch paraphernalia. One could buy a full set of Chudley Cannon robes, a League broom or regulation Quidditch balls there. This was the shop that first had the Firebolt prototype on display in Aug 1993.

Second-Hand Robe Shop: Located in Diagon Alley. Molly gets robes for her children here. She bought Ron's dress robes here in 1994. They were 100 years old and way out of fashion, so obviously the shop keeps things for a long time.

Stationary Store: Located in Diagon Alley beside Quality Quidditch Supplies, the store is unnamed. They carry all manner of stationary supplies including Hermione's study planner that keeps giving annoying advice and pointed reminders to study every time it's opens. They sell parchment, quills and even ink that changes color as one writes (Harry bought some in 1991). Wizards usually develop a favorite color of ink they like to use Snape likes black ink, Lockhart lilac, Hogwarts mail always use green,

Harry uses red. But whether that's a preference or because he's in Gryffindor and students are supposed to use their house color (Gryffindor red, Ravenclaw blue, Slytherin green, Hufflepuff black) is unknown.

Weasleys' Wizarding Wheezes: Located in 93 Diagon Alley, this is Fred and George's joke shop. They started as as mail-order business selling trick sweets and assorted joke items they had created and expanded to the shop with Harry's 1,000G financial backing. The shop opened in May 1996 after Fred and George suddenly left school. It became highly successful within just 6 weeks. The twins seem to be on speaking terms with Molly so she must approve and be glad for them and allows them to continue living at home.

WhizzHard Books: Located in 129B Diagon Alley, it is the publisher of Kennilworthy Whip's *Quidditch Through the Ages.*

HOGSMEADE

Dervish and Banges: Located in Hogsmeade's High Street, it is a wizarding equipment shop that sells magical instruments. It can also check and repair malfunctioning instruments.

Gladrags Wizardwear: Located in London, Paris, and Hogsmeade according to their advert at QWC 1994, it is located in Hogsmeade's High Street. Harry bought Dobby some lurid socks there for helping him with the TT Task 2, including a pair with flashing gold and silver stars and another that screamed loudly when they became too smelly.

High Street: The main street of Hogsmeade village. Dervish and Banges, Gladrags Wizardwear, Honeydukes, the Post Office, the Three Broomsticks and Zonko's are all on the High Street.

Hog's Head: Located on a side street in Hogsmeade, it's 1 of 2 village pubs. It has the reputation for playing host to strange, secretive or weird folk and illegal doings. Hagrid got his illegal dragon egg gambling with a hooded stranger here. It is the least expensive inn in town, so sometimes the broke are here as well, like Sybill in 1979. It is the fashion for patrons to keep their hoods up at all times and never introduce themselves. Anonymity is the Hog's Head's specialty. The pub doesn't get a lot of student traffic, but it is ok for students to go to this pub. Pr Flitwick suggests students bring their own glasses. Butterbeer is 2S a bottle at the Hog's Head.

A battered and creaky wooden sign, hung from a rusty bracket outside the pub, depicts a decapitated wild boar's head leaking blood onto a white cloth around it. Inside it's a small dingy one room pub that is very dirty and stinks of goat. The bay windows are encrusted with grime and very little light gets in. Stubs of candles flickering low on rough wooden tables provide the only, rather shadowy, light. The floor appears to be earthen, but is actually stone with centuries of accumulated filth on top. An ancient wooden till with a slide drawer that opens automatically sits on the countertop. The Hog's Head barman is possibly Aberforth Dumbledore. His description fits Dumbledore, Harry thinks he looks vaguely familiar and Dumbledore's brother is apparently a slightly shady character himself who was in trouble once for doing charms on goats.

Hogsmeade: Established prior to the 1600s, it is Britain's only 100% wizarding population village. A village inn (probably at the Hog's Head) was used the headquarters for the 1612 Goblin rebellion. It's located within walking distance of Hogwarts. Third years and above can visit Hogsmeade on certain Saturdays during the school year if they have a permission slip signed by a parent or guardian. The village is

ACASCIAS RIPHOUSE

a sanctuary for hags, vampires and other beings that just don't quite fit in a enough to be able to live in a Muggle town. The village is very quaint with thatched cottages and a High Street lined with interesting shops. It is especially attractive at Christmas when decorated for the holidays and covered in a crisp layer of snow. See schematic Z for details.

Hogsmeade Hiding Place: Located just outside Hogsmeade. Sirius stayed here at Dumbledore's request during the TT. To reach it one must pass through the town on the High Stree and go up a winding lane where the countryside is wild and there are only a few cottages with large gardens. Going up the mountain in whose shadow Hogsmeade lay, turn a corner and pass a turnstile at the end of the lane. Proceed up the scrubby, rocky mountain steppes along the steep, winding path up until a narrow fissure appears in the rock face. The fissure is the entrance to a cool dimly lit, rather roomy, cave.

Hogsmeade Post Office: Located on the High Street, across from the Three Broomsticks. It's an interesting place to visit just to look at. They have about 300 owls on the shelves, all of which are color coded by speed of delivery. From great grey owls that could haul something across the Continents to tiny scops owls that only do local deliveries, the Post Office has them all.

Hogsmeade Station: The Hogwarts Express stops at the Hogsmeade village's tiny platform and station house. Usually no one sees the town when they arrive in the night as a hill blocks it. At night the station keeps its windows glowing, providing a dry well-lit place for students to pause in before continuing on. Outside the Hogsmeade Station is a dirt track where the thestral-drawn stagecoaches pick up students who are in their 2nd year and above. First years follow Hagrid from the platform down the path through the pine forest that leads to the Lake. When pulling out of Hogsmeade station, it quickly disappears behind the mountains.

Honeydukes: Located in the High Street, it is a famous sweet shop. It has everything imaginable in wizarding as well as normal candies. It is a favorite stop for Hogwarts' students. The shop is run by Mr and Mrs Honeydukes who work the floor and live above shop. The shop has mullioned windows and a bell on the door in case someone is in the cellar or upstairs when a customer turns up. A wooden staircase leads down into the cellar which is loaded with wooden crates and boxes of candies stacked all around on the dusty floor. The cellar has a trapdoor which leads to a tunnel that leads to the inside of a statue on the 3rd floor of Hogwarts castle. Mr and Mrs Honeydukes must know about the trapdoor and tunnel. After all they must have wondered how Fred and George show up in the shop for sweets after the shop was closed. Probably they don't really mind because a sale is a sale no matter the time and they want to maintain a good relationship with the students.

Madam Puddifoot's Coffee Shop: Located on a side road off the High Street, it is a cramped, steamy little place where everything is decorated in frills or bows including the napkins. Frequented by Hogwarts students who are in relationships or dating, it serves coffee but it's really more of a tea shop. Harry was there once and will probably never return. On Valentine's day, the shop becomes even more lurid with golden cherubs hovering over the small circular tables and occasionally throwing pink confetti at the patrons below. It was the scene of Harry's disastrous first date-breakup with Cho in Feb 1996.

Scrivenshaft's Quill Shop: Located in the High Street just before turning the corner to go up the side street to the Hog's Head, it's the local stationary store. They have a display of handsome pheasant quills in the front window. They keep their quills displayed in copper pots. Hermione bought a long black and gold quill there for 15S 2K.

Shrieking Shack: It is supposedly the most severely haunted building in Britain, but Dumbledore created its reputation in the 1960s. There is a very low underground tunnel leading to the Shrieking Shack from the base of the Whomping Willow. Harry at 13 has to almost double over to get through it. The tunnel is probably about 3' tall. Located up a slope reachable by a track running just past the Three Broomsticks, it stands a little ways above the rest of the village and is a slightly creepy place with boarded up windows and a dank overgrown garden. Even the Hogwarts' ghosts avoid it. Fred and George of course tried to get in the shack, and failed. No one can get in as all the entrances have been magically sealed shut (by Dumbledore who secretly created the Shrieking Shack as a safe space for Remus Lupin to transform when he was a student at Hogwarts). James, Sirius and Peter all used to hang out there (as animals) when Lupin was in a wolf form.

The Shrieking Shack is 2 stories tall. On the ground floor there is a dusty ransacked room with peeling wallpaper, stains on the floor and furniture that is broken. The boarded-up windows are all smashed. All the signs of a doglike creature being there are prevalent, right down to a wooden chair with a leg ripped off and another with chunks torn out of it. It is this room that the willow's tunnel leads to. A door to the right of the tunnel's entrance into the dusty room leads from the room to a hallway. From the hallway one can reach the crumbling staircase. From the upper landing, there are a few doors visible. One bedroom upstairs is furnished with a magnificent four-poster bed with dusty hangings. It was here in this room that Sirius and Lupin had it out with Peter in front of Harry, Hermione and Ron in Jun 1994.

The Three Broomsticks: Located in the High Street across from the Post Office, it is the place where the decent wizarding folk hang out. Run by owner Madam Rosmerta for over 20 years, but around for several 100 years at least, they may not get Dark wizards, but they get just about everything else, hags, vampires, goblins, etc. Ron claims he saw an ogre there once. Purveyor of hot and cold foaming butterbeer, it is a favorite drinking spot of Hagrid's as well as the teachers and students of Hogwarts. In addition to the main bar, the front room has several tables, loads of bright windows and a blazing hearth. It is clean, cheerful and friendly that also rents rooms, at a slightly higher price than the Hog's Head.

Zonko's Joke Shop: Located in the High Street, it is a much-loved joke shop. Fred and George used to visit it at every opportunity to stock up on such things as Stinkpellets which Fred liked, as well as Belch Powder, Dungbombs, Nose-Biting Teacups, Hiccup Sweets, Frog Spawn Soap and Whizzing Worms. It's a dangerous but rather inspirational shop for future joke makers of the wizarding world.

OTHER WIZARDING PLACES

Appleby: England, has the Arrows.

Azkaban: Located offshore from southern England (possibly on the Isles of Scilly), it is a fortress on a tiny island for criminal prisoners of the wizarding world. It had never had a breakout until Jul 1993 and was thought till then to be inescapable. In reality, Barty Jr had escaped in 1983 with the help of his mother and Polyjuice Potion, Sirius escaped in Jul 1993 by transforming into a dog and a whopping 10 Death Eaters escaped in Jan 1996 by means unknown. One presumes the Death Eaters were let out by dementors who were probably in negotiations with the Voldemort at the time and Voldemort had asked for a show of good faith. The dementors however did jump the gun by leaving their post in Jun, thinking Voldemort had pulled off the MoM raid with his Death Eaters, which they had not.

January 1996 Prison Break, Death Eater Escapees:
>**Unknown Death Eater.** Escapee 1: Death Eater wizard escaped from Azkaban Jan 96 Unknown crime/name. Still at large.
>**Unknown Death Eater.** Escapee 2: Death Eater wizard escaped from Azkaban Jan 96 Unknown crime/name. Still at large.
>**?? Travers.** Escapee 3: Death Eater wizard escaped from Azkaban Jan 96 Unknown crime/name. Still at large.
>**?? Mulciber.** Escapee 4: Death Eater wizard escaped from Azkaban Jan 96 Unknown crime. Recaptured Jun 1996.
>**?? Jugson.** Escapee 5: Death Eater wizard escaped from Azkaban Jan 96 Unknown crime. Recaptured Jun 1996.
>**Rastaban Lestrange.** Escapee 6: Death Eater wizard escaped from Azkaban Jan 96 Brother of Rodolphus. Responsible for the Longbottoms madness. Recaptured Jun 1996.
>**Rodolphus Lestrange.** Escapee 7: Death Eater wizard escaped from Azkaban Jan 96. They tortured and permanently incapacitated Frank and Alice Longbottom. Recaptured Jun 1996.
>**Antonin Dolohov.** Escapee 8: Death Eater wizard escaped from Azkaban Jan 96. Killer of Gideon and Fabian Prewett. Recaptured Jun 1996.
>**Augustus Rookwood.** Escapee 9: Death Eater wizard escaped from Azkaban Jan 96. He leaked MoM secrets to Voldemort. Recaptured Jun 1996.
>**Bellatrix Black Lestrange.** Escapee 10: Death Eater Witch escaped from Azkaban Jan 96. She tortured and permanently incapacitated Frank and Alice Longbottom. Still at large.

Dementors guarded the prison for the MoM because it gave them people 200+ they could legally feed off. Dementors don't care whether their charges are innocent or guilty, that's for the MoM to decide, they just want to eat and live. The MoM was in control of the dementors until Jun 1996 when the dementors left Azkaban to join Voldemort, their natural ally.

There are cells for prisoners, but bars aren't really needed. Prisoners become trapped in their own minds, incapable of a single cheerful thought. Most of the prisoners start out screaming and after a few weeks begin sitting and muttering to themselves in the dark. Most go mad in weeks and every one of them goes quiet in the end, except for when they shriek in their sleep. Hagrid says one can't remember who one is after awhile and subsequently can't see the point in living. Sirius said most people go mad and stop eating in the end because they lose the will to live. At which point, when prisoners are about to die, the dementors can sense it and get excited.

Prisoner are buried outside the fortress. Sirius could see the graveyard from his cell window. The MoM sends both short-term and long-term prisoners to Azkaban, as well as suspected criminals (as in Hagrid's case in 92/93 school year). There are minimum-security and maximum-security cells. Minimum-security cells have no bars, maximum-security cells have bars and had 2 dementors outside the door day and night. It is unclear what the MoM will do now the dementors have left. One expects wizarding guards on the whole would do a better job.

Ballycastle: North Ireland, has the Bats, a really beautiful city and a great annual faire!
Beauxbatons Academy of Magic: aka Beauxbatons. A French wizarding school, the precise location of which is unknown. Its students wear pale blue silk robes and tend to

be a bit emotional and a bit stuck up. At Christmas the school's dining room is surrounded by ice sculptures that don't melt and choirs of wood nymphs serenading the diners. Students don't sit down before their Head, Madame Olympia Maxime, does. The school has always been a part of the TT since its inception, making it over 700 years old. For the TT in 1994, 12 students came from Beauxbatons hoping represent their school. Fleur Delacour was ultimately picked by the Goblet of Fire and did the worst of all 4 of the champions.

Beauxbatons Crest: Located on the door of Olympia Maxime's coach, it consists of 2 gold wands crossed, emitting 3 gold stars each, on a pale blue background.

The Burrow: Located just outside the village of Ottery St Catchpole in an rural area with patchwork fields and lots of trees, the Burrow is the home of the Weasleys. See schematic Za for details. The Otter River is in Devon. So possibly it is in somewhere in Devon, this would line up with the fact that Molly said from the Burrow to Little Whinging is half way across the country. On the other hand, Molly took the kids from the Burrow to King's Cross Station in Muggle taxis, which would be very expensive not to say impractical from Devon. The Burrow is Harry's first experience of a wizard house. The house looks like a large stone pigpen, is 7-stories high, including the attic, and so crooked that it's probably only held up by magic. There are 4-5 chimneys perched on top of its red (probably clay tile) roof indicating there is probably a fireplace in every room.

Near the entrance is a lopside sign stuck in the ground which says "The Burrow." Around the front door are a bunch of rubber boots and a very rusty cauldron. The house has a ramshackle garage which formerly housed the bewitched Ford Anglia till it ended up in the Forbidden Forest. There is a small frontyard with a shed where several fat brown chickens like to scrtach around. The shed is Arthur's and full of Muggle objects which Arthur likes to take apart, enchant and then put back together. Molly tries to ignore the shed and what Arthur does in it. The back garden is large with plenty of weeds and tall grass and and a big green pond full of frogs. There are many unusual plants bursting from every flower bed including honeysuckle, rosebushes and a peony bush. Gnarled tress grow all around the walls and a field is just over the hedge of the backyard, very convenient for throwing gnomes into when degnomeing.

The kitchen is small and cramped with a scrubbed wooden table and probably 10 chairs in the middle. Copper pans hang from the ceiling or rest on the wood burning (probably Victorian) stove. Errol has a perch by the door, but ends up on the drying board regularly. A radio sits next to the sink that plays the WWN station. Floo Powder is kept in a flowerpot on the kitchen mantle as are books, stacked 3 deep, on how to cook. The mirror over the kitchen mantle shouts helpful comments to passers-by. The clock on the wall opposite the door has various housewitch reminders on it rather than numbers. From the kitchen, one can go down a narrow passageway, to an uneven staircase that leads to the upper floors.

The staircase zigzaggings up as far as Ron's Room. See the schematic Za for who sleeps on what floor. Apparently there is only one bedroom on each floor. On the 5th floor is a door with peeling paint (probably violent orange) and a small plaque that says "Ronald's Room." Ron's room has a steeply sloping ceiling which almost touches Harry short, 12-year-old head. Almost everything in the room is a violent shade of orange including the ceiling and bedspread. Most of the shabby wallpaper is covered by the 7 witches and wizards of the Chudley Cannons who are wearing bright orange robes, carrying broomsticks and waving energetically. Ron is so devoted to the Cannons his orange bedspread even has the Cannon's insignia.

ACASCIAS RIPHOUSE

Ron's room is rather messy. He throws his schoolbooks in a corner next to a pile of comics, leaves his wand on top of a fishtank full of frog spawn on the windowsill and self-shuffling playing cards lying on the floor. Either his mother doesn't clean his room or he doesn't let her clean it. He has 1 tiny window that overlooks the field. The room is smaller than Harry's at Dursleys, which is quite small, and it's right underneath the ghoul in the attic who is always banging on the pipes and groaning when it gets too quite, but Harry loves it. There are usually 2 beds crammed into the room when Harry visits, so perhaps at those times Molly puts and expanding charm on the room so they fit.

The living room is very cozy. There is a warm fireplace with a hearth rug at the far end of the room and a grandfather clock tucked in the corner. The clock has 9 golden hands, one for each member of the family, and where numbers should be it has inscriptions like school, lost or mortal peril. The clock belongs to Molly and has apparently been in her family for some time. The Weasleys also own a small paddock up on a hilltop near the house. It is also called an orchard because of the apple trees surrounding it, which block it from view of the village below to the east. The boys play Quidditch there, but don't fly too high, and use apples for balls since they wouldn't be dangerous to Muggles if they got away.

Caerphilly: Wales, has the Catapults. "Dangerous" Dia Llewellyn played here.

Chudley: England, has the Cannons, Ron's team.

Durmstrang: A magical secondary school like Hogwarts except it actually teaches its students the Dark Arts, doesn't admit anyone but purebloods and has a terrible reputation. It is over 700 years old and along with Hogwarts and Beauxbatons, has always been a part of the TT since its inception. Apparently the school is very basic as students from this school were interested in Hogwarts and impressed by the gold plates and goblets. Igor Karkoff brought 12 students to Hogwarts for the TT but only entered Viktor's name. Igor, a former Death Eater, was the Head till he left Hogwarts, and his students, in a panic when the Dark Mark activated in Jun 1995. The students didn't like him much and it's unclear who has replaced him.

All magic schools conceal themselves so no one can steal their secrets and Durmstrang is no exception. Durmstrang students have shaggy matted fur capes as part of their uniform, so it must be quite cold, and the school is believed to be located in the far North, perhaps in Russia, but the exact location is unknown. Judging by Viktor's skill level, the quality of education there is not very good. According to Viktor, the castle is not as big as Hogwarts, having only 4 floors, fires are only lit for magical purposes and in winter there is little daylight and students don't enjoy it much. On the plus side, summer days are really long and they spend them flying every day out over the lakes and mountains, which implies there is year-round school, students stay there during holidays and summer, and cirriculum is mostly outdoor classes like flying and Quidditch. All the students are built along the lines of Crabbe and Goyle and wear blood-red robes.

Falmouth: England, has the Falcons.

Godric's Hollow: A Muggle village probably located in Wales and named after Godric Gryffindor. Wizards have lived here since at least the 1300s. Lily and James Potter lived here in a cottage for a couple of weeks before their death Oct 31, 1981. Harry was found there by Hagrid. Since Hagrid, coming from Godric's Hollow, had to fly over Bristol to arrive in Little Whinging, Gryffindor is a Welsh name, Lily's maiden name, Evans, is also Welsh, and leeks, the Welsh national symbol, have come up in connection with Gryffindor House, one presumes the Hollow to be in the South of Wales somewhere.

The Harry Potter Companion

The Green Dragon: A pub whose location is unknown. The landlady was the object of Janus Thickey's affections, with unforeseen and awful results. See entry in Magical Beings for Janus Thickey, and the Janus Thickey Ward under St Mungo's in this section.

Headquarters: aka Sirius Black's House, 12 Grimmauld Place. Located in London this dwelling is Unplottable and its exact address is now in the soul possession of Dumbledore, the OoP's Secret-Keeper. Mr Black, Sirius' father, put every possible security measure known to wizardkind on his home. Sirius, as the last Black left, inherited the house in 1985 after his mother died. Sirius offered it to Dumbledore as a headquarters for the Order in 1993. See schematic Y for a layout of the ground floor and basement kitchen. The schematic of the various floors should suffice to show where everyone slept. This is a very basic schematic and doesn't show every portrait of stuffed house-elf.

For those wishing to suss out it's actual location, I can only give 4 clues: it is a 20-minute walk from the house to Kings Cross Station; it is 4 stops on the Underground from the MoM; the house is between 2 odd numbered house, 11 and 13; and the house faces a small square with unkempt grass and rather grimy looking houses all around it, some of which have doors with peeling paint, broken windows and or heaps of rubbish outside their sets of steps. Of course even if one could figure out the general area it might be in, the house can't be found unless Dumbledore himself gives one the address personally because it's Unplottable.

The front of the house has worn stone steps and a shabby, scratched and battered black frontdoor with a silver knocker in the form of a twisted serpent. There is no keyhole or letterbox on the door as the Blacks apparently didn't want any means of entry on their door. Tap the door with a wand and its many locks will hopefully unlock, the chain will slide off the door and it will open. If the doorbell is rung, the portrait of Mrs Black, which hangs nearby between some moth-eaten velvet curtains in the hallway, goes off and she subsequently sets off all the other portraits. The front hall is damp, dusty and has a sweetish smell like rotting wood. A large, troll's leg umbrella stand is in the corner by by frontdoor. The long gloomy hall has a snake-shaped chandelier, age-blackened portraits and a rickety table on which is a matching snake-shaped candelabra.

The soft hissing of gas lighting, as well as the scuttling of rats, sounds throughout the house. Every room has peeling wallpaper, threadbare carpet and moth-eaten drapes. The whole place is in very shabby condition because no one lived in it from 1985-1993 except Kreacher the house-elf. Lupin moved in late Jun 1993, but he couldn't give Kreacher orders as he wasn't his master. At the back of the main hallway is the door to a flight of narrow stone steps that go down to the basement kitchen, pantry and boiler room.

The kitchen is a gloomy cavernous room with rough stone walls and no windows and heavy iron pots and pans hanging from the dark ceiling. A long wooden table with many chairs around it sits in the middle of the room. An ancient dresser, with the plates on the upper shelves and cutlery in the drawers, stands against one wall. There is a space under the dresser large enough to fit a big cat (Crookshanks went under it once). There is a pantry off the kitchen, its door is opposite the door to the boiler room, which is on the other side of the kitchen. Kreacher has a nest under the large old-fashioned boiler.

The dining room is on the ground floor, just next to the drawing room and above the kitchen. This arrangement also probably made it easier for the resident house-elf to send the food up without being noticed. The dining room is where the the Black family goblets, the finest 15th-century goblin-wrought silver, embossed with the Black family crest, were before they ended up in the kitchen. There was china with the Black crest and motto on it here as well, till Sirius threw it out. The drawing room is a long room with a high ceiling. It has olive green walls covered in dirty tapestries. The carpet exudes dust when steeped on. Long moss-green velvet curtains, formerly buzzing with doxies, cover the windows. Photos of Black family members, in silver glass-faced frames, were in this room, till Sirius threw them out.

The drawing room had the best furnishing of the house including a couch, armchairs, a spindly legged table and a writing desk with the tall cabinet (probably a secretary desk) where Molly found the boggart. On either side of the fireplace are dusty glass-fronted cabinets with shelves. The shelves had all manner of extremely nasty Dark Arts items, such as rusty daggers, claws, coiled snakeskins, silver boxes engraved with foreign languages containing things like Wartcap Powder and an ornate crystal bottle full of a blood-colored liquid. An Order of Merlin, 1st class that had been Sirius' grandfather's for services to the ministry (ie, he gave them a lot of gold) was also kept there. All these things were unceremoniously chucked by Sirius.

The Black family tapestry, in the family since about 1295, is hung the length of a wall in the drawing room. It's old, faded and doxy gnawed. Bright golden threads of the embroidered names give the sprawling family tree back to the Middle Ages. The Noble and Most Ancient House of Black with the faimly motto "Toujour Pur" (Always Pure), is embroidered at the top. Toujour Pur is French, so distantly the Blacks must be as well or they'd have chosen a Latin motto, more traditional for British families. There are some gaps in the genealogy. Mrs Black burned off people she didn't like, like Sirius when he ran away from home, Tonks for being an Auror, Andromeda for marrying a Muggle born and Uncle Alphard for giving a 17-year-old Sirius an inheritance to live off. Attached by a Permanent Sticking Charm, the tapestry is impossible to remove. How names are added to it, if it's attached to the wall, is a mystery. It must be magically embroidered or self-embroidering.

Going up the dark staircase, past the row of snout-nosed house-elf heads mounted on plaques, on the 1st landing was Ginny and Hermione's room. From this landing one can look into the hallway to the front door and watch the goings on. On the 2nd landing, the door to the right, with a knob in the shape of a serpent's head, was Ron and Harry's room. Fred and George's room was on the 3rd landing. Everyone had to keep their bedrooms bolted shut at night or Kreacher would wander in. This was only slightly worse than having a smirking portrait in one's room as Ron and Harry did. Ron and Harry's room had a high ceiling, twin beds and a wardrobe with clawed feet that Hedwig and Pig like to sit on top of. It was dank and dark with peeling walls and a grimy window. The wastepaper basket burped and coughed up anything put in it, the bedcovers were moth eaten and the ornately framed portrait of Phineas Nigellus was usually blank because he was spying on the room's occupants. It's the sniggering Phineas does that was most irritating.

Hard to say who owns the house now. Since Dumbledore is the Secret-Keeper, no one looking for it can find it except Kreacher. But if Sirius didn't leave a will, it should go to Andromeda the closest eldest living, non-escaped or convicted felon. If Sirius did leave a will, possibly he left the house to Dumbledore, or more likely Harry, or Dumbledore in trust for Harry. One would guess Lupin will continue to live in the house, being a destitute undesirable in his own community. An interesting thing to consider while speaking of legal matters is that the Potters left a will making Sirius Harry's legal guardian, so technically Sirius had a right and a duty to will the guardianship on to someone else. One expects that Dumbledore would still send Harry to the Dursleys, even if he was now Harry's guardian. But of course it's entirely possibly Sirius never thought to write a will, in the absence of which, the wizard court would make Harry a ward unless Petunia, Harry's only relation, petitioned and was allowed to become his guardian.

Holyhead: Wales, has the Harpies.
Kenmare: Ireland, had the Kestrels, Seamus' team.
Little Red Books: Probably located in Diagon Alley, it is the venerable old publishing house that produced *A History of Magic,* and *Home Life and Social Habits of British Muggles.*
Montrose: Scotland, has the Magpies.
Ottery St Catchpole: A village just east of the Burrow. It has post office with a telephone that Molly occasionally uses to call cabs. There are 4 wizarding families live in the area: Diggory, Weasley, Lovegood and Fawcett.
Platform Nine and Three Quarters: Located in King's Cross Station, London, between Muggle Platform 9 and 10, it's the place from which students catch the Hogwarts Express. It can be reach by walking straight through the brick and steel barrier between Platforms 9 and 10 at King's Cross station London on Sep 1 before 11am. Once through, if one looks back, an archway of wrought iron with *Platform Nine and Three-Quarters* written on it can be seen. There is a sign that says Hogwarts Express with a clock giving the time above the platform. Ticket are available for purchase on the platform. There is a station guard, a wizened old wizard, standing at the ticket barrier who oversees people leaving the platform when the Express makes its return journey. He lets people through slowly in 2s or 3s so as not to attract attention on the Muggle side of the station.
Portree: Isle of Skye, Scotland, has the Pride of Portree.
Puddlemere: England (or maybe Wales), has Puddlemere United. Oliver Wood started on their reserve team in 1994 after graduating Hogwarts. It is Dumbledore's favorite team.
Purge and Dowse Ltd: Located in the very heart of London, it is the entrance to St Mungo's. From Headquarters it is one stop away via the Underground. The storefront can be found on a busy shopping street near an electronics store. Housed in a large old-fashioned red brick department store, Purge and Dowse Ltd has a shabby miserable air. The display window features chipped dummies with wigs askew standing at random and modeling clothes from the 1980s. A large sign on the dusty doors explains the place is closed for refurbishment. It's never open to the Muggle public because it is actually a portal for wizards into St Mungo's lobby.

The very ugly, dumpy female mannequin with peeling false eyelashes and a green nylon pinafore is actually the entrance keeper. By telling her who in St Mungo's the visitor wants to see, she will, if the person is there, nod and beckon with her jointed finger. At that point the visitor can step through the window's glass. As one steps through the glass, one will vanish to the hospital's reception area. Going through the glass is like passing though a sheet of cool water but one arrives at the other side warm and dry. It is not clear if people exit in a similar fashion or not. They don't seem to use the Floo Network at St Mungo's, so one assumes one does have to go back out through the window if one can't Apparate.

Queerditch Marsh: An important historic Quidditch site. See QTA.
St Mungo's Hospital for Magical Maladies and Injuries: aka St Mungo's. Located in central London. See schematic Zb for detailed floor information. See Purge and Dowse Ltd for entrance information. A crowded reception room filled with rows of wizards with odd difigurements sitting on rickety wooden chairs reading outdated

magazines is usually what one sees upon entering St Mungo's. Healers at St Mungo's wear lime-green robes with a crossed wand and bone emblem embroidered on the chest. They have no doctors, only Healers. Wizarding medicine doesn't practice body-invasive techniques like surgery, stitches, etc, which don't usually work on wizards anyway. However, some Healers are willing to try Muggle therapies (called complimentary medicine) if their patients are open to them.

The reception desk has slogans behind it advocating preventative health measures and also a picture of Dilys Derwent, a famous Healer who went on to become Headmistress of Hogwarts later in life. Although wizards are the most frequent patients, Muggles are sometimes brought to the hospital for treatment and memory modification if they have suffered some really heinous magical accident (eg, being bitten by a dragon). The hospital has a spokeswizard that handles the press when matters like the murder of Derrick Bode come up. But generally St Mungo's is very good with patients and manages to cure the large majority. For those that aren't considered curable or quickly curable, the hospital has a special ward where Healers do keep trying to work with them, through a course of various potions over a long period of time.

Interestingly enough, St Mungo's has no obstetrics ward. Whether this is because witches prefer to have their babies at home with the help of a midwitch, is difficult to determine. Other missing wards include, practically anything normal, like cardiology, pediatrics, othopedics or internal medicine. But wizards may either treat these problems at home, don't believe in treating them or can't treat them. Like most hospitals, it does all it can to make the wards comfortable and cheerful. St Mungo's always decorates for Christmas. The usual crystal orb lighting that runs throughout the hospital is magically changed to glow red and gold. Holly is put around the doorways, Christmas trees are set up in the lobby covered with magical snow and icicles and each topped with a golden star.

The "Dangerous" Dai Llewellyn Ward: This ward is located on the 1st floor, 2nd door on the right, and is for those with serious bites. This is where Arthur was treated after his Nagini (Voldemort) bite. It is a small, dingy room with only 1 narrow window set high in the wall at the far end of the room facing the door. Lighting is primarily from shining crystal bubbles or orbs clustered in the middle of the ceiling. Walls are oak paneled and a portrait of Urquhart Rackharrow is the main decoration of the room. When Arthur was there there were 2 other patients in the ward. Down the corridor from the ward is a pair of double doors and a rickety staircase lined with more portraits of brutal or vicious looking Healers. Up the staircases one will find more sets of double doors each with a small window and a sign marking what they treat. On the fourth floor is Spell Damage.

The Janus Thickey Ward: aka Ward 49. Located on the 4th floor of St Mungo's (probably in Room 9), it is a locked ward for the treatment and care of people who have suffered major, possibly irreversible, spell damage. Miriam Strout is the Healer in charge of this ward and administers the intensive treatment regimes for about 5-6 people. Gilderoy Lockhart has been here since his Memory Charm accident in 1993 and seems to be making progress. The Longbottoms have been there since 1982 and don't seem to be making progress. Broderick Bode was making progress till he was murdered. Agnes seems to have had a Transfiguration go astray. All the beds have armchairs beside them. Most people have more personal items there, pictures, knickknacks, calendars, plants, etc. There are flowery curtains visitors can draw around each bed for privacy. The ward does allow, encourage and welcome visitors but they have to be let in by the Healer on duty.

Stoatshead Hill: A hill just East of Ottery St Catchpole. It is a part of the village. It was where Amos and Cedric Diggory, Arthur, Ron, Ginny, Fred and George Weasley, Hermione Granger and Harry Potter took the Portkey to QWC 1994.
Tutshill: England, has the Tornados, Cho's team.
Wigtown: Scotland, has the Wanderers, K. Whisp's team.

LITTLE HANGLETON

The Hanged Man: Little Hangleton's village pub. In the 1940s it had a female owner that was sympathetic toward Frank Bryce.
Great Hangleton: The larger town neighboring Little Hangleton. It has a police station which services Little Hangleton as well.
Little Hangleton: The village where Tom Riddle Sr's house is.
Little Hangleton Churchyard: An overgrown valley set cemetery with a small church. A large yew tree grows among the graves. Looking from the yew tree toward the right is the church and to the left is a hill where Riddle House can be seen. The cracked but otherwise towering marble headstone belongs Tom Riddle Sr. All the Riddles are buried in the churchyard.
Riddle House: A fine old house that once belonged to Voldemort's grandparents. His father also lived at the house. It sits on a hill overlooking Little Hangleton and has a view of the village church and cemetery. One can see Frank's kitchen window from the house as his cottage is on the property. Once the finest, largest, grandest looking house for miles its windows are now broken and boarded up, some of the rooftiles are missing and ivy is running rampant on the house and fence. It is damp, derelict, and unoccupied.

After the Riddles died in 1944, the house then went through 2 short-term owners before arriving at its current owner, a rich man who has never lived there and never does anything with the house but keeps it anyway for tax purposes. The Riddles died in the upstairs drawing room which is still much like they died in it. The drawing room has a fireplace at the end opposite the door. The shabby furnishings include an ancient armchair and rotting hearth rug. It was in this room that Voldemort, during his stay there in Aug 1994 after he'd returned from Albania, also killed Frank Bryce. See schematic X for details.

LITTLE WHINGING

Alley: Located between a high fence and a garage, it leads from Magnolia Crescent to Wisteria Walk. See schematic W. The alley has no streetlights. It was here that Harry first saw Sirius (as a dog) in Aug 1993, and where the 2 dementors, coming from opposite ends of the alley, tried to trap and Kiss Dudley and Harry in Aug 1995.
Little Whinging: Located in Surrey, it is a town of identical large square houses owned by large square men. The people like to wash their new cars and mow their manicured front lawns on weekends. It is upper-middle class and seems to be entirely White. People of this community don't like people who make noise or who are scruffy looking (like Harry) and believe in the use of capital punishment for both types of offenders.
Magnolia Crescent: Located several streets away from Privet Drive, it is connected to Wisteria Walk by an alley (see Alley). The alley from Magnolia Crescent to Wisteria Walk is between Number 2 Magnolia Crescent's pebble-washed garage wall on one side a high fence on the other. Crossing Magnolia Crescent one can then turn into Magnolia Road.

ACASCIAS RIPHOUSE

Magnolia Road: Across from Magnolia Crescent, Magnolia Road leads to a play park. There's a lilac tree on it within view of the alley.
The Play Park: Located at the end of Magnolia Road, its gate is generally locked at night. It has some swings and seems to be for younger children.
Privet Dr, Nextdoor: Apparently at least one neighbor, at Number 2 or 6, is a gardener and has runner beans growing in a vegetable plot in the backyard. Another has a dog.
Privet Drive, Number 4 : See schematics V1 and V2 for the layout of the house, including Harry's bedroom. The expensive square 4-bedroom, 2-bath, 2-story home of the Dursleys, Number 4 is located not far from the corner of the street. There are 14 streetlights on Privet Dr and Number 4 is 2 streetlights from the end. There are streets in back of the house. The house itself faces due east. The house has a manicured lawn with a low garden wall in the front and a gravel driveway at the side. The front door has a brass number 4 on it, a mail slot and rippled glass in it. The door is elaborate having little pieces of glass at the top of the door above the larger central piece of glass.

There is a doorbell that rings rather than a knocker, and a doorstep where Petunia puts the milk bottles out. Inside the frontdoor is an indoor doormat and next to the door is a hook for Vernon's car keys. The cupboard that was Harry's first bedroom is under the stairs. It is very small, dark and a bit spider-ridden. The bottom step of staircase creaks. Across from the cupboard is the living room or "lounge" as Petunia calls it. It has a fireplace with a mantle covered in Dudley's most recent pictures. These pictures are updated every year but there are no pictures of Harry or his family in the entire house.

The living room fireplace is boarded up with a fake electric coal fire plugged in the front of it, a standard part of most British homes. Net curtains, a popular item on Privet Dr, are in the living room windows. There is a sideboard with a collection of china figurines in it, some armchairs, a sofa with cushions strew over it and a coffee table. The living room has the stereo and TV as well as the only phone in the house. There is a dining room is just off the living room. It gets used for dinner parties but not much else it would seem. All the windows downstairs open outward like pairs of doors, but all the windows upstairs are sash windows. There is carpet in the downstairs hallway and downstairs but the upstairs it's all wood flooring.

The kitchen is kept scrupulously clean. It has a table and 4 chairs, a food processor, stove, microwave, and large top-of-the-line fridge with Dudley's diet on it. A draining board stands by the sink, even though they have a dishwasher. The large room has multiple windows, a widescreen TV and even a fireplace. There is a door between the kitchen and carpeted hallway and a door from the kitchen into the backyard. The inner kitchen door has a keyhole and a gap between the floor and the door bottom.

Out the backdoor, there is a lawn and a garden bench at the back near some bushes. There is also a glass greenhouse, hopefully repaired since 1991 when Dudley threw his tortoise through its roof. The backyard has fences around it which Petunia is always craning her neck to spy look over. There are several flowerbeds and rosebushes. At the very back of the garden there are bushes and trees and a garden shed.
Harry's Room: The smallest bedroom in the house, it was Dudley's second bedroom till Jul 1991. Harry's room has a doorhandle not a knob and shares a wall with the Dudley's bedroom. It has 2 windows, one over the desk and one the over bed. Hedwig's cage is usually on the desk by the window and open so she can come and go as she likes but occasionally Harry sticks it in his wardrobe. The door has an external lock on it and a catflap cut into it. At one point Harry had bars on his windows but the

set over the chest of drawers was ripped off by Fred and the flying Ford Anglia. One would assume Vernon took them off the other window as well, probably at Petunia's insistence because they looked unattractive.

Stonewall High: The local public secondary school. Its uniforms are grey. This is where Harry was going to planning to go to school until the Hogwarts' letter came. Interestingly enough, that Harry would have gone to Stonewall High indicates that the Dursleys would rather have continued to live with Harry than pay for him to go to a school where he would have to board.

Wisteria Walk: Located a short distance from Privet Dr, it is where Mrs Figg lives with her cat. There is a corner shop nearby where Mrs Figg gets her cans of cat food.

LONDON AREA

London is a large city with many suburbs and sections. Little Whinging is not too far from London. It is about a 3.25 hours drive to London. But it's probably easier to catch the train from Little Whinging. Petunia goes up to London as a shopping day trip. She took Dudley there to get his Smeltings uniform and Vernon and Petunia took Dudley to a private hospital in London for tail removal.

Bethnal Green: A suburb of London, it is the location where Wily Widdershins created the 3rd regurgitating toilet.

Charing Cross Road: The Knight Bus arrives here to reach the Leaky Cauldron. It is a one-way road.

Elephant and Castle: A suburb in London, it is where Wily Widdershins created a 2nd regurgitating toilet.

King's Cross Station: A central train station, arguably the most important in London. On either side of the station are dirty buildings and the Post Office is nearby. It has a shiny floor, free luggage trolleys and male guards. There are large plastic numbers over the platforms and a large arrivals and departures board. There is a ticket inspector's stand between platforms nine and ten that is also the metal and brick barrier that's the entrance to the Platform Nine and Three-Quarters. There is a dividing barrier between the platforms usually lined with plastic seats that are attached to it.

London Post Office: aka the Mount Pleasant Post Office. Ron flew the Ford Anglia over its tower and two Muggles spotted it. It's the central post office for the city of London.

Ministry of Agriculture, Fisheries and Food: aka the Ministry of Agriculture and Fisheries. A British government ministry located near Charing Cross Station.

Paddington Station: A train station where Harry caught a train to Little Whinging after having a hamburger with Hagrid in 1991. It has plastic seats and fast food restaurants.

(Unknown) Private Hospital: This is where Dudley had his tail removed in 1991.

Vauxhall Road: South of Buckingham Palace, East of Victoria Station, this is where Tom Riddle's Diary was printed in 1942.

Wimbledon: A suburb of London where the annual eponymous tennis cup matches held. Wily Widdershins 1st created a regurgitating toilet here.

OTHER MUGGLE PLACES

Aberdeen: Scotland, a Knight Bus stop during Harry's 1st ride on it.

Abergavenny: Wales, where the elderly Madam Marsh got off the Knight Bus during Harry's 1st ride on it.

ACASCIAS RIPHOUSE

Albania: Where Voldemort keeps going to hide.
Anglsea: Wales, a Knight Bus stop during Harry's first ride on it.
Argyllshire: Scotland. The Fat Lady hid in a map of this area after being attacked by Sirius.
Armenia: Where Lockhart claimed another wizard's credit for ridding a village of a werewolf.
Assyria: Now Iraq, it's where Neville's Mimbulus mimbletonia came from. Shrivelfigs also come from this area.
Bandon: Ireland, where the banshee that Lockhart supposedly banished was acting up.
Barnsley: in Gloustershire, England, where the Five Feathers is and Bungy lives.
Bath: England, a spa town where an old witch had a book one could never stop reading.
Birmingham: England, Harry's 2nd trip on the Knight Bus included a stop here.
Black Forest: Germany, where vampires supposedly turned Pr Quirrell into a trembling coward.
Blackpool: England, where Neville's Great Uncle Algie pushed him off the pier, hoping to force magic out of him.
Brazil: Where the boa constrictor Harry set free planned to go and where Bill had a very nasty penfriend once.
Britain: Includes England, North Ireland, Scotland, Wales.
Bristol: England, Hagrid passed over this city en route from Godric's Hollow to Little Whinging.
Bulgaria: The national team was in QWC 1994. Viktor Krum is Bulgarian. Possibly Hermione has been there as she was invited to visit by Viktor in 1995.
China: Fireball dragons are native here.
Cokeworth: A large city in England where the Railview Hotel is located.
Cornwall: A part of Britain. Pixies come from here.
Devon: England, where Nicolas and Perenelle Flamel lived for several hundred years.
Didsbury: England, where wizard D. J. Prod is from.
Dijon: France, where Hermione has been on vacation in the summer of 1994 and Hagrid and Olympia passed through on their way to the giants Abroad in the summer of 1995.
Dorset: England, where Newt Scamander lives with his wife and 3 kneazles.
Dundee: Scotland, where magical shooting stars were seen after Voldemort's defeat in 1981.
Egypt: Where Bill worked for Gringotts as a curse breaker till 1995 and where all the Weasleys went after Arthur won the drawing in summer 1993.
England: The national team lost to Transylvania in QWC 1994 playoffs.
Eton: England, a top-drawer secondary school Justin's parents were going to send him to before the Hogwarts' letter arrived.
The Five Feathers: A pub or inn in Barnsley where Bungy lives.
France: Where Hermione vacationed in summer 1993 and where Beauxbatons Academy of Magic and ICW headquarters probably are. Olympia Maxime and Fleur Delacour French speaking and probably from France, but they could be Belgian, Swiss or Luxemburgers as they all also speak French.
Greece: Where all the really dangerous magical beasts seem to come from and "Dangerous" Dai died.
Grunnings: A drill manufacturing company where Vernon Dursley works. It is about an half hour from Vernon's home. It has at least 9 floors and a parking lot. Vernon

works on the 9th floor where he has a window office and a secretary outside his door. Across the street is a bakery. Vernon is the company's Director of Sales. A normal morning at Grunnings' for Vernon includes yelling at 5 people at work, making several important phonecalls and yelling some more. It must be a really terrible place to work.
Hungary: Horntail dragons are native here.
Hut-on-the-Rock: The Sea. Just off a small town with a train station and reachable only by rowboat from harbor with the stone steps, it is a miserable shack on a small rocky island in the middle of the sea. The ramshackle house seems to be a crude shelter for the occasionally stranded sailor. It smells of seaweed and has gaps in the walls but the fireplace works and there is a bedroom as well as a front room. The front room had a moth-eaten sofa and the sideroom a lumpy bed but there were sheets (moldy ones) and blankets (thin and ragged). When stormy, the spray from high waves splatters the walls of the house and wind rattles its filthy windows. Hagrid's head, at about 12', just brushes the ceiling. He ripped the frontdoor off its hinges coming to give Harry his Hogwarts letter.
Ireland: Where Seamus Finnigan is from. Their national team won QWC 1994. This is the country of Ireland. A separate nation from Britain. North Ireland is a part of Muggle Britain and a section of the island called Ireland.
Isle of Wight: England, a small island off the south end of England, near Portsmouth. Marge Dursley vacationed here in July 1991.
Kent: England, where the Wailing Widow is from and Dedalus Diggle lives and set off magical shooting stars in 1981.
Liechtenstein: Wizards of this nation contested Pierre Bonaccord's appointment to Supreme Mugwump of the ICW because of his stand on various troll-related issues.
Little Norton: England, where Doris Purkiss and Stubby Boardman live.
Loch Ness: Scotland, an ongoing problem area for the ICW.
Luxembourg: Their national team was in QWC 1994 playoffs.
Majorca: Where Yvonne, Petunia's friend, vacations and where Vernon wants to get a vacation home.
Minsk: Russia, where Hagrid got into a fight at a pub on his way to the giants.
Mongolia: Where Pr Snape, incorrectly, thinks kappas are from.
Norfolk: England, where a Hetty Bayliss saw the Ford Anglia flying.
Norway: Where the dragon dung fertilizer sample Percy received was supposed to be from. It has a native dragon.
Nottinghamshire: England, where Kennilworthy Whisp lives and a goblin family was murdered by Voldemort's Death Eaters.
Peebles: Scotland, where Angus Fleet saw the Ford Anglia flying.
Peru: Their national team beat Ireland in the semifinals of QWC 1994.
Poland: Where Hagrid and Olympia ran into mad trolls on their way to the giants.
Railview Hotel: A gloomy looking hotel on the outskirts of Cokesworth, it is wher Dudley and Harry had to share Room #17. Harry's room had twin beds with damp musty sheets but a window with a view to the street. The owner of the hotel is a woman. She tried to bring Harry his Hogwarts' letter, 1 of 100 that had arrived at the front desk. It has a dining room but not very good food.
Romania: It is where the dragon reserve is that Charlie works at and where Norbert is living. It has a native dragon.
Russia: Probably where Durmstrang is and where Igor Karkoff's father was probably from before marrying an Englishwoman and immigrating to Britain.
St Brutus's Secure Center for Incurably Criminal Boys: A possibly fictional first-rate English institution for hopeless cases. This is where Vernon tells Marge, and all of

ACASCIAS RIPHOUSE

Little Whinging, that Harry goes to school. It can't be a local school because the Dursleys' explain Harry's absences this way.
Salem: Massachusetts, USA. Where the Salem Witches' Institute is.
Scotland: Their national team lost to Luxembourg in QWC 1994 playoffs. But at least they didn't lose to Faeroe Islands.
Smeltings: Vernon's old private secondary school. This is where Dudley and Piers now attends. One presumes it's posh and expensive since the Dursleys seem always to have had money. The uniform is maroon tailcoat, orange knickerbockers, a flat straw hat (called a boater) and a knobbly stick used for hitting other students while teachers aren't looking, which is supposed to be good training for adulthood.
Spain: Where the baggage handlers went on strike in the summer of 1995 for at least 2 week.
Surrey: The English county that Little Whinging is in, just south of the Thames River.
Sweden: It has a native dragon.
Tibet: An ongoing problem area for the ICW. Where the MoM believed Sirius to be for many months.
Topsham: England, where Madam Z Nettles is from.
Transylvania: A region in Romania, where Lockhart claimed to cure a man of Babbling Curse. Their "national" team was in the first QWC in 1473 and in QWC 1994 playoffs.
Turkey: Ludo played against their national team in 1981 or 1982. His excellent work as Beater for England during this game got him acquitted of being a Death Eater.
Uganda: Africa. Their national team was in QWC 1994 playoffs.
Waga Waga: New South Wales, Australia, where Lockhart claimed to cure a man of being a werewolf.
Wales: Where Godric's Hollow probably is and Godric Gryffindor was from. Their national team lost to Uganda in QWC 1994 playoffs.
Wiltshire: England, here the Malfoys have their mansion.
Wimbourne: England, where Ludo's old team the Wasps are based.
Woodcroft: Gloustershire, England, where the great wizard Hengist was from.
Yorkshire: England, a place magical shooting stars were seen after Voldemort's defeat in 1981.
Zoo: Where Dudley went for his birthday in 1991. One can drive to it from Little Whinging in an hour or so. It has a restaurant on the premises serving meals and deserts like knickerbocker glory. There are stands throughout the park, which serve lemon ice pops and chocolate ice creams among other things. The zoo has assorted creatures including gorillas and a reptile house replete with cobras, pythons, boa constrictors, and lizards. The reptile house is cool and dark with lighted windows all along the walls. This is where Harry accidentally set the boa constrictor free and the first place Harry ever went that wasn't the cupboard, school, or Mrs Figg's.

Timeline of Events*

1000 BC – July 1, 1996

1000 BC
Circe begins Transfiguring sailors into animals.
382 BC

The Harry Potter Companion

Ollivander's wandmakers shop opens. Probably in Roman Londinum.
100 AD
Ptolomey is born.
300
Cliodna works her healing magic among the Celts.
400
Hengist of Woodcroft comes to Britain.
500
Merlin works with King Arthur, and Morgana works against him.
c 900
Slytherin, Gryffindor, Hufflepuff and Ravenclaw team up and start to create Hogwarts.
c 925
Slytherin builds the Chamber of Secrets and sticks a basilisk (egg) in it.
c 950
Some point after Hogwarts is up and running, Slytherin leaves after a final quarrel with Gryffindor.
c 1000
An early form of Quidditch is played on Queerditch Marsh.
1100
Gregory the Smarmy is born.
1112
Wilfred Elphick born (probably Wilfred the Wistful).
1199
Wilfred Elphick dies (probably Wilfred the Wistful).
1280
The Medieval Assembly of European Wizards meets.
1289
The International Warlock Convention happens.
1294
The Triwizard Tournament with 3 competing schools. Hogwarts, Beauxbatons and Durmstrang, is started.
1296
A manticore savages someone but is let off because no one wanted to go near it.
c 1300
British witches presumably get the right to vote and hold office since later one actually turns up as Chief of the Wizards' Council.
1312
Wendelin the Weird starts getting herself burned at the stake in different disguises, 47 times.
1327
Nicolas Flamel is born.
1334
Perenelle (Flamel) is born.
1350
Elfrida Clagg becomes Chieftainess of the Wizards' Council.
1473
Transylvania v. Flanders in the 1st QWC. Over 700 types of foul are committed with many never before seen fouls and is considered the most violent game of all time.
1486
Agrippa is born.

1492
Oct 31
Sir Nicholas de Mimsy-Porpington is nearly beheaded
1493
Paracelsus is born.
1535
Agrippa dies.
1556
Gunhilda of Gorsemoor is born.
circa 1600
The MoM system is developed and Britain establishes its MoM in London. At this time Scotland was separate country, but later, probably after 1701 and the Act of Union, united its MoM with the London. See Note 1.
1612
An Hogsmeade inn becomes the headquarters for the 1612 goblin rebellion.
Urquhart Rackharrow born.
1637
Werewolf Code of Conduct is written and adopted.
1650
The British Dept of Magical Games and Sports is established. See Note 1.
1652
1st Quidditch European Cup match played.
1662
Gryffindor House suffer a crushing defeat, the like of which will not happen again for another 300 years.
1663
Gunhilda of Gorsemoor dies.
1674
The British and Irish League was established with 13 teams. See Note B.
1692
Pierre Bonaccord becomes 1st ICW Supreme Mugwump.
The International Statute of Wizarding Secrecy of 1692 goes into effect.
1697
Urquhart Rackharrow, inventor of the Entrail-Expelling Curse, dies.
c 1700
Goblin riots and rebellions break out throughout the 18th century.
1709
The Warlocks' Convention outlaws dragon breeding.
1712
A hippogriff is convicted and executed of an unknown crime.
1722
Dilys Derwent becomes Head Healer at St Mungo's.
1741
Dilys Derwent leaves St Mungo's to become Head of Hogwarts.
1740
A spectacular breach of the Statute of Security occurs.
1750
Clause 73 is inserted in the International Code of Wizarding Secrecy, making MoMs responsible for magical creatures in their territories.
1768

The Harry Potter Companion

Dilys Derwent retires from Hogwarts (or possibly dies).
1792
A cockatrice goes on a tear and injures all three school judges on the panel for the TT. The TT is henceforth suspended.
1803
Alberic Grunnion is born.
1814
The Banchory Bangers incident. See Note B.
1835
Bertie Bott is born. See Note A.
1860
Bertie Bott invents the Every Flavor Bean.
1870
Armando Dippet is born.
1875
The Decree for the Reasonable Restriction of Underage Sorcery is passed.
1882
Alberic Grunnion dies.
1892
Chudley Cannons win the League win and henceforth starts 100+ years of losing the League.
1897
Newt Scamander born.
1900
Bathilda Bagshot is born.
1908
Newt Scamander starts Hogwarts.
1915
Albus Dumbledore is born. See Note 2.
Newt Scamander gets a job with the MoM.
1917
Frank Bryce and Aberforth Dumbledore are born.
1918
Augustus Worme asks Newt Scamander to write a book on magical creatures.
1920
Minerva McGonagall is born.
1921
Miranda Goshawk is born.
1926
Dumbledore starts Hogwarts.
1927
Tom Marvolo Riddle born and is put in Muggle orphanage.
Tom's mother, (Unknown) Marvolo, dies.
Mr Hagrid marries Fridwulfa.
Newt Scamander's *Fantastic Beasts and Where to Find Them* is published and adopted at Hogwarts.
1929
Rubeus Hagrid born.
1930
Barty Crouch Sr is born.

1932
Giantess Fridwulfa Hagrid leaves son Rubeus Hagrid and wizard husband Mr Hagrid.
1933
Jun
Dumbledore graduates Hogwarts and is given the job of teaching Transfiguration there.
1935
The first Transatlantic broom crossing.
1938
Tom Riddle start Hogwarts and starts trying to find out about the Chamber of Secrets.
Armando Dippet is made Headmaster.
1939
Frank Bryce participates in WWII.
1940
Hagrid starts Hogwarts.
1941
Frank Bryce is wounded and hospitalized.
1942
Frank Bryce goes home to become the Riddle's gardener.
Hagrid's father dies.
The Chamber of Secrets is opened by Tom Riddle.
Tom starts to fancy himself Lord Voldemort.
Albus Dumbledore is at Hogwarts teacher of Transfiguration.
1943
Jan
Tom Riddle cooks up the enchanted diary.
Jun 10
Moaning Myrtle dies in a basilisk attack.
Jun 13
Prefect Tom Riddle gets Hagrid expelled over Aragog.
Aragog takes up life in the Forbidden Forest.
Jun 14
Myrtle's parents come for her body.
Jun 25
Tom gets a School Service award and gets to stay at Hogwarts during his summer holidays from now on.
Dumbledore convinces Dippet to let Hagrid stay.
Hagrid becomes Gamekeeper in training.
Sep
Arthur Weasley is born.
1944
Molly (Weasley) is born.
Jul
Tom Riddle Jr murders Tom Riddle Sr and paternal grandparents Mr and Mrs Riddle in the village of Little Hangleton.
Sep 1
Tom Riddle becomes Head Boy.
1945
Jun 26
Tom Riddle graduates and begins to travel the world in search of immortality and power through the use of Dark Arts and dangerous experimental magical practices.

Dumbledore leaves Hogwarts and travels a bit himself.
Nov
Dumbledore defeats Grindelwald.
1946
Dumbledore begins to work with Nicolas Flamel on alchemy projects.
1947
Broderick Bode is born.
Newt Scamander gets the Werewolf Registry established.
Bathilda Bagshot publishes *A History of Magic*.
1950
Augustus Rookwood and Mr (Unknown) Nott are born.
1951
Mr (Unknown) Mulciber, Rita Skeeter, Rodolphus Lestrange, Mr Death Eater 1 and Bertha Jorkins are born.
1952
Mr (Unknown) Wilkes, Mr (Unknown) Jugson, Marge Dursley are born.
1953
Lucius Malfoy, Walden Macnair, Evan Rosier and Antonin Dolohov are born.
1954
Vernon Dursley, Petunia Evans, Mr (Unknown) Avery, Andromeda Black, Mr (Unknown) Stebbins, Severus Snape and Igor Karkoff are born.
1955
Universal Brooms Ltd. releases the Shooting Star.
Mr (Unknown) Crabbe, Mr Death Eater 2, Peter Pettigrew, James Potter, Remus Lupin, Lily Evans and Sirius Black are born. See Note 3.
Sep
Pr Binns starts teaching at Hogwarts. See Note C.
Arthur Weasley and Molly start Hogwarts.
1956
Narcissa Black, Rastaban Lestrange and Mr (Unknown) Goyle are born.
Sep
Minerva McGonagall is hired to teach Transfiguration at Hogwarts.
Hagrid becomes Gamekeeper and Keeper of Keys at Hogwarts.
1957
Sturgis Podmore, Regulus Black and Mr (Unknown) Travers are born.
1960
Millicent Bagnold is elected Minister of Magic.
1962
Remus Lupin gets bitten by a werewolf.
Jun
Arthur Weasley and Molly graduate Hogwarts.
Sep
Augustus Rookwood, Mr Mulciber and Mr Nott start Hogwarts.
1963
Barty Crouch Jr is born.
Bertha Jorkins, Rita Skeeter, Bellatrix Black, Rodolphus Lestrange and Mr Death Eater 1 start Hogwarts
Arthur gets a job at the MoM.
1964
Mr Wilkes, Evan Rosier, Mr Jugson and Antonin Dolohov start Hogwarts.

450

Armando Dippet retires as Headmaster of Hogwarts.
1965
Newt Scamander gets the Ban on Experimental Breeding passed.
Dumbledore becomes Head of Hogwarts.
Sep
Lucius Malfoy, Andromeda Black and Walden Macnair start Hogwarts.
1966
Pr Binns dies but goes on teaching.
Sep
Lily, James, Sirius, Remus, Peter, Mr Stebbins, Mr Avery, Igor and Severus start Hogwarts.
James, Sirius and Peter realize Remus is a werewolf and begin to study how to become Animagi with an eye toward joining Remus during his wolf periods.
1967
Arthur Weasley marries Molly.
Sep
Rastaban Lestrange, Mr Crabbe, Mr Goyle and Mr Death Eater 2 start Hogwarts.
1968
Sep
James joins Gryffindor Quidditch team.
Regulus Black, Mr Travers and Narcissa Black begin Hogwarts.
Bertha Jorkins gets hexed and ends up in Dumbledore's office.
1969
Sirius and James become Animagi.
Bill Weasley is born.
Jun
Augustus Rookwood, Mr Mulciber and Mr Nott graduate Hogwarts.
Sep
James becomes Captain and Seeker for the Gryffindor Quidditch Team.
1970
Voldemort begins his rise to power.
Barty Crouch Sr is made Head of Dept of Magical Law Enforcement.
Dumbledore forms the OoP.
Arthur joins the Order, but Molly does not.
Bertha Jorkins, Rita Skeeter, Bellatrix Black, Rodolphus Lestrange and Mr Death Eater 1 graduates Hogwarts.
Bellatrix, Rodolphus and Mr Death Eater 1 become Death Eaters.
Sep
Remus is made a Prefect in hopes of reigning in Sirius and James.
Lily Evans is probably made a Prefect as well.
1971
Peter manages to become an Animagi.
Jun
James and Sirius humiliate Severus in front of Remus and only Lily tries to stop them.
Mr Wilkes, Evan Rosier, Mr Jugson and Antonin Dolohov graduate Hogwarts and become Death Eaters.
Jul
Sirius runs away from home and never goes back.
Oct

The Harry Potter Companion

Sirius tries to get Severus killed or bitten by Remus, who is in a wolf state, but James saves him.

1972
Charlie Weasley is born.
Jun
Lucius Malfoy, Andromeda Black and Walden Macnair graduates Hogwarts.
Lucius and Walden become Death Eaters.
Sep
Lily Evans and James Potter become Head Girl and Head Boy.
1973
Lily and James start dating.
Janus Thickey fakes his death.
Jun
Lily, James, Sirius, Peter, Remus, Mr Stebbins, Igor, Mr Avery, Severus graduate Hogwarts.
Severus, Igor and Mr Avery become Death Eaters.
Jul
Sirius' Uncle Alphard dies leaving him money and Sirius gets his own place.
1974
Lily, James, Sirius, Peter and Remus all join the OoP and get day jobs as well.
June
Rastaban Lestrange, Mr Crabbe, Mr Goyle and Mr Death Eater 2 graduate Hogwarts and become Death Eaters.
1975
Mundungus Fletcher is banned from the Hog's Head by the barman.
Percy Weasley, Marcus Flint, Oliver Wood and Viktor Krum are born.
Lily Evans marries James Potter.
Jun
Petunia marries Vernon Dursley.
Regulus Black and Mr Travers graduate and become Death Eaters. Narcissa Black graduates. See Note D.
1976
Penelope Clearwater, Fleur Delacour and Mr (Unknown) Bole are born.
Lily's parents, the Evans, die. See Note E.
1977
Lily and James survive an attempt on their lives by Voldemort.
Mr (Unknown) Derrick, Lee Jordan, Patricia Stimpson, Kenneth Towler and C Warrington are born.
Oct 24
Angelina Johnson is born.
1978
Katie Bell, Alicia Spinnet, Roger Davies, Miles Bletchley, Cedric Diggory and Marietta Edgecombe are born.
Universal Brooms Ltd. goes out of business and the Shooting Star ceases to be made.
Lily and James survive a 2nd attempt on their lives by Voldemort.
Apr
Fred and George Weasley are born.
Sep
Angelina Johnson is born.
1979

ACASCIAS RIPHOUSE

Newt Scamander gets the Order of Merlin, 2nd class.
Lily and James survive a 3rd attempt on their lives by Voldemort.
Cho Chang, Eddie Carmichael, Vincent Crabbe and Gregory Goyle, Michael Corner, Justin Finch-Fletchley, Ernie Macmillan, Eloise Midgen, Seamus Finnigan, Theodore Nott, Parvati and Padma Patil, Sally-Anne Perks, Morag MacDougal, Dean Thomas, Lisa Turpin and Blaise Zabini are born.

Jun
Rodolphus Lestrange marries Bellatrix Black.

Nov
Lily becomes pregnant with Harry.
Alice Longbottom becomes pregnant with Neville.

Dec
Dumbledore hires Sibyll Trelawney to teach Divination after she gives a real prophecy about Voldemort's defeat.
One of Voldemort's spies hears a part of the prophecy.

1980
Draco Malfoy, Ron Weasley, Hannah Abbot, Susan Bones, Terry Boot, Lavender Brown, Millicent Bulstrode, Anthony Goldstein, Daphne Greengrass, Eloise Midgen, (Unknown) Moon, Pansy Parkinson and Mandy Brocklehurst are born.
Regulus Black is killed by Death Eaters for failure to comply.
Edgar Bones and family are killed by Death Eaters.
Peter Pettigrew gets leaned on by Voldemort, who suspects Lily to be carrying the child that will destroy him, and Peter begins passing information about the Potters to Voldemort.
Stubby Boardman gives up singing with the Hobgoblins.

May
Dumbledore suspects someone close to the Potters of betraying them.
Carardoc Dearborn disappears.

Jun 24
Dudley Dursley is born.

Jul
At the end of Jul Neville Longbottom is born.

Jul 31
Harry James Potter born.

Aug 27
Sirius becomes Harry's godfather.

Sep
Hermione Granger is born.

1981
Ginny Weasley, Luna Lovegood and Colin Creevey are born.
James Potter's parents die. See Note F.
Benjy Fenwick is killed by Death Eaters.

Sep 1
Bill starts Hogwarts.

Sep 15
Dumbledore offers to be the Potter's Secret-Keeper but Lily and James insist on using Sirius Black.

Oct 24
James and Lily make Peter Pettigrew their Secret-Keeper at Sirius' request and go into hiding at Godric's Hollow.

453

Sirius Black goes into hiding as well, to keep up the illusion that he is the Potter's Secret-Keeper.

Peter betrays Lily and James to Voldemort.

Book 1 *Harry Potter and the Sorcerer's Stone* timeline begins

1981

Oct 31

James tries to hold Voldemort off so Lily can make a run for it with Harry but James is mortally wounded by Voldemort.

Voldemort doesn't want to kill Lily, but Lily throws herself in the way so Voldemort has to kill her, thus giving Harry a very strong protection against Voldemort.

Lily dies from the Avada Kedavra curse.

James dies of his wounds.

Voldemort tries to kill Harry but fails, gets vaporized and flees to Albania.

Harry lives but is wounded (this wound eventually becomes his scar).

Nov 1

Owls and shooting stars appear in the daytime.

Hagrid picks up Harry and Sirius loans him his flying motorcycle.

Hagrid hides all during the day, because he can't use the flying motorcycle in daylight and besides, he has to feed and change Harry.

Sirius Black attempts to catch Peter Pettigrew.

Peter kills 12 Muggles, fakes his death and escapes as a rat down the sewer line he cracked open with the murderous blast.

Fudge, then Junior Minister at the DMAC, is first on the scene.

Sirius gets the blame and is sent to Azkaban by Barty Sr without a trial.

The MoM disseminates a lie saying the incident was caused by a gas explosion.

Night falls and Hagrid brings Harry to Dumbledore.

Harry is left at the Dursley's just about midnight.

Nov 2

Harry is found on the doorstep by Petunia Dursley with a letter from Dumbledore explaining how Harry will be safe as long as he can stay with her. She screams.

Nov 25

Severus Snape is cleared of any wrongdoing after Dumbledore vouches for him.

Dec

Severus Snape starts teaching at Hogwarts. See Note 4.

1982

Emma Dobbs, Laura Madley, Natalie McDonald, Graham Pritchard, Kevin Whitby and Rose Zeller are born.

Jan

Death Eaters Mr Rosier and Mr Wilkes are killed by Aurors.

Feb

Death Eater Mr Avery escapes prosecution by claiming Imperius Curse.

Mar

Death Eater Igor Karkoff rats out other Death Eaters, including Mr Rookwood, is set free and leaves Britain.

Mr Rookwood is sent to Azkaban.

Ludo Bagman plays Beater for England.

Ludo is tried for being a Death Eater but gets off.

Apr

ACASCIAS RIPHOUSE

Frank and Alice Longbottom are tortured to insanity by the Rodolphus, Bellatrix and Rastaban Lestrange and Barty Jr in an attempt to find Voldemort, whose whereabouts they thought the Longbottoms knew.
Neville Longbottom becomes Gran Longbottom's ward.
Aug
Bellatrix, Rodolphus and Rastaban Lestrange and Barty Jr go to Azkaban for torturing the Longbottoms.
Barty Crouch Sr disowns his son.
1983
Dennis Creevey, Stewart Ackerley, Malcolm Baddock, Owen Cauldwell, Eleanor Branstone and Orla Quirke are born.
Amelia Bones takes over as Head of the DMLE.
Barty Crouch Sr becomes Head of the DIMC.
Barty Crouch Jr is replaced in Azkaban by his mother, who dies shortly afterwards.
Barty Jr lives with his father under Winky's strict supervision and his father's Imperius Curse.
Sep 1
Charlie starts Hogwarts.
1984
Euan Abercrombie is born.
Sirius' father dies.
Jul
Fred turns Ron's teddy bear into a spider giving Ron a lifetime phobia.
Sep
Charlie becomes Seeker for Gryffindor Quidditch Team.
1985
Sirius Black's mother dies and the house at 12 Grimmauld Place sits empty but for Kreacher.
May
Gryffindor wins the Quidditch Cup, then goes on a long losing streak. See Note 5.
Jun 24
At Dudley's birthday party, Marge Dursley beats Harry's shins with her walking stick so Dudley can win at musical statues.
Aug
Bertha Jorkins, while working for Barty Crouch Sr at the DMLE, discovers Barty Jr is alive and out of prison.
Barty Sr gives her an overly strong Memory Charm.
Sep
Pr Quirrell starts teaching at Hogwarts.
1986
Gabrielle Delacour is born.
Jun 24
Dudley gets a new red bike and Harry is consumed with jealousy.
Sep
Marcus Flint starts Hogwarts.
1987
Fred gives Ron an Acid Pop and it burns a hole through his tongue.
Wilhelm Wigworthy publishes *Home Life and Social Habits of British Muggles*, which is subsequently adopted as the Muggle Studies' textbook at Hogwarts.
Jul 31

THE HARRY POTTER COMPANION

Harry ceases to get pocket money from the Dursleys.
Sep 1
Percy Weasley, Mr Bole, Mr Derrick, Penelope Clearwater, Marcus Flint and Oliver Wood start Hogwarts.
Viktor Krum starts Durmstrang.
Harry and Dudley start grammar school.
Harry gets fairly good grades and Dudley gets a gang.
1988
Harry is made to stand in a toilet by Dudley and his gang.
Jun
Bill Weasley leaves Hogwarts and gets a job with Gringotts.
Sep
Harry accidentally magically turns a teacher's wig blue.
Harry is punished, a week in the cupboard.
Fleur Delacour starts Beauxbatons.
Dec 25
Marge gives Dudley a computerized robot and Harry dog biscuits.
1989
Harry accidentally magically shrinks an old brown sweater with orange fluff balls on it to hand-puppet size.
Sep 1
Fred and George, Lee Jordan, Angelina Johnson, Katie Bell, Roger Davies, C Warrington and Alicia Spinnet start Hogwarts.
1990
Jan
Harry is given a really bad haircut but it all grows back overnight.
Harry is punished, a week in the cupboard.
Jun
Charlie Weasley graduates Hogwarts. See Note 6.
Marge allows Ripper to tree Harry for almost a day after he accidentally steps on the dog's tail.
Jul
Hagrid buys Fluffy from a Greek man in a pub.
Sep
Pr Quirrell goes on a sabbatical to do vampire research and ends up meeting Voldemort.
Miles Bletchley, Eddie Carmichael, Roger Davies, Cho Chang, Cedric Diggory and Marietta Edgecombe start Hogwarts.
Nov
Harry tries to jump behind some big trash cans to escape Dudley and his gang but suddenly finds himself sitting on the chimney on the roof of the school kitchens.
Harry is punished, locked in the cupboard.
Dec
Millicent Bagnold retires and Cornelius Fudge becomes Minister of Magic.
Mrs Lovegood has a fatal experimental spell accident in front of Luna.
1991
Jun 21
Harry and Dudley graduate from primary school.
Jun 23
A wizarding stranger in a long purple coat shakes Harry's hand in the street.

Jun 24
Dudley's birthday, on which he gets 39 presents.
Harry goes to the Zoo, talks to a boa constrictor then accidentally does magic.
Harry is sent to the cupboard for punishment for 2 weeks.
Jul 12
Percy is made a Prefect and gets Hermes the owl as a present from his parents.
Percy finds out he got 12 OWLs.
Penelope Clearwater is made a Prefect.
Jul 23
Petunia and Dudley go up to London to get a uniform for Smeltings.
Harry is left at Mrs Figg's house.
Marge gets ill on a bad whelk while vacationing on the Isle of Wight.
Jul 24
Petunia dyes Dudley's clothes grey for Harry to wear to Stonewall High.
Harry's 1st Hogwarts' letter arrives along with Marge's vacation postcard from Isle of Wight.
Vernon's first visit ever to Harry's cupboard.
Harry is moved to a bedroom upstairs.
Jul 25
A 2nd Hogwarts' letter arrives.
Dudley throws his tortoise through the greenhouse roof.
Jul 26
3 Hogwarts' letters arrive.
Vernon stays home from work that day to board up the mail slot.
Jul 27
12 Hogwarts' letters arrive.
Vernon nails up the house.
Jul 28
24 Hogwarts' letters arrive rolled up in 2 dozen eggs.
Jul 29
Over 40 Hogwarts' letters come out of kitchen fireplace.
Vernon packs up the family and flees the house.
The Dursleys and Harry stay the night at the Railview Hotel in Cokeworth.
Jul 30
About 100 Hogwarts' letters arrive at front desk of the Railview Hotel.
Vernon drives to the coast and rows the family out to Hut-on-the-Rock.
The Great Humberto is on TV.
Jul 31
Hagrid appears at midnight to hand deliver Harry's Hogwarts' letter.
Hagrid sends reply owl to Dumbledore and tells Harry all about his family and his being a wizard while making him dinner.
Harry leaves with Hagrid to go to Diagon Alley but not before Hagrid fights with Vernon and gives Dudley a pig's tail.
Harry meets Dedalus Diggle, Doris Crockford, Pr Quirrell and Tom the barkeeper at the Leaky Cauldron.
Harry discovers he's rich.
Hagrid collect the Sorcerer's Stone.
Harry meets Draco Malfoy in Madam Malkin's then gets all his school supplies.
Hagrid gives Harry a snowy owl (Hedwig) for is birthday.
Harry returns to Dursley's.

THE HARRY POTTER COMPANION

An attempt to break into Vault 713 and steal the Sorcerer's Stone is made by Pr Quirrell.

Aug 1
The Dursley's completely ignore Harry for the next 30 days.
Petunia stops vacuuming his room – the ultimate snub in her book.

Aug 5
Harry names his snowy owl Hedwig after someone in *A History of Magic*.
Pr Quirrell returns to Albania with bad news for Voldemort.

Aug 31
Harry tells Vernon and Petunia he needs to go to London.
Vernon and Petunia are going anyway to take Dudley to private hospital for tail removal.
Pr Quirrell returns to Hogwarts with Voldemort in his head.

Sep 1
Harry arrives at King's Cross Station and is dumped by the Dursleys.
Dudley checks into private London hospital for pig's tail removal.
Harry asks Molly Weasley for help and becomes acquainted with Percy, Fred, George, Ron, Molly and Ginny Weasley.
Lee Jordan is on the platform with his tarantula.
Fred and George help Harry with his trunk.
On the Hogwarts Express he befriends Ron and meets Neville Longbottom, Hermione Granger, Draco Malfoy, Vincent Crabbe and Gregory Goyle.
Harry decides he dislikes Draco, Crabbe and Goyle.
Harry is sorted into Gryffindor because he refuses to be a Slytherin.
At the Start of Term Feast Dumbledore warns everyone off the 3rd floor right-hand corridor.
Harry becomes a roommate of Ron, Seamus Finnigan, Dean Thomas and Neville Longbottom.

Sep 2
Classes begin.
Harry, Ron Weasley, Hannah Abbot, Susan Bones, Mandy Brocklehurst, Terry Boot, Lavender Brown, Millicent Bulstrode, Michael Corner, Vincent Crabbe, Justin Finch-Fletchley, Seamus Finnigan, Anthony Goldstein, Hermione Granger, Neville Longbottom, Draco Malfoy, Eloise Midgen, Theodore Nott, Morag MacDougal, Dean Thomas, Lisa Turpin, Blaise Zabini, Daphne Greengrass, Ernie Macmillan, ? Moon, Pansy Parkinson, Parvati and Padma Patil, Sally-Anne Perks start Hogwarts.

Sep 6
Harry meets Pr Snape during Potions class with the Slytherins.
Harry has tea with Hagrid.

Sep 12
Neville gets a Remembrall.
Harry finds he's good at flying.
Pr McGonagall gets Albus to bend the House team rules so Harry can play.
Harry meets Oliver Wood and makes the Gryffindor Quidditch team as the youngest Seeker in a century.

Sep 13
Harry is challenged Draco to a midnight wizard's duel in the Trophy Room but Draco never shows up.
Ron, Hermione, Harry and Neville find Fluffy.
Hermione sees the trapdoor Fluffy is guarding.

Sep 18
Harry's Nimbus 2000 arrives, a gift from Pr McGonagall.
Harry has his first secret practice with Wood and spends it catching golf balls.
Hermione stops speaking to Ron and Harry.
Oct 31
Ron insults Hermione to tears over her lack of friends.
A mountain troll attack occurs during Halloween Feast.
Pr Quirrell tries to lure all the teachers to the dungeons.
Pr Snape outwits Pr Quirrell but is bitten in the leg by Fluffy (apparently Pr Snape isn't musical).
Hermione, Harry and Ron defeat the mountain troll and become firm friends.
Nov 8
Pr Snape takes Harry's Library copy of *Quidditch Through the Ages.*
Harry sees Snape's bitten leg.
Nov 30
Harry plays the Gryffindor v. Slytherin game and discovers he loves Quidditch.
Pr Quirrell attempts to jinx Harry's broom but Pr Snape stops him.
Harry has tea with Hagrid and hear about Nicolas Flamel.
Dec 7
Harry, Ron and Hermione start looking for Nicolas Flamel in the Library.
Dec 9
Pr McGonagall comes around, 2 weeks before Christmas vacation, taking names of the students staying.
Harry, Ron, Percy, Fred and George opt to stay.
Dec 15
Several feet of snow falls and the lake freezes.
Dec 20
Pr McGonagall and Pr Flitwick begin the decoration of the Great Hall.
Hagrid brings in the 12 Christmas Trees.
Dec 22
Three-week Christmas holidays start.
Dec 25
Arthur and Molly visit Charlie in Romania.
Harry wakes up to presents, including an Invisibility Cloak.
Christmas Feast is held at lunchtime.
Harry has an afternoon snowball fight with Weasley boys.
Harry finds the Mirror of Erised.
Dec 26
Harry shows Ron the Mirror of Erised.
Ron decides it's a Dark object.
Dec 27
Harry returns to the Mirror of Erised and meets Dumbledore there.
Dec 28
The Mirror of Erised is moved.
Dec 29
Harry begins to have nightmares about his parents' death.
1992
Bertha Jorkins starts working for Ludo at the DMGS.
Jan 12
Hermione returns to school.

The Harry Potter Companion

Jan 13
Second Term starts.
Quidditch practices starts again.
Feb 4
Neville gets cursed by Draco and uncursed by Hermione.
Flamel is found on a Chocolate Frog trading card.
Feb 10
Pr Snape starts stalking Harry to protect him from Pr Quirrell.
Feb 21
Pr Snape referees a rare afternoon Quidditch match Gryffindor v. Hufflepuff and Dumbledore attends.
Ron attacks Draco and Neville attacks Crabbe and Goyle.
Pr Snape confronts Pr Quirrell in the Forbidden Forest and is overheard by Harry.
Mar 29
Hermione starts drawing up study schedules.
Apr 12
Three-week Easter holidays start.
Most everyone stays at school.
There is lots of homework.
May 3
Lucius Malfoy begins to cook up an idea to discredit Arthur Weasley and get the Muggle Protection Act Arthur is working on scrapped.
Dobby overhears his plans and worries about Harry Potter being hurt by it all.
May 4
Easter Holidays end.
The Third Term starts.
May 5
Hagrid steals books on dragons from the Library.
Harry, Hermione and Ron discover Hagrid has acquired a dragon's egg.
May 11
Hermione starts making study schedules for Ron and Harry.
May 14
Norbert hatches.
May 21
Ron asks Charlie to take Norbert via Hedwig.
May 27
Ron is bitten by Norbert.
Charlie's reply arrives.
May 28
Ron is hospitalized and Draco steals Charlie's letter.
May 30
At midnight, 4 of Charlie's friends pickup Norbert from the Tallest Tower (Astronomy Tower).
Harry, Neville and Hermione lose Gryffindor 150 points and get detentions.
Draco gets a detention.
Harry loses his Invisibility Cloak.
Jun 1
All the Gryffindors, Hufflepuffs and Ravenclaws stop speaking to Harry.
Jun 3
Harry serves his detention with Hagrid in the Forbidden Forest.

Harry meets the centaurs: Firenze, Ronan and Bane.
Harry sees a dead unicorn, then Voldemort and his scar starts to hurt.
Firenze saves Harry.
Jun 4
Harry gets his Invisibility Cloak back thanks to Dumbledore.
Harry's scar continues to hurt and he starts having bad dreams.
Jun 8-13
Exam week.
Harry's scar continues to hurt and he keeps having bad dreams.
Jun 13
The last exam ends and Harry, Hermione and Ron try to save the Sorcerer's Stone since Dumbledore is away at the MoM.
Neville is petrified by Hermione.
Harry defeats Fluffy, Hermione the devil's snare, Harry the winged keys, Ron the wizard's chess, Pr Quirrell had already knocked out the mountain troll, Hermione solved the potions puzzle, Harry gets the stone from the Mirror of Erised.
Harry is attacked by Voldemort.
Dumbledore saves Harry and Voldemort escapes back to Albania.
Pr Quirrell dies when Voldemort leaves his body.
Jun 14
Gryffindor v. Ravenclaw Quidditch match in which Gryffindor plays even though they have no Seeker and Ravenclaw wins giving Gryffindor its worst defeat in 300 years.
Slytherin wins the House Cup and the Quidditch Cup.
Harry is in a coma.
Jun 15
Student have this week after exams off.
Jun 17
Harry wakes up from his coma.
Hagrid gives him a photo album with pictures of his parents.
Jun 18
At the End of Year Feast, last minute points are awarded by Dumbledore.
Gryffindor upsets Slytherin and wins the House Cup.
Jun 21-25
Normal classes resume.
All of the Gryffindors get passing grades.
Hermione is the top of her class in everything.
Jun 27
The Hogwarts Express takes everyone home for the Jul-Aug summer vacation.
Harry's school things are locked in the cupboard under the stairs.
Hedwig is padlocked in her cage.
Jun 28 - Jul 31
Dobby stops Harry's mail, including Ron's 12 letters.
Percy writes to Penelope Clearwater all summer.
Book 2 *Harry Potter and the Chamber of Secrets* timeline
1992
Jul 17
The Dursleys start talking about a dinner party with the Masons on Jul 31.
Jul 31
Harry's 12th birthday.

THE HARRY POTTER COMPANION

Dobby admits to stealing Harry's letter and tries to force him not to go back to Hogwarts.
The Masons come to dinner.
Dobby Hover Charms then wrecks a desert.
Harry is warned about using magic by Mafalda Hopkirk of the MoM.
Vernon finds out Harry can't use magic outside of school.
Vernon decides Harry won't return to Hogwarts.

Aug 1
Vernon pays a man to fit bars on Harry's windows and a catflap in the door.
Harry is let out of his room only twice a day to use the bathroom.

Aug 3
Arthur hears about the warning Harry got from the MoM and tells his family.

Aug 4
Ron, Fred and George break Harry out using Arthur's flying Ford Anglia.
Arthur conducts 9 raids, including one on Mundungus Fletcher's place.

Aug 5
Harry arrives at the Burrow and meets Molly, Arthur and Ginny.
Bill and Charlie are overseas.
Harry and the Weasley boys degnome the Burrow's garden.

Aug 12
Hogwarts' letters arrive with supply and book lists.
Ginny is accepted to Hogwarts.
Hermione writes Ron and Harry to arrange a meet in Diagon Alley.
Percy starts wearing his Prefect badge everywhere.
The Harry and the Weasley boys play Quidditch in the back paddock.

Aug 19
Harry uses Floo Powder, breaks his glasses and ends up in Knockturn Alley.
Harry overhears Lucius Malfoy selling Dark Arts things.
Hagrid, buying slug repellent in Knockturn Alley, finds and rescues Harry.
The Weasleys, the Grangers and Harry all meet at Gringotts.
Gilderoy Lockhart, while doing a book signing at Flourish and Blotts, announces his new position as teacher of DADA at Hogwarts.
Arthur and Lucius Malfoy have a fistfight in Flourish and Blotts and Hagrid breaks it up.
Lucius secretly puts Tom Riddle's Diary in Ginny's used Transfiguration book.

Aug 20
Ginny begins writing in Tom's Diary and getting answers back.

Aug 31
Molly makes all Harry's favorite foods for a going away party.

Sep 1
Arthur drives everyone to King's Cross Station in the Ford Anglia.
Dobby prevents Harry and Ron from getting to the Hogwarts Express.
Harry and Ron fly the Ford Anglia to Hogwarts, get stuck in the Whomping Willow then are caught by Pr Snape.
Ron's wand in broken almost in half.
Dumbledore writes to Ron's and Harry's families and they get detentions.
Ginny is sorted into Gryffindor.
Colin Creevey and Luna Lovegood start Hogwarts.

Sep 2
Ron gets a Howler from Molly.

Pr McGonagall hands out class schedules to her House.
Harry meets Colin Creevey and his camera at lunch.
Sep 4
Ron accidentally hits Pr Flitwick with a spell from his wonky wand.
Sep 5
Slytherin House team members all get Nimbus 2001s, paid for by Lucius.
Slytherin makes Draco Malfoy the team Seeker.
Draco calls Hermione a Mudblood and Ron ends up barfing slugs after his curse backfires.
Hagrid's rooster is killed (by Ginny)
Harry and Ron do their detentions: Harry helps Pr Lockhart address envelops for fan mail, Ron helps Filch polish silver in the Trophy Room.
Harry hears the basilisk speaking while at Pr Lockhart's office.
Oct 1
Madam Pomfrey treats students and staff for colds.
Oct 28
Harry is caught by Filch, dripping in the castle, but saved by Nearly Headless Nick's diversionary tactics.
Harry finds out about Filch taking a Kwikspell course.
Nearly Headless Nick asks Harry to his 500th Deathday Party.
Fred and George set off a salamander by feeding it a firework.
Oct 31
Harry, Ron and Hermione attend Nearly Headless Nick's Deathday Party in Dungeon 5.
Harry meets Moaning Myrtle.
Harry hears the basilisk in the dungeon walls and follows it up to the 1st floor, then the 2nd floor, where he finds the writing on the wall left by Ginny and a Petrified Mrs Norris.
Harry finds out Filch is a Squib, and what a Squib is.
Nov 1
Filch tries to remove message, begins to guard the scene of the crime and becomes really hostile to students.
Nov 3
Ginny is very disturbed by recent events.
Nov 11
Hermione confronts Pr Binns about the Chamber of Secrets.
People begin avoiding Harry because they think he's the Heir of Slytherin.
Harry, Ron and Hermione find scorch marks and spiders in the corridor where Mrs Norris was attacked, the same corridor Moaning Myrtle's bathroom is on.
Hermione suggests the use of Polyjuice Potion to get a confession from Draco.
Nov 17
Pr Lockhart gives Hermione a note to check out *Moste Potente Potions* from the Library's Restricted Section.
Nov 14
During the Gryffindor v. Slytherin Quidditch match Dobby's rouge Bludger goes after Harry.
Harry breaks his arm and Pr Lockhart debones him.
Madam Pomfrey keeps Harry in the Hospital wing to regrow his 33 arm bones.
Dobby visits Harry and reveals the Chamber has been opened before, 50 years ago.
Colin is found Petrified on the stairs by Pr McGonagall.

THE HARRY POTTER COMPANION

Nov 15
Harry leaves Hospital.
Ron and Hermione have started working on the Polyjuice Potion in Myrtle's bathroom.
Nov 16
Everyone discovers Colin's been attacked.
First years start moving around in groups for protection.
Ginny begins having nightmares.
A black-market trade in protective devices springs up among students.
Neville buys things even though he's a pureblood.
Dec 7
Pr McGonagall collects names of students staying for Christmas.
Draco, Crabbe, Goyle, Ron, Percy, Fred, George, Ginny, Harry and Hermione stay.
Dec 10
Harry creates a distraction while Hermione steals potion ingredients from Pr Snape's private store cupboard during Potions class.
Dec 17
The Dueling Club in the Great Hall starts, led by Pr Lockhart.
Pr Snape tells Draco to use a snake against Harry in a duel.
Harry speaks Parseltongue but his actions are misinterpreted.
Dec 18
Herbology is canceled so Pr Sprout can sock and scarve the mandrakes.
Harry overhears Ernie and Hannah saying evil things about him in the Library.
A 2nd rooster of Hagrid's is killed (by Ginny).
Justin and Nearly Headless Nick are found Petrified, by Harry.
Harry is taken to Dumbledore's office and retries the Sorting Hat.
The Sorting Hat stands by what it said.
Fawkes bursts into flame and is reborn.
Dec 19
Fred and George walk around announcing Harry everywhere he goes as the Heir of Slytherin.
Ginny is upset by Fred and George's behavior and Percy threatens to write Molly about it.
Dec 20
Christmas holidays begins.
All the Weasley boys (except Percy) play Exploding Snap, practice dueling.
Arthur and Molly visit Bill in Egypt.
Dec 25
The Polyjuice is ready.
Harry gets presents and Hedwig even brings a present from the Dursleys.
After Christmas Feast, Hermione drugs Crabbe and Goyle.
Percy and Penelope are in the dungeons kissing.
Harry and Ron interrogate Draco to no avail.
Hermione's potion goes awry and she goes to Hospital wing looking rather like a cat.
The Daily Prophet reports on Arthur being fined 50G's for flying car.
1993
Jan 11
Second Term begins.
Hermione is still in Hospital.
Jan 18
Harry and Ron find Riddle's 1943 diary in Myrtle's bathroom.

ACASCIAS RIPHOUSE

Feb 1
Hermione is released from Hospital.
Hermione tries various things on Tom's Diary to get it to reveal itself but to no avail.
Feb 2
Harry goes to the Trophy Room to find out more about Tom Riddle.
Feb 14
Pr Lockhart annoys the entire school by setting up a St Valentine's Day event.
Ginny sends Harry a singing Valentine.
Harry discovers how the Diary works.
Harry is shown Riddle's memory of the events of Jun 13, 1943 - regarding Hagrid and Aragog, and Aragog's escape.
Mar 28
Easter holiday starts.
Second years have to think about electives for their 3rd year now.
Apr 18
Easter holidays ends.
Apr 19
Third Term begins.
Gryffindor begins Quidditch practices every night after dinner until the big game on May 8.
Apr 30
Ginny trashes Harry's room to get the Tom Riddle's Diary back.
May 8
Gryffindor v. Hufflepuff Quidditch match is canceled just before it starts by Pr McGonagall after Hermione and Penelope are found Petrified near the Library.
Emergency measures are put into action.
Harry and Ron go to see Hagrid and Hagrid tells them the spiders are a clue.
Hagrid is arrested and sent to Azkaban for protective custody by MoM head Cornelius Fudge and School Governor Lucius Malfoy, against Dumbledore's wishes.
Dumbledore is suspended as Head of Hogwarts.
Pr McGonagall becomes acting Head of Hogwarts.
May 10
Visitors are banned from the Hospital wing.
May 24
Draco says he'll recommend Pr Snape for Headmaster during Potions class.
May 25
Ron and Harry go to visit Aragog and discover Hagrid was innocent in 1943. They are then attacked by the spiders but rescued by the feral Ford Anglia.
Harry realizes Myrtle was the person killed in 1943.
Exams are announced by acting Headmistress McGonagall.
May 29
The mandrakes are ready for use.
Harry and Ron visit Hermione and discover she has solved the mystery of the monster, that it is a basilisk in the pipeworks.
Ginny is taken hostage by Tom Riddle.
Students are ordered to pack up as the school is closing immediately.
Pr Lockhart attempts to flee rather than face the basilisk.
Harry, Ron and Pr Lockhart all set out to stop the basilisk.
Pr Lockhart loses his memory trying to rid Ron and Harry of their's

The Harry Potter Companion

Harry defeats the basilisk and Tom Riddle with the help of Fawkes and the Sorting Hat.
Ginny is saved.
Dumbledore returns to Hogwarts as Head.
Hagrid is finally cleared of the crime that got him expelled from Hogwarts in 1943.

May 30
A midnight feast of celebration ensues.
All the Petrified are restored to normal.
Hagrid returns.
Gryffindor wins the House Cup.
Harry gets Dobby set free.
Lucius is sacked as a school governor.

May 31
DADA classes canceled for the rest of the term.
Ginny returns to normal.

Jun
Exams are canceled.
Everyone gets a pass.

Jun 26
Harry returns to the Dursleys.
His school things are locked in the cupboard.

Book 3 *Harry Potter the Prisoner of Azkaban* timeline begins
1993
Jun 28
Vernon gets a new company car.
Harry picks the lock on the cupboard, gets his school supplies out and hides them in his room.

Jul 1
Viktor Krum is asked to play Seeker for Bulgaria and takes a year off school to do so.

Jul 2
Ron tries to call Harry on the telephone but gets Vernon.

Jul 28
Hedwig flies off to make the rounds of Harry's friends to insure that his birthday isn't forgotten.

Jul 16
Arthur Weasley wins the 700G purse in *The Daily Prophet* Grand Prize Galleon Drawing and decides to take the family to visit Bill in Egypt for a month.

Jul 19
Percy Weasley is made Head Boy.

Jul 23
The Weasleys go to Egypt.

Jul 24
The Weasleys are in *The Daily Prophet.*
Sirius Black sees the picture of Ron with Peter (as Scabbers) in *The Daily Prophet* Fudge gives him.
Sirius realizes that Ron and Harry are both at Hogwarts, and that Peter is there too, probably waiting to do Harry harm as soon as Voldemort reappears.
Sirius wants to find Peter to kill him, but also to protect Harry and explain to him what happened to his parents.
Sirius alone knows that Peter is Voldemort's servant and would harm Harry.

Cedric Diggory becomes a Prefect.
Jul 31
Sirius escapes from Azkaban as Snuffles and journeys to Little Whinging to find Harry.
Harry gets birthday presents, cards and a Hogwarts' letter.
Muggle news reports the escape of Sirius Black.
Aunt Marge arrives by train for a week's visit.
Harry sends Hedwig with Errol to Ron's house.
Aug 3
Marge insults Harry's mother at lunch and he unintentionally magically causes her wineglass to shatter.
Aug 7
After dinner Marge continues to insult Harry's family till he unintentionally magically causes her to swell up like a balloon and float to the ceiling.
Harry unintentionally magically opens the cupboard door, grabs all his stuff and runs off into the night.
Harry sees Sirius, as a Snuffles, and gets picked up by the Knight Bus.
Harry meets Cornelius Fudge and books in at the Leaky Cauldron for his remaining vacation.
Hedwig joins Harry at the Leaky Cauldron.
Aug 8
Harry spends the rest of his vacation as a resident at the Leaky Cauldron, Room 11.
Harry hangs out every day in Diagon Alley.
Aug 9
Harry strikes up a friendship with Florean Fortescue, owner of an ice cream parlor, who helps him with his History of Magic homework as well as gives him free sundaes.
Aug 16
Harry sees the Firebolt in the window at Quality Quidditch Supplies and goes back every day afterwards to look at it.
Aug 18
Harry picks up potion supplies, a new set of robes and books for the coming year.
Harry is worried that he might have seen the Grim, which looks very similar to Snuffles.
Aug 21
The Weasleys return from Egypt.
The MoM pulls everyone off their regular jobs to look for Sirius Black, without any luck.
Aug 24
Harry runs into Seamus Finnigan and Dean Thomas looking at the Firebolt.
Aug 26
Harry runs into Neville and Gran Longbottom outside Flourish and Blotts.
Aug 31
Ron gets a new wand.
Harry meets Ron and Hermione sitting outside Florean Fortescue's Ice Cream Parlor.
Hermione buys Crookshanks.
The Weasleys and Hermione stay at the Leaky Cauldron, and have a 6-course going away dinner.
Harry overhears Molly and Arthur in a private parlor saying Sirius Black is out to get him.
Sep 1

THE HARRY POTTER COMPANION

Harry, Hermione and the Weasleys go to King's Cross Station in 2 MoM cars.
Dementors are stationed around Hogwarts' entrances.
Arthur discovers Harry knows about Sirius looking for him.
The dementors board the train and Harry faints at the sight of them.
Remus Lupin performs the Patronus Charm.
Harry recovers and he, Hermione, Ron, Ginny and Neville meet Pr Lupin, who gives everyone chocolate.
Pr McGonagall give Hermione a MoM Time-Turner.
Harry misses the Sorting for the second year in a row.
Pr Lupin is the new DADA teacher.
Hagrid is announced as the new Care of Magical Creatures teacher.

Sep 2
At Divination class, Harry's death is predicted.
Pr McGonagall turns into a cat and discusses Animagi in Transfiguration.
Draco get a slash to his right arm from Buckbeak during the first Care of Magical Creatures class and ends up in Hospital.
Hagrid starts drinking after the accident with Draco and Buckbeak because he fears being fired.

Sep 3
Draco announces his father has complained to the School Governors and the MoM about Hagrid.
Sirius is sighted near the school.
Pr Lupin teaches the coolest DADA class ever.

Sep 5
Dolores Umbridge drafts anti-werewolf legislation that makes it almost impossible for a werewolf to get work (which probably passed rather quickly after Pr Lupin was ratted out of Hogwarts).

Oct 15
Oliver Wood calls a meeting of the House team.
Crookshanks attacks Scabbers.

Oct 16
Lavender Brown gets word her rabbit Binky was killed by a fox.

Oct 31
Ron and Hermione go to Hogsmeade while Harry stays and visits with Pr Lupin.
Pr Lupin gets a grindylow, says Lord Voldemort and drinks a smoking Wolfsbane Potion Pr Snape gives him to prevent the worst of the werewolf symptoms, loss of his human mind.
The Fat Lady's portrait is found slashed by Sirius Black after the Halloween Feast.
The entire school is forced to sleep in the Great Hall in squashy purple sleeping bags while the building is searched.

Nov 1
The teachers and Percy start escorting, or tailing, Harry every where he goes.

Nov 10
Pr McGonagall lets Gryffindor practices continue but only with Madam Hooch there.

Nov 12
Wood finds out that Gryffindor is playing Hufflepuff rather than Slytherin.

Nov 19
Pr Lupin is absent and Pr Snape takes his place and teaches on werewolves instead of hinkypunks.

Pr Snape demands an essay on werewolves in an attempt to force all the DADA students to realize Pr Lupin is one.
Ron does a detention and finds that Pr Lupin was not sick in the Hospital.
Nov 20
The Gryffindor v. Hufflepuff match takes place in a gale force storm.
Harry see the Grim (Snuffles) in the empty topmost seats of the Quidditch stadium.
Dementors appear on the pitch and Harry falls 50' off his broom.
Hufflepuff wins the match.
Harry ends up in the hospital wing.
Harry's Nimbus 2000 is destroyed by the Whomping Willow.
Nov 22
Draco takes his bandages off.
Pr Lupin returns to class and promises to teach Harry how to fight dementors.
Only Hermione realizes, from doing Pr Snape's essay, Pr Lupin is a werewolf, but she says nothing.
Nov 27
Ravenclaw beats Hufflepuff in Quidditch.
Dec 5
Pr Flitwick decorates his classroom with fairies.
Hermione and Ron decide to stay over the Christmas holiday to keep Harry company.
Pr McGonagall organizes a list of people going home for Christmas.
Dec 11
Christmas holidays start.
Percy goes home for Christmas.
Fred and George give Harry the Marauder's Map so he can get to Hogsmeade.
Harry overhears that Sirius Black was responsible for the death of his parents.
The MoM has dementors patrolling the streets of Hogsmeade after sunset.
Fudge admits he does believe that Voldemort is back and publicly says he's worried what will happen if he gets his most devoted servant (Sirius Black) back.
Fudge dines with Dumbledore.
Fred and George set off 12 Dungbombs.
Dec 13
Hermione starts doing homework while Ron relaxes by the fire.
Harry confesses to Ron and Hermione that he hears his parents dying moments when dementors are near.
Harry, Ron and Hermione go to see Hagrid and find him weeping over a MoM letter saying Buckbeak must have a hearing and will likely be destroyed.
Hermione offers to look up legal cases on hippogriffs.
Harry volunteers himself and Ron to be witnesses.
The flobberworms are dead from overdosing on lettuce.
Dec 14
Harry, Ron and Hermione begin the library research on Buckbeak's defense.
Dec 24
Scabbers smells so much good cooking he finally pokes his nose out.
Dec 25
Harry gets a Firebolt anonymously, from Sirius.
Crookshanks scares Scabbers out of Ron's pocket.
Harry's Pocket Sneakoscope goes off.
Scabbers is very skinny with patches of skin showing.

Everyone eats the Christmas Feast at one table since so few stayed: Dumbledore, McGonagall, Snape, Sprout, Flitwick, Filch; 2 nervous 1st years, a sullen 5th year Slytherin, Harry, Ron and Hermione.

Pr Trelawney joins the feast late making 13.

Ron and Harry leave the table together making the "1st to leave dies curse" a little tricky.

Hermione rats Harry out thinking the Firebolt might be a booby-trapped gift from Sirius.

Pr McGonagall takes the Firebolt for jinx inspection by Madam Hooch and Pr Flitwick.

Dec 26

Hermione avoids Ron and Harry and studies in the Library instead of common room as they are no longer speaking.

1994

Jan 2

Wood considers dropping Harry from the team due to his dementor problems but decides to keep him after Harry tells him he will be getting anti-dementor lessons from Pr Lupin and has a Firebolt.

Wood talks to Pr McGonagall about returning Harry's Firebolt.

Hermione starts visiting Hagrid because she's lonely.

Jan 3

The Second Term begins.

Hagrid uses salamanders in class.

Jan 6

Harry's first anti-dementor lesson with Lupin in the History of Magic classroom doesn't go too well.

Using a boggart, Harry tries to learn the Patronus Charm.

Pr Lupin admits to Harry that he knew James and Sirius.

Jan 15

Slytherin beats Ravenclaw in a Quidditch match.

Hermione begins to crack under the pressure of too many classes.

Pr McGonagall is still not returning the Firebolt and yells at Wood for asking about it.

Jan 18

Harry starts asking for his Firebolt back after every Transfiguration class.

Feb 1

Fred and George start developing Ton-Tongue Toffees.

Apr 7

Harry is still not able to produce a proper Patronus.

Pr McGonagall gives back Harry's broom.

Neville has his list of passwords stolen by Crookshanks, for Sirius.

Harry and Ron try to make up with Hermione.

Scabbers fakes his own death, implicating Crookshanks.

The Ron-Hermione friendship seems at an end.

Apr 8

Harry lets Ron try his broom at Quidditch practice as Madam Hooch oversees because of Harry.

Harry spots the Grim's (Snuffle's) eyes, but only finds Crookshanks prowling around the grounds in the undergrowth.

Apr 9

Percy bets Penelope Clearwater 10G Gryffindor will win the match against Ravenclaw to impress her.

Harry shoots a huge Patronus at Marcus Flint, Crabbe and Draco on Goyle's shoulders who are pretending to be 3 dementors.
Gryffindor wins the match.
Apr 10
The Gryffindor party is shut down at a 1am by Pr McGonagall.
Hermione continues struggling through 422 pages of *Home Life and Social Habits of British Muggles.*
Sir Cadogan lets Sirius into Gryffindor Tower.
Sirius slashes Ron's curtains, thinking Scabbers was in Ron's bed, and Ron wakes up screaming.
Sirius escapes.
Pr McGonagall discovers Neville wrote down his passwords.
Pr Flitwick teaches the frontdoors to recognize Sirius.
Filch boards up all the cracks and mouseholes in the castle.
The Fat Lady returns to her job with security trolls to protect her.
Ron experiences instant celebrity.
Apr 12
Gran Longbottom sends Neville a Howler.
Harry and Ron go to Hagrid's for tea at 6 pm.
Hagrid says he's going to London on Friday for Buckbeak's hearing.
Hagrid asks Ron and Harry to make up with Hermione.
Hermione threatens to tell about the Marauder's Map.
Apr 19
Buckbeak and Hagrid go to London on the Knight Bus.
Apr 20
At Buckbeak's hearing, Lucius says Draco couldn't use his arm for 3 months.
Apr 21
Harry (in his Invisibility Cloak) and Ron go to Hogsmeade.
Draco sees Harry's head at the Shrieking Shack and bolts to Pr Snape.
Harry makes it back to Hogwarts but leaves his Invisibility Cloak in the secret passageway.
Pr Lupin takes the Marauder's Map.
Buckbeak looses his case but appeals.
Hermione and Ron make up.
Apr 23
Hermione, Harry and Ron promise to help Hagrid with the appeal for Buckbeak.
Hermione slaps Draco for insulting Hagrid and forgets to go to Charms because she's cracking under pressure (but let's face it, it's Draco. Who wouldn't slap him?).
Hermione drops Divination rather flamboyantly.
Apr 26 - May 15
Easter holidays.
Everyone has homework.
Ron works on Buckbeak's appeal.
Quidditch practice runs every day for Harry.
May 16 -20
The Third Term starts.
Harry is escorted to all his classes so he doesn't get beat up before the game by Slytherins.
May 21

Harry sees the Grim (Snuffles) and Crookshanks together at the edge of the Forbidden Forest in the wee hours of the morning.
Gryffindor beats Slytherin and wins the Quidditch Cup.
May 23
Hagrid sends word that Buckbeak's appeal is on Jun 6.
May 24-Jun 1
Everyone is studying for exams.
Jun 3
Exams begin.
Monday 9-12: Transfiguration (Arithmancy); 1-4: Charms (Ancient Runes).
Jun 4
Tuesday 9-12: Care of Magical Creatures; and 1-4: Potions exams.
Jun 5
Wednesday midnight: Astronomy; 9-12: History of Magic; 1-4: Herbology exams.
Jun 6
Thursday in the 9-12: DADA; 1-4: Divination (Muggle Studies).
Pr Trelawney gives a real prophecy while Harry is at his Divination exam but she doesn't remember it afterwards.
Buckbeak looses the appeal.
Hermione retrieves the Invisibility Cloak for Harry.
Harry, Ron and Hermione go to visit Hagrid before the execution.
Hermione finds Scabbers hiding in a cupboard.
Pr Lupin sees Peter Pettigrew's name on the Marauder's Map and realizes Sirius has been innocent all along.
Sirius jumps Ron (who has Scabbers in his pocket) and drags him under the Whomping Willow to the Shrieking Shack.
Ron's leg is broken by the willow.
Crookshanks opens the passage for Harry and Hermione.
Harry, Ron and Hermione confront Sirius, and Pr Lupin joins them.
Hermione exposes Pr Lupin for a werewolf.
Pr Snape hears the truth about Peter Pettigrew but doesn't believe it.
Pr Snape is knocked out by Ron and Hermione.
Peter is returned to a human state by Sirius and Pr Lupin.
While chained to Ron, Pr Lupin turns into a werewolf because of the full moon and forgetting to take his potion.
Peter escapes as a rat.
Sirius goes after Pr Lupin as Snuffles but is trapped as a man by the dementors by the Lake with Hermione and Harry.
Harry and Hermione save themselves, Sirius and Buckbeak by going back in time with Hermione's Time-Turner - at Dumbledore's suggestion.
Sirius escapes on Buckbeak and goes into hiding.
The dementors are sent back to Azkaban.
Jun 7
Harry, Hermione and Ron leave the Hospital.
Peter goes to Albania looking for Voldemort.
Jun 8
Harry, Ron and Hermione stay at Hogwarts rather than go to Hogsmeade.
Pr Lupin hurriedly resigns and leaves the school because Pr Snape told all the Slytherins he was a werewolf.
Pr Lupin gives back Harry's Invisibility Cloak and the Marauder's Map.

Sirius allows Dumbledore to use his house as the Order's Headquarters.
Pr Lupin goes to live at Sirius Black's house at 12 Grimmauld Place, London.
Jun 9 - 16
There is no class.
Jun 19 - 26
Classes resume.
Jun 26
Exam results come in and everyone passes.
Percy receives top grades in his NEWTs.
Fred and George get 3 OWLs a piece.
Gryffindor wins the House Cup for the 3rd year running.
Jun 27
Summer holidays begin.
Percy Weasley, Marcus Flint, Oliver Wood, Mr Derrick, Mr Bole and Penelope Clearwater graduate.
Everyone takes the Hogwarts Express home.
Hermione drops Muggle Studies but keeps Ancient Runes, Arithmancy and Care of Magical Creatures.
Ron promises to have Harry come and stay so they can go to QWC 1994.
Sirius sends Harry a tiny owl with a signed Hogsmeade permission slip.
The tiny owl is a gift for Ron to replace Scabbers and Ron ends up naming him Pig.
Harry tells Vernon that he has a convicted murderer for a godfather and that he's very interested in his well being so they better not mistreat him.
Book 4 *Harry Potter and the Goblet of Fire* timeline begins
1994
Jun 26
Harry gets to keep all his school stuff in his room under threat of Sirius finding out he's unhappy at the Dursleys' house.
Smeltings' nurse says Dudley must be put on a diet.
Everyone in the house must diet too.
Jun 28
Harry asks friends to send him food.
Jun 30
Hermione sends sugar-free snacks via Hedwig.
Sirius writes.
Bertha Jorkins goes on vacation to Albania to visit family members.
Jul 5
Hagrid send rock cakes via a school owl.
Jul 10
Molly sends assorted meat pies and a large fruitcake via Errol.
Jul 15
Peter meets Bertha Jorkins in Albania and brings her as a hostage to Voldemort.
Errol is finally able to fly back home.
Jul 16
Voldemort finds out a lot of information from Bertha, including that Barty Crouch Jr is out of Azkaban, QWC 1994 is being held in Britain, Moody will be teaching DADA at Hogwarts and the TT will be held at Hogwarts, then he kills her.
Jul 15
Bertha Jorkins fails to return to work at the MoM's DMGS.
Ludo Bagman, Bertha's boss, doesn't look for her.

Jul 20
Voldemort, having formed a plan, gets a body and returns to England with Peter's help.
Jul 31
Ron, Hermione, Hagrid and Sirius send Harry birthday cards and birthday cakes.
Sirius sends a letter by a very large tropical bird.
Aug 1
Dumbledore attends the International Confederation of Wizards' Conference.
Rita Skeeter writes a nasty piece about him.
Aug 3
Percy Passes his Apparition Test.
Tonks becomes an Auror.
Aug 18
Voldemort and Peter arrive at Riddle House and stay there till after QWC 1994.
Voldemort promises Peter will be given an honor and a task most followers would give their *right hand* for.
Harry, starting to see into Voldemort's mind, sees Voldemort kill Frank Bryce and wakes up with his scar hurting.
Molly's letter arrives via Muggle Post at the Dursley's asking Harry to QWC 1994 on Aug 20.
Ron's letter arrives.
Hermione arrives at the Burrow.
Percy gets a job with the DIMC.
Harry sends a letter to Sirius via Hedwig about his scar.
Aug 19
The Weasleys pick up Harry via the Floo Network.
Arthur, Fred, George and Ron get stuck in the Dursley's fireplace, so Arthur blows it up to get out.
Dudley eats a Ton-Tongue Toffee.
Harry meets Bill and Charlie Weasley for the first time.
By this time the competing schools in the TT have signed an agreement to play and to play at Hogwarts, the DMGS and the DIMC are jointly responsible for this event.
Aug 20
Fred and George are caught with Ton-Tongue Toffees.
Molly goes to Diagon Alley to get everyone's school supplies.
Amos and Cedric Diggory, Harry, Hermione and Arthur, Ron, Fred and George Weasley catch the 5:07am Portkey to QWC 1994: Ireland v. Bulgaria.
Basil is working the Portkeys.
Harry meets Dean Thomas, Seamus and Mrs Finnigan, Oliver Wood, Cho Chang and Ernie Macmillan at the campsite.
Harry discovers there are wizards and wizarding schools everywhere in the world.
Barty Crouch Jr takes Harry's wand while in the Top Box.
Harry sees Viktor Krum and professional Quidditch for the first time.
Ireland wins QWC 1994.
Aug 20
Former Death Eaters, including Lucius Malfoy, assault the Roberts family, owners of Harry's campsite.
Barty Crouch Jr lights up the Dark Mark with Harry's wand and escapes from Winky.
Winky is caught with a wand and fired.
The idea for SPEW begins to form in Hermione's mind.
Aug 21

Everyone returns to the Burrow.
Arthur and Percy go to work.
Arthur is supposed to be on holiday but the MoM needs people to investigate and field questions about the occurrence of the Dark Mark at QWC 1994.
Harry tells Ron and Hermione about his scar hurting.
The boys go play Quidditch in the upper paddock.
Aug 22 - 27
Arthur and Percy are busy at the MoM working long hours to try and calm people down and reassure them Voldemort is nowhere near Britain.
Barty Crouch Sr is put under an Imperius Curse by Voldemort.
Aug 28
Rita Skeeter finds out Bertha Jorkins is missing.
Ron gets a look at his ancient dress robes while packing.
Aug 29
Moody is attacked by Barty Jr, put under the Imperius Curse and locked in his own magical trunk.
Barty Jr takes Moody's place using Polyjuice Potion.
Sep 1
Amos Diggory gets Arthur to handle the exploding dustbin affair.
Harry learns about using a floo phone and about "Mad-Eye" Moody.
Bill, Charlie and Molly see everyone off on the Hogwarts Express.
Dennis Creevey, Kevin Whitby, Stewart Ackerley, Graham Pritchard, Malcolm Baddock, Mandy Brocklehurst, Owen Cauldwell, Emma Dobbs, Laura Madley, Eleanor Branstone, Orla Quirke and Natalie McDonald start Hogwarts.
Hermione discovers Hogwarts has house-elves.
Dumbledore announces Moody (actually Barty Jr) is taking the DADA job and the TT will be happening at Hogwarts so Quidditch is canceled.
Sep 2
Hagrid introduces the blast-ended skrewts project to his horrified class.
Arthur Weasley ends up in *The Daily Prophet* thanks to Rita Skeeter finding out about Moody's dustbin problems.
Pr Moody (Barty Jr) turns Draco into a ferret and bounces him around the entrance hall till Pr McGonagall stops him.
Sep 4
Neville gets detention for melting his 6th cauldron in Potions.
Pr Moody (Barty Jr) teaches on the Unforgivable Curses.
Pr Moody (Barty Jr) gives Neville a book that contains the answer to one of the TT tasks.
Ron and Harry start making up their Divination homework and Sybill doesn't notice.
The Weasley twins write a letter to Ludo Bagman trying to get their winnings from the QWC 1994 bet they placed with him.
Hermione starts SPEW.
Hedwig returns with Sirius letter and gets offended by Harry.
Sep 5
Harry sends Sirius a retraction letter hoping he won't come to Britain and get caught.
Sep 23
Pr Moody (Barty Jr) preforms the Imperius Curse on each student in DADA class.
Only Harry can throw the Imperius Curse off.
Oct 24
Hagrid has students come to his cabin on alternate nights to observe skrewt behavior.

THE HARRY POTTER COMPANION

Oct 25
Filch cleans the whole castle and scrubs all the portraits for the upcoming arrival of the Beauxbatons and Durmstrang students and their respective Heads.

Oct 30
Hedwig arrives with a letter from Sirius who insists on coming back to Britain to be near Harry.

The delegations of shortlisted students from Beauxbatons (12) and Durmstrang (12) appear with their Heads.

Hagrid is hurt by a skrewt.

People are given 24 hours to enter the TT.

Durmstrang enters only Viktor Krum, though 12 students total arrive from the school.

Harry is entered by Pr Moody (Barty Jr) under a fourth school's name.

Oct 31
Fred and George and S. Fawcett and Stebbins try to cross the Age Line and end up with beards.

Angelina Johnson enters.

All the Beauxbatons enter.

The skrewts are now 3' long and killing each other. Only 20 are left.

Hagrid refuses to join SPEW.

Viktor, Fleur, Cedric and Harry are chosen to compete by the Goblet of Fire.

Harry is obliged to compete.

Pr Moody (Barty Jr) suggests that someone is trying to kill Harry via the TT.

Everyone in Gryffindor is happy about Harry's entry but Ron.

Ron begins to snub Harry.

Nov 1
Hermione knows Harry didn't enter himself and explains that Ron is having a jealous fit.

Harry writes to Sirius about being entered, via a school owl, and Hedwig goes into a jealous fit as well.

Nov 3
All the Hufflepuffs, Ravenclaws and Slytherins turn cold toward Harry for trying to steal Hufflepuff's glory.

Hagrid believes Harry didn't enter his name.

Nov 6
The Slytherins break out anti-Potter badges.

Harry and Draco get into a wand fight hurting Hermione and Goyle.

Harry and Ron get detentions.

The Wand Weighing ceremony occurs.

Harry has a photo shoot and interview with Rita Skeeter.

Sirius' letter arrives.

Nov 7
Hermione's teeth are now smaller and straighter than they originally were thanks to Madame Pomfrey.

Nov 12
Rita Skeeter publishes a highly colored version of Harry's life in *The Daily Prophet* implying Hermione is his girlfriend.

Nov 13
Harry and Ron do detentions in Pr Snape's dungeon.

Victor Krum starts stalking Hermione in the Library because he likes her.

Nov 21

Harry (in his Invisibility Cloak) and Hermione go to Hogsmeade.
Pr Moody (Barty Jr) and Hagrid go to the Three Broomsticks.
Pr Moody (Barty Jr) sees Harry with his magical eye and joins Hermione's table.
Rita Skeeter is staying in Hogsmeade for the TT.
Nov 22
Hagrid shows Harry and Madam Olympia Maxime the dragons.
Igor Karkoff sneaks off and sees the dragons.
Sirius speaks to Harry via the fire in the common room and tells him Karkoff was a Death Eater.
Harry gets violent with Ron.
Hermione and Harry spend time in the Library trying to find something to use on dragons.
Nov 23
Harry tells Cedric about the dragons.
Pr Moody (Barty Jr) advises Harry to play to his strengths (flying) and use a simple spell (Accio) to get what he needs (broom) to play to his strengths with Task 1 of the TT.
Harry spends his lunch and most of the night practicing Summoning Charms.
Nov 24
Task 1 of the TT begins at noon, and classes are stopped early so everyone can go.
Ludo commentates the action for the spectators.
Ron and Harry make up.
Harry ties with Krum for first place with 40 points.
Ron sends Molly an owl with the outcome.
Harry sends a letter with Pig to Sirius.
TT competitors discover they must use what's inside the golden eggs as the clue to solving Task 2.
Dumbledore bans Rita Skeeter from the Hogwarts' grounds.
Dec 2
Dobby and Winky start work at Hogwarts.
Dec 5
Rita Skeeter spies on Hagrid and the Care of Magical Creatures class.
Harry, Ron and Hermione visit the Kitchens.
Dobby and Winky are in the Kitchens.
Ron offers to give Dobby his mother's maroon Christmas sweater.
Harry gives Dobby permission to come and see him sometimes.
Dec 8
Pr McGonagall announces the Yule Ball. She tells Harry he has to bring a date to the ball and dance to open the ball, even though Harry has never learned to dance.
Dec 9
Hagrid gives Rita an interview at the Three Broomsticks.
Dec 10
People start to leave Harry alone, probably due to Cedric's intervention.
Dec 14
Ron and Harry still don't have dates for the Yule Ball.
Fred and George are still writing Ludo for their winnings.
Fred asks Angelina to the Yule Ball.
Dec 16
Harry discovers that Cho is going with Cedric to the Yule Ball.
Hermione refuses to say she's going with Viktor.

THE HARRY POTTER COMPANION

Harry asks Parvati.
Ron is set up with Padma.
Ginny goes with Neville just so she can attend.
Lavender goes with Seamus.
Dec 18
Christmas holidays start.
Hardly anyone goes home this year because of the Yule Ball.
Dec 19
Ali Bashir gets caught trying to smuggle flying carpets into the UK.
Dec 20
Harry and Ron notice that Hermione's front teeth are all straight and normal sized.
Pig arrives with Sirius' letter.
Ron and Harry play wizard's chess instead of Harry working on his egg.
Pr Moody (Barty Jr) tells Cedric how to work the egg knowing he'll tell Harry.
Dec 25
Dobby wakes Harry with a Christmas present.
The Christmas Feast precedes the Yule Ball.
Percy attends the ball for Barty Sr, who has left Percy in charge of the office.
Dumbledore talks about the Room of Requirement.
Pr Snape and Karkoff are overheard by Harry and Ron in the fairy grotto.
The Dark Mark is getting clearer and more vivid.
Harry and Ron hear Hagrid and Madam Maxime fight about her being a half-giant.
Rita Skeeter overhears Hagrid because she's there as a beetle.
S. Fawcett and Stebbins are caught in the bushes by Pr Snape.
Cedric tells Harry how to get the clue from the egg.
Ginny gets over Harry and takes up with Michael Corner.
Dec 26
Ron and Hermione have a tiff about her going to the ball with Viktor.
Cedric and Cho become boyfriend and girlfriend and Harry is jealous.
Harry finds an arm from Ron's Krum figurine under his bed.
People begin to suspect that Barty Sr has gone missing.
1995
Jan 9
The Second Term starts.
Rita Skeeter's article on Hagrid comes out in *The Daily Prophet* exposing him as a half-giant and as breaking the Ban on Experimental Breeding by creating the blast-ended skrewts.
Hagrid goes into hiding in his cabin.
Jan 10
Pr Grubbly-Plank takes over Hagrid's classes.
Harry, Ron and Hermione attempt to see Hagrid, but he won't open the door.
Jan 18
Hogsmeade Saturday.
Harry, Ron and Hermione go to look for Hagrid.
Viktor is swimming in the Lake in nothing but swim trunks.
Ludo is in trouble with goblins and gets cornered by them at the Three Broomsticks.
Ludo says Barty Sr has been missing for a couple of weeks and people are looking for him and Bertha Jorkins.
Ludo offers to help Harry cheat on Task 2 but Harry refuses to accept his offer.
Ludo runs off to avoid confronting Fred and George and the goblins follow him.

Ludo is in debt from gambling on the QWC 1994 and is trying to make good his losses by betting on Harry to win the TT.
Hermione publicly insults Rita Skeeter.
Harry, Ron and Hermione try, with Dumbledore, to convince Hagrid to ignore Rita's article.
Dumbledore refuses to accept Hagrid's resignation.

Jan 20
Hagrid returns to teaching.

Jan 24
Harry cracks the secret of the egg, with help from Moaning Myrtle.

Jan 25
Pr Moody (Barty Jr) is in Pr Snape's office but Harry thinks it's Barty Sr.
Pr Moody (Barty Jr) borrows the Marauder's Map because he sees his name as Bartemius Crouch on it.

Jan 26
Harry writes to Sirius about the previous night.

Jan 27
Harry gets permission from Pr McGonagall to search books in the Library's Restricted Section for a charm that will help him with TT Task 2.

Feb 22
A letter from Sirius arrives asking for the next Hogsmeade weekend date so he can meet with Harry.
Only 2 skrewts are left now.
Hagrid continues lessons on unicorn.

Feb 23
Cho, Hermione and Ron are used as hostages for Cedric, Viktor and Harry, respectively.
Harry spends all night looking for a charm that will let him breathe underwater.

Feb 24
Pr McGonagall and Pr Moody (Barty Jr) talk about the use of gillyweed in Dobby's hearing.
Pr Moody (Barty Jr) does this intentionally, knowing Dobby will help Harry.
Dobby gives Harry gillyweed he stole from Pr Snape's private store cupboard.
TT Task 2 takes place at the Lake.
Percy is there in place of Barty Sr.
Rita Skeeter is there as a beetle.
Dumbledore explains why Harry was outside the time limit.
Fleur becomes friends with Harry and Ron for saving Gabrielle.
Viktor invites Hermione to Bulgaria during the summer holidays.
Harry's watch stops working.

Feb 25
Ron gains popularity from being a part of TT Task 2.

Mar 5
Sirius' reply letter arrives arranging a meeting with Harry.
Sirius will come to Hogsmeade.
The *Witch Weekly* article Rita Skeeter wrote as revenge on Hermione comes out.
Ron discovers Viktor has asked Hermione to Bulgaria.
Karkoff talks to Pr Snape about the Dark Mark.

Mar 6
Hogsmeade weekend.

The Harry Potter Companion

Harry buys socks for Dobby for helping with the TT Task 2.
Harry, Ron and Hermione meet Sirius and go to his and Buckbeak's hideout in a mountain cave outside of town.
Sirius doesn't like Barty Sr because he sent him to Azkaban without a trial.
Sirius requests to be called Snuffles as a protection of his identity and continues acting the lovable stray in town to stay near Harry.

Mar 7
Ron writes to Percy about Barty Sr.
Harry, Ron and Hermione visit Dobby and give him his socks.
Harry sends food to Sirius and Buckbeak.
Winky is drunk and pining for Crouch Sr and her old home.
The house-elves are offended by SPEW and physically push Hermione, along with Ron and Harry, and out of the Kitchens.
Hagrid buries leprechaun gold coins in his garden and brushes off Madam Maxime who is trying to make up to him by telling him about TT Task 3, to no avail.

Mar 8
Hermione becomes a subscriber to *The Daily Prophet* and begins to get hate mail from *Witch Weekly* readers - including booby-trapped hate mail.
Hagrid starts lessons on nifflers.

Mar 15
Hermione continues to get hate mail and Howlers.
Hermione begins to work out how Rita Skeeter is getting information from inside Hogwarts.

Apr 13
3-week Easter holidays start.
Harry is regularly sending food to Sirius and notes.

May 5
The Third Term starts.
Percy's response arrives with Easter Eggs from Molly full of homemade toffee.
Hermione's egg from Molly is smaller than Harry's - because Molly believes the *Witch Weekly* article.
Percy admits he hasn't seen Barty Sr in a while but he claims to know his handwriting.

May 19
Barty Sr escapes the Imperius Curse and tries to get to Hogwarts to tell Dumbledore about his son's doings.

May 25
Harry learns more about TT Task 3 from Ludo on the Quidditch field which is being turned into a maze.
Viktor confronts Harry about Hermione near the Forbidden Forest.
Barty Sr stumbles out of the woods asking for Dumbledore.
Harry goes to get Dumbledore but Viktor is Stunned by Pr Moody (Barty Jr) and Barty Sr vanishes.
Pr Moody (Barty Jr) appears and goes into the forest, supposedly to look for the perpetrators but actually to kill Barty Sr. He Transfigures the body into a bone, and buries it.
Karkoff flies off the handle in paranoia.
Hagrid takes Harry back to Gryffindor Tower.

May 26
Harry, Ron and Hermione overhear Fred and George in the Owlery talking of blackmail while they are there sending a letter to Sirius.

Ron says they really want to start a joke shop of their own and are obsessed with money.
May 28
Sirius sends a reply letter.
May 29 - Jun 1
Harry Ron and Hermione spend all their free time looking up hexes and practicing Stunning and Disarming Spells that might help Harry with TT Task 3.
Jun 10
Harry falls asleep and has a Voldemort dream in class, Rita is there as a bug and sees all.
Harry goes to Dumbledore's office and finds Pr Moody (Barty Jr) and Fudge.
Harry sees the confession of Karkoff and the trials of Ludo Bagman, Bellatrix, Rodolphus and Rastaban Lestrange and Barty Crouch Jr in the Pensive.
Harry sends Sirius another owl.
Jun 11
Harry, Ron and Hermione spend all their time getting Harry ready for TT Task 3.
Pr McGonagall gives them use of the Transfiguration classroom at lunchtimes.
Jun 13
Ron, Hermione and Harry see Draco outside talking into his hand - actually Rita in her beetle form.
Jun 15
Sirius sends daily owls now.
Jun 20 - 24
Exams for the school begin.
Harry is exempt because he's in the TT.
Jun 23
Pr Moody (Barty Jr) turns the TT Cup into a Portkey and takes it into the maze.
Jun 24
The Daily Prophet says Harry is dangerous and disturbed - a Rita Skeeter article.
Molly and Bill come as Harry's family to watch Task 3.
Fleur sees Bill and really taken with him.
Molly realizes she's mistaken about Hermione.
Hermione realizes Rita is an illegal Animagus - a beetle.
During Task 3 Cedric dies.
Peter cuts off his right hand with which Voldemort is reborn and give Peter a new magical hand.
Voldemort duels with Harry to prove there is nothing special about him.
Harry escapes via the Portkey with Cedric's body.
Pr Moody (Barty Jr) gives Harry Veritaserum to try to find out what happened to the Death Eaters when Voldemort showed up.
Pr Moody (Barty Jr) is revealed to be Barty Crouch Jr and apprehended.
The real Moody is released from the magical trunk.
Harry is healed by Fawkes.
The Dementor's Kiss is given to Barty Jr without anyone's order.
Fudge refuses to believe Voldemort is back.
Harry is given the 1,000G prize.
Dumbledore restarts the OoP and forces Sirius and Pr Snape to shake hands.
Hermione captures Rita Skeeter in beetle form and puts her in an unbreakable glass jar.
Jun 25
Fudge begins leaning on *The Daily Prophet.*

THE HARRY POTTER COMPANION

Harry meets with Mr and Mrs Diggory who tell him to keep the prize money.
Bagman goes on the run from the goblins he owes money because technically Harry didn't win, Harry and Cedric won.
Jun 26
Harry visits Hagrid during the DADA lessons that are now canceled.
Hagrid admits he has been expecting Voldemort's return.
Hagrid and Olympia are asked by Dumbledore to go talk to the giants Abroad.
Dudley becomes Junior Heavyweight Inter-School Boxing Champion of the Southeast.
Jun 29
During the Leaving Feast Cho cries for the loss of Cedric.
Dumbledore tells everyone that Cedric was killed by Voldemort, that Voldemort has returned and that Harry escaped him and brought back Cedric's body.
Jun 31
Start of Summer holidays.
Ron finally asks for Viktor's signature.
Fleur says she will get a job in Britain to improve her English.
Hermione tells Ron and Harry that Rita Skeeter is an illegal Animagus, and has her in her beetle form in a jar with an Unbreakable Charm on it.
Draco, Crabbe and Goyle are hit with multiple curses.
Harry secretly gives Fred and George his 1,000G prize money to them for their joke shop and tells them to buy Ron some decent dress robes.
Molly kisses Harry on the cheek.
Hagrid and Olympia start off to the giants Abroad.
Hagrid and Olympia are tailed by some MoM people.
Book 5 *Harry Potter and the Order of the Phoenix* timeline begins
1995
Jul 1
Harry is being watched 24/7 by members of the Order but doesn't know it.
Jul 2
Harry starts getting *The Daily Prophet* delivered to find out what's happening.
Fudge tries to make sure that no one at the MoM has contact with Dumbledore and starts firing those who believe Dumbledore.
Jul 3
The Daily Prophet begins to mention Harry a couple times a week in unflattering terms to discredit him - at Fudge's order.
Fred and George start work on Skiving Snackboxes.
Jul 4
Sirius writes, but doesn't really say anything.
Fred and George pass their Apparition Test with distinction.
Percy is promoted to Junior Assistant to the Minister of Magic then falls out with Arthur.
Percy moves out of the house to a flat in London and cuts all ties with his family.
Hagrid and Olympia give the MoM people the slip in Dijon, France and make for Poland.
Jul 5
Mrs Figg starts inviting Harry to tea every time she sees him - to keep an eye on him for the Order.
Harry begins a summer of reading newspapers and trying to listen for any news that would indicate Voldemort's activities.
Jul 7

482

Molly tries to visit Percy to talk and has the door slammed in her face.
Sirius goes into hiding at 12 Grimmauld Place, London
Molly, Arthur, Ron, Hermione, Fred, George and Bill are all spending a lot of time at the Headquarters.
Dumbledore has forbidden anyone to tell Harry anything, suspecting Harry and Voldemort might have a mindlink of some kind.
Sirius and the Weasleys spend their time decontaminating the Headquarters.
Hermione goes to Bulgaria to visit Viktor Krum.

Jul 8
Dudley and his gang begin a summer of vandalizing parks, smoking on corners and throw stones at passing cars and children.
Bill comes home from Egypt to work with the Order.
Bill takes a job with Gringotts in London and starts dating Fleur Delacour who is also working there.
Charlie stays in Romania to recruit foreign wizards into the Order on his days off.
Hagrid and Olympia run into problems at the Polish border.

Jul 10
Voldemort begins to consider going after the prophecy about himself - knowledge is power - kept in the DoM at the MoM.

Jul 15
Hermione and Ron write, but don't say much.
Hagrid and Olympia run into trouble in Minsk.

Jul 20
Hagrid and Olympia reach the giants.

Jul 21
Hagrid and Olympia give Gurg Karkus the branch of Gubraithian fire.
Hermione returns from Bulgaria and turns up at Grimmauld Place.

Jul 22
Hagrid and Olympia give Gurg Karkus the indestructible goblin-made helmet and tells him all about Dumbledore arguing against killing the giants or sending them into exile.

Jul 23
Gurg Karkus is killed and Gurg Golgomath takes over.
Hagrid give Golgomath a present of dragon hide but is attacked by the giants.
Olympia saves Hagrid and they go into hiding.
Some giants to into hiding in caves, afraid of Golgomath.

Jul 24
Macnair and another Death Eater are visiting Gurg Golgomath with gifts every day.

Jul 26
Macnair and another Death Eater begin hunting in the caves at night to find and kill Hagrid and Olympia.
Hagrid and Olympia begin visiting other caves and tending to the wounded giants and tell them about Dumbledore in an attempt to make them aware of wizards that want to help them and want a better life for them.

Jul 28
Spanish baggage handlers go on strike.
Hagrid discovers Grawp is his half-brother and that his mother Fridwulfa died many years ago.

Jul 29
Fred and George start advertising in *The Daily Prophet* without Molly's knowledge.

Jul 30

Dumbledore loses the Chairmanship of the ICW.
Dumbledore is removed as Chief Warlock on the Wizengamot.
Jul 31
Harry's gets birthday cards and presents, but not much information.
Ron and Hermione are at the Headquarters of the OoP.
Harry starts having mood swings based on his own feelings and Voldemort-influenced ones.
Aug 1
Dudley and gang beat up Mark Evans.
Hagrid and Olympia have convinced 6-7 giants to Dumbledore's side, but Golgomath raids the caves killing some which convinces others to have nothing to do with Dumbledore's emissaries.
Hagrid decides to bring Grawp home with him because he was being picked on for being small.
Aug 2
Dudley hears Harry pleading for Cedric's life and his dad's help during a nightmare.
Southeast England is having a drought.
The Spanish baggage handlers are still on strike.
Mundungus "Dung" Fletcher Disapparates from his post to handle some shady doings.
Harry unintentionally magically electrocutes Vernon.
Dudley hits Harry.
Dementors attack Harry and Dudley but Harry saves the day by using magic.
Mrs Figg is found to be a Squib and takes Harry and Dudley to safety.
Harry gets several owls about his using magic: Mafalda Hopkirk of the MoM's Improper Use of Magic Office, Arthur, Mafalda again and Sirius.
Petunia get an owl with a Howler from Dumbledore and lets Harry stay despite Vernon's objections.
Harry sends letter to Ron, Hermione and Sirius via Hedwig demanding a response.
Aug 3
Harry stays in his room again except to go to the bathroom and food is sent in through the catflap.
Aug 6
The Dursley go out in the evening on a ruse of being shortlisted for the All-England Best-Kept Lawn Competition.
Members of the Order break in through the kitchen door and take Harry back to the Headquarters.
Pr Snape is at an Order meeting giving a report.
Harry, Molly, Fred, George, Ginny, Ron, Hermione, Bill, Arthur, Sirius, Dung, Lupin and Tonks all have dinner at the Headquarters.
Harry finds out a little of what Voldemort and the Order have been up to.
Aug 7
Harry meets Mrs Black.
Hestia Jones relieves Kingsley on guard duty at the MoM so she is now wearing Moody's Invisibility Cloak.
Kingsley Shacklebolt leaves a report for Dumbledore with Sirius.
The Order is guarding the DoM, specifically the prophecy about Harry defeating Voldemort.
Dung tries to stash stolen cauldrons at Sirius' house.
Harry meets Kreacher and finds out about Sirius' family tree.
Aug 8

Dumbledore is having real difficulty finding someone to teach the DADA class.
Aug 10
Sirius' drawing room is decontaminated but for the boggart in the writing desk and tapestry.
Sirius is forbidden to accompany Harry to the MoM hearing.
Aug 11
Harry, Hermione and Molly and the Weasley kids start decontaminating Sirius' dining room.
Aug 12
Arthur takes Harry to work early for his hearing.
Willy Widdershins creates a regurgitating toilet in Bethnal Green.
Kingsley gives Arthur the Sep *The Quibbler* with an article about Sirius in it.
The hearing time and place are changed to 8am Courtroom 10 to throw off everyone.
Harry discovers he's being tried by a full Wizengamot in a high-security courtroom.
Dumbledore and Arabella testify on Harry's behalf.
Dumbledore never looks at Harry.
Lucius is in the DoM corridor with Fudge.
Aug 15
Harry et al continue to clean the Headquarters
Sirius goes a bit moody and starts spending a lot of time in Buckbeak's room.
Aug 20
Hagrid and Olympia part ways so she can return to her school in time for the start of term.
Hagrid continues alone with an unwilling Grawp.
Aug 30
Educational Decree 22 is passed giving the MoM control to appoint staff to any vacant positions that Dumbledore can't fill at Hogwarts.
Aug 31
Book lists arrive from Hogwarts.
Ron and Hermione; Hannah and Ernie; Anthony Goldstein and Padma Patil; and Draco Malfoy and Pansy Parkinson are made Prefects.
Molly goes to Diagon Alley to get everyone's books and Ron a Cleansweep 11.
Molly has a party for Ron and Hermione.
Moody shows Harry a picture of the former members of OoP members from circa early 1980.
Molly has a melt down dealing with the boggart.
Sturgis is arrested at the MoM for trying to break into the DoM, but he is acting under the Imperius Curse of Lucius Malfoy.
Sep 1
Moody, Lupin and Tonks take Harry to King's Cross Station.
Sirius goes as a dog but is spotted by Lucius and Draco.
Harry meets Luna Lovegood and discovers *The Quibbler*.
Pr Grubbly-Plank is filling in for Hagrid who is still on his mission.
Harry discovers he and Luna can see the thestrals.
Dolores Umbridge is the new DADA teacher.
Everyone is scared of Harry because of *The Daily Prophet* articles.
Harry and Seamus have a fight about Seamus' mom.
Sep 2
Ron accuses Cho of being a false supporter of the Tornados.
Harry gets a detention for insisting Voldemort is back.

The Harry Potter Companion

Fred and George start using 1st years as candy testers.
Hermione starts leaving badly knitted hats for house-elves lying about the common room in hopes they will accidentally free themselves and ends up offending them instead.
Harry starts a week's detention.

Sep 3
Draco seems to know that Hagrid is with the giants.
Luna publicly professes her support for Harry's version of what happened to Cedric and Ernie then does the same.

Sep 4
Harry gets chewed out by Angelina for not showing up to tryout, despite his detention.

Sep 5
Harry discovers Ron is going to try out for Keeper on the Gryffindor team.

Sep 6
Ron gets the Keeper position even though he's not very good.
Hermione's magical knitting improves.

Sep 7
Harry gets Hedwig to take a message to Sirius and meets up with Cho before Filch can intercept him on Pr Umbridge's behalf.
Lucius has tipped off the MoM that Sirius is in London.
The Gryffindor team holds a practice that's interrupted by Slytherin watchers.

Sep 8
Percy sends a letter to Ron telling him to avoid Harry and Dumbledore.
Hermione offers to correct Ron's and Harry's homework.
Sirius' contacts Harry via the Floo Network.
The MoM passes new legislation to give itself control over Hogwarts.

Sep 9
Educational Decree 23 is passed.
Dolores Umbridge becomes Hogwarts High Inquisitor.
Harry gets another week of detention.

Sep 10
Harry gets another night of detention.
Hermione prepares a murtlap solution and she and Ron suggest that Harry teach a DADA club secretly.
Hermione says the name Voldemort for the first time.

Sep 24
Hermione again suggests Harry teach DADA classes.
Harry agrees.
Hermione and Ron start secretly spreading the word about a meeting in Hogsmeade for those interested in a DADA club.

Oct 7
Hogsmeade weekend.
The DADA club organizes and members sign a magical contract on a jinxed parchment.
Dung listens in while disguised as a witch.
Willy Widdershins listens in from under his bandages.
Cho is warming up to Harry.
Ron discovers Ginny is seeing Michael Corner.

Oct 9
Educational Decree 24 is passed.

Hedwig brings Harry a letter from Sirius, but she is injured by someone trying to intercept her.
Pr Grubbly-Plank takes Hedwig and treats her damaged wing.
Pr Umbridge lets the Slytherin Quidditch team keep playing.
Sybill gets put on probation.
Fred and George make money selling Puking Pastilles, about 26Gs worth.
Oct 10
Sirius contacts Harry through the Floo Network.
Pr Umbridge is watching the Floo Network in Hogwarts.
Pr McGonagall gets Dumbledore to allow Gryffindor's Quidditch team to play.
Dobby returns Hedwig all healed up to Harry.
All the house-elves except Dobby refuse to clean Gryffindor Tower because of Hermione's knitted items which they find insulting.
Dobby tells Harry how to find the Room of Requirement.
Oct 11
The first DADA club meeting elects Harry leader and names the organization Dumbledore's Army (DA).
They decide meetings at least once a week, but always on different days.
Oct 20
Derrick Bode is injured at the MoM by Lucius Malfoy's Imperius Curse trying to force him to get him to take down a prophecy in the DoM and bring it to him.
Nov 5
The Slytherin v. Gryffindor Quidditch match.
Slytherins show up wearing badges and singing a nasty song Draco wrote to unnerve Ron, which it does.
George and Harry jump Draco for insulting the Weasleys and get a week detention.
Educational Decree 25 is passed.
Pr Umbridge gives Fred, George and Harry a lifetime ban on Quidditch playing and confiscates their brooms.
Hagrid returns to Hogwarts very beat up.
Hagrid ties up Grawp in the Forbidden Forest.
Harry, Ron and Hermione go to visit Hagrid.
Pr Umbridge confronts Hagrid about his absence.
Nov 6
Hermione tries to convince Hagrid to stick to Pr Grubbly-Plank's lesson plans, without success.
Nov 7
Hagrid teaches on thestrals while the class is inspected by Pr Umbridge.
The Slytherins make out that Hagrid is a bad teacher.
Dec 7
Prefects have to oversee the Christmas decorating of the castle.
Dec 19
Dobby decorates the Room of Requirement.
The last DA meeting reviews the Impediment Jinx and Stunning.
Cho cries over Cedric, then kisses Harry (his first).
Hermione says Cho cries all the time these days.
Harry sees into Voldemort's mind which is possessing Nagini and sees Nagini bite an Invisibility Cloaked Arthur in the MoM near the door to the DoM.
Harry tells Pr McGonagall and Dumbledore what happen to Arthur.
The portraits step into action to save Arthur.

Voldemort becomes aware Harry is looking into his mind.
Dumbledore's machine informs him Harry and Voldemort are pretty much 2 entangled halves of 1 soul.
Harry wants to kill Dumbledore when he looks at him because a part of Voldemort's mind is lurking in Harry's.
Dumbledore Portkeys Harry and the Weasleys to Headquarters and Sirius before Pr Umbridge can find out what's going on.
Sirius accidentally dismisses Kreacher by saying get out.
Kreacher goes to Narcissa Black Malfoy and thus begins a plot to get Harry to get the prophecy for Voldemort.
Molly goes to the hospital to see Arthur.

Dec 20
Arthur survives and Molly thanks Harry for saving him.
Sirius has everyone to stay for Christmas.
The Hogwarts trunks and animals arrive at Headquarters.
Harry and the Weasleys, under escort from Tonks and Moody, go to St Mungo's to see Arthur and find that Arthur can't stop bleeding.
The Extendible Ears prove a bit too revealing for Harry.
Harry thinks about bolting but Dumbledore via Phineas stops him.

Dec 21
The Christmas holidays start.
Sirius et al start decorating Headquarters for Christmas.
Harry retreats from company to Buckbeak's room.
Hermione decides not to go skiing with her parents and turns up at Headquarters via the Knight Bus.
A group intervention ensues with Ron, Ginny and Hermione convinces Harry he isn't possessed by Voldemort after all.

Dec 22
Mundungus brings a Christmas Tree to Sirius et al.

Dec 24
August Pye tries stitches on Arthur.

Dec 25
Percy sends back his Molly's annual Weasley sweater Christmas gift.
Hermione leaves Kreacher a quilt in his nest.
Dung steals a car so everyone can visit Arthur at St Mungo's.
Molly and Arthur have a fight.
Lupin visits with the werewolf in Arthur's ward.
Harry, Ron, and Hermione find Gilderoy Lockhart, and Neville, Gran, Frank and Alice Longbottom, in the Janus Thickey Ward at St Mungo's.

Dec 27
Kreacher is found in the attic by a slightly panicked Sirius, but Harry thinks Kreacher is up to something all the same.
Sirius starts to go uncommunicative and grumpy, withdrawing to Buckbeak's room for hours at a time.

1996
Jan 3
Pr Snape shows up at Headquarters.
Dumbledore has ordered Pr Snape to give Harry secret occlumency lessons.
Pr Snape gets in a fight with Sirius but it's interrupted before the fur flies.
Arthur returns to Headquarters completely cured.

Dung and Moody come to dinner.
Jan 4
Sirius gives Harry an old two-way mirror that was James' so they can stay in touch.
Fred, George, Ginny, Harry, Hermione and Ron take the Knight Bus back to Hogwarts escorted by Lupin and Tonks.
Ron has never been on the Knight Bus and will never go on it again.
Jan 5
Harry invites Cho to Hogsmeade on Valentine's Day.
Pr Snape removes some thoughts to the Pensive before giving Harry occlumency lessons.
Harry realizes what Voldemort wants is beyond the door of DoM, where Sturgis had tried to break in and Arthur had been attacked.
Fred and George come up with Headless Hats.
Harry passes out and comes to realizing that Voldemort is really happy (because of mass prison break out by the Death Eaters from Azkaban).
Jan 6
The Daily Prophet reports that 10 Death Eaters have broken out of Azkaban.
Derrick Bode is murdered.
Hagrid is put on probation by Pr Umbridge.
Jan 16
Educational Decree 26 is passed.
Jan 21
All Care of Magical Creatures and Divination classes are conducted with Pr Umbridge watching. See Note G.
Jan 30
Neville improves at an amazing rate in DA club classes.
Only Hermione learns faster than Neville now.
Harry's scar prickles all the time and his moods are constantly affected by Voldemort's.
Harry is failing at occlumency.
Feb 14
Harry takes Cho to Hogsmeade and they break up.
Hermione arranges a meeting with Harry, Rita Skeeter and Luna Lovegood to tell Harry's story to the world through *The Quibbler*.
Ron continues to do badly at Quidditch practices.
Feb 16
Hermione explains female psychology and beginner's dating tactics to Harry.
Feb 21
Hufflepuff v. Gryffindor Quidditch match, Gryffindor loses by 10 points.
Feb 23
The Quibbler runs Harry's interview in its Mar edition, complete with the names of Death Eaters he saw.
Pr Umbridge revokes Harry's Hogsmeade weekends privileges, among other punishments.
Educational Degree 27 appears.
Feb 24
Harry makes up with Cho (as a friend) and Seamus.
The Quibbler runs a 2nd edition to keep up with demand.
Harry ends up in Voldemort's head again. He sees Rookwood talking but then Harry sees Voldemort seeing Harry in his own eyes.

THE HARRY POTTER COMPANION

Mar 3
Harry is becoming obsessed with the DoM corridor and door dream.
Mar 23
Harry gets beyond the black door into the circular room in his dream.
Sybill Trelawney loses her job and is almost thrown out of Hogwarts by Pr Umbridge, but she is allowed still to live at Hogwarts by Dumbledore.
Hagrid saves Firenze from being kicked to death.
Dumbledore hires Firenze to teach Divination.
Mar 24
Firenze asks Harry to pass on a message to Hagrid about Grawp.
Apr 15
The DA club starts working on Patronuses.
Seamus comes to his first DA club meeting.
Dobby alerts the DA club Pr Umbridge is on the way but Harry fails to get away.
Kingsley uses a Memory Charm on Marietta.
Dumbledore takes the fall for the DA club and goes on the lam from the MoM with Fawkes' help.
Apr 16
Educational Decree 28 is passed.
Fudge makes Pr Umbridge Head of Hogwarts.
The Inquisitorial Squad is formed.
Pr Umbridge is locked out of Dumbledore's office which begins to repair itself.
Montague ends up in the Vanishing Cabinet.
Fred and George launch a full scale anti-Umbridge campaign aided and abetted by Peeves, students and other teachers.
Pr Umbridge wants Fudge to sign an order removing Peeves and a decree giving Filch permission to use torturous punishments.
Pr Umbridge tries to give Harry Veritaserum but Pr Snape intentionally gave her fake Veritaserum.
Apr 18
Harry fights with Cho, again.
Draco discovers Harry is taking Remedial Potions.
Montague is found jammed inside a toilet on the 4th floor.
Harry looks into the Pensive and Snape's memories and sees some unpleasant things about his father.
Pr Snape refuses to give Harry anymore occlumency lessons.
Apr 20
The Easter holidays start.
Hermione draws up color-coded study schedules for Harry and Ron.
May 13
Educational Decree 29 is passed.
Pr Snape ignores Harry completely.
Pr McGonagall talks to Harry about being an Auror.
Fred and George set off a diversion so Harry can talk to Sirius via Pr Umbridge's fire.
Kreacher has disappeared again.
Lupin and Sirius talk to Harry about James and occlumency.
Filch finally gets the Approval for Whipping.
Fred and George leave school for good.
Peeves takes up the good fight.
May 14

490

Filch goes around with a horsewhip.
Peeves leads a ongoing campaign of harassment and destruction and mayhem against Pr Umbridge.
May 15
Students start setting off random Dungbombs and Stinkpellets.
Wearing a bubble over one's head becomes fashionable.
May 16
Lee Jordan puts a niffler in Pr Umbridge's office.
Members of the Inquisitorial Squad start having a series of odd accidents.
May 17
Umbridge-itis sets in.
May 18
Filch is put in charge of punting people across the 5th-floor corridor swamp.
Pr Umbridge gets a new office door.
Harry's broom is moved to the dungeons.
May 19
Ron tells Hermione that Harry is continuing to dream about the DoM corridor but Harry denies it.
Mr and Mrs Montague show up to complain about their son's treatment.
Harry finally admits to Ron and Hermione that he gave Fred and George the TT winnings to start a shop.
Ron tells Molly about Harry's doings with Fred and George.
May 21
The Gryffindor v. Ravenclaw Quidditch game goes on while Harry and Hermione are taken to meet Grawp by Hagrid.
Hagrid is persona non grata with centaurs for saving Firenze.
Magorian warns Hagrid off but lets him go because of the children.
Ron finally pulls it off and Gryffindor wins the game and the Quidditch Cup.
May 22
Harry and Hermione tell Ron about Grawp.
Jun 2
Ernie goes manic about study schedules.
A trade in brain stimulants springs up among 5th and 7th years.
Jun 9
Hermione is starting to show signs of extreme stress about OWL exams.
The examiners from the Wizarding Examinations Authority arrive.
Jun 10
OWLs begin with the OWL in Charms.
Jun 11
OWL in Transfiguration.
Jun 12
OWL in Herbology.
Jun 13
OWL in DADA.
Jun 14
OWL in Ancient Runes for Hermione.
Lee Jordan puts another niffler in Umbridge's office.
Jun 17
OWL in Potions.
Jun 18

THE HARRY POTTER COMPANION

OWL in Care of Magical Creatures.
Jun 19
OWL in Astronomy, written;
Divination written and practical
For Hermione Arithmancy written and practical; Astronomy, practical.
During the Astronomy practical the MoM tries to arrest Hagrid, Fang is stunned.
Hagrid escapes with Fang to hide in the mountain cave outside Hogsmeade but Pr McGonagall is severely injured by multiple simultaneous Stunning Spells to the chest.
Lee admits to all the Gryffindors that he put the nifflers in Pr Umbridge's office by levitating them in through an open window.
Jun 20
OWL in History of Magic, written.
Harry thinks he sees Sirius being tortured by Voldemort in the Hall of Prophecy room at the MoM and passes out.
Pr McGonagall is transferred to St Mungo's.
Hermione utters some words of wisdom about the situation and Harry's need to save people.
Harry refuses to believe he has a savior complex or that Voldemort might be playing on it.
Ron, Ginny, and Luna help Harry and Hermione break into Pr Umbridge's office to attempt to contact Sirius.
Kreacher tricks Harry into thinking Sirius is at the MoM.
Everyone gets caught, including Neville who tried to help Ginny.
Pr Snape is put on probation but takes Harry's warning and contacts Dumbledore and the Order about Sirius.
Pr Umbridge is lured into the Forbidden Forest and carried off by centaurs.
Grawp saves Hermione and Harry and apparently has learned to speak English.
Neville, Ginny, Luna, Ron, Harry and Hermione fly thestrals to the MoM to rescue Sirius.
Realizing that Harry et al are gone, Pr Snape tells the Order.
Death Eaters Bellatrix, Lucius, Rastaban, Rodolphus, Crabbe, Jugson, Dolohov, Macnair, Avery, Rookwood, Nott and Mulciber try to jump Harry et al to get the prophecy.
Dumbledore gets the truth out of Kreacher and he and the Order go and check on the MoM Hall of Prophecy.
Jun 21
After Harry et al up a very good fight, Sirius, Remus, Moody, Tonks and Kingsley arrive and join the fray.
Dumbledore arrives but Sirius is killed and Tonks is injured.
Voldemort shows up in the MoM and duels with Dumbledore in front of Fudge and others.
Fawkes helps Dumbledore by swallowing the Avada Kedavra curse of Voldemort.
Voldemort and Bellatrix escape but the other Death Eaters are caught.
Harry returns to Hogwarts.
Dumbledore explains the prophecy that was lost and why he's been avoiding Harry.
Jun 22
Pr Umbridge is rescued from the centaurs by Dumbledore and is hospitalized for shock.
The Death Eaters are put in prison, including Lucius Malfoy, Mr Nott and Mr Crabbe.
Jun 23
The MoM finally tells people Voldemort is back.

ACASCIAS RIPHOUSE

The dementors revolt and join Voldemort.
Dumbledore is reinstated as Headmaster, Supreme Mugwump and Chief Warlock.
Mr Lovegood sells Harry's interview to *The Daily Prophet* which runs it.
Harry is threatened by Draco.
Pr McGonagall returns from St Mungo's walking with a cane.
Jun 26
Ron and Hermione leave the Hospital wing cured.
Jun 28
Pr Umbridge leaves Hogwarts suddenly, probably to avoid arrest.
Harry gets some advice on death from Nearly Headless Nick.
Luna comforts Harry about the afterlife.
Jun 29
Lee Jordan, Angelina Johnson, Katie Bell, Roger Davies, C Warrington and Alicia Spinnet graduate Hogwarts. Draco, Crabbe and Goyle get hit with multiple hexes by DA members and are turned into giant slugs.
Marietta is still covered in pustules.
Harry is met at the station by Tonks, Moody, Lupin, Arthur, Molly, Fred and George.
The Grangers and Dursleys are there too, but not Percy.
Fred and George are doing very well with their joke shop.
Moody warns the Dursleys not to mistreat Harry.
Moody tells the Dursleys that he or one of his comrades should get a letter from Harry every 3 days or else they will show up in Little Whinging to find out what's wrong.
Jul 1
Luna and her father go to Sweden to look for Crumple-Horned Snorkacks.

Book 6 *Harry Potter and the ?????* timeline begins

Book 7 *Harry Potter and the ?????* timeline begins

Notes
* There is an authorized timeline, which can be found I'm told on CDs related to theatrical versions of Harry's tale. It differs in many respects to the timeline presented here and it is up to readers to decide which they prefer. This alternative version was developed because the official timeline, as it was described to me, seemed to have several places where logically it broke down or had been bent to fit into Muggle calendars. This timeline seeks to restore logic and the relationship of the days, regardless of Muggle calendars.

So, if 2 days are said to pass, on this timeline, 2 days pass. If Christmas vacation occurs at a strange time, then so it is. If vacations are 3 weeks, they are 3 weeks. If Easter break always seems to occur at the very end of Apr, then irregardless of the actuality date of Easter each year, this calendar reflects a break at the end or Apr, running into May. If something occurs on a specific date, Apr 20, that's when it's shown to occur. If exams are week late as was true in 91/92, that's how it's been shown here. Factors such as Harry's 11th birthday, in 1991, which is said to be on a Tuesday but on Muggle calendars for 1991, Jul 31 actually fell on a Wednesday, are irrelevant to the purposes of this timeline.

In only one place did a snag with the text occur in developing this timeline. Harry cannot leave his home in the first week of August 1993 and subsequently spend only 2 weeks at the Leaky Cauldron before Sep 1 occurs. So, sticking with the relationship of days as primary, this calendar shows Harry at the Leaky Cauldron for 3 weeks. This was the only case where conflict with the text occurred. In all other instances where some have found discrepancies, I have found perfectly logical explanations for the timeline to be as it has been stated in the books on Harry.

For example, some individuals believe it couldn't possibly take 2 days from Harry's home being destroyed in Godric's Hollow to the time Petunia finds him on her doorstep and screams. But in point of fact, it very easily could. If Voldemort is vaporized at 11pm Oct 31 and Harry is not found until dawn, about 4am, Nov 1 by Hagrid and Sirius. Since Harry is a small infant that has only just survived a curse and suffered a long cold night alone in a destroyed house, he needed care. Also, Hagrid couldn't fly Sirius' motorcycle unnoticed in the daytime. So, Hagrid got Harry cleaned up, fed and rested, then waited for nightfall before going to Little Whinging.

Depending on how often he had to stop and change or feed Harry, and the speed of the flying motorcycle, Harry arrives at 4 Privet Dr, just before midnight Nov 1. The elapsed time is 24 hours place to place and with a 1 year old child in the care of Hagrid, that's amazingly good. It is perfectly reasonable then that Harry is placed on the doorstep and not found for about 6 hours, approximately 6 am, when Petunia sets her bottles out. In days, Oct 31-Nov 2 it seems as though 72 hours has elapsed, but in fact it is more along the lines of 26 hours. So the text is correct, and logic and reason proves it so.

Of course in some cases exact dates are missing, and months have been suggested, but in many cases at least a month is known. For instance, Fred and George say their birthday is in Apr. Angelina says her birthday is a week before Oct 31, counting back 7 days makes it Oct 24. Deductive reasoning can fill in many gaps. Students can only join the House teams in Sep. One can only become a Prefect in one's 5th year. Every event must harmonize with every other event. Dumbledore cannot eat a candy in his youth if it was not invented until he was well past 120 years old. Either Dumbledore is younger than he appears, the candymaker is older than suspected previously, or both.

Finally, at a certain point it seemed foolish to continually explain the logic of this particular timeline. Readers are after all very clever and many I'm sure have already realized the flaws of the official time and will immediately comprehend the reasons behind why things are laid out on this timeline as they are. After 12 notes, it seemed the credible proofs for my deductive reasonings were sufficiently exposed and, as it was never my intention to plague readers with excruciating or unnecessary detail, I left off.

Note 1: A date of 1750 is given by K. Whisp, in *Quidditch Through the Ages*, for the formation of the British MoM's DMGS. However the date makes no logical sense.

Who pared down and established the Leagues 13 teams if not the British MoM in 1672?

Who set up the first Eurocup in 1652 if not the very nation that invented it?

Why would an existing British MoM would wait nearly 60 years after the ICW decision (1692) to establish a Dept of Magical Games and Sports (1750), for a game that was invented 500 years earlier in that MoM's own country?

My feeling is that the MoM in Britain was established in 1650 (not 1750) and its Dept of Magical Games and Sports was immediately organized at the same time in an effort to deal with the 1st European Cup, which was held in 1652. It would then make sense for the DMGS to establish its Quidditch League in 1674, and be made (via its MoM) responsible for games played in its territory by the ICW in 1692.

Note 2: In theory wizards are as human as everyone else, so the idea that a wizard not using magical means would survive 150 years is a bit ridiculous. Even the Hunza people only live to 130, and he's certainly no Hunza. It is quite reasonable however for Albus to be Headmaster at 80, and the person who did his NEWT exams to still be alive to do Harry's, making Madam Marchbanks about 100 years old.

Note 3: Why are James et al born so early? First of all, consider Severus Snape's relationship with Lucius. He is said to be Lucius' lapdog. Based on the fact that Harry doesn't give the time of day to anyone outside his grade that isn't a Weasley, or Cho, my feeling is that Lucius would only know Severus if he was 1 grade lower. Any greater age difference would be unrealistic. If Snape was 11 and Lucius 17 or 18, how ridiculous would that be? Most 17-year-old males wouldn't be caught dead with an 11-year-old even if that 11-year-old was related to them. So, for starters, Severus and Lucius had to be only 1 year apart.

But does that work for Lily and James as well? Yes. Lily only started dating James in her final year and that took some doing, because she had to overcome her "James is an arrogant bully" image of him that she'd lived with for the past 7 years. In addition, Lily is white, middle-class and well educated, as is James. They would never in 1970s bolt to an early marriage at 18 with the world open to them as it was. And look at all the money they left Harry. Does anyone know 2 married with children 20-year-olds that have wads of cash? No. Because they don't exist. So, Lily and James had to have spent a number of years after graduating doing paid work as well as being in the OoP.

Also, both sets of parents, the Evans and the Potters, were dead by the time Harry was orphaned. Did they suddenly all die in 18 months? Rather ridiculous. So there should be time for both sets of parents to die. We know that Lily brought James home to meet her parents while Petunia was still living there. So the Evans were alive then. Sirius says he used to go to lunch at the elder Potters after graduating, so they were still alive as well. Petunia says she hadn't spoken to Lily in *several years* as of 1981. She can't possibly have been living with Lily till she was 17 and not have spoken to her. If Lily dies at 20, only 20 months have passed. Presuming they met at weddings and funerals, that would mean even less time passed between the time they last spoke and Lily died.

It is hardly likely that Lily dated in her 7th year, graduated, got married, had an attempt on her life, attended her parents funeral, had an attempt on her life, gone to her in-laws funeral, had an attempt on her life, become pregnant, set aside a wad of cash from unknown sources, had a baby which she raised for over a year before her death, and had several years pass since Lily and Petunia have spoken, all in a under 2 or 3 years. Lily would have died of stress long before Voldemort ever got her with these sorts of circumstance.

The books state "several years," meaning at least 4 at a minimum, pass between the time Petunia and Lily last speak and Harry's arrival at Petunia's doorstep. If Harry arrives in 1980, Petunia must last have spoken to Lily in 1977 or 1978 at a minimum. So in this timeline a reasonable 5+ years is allotted.

Note 4: Even though Severus is a spy against Voldemort, he can't be seen to be acting against Voldemort before his disappearance. So, he can't be hired before Nov 1. My feeling is Severus got Lucius, as an influential person, to ask Dumbledore to hire him, even though Dumbledore was more than willing to hire Severus. The reason for this circuitous route is that Severus must make it look like he's insinuating himself into Dumbledore's staff as a means of saving himself to maintain his Death Eater image. He must keep up the pretense of being a Death Eater because Dumbledore knows for a fact, given Sybill's prophecy, that it's not over for Voldemort till Harry kills him, which means Severus will be needed again as a spy and can't be blowing his cover with Voldemort or other Death Eaters.

Note 5: McGonagall tells Harry the team has lost 6 years in a row and *if* they don't win in 91/92 it will be the 7th year in a row they've lost. This makes 84/85 the last year the Gryffindor team won and Jun 1985 when the trophy would have been awarded.

Note 6: Bill says in 1995, he hasn't been to Hogwarts in 5 years. Assuming the last time he saw it was Charlie's graduation, not his own, just before he went to Egypt, and factoring in the last time Gryffindor won a cup (before Harry was on the team), Charlie's last year has to be 89/90. This is presuming there is a graduation. No one ever seems to talk about any graduation ceremony, but it would be very odd that they didn't have one. At what point would one be presented a Medal for Magical Merit, but at a year-end graduation ceremony?

Note A: Although some sources say Bertie was born in 1935 this cannot be correct. If Dumbledore was born in supposedly in the 1840s as some sources report, he would be well over 150 by the time Bertie finally invents his famous Every Flavor Beans. Dumbledore clearly states, he tried one in his youth. How could he have done that if Bertie wasn't even alive during Dumbledore's youth? He couldn't. It makes more sense that Bertie was born in 1835, when the name Bertie was popular due to Queen Victoria's husband Prince Albert (Bertie), and then invented his candy between 1860-1880. It would then be an established favorite by the time Dumbledore's youth occurred in the 1910s.

Note B: All other professional teams voluntarily disbanded, except the Banchory Banger who apparently refused. They were not considered a League team except in their own minds. In 1814, almost 150 years after they were tossed out of the League, they were forced to disband after an unusual incident involving Bludgers and dragons. See QTA for details.

Note C: Pr Binns must have joined the staff a long while after 1942/43 attack because he doesn't initially think the Chamber is real.

Note D: Narcissa Black might not be a bona fide Death Eater because she didn't show up when the Dark Mark went active in Jun 1995. Voldemort didn't comment on her missing and didn't ask Lucius why she wasn't there. Although she clearly has Voldemort sympathies, she must not have the Dark Mark.

Note E: Because Petunia's excuse for Lily's death as car crash is so swift it's like she didn't have to think about it one would assume it was actually her parents, the Evans, that died in a car crash. Their funeral would be the last time Petunia ever sees or speaks to Lily.

Note F: Because only a part of Sybill's prophecy was heard, Voldemort is under the impression he has to get rid of blood-born Potters. He says as much when he tell Lily he doesn't want to kill her, just Harry, after he thinks he has already killed James (but who in fact is still dying in the other room). Voldemort probably had James' parents killed, either because he believed he needed the Potter's dead, or just out of sheer frustration at missing Lily and James all the time.

Note G: Even if Pr Umbridge were able to teach all the DADA classes, which she can't possibly, how on earth does she watch all the Care of Magical Creatures and Divination classes as well? Both the electives have classes for years 3-5 and NEWT levels for years 6 and 7, which means they run all day. She must only go to Harry's classes. Even at that, she'd have had to hire a 4th DADA teacher to cover her classes.

Part VII.
Schematics

THE HARRY POTTER COMPANION

Schematic A
A History of Wizarding Government

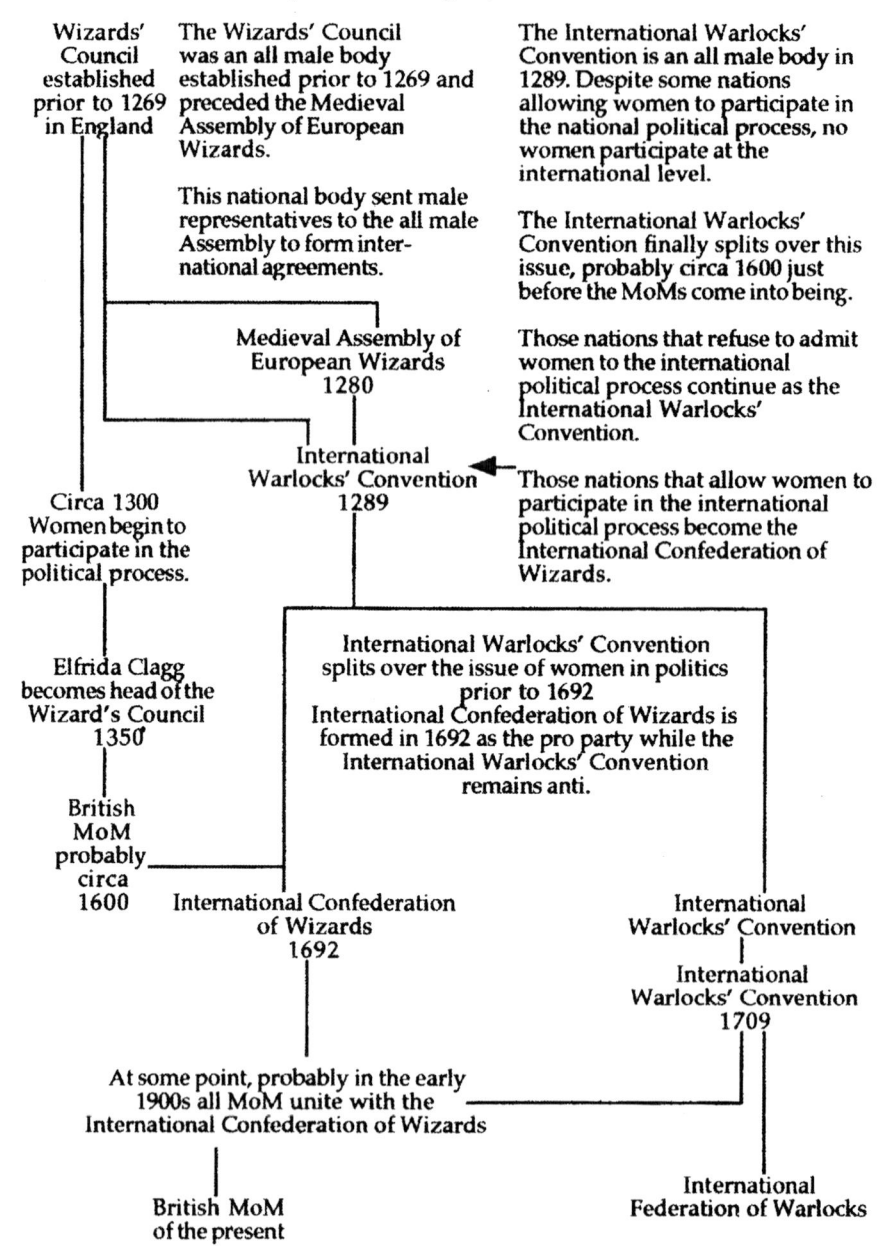

Wizards' Council established prior to 1269 in England

The Wizards' Council was an all male body established prior to 1269 and preceded the Medieval Assembly of European Wizards.

This national body sent male representatives to the all male Assembly to form international agreements.

The International Warlocks' Convention is an all male body in 1289. Despite some nations allowing women to participate in the national political process, no women participate at the international level.

The International Warlocks' Convention finally splits over this issue, probably circa 1600 just before the MoMs come into being.

Medieval Assembly of European Wizards 1280

Those nations that refuse to admit women to the international political process continue as the International Warlocks' Convention.

International Warlocks' Convention 1289

Those nations that allow women to participate in the international political process become the International Confederation of Wizards.

Circa 1300 Women begin to participate in the political process.

Elfrida Clagg becomes head of the Wizard's Council **1350**

British MoM probably circa 1600

International Warlocks' Convention splits over the issue of women in politics prior to 1692
International Confederation of Wizards is formed in 1692 as the pro party while the International Warlocks' Convention remains anti.

International Confederation of Wizards 1692

International Warlocks' Convention

International Warlocks' Convention 1709

At some point, probably in the early 1900s all MoM unite with the International Confederation of Wizards

British MoM of the present

International Federation of Warlocks

Post union, the International Warlocks' Convention adopts the name the International Federation of Warlocks. It remains an all male body but is not a political body. The new ICW has all the political power, but the IFW is influential and many powerful warlocks, who are in the ICW, belong to it.

498

ACASCIAS RIPHOUSE
Schematic Ab
Wizarding Governmental Structure:
From International Level to MoM Level

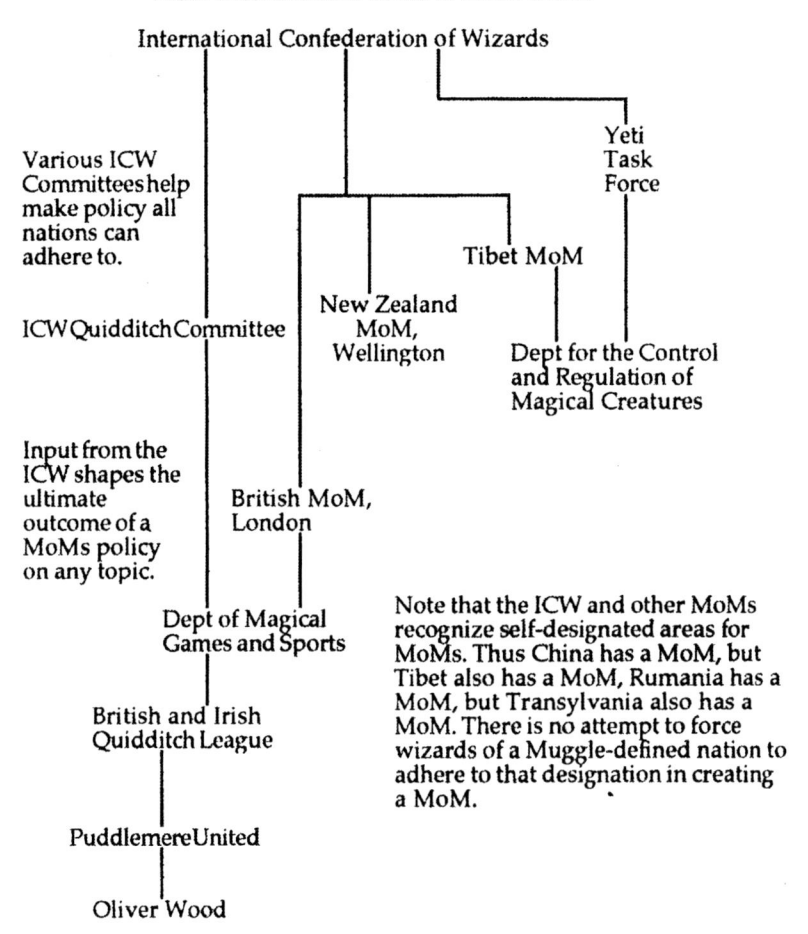

International Confederation of Wizards

- Yeti Task Force

Various ICW Committees help make policy all nations can adhere to.

- Tibet MoM
  - Dept for the Control and Regulation of Magical Creatures

- New Zealand MoM, Wellington

ICW Quidditch Committee

Input from the ICW shapes the ultimate outcome of a MoMs policy on any topic.

- British MoM, London
  - Dept of Magical Games and Sports
    - British and Irish Quidditch League
      - Puddlemere United
        - Oliver Wood

Note that the ICW and other MoMs recognize self-designated areas for MoMs. Thus China has a MoM, but Tibet also has a MoM, Rumania has a MoM, but Transylvania also has a MoM. There is no attempt to force wizards of a Muggle-defined nation to adhere to that designation in creating a MoM.

The Harry Potter Companion

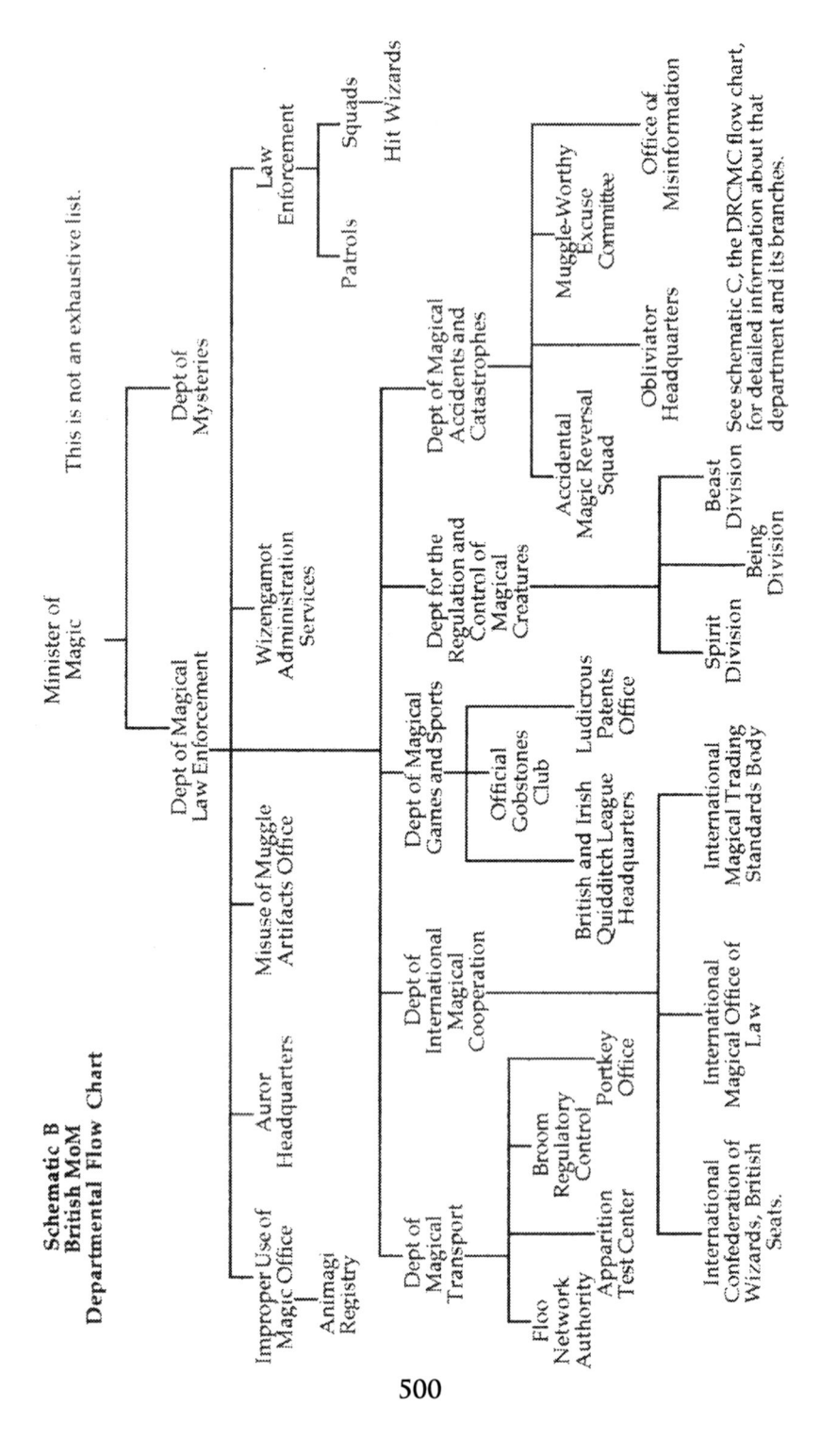

Schematic B
British MoM Departmental Flow Chart

This is not an exhaustive list.

- **Minister of Magic**
  - **Dept of Magical Law Enforcement**
    - Improper Use of Magic Office
    - Animagi Registry
    - Auror Headquarters
    - Misuse of Muggle Artifacts Office
    - Wizengamot Administration Services
    - Dept of Mysteries
    - Law Enforcement
      - Patrols
      - Squads
      - Hit Wizards
  - **Dept of Magical Games and Sports**
    - Official Gobstones Club
    - Ludicrous Patents Office
    - British and Irish Quidditch League Headquarters
  - **Dept for the Regulation and Control of Magical Creatures**
    - Spirit Division
    - Being Division
    - Beast Division
  - **Dept of Magical Accidents and Catastrophes**
    - Accidental Magic Reversal Squad
    - Obliviator Headquarters
    - Muggle-Worthy Excuse Committee
    - Office of Misinformation

    See schematic C, the DRCMC flow chart, for detailed information about that department and its branches.

  - **Dept of International Magical Cooperation**
    - International Magical Trading Standards Body
    - International Magical Office of Law
    - International Confederation of Wizards, British Seats.
  - **Dept of Magical Transport**
    - Broom Regulatory Control
    - Portkey Office
    - Apparition Test Center
    - Floo Network Authority

ACASCIAS RIPHOUSE

Schematic C
Dept for the Regulation and Control of Magical Creatures
Flow Chart

This is not an exhaustive list.

- Dept for the Regulation and Control of Magical Creatures
  - Spirit Division
  - Being Division
    - Office for House-Elf Relocation
    - Werewolf Support Services
    - Goblin Liaison Office
  - Beast Division
    - Committee for the Disposal of Dangerous Creatures
    - Pest Sub-Division
      - Pest Advisory Bureau
      - Ghoul Task Force
    - Dragon Research and Restraint Bureau
    - Centaur Liaison Office
    - Werewolf Registry
    - Werewolf Capture Unit

The Harry Potter Companion
Schematic D
Ministry of Magic Levels Guide

← Ministry of Magic Visitors' Entrance Phonebooth at Muggle street level

MoM interior elevators to Levels 1-9 only ↓

Level 1 Offices of the Minister of Magic?
Level 2 Dept of Magical Law Enforcement, Improper Use of Magic Office, Auror Headquarters, Wizengamot Administration Services, Misuse of Muggle Artifacts Office
Level 3 Dept of Magical Accidents and Catastrophes, Accidental Magic Reversal Squad, Obliviator Headquarters, Muggle-Worthy Excuse Committee
Level 4 Dept for the Regulation and Control of Magical Creatures, Beast, Being and Spirit Divisions, Goblin Liaison Office, Pest Advisory Bureau, House-Elf Relocation Office
Level 5 Dept of International Magical Cooperation, International Magical Trading Standards Body, The International Magical Office of Law, The International Confederation of Wizards, British Seats
Level 6 Dept of Magical Transport, Floo Network Authority, Broom Regulatory Control, Portkey Office, Apparition Test Center
Level 7 Dept of Magical Games and Sports, including British and Irish Quidditch League Headquarters, Official Gobstones Club, Ludicrous Patents Office
Level 8 Main Entrance, Security Desk, Fountain of Magical Brethren, Lifts to levels within the MoM building
Level 9 Dept of Mysteries   There is a staircase between Level 9 and Level 10. Lifts do not go beyond Level 9.
Level 10 Courtroom 10 and various prison cells for prisoners awaiting trial. This is a high-security area.

↑ Shaft down to Level 8 and the Main Entrance to the MoM

Trolls to work the lifts in this area →

ACASCIAS RIPHOUSE
Schematic E
MoM Level 2

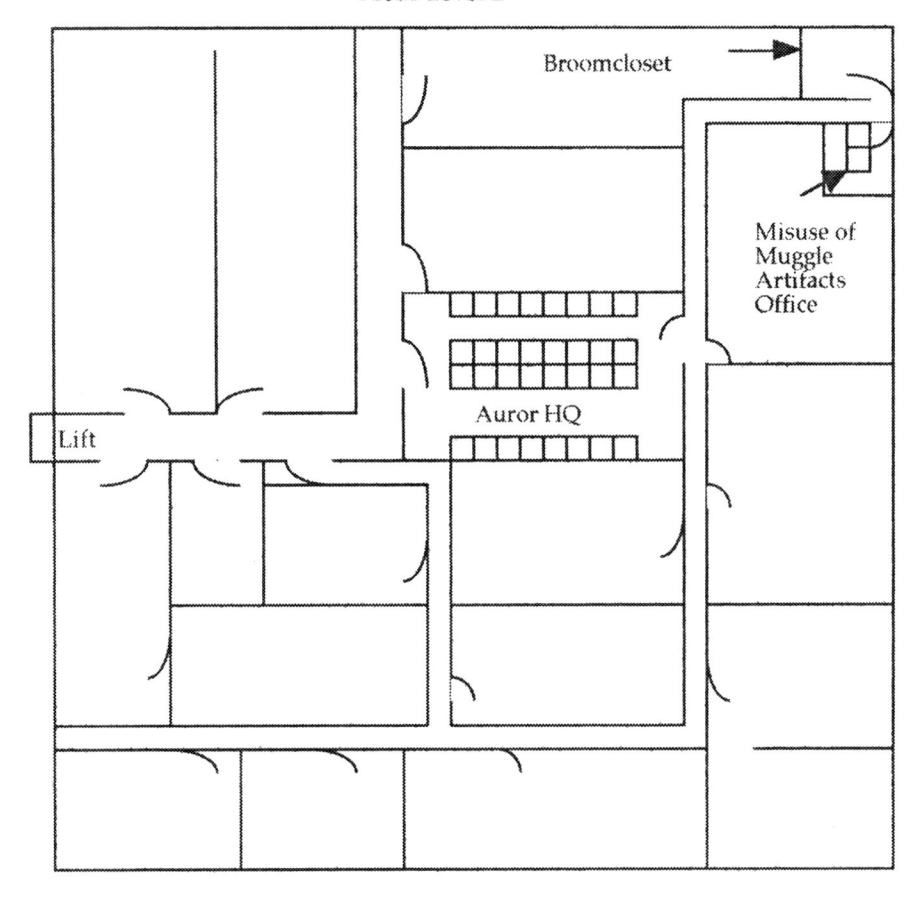

Broomcloset

Misuse of Muggle Artifacts Office

Lift

Auror HQ

The Harry Potter Companion

Schematic F
MoM Level 9
Dept of Mysteries

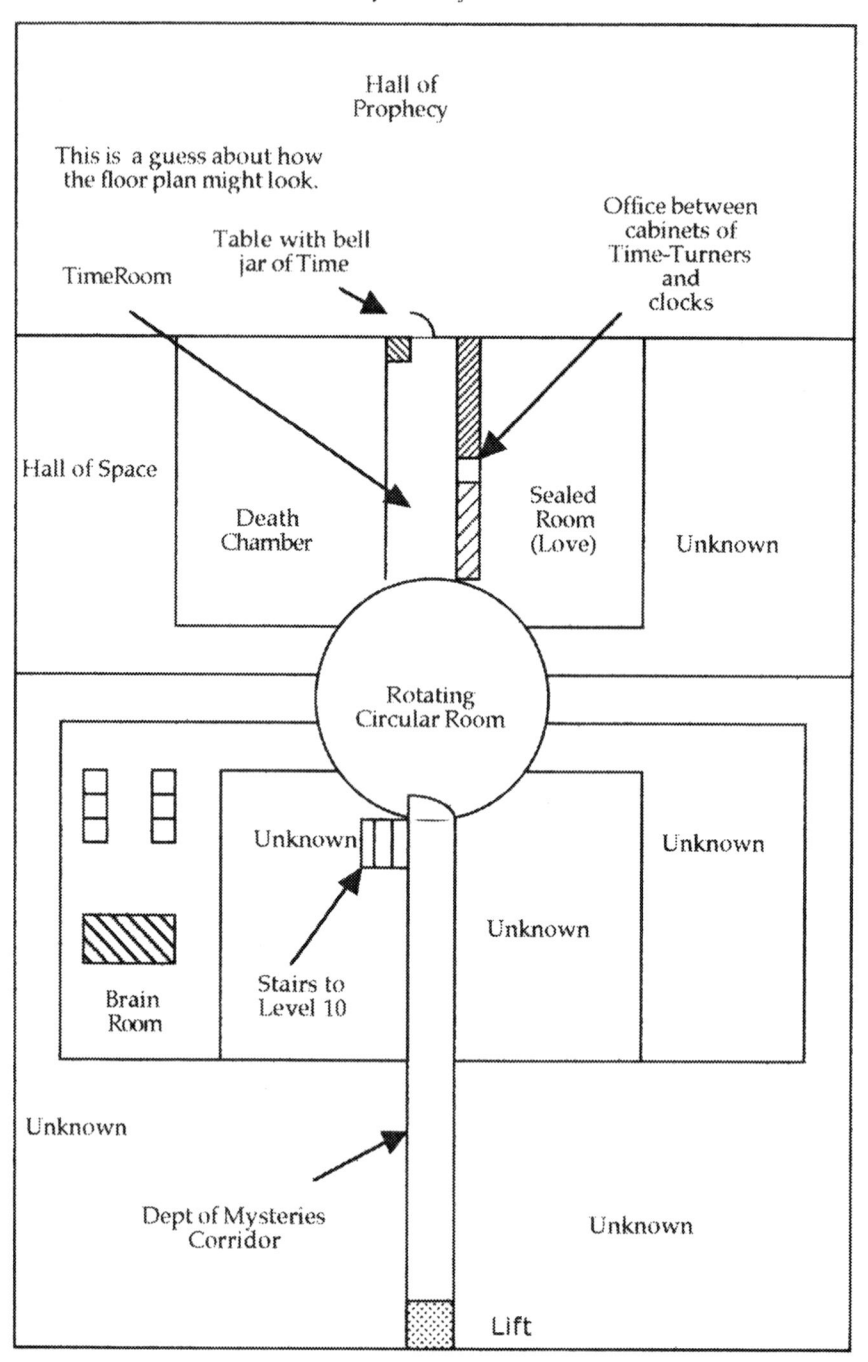

Hall of Prophecy

This is a guess about how the floor plan might look.

Table with bell jar of Time

Office between cabinets of Time-Turners and clocks

TimeRoom

Hall of Space

Death Chamber

Sealed Room (Love)

Unknown

Rotating Circular Room

Unknown

Unknown

Unknown

Brain Room

Stairs to Level 10

Unknown

Unknown

Dept of Mysteries Corridor

Unknown

Lift

504

Acascias Riphouse

Schematic G
Level 10
High Security Courtroom and Environs

- Courtroom 10
- Jury Box
- Judge's Bench
- Chair with chains
- Cells
- Level 10
- Room for guards, witnesses, etc
- Stairway to Level 10
- Level 9
- Door to the Dept of Mysteries
- Lift

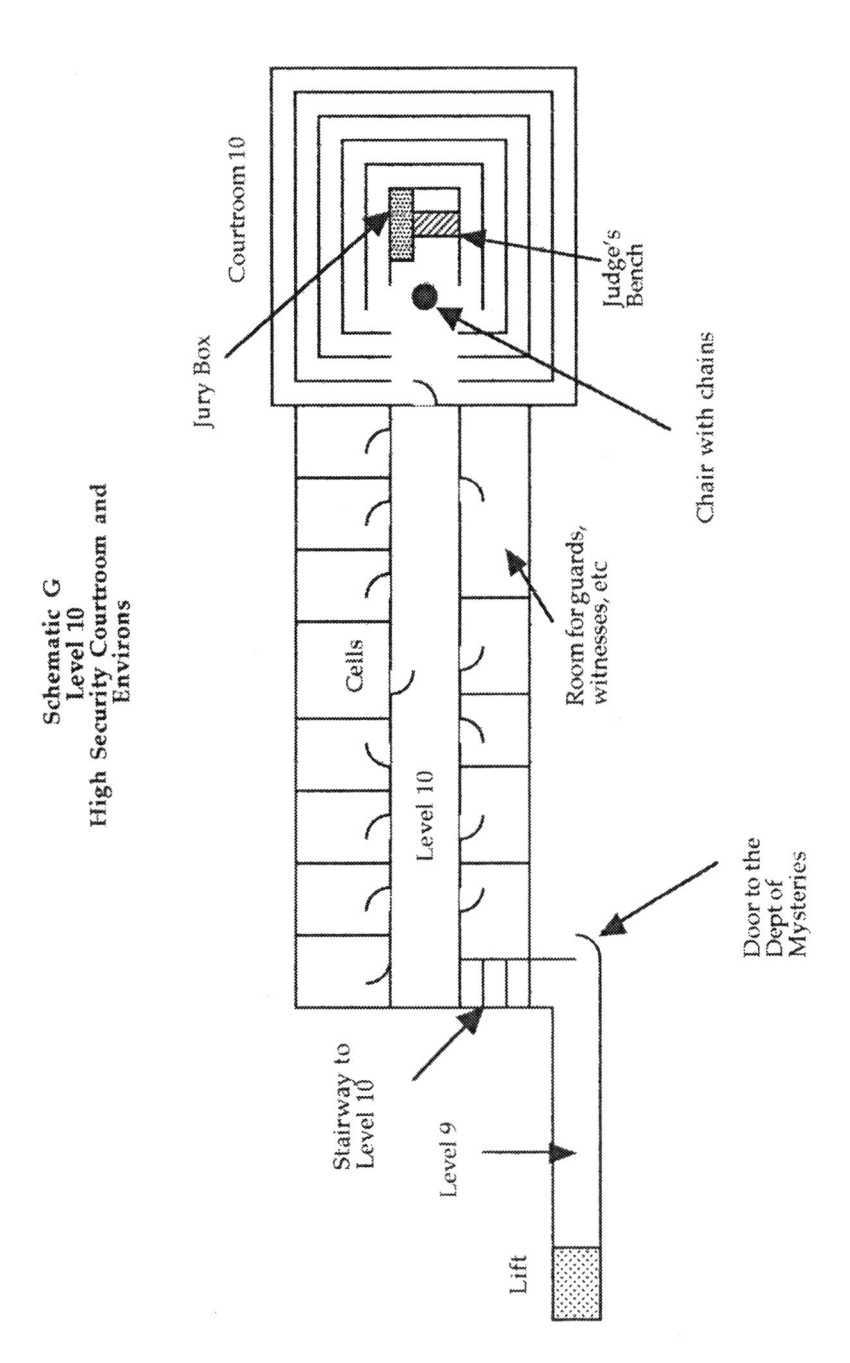

The Harry Potter Companion

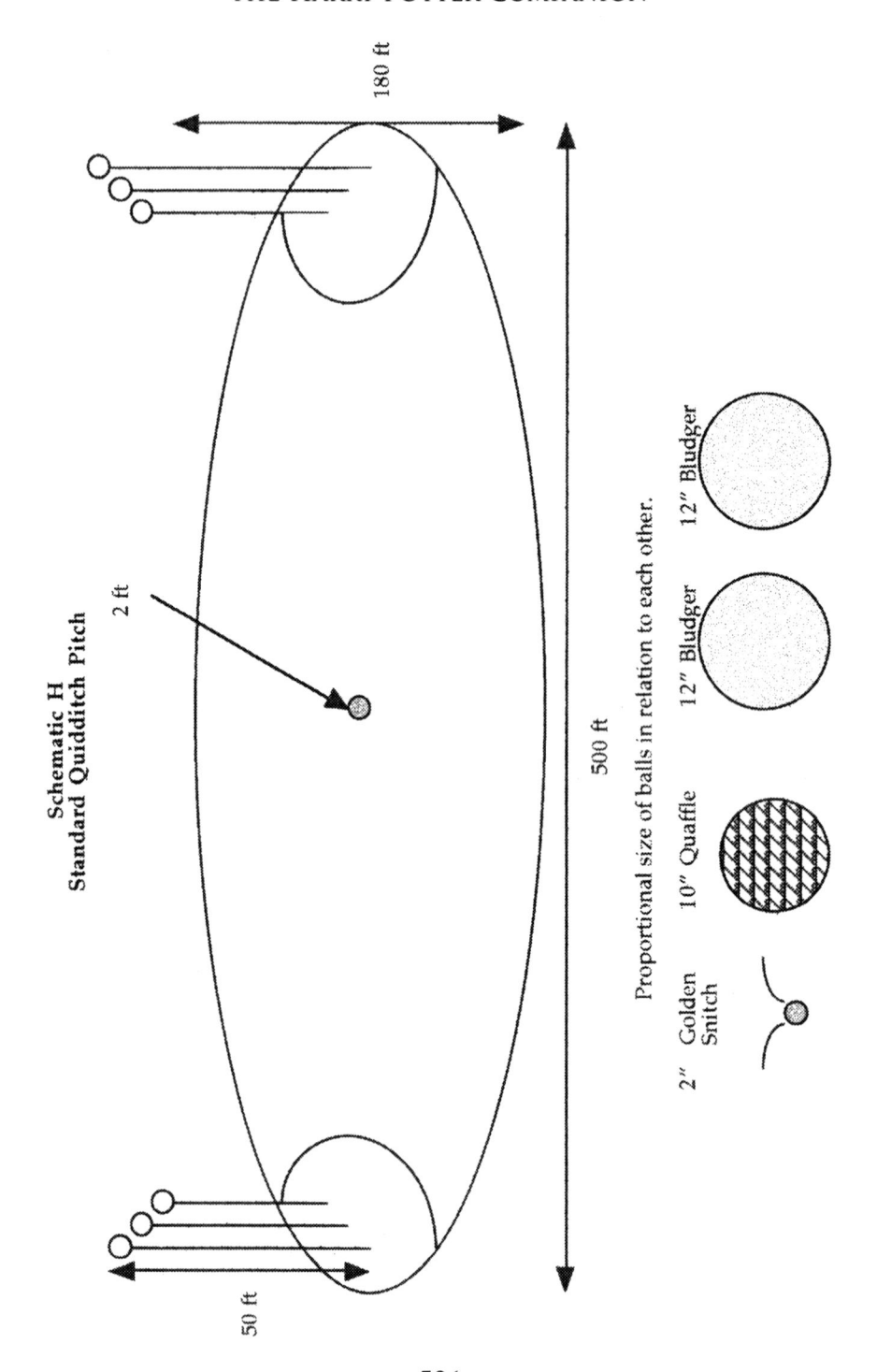

**Schematic H
Standard Quidditch Pitch**

180 ft

500 ft

50 ft

2 ft

Proportional size of balls in relation to each other.

2" Golden Snitch   10" Quaffle   12" Bludger   12" Bludger

ACASCIAS RIPHOUSE

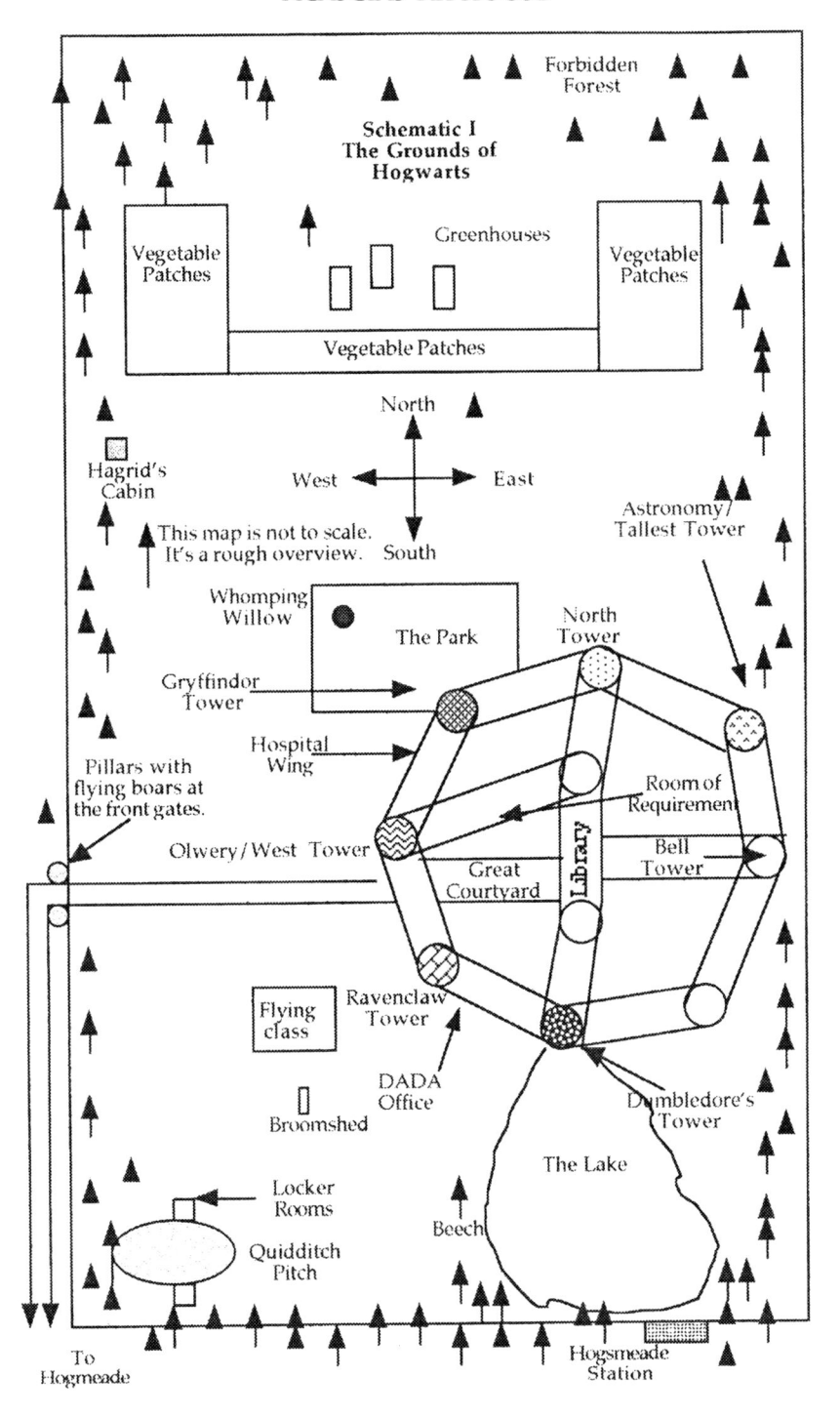

**Schematic I
The Grounds of Hogwarts**

Forbidden Forest

Vegetable Patches

Greenhouses

Vegetable Patches

Vegetable Patches

North / West / East / South

Hagrid's Cabin

This map is not to scale. It's a rough overview.

Astronomy/ Tallest Tower

Whomping Willow

The Park

North Tower

Gryffindor Tower

Hospital Wing

Room of Requirement

Pillars with flying boars at the front gates.

Olwery/West Tower

Great Courtyard

Library

Bell Tower

Flying class

Ravenclaw Tower

DADA Office

Broomshed

Dumbledore's Tower

The Lake

Locker Rooms

Beech

Quidditch Pitch

To Hogmeade

Hogsmeade Station

THE HARRY POTTER COMPANION

Schematic J
Hogwarts Floor Guide

Floor	Rooms
7	Room of Requirement / Barnabas the Barmy / Pr Flitwick's Office / Sinister Looking Monks Painting / Entrance to Gryffindor Tower / The Fat Lady / Lachlan the Lanky / Entrance to North Tower / Divination Classroom and Pr Trelawney's Quarters
6	Sir Cadogan's Painting / Wolfhound Painting / Staircase to Entrance of the North Tower
5	Boris the Bewildered / Prefects Bathroom / Gregory the Smarmy / Entrance to a Collapsed Passageway Out of Hogwarts
4	Classroom Where Mirror of Erised Was / Bathrooms
3	Charms Classroom & Corridor / Fluffy's Room / Armor Display Corridor / Trophy Room / Hump-Backed Witch Statue & Passageway to Honeydukes / Hospital Entrance / DADA Office
2	DADA Classroom / Moaning Myrtle's Bathroom / Transfiguration Classroom / Staffroom / Library Entrance / Gargoyle Entrance to Dumbledore's Office / Vanishing Cabinet
1	Pr McGonagall's Quarters & Office / Muggle Studies Classroom / History of Magic Classroom
G	Filch's Office / Broom Closet / Classroom 11 / Staffroom / Pre-Sort Room / Entrance Hall / Great Hall / Entrance to Dungeons / Vi's Chamber / Courtyard / Kitchens and Hufflepuff House / Corridor to Entrance of Hufflepuff House
LL	Kitchens
UL1	Pr Snape's Quarters & Office / Aragog's Old Cupboard & Now Pr Snape's Potions Classroom / Dungeons 1, 2 & 32
UL2	Entrance to Slytherin House / Slytherin House
UL3	Dungeon 4 / Dungeon 5
SSL	Chamber of Secrets / Multiple Rooms Connected with the Sorcerer's Stone

G = Ground Floor
LL = Lower Level
UL1 = Underground Level 1
UL2 = Underground Level 2
UL3 = Underground Level 3
SSL = Salazar's Secret Level

Like most schools, teachers tend to move classrooms with each bell. They may have a usual classroom but it doesn't prevent them from using any classroom that suits their purpose.

Europeans do not count the ground floor as the first floor as Americans do.

This chart reflects Hogwarts floors in the European fashion as is used in the books.

It's unclear where the entrance to the Owlery Tower and Ravenclaw Tower are so I've elected not to show them.

There are many options when picking what floor something may be on. This is a best guess based on 2 or more references confirming a place to be on the same floor. A single conflicting reference was therefore disregarded.

ACASCIAS RIPHOUSE

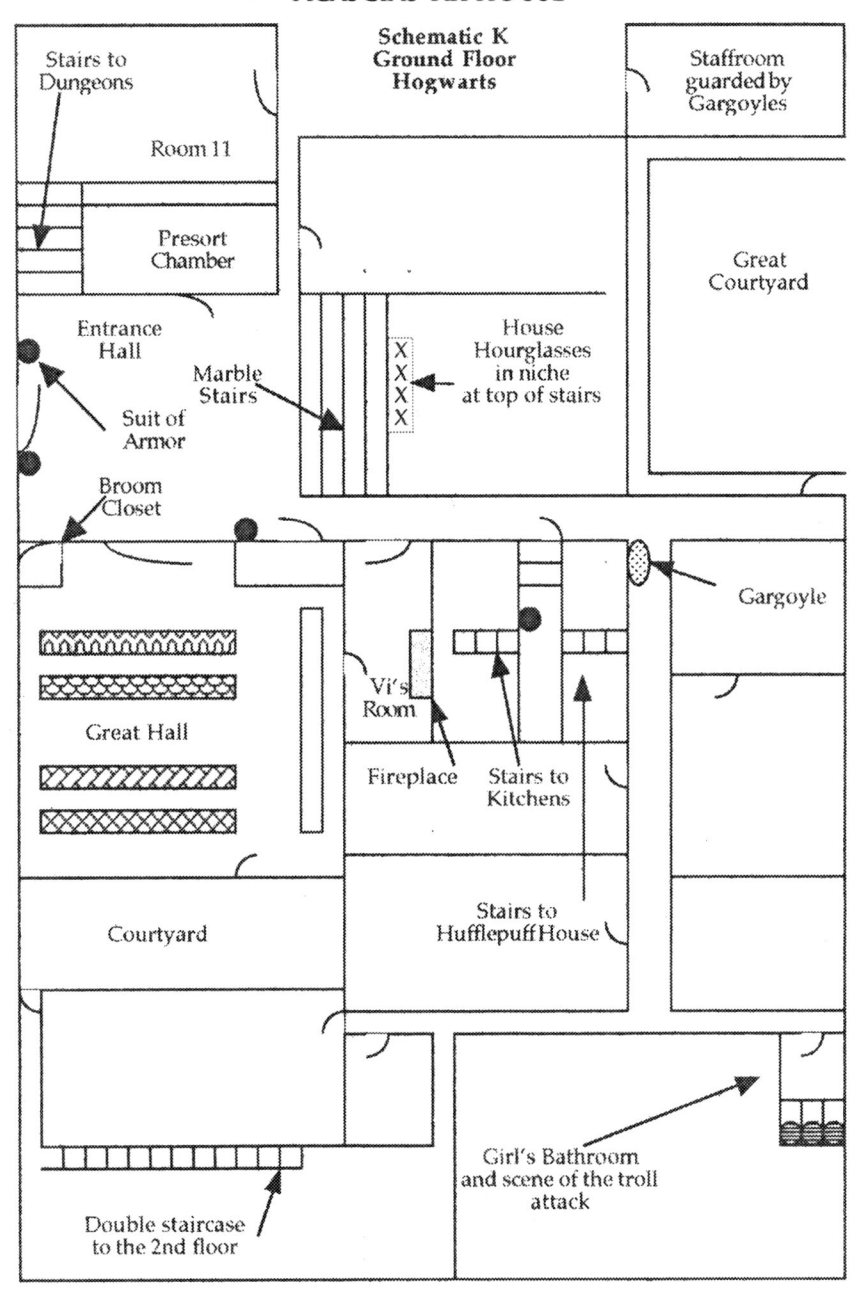

**Schematic K
Ground Floor
Hogwarts**

Stairs to Dungeons

Room 11

Presort Chamber

Staffroom guarded by Gargoyles

Great Courtyard

Entrance Hall

Marble Stairs

House Hourglasses in niche at top of stairs

Suit of Armor

Broom Closet

Gargoyle

Great Hall

Vi's Room

Fireplace

Stairs to Kitchens

Courtyard

Stairs to Hufflepuff House

Double staircase to the 2nd floor

Girl's Bathroom and scene of the troll attack

The Harry Potter Companion

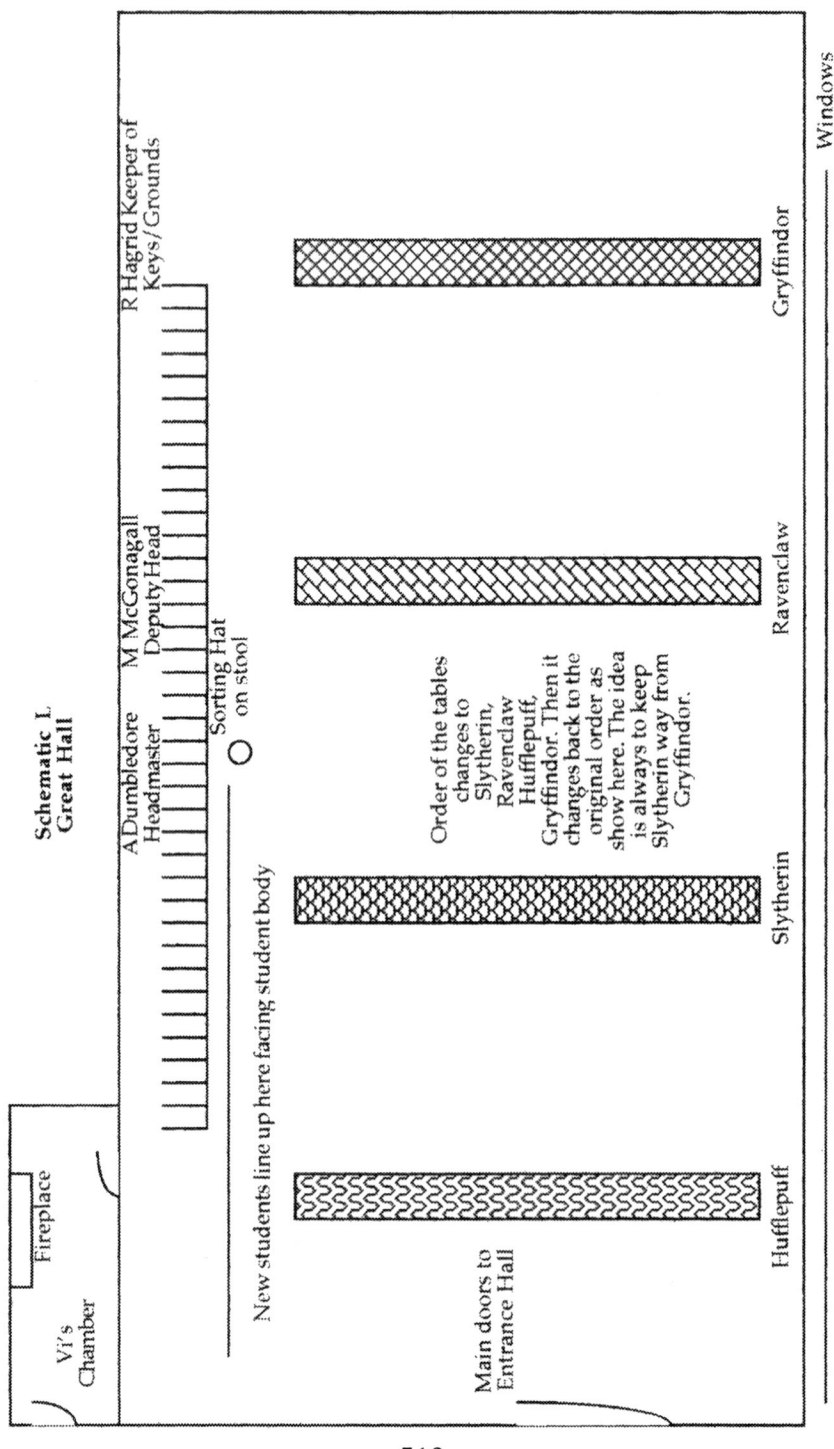

**Schematic 1.
Great Hall**

A Dumbledore
Headmaster

M McGonagall
Deputy Head

R Hagrid Keeper of
Keys/Grounds

Sorting Hat
on stool

New students line up here facing student body

Vi's Chamber

Fireplace

Main doors to Entrance Hall

Hufflepuff

Slytherin

Ravenclaw

Gryffindor

Windows

Order of the tables changes to Slytherin, Ravenclaw, Hufflepuff, Gryffindor. Then it changes back to the original order as show here. The idea is always to keep Slytherin way from Gryffindor.

ACASCIAS RIPHOUSE

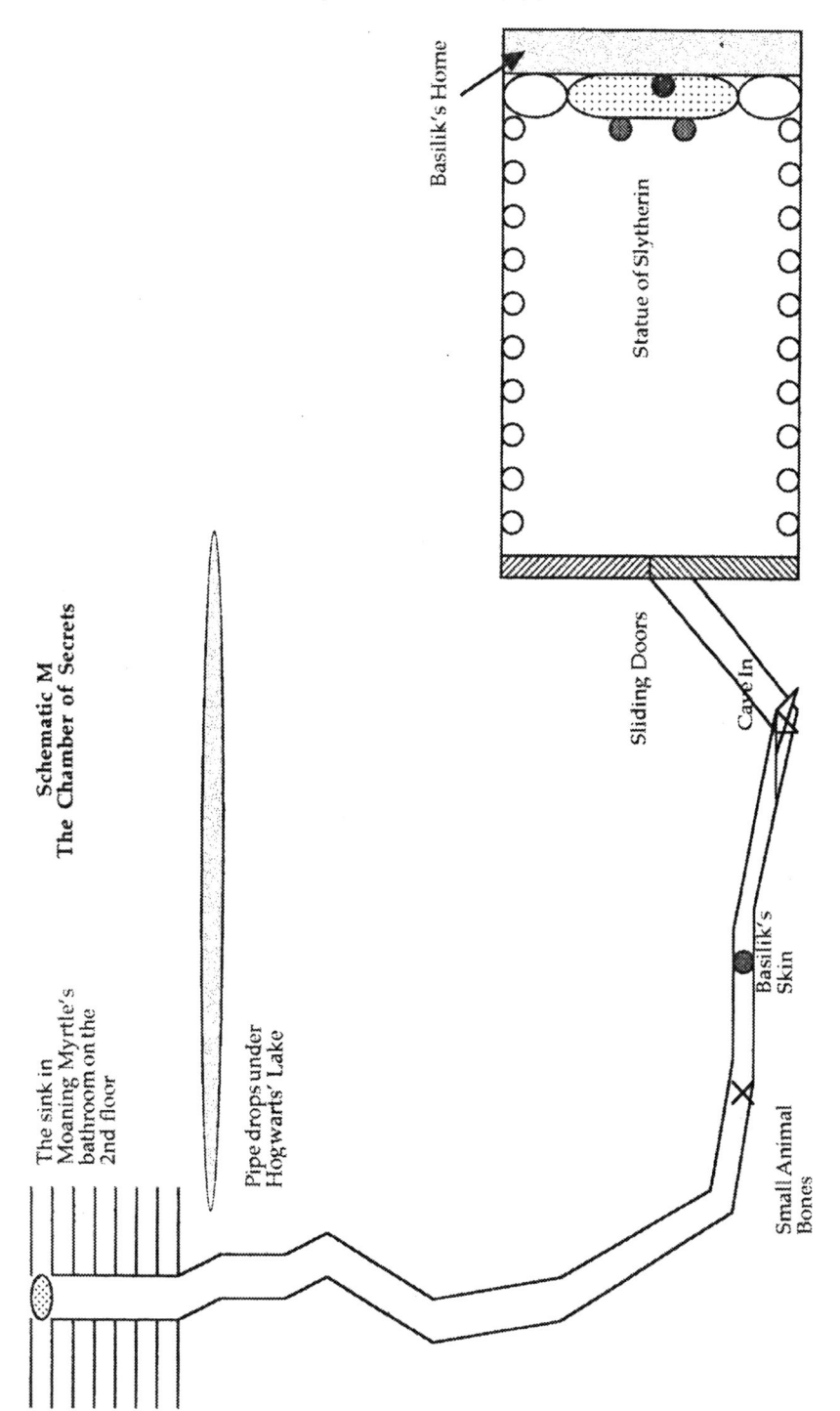

Schematic M
The Chamber of Secrets

- The sink in Moaning Myrtle's bathroom on the 2nd floor
- Pipe drops under Hogwarts' Lake
- Small Animal Bones
- Basilik's Skin
- Cave In
- Sliding Doors
- Statue of Slytherin
- Basilik's Home

The Harry Potter Companion

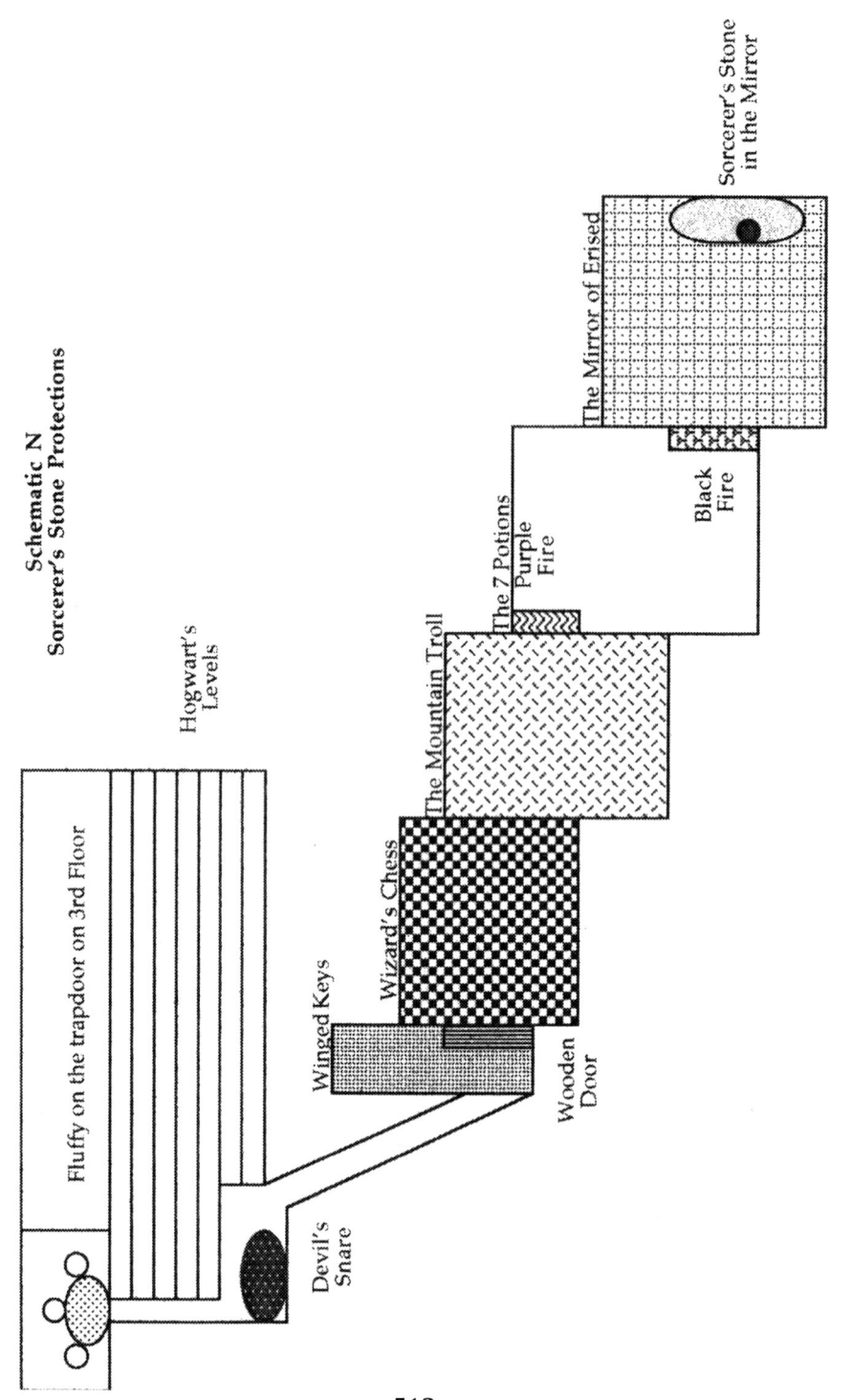

Schematic N
Sorcerer's Stone Protections

- Fluffy on the trapdoor on 3rd Floor
- Devil's Snare
- Hogwart's Levels
- Winged Keys
- Wooden Door
- Wizard's Chess
- The Mountain Troll
- The 7 Potions
- Purple Fire
- Black Fire
- The Mirror of Erised
- Sorcerer's Stone in the Mirror

This Page Has Been Intentionally Left Blank

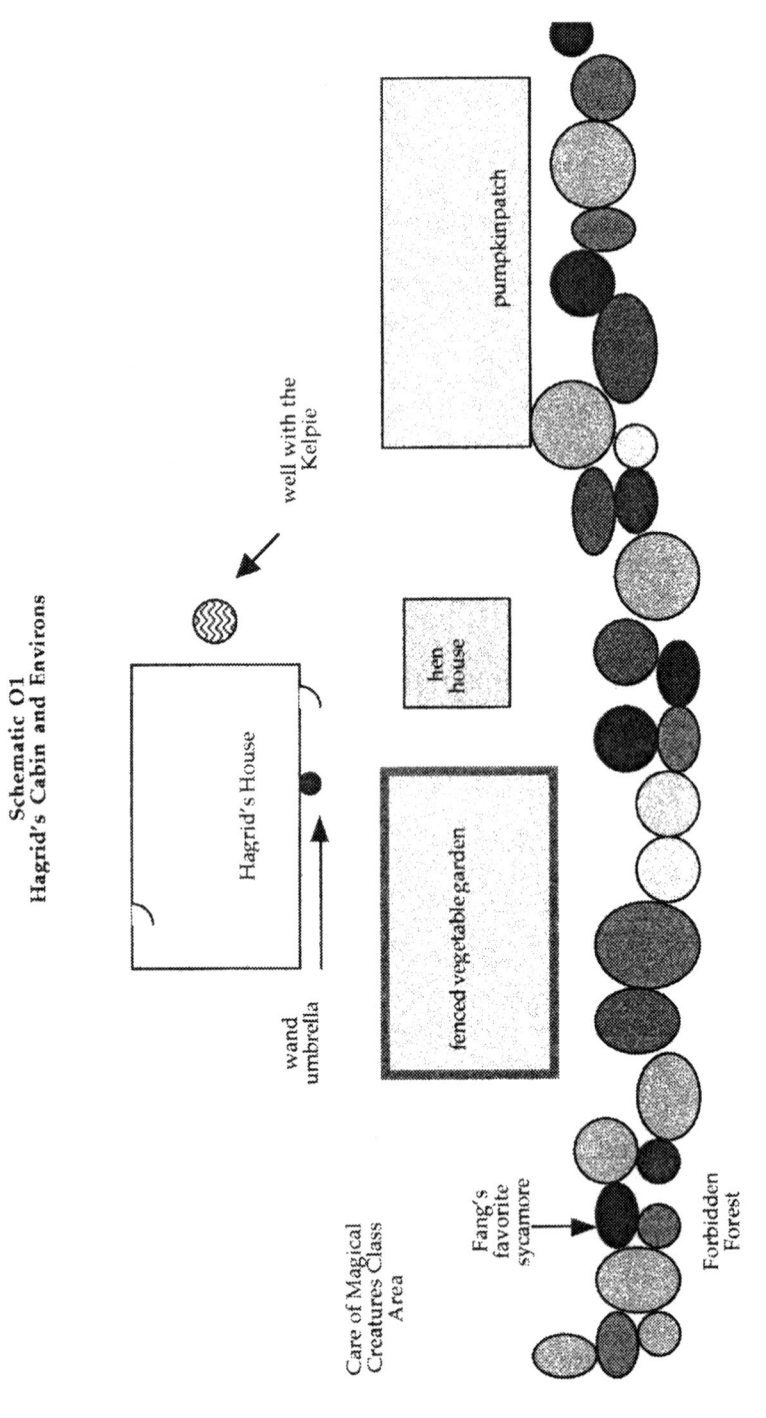

Schematic O1
Hagrid's Cabin and Environs

- pumpkin patch
- well with the Kelpie
- Hagrid's House
- hen house
- wand umbrella
- fenced vegetable garden
- Care of Magical Creatures Class Area
- Fang's favorite sycamore
- Forbidden Forest

ACASCIAS RIPHOUSE

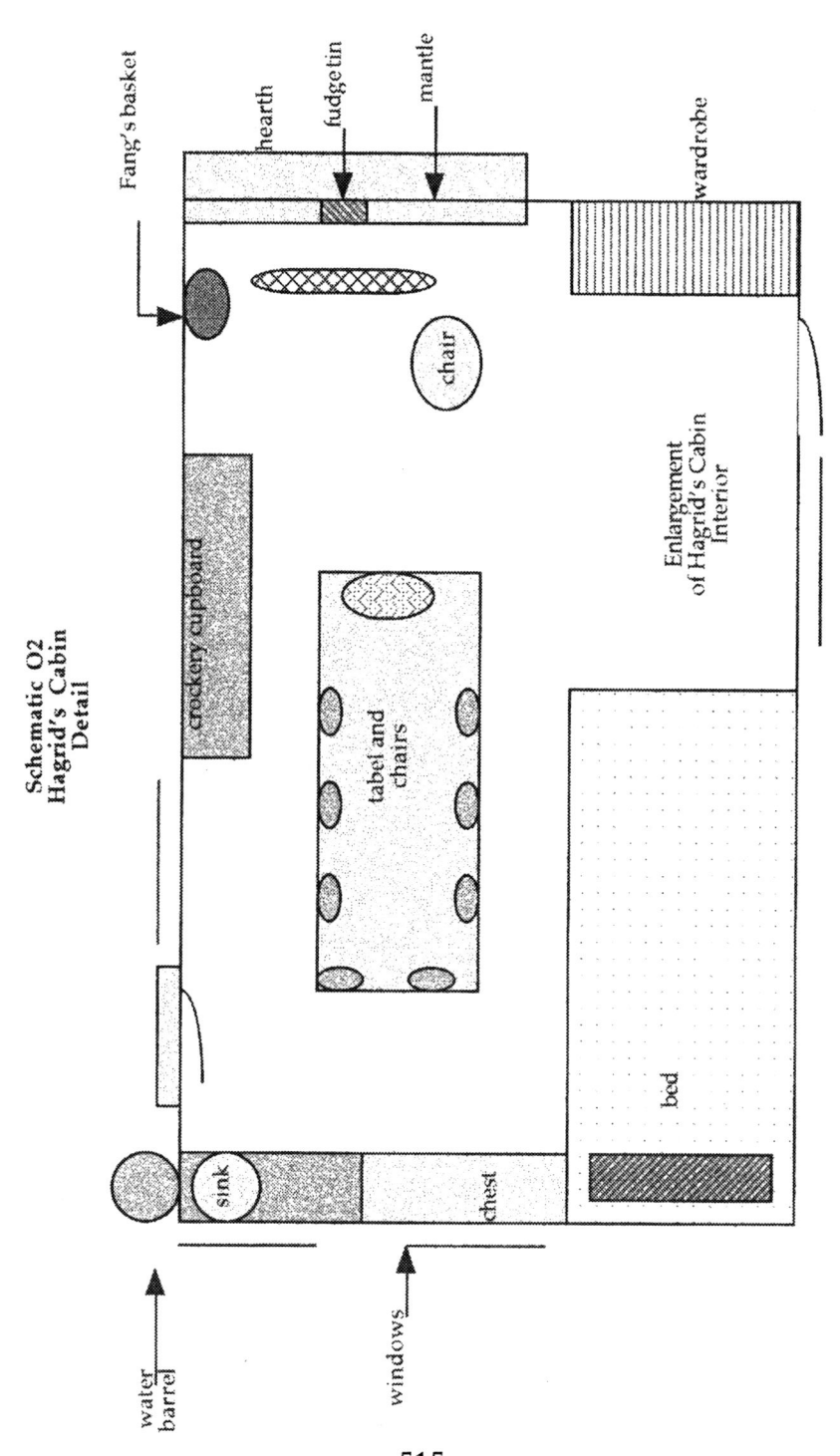

Schematic O2
Hagrid's Cabin
Detail

Enlargement of Hagrid's Cabin Interior

Fang's basket — hearth — fudge tin — mantle — wardrobe — chair — crockery cupboard — tabel and chairs — bed — sink — chest — water barrel — windows

Schematic P
Filch's Form

Incident Report Form

Name: Harry Potter

Crime: Befouling the Castle

Suggested Sentence: Hanging by the ankles from the ceiling of Dungeon 4 for a period of not less than 7 days.

Signed: Argus Filch,

Date: April 10, 1994

Acascias Riphouse
Schematic Q
Harry's Tower Room

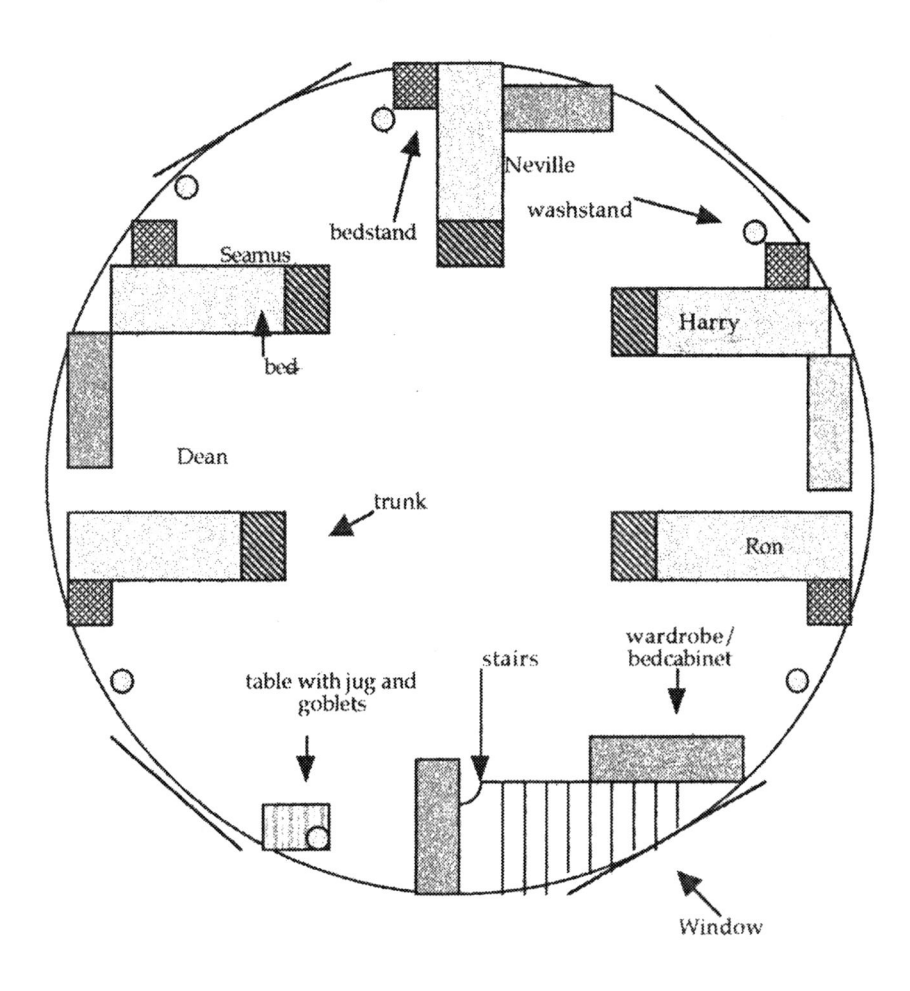

Neville
bedstand
washstand
Seamus
Harry
bed
Dean
trunk
Ron
table with jug and goblets
stairs
wardrobe/ bedcabinet
Window

THE HARRY POTTER COMPANION

Schematic R
Family Trees

Harry Potter's Family Tree

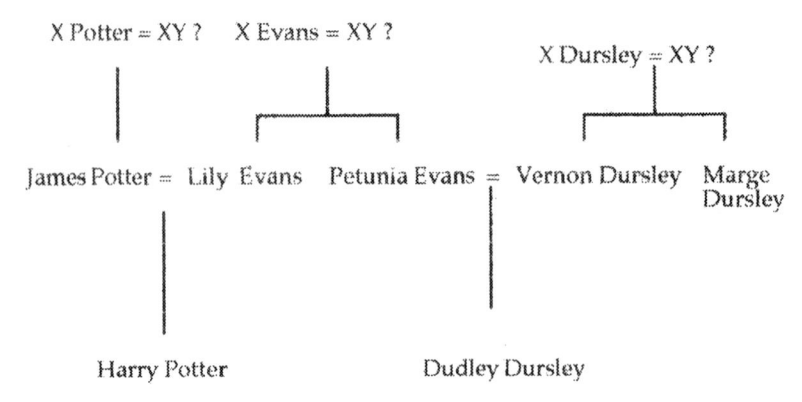

```
X Potter = XY ?    X Evans = XY ?
     |                  |                    X Dursley = XY ?
     |            ┌─────┴─────┐                    |
James Potter = Lily Evans   Petunia Evans = Vernon Dursley   Marge Dursley
         |                         |
     Harry Potter              Dudley Dursley
```

X = male
XY = female
? = unknown last name

Voldemort's Family Tree

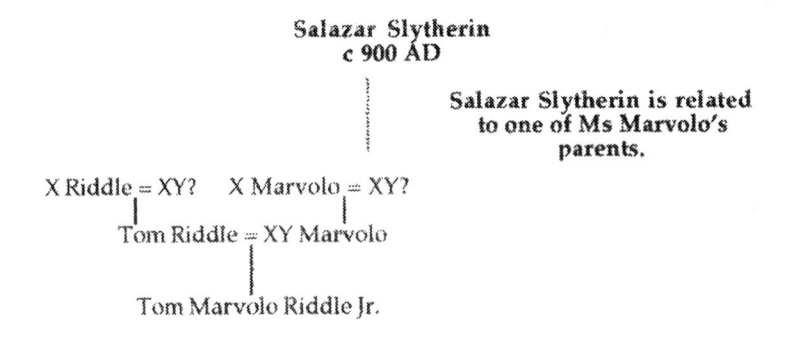

Salazar Slytherin
c 900 AD
|
| Salazar Slytherin is related
| to one of Ms Marvolo's
| parents.

X Riddle = XY?   X Marvolo = XY?
     | |
   Tom Riddle = XY Marvolo
              |
     Tom Marvolo Riddle Jr.

ACASCIAS RIPHOUSE
Schematic S
More Family Trees

Susan Bone's Family Tree

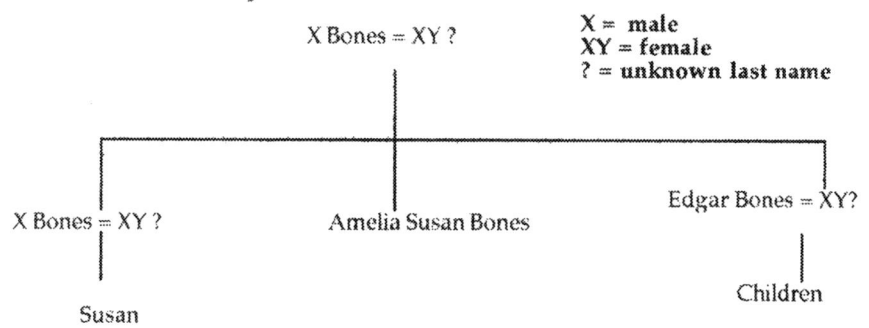

X Bones = XY ?

X = male
XY = female
? = unknown last name

X Bones = XY ?   Amelia Susan Bones   Edgar Bones = XY ?

Susan

Children

Ludo Bagman's Family Tree

X Bagman = XY ?

Ludovic   Otto

Dumbledore's Family Tree

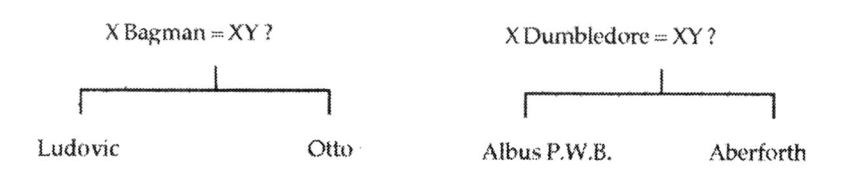

X Dumbledore = XY ?

Albus P.W.B.   Aberforth

Neville's Family Tree

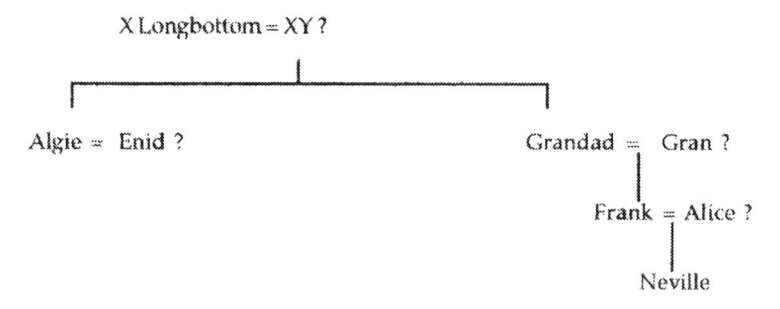

X Longbottom = XY ?

Algie = Enid ?   Grandad = Gran ?

Frank = Alice ?

Neville

THE HARRY POTTER COMPANION

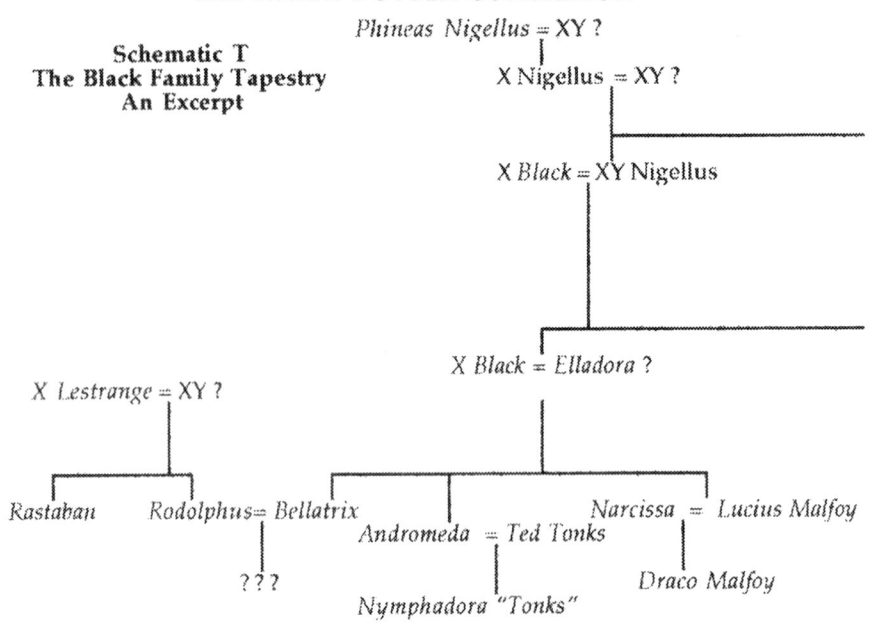

Schematic T
The Black Family Tapestry
An Excerpt

Phineas Nigellus = XY ?
│
X Nigellus = XY ?
│
X Black = XY Nigellus
│
X Black = Elladora ?

X Lestrange = XY ?
│
Rastaban   Rodolphus = Bellatrix   Andromeda = Ted Tonks   Narcissa = Lucius Malfoy
                 │   │   │
            ? ? ?   Nymphadora "Tonks"   Draco Malfoy

Molly has a second cousin that's an accountant, a descendant of her father's grandfather probably.

For Molly to be cousin by marriage to Sirius, one of her parents must have made a second marriage to an aunt/uncle of Sirius.

I'm presuming Molly's mother married Alphard Melifula as her second husband since he seems to be the only decent one in the family.

X or XX = male
XY = female
? = name unknown
??? = may or may not have children, or additional children
Italics indicate certainties - there are so few in life!

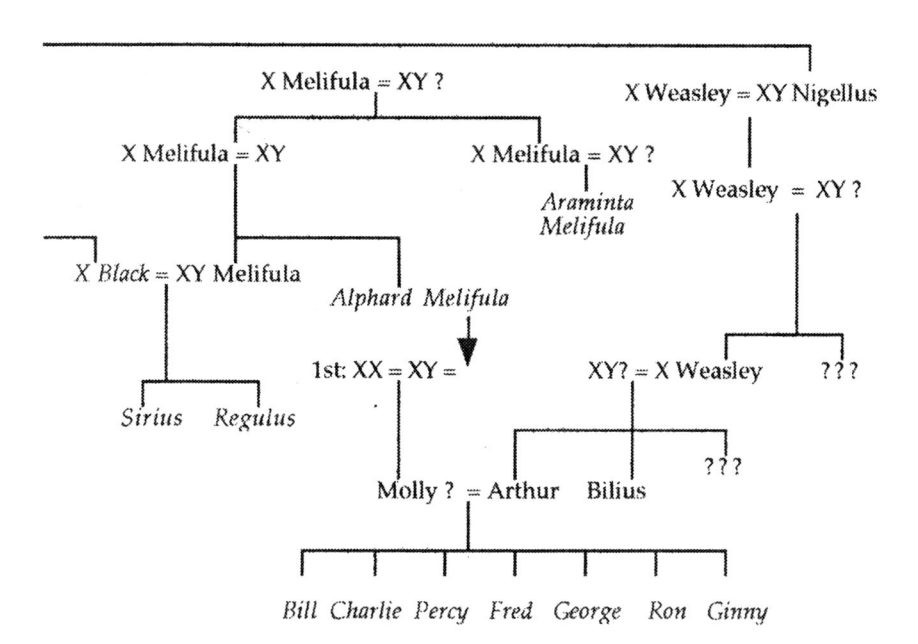

```
                    X Melifula = XY ?                    X Weasley = XY Nigellus
         X Melifula = XY      X Melifula = XY ?                    |
                                      |                    X Weasley = XY ?
                                 Araminta
                                 Melifula
    X Black = XY Melifula
                              Alphard Melifula
                          1st: XX = XY =          XY? = X Weasley       ???
                                                                    ???
       Sirius   Regulus
                             Molly ? = Arthur   Bilius

                     Bill  Charlie  Percy  Fred  George  Ron  Ginny
```

It is unknown if Uncle Bilius is a Arthur or Molly's brother - Ron doesn't say.
one would assume Arthur's from the number of 2 boys only wizard families seem to produce.

Even though Arthur is older than Sirius, Sirius belongs the genealogical generation preceding Arthur, probably because Arthur's ancestors married younger and his great-grandmother was much older than her Nigellus sister who married Black.

The Harry Potter Companion

Schematic U
Muggle Games

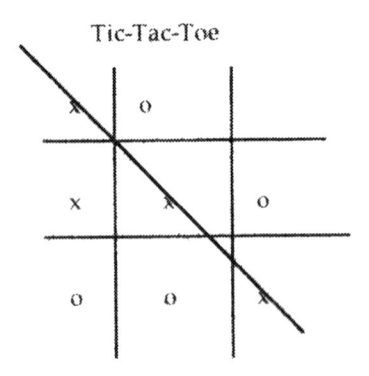

Tic-Tac-Toe

Hangman

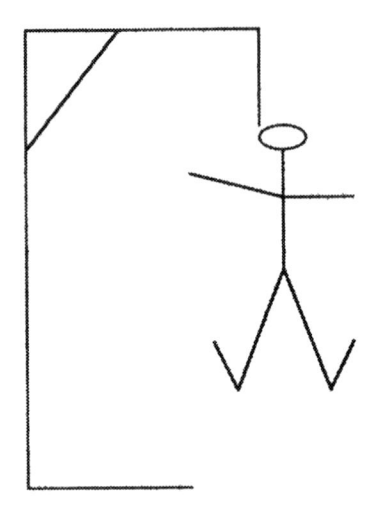

_ _ _ _ n _ _ _ r _ b _ _ _ _ r _

n e k s b m a u l o p h k y

THIS PAGE HAS BEEN
INTENTIONALLY
LEFT BLANK

The Harry Potter Companion

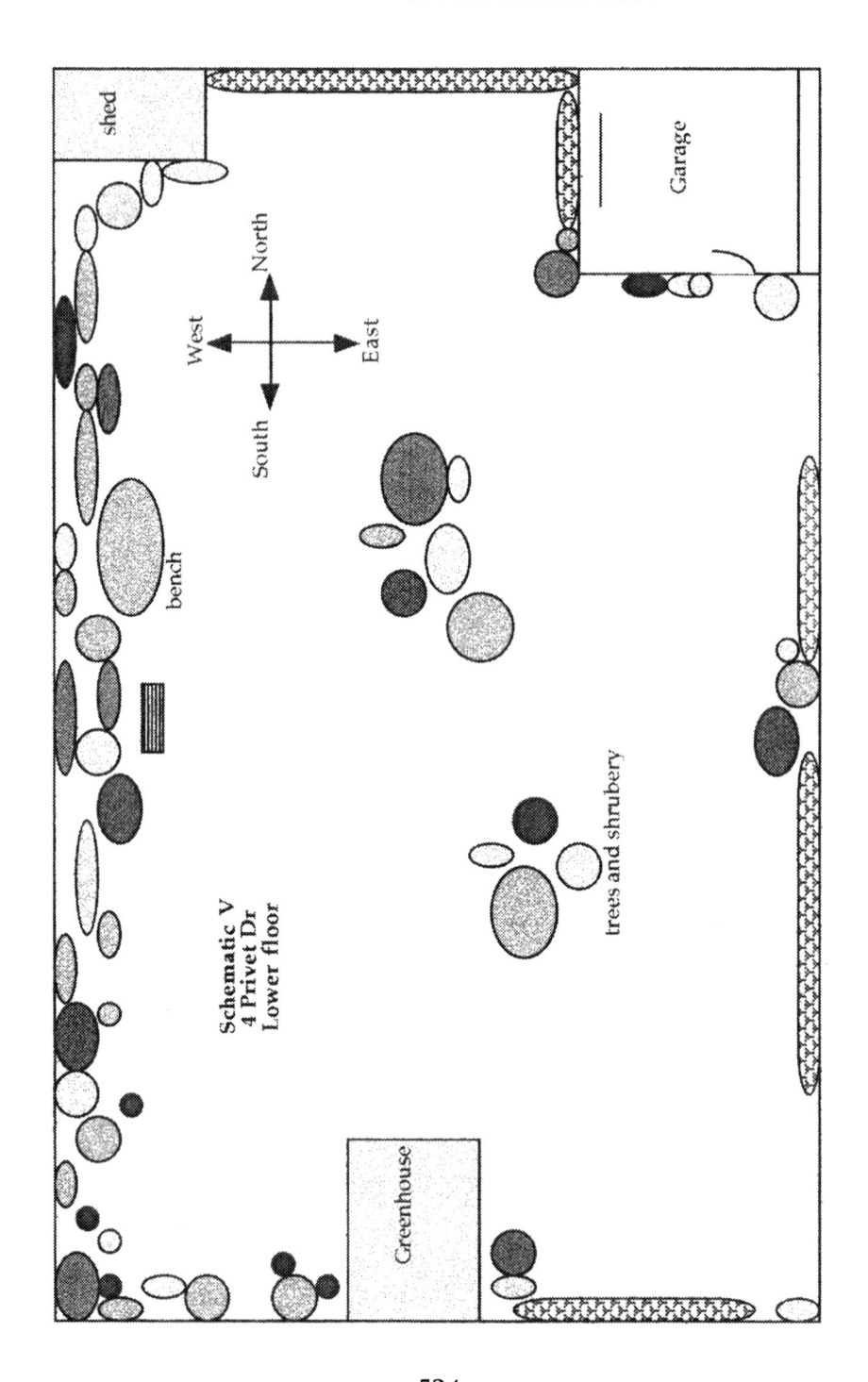

North / South / West / East

shed

Garage

bench

trees and shrubery

Greenhouse

Schematic V
4 Privet Dr
Lower floor

Acascias Riphouse

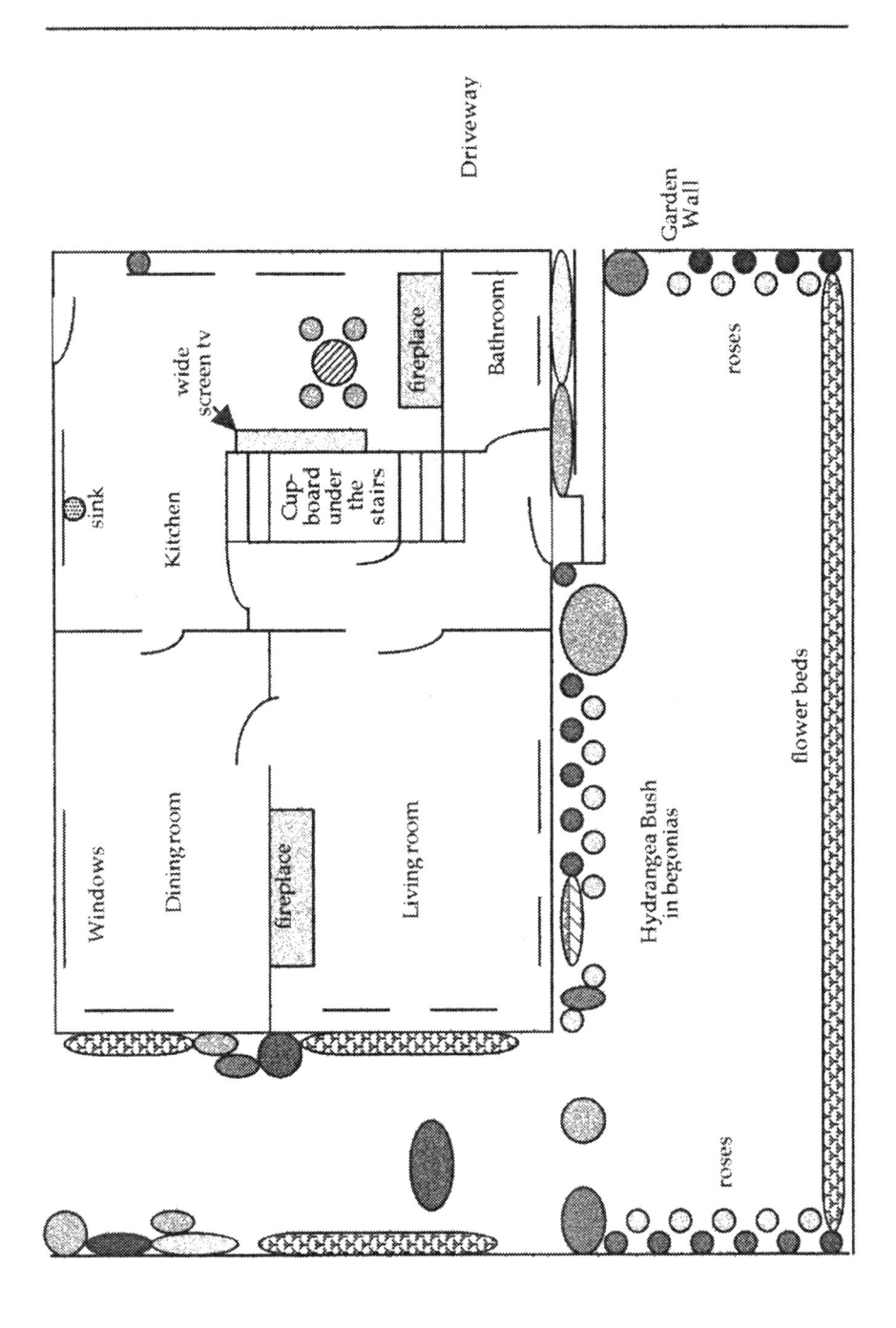

The Harry Potter Companion

4 Privet Dr
Upper floor

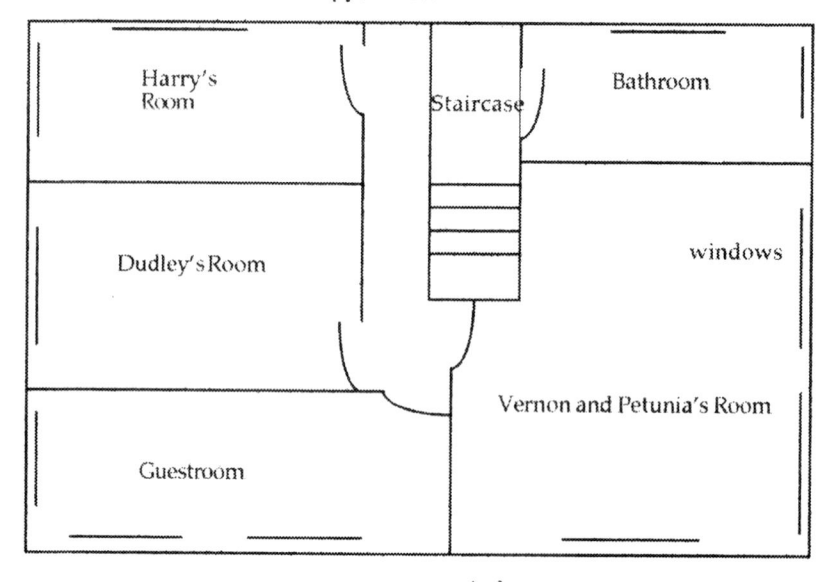

[Floor plan of upper floor showing: Harry's Room (upper left), Bathroom (upper right), Staircase (center), Dudley's Room (middle left), windows (middle right), Guestroom (lower left), Vernon and Petunia's Room (lower right)]

[Floor plan of Harry's Bedroom showing: windows (top), book shelves, lamp, desk, Hedwig, chest of drawers (left), chair, door (right), lamp, nightstand, loose floorboard, Harry's bed, school trunk, wardrobe with interior mirror on the door]

The fact that Harry can pull up a floorboard suggest that he has wood flooring in his entire room.
The book shelves have been hanging on the wall since it was Dudley's second bedroom, complete with books.
Harry keeps his school trunk at the foot of his bed and Hedwig's cage on his desk.

ACASCIAS RIPHOUSE
Schematic W
Privet Dr and Environs
Little Whinging

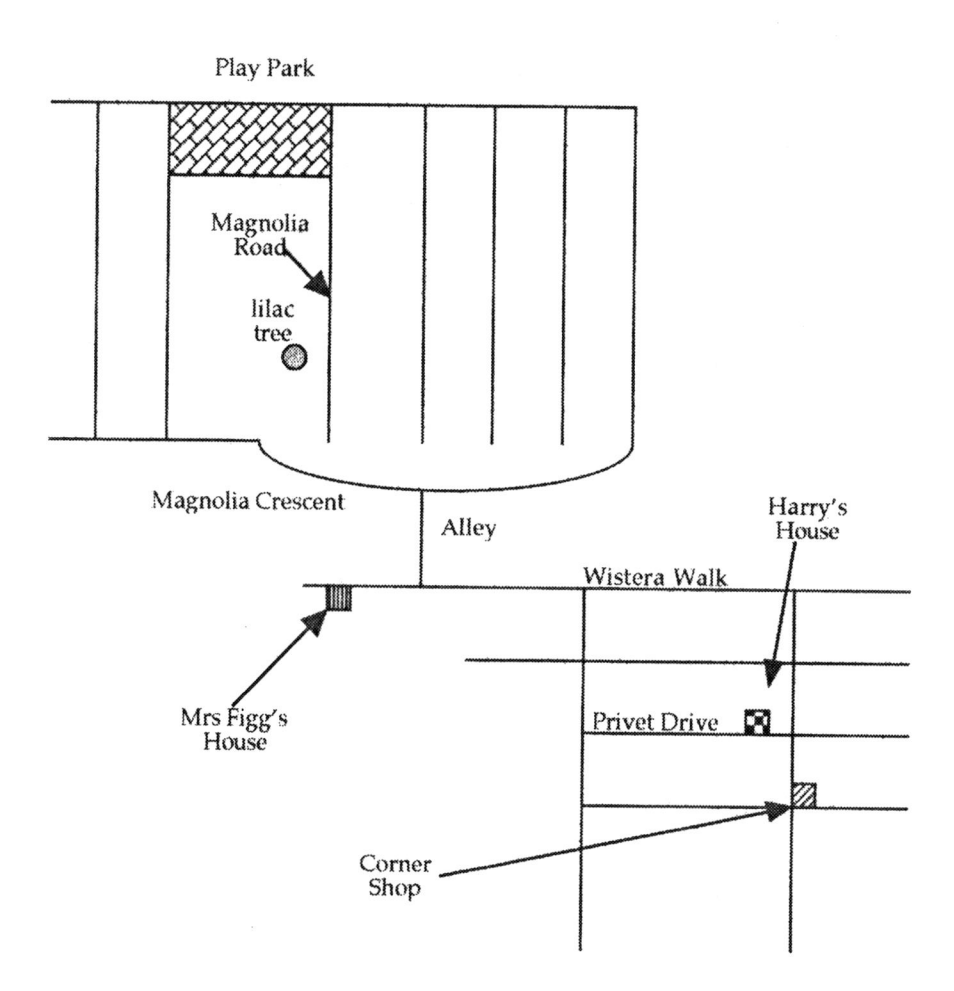

Play Park

Magnolia Road

lilac tree

Magnolia Crescent

Alley

Harry's House

Wistera Walk

Mrs Figg's House

Privet Drive

Corner Shop

The Harry Potter Companion

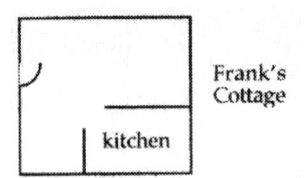

Frank's Cottage

**Schematic X
Riddle House and Property**

Riddle House

1st floor

There is probably a second floor where the bedrooms are.

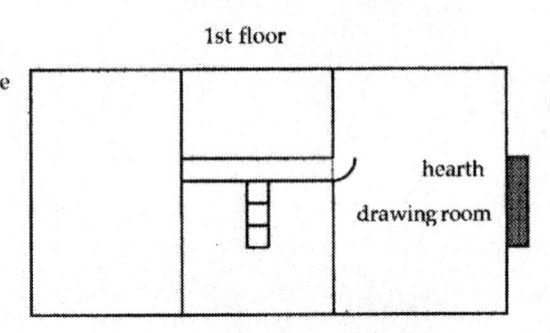

hearth

drawing room

ground floor

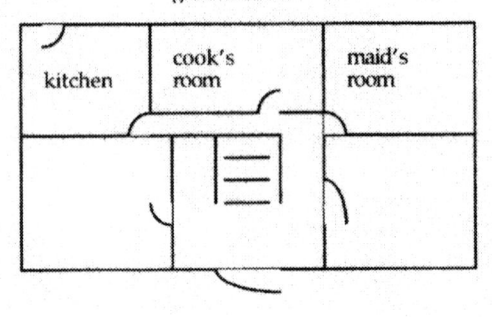

kitchen | cook's room | maid's room

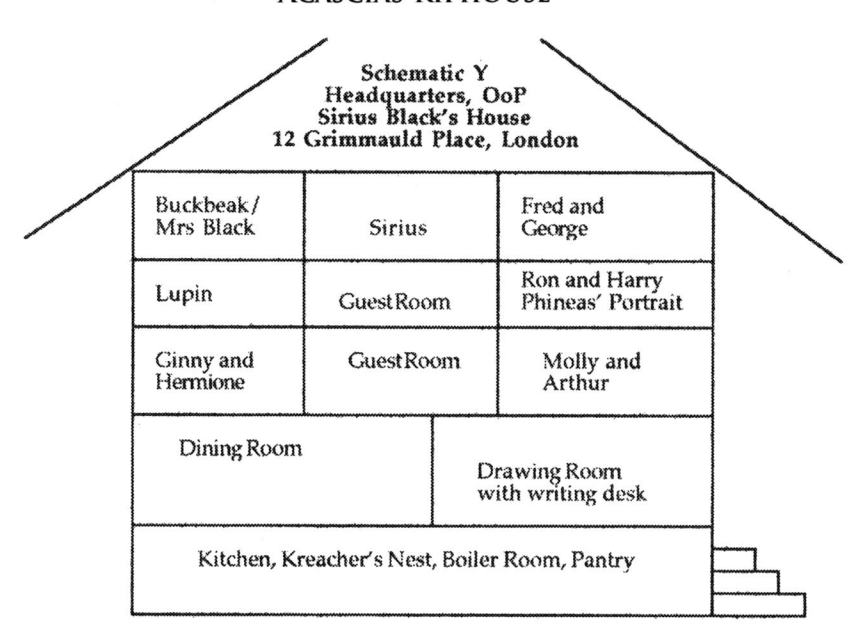

ACASCIAS RIPHOUSE

Schematic Y
Headquarters, OoP
Sirius Black's House
12 Grimmauld Place, London

Buckbeak/ Mrs Black	Sirius	Fred and George
Lupin	Guest Room	Ron and Harry Phineas' Portrait
Ginny and Hermione	Guest Room	Molly and Arthur
Dining Room	Drawing Room with writing desk	
Kitchen, Kreacher's Nest, Boiler Room, Pantry		

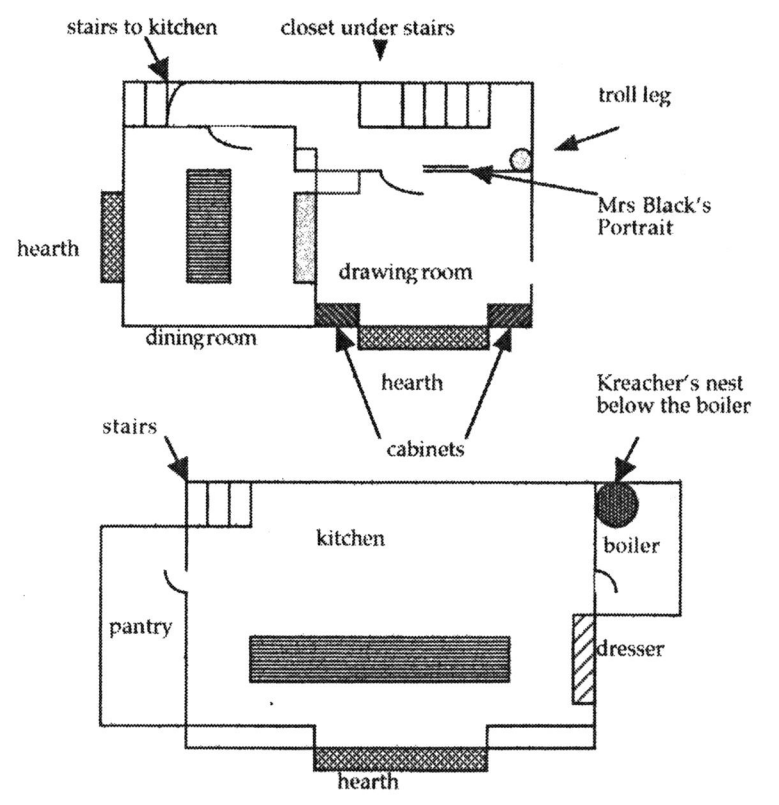

- stairs to kitchen
- closet under stairs
- troll leg
- Mrs Black's Portrait
- hearth
- drawing room
- dining room
- hearth
- cabinets
- Kreacher's nest below the boiler
- stairs
- kitchen
- boiler
- pantry
- dresser
- hearth

The Harry Potter Companion

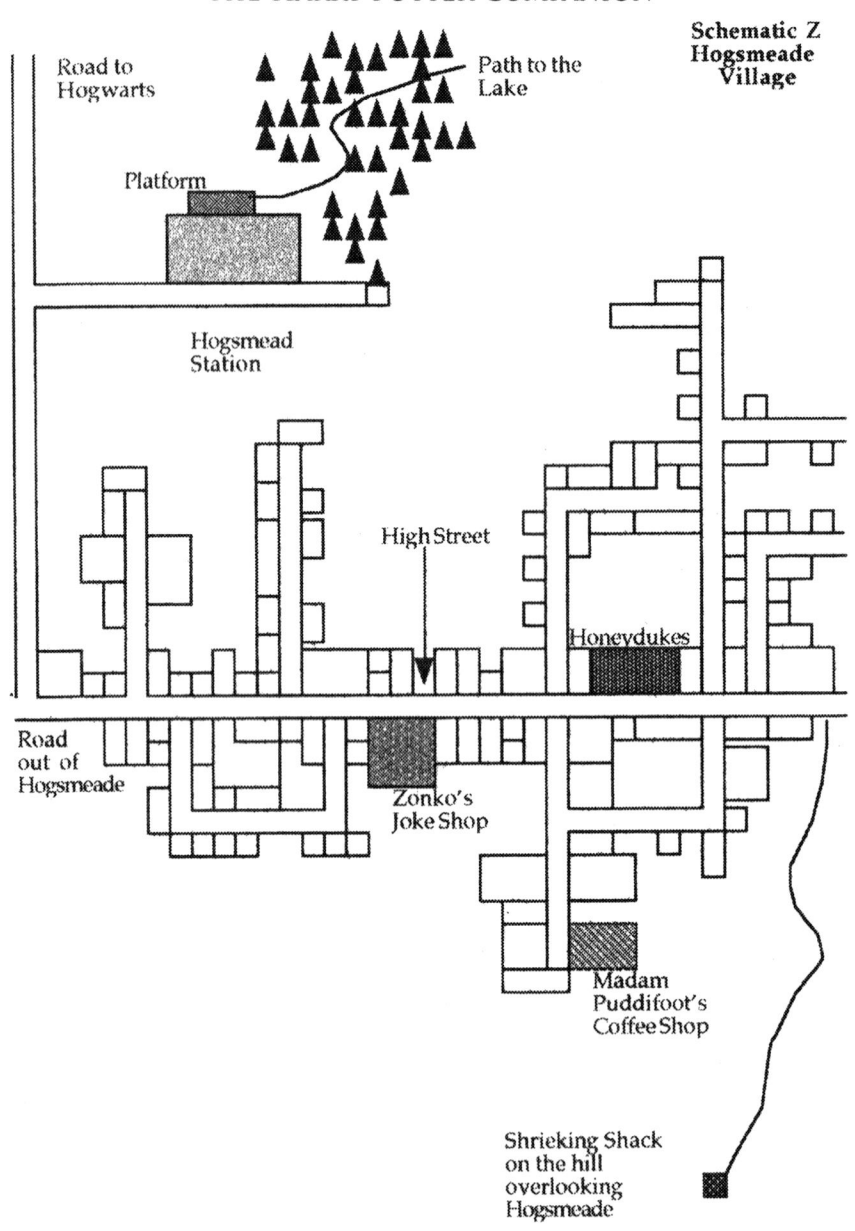

**Schematic Z
Hogsmeade Village**

Road to Hogwarts

Path to the Lake

Platform

Hogsmead Station

High Street

Honeydukes

Road out of Hogsmeade

Zonko's Joke Shop

Madam Puddifoot's Coffee Shop

Shrieking Shack on the hill overlooking Hogsmeade

ACASCIAS RIPHOUSE

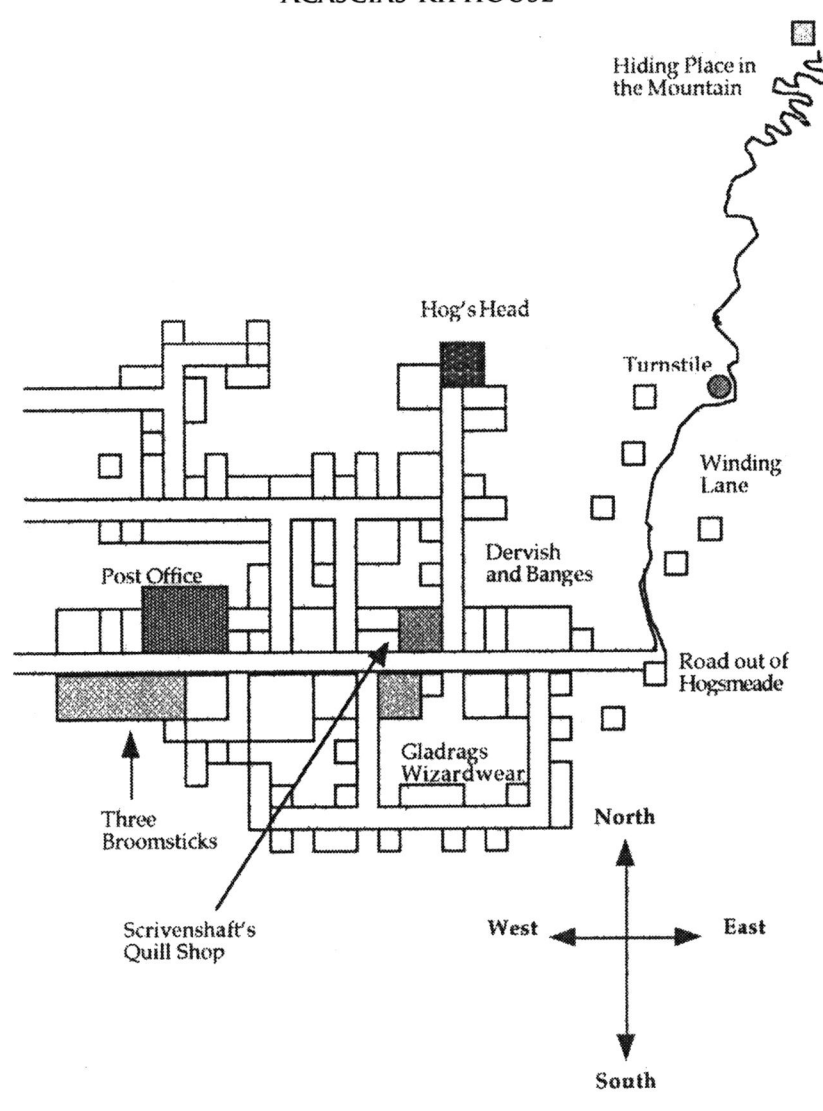

Hiding Place in the Mountain

Hog's Head

Turnstile

Winding Lane

Dervish and Banges

Post Office

Road out of Hogsmeade

Three Broomsticks

Gladrags Wizardwear

Scrivenshaft's Quill Shop

North
West ←→ East
South

THE HARRY POTTER COMPANION

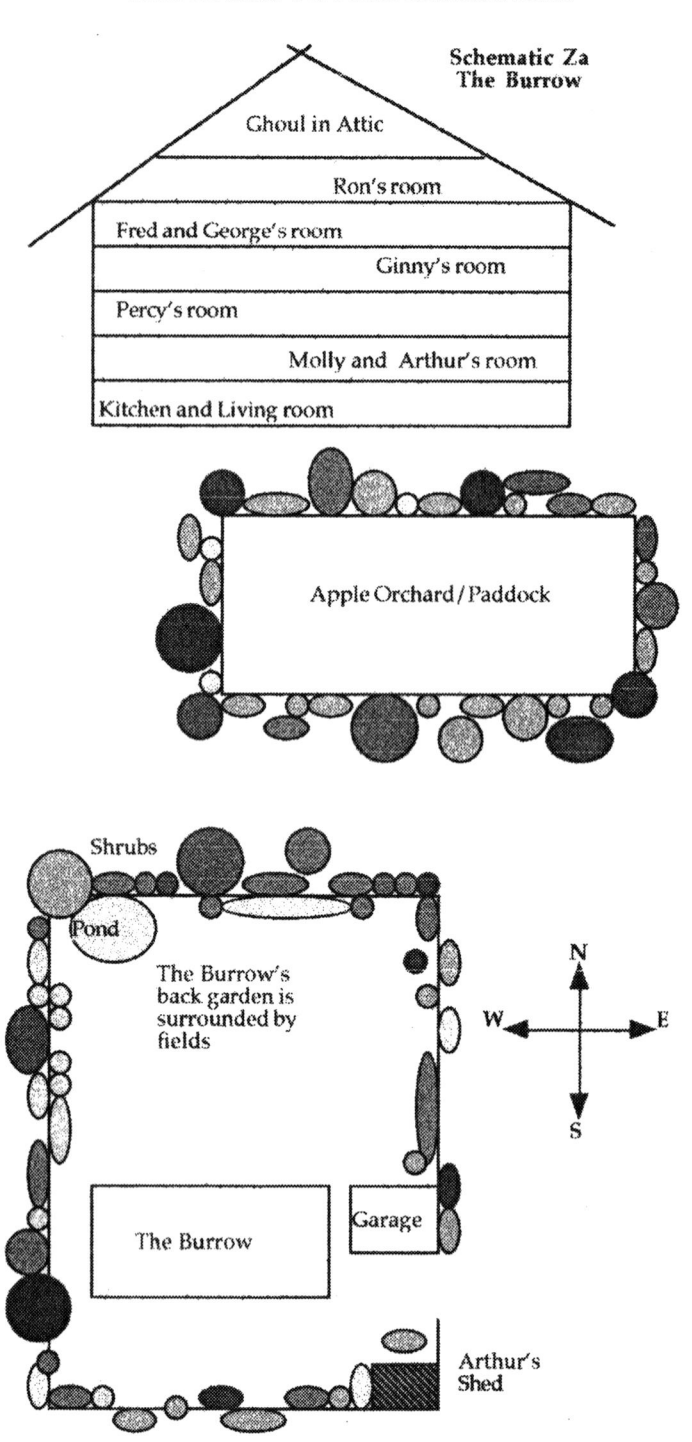

**Schematic Za
The Burrow**

| Ghoul in Attic |
| Ron's room |
| Fred and George's room |
| Ginny's room |
| Percy's room |
| Molly and Arthur's room |
| Kitchen and Living room |

Apple Orchard / Paddock

Shrubs

Pond

The Burrow's back garden is surrounded by fields

N / W / E / S

The Burrow

Garage

Arthur's Shed

ACASCIAS RIPHOUSE
Schematic 2b
St Mungo's Hospital for Magical Maladies and Injuries

Visitors' Tearoom and Hospital Shop	5th Floor

Spell Damage — 4th Floor

e.g., combining Jelly-Legs + Furnuculus Curses, hitting an older person with multiple Stunning Spells, overstrong Memory Charm.

The Janus Thickey Ward (Ward 49) is located here also.

Potions and Plant Poisoning — 3rd Floor

e.g., Polyjuice Potion made with cat fur, overstrong Draught of Peace, eating Alihotsy leaves.

Magical Bugs — 2nd Floor

Any type of contagious sickness with a magical origin.

Creature-Induced Injuries — 1st Floor

e.g., Doxy bites, dragon scratches, petrification by a Basilisk.

The "Dangerous" Dai Llewellyn Ward is located also here.

Artifact Accidents — Ground Floor

Anything involving a magical object or object used in doing magic causing injury, i.e., a Quodpot ball exploding too strongly, or a wand backfiring

The Reception Desk is located here also.

staircases

The Harry Potter Companion

Schematic Zc
Map of the London Underground
Dumbledore's Left Knee Scar

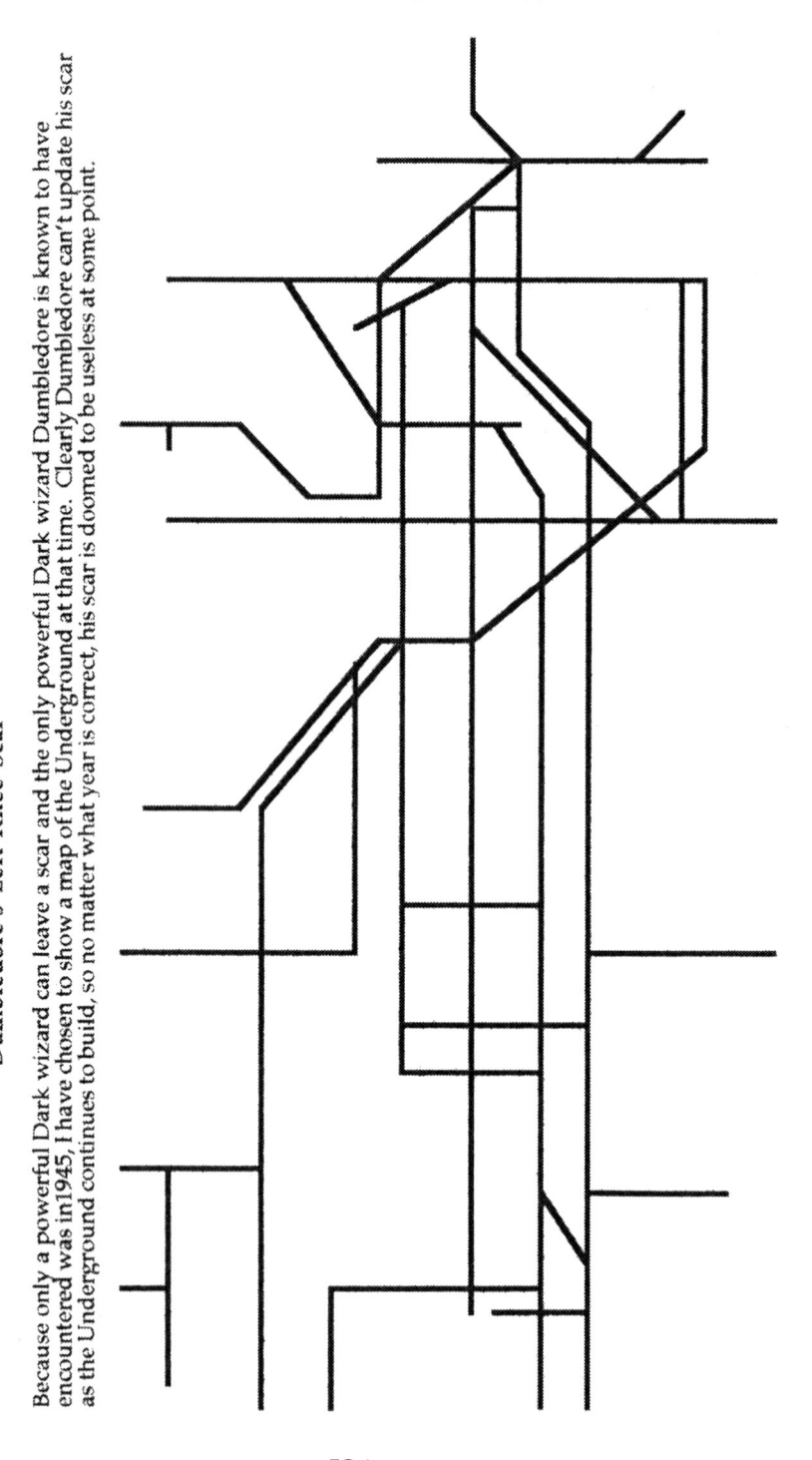

Because only a powerful Dark wizard can leave a scar and the only powerful Dark wizard Dumbledore is known to have encountered was in 1945, I have chosen to show a map of the Underground at that time. Clearly Dumbledore can't update his scar as the Underground continues to build, so no matter what year is correct, his scar is doomed to be useless at some point.

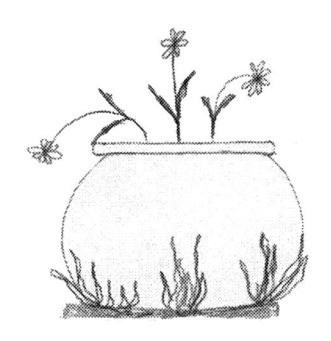

ACKNOWLEDGEMENTS

THE MAKING OF THIS BOOK would of course never have been possible without JK Rowling and her wonderful Harry Potter series. So, first and foremost and with great respect I would like to acknowledge JK Rowling. This aside, the material in this book was created with great appreciation for the work of, but without the consent, approval or even knowledge of, JK Rowling or the Warner Brothers. All characters are property of JK Rowling, Warner Brothers and their designees. Thoughts and opinions expressed are purely my own and no blame should be attached to any of these fine people or institutions.

Quidditch Through the Ages and *Fantastic Beasts and Where to Find Them* were especially helpful resources but it's presumed most readers have these books and if not, they can and will buy them. Information from these books was intentionally skipped over because they are for charity. Incorporation of all the details of these fine book would defeat the purpose of JK Rowling and be stealing from charity. While some websites have chosen to publish the entire contents of these works without a second thought, this practice seemed unacceptable, not to mention illegal, to me. Of the author's profits, 10% will be joyfully donated to Comic Relief UK's Harry's Books Fund.

Other individuals whose work and knowledge have contributed to this effort and who deserve hearty thanks are Fergus Beeley, noted naturalist and filmmaker, and the World Owl Trust of the UK for their insights into owls and owl behavior (www.owls.org); Bernhard Graf, gem expert, historian and author of *Gems: The World's Greatest Treasures and Their Stories*; Francis Bridger, for his insightful look at Harry and Christianity: *A Charmed Life*; Botanical.com for publishing Mrs M. Grieve's text of *A Modern Herbal* (c 1900) on the uses of various plants; and, the London Underground for keeping all their maps back to the 1930's and making them available to the public. My illustrator Henry Starbright also has my high praise and admiration for taking a jumble of thoughts and turning them into fine and meaningful art.

On a lighter note, I'd liked to thank my mother Irene, a great writer and constant encouragement, my father Harry, a great story teller and the beautiful of the great state of Tasmania, who gave me not only inspiration, but motivation to write. Pr W. Randolph Griffith, who trained me in historical research, gave me the means to embark on a 2,000+ page expedition and deserves both thanks and praise. Sirius Black, who gave me the idea for this project, will be remembered with fondly. The authors of *Blood and Swash,* "Legs" Lovick, C. B. Vale, C. M. Barton and Thomas and Kitty

Cochrane encouraged and inspired me when hope and health flagged, and Carlotta Pinkstone has been a guiding light to all my thoughts. Finally, I'd like to acknowledge Dr Stuart Grant, who gave me back my eyesight after this project nearly sent me blind!

About the Author

Acascias "Sphinx" Riphouse is a nameless research historian and the author of several works including a biography of *Anonymous Tunes: Itinerant 18th-Century Scots Fiddler,* the award-winning *Forgotten Battles: Amnesiac Poet-Soldiers in the 30 Years War and Old What's-his-name: Lost Flemish Masters & Their Unknown Art.*

Acascias Riphouse lives with a countless collection of nameless oddities at the San Damiano Bowtruckle Rescue Center. Her hobbies include cider making, competitive bonsai and avidly supporting the Triabunna Thylacines.